AF335312

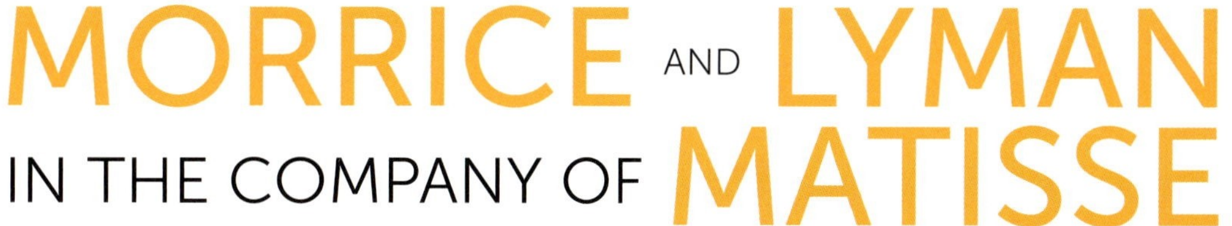

MORRICE AND LYMAN
IN THE COMPANY OF MATISSE

This volume accompanies the exhibition *Morrice and Lyman in the Company of Matisse*, organized and circulated by the Musée national des beaux-arts du Québec with the generous support of the Montreal Museum of Fine Arts and the National Gallery of Canada.

Musée national des beaux-arts du Québec, Quebec City, Quebec
May 8 to September 7, 2014

McMichael Canadian Art Collection, Kleinburg, Ontario
October 4, 2014, to January 4, 2015

The publishing of the English edition of this book was made possible through the generous contribution of A. K. Prakash Foundation, Toronto, Galerie Alan Klinkhoff, Montreal, Galerie Jean-Pierre Valentin, Montreal, Masters Gallery, Calgary, and donors who wish to remain anonymous.

A French version has been published under the title
Morrice et Lyman en compagnie de Matisse.

MORRICE AND LYMAN
IN THE COMPANY OF MATISSE

Essays by Lucie DORAIS, Richard FOISY, François-Marc GAGNON,
Marc GAUTHIER, Michèle GRANDBOIS & John O'BRIAN

FIREFLY BOOKS

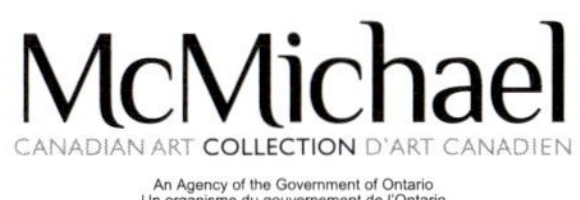

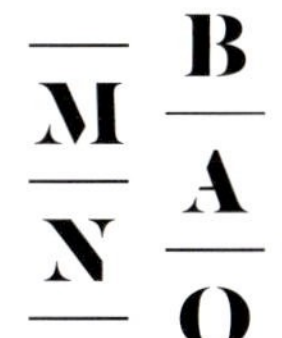

Musée national
des beaux-arts
du Québec

Québec

TABLE OF CONTENTS

FOREWORD

A THREE-SIDED CONVERSATION

Situating the careers of artists from Quebec and Canada within a wider international context has been a goal of the Musée national des beaux-arts du Québec since its foundation over eighty years ago, and a similar ambition drives the McMichael Canadian Art Collection. However, the scale of the research project whose results are presented here is virtually unequalled in the historiography around the emergence of modernity in Canada. It was in the fall of 2011 that Michèle Grandbois, Curator of Modern Art at the Musée national des beaux-arts du Québec, first began work on the major research project that has culminated in the publication *Morrice and Lyman in the Company of Matisse* and its accompanying exhibition.

Retrospective exhibitions of the work of the painters James Wilson Morrice (1865-1924) and John Lyman (1886-1967), both from Montreal, have not been held since 1985 and 1986 respectively. Yet both artists occupy an important place not only in the development of modern Canadian art but also in the nation's public collections. The Musée national des beaux-arts du Québec became the fortunate beneficiary of Lyman's works in 1970 by the bequest of his widow, while the Montreal Museum of Fine Arts holds a major corpus of works by Morrice (whose father, David, was an active supporter of the Art Association of Montreal). In 1992, the National Gallery of Canada received a remarkable donation from G. Blair Laing consisting of eighty-three works by Morrice. Finally, in 2009, the McMichael Canadian Art Collection acquired an important Morrice painting in order to enhance its collection of Quebec art.

Having relocated to Paris, first to study and later to pursue a career in art, both Morrice and Lyman came into contact with their French contemporary Henri Matisse (1869-1954) on a number of occasions during the first two decades of the twentieth century. Disappointed by the reception afforded their works by their compatriots, they found affinity with Matisse's views on artistic practice and saw him as representing—even before his confirmation as the leader of a new form of modernity—a world of new possibilities and a promise of freedom.

With this context in mind, the pertinence of documenting the development of the careers of these two major artists in relation to Matisse was evident. Morrice, a very private person who left virtually no personal papers and who was reluctant to enter into personal or professional relationships, successfully forged a place for himself as a painter of note in the extremely competitive Parisian art scene of the period. An insatiable traveller, whose work was admired by his peers and collected by European museums and art lovers from Russia, Britain and France, Morrice was also known for his wit and sense of humour. As we learn from the catalogue of the exhibition held at the Galeries Simonson in Paris a few months after the Canadian artist's death in 1926, these aspects of his personality—along with his "delicate eye"—were also appreciated by Matisse when the two were together in Tangier in 1912 and 1913.

Younger, more introverted and more intellectual than Morrice, Lyman nevertheless followed a similar path. Having left Montreal to escape the prevailing academicism of its art scene, he moved to Paris in 1907 with the aim of becoming a professional painter. Upon spending a few months at the Académie Matisse in 1910, he was impressed by "the classicism, the measure, the order, especially the balance" of the master's approach. Just as indefatigable a traveller as Morrice, dividing his time between Europe (he encountered Matisse again in Nice in the early 1920s), North Africa, Canada and the West Indies, Lyman would maintain throughout his life an unfailing admiration for his two friends and mentors, as evidenced by his decidedly independent work as a painter and as an art critic.

This exhibition invites visitors to tread the hitherto unexplored byways of the unique artistic nexus that linked Morrice, Lyman and Matisse. Transgenerational and transatlantic, this singular set of connections spanned several decades. More than simply anecdotal, the narrative that emerges illustrates the similarities between three men who were equally resistant to any rigid definition of painting, and who embarked upon the same quest for harmony and mastery of the means to express their own individuality. Conceived by the exhibition's curator and organizer, Michèle Grandbois, as a dialogue rather than an exposition, both exhibition and catalogue aim to reveal influences, convergences and dissonances that highlight the creative sensibilities of each artist—a conversation in three voices.

In bringing this significant undertaking to fruition, Michèle Grandbois has had the support of a number of enthusiastic and knowledgeable collaborators. First, the art historians Lucie Dorais, Richard Foisy, François-Marc Gagnon, Marc Gauthier and John O'Brian opened their archives and shared their research with remarkable magnanimity. We are particularly indebted to them for their enlightened and original accounts of the relationships between the three artists. This catalogue, co-published in English with Firefly and in French with Les Éditions de l'Homme, represents a vital step in our understanding of the genesis of modernity in Canada. We would also like to thank the Montreal and Toronto donors who have made the production of the English edition possible.

The outstanding generosity of numerous private collectors from Canada and abroad proved equally crucial, for few Canadian artists are displayed on the walls of private homes as frequently as Morrice and Lyman. We are grateful to these discerning art lovers—from Calgary, Alberta, to London, England, from Burnaby, British Columbia, to Loretteville, Quebec—who, eager to share their appreciation of the two artists' work, responded so positively to our wish to demonstrate Morrice and Lyman's artistic kinship with Matisse. Without their openness and their many loans, the exhibition would simply not have become a reality.

We have received the support, of course, of a number of institutions. In Canada, we gratefully acknowledge all those colleagues at the Musée d'art contemporain de Montréal, the Montreal Museum of Fine Arts, the National Gallery of Canada and the Art Gallery of Ontario, who responded so obligingly to our many requests for loans and information. Overseas, we extend warm thanks to the Musée des beaux-arts de Lyon and the Tate Modern in London, who have allowed us to present two paintings by Morrice that have not been exhibited in Canada since 1937 and 1985 respectively.

Particular mention must be made of the National Gallery of Art in Washington, the Detroit Institute of Arts and the Norton Museum of Art in West Palm Beach, who have demonstrated their confidence in the exhibition by agreeing to the loan of major paintings by Matisse from their permanent collections. While we have also been able to count on loans of works by the French painter from Canadian collections, the support of these American institutions has been especially precious, in part because of our plan to present Matisse's work in an unusual context—on the same footing as that of contemporary Canadian artists little known south of the border—and in part because competition for loans is at the moment particularly fierce, owing to the many monographic projects underway. We are grateful to them for supporting our effort to add significantly to the history of Canadian art.

Finally, we salute the superlative work of Michèle Grandbois, accomplished with her unfailing vision, meticulousness and passion, and of the Musée national des beaux-arts du Québec's diverse teams under the judicious direction of Anne Eschapasse. As far as the circulation of the exhibition to Ontario is concerned, we are delighted to continue the fruitful collaboration between our two institutions, following the success in 2010 of *Marc-Aurèle Fortin: The Experience of Colour*, and to present this project to a wider public. Our thanks to Katerina Atanassova, Jennifer Withrow and the rest of the McMichael team for their diligence and commitment. We would also like to acknowledge the vital role played by the Government of Ontario, the City of Vaughan, and sponsors from Toronto and the surrounding area whose generous support has made the presentation of this magnificent exhibition at the McMichael possible.

In his "Notes of a Painter," published in 1908, Matisse dreamed of "an art of balance, of purity and serenity . . . a mental soother, something like a good armchair." We offer here the chance to be seduced by the light and colours of the Mediterranean, the West Indies and Canada, to delight in the chromatic harmonies created by these artists and to be moved by this most singular narrative of art and life.

LINE OUELLET
Director and Chief Curator
Musée national des beaux-arts du Québec

Dr. VICTORIA DICKENSON
Executive Director and Chief Executive Officer
McMichael Canadian Art Collection

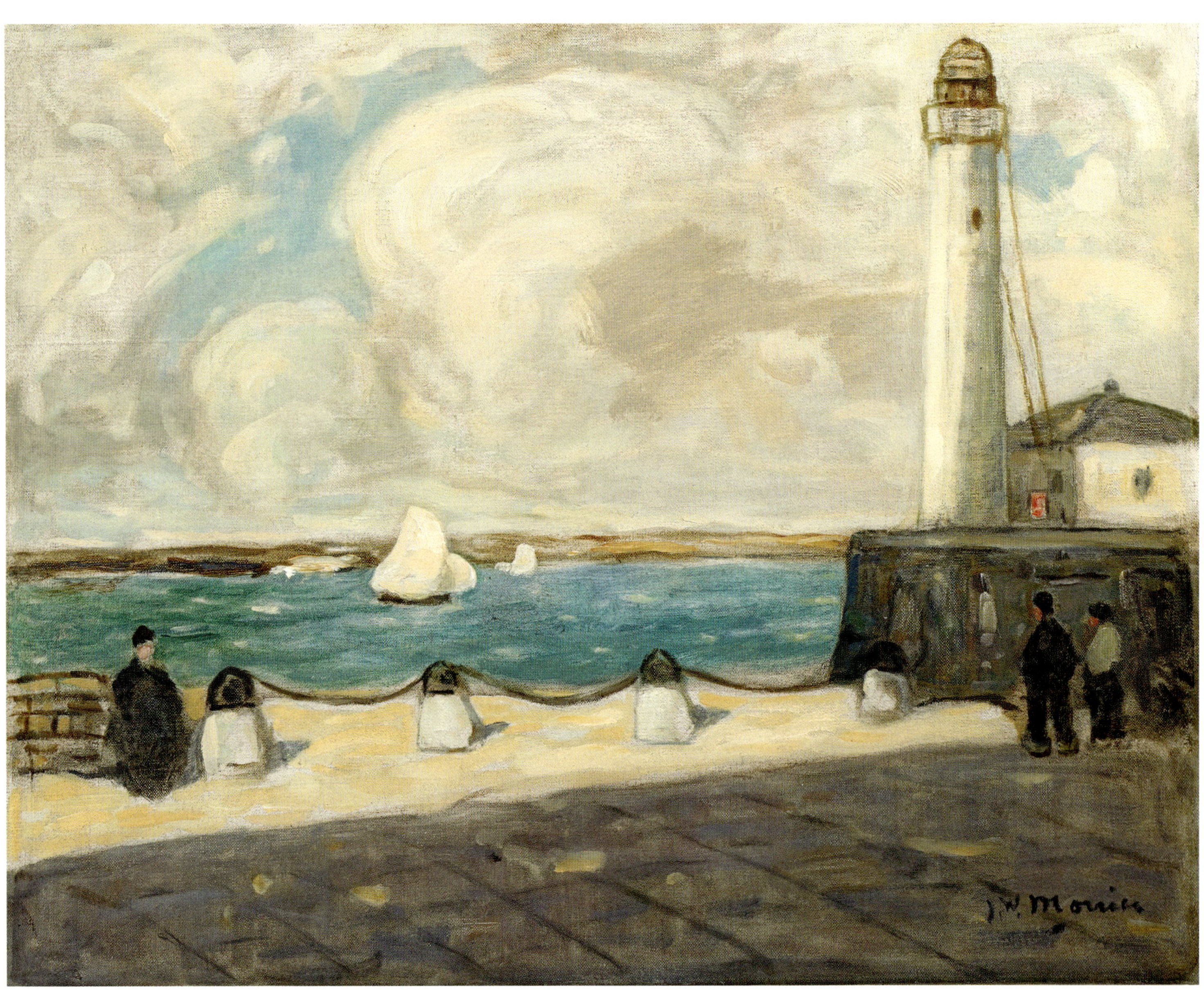

James W. Morrice
Le Havre
1909

A WORD FROM OUR PATRON

Artistic dialogues are subtle events. They involve place, aesthetics and personalities. For Canadian painters James Wilson Morrice and John Lyman the influence of the French modernist master Henri Matisse is sometimes loud and sometimes a whisper.

The A. K. Prakash Foundation is pleased to be Exhibition Patron of the McMichael Canadian Art Collection's presentation of *Morrice and Lyman in the Company of Matisse* and to have contributed to the publishing of the English edition of this book. The Foundation's mission is to advance the scholarship, appreciation and under-standing of Canadian historical art and to improve health outcomes and quality of life in Canada and abroad. We address these two foci through strategic programs with key charity partners. This exhibition and catalogue is an example of the former; an international surgical training and global health program with the University of Toronto is an example of the latter.

This exhibition allows a new generation to explore the paintings of these three artists in a fresh context. We are confident that new insights will be revealed, the least of which is the quality of the Canadian painters—especially Morrice—when placed beside the giant Matisse. It is our hope that the images in this catalogue will provide the context and insights to complement the viewing experience. We are delighted to play a part in providing Canadians with this opportunity of discovery and rediscovery.

A. K. PRAKASH
Chairman, A. K. Prakash Foundation

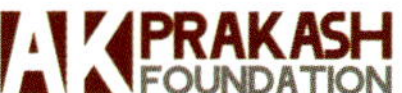

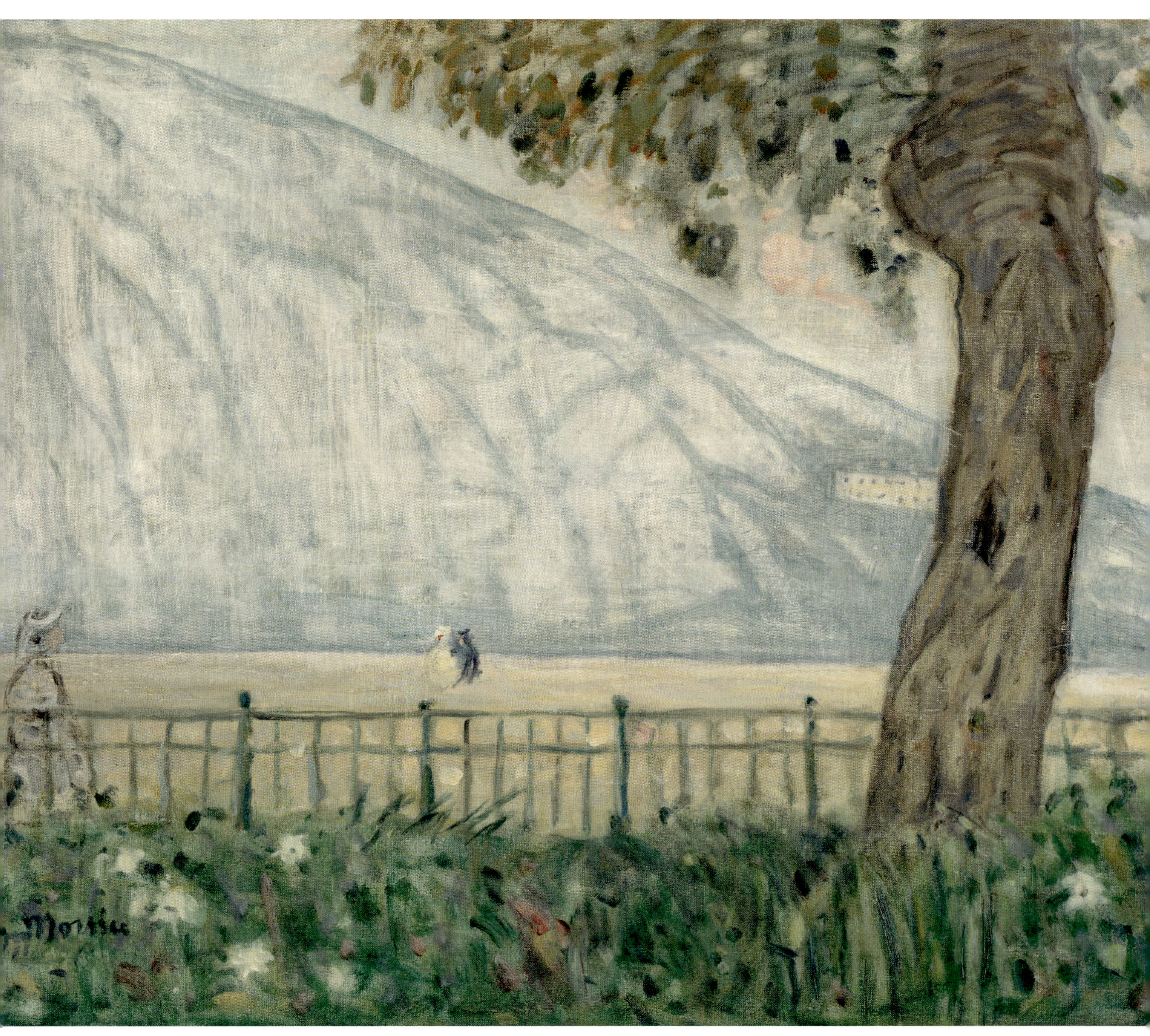

/ **CAT. 1** James W. Morrice
Rock of Gibraltar
1913

LENDERS

We wish to express our gratitude to the many collectors and institutions without whose support this exhibition would not have been possible.

PUBLIC COLLECTIONS
Agnes Etherington Art Centre, Queen's University, Kingston
Art Gallery of Hamilton
Art Gallery of Ontario, Toronto
Detroit Institute of Arts
Montreal Museum of Fine Arts
Musée d'art contemporain de Montréal
Musée des beaux-arts de Lyon
Musée national des beaux-arts du Québec, Quebec City
National Gallery of Art, Washington
National Gallery of Canada, Ottawa
Norton Museum of Art, West Palm Beach, Florida
Tate Gallery, London
Thomson Collection at the Art Gallery of Ontario, Toronto
Vancouver Art Gallery
Winnipeg Art Gallery

PRIVATE AND CORPORATE COLLECTIONS
A. K. Prakash
Gordon Lenko and Lucie Charbonneau
Jean-Pierre Valentin
LMC Health Care
Pierre Lassonde
Power Corporation of Canada
Richard Renlund
Succession Michel Doyon

And those who wish to remain anonymous.

ACKNOWLEDGEMENTS

My thanks go first to Paul Bourassa, who, as interim Director of Exhibitions and Publications, offered warm encouragement when I first submitted the exhibition concept in the fall of 2011, and who has remained steadfastly supportive throughout. I am also indebted to his successor, Anne Eschapasse, whose conviction, determination and enthusiasm have provided a solid defence against the snags that arise in the course of any large-scale project. I am most grateful to her.

Before taking the form of an exhibition and a catalogue, *Morrice and Lyman in the Company of Matisse* was an intensive research undertaking that benefited from the contributions of two learned collaborators. Lucie Dorais, an independent researcher and specialist on the work of James Wilson Morrice, has accompanied me on my venture, generously sharing her extensive documentation and vast knowledge. Her expertise and commitment are reflected throughout this volume. I also salute Charles C. Hill, Curator of Canadian Art at the National Gallery of Canada in Ottawa, who has once again allowed me access to his impressive research resources and who helped in identifying works in private collections. Working with these scholars has been an honour.

Without the attentive response of numerous private lenders and of those responsible for public collections, the exhibition and the catalogue would not be what they are. I would like all the collectors and colleagues who I met in their homes or at their respective institutions—museums, universities, university galleries and libraries, in Canada and France—to know just how enriching and stimulating I found each encounter. Their interest in the project has been enormously gratifying. My thanks go first to the following individuals: Jacques Des Rochers, Danielle Blanchette, Anne Grace and Nathalie Bondil, of the Montreal Museum of Fine Arts; Charles C. Hill and Julie Nash, of the National Gallery of Canada; Greg Humeniuk and Georgiana Uhlyarik, of the Art Gallery of Ontario; Annick Lapôtre, of the Thomson Collection; Josée Belisle, Julie Rivest and Anne-Marie Zeppetelli, of the Musée d'art contemporain de Montréal; Alicia Boutilier, of the Agnes Etherington Art Centre, Kingston; Tobi Bruce and Louise Dompierre, of the Art Gallery of Hamilton; Ian Thom and Daina Augaitis, of the Vancouver Art Gallery; Andrew Kear, of the Winnipeg Art Gallery; Paul Maréchal, of Power Corporation of Canada; Mélanie Rainville, of the Leonard & Bina Ellen Art Gallery, Concordia University; Louise Grenier, of the Université de Montréal; and Gilles Daigneault, of the Fondation Molinari in Montreal.

During two missions to France the state of research was considerably advanced by the expertise and obliging collaboration of Elsa Badie-Modiri and the assistance of Véronique Beauregard, at the library of the Musée d'Orsay, and the help of Magali Lalousse, at the Archives nationales de France. I also wish to acknowledge the contribution of Wanda de Guébriant, Director of the Archives Matisse, in Issy-les-Moulineaux, who allowed us to trace extracts of Matisse's correspondence that relate to Morrice. My thanks as well, for their kind cooperation, to Patrice Deparpre, of the Musée Matisse in Cateau-Cambrésis; Claudine Grammont, of the Archives Camoin; and Cécile Debray, of the Musée national d'art moderne, Centre Pompidou. Marie-Christine Maufus, of the Institut Wildenstein, responded diligently to my inquiries. Supporting those listed here are the many other dedicated individuals who have facilitated the exchange of knowledge and thereby ensured the high quality of this ambitious project.

One of the high points during the months it took to prepare the exhibition was the moment when we secured the loan of the extraordinary painting *Palm Leaf, Tangier,* by Henri Matisse. I would like to express my most sincere gratitude to Harry Cooper, Curator and Head of Modern Art, and Earl A. Powell III, Director, of the National Gallery of Art in Washington. Among the other colleagues in the United States who lent me their assistance, I also warmly thank Rebecca Rabinow, of the Metropolitan Museum of Art in New York.

The generous help of Canadian art dealers and independent consultants in tracking down works in private collections has been particularly appreciated. My sincere thanks to Alan Klinkhoff, Michel Moreault, Jean-Pierre Valentin, Robert Remue and Simon Blais of Montreal; Ash Prakash and David Silcox of Toronto; Rod Green of Calgary; and Grégoire Billault and Simon Shaw of Sotheby's in New York.

The exchanges I had with Anatoly Ciacka, in Burnaby, and with Victor Isganaïtis, René Viau and his mother, Suzanne Viau, in Montreal, considerably enhanced my understanding of John Lyman and his works. I thank them for the precious time I was able to spend with them.

The enthusiasm with which the authors agreed to take part in the project was both stimulating and reassuring, and I am most grateful for the exceptional quality of their contributions. I also acknowledge with much affection the friends and colleagues who have offered advice at various stages: Eve-Lyne Beaudry, Mario Béland, Marie Bellemare, Denis Castonguay, Daniel Drouin, Richard Foisy, Thérèse Labbé, Jean-Pierre Labiau, Laurier Lacroix, Pierre B. Landry, Anne Leahy, P. E. Lépine, Sarah Mainguy, Martin Rhainds and Louise Simard. The invigorating presence of Philippine Lefas, an intern in the exhibitions department, proved valuable during the summer and fall of 2013, a crucial period when the project shifted from research into production.

Once again, the personnel of the Musée national des beaux-arts du Québec have shown proof of efficiency, diligence and good nature. I thank my colleagues in the Library, Lina Doyon, Nicole Gastonguay and Hélène Godbout; in the Archives and Photography sectors, Caroline Gauthier, Idra Labrie, Marie-France Laflamme, Denis Legendre, Catherine Perron, Dyan Royer, Phyllis Smith and Nathalie Thibault; in Exhibitions and Publications, Marie-Claude Boily, Anne Gagnon, Marie-France Grondin and André Sylvain; in Collections and Research, Julie Bélanger, Linda Boucher, Laetitia Jugnet, Nassima Kebbas and Christine Parent; in Arts Outreach and Communications, Julie Bigaouette, Dominique Potvin and Linda Tremblay; along with all the members of the exhibition committee. Finally, I extend warm gratitude to the directorial staff of the Musée, whose members have given this fascinating project their unflagging support.

The creativity and vision of Guillaume Lord, responsible for the design of the exhibition in Quebec City, have done splendid justice to the works. Thanks go too to Étienne Paquette for his video, which provides the perfect complement to a tour of the exhibition. The quality of this catalogue owes much to our managing editor André Gilbert, who has harmonized with characteristic skill and refinement the sum of information presented in its pages. The book's elegant design is the work of Christine Hébert, of Les Éditions de l'Homme.

In these final lines I would like to pay tribute to two people who are dear to me and who have long been my guides, in life and in writing: Claude Lépine and Monique Désy Proulx.

M. G.

INTRODUCTION

The protagonists of our story are two iconic figures of Canadian modern art, James Wilson Morrice and John Lyman, and the great French painter Henri Matisse. The three men encountered one another during the early twentieth century in Paris, then a cauldron of avant-garde activity in which Matisse was playing a vital role. Although they did not spend all that much time together—a total, as far as we know, of around four and a half months—these meetings resulted in a creative surge that had a powerful impact on the conventional Canadian art milieu of the time. When John Lyman exhibited his paintings in Montreal in 1913, they caused a scandal. Their bold new look reflected an aesthetic language shaped by lessons learned in Paris, notably at the Académie Matisse in 1910. This critical event was the catalyst for an irreversible move forward that would be manifested over the next three decades in the formation of a variety of artists' associations dedicated to a modern, universal creative approach, free of any nationalist or regionalist ambition. These collectives included the Beaver Hall Group, the Atelier, the Contemporary Arts Society of Montreal, the artists linked to Alfred Pellan and the Prisme d'Yeux manifesto, and of course Paul-Émile Borduas and the Automatistes, source of the highly critical *Refus global*, which became a crucial factor in the Quiet Revolution that would transform Quebec during the 1960s.

It was admittedly a bold move to bring together three men whose paths were so different, particularly since they left relatively little contemporary written evidence of their meetings. In the case of James Wilson Morrice, the only direct proof we have that he knew Matisse takes the form of two notes in a sketchbook dating from 1920-1922 that mention his name. But then Morrice left just as few clues to his encounters with his compatriot Lyman. Henri Matisse, on the other hand, was more communicative about Morrice. In letters to his wife, Amélie, he mentions on several occasions having spent time with him in Tangier in April 1912. A few months after the Canadian's death, Matisse recalled their two trips to Morocco during the winters of 1912 and 1913: "You know the artist with the delicate eye who delighted in interpreting landscapes of closely related values in soft and muted hues. As a man, he was a true gentleman, a good companion, with great wit and humour." These lines by the French artist, published in the catalogue of the posthumous Morrice exhibition organized by the Galeries Simonson in Paris, in January 1926, have been invoked regularly by specialists, biographers, critics, art historians and museologists interested in the Montreal painter. Matisse's affection for him was confirmed on other occasions and documented by Morrice's biographer, Donald W. Buchanan, who interviewed Matisse twice to discuss their relationship. And in a letter to the curator of the Art Gallery of Toronto (now the Art Gallery of Ontario), Pierre Matisse, the artist's son, affirmed that the Canadian was "a very good friend" of his father.

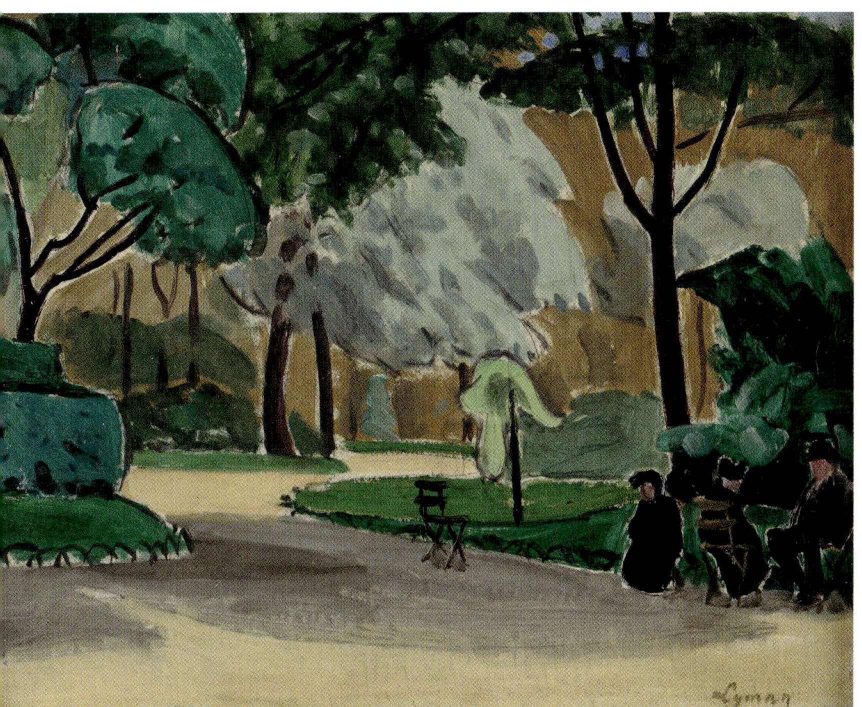

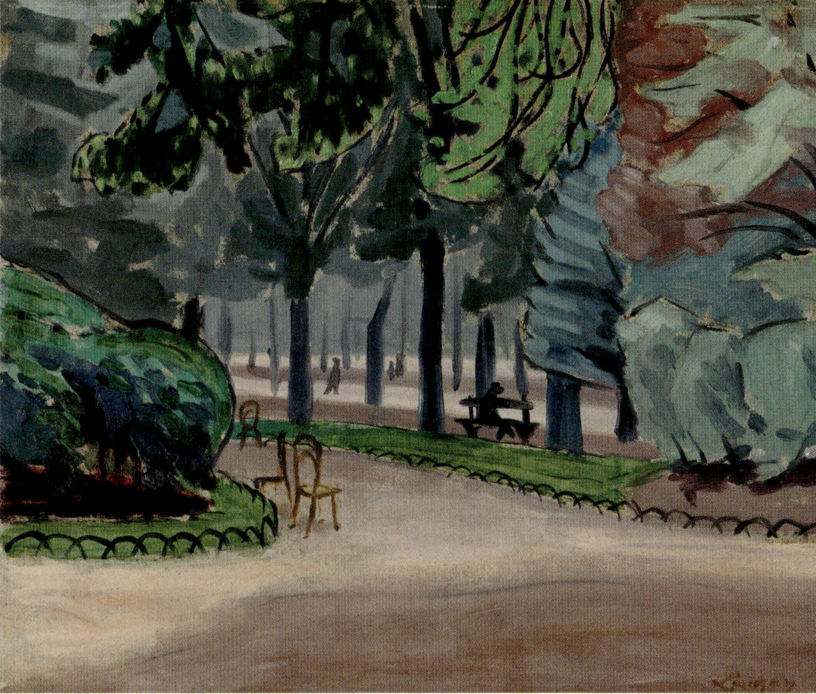

Of the three artists, it is John Lyman whose writings are the most illuminating. Although the painter made little mention of the Académie Matisse in the letters written to his father while he was there, he defended his former teacher vigorously in 1913, when Montreal journalists criticized his work, claiming it had been corrupted by Matisse's teaching and influence. In the diary Lyman kept from 1927 to 1963 and in the articles he published in *The Montrealer* between 1936 and 1942, he acknowledged his debt to Cézanne and Matisse and declared his admiration for Morrice, whose work he helped promote with his 1945 monograph on the painter— the first ever in French. But the two richest sources of aesthetic, factual and anecdotal information concerning Lyman's relations with Matisse and Morrice are probably the documentary *John Lyman, peintre*, produced by the National Film Board of Canada in 1959, and the handwritten notes by Guy Viau in which he recorded his memories of the painter. All this documentation attracted the attention of art historians, and several monographic studies of the two Canadians would appear, accompanied in 1985 and 1986 by retrospective exhibitions.

But aside from material research into the connections between the three painters, it was above all their art that showed us the direction our project should take. Were Morrice and Lyman working as the disciples of a master, or were we

/ CAT. 2 John Lyman
Jardin du Luxembourg
About 1923

/ CAT. 3 John Lyman
Jardin du Luxembourg II
About 1923

dealing with an aesthetic kinship between three distinct personalities? The answer lies in the absolute freedom manifested in the production of the two Montreal painters. If there was a single principle that Henri Matisse held dear, it was the idea of creative authenticity, the need for artists to define their own path, regardless of institutional or commercial considerations. The interweaving of art and life was the basis of the liberty expressed by these three artists and of their capacity to appreciate the present moment.

So as we follow the careers of Morrice, Lyman and Matisse, it is a narrative of artistic fraternity that emerges—one composed of life stories and travelogues, and of aesthetic explorations spanning over eighty years, conducted in Canada and abroad. Morrice and Lyman's encounters with Matisse, though referred to in articles and specialized studies, had not hitherto been taken beyond the level of human interest and anecdote, and the data remained scattered and fragmented. Now, at last, the three artists have been brought together in an exhibition and a catalogue that offer a far more complete picture of a fundamental episode in the history of Canadian art.

We have concentrated on the paintings, reluctantly leaving aside the many works on paper—drawings and watercolours—that would have further supported our argument. More specifically, we have focused on the three painters' shared view of "colour-light" as the expression of an aesthetic approach aimed at essential form, form that—as Lyman (echoing Matisse) wrote—is "below the surface, beyond appearances . . . permanent and durable."

This catalogue testifies to the interest our project has generated among seasoned art historians. Three of the six essays it includes offer an in-depth exploration of relations between two of the artists. In "Morrice and Lyman: The Light of Exile," for example, I have traced the careers of the two Canadian painters abroad. The emancipation and freedom they embodied proved richly instructive. The essay also examines the vitality of Paris and its Salons (in which the artists participated), their aesthetic discoveries and the critical reception afforded their work, in France and in Canada. Their practice of art, so closely connected to their moves and travels, takes us to the countries of North Africa and to the islands of the Caribbean.

In an essay entitled "Morrice and Matisse: Bedfellows Under the Sign of Modernism," John O'Brian examines the personal relationship between the two artists, as well public reaction to their respective oeuvres. Author of *Ruthless Hedonism* (1999), a remarkable book on the American reception of Matisse's work, the art historian begins by reviewing the two painters' historiography. He then goes on to discuss their encounters in Tangier and elucidate their painting procedures, ending with a fascinating account of the acquisition of works by Matisse in Canada.

With his contribution, "Lyman's Encounter with Matisse," François-Marc Gagnon offers an illuminating view of the relationship between John Lyman and the Fauve aesthetic. He examines the time the Montreal painter spent at the Académie Matisse and his visits to the Steins, as well as his meetings with Matisse in Nice. Having considered the impact of the French artist on Lyman's work as a critic, the author clarifies the distinction between the notions of the "picturesque" and the "pictorial," and explains by means of examples how they and the concept of the "decorative" relate to the two artists' work.

The essay by Lucie Dorais looks at Morrice's trips to North Africa, which occurred over a period of more than a decade. She takes us first to the Tangier of 1912 and 1913, where the Canadian painter spent several weeks in Matisse's company. Through the intermediary of Morrice's works, we stroll along the beach, linger in the places that caught his eye and follow him into the medina, whose gates inspired a number of luminous pochades. Our next stop is Tunis, where Morrice spent the winter of 1914. And finally, after the war, Algeria, which the painter visited in 1922 and 1923, less than a year before his death in the region that had so inspired him.

In order to gain a better sense of the Canadian art milieu from which our painters emerged, we felt it important to examine the diffusion of French art in this country. We therefore asked Marc Gauthier to share his previously unpublished research on an exhibition held in Montreal in 1906, *Some French Impressionists*, which inspired the young Lyman to embark on a career as a painter.

Complementing these various studies is a chronology entitled "Morrice, Lyman, Matisse: Intertwining Journeys," which details the three artists' intersecting paths. The product of research undertaken by Richard Foisy and myself, it includes numerous quotes, creating "conversations" that add a lively dimension to the most significant aspects of their encounters and their artistic affinities.

Finally, four richly illustrated portfolios mirroring the circuit of the exhibition itself focus on decorative painting, the particular quality of Mediterranean and Caribbean light, and the allure of water. Taken together, these texts illuminate a facet of our history that has remained in obscurity for over a century.

MICHÈLE GRANDBOIS
Curator of the Exhibition

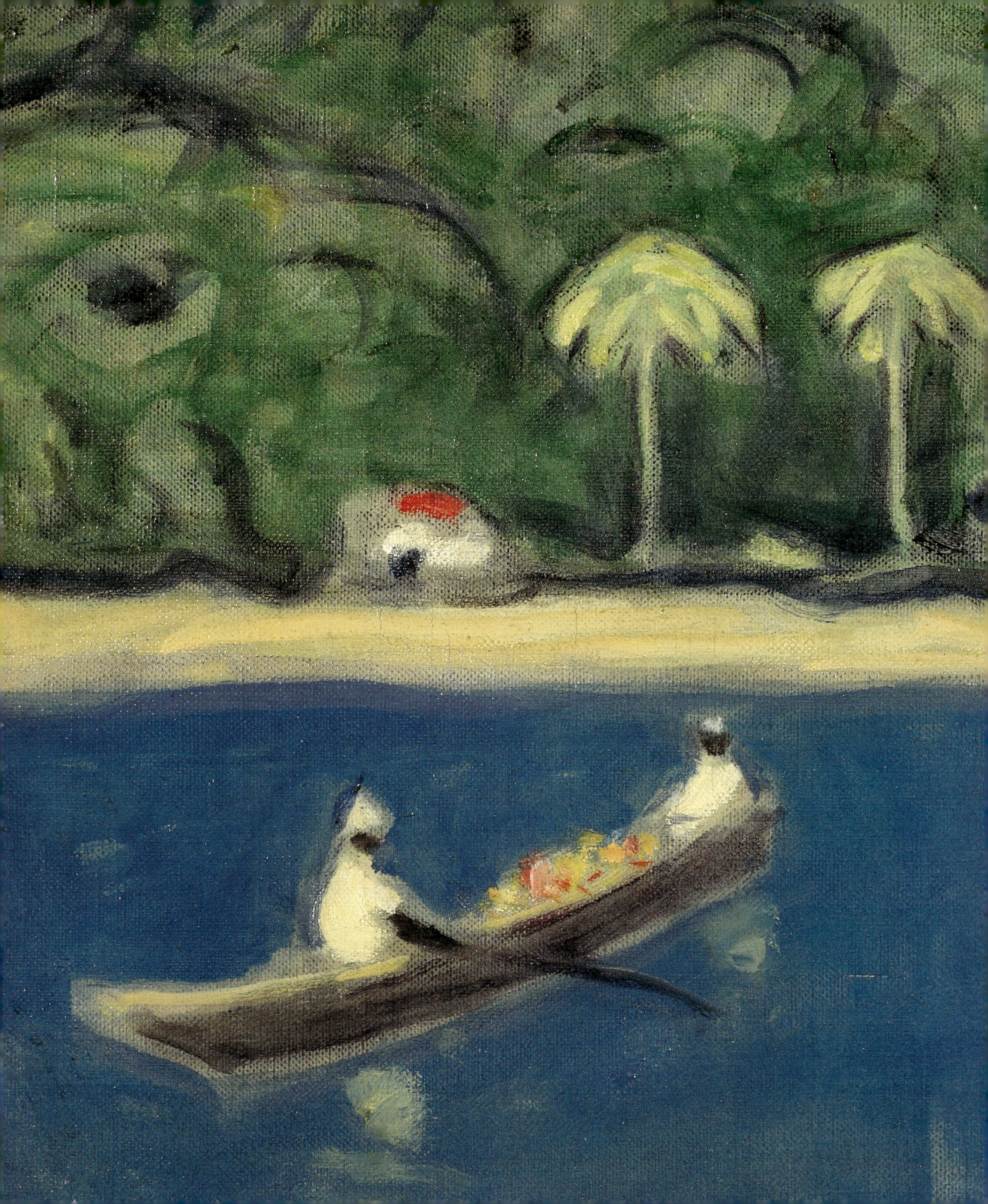

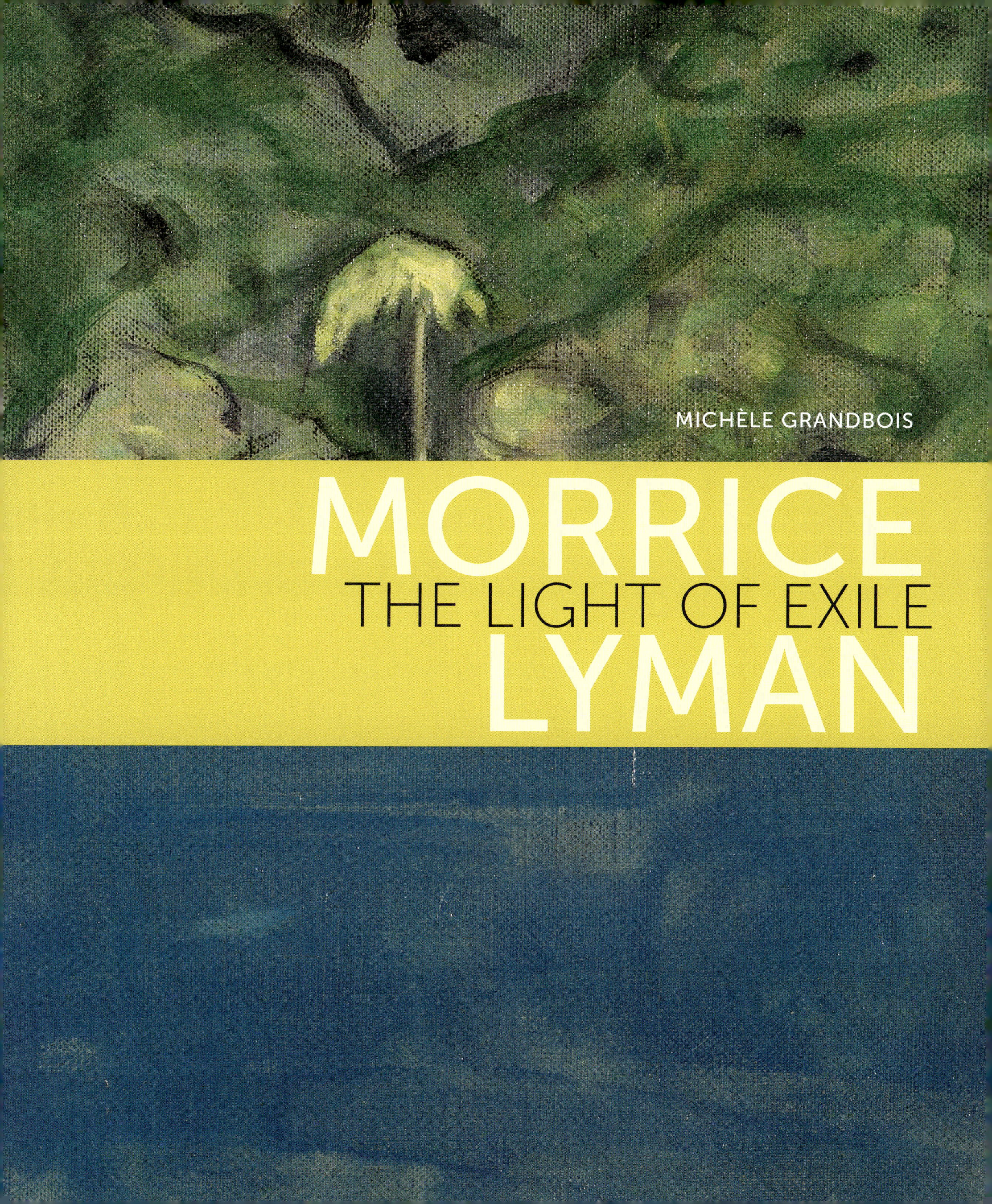

MICHÈLE GRANDBOIS

MORRICE

THE LIGHT OF EXILE

LYMAN

TWO GENTLEMEN BORN ON "EASY STREET"

There are many kinds of exile. For James Wilson Morrice[1] and John Lyman, exile encompassed the lure of faraway places, the need to travel and a feeling of exclusion, all at the same time. The lives of these two painters have in common the comfortable wanderings of well-born sons of good families, from an affluent Anglo-Montreal middle class that had made its fortune in textiles and pharmaceuticals during the industrial era. Money was never a problem for these artists, both of whom spent almost thirty-five years of their active lives outside Canada. Elegantly dressed and distinguished in manner, their gentlemanly bearing left no doubt as to their upper middle-class origins. They moved as easily in the higher echelons of society as among groups of artists, in both Canada and France. Their free spirits and cultivated minds, in one tinged with humour and lightheartedness, and in the other with conviction and irony, made them popular with their contemporaries. Morrice, naturally reserved, avoided social events. Somewhat reluctant to reveal himself though words, he left us his paintings as the key to his mystery. Lyman, on the other hand, enjoyed an active social life. Perfectly bilingual, he used words gracefully and effectively. In many writings, both private and public, he set out his beliefs about life and art. Despite their very different temperaments, the two men shared travels that led them far and wide, to many and varied places.

    James Wilson Morrice chose exile as a way of life. He left Montreal when he was twenty-five and only returned ten or so times, to visit his family.[2] Although immersed in the artistic excitement of Paris during the Belle Époque, he remained interested in Canada as a subject, bringing back from his trips many sketches and copying them onto canvas in his studio on the Quai des Grands-Augustins in Paris. His regular participation in exhibitions in Montreal and Toronto showed his attachment to Canada. After his parents' deaths in the fall of 1914, his sojourns in Canada became less frequent. He died in Tunis at the age of fifty-eight. In the end, Morrice would spend more years of his life abroad than in Canada.

Previous double page:

/ **CAT. 26 (DETAIL)** James W. Morrice
Fruit Boat, Trinidad
1921

In the remarkable monograph John Lyman devoted to him in 1945, he described Morrice's disillusion with regard to his country, a regret he witnessed during the accidental encounters that brought them together in the course of their nomadic lives: "Whether in a café, on a cruise ship, at his home, in the Restaurant de la Marine, which appealed to the perpetual traveller he was . . . on each of these occasions, Canada, so inhospitable to artists, was present in his mind."[3] The lack of recognition Morrice claimed he was a victim of had fed a growing resentment in him over the years. Furthermore, the rise in Canadian nationalism in painting, which found its voice with the creation of the Group of Seven in 1920, added to his disillusionment. A voluntary exile, he felt excluded by the artistic community in his own country. "During one of his visits to me," Lyman wrote, "just before boarding a boat for Tunis, where he had to be laid dying on the ground, he spoke with bitterness of the lack of attention his fellow Canadians paid to his work."[4] Morrice had clearly shared this painful feeling with the painter Henri Matisse, who, in 1950, asked about the treatment then being given to his friend's work in Canada.[5]

The third of seven children, James had travelled very little before arriving in Paris in 1890. His first experience of being in unfamiliar surroundings outside the country had been holidays by the seaside in the state of Maine with his family, with later visits to Quebec City and the Toronto area, where he studied law. Later on, when Henri Matisse recalled Morrice, he spoke of a "migrating bird . . . always travelling over hill and dale . . . with no fixed landing place."[6] It is true that the Canadian's trunk was never far from the door of his dwelling, even though Paris did become his anchor point, the longest-lasting of his life.

As for John Lyman, who was twenty years younger than Morrice, he very early on felt himself exiled in his own country, where academic art dominated cultural and artistic life. For him, as for the older artist, there was no choice but to leave Canada.

In 1900, the Lymans left for Europe, as was common at the turn of the twentieth century and during its first decades among Montreal's prosperous bourgeois society. John was then fourteen years old, and the little family—consisting only of father and son since the death of John's mother when he was three—began its Grand Tour: Naples, Rome, Florence, Paris and London. The World's Fair was underway in the French capital, and the adolescent was especially impressed by the paintings of nudes he saw there. Did he visit the Alma Pavilion, where Auguste Rodin had organized his own retrospective, attracting a large international clientele already collecting his works? Lyman does not say. Nor does he speak about the Centennale de l'art français exhibition prepared by critic Roger Marx; this exhibition had given pride of place to the Impressionist painters, who were from then on officially recognized by the government. What we do know for sure is that this light-filled painting style would have its effect on Lyman six years later when he saw the *Some French Impressionists* exhibition in the rooms of the Art Association of Montreal.[7] "The treatment of light, this extraordinary quality of light"[8] emanating from the paintings of Monet, Renoir, Sisley or Pissarro would make him realize how much Montreal was isolated from major trends in modern painting.

In 1907, Lyman returned to Paris, which was destined to become his home base for the next twenty-five years. The young man became part of the group of expatriate students in Paris and finished his training there at the Académie Matisse. Back in Montreal in 1913 to show his work, he encountered the press's brutal and irrevocable reaction to the modernism of his paintings. He was thus forced to leave, and it was not until eighteen years later that he returned to settle in Canada.

Toward the end of his European adventure, John Lyman made a heartfelt plea to his father in favour of financial independence for the artist. While this was not, of course, a guarantee of success, he wrote, it served as a rampart to safeguard the artist's integrity, often undermined by commercial success:

> I have often thought of selling my painting, as you saw in my last letter, but I hope I may never think of "commercializing my abilities." I see too often the results of that, men abandoning their artistic integrity from necessity or from the lure of success. I could name several of great promises who lost the real incentive as soon as that of success came to them. But of course it is a satisfaction to sell to people of discrimination. Perhaps that is what you mean? . . . What are "the great laws" that rule humanity? Cézanne was a millionaire, never had to earn a centime, yet he was the hardest worker that ever lived and became one of the greatest painters. How do you explain it? And a dozen other great painters who were born on Easy Street? How do you explain them? [9]

Beginning in 1931, when he was in his mid-forties, John Lyman led an unrelenting crusade in Montreal in defence of modern Canadian art. Then, at the end of the 1950s, he again experienced the old feeling of being exiled in his own country, but for reasons opposite to those that had motivated his departure fifty years earlier: this time, Lyman would feel he had been left behind by advances in lyrical and geometric abstraction in the 1950s. The seventy-year-old painter took refuge in Barbados, where he produced his last dazzling paintings. He died there at the age of eighty-one.

James Wilson Morrice and John Lyman, both born on "Easy Street," embodied emancipation and freedom at a time when Canadian art was still subject to the restrictive rules of the Royal Canadian Academy of Arts and the Art Association of Montreal. Their lives unfolded on the fringes of their family circle and their country's official art world. The voluntary exile they experienced, each in his own way, was the source of a wealth of lessons, each one a beacon shedding light on the Canadian artistic landscape and setting it on the path toward modernism.

Their adventure began in Paris.

PARIS AND ITS SALONS

At the time Morrice and Lyman were living in Paris, the city was the cultural centre of the western world and deserved more than ever to be called "The City of Light," as it had been since the eighteenth century. On the one hand, there was the taste for official art, supported by the government, quietly traditional, to the point of being academic. On the other, there was the avant-garde explosion of the Post-Impressionist, Fauvist, Cubist and Abstractionist revolutions that caused so many scandals and upheavals. The many events on the cultural calendar reflected this profusion of trends and ideas: the most spectacular were, beyond any doubt, the Salons of the artists' societies.

In the spring every year, in March and April, the season began with the Salon de la Société des Artistes indépendants. In April and May, it was the turn of the Salon de la Société nationale des beaux-arts, and then, in May and June, of the Société des Artistes français. The last two attracted tens of thousands of visitors, both French and foreign, to the Palais des beaux-arts on the Champ-de-Mars and the Palais de l'industrie on the Champs-Élysées, before becoming permanently established beneath the glass roof of the Grand Palais at the beginning of the twentieth century. All of these buildings dedicated to the glory of art were filled with a large number of works carefully chosen by official juries, whose members advised the government on what to buy to add to the national collections. The Salon d'Automne acted as a counterbalance to this very packed spring calendar.

Before going further, a few lines of introduction are needed to fully grasp the issues raised by these events for Morrice and Lyman.

THE SALONS DES ARTISTES FRANÇAIS AND DES INDÉPENDANTS

Of the four societies, the oldest was the Artistes français, created in 1881. Its salon, crammed with several thousand works, carried on in the tradition of the official salons overseen since the seventeenth century by the Académie des beaux-arts. It was under the overbearing influence of Alexandre Cabanel, Jean-Léon Jérôme and William Bouguereau, academicians and professors at the École des beaux-arts. This was the salon where Canadians exhibited in greatest numbers between 1882 and 1914.[10]

Right from the beginning, the jury of the Salon des Artistes français exercised great authority, scrupulously applying the conventions passed down by institutions like the Académie and the École des beaux-arts. This caused the most progressive artists to react: in 1884, Paul Signac, Georges Seurat and other members of the Neo-Impressionist circle founded the Société des Artistes indépendants, which would have no admissions jury; Signac was its president for many years. The openness of the Indépendants made for an extremely lively and inclusive group. Its salon was eclectic, a large melting pot where ideas were exchanged.[11] This stimulating locale welcomed most of the main representatives of modern art, from the Neo-Impressionists (Signac, Seurat, Pissarro) to the Cubists (Braque, Laurens, Lhote, Léger, Gleizes, Zadkine), along with the Nabis (Denis, Bernard, Sérusier, Vuillard, Bonnard), the Fauves (Marquet, Friesz, Derain, Manguin, Puy, Valtat, Van Dongen, de Vlaminck, Rouault, Matisse) and many more. The Indépendants also offered space to foreigners (Munch, Chagall, Kandinsky, Archipenko, de Chirico, Modigliani, Sickert, Zadkine, Mondrian, Zuloaga and Valloton) and to the great Post-Impressionist painters (Cézanne, Van Gogh, Gauguin, Toulouse-Lautrec, Le Douanier Rousseau, Valadon, Dufy).

The Salon des Indépendants welcomed relatively moderate Canadian artists—sensitive and somewhat traditional landscape and portrait painters. Henri Beau (1863-1949), a native of Montreal, exhibited some thirty of his drawings and paintings there between 1897 and 1914. A more daring artist, painter Randolph Stanley Hewton (1888-1960), born near Lake St. Louis on Montreal's south shore, participated in this salon in 1911 and 1912. A few years earlier, from 1906 to 1911, the salon had also exhibited some forty works by landscape painter Frederic Charles Vincent Ede (1865-1913?), originally from Montana, who had studied in Toronto and Montreal before settling in the Loing region of France.[12]

THE SALONS DE LA NATIONALE AND D'AUTOMNE

The Salon de la Société nationale des beaux-arts, commonly referred to as the "Nationale," provided a showcase for "the happy medium," between the Salon des Artistes français and the Salon des Indépendants. This society was born out of a split in the Artistes français that pitted the hard-line academicians, the "Bouguereauistes," against the more liberal artists gathered around Éric Meisonnier, the "Meissonieristes."[13] In 1889, exasperated by the systematic obstruction of the juries by the parent society, which refused entry to all talented young painters, Puvis de Chavannes and August Rodin founded this new society, remaining nonetheless highly dependent on the government.

The Salon d'Automne was the creation of architect and art critic Frantz Jourdain, and took place in October and November. From 1903 to 1945, it provided a counterweight to the heavy schedule of spring shows by the Indépendants, the Nationale and the Artistes français. The Société du Salon d'Automne was also a dissenter from the official salon; it defended contemporary art and differentiated itself by presenting the avant-garde in every form (fine arts and decorative arts, as well as urban planning, photography, book illustration, book-binding, music, film, literature), while honouring past masters and artistic endeavours from other countries. For example, retrospectives were dedicated to El Greco, Ingres, Delacroix, Manet, Cézanne, Renoir, Gauguin and Daumier, and national exhibitions were held, highlighting recent work from various countries, including Germany, Belgium, Spain, Great Britain, Finland, Italy and Japan. Music held a special place; and the series of concerts that marked the 1905 salon featured Claude Debussy, Gabriel Fauré, César Franck and Maurice Ravel. This salon covered a wide range: in 1909, a room was devoted to children's drawings. In contrast to the Salon des Indépendants which, twenty years earlier, had abolished both juries and prizes, this salon did not open its doors to everyone. A jury was formed, but it was chosen by drawing lots among the members of the Société.[14] We should add that the choice of autumn as their exhibition season was strategic; not only did this re-establish balance in Paris's annual calendar of major artistic events, it also allowed artists to show what they had produced during the spring and summer and to position themselves on the cutting edge of artistic trends.

MORRICE AND THE SALONS: AN UNUSUALLY WIDE CIRCULATION

Morrice was a fixture at the Salon de la Nationale from 1896 to 1911, and again in 1920, as well as at the Salon d'Automne from 1905 to 1923, exhibiting over a hundred works; this gave him prominence in Paris and internationally, a unique phenomenon in the history of Canadian art.[15] Of all the Canadians who participated in the salons of the four Parisian artists' societies, he was the only one to have exhibited for so long and at such a regular rate.[16]

Participating in the salons, especially if you were noticed, ensured public recognition, essential for any artistic career to flourish. Morrice immediately understood that circulating his works widely was vitally important. Before leaving Canada, he had exhibited in the salons of the country's two main artists' associations, the Royal Canadian Academy of Arts and the Art Association of Montreal. In 1888 and 1889, the Toronto public had also been able to see a few of his works at the Ontario Society of Artists exhibition. His constant presence in the Parisian salons was indicative of an entrepreneurial and ambitious temperament, complementing the image of the sensitive, reserved and nomadic artist that he has often been portrayed as. In fact, it would be a misreading of this prosperous merchant's son to underestimate his acute sense of marketing and the ease with which he mingled in the influential circles of the international art network.

Like the innumerable threads of a spider's web, the art world was a tangle of relationships among artists, societies, dealers, collectors, critics and exhibition organizers. Morrice wove so many connections in this Parisian web that it is difficult to untangle them. Among others, he maintained relations with Americans living in Paris, like Robert Henri and Maurice Prendergast, who familiarized him not only with the best places to exhibit on the other side of the Channel—such as the New Gallery in London—but also on the other side of the Atlantic, at the Pennsylvania Academy of Fine Arts in Philadelphia[17] and the Carnegie Institute in Pittsburgh. He also participated in exhibitions at La Libre Esthétique in Brussels, at the invitation of Octave Maus of the International Society of Sculptors, Painters and Gravers of London (ISSPG) and at the Société Nouvelle.[18] Finally, he made many contacts in Auguste Rodin's circle of friends and among his collectors,[19] as well as with artists in Georges Petit's gallery in Paris. The Société Nouvelle, which Morrice belonged to from 1908 to 1914, actually held its salon in this gallery. It brought together, he wrote, "the most eminent artists in Paris" (Jacques-Émile Blanche, Charles Cottet, René Ménard and Lucien Simon).[20] The Société Nouvelle sent touring exhibitions to the United States, as did the International Society of London, which he belonged to from 1900 onward. In 1904, Morrice's works were seen in Philadelphia, Pittsburgh, Cincinnati, Chicago, Buffalo, Boston and St. Louis. Several artists associated with the International Society and the Société Nouvelle also exhibited at the Venice Biennale, in 1903 and 1905,[21] where Morrice was the only Canadian to participate. That year, visitors to the Biennale saw his works hanging in the "foreign artists'" room, near those of James McNeill Whistler and the Scottish painter John Lavery.

In 1905, Morrice was forty. He had been living in Paris for fifteen years, felt completely at home there and had achieved enviable fame, as evidenced by the interest shown in him by the French government[22] and art critics. As proof, there is

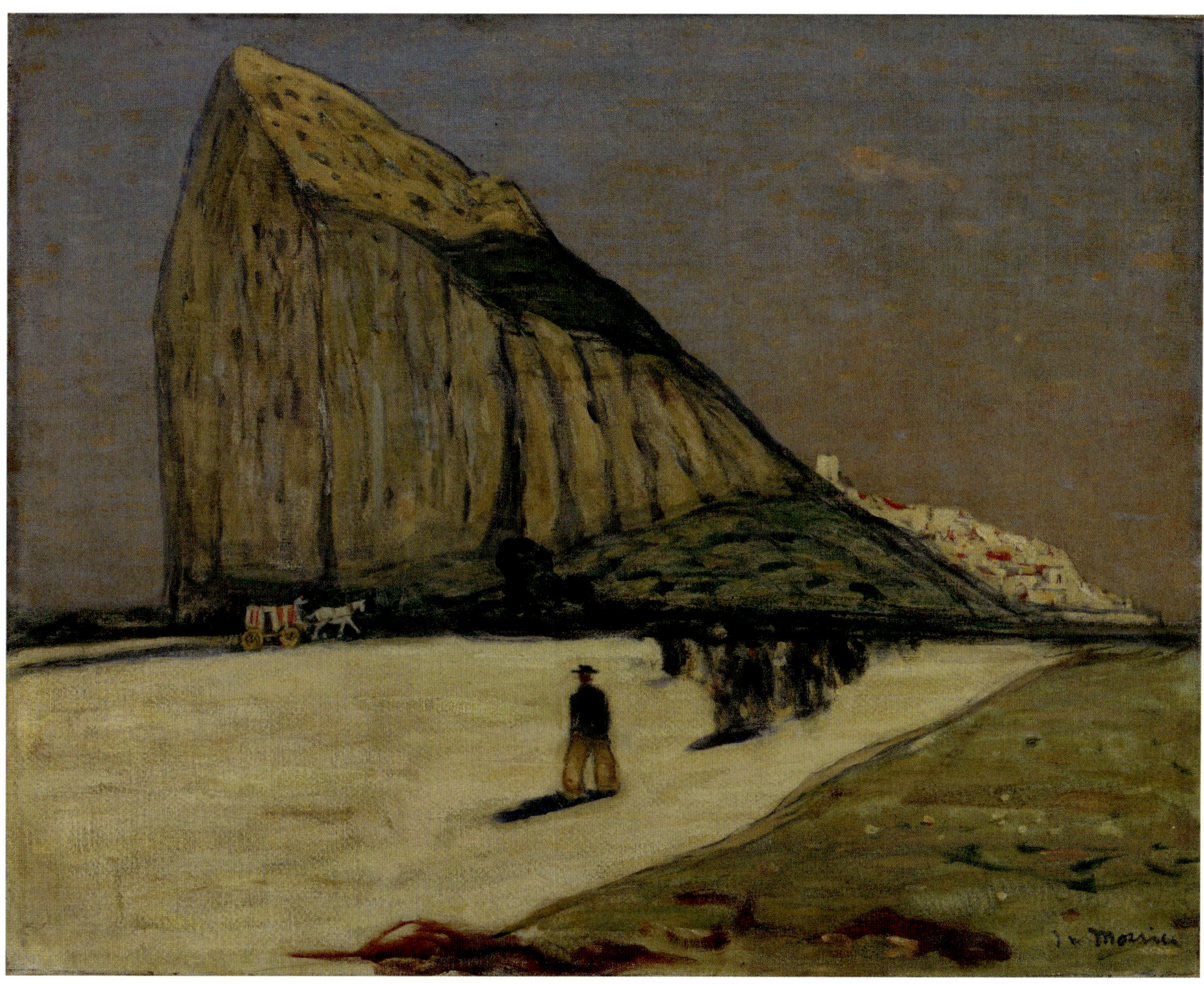

the considerable press review compiled by the art historian Ghislain Clermont for that year: his participation in 11 exhibitions in 5 countries generated references and comments in some 122 articles published in French, Belgian, British and American art journals and magazines.[23]

At the time, he was exhibiting at the Salon de la Société des Peintres orientalistes français, founded in 1893, some sixty years after Eugène Delacroix's travels in North Africa. This society had been established by Léonce Bénédicte, an art historian with a passion for the Orient and curator at the Musée du Luxembourg, to promote the study of art inspired by the countries and civilizations of the East and Far East. The society's field of interest also extended to regions that had simply experienced contact with and the influence of eastern civilizations;[24] Morrice was thus able to present six scenes of Venice at the salon, in 1904 and 1905.[25] Some years later, in 1912 and 1913, the painter was to visit Tangier twice, on journeys that became

/ CAT. 4 James W. Morrice
Gibraltar
1913

famous for giving him the opportunity to spend time with Henri Matisse. Morrice brought back sketches that formed the basis of remarkable paintings done in his studio not long before being exhibited: ten works inspired by the light, landscapes and people of Morocco and Gibraltar (CAT. 4) that were shown, not at the Salon des Orientalistes, but at the two exhibitions of the Salon d'Automne, which Morrice felt was the most stimulating in the Parisian calendar.[26]

On January 30, 1909, while Morrice was especially busy in Paris, a major *Exposition d'art français* opened at the Art Association of Montreal.[27] This was the second French artistic event in Montreal, coming after *Some French Impressionists*, which had been organized in 1906 by the Galerie Durand-Ruel in Paris. This time, the exhibition was of an official nature, occurring at a time when diplomatic ties between France and Canada were becoming stronger, notably with the creation of the Comité France-Québec. The Comité was an influential private organization composed of a group of business people, intellectuals and statesmen, among whom was Sir William Van Horne, President of the Canadian Pacific Railway, a major collector of Flemish, Dutch, French and English masters, and a friend of the Morrice family.[28] Not only had Van Horne been the first to acquire a painting by Morrice at the end of his studies in Toronto, but in a way it was also to him that the young Montrealer passionate about art owed his career, for Van Horne had managed to convince his father to allow him to go and study painting in Paris.

To oversee this eclectic and rather conservative exhibition, the French government had chosen three artists' societies—the Société des Artistes indépendants had not been selected—and appointed four leading figures to represent them in Quebec: René Lalique (Société des Artistes français), Albert Besnard and Auguste Rodin (the Nationale), and Frantz Jourdain (Société d'Automne). The exhibition brought together 300 works (paintings, sculptures, engravings and decorative arts) by 150 French artists, including the first showing in Montreal of a sculpture by Rodin, *The Thinker*.[29] However, not one of the leading lights of the Parisian avant-garde was represented at this event, whose goal was to open up the Canadian market to contemporary French art and where all the works were for sale.[30] It was a huge success, as shown by the 11,500 people who visited the exhibition and the 151 sales that were negotiated with 27 collectors, half of whom were members of the Art Association.[31] Louis Vauxcelles, the author of the exhibition catalogue's introduction, was an ardent admirer of Morrice, and the influential art critic was in the middle of preparing the first feature article to appear on Morrice in a Canadian art journal for the month of December 1909.[32]

For all of these reasons, and considering Morrice's regular participation and wide circulation in the Paris art world, it is surprising to note that he did not attend this major event, despite the fact that it included artists he had been exhibiting with in Paris for more than twenty years.[33] It is true that Morrice was part of the contingent of foreigners in France and was viewed as such by the critics. And of course the exhibition aimed to introduce French art to Montrealers. Since he was not participating in it, might he have helped organize the exhibition in Montreal? A journalist from *La Presse* reported having seen him meandering through the rooms of the Art Association a few days before the exhibition opened.[34] In any event, if he was closely or distantly connected to this event, it was under a cloak of anonymity, as there are no documents to confirm this.

However, his works were presented in the main Canadian exhibitions: at the Spring Exhibition of the Art Association of Montreal, as well as in Toronto, at the annual exhibition of the Royal Canadian Academy of Arts and at the Canadian Art Club. The painter was a founding member of this latter group of artists, created in 1907 and chaired by his friend Edmund Morris. He also exhibited at the Arts Club of Montreal, which included two of his works in its inaugural exhibition in 1913, one of which was *Entrance to a Quebec Village* (CAT. 7). The Montreal club dedicated a solo exhibition to him in 1914. Morrice's participation in Canadian exhibitions thus added to the wide network he was involved in.

In fact, in addition to his travels and his studio work, Morrice participated in eight annual exhibitions on average up to the beginning of the First World War. This forced him to organize his work meticulously to allow for creation, production and circulation, in an annual schedule that also had to take into account the shipping of his works. His exhaustion was palpable in the letters he sent to Edmund Morris and Newton MacTavish in Canada: "I'm working like a slave now for the Autumn Salon which opens next month."[35] The pace was sometimes so fast that it caused him to neglect his participation in Canadian exhibitions, as was the case in February 1911 for the Canadian Art Club exhibition in Toronto: "It will be impossible for me to send over six of my best pictures as you suggest. I have just sent two to Bordeaux and two to Nantes and I have to send to the Société Nouvelle next month (this is always my most important exhibition) also to the International in London and afterwards the Salon."[36] It was the same story at the end of the year: "Brymner wrote & asked me to send to the Academy exhibition in Toronto but I have nothing ready. So many exhibitions to send to. Too many!!"[37]

MORRICE: A MIRROR FOR LYMAN

In 1907, John Lyman left to study painting in Paris, initially finding a place in the small studio of Pierre-Amédée Marcel-Béronneau, a friend and disciple of symbolist painter Gustave Moreau. Then, wanting to please his father, he enrolled in architectural drawing at the Royal College of Art in South Kensington, London, which he left without regret at the beginning of 1908 to return to Paris. He then began to attend the Académie Julian every morning until January 1910.[38] Lyman really did not seem very happy there.[39] He did not like the critiquing sessions with Jean Paul Laurens, the archetype of the official artist, an academician and well-known representative of historical painting. He confided this to his father in November 1909:

> My last esquisse at Julian's took about 37e place, next to the last. You
> know Jean Paul's esquisse judging is notoriously humorous to all except
> the old standbys who have been at the academy for the last 10 or 15 years
> & have driven themselves into his rut . . . Anything high in key invokes his

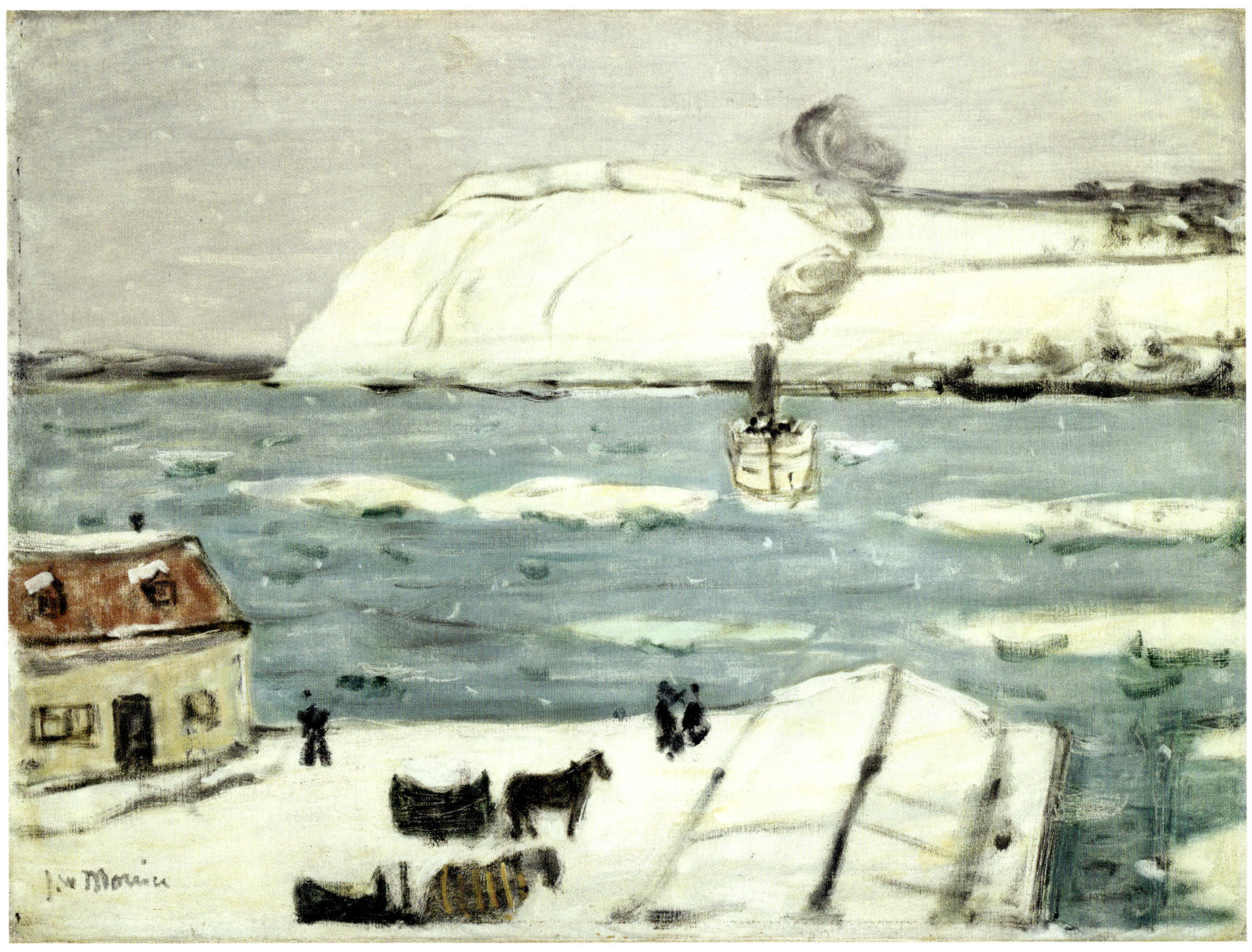

/ **CAT. 5** James W. Morrice
The Ferry, Quebec
1907

censure to such a degree that he doesn't even criticize its composition; air and light in an esquisse are sufficient to make him throw it on the floor and sunlight in a canvas gives him an apoplexy . . . It is my business to try to develop my personality rather than to repress it every time it comes into play.[40]

The student identified more with the painting of his fellow Canadian Morrice, which he had discovered on his arrival in Paris two years earlier. This happened during a visit to the Salon de la Nationale with a friend—"an American painter," he wrote, without identifying him—and the latter had drawn his attention to a small group of paintings. In contrast to Lyman, who knew nothing about Morrice, his friend seemed to know him well. The two visitors then discussed whether living the life of an "artiste maudit"—a tragic cursed figure—was a requirement for success. Absorbed by this question, the friend had studied the careers of a few great masters of painting to finally conclude that it was not necessary to live a life of debauchery to become a great artist. However, looking at Morrice's works, he exclaimed that he would be perfectly prepared to take up whiskey if that was what it took to paint as well as the Canadian. Much later, Lyman recounted this anecdote, concluding, not without irony: "Each man followed his destiny. My friend remained abstemious, and Morrice became a great painter."[41]

From then on, John Lyman expressed unconditional admiration for James Wilson Morrice. He described one of the six paintings exhibited in 1907 at the Salon de la Nationale that so impressed him: "It was a view of the St. Lawrence during the spring ice break-up, with the water sweeping the chunks of ice along. It looked almost clumsy, unfinished in contrast to paintings in this salon. And yet, this was the only memory that stayed with me."[42] Identified as *Le Bac* in the salon catalogue **(CAT. 5)**, the painting was inspired by a small study in oils that Morrice had painted ten years earlier in 1897, during a stay in the Quebec City region with his friend Maurice Cullen.[43] The painting is of the ferry that connects Lévis to Quebec City, at the crossing's halfway point, steaming forward, its smokestack puffing, through the ice floes blocking its passage. The composition revisits a scene made famous many times since the eighteenth century by Canadian and foreign painters because of its picturesque character. Morrice emphasized the spectacular effect of Cap Diamant in Quebec City, the "Gibraltar of North America," by apparently reorganizing the setting to balance the coloured shapes.[44] The painting retains the essential aspects of the elements in the study: the organization of the space into four horizontal bands, depicting, from bottom to top, first the banks of the south shore dotted with people, sleighs drawn by horses and ferry terminal buildings that create the only diagonal lines in the painting. These lines lead the eye toward the river and the ferry. The cloud of swirling black smoke crosses the third band showing Quebec City buried in snow, and connects the river to the greyish band of a March sky, at the top of the composition, from whence heavy flakes fall on this surprisingly luminous landscape.

Some motifs are just signs, dark marks that nonetheless manage to evoke the passengers waiting for the ferry on the Lévis wharves. The black lines and grey strokes roughly denote the vast space which, instead of suggesting remoteness, is overshadowed by the foil effect of the promontory's white shape. For his large composition, the painter preferred a light application of colour to the impasto technique used in the study, creating a transparent and fluid effect and hinting at the primed canvas beneath the colourful surface. Morrice used this technique to emphasize the radiant whiteness of the snow and ice.

The effect of *The Ferry* is far removed from that of the "quiet" Impressionism with Whistlerian touches that made Morrice well-known among Paris's collectors and critics. *Autumn* **(CAT. 9)**, exhibited near *The Ferry* at the Salon de la Nationale in 1907, corresponds more closely to this tried and true style. Its light gives a delicate iridescence, by means of countless scattered strokes, to the trees lining one of the pathways in the Jardin du Luxembourg. The work was noticed by critic Maurice Guillemot, who had only these words for the Canadian at this salon: "By Morice *[sic]*, a path in the park, very delicate in feeling."[45]

Beginning in 1899 and up to 1911, the Salon de la Nationale exhibited snow scenes by Morrice, slightly more than a dozen winter compositions, with the majority shown between 1906 and 1909. At the 1906 salon, the artist was nicknamed "Our Lady of the Snows," as he exhibited only "snow effects."[46] When the event was over, one of his paintings, *Snow Effect (Sleigh)* (**CAT. 6**), went to the Musée des beaux-arts de Lyon. The work would only cross the Atlantic for display in Canada twice: for the commemorative exhibition organized by the National Gallery of Canada in 1937-1938,[47] and in 2014, for our own exhibition *Morrice and Lyman in the Company of Matisse*.

During the winter of 1905-1906, an especially cold winter in Montreal and Quebec City, the artist did several oil sketches on this theme, including a night scene with sleigh.[48] The Montreal art dealer William Watson would later remember Morrice complaining about how difficult it was to paint outdoors in the cold, and about stiffening paint and numb hands, to the point where "one could hardly feel what was being painted."[49] Yet the winter scene entitled *Snow Effect (Sleigh)*, unidentifiable and highly simplified, gives the impression that Morrice actually imagined the sketch in his Paris studio, inspired by his drawings.[50] This studio creation marked the rebirth of pictorial space in Morrice's work. A very powerful blue, its effect heightened by its proximity to the snow-covered ground, with opalescent strokes here and there, almost makes us forget the house and sleigh motifs and focus entirely on the painting's formal qualities, its chromatic structure, and the fluidity and density of the medium.

In 1907, looking at *The Ferry, Quebec*, Lyman discovered a composition in which the effects of synthesis and permanence contrasted with the Impressionist painting that had so fascinated him in Montreal the year before, with its multitude of small, thick and light-filled strokes trying to capture the moment. Without doubt, Lyman found something of himself in this winter scene. However, rather than savouring its picturesque regionalism, he was especially intrigued by its cursory style, which perfectly communicated "the dull poetry of the Quebec winter."[51] Lyman realized that simplifying and balancing coloured shapes in a landscape in no way lessened a painter's feelings about his subject.

He was not the only one to be charmed by Morrice's snow scenes in Paris. Another Canadian, Clarence Gagnon,[52] who had arrived in the capital in 1904, was greatly impressed by the delicacy of the sketches he had seen in the Paris salons and the painter's studio. Gagnon's fascination with Morrice's work is glimpsed in his own colourful studies, impressions delicately recorded on small wooden panels while he was walking and strolling around Paris and Venice. In Canada, Clarence Gagnon would become the painter of winter's brilliant light, like Marc-Aurèle de Foy Suzor-Coté and Maurice Cullen, who chose this season to express their Impressionist vision of the Canadian landscape.

/ CAT. 6 James W. Morrice
Snow Effect (Sleigh)
1906

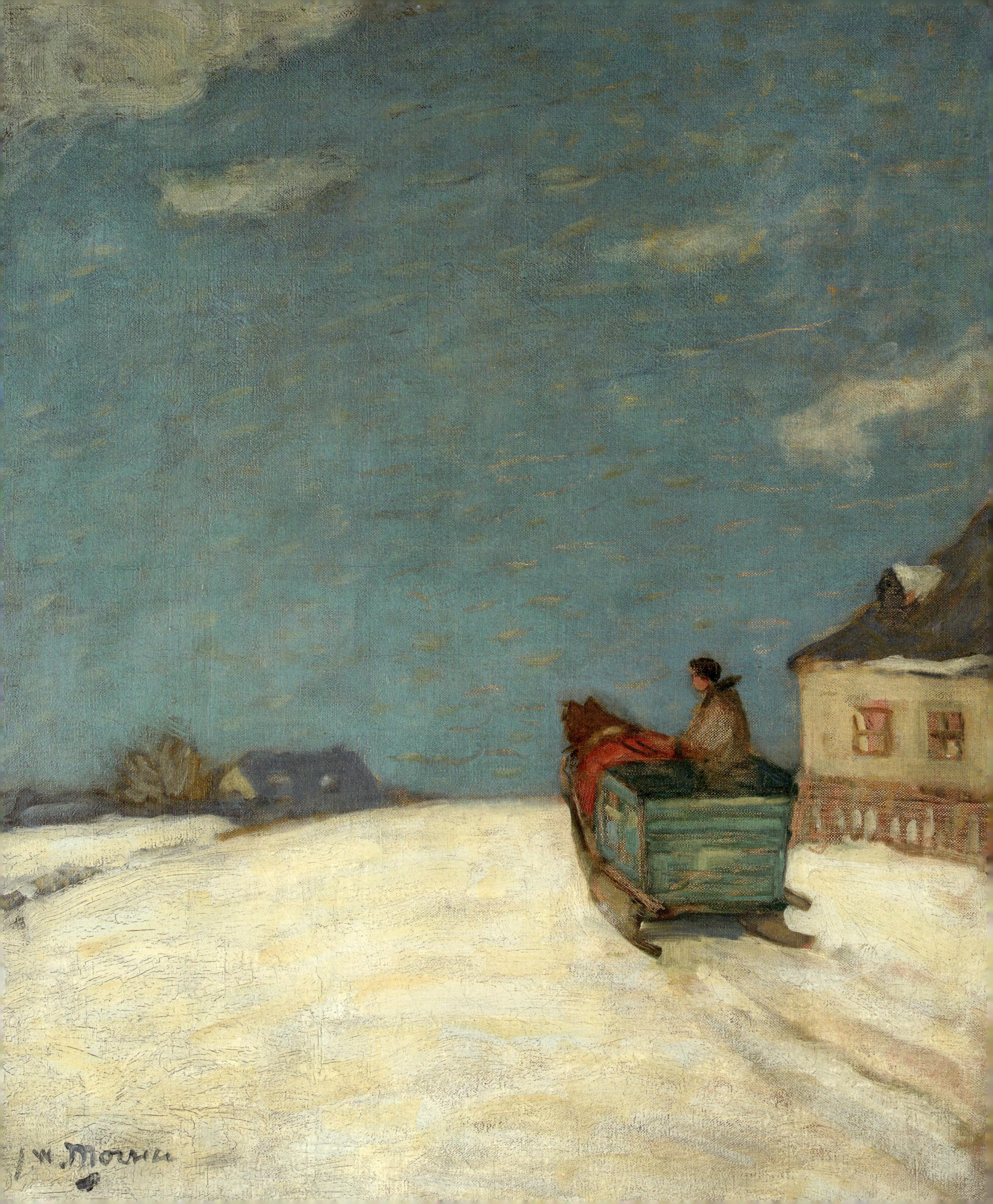

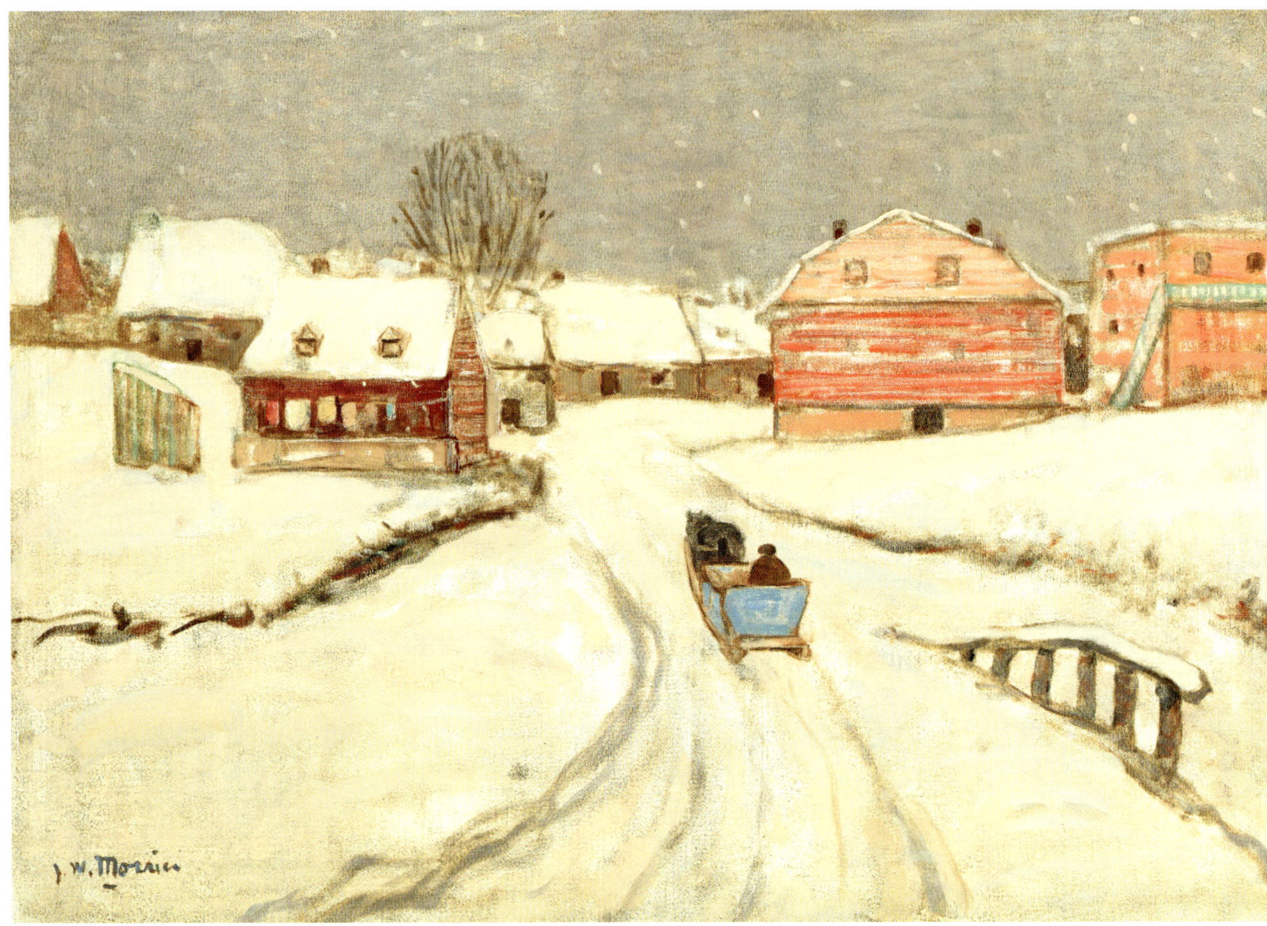

Lyman continued to make the rounds of the salons, which encouraged his tendency toward expression and simple techniques, qualities he had appreciated in Morrice's art. In the spring of 1909, the powerful intensity of the painting in a composition by Henri Matisse also fascinated him. *Autumn Landscape: Forest of Fontainebleau* (**FIG. 23**), shown at the Salon des Indépendants, haunted his dreams. He later wrote, "I'd already heard about Matisse, but it was the first time I'd seen any of his paintings, and I was by myself when I saw them . . . It gave me nightmares, I dreamt about it all night afterwards."[53]

That same year, at the Salon de la Nationale, Lyman again fell under the spell of Morrice's winter scenes. In a letter he sent to his father, he said nothing about his visit to the Indépendants, nor about the revelation he had experienced while looking at Matisse's landscape a few weeks earlier. The two salons he mentioned in his letter were the Artistes français and the Nationale: "For myself, I enjoy J. W. Morrice's exhibit *more than anything else in the two Salons* [the emphasis is Lyman's]. One is a picture of a Canadian village in winter in a tone of remarkable perfection in a pearly-pink note, perhaps the most pleasurable thing of his I have seen; another looking across from Quebec to Levis in winter, in wonderful blues."[54]

These works by Morrice had also attracted the attention of Paris critics. In *La Nouvelle Revue*, Henri Chervet agreed with Lyman that *Entrance to a Quebec Village* (**CAT. 7**) was very appealing, "with its houses so wonderfully pink."[55] Maurice Hamel, in *Les Arts*, was equally delighted by the "soft whiteness" of the snow contrasting with the "singing blues of the waterways flowing through Quebec."[56]

/ **CAT. 7** James W. Morrice
Entrance to a Quebec Village
1909

/ **CAT. 8** James W. Morrice
View towards Lévis from Québec
1909

For his part, Louis Vauxcelles described as "jewels Morrice's Canadian and Parisian settings, whose freedom, still, seems out of place here."[57] The critic admired the delicate pictorial qualities in Morrice's art. The same year in which he disparagingly characterized Room VII at the 1905 Salon d'Automne as "la cage aux fauves"—the cage of wild beasts—in reference to the outrageously colourful paintings on exhibit, he had noticed in the room next door the Canadian's "three small paintings," which he compared to "jewels that Boudin would have liked."[58]

The painting entitled *Québec*, and known today as *View towards Lévis from Québec* (**CAT. 8**), expresses freedom, a quality that did not escape Vauxcelles' notice. As with *The Ferry, Quebec*, which is approximately the same size, this painting glorifies the "magnificent" blues of the St. Lawrence, filling the middle ground of the composition. Morrice painted his sketch on Dufferin Terrace, on Quebec's north shore, choosing a point of view across from that of the 1907 scene. The view of the less rugged heights of the Lévis landscape inspired a simple formal organization, marked by wide horizontal bands. These extend beyond the limits of the painting, crossing it from one side to the other, to left and right, giving the impression of virtually extending the landscape. Aside from two people and their footprints in the snow, the rare motifs evoking human presence are limited to smoking chimneys and St. Joseph's Church at the summit of the Lévis skyline.

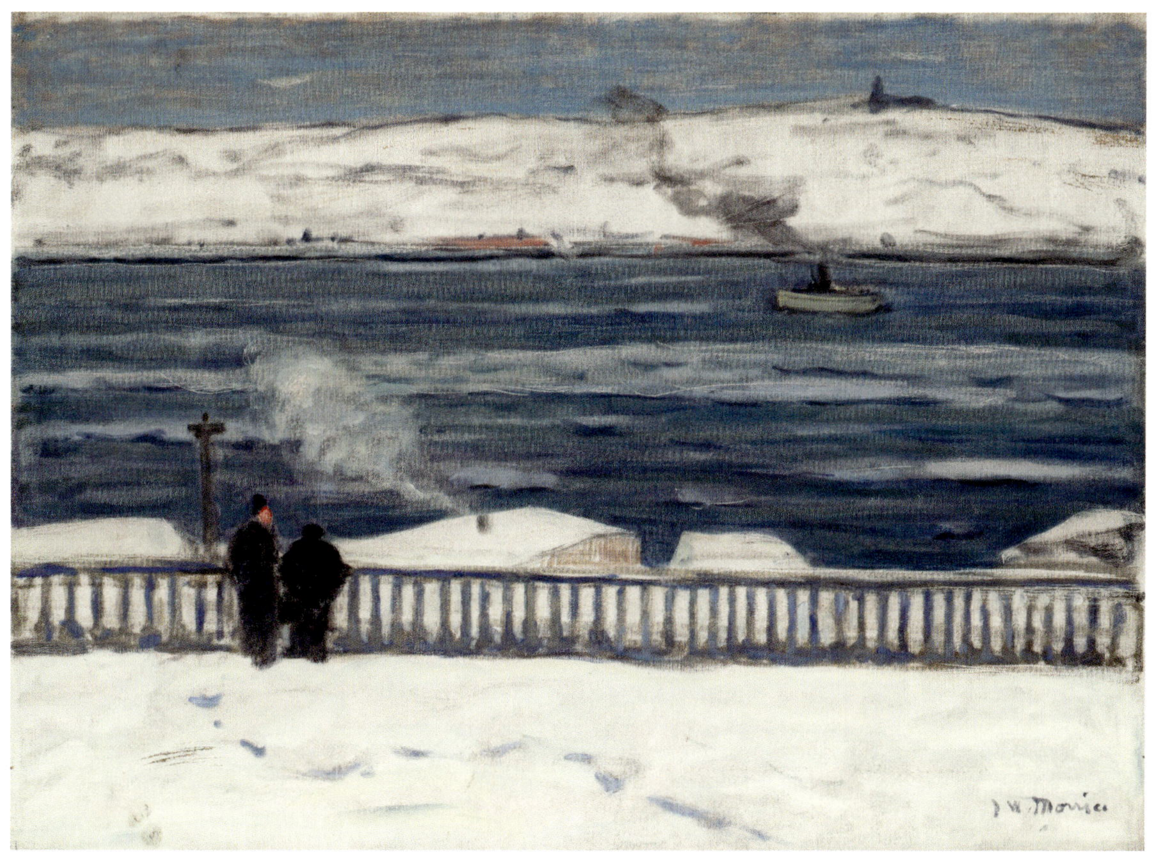

When Vauxcelles wrote that Morrice "is out of place here," it may be supposed that he was wondering whether the Canadian was suited to the Salon de la Nationale; this salon, in 1909, no longer showed the same openness as when it was founded in 1890, and it was clearly out of touch with new trends that had found a home at the Salon des Indépendants and the Salon d'Automne. Did Vauxcelles feel that Morrice's work more closely resembled works currently being shown in these two salons?

At this point in our story, it's time to determine Morrice's place in the rich and diverse landscape of the avant-garde movements.

MORRICE'S CONNECTIONS TO WHISTLER, CÉZANNE, BONNARD AND MATISSE

Morrice's modernism was in line with movements developing in artistic circles at the turn of the century and in the pre-war period. Unfortunately, the painter never spoke out publicly about his own conception of his art, leaving it to his work to express "his sensitive and poetic discoveries," as John Lyman later wrote.[59] In the 1890s, Morrice's paintings displayed the sober harmonies and refined aesthetic of Whistler, followed by, in the first decade of the twentieth century, the use of rich and contrasting colours applied in thin layers, as seen in *Red House, Venice* (CAT. 10).

CONNECTIONS TO WHISTLER

As a young artist working in Paris at the end of the nineteenth century, Morrice was won over by Whistler's doctrine of "art for art's sake," which considered figurative motifs like so many harmonic arrangements of tones, while remaining faithful to painting's unique means of expression. This idea echoed the synthetism of Paul Gauguin and the Nabis,[60] who had decreed—with Maurice Denis as the mouthpiece—that a painting was essentially "a flat surface covered with colours assembled in a particular way." The first lines of an article by Louis Vauxcelles, in December 1909, pointed to Morrice as Whistler's successor: "Since the death of James McNeill Whistler, Morrice is unquestionably the American painter . . . who has achieved . . . the most notable and well-merited place in the world of art."[61] The Canadian rejected this comparison, calling it absurd.[62] On reading the article, we understand it is to Morrice's "eminently personal" freedom of expression that Vauxcelles is paying homage, and to his painting, which "focusses on the essential." This is what makes him "neither a portraitist nor a landscapist—simply a painter, and one of the best of to-day."[63]

CONNECTIONS TO CÉZANNE

A few terse comments by Morrice give us insight into his artistic preferences. For example, the work of Paul Cézanne inspired him in 1910 to make this incisive remark: "Fine work almost criminally fine."[64] He admitted at the same time that at one point he did not like Cézanne's paintings, but that now he "liked them all."

/ **CAT. 9** James W. Morrice
Autumn
1906-1907

Next double page:

/ **CAT. 10** James W. Morrice
Red House, Venice
About 1906

/ **CAT. 11** James W. Morrice
Venice at the Golden Hour
About 1901-1902

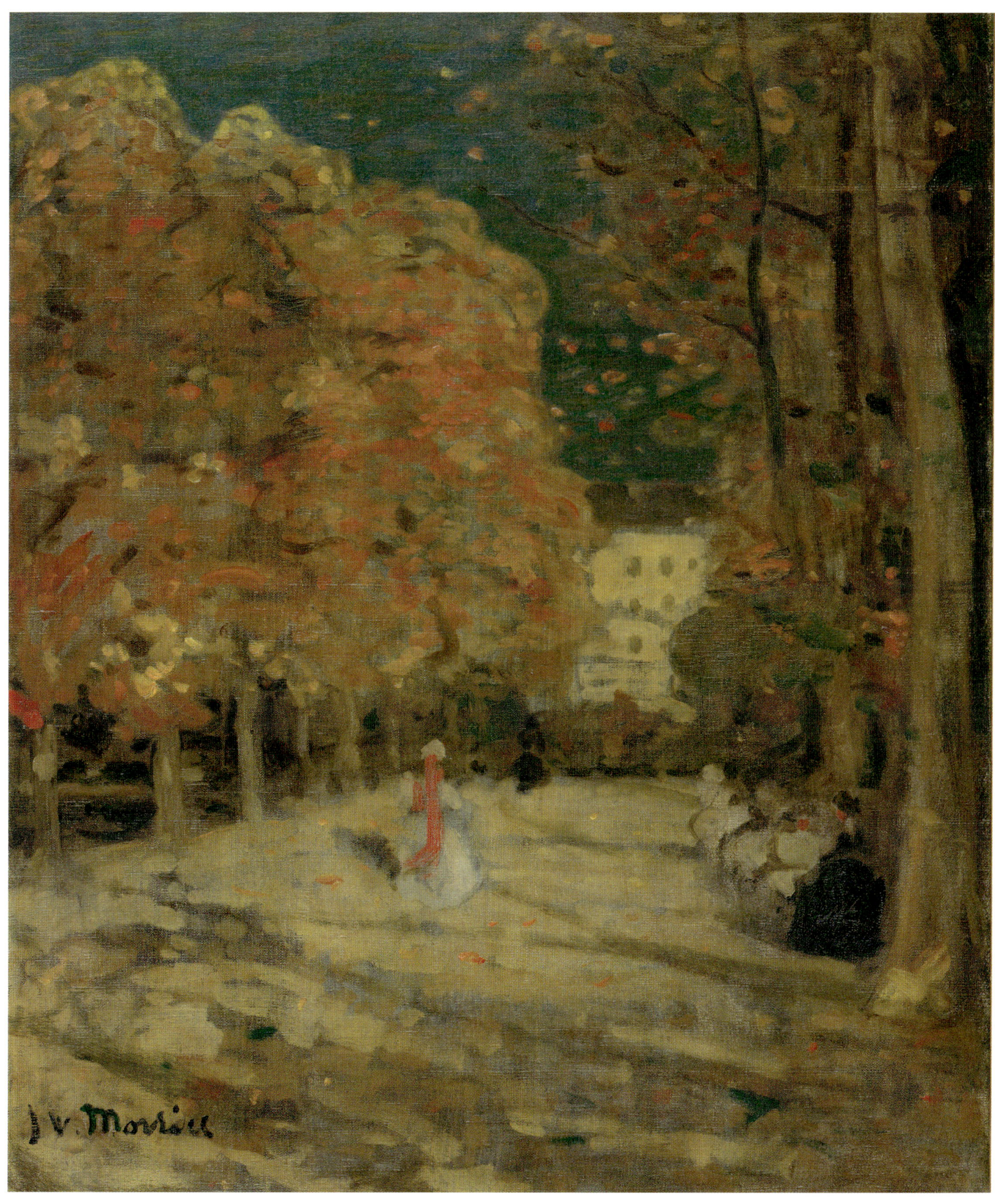

J. V. Morice

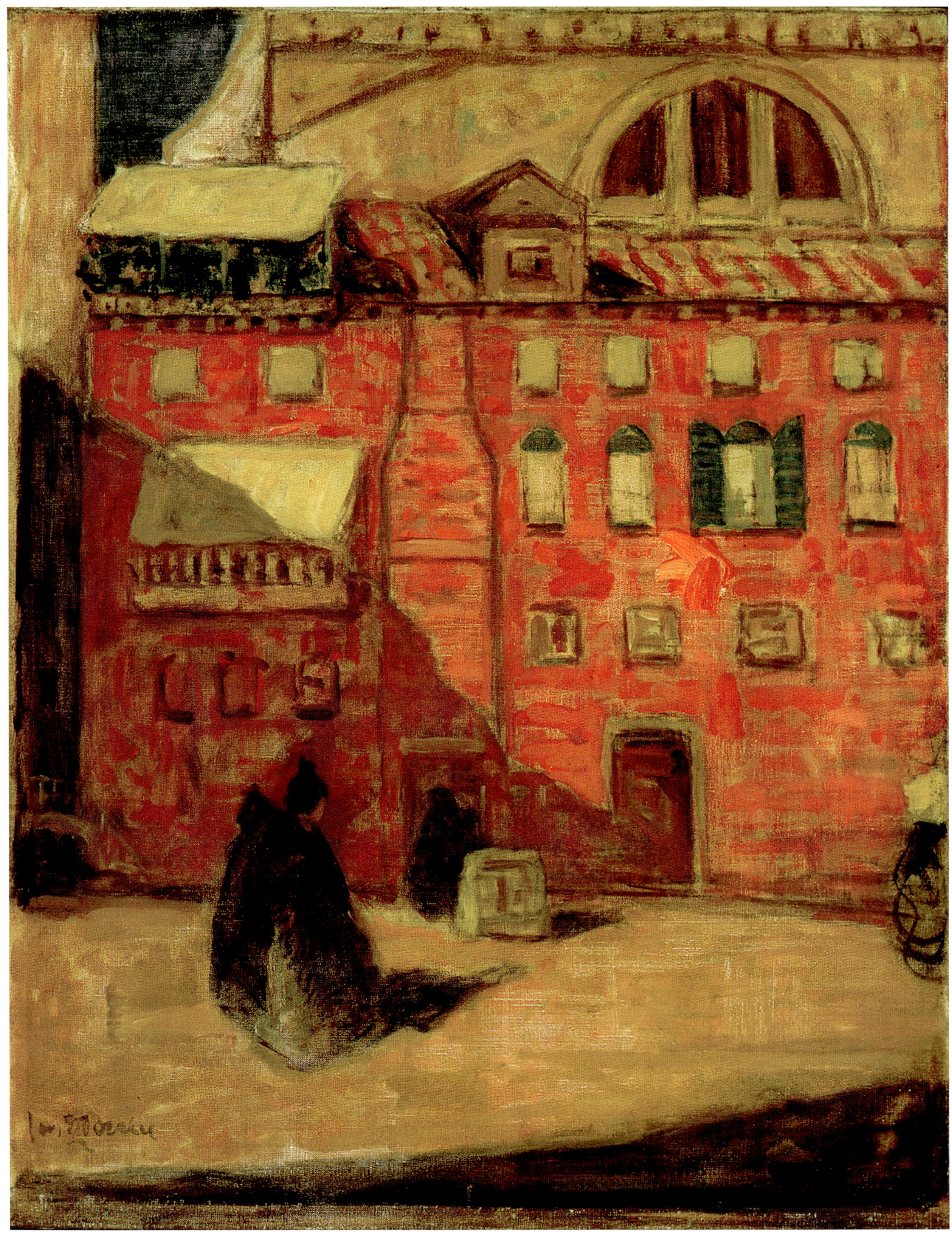

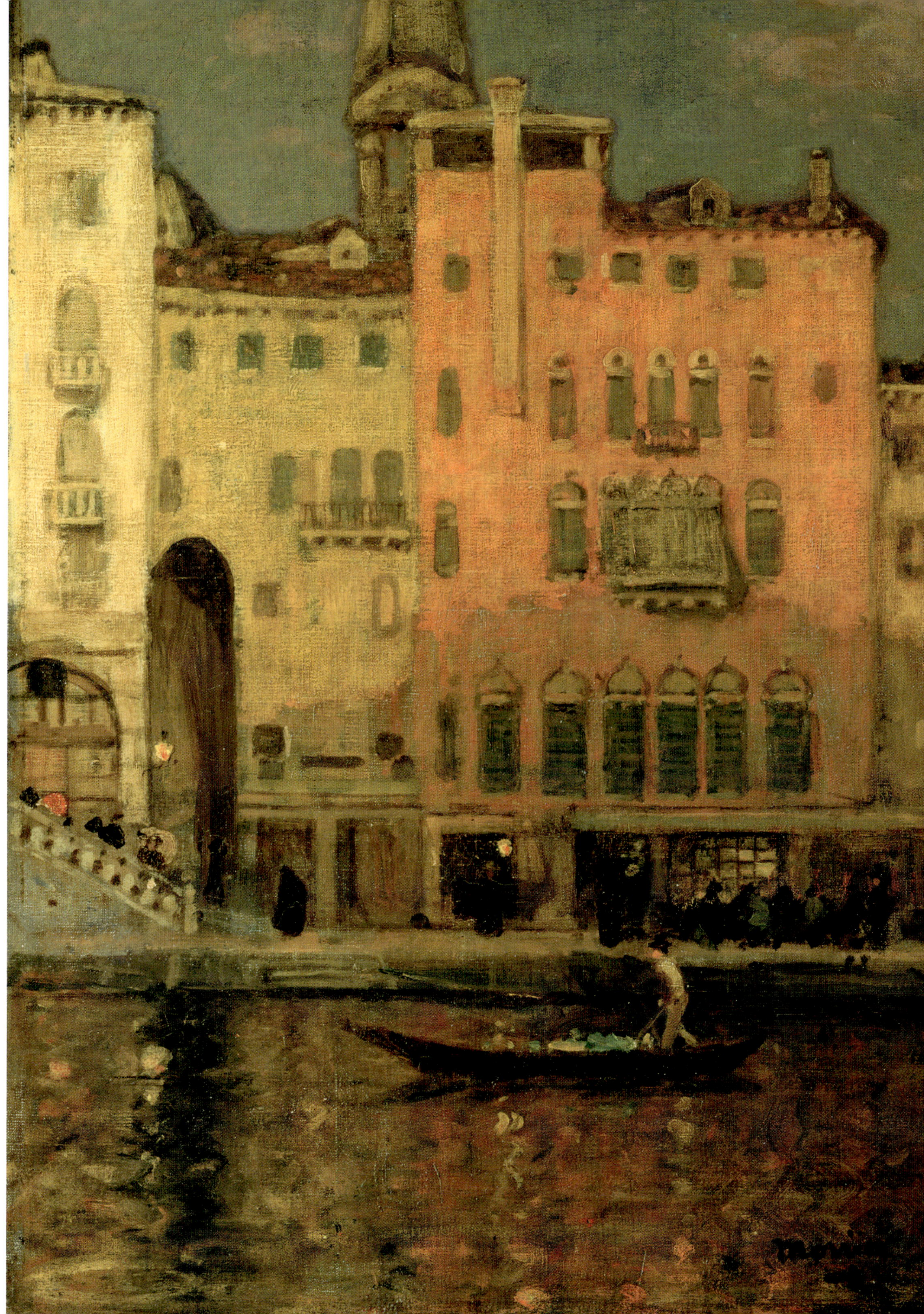

In 1906, following the death of the master from Aix, a series of exhibitions were held in the capital to pay homage to the artist, the central figure of Post-Impressionism. This movement soon found expression in two large exhibitions organized by British artist and critic Roger Fry, assisted with the second by Clive Bell, and presented in 1910 and 1912 at the Grafton Galeries in London.[65] The exhibition brought together various turn-of-the-century movements that looked beyond the fleetingness of appearances—glorified by Impressionist painting and its changing light—and paved the way for new aesthetic approaches. Although Morrice did not participate in these exhibitions, he remarked briefly on the reception given to the first: "There was some excitement in London last month over the exhibition called the *Post Impressionists*. Everybody laughed and jeered." He continued by saying that "with a few exceptions it consisted of good things. Art that will last."[66] This recognition of Cézanne's work may be taken as the point of departure for our reflection on the Canadian artist's modernism.

Paul Cézanne had always taken counsel from nature, paying attention to the lessons painting could learn from it, and to the need for the painter to organize his own sensations with respect to it. His famous saying, "treat nature by means of the cylinder, the sphere, the cone," made him the precursor of Cubism. Furthermore, the determining influence he had on Henri Matisse and, by extension, on Fauvism cannot be ignored. Indeed, Matisse had observed Cézanne's work with admiration, long before his death. In 1899, while barely earning enough from his art to live on, he allowed himself to buy his *Three Bathers*, which he kept all his life. In "Notes of a Painter," first published by Matisse in 1908, in which he set out his artistic approach,[67] there are many references to the painter of Mont Sainte-Victoire. Like Cézanne, Matisse stressed the importance of observing nature: "Those who work . . . deliberately turning their back on nature, are in error." He shared his admiration for the qualities of order and clarity of the master from Aix: "All is so well arranged in them that no matter how many figures are represented and no matter at what distance you stand, you will be able always to distinguish each figure clearly and you will always know which limb belongs to which body." These qualities must pre-exist in the painter's mind; from the moment he imagines his painting, the artist must be aware of them. Matisse also opposed to the changing appearance of nature and the fleeting sensations of Impressionist painting his more lasting interpretation of reality, based on the true and essential character of beings and things.

CONNECTIONS TO MATISSE AND THE 1908 SALON D'AUTOMNE

Clive Bell, a London art historian and influential critic of the avant-garde, wrote in his memoirs that it was to Morrice he owed his having noticed Matisse,[68] when he was studying in Paris. Morrice was therefore aware of Matisse's modernism as early as the first decade of the century. While there is no written text to tell us what he thought of the French painter, there is, on the other hand, one event that lets us shed light on the relationship the Canadian had with Matisse, with whom he would spend time in North Africa a few years later. The year 1908 was a busy one for the French painter, a pivotal year,[69] in which he opened his academy, published "Notes of a Painter" and exhibited some thirty works at the Salon d'Automne (paintings, drawings and sculptures).[70] A few months earlier, in April 1908, Matisse and Morrice

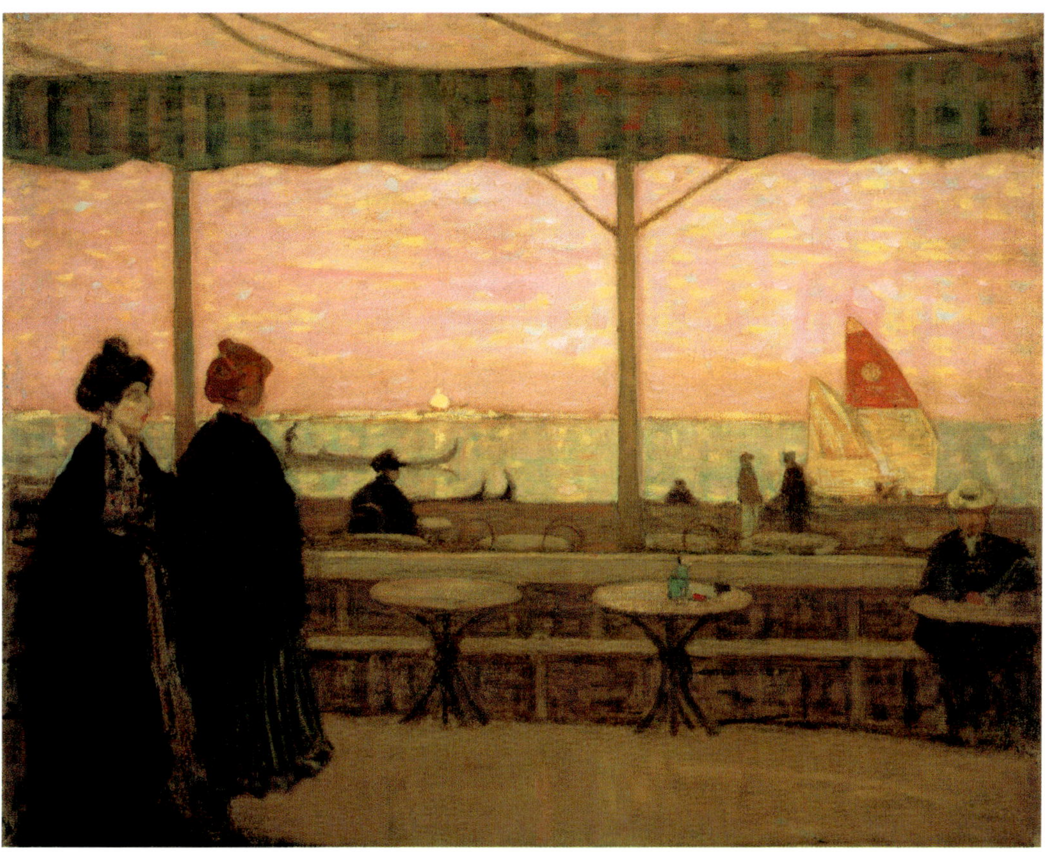

had both been elected, by lottery, as members of the salon's jury.[71] They thus found themselves at the same table in September, alongside the twenty-two other jury members in the painting section; this section had the most members, compared with the sculpture, architecture, drawing, engraving and decorative arts sections. Under the chairmanship of Henri Lebasque, a Post-Impressionist painter whose career had been followed for several years in the capital's various salons, Morrice and Albert Marquet served as vice-presidents of the jury, while John Lavery, Henri Matisse[72] and Georges Rouault were among the members in the painting section.

What kind of relationship existed between Morrice and Matisse at that time? Did they discuss their painting with each other? Did they only exchange a few words? There is no mention whatsoever. All we have is a list in the catalogue, with their names one after the other. Some twenty days after the salon opened, Morrice wrote to Edmund Morris: "I was on the jury this year. There are a few good things but a frightful amount of trash. Henri's pictures were refused. This will be an awful blow to New York."[73] More concerned by the rejection of works by his American friend Robert Henri, Morrice said nothing about the dramatic gesture by Georges Braque, who, when the jury turned down a composition he had painted at l'Estaque, withdrew all of his works from the exhibition. His protest would crystalize the hostility between "Picassoists" and "Matissists," as Gertrude Stein liked to call them.[74] The day after the salon ended, Braque presented twenty-seven paintings to Henry Kahnweiler's gallery, thus signalling the beginnings of Cubism.

In reality, there is no factual basis for dwelling on the relationship between Morrice and Matisse before their sojourn in Tangier in 1912. If there is any connection to be made before that year, it is found in the paintings themselves, even though their styles seem very far apart, as evidenced by the images in the paintings done by

/ **CAT. 12** James W. Morrice
Venice, Looking Out over the Lagoon
About 1904

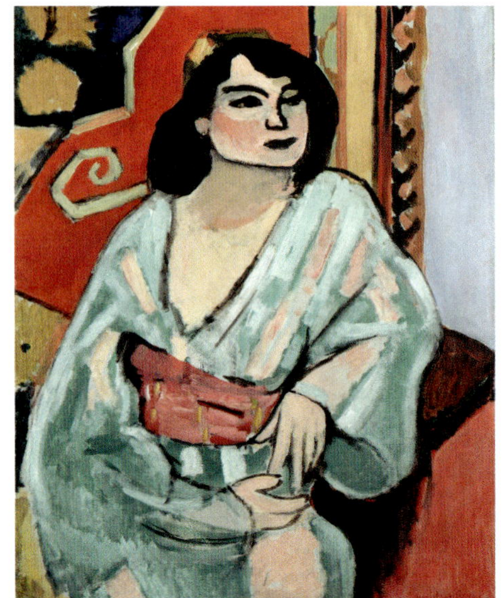

Matisse from 1906 to 1908 to illustrate "Notes of a Painter": *The Reader*, three female nudes, their bodies outlined in large brushstrokes, *Portrait of Greta Moll* and *Game of Bowls* **(FIG. 2)**. The highly modernist expression of the landscape and bodies in the latter painting foreshadow Matisse's work on the large decorative compositions *Dance* and *Music*, painted in the subsequent two years to fulfill a commission from the Russian businessman and art collector Sergei Shchukin, for his palatial residence in Moscow. At the time Matisse was carrying out these commissions, Morrice was a thousand miles away from monumental art; he was still excelling in the small-sized works that had made his reputation on the European scene. He would always confine himself to easel painting, with the exception of one mural he was commissioned to do in 1917, in the context of Canada's War Memorial program.

This was certainly not the only aesthetic difference between the Canadian's work and that of the Frenchman before their meeting in Tangier in 1912, where Morrice's painting would become brighter than it had ever been. For several years, however, Morrice had been experimenting with more permanent plastic signs and decorative unity in his painting, qualities that had been present since 1904, in *Venice, Looking Out over the Lagoon* **(CAT. 12)**, for example, or in *Dieppe* from about 1906 **(CAT. 106)**. Heading into the second decade of the century, Morrice painted a few portraits that hinted at Matisse's influence and the thoughts Matisse had expressed in 1908 concerning his approach and understanding of the aesthetic of his era. The French painter was then at a crossroads in his development; he had been profoundly shaken by the emergence of Cubism, a new movement about which Morrice admitted he could understand nothing.[75] Matisse's thinking was rooted in the idea that a painting must above all embody the relationship between the painter and nature, by erasing any distinction between his feelings about life and the way he portrays them. Using only the techniques of painting, the work should try to express a holistic harmony to transmit the intensity of the many sensations that inspired the artist. "The simplest means are those which enable an artist to express himself best," he wrote in "Notes of a Painter."

Despite the distance between them, Morrice was drawing closer to Matisse and his principles by observing the work of the Nabi Pierre Bonnard.

CONNECTIONS TO BONNARD

Morrice admired not only Matisse and Cézanne but also Bonnard, sharing with all of them the idea that artistic expression should be lasting and permanent. A Nabi, to convey his feelings toward his subject, claimed to have to get away from it and reconstruct it from a distance, "sheltered by his recollection of it."[76] Immediately after Fauvism's peak in 1905, Pierre Bonnard had drawn closer to Matisse. His work at the time is illuminated by a shimmering and unifying light, penetrating interiors through recurring open doors and windows. The luminous and sensual materials thus project a feeling of sumptuousness and decorative proliferation. This was the effect of the two nudes Bonnard submitted to the Salon d'Automne jury in 1908: *Nude against Daylight* and *Mirror on the Wash Stand*. Morrice, a member of this jury, was able to examine these compositions, both awash in diffuse light, closely. He had apparently not forgotten the nude seen from the back reflected in the mirror when he painted, some years later, his *Standing Nude, from the Back*, now part of the Art Gallery of Ontario collection.

/ **FIG. 1** Henri Matisse
Algerian Woman
1909

/ **CAT. 13** James W. Morrice
Olympia
About 1912

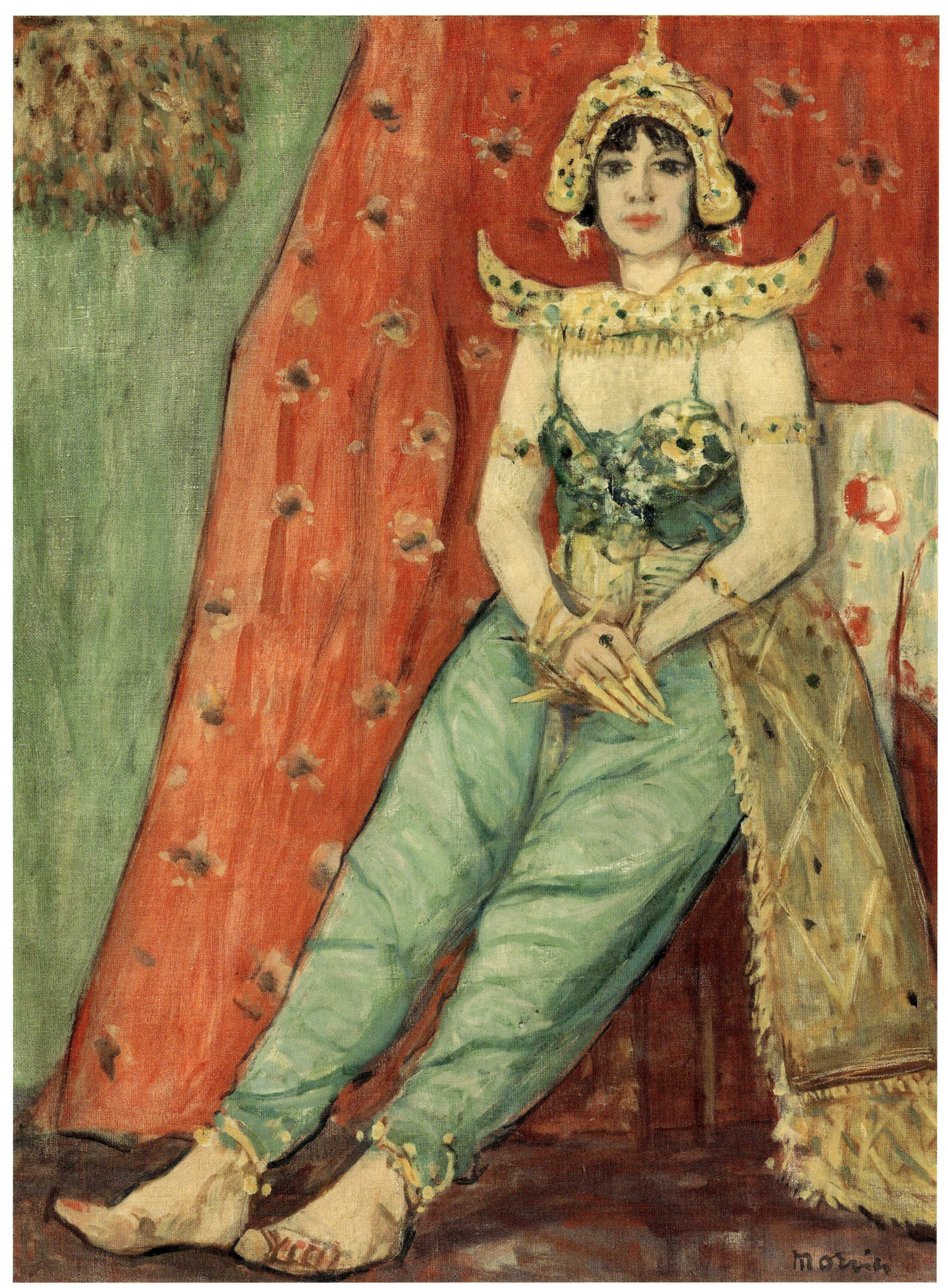
Morrice

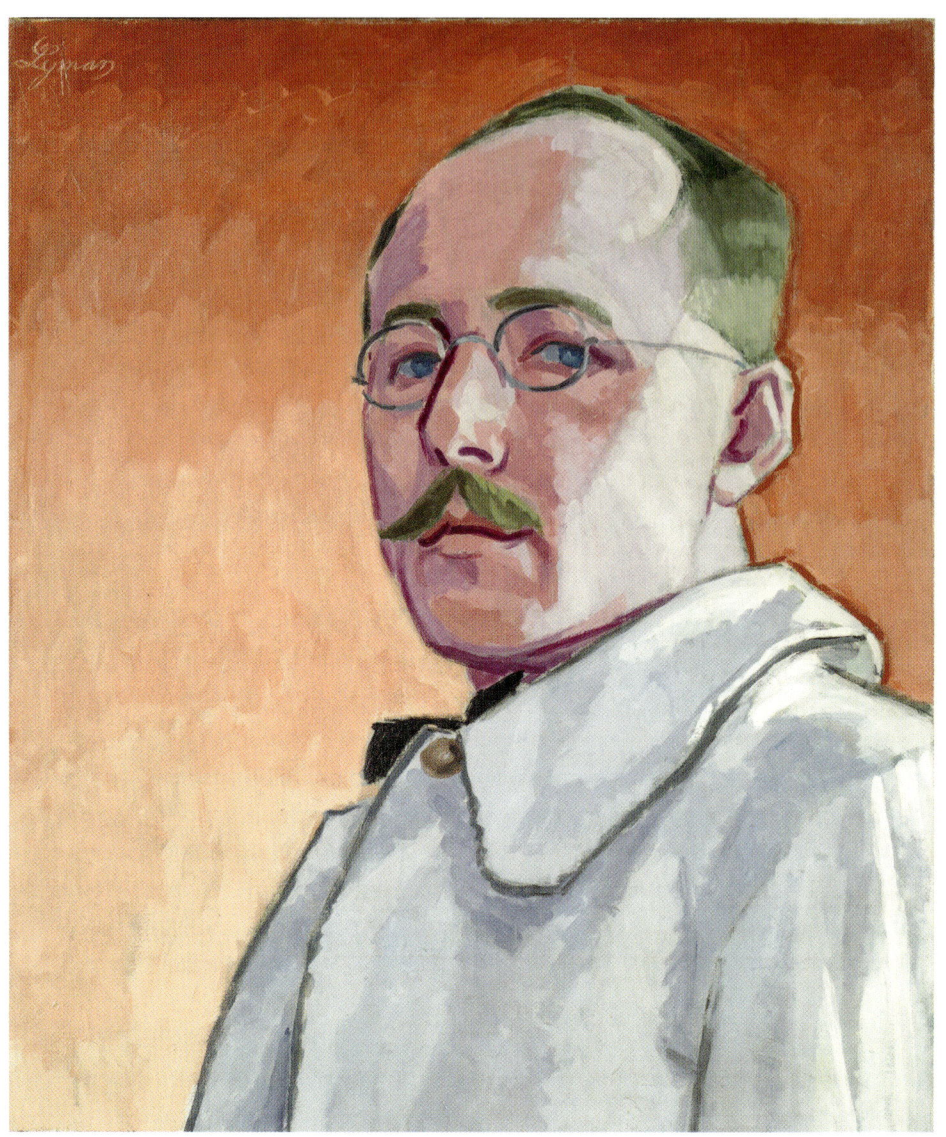

/ **CAT. 14** John Lyman
Self-portrait
1918

In May and June 1911, the Galerie Bernheim-Jeune exhibited twenty-eight of Bonnard's paintings. The exhibition filled Morrice with enthusiasm and he wrote to his friend Edmund Morris: "[Bonnard] is the best man here now, since Gauguin died."[77] At the time, Morrice's style converged with that of Bonnard in several compositions of figures and in an intimist and decorative still life (**CATS. 67, 68, 100** and **101**). His approach can be examined by looking first at two portraits painted at a time when his palette was becoming vibrantly brighter, as a result of his use of complementary colours. The crimson backdrop in *Nude with a Feather* (**CAT. 101**) presents a perfect synthesis of everything the Canadian had learned during two decades of exile in the French capital. With touches of Japonisme and Whistlerian refinement, the work projects a feeling of intimacy and reminds us somewhat of the interiors done by the Nabi painters, Bonnard among them. We note the way the painting's harmony echoes this very private character that everything seems to accentuate, from the tight frame around the model, to her pose, in which she is entirely absorbed by her gesture, and including the warm, matte colours. Flower and butterfly motifs enliven the vertical bands in the background and highlight the ornamental setting, also reflected in the red garment covered in formless shapes. The dressing gown sliding off the model's shoulders reveals the whiteness of flesh tones against a spotless veil, on the lower half of the body. And as though the painting's coloured paste were not enough to capture the light, the painter turned his brush over and scraped away the thinly applied medium, to reveal the underlying luminosity.

In the painting entitled *Olympia* (**CAT. 13**), which specialists date from several months after *Nude with a Feather*, the subject emerges from private space to show a dancer wearing a Siamese costume. To make this portrait appear more official, Morrice presents his model standing up, lightly supported by what we imagine to be a chair, her face turned toward the viewer. The setting's flamboyant fabrics, enhanced with embroidery and satiny effects, create a sensuous surface for the eye, as do the dancer's costume and sparkling accessories. Despite the predominance of this decorative fantasy, in which Bonnard's influence can be seen, there is a sense of solidity in the composition, stemming from the even balance of chromatic areas and the outline around the figure that separates it from the background. With *Olympia*, Morrice's painting sets off in a new direction: toward Matisse. Had he seen the paintings the French master had painted in 1909 and 1911, *Algerian Woman* (**FIG. 1**), *Spanish Woman with a Tambourine* and *Madame Matisse with Manila Shawl*, as art historian Nicole Cloutier suggests?[78] It cannot be denied that Morrice's style is similar to that of Matisse, with the painting's shapes mainly enlivened by colour.

LYMAN: "PARIS HAS MADE ME"

In the three years he had been living in Paris, John Lyman had written in his letters to his father about the admiration he felt for Morrice. This correspondence also sheds light on his evolution in the world of modern Parisian painting. The letters written at the end of the few weeks he spent at the Académie Matisse in May 1910 are sprinkled with passages forcefully defending the innovative values of painting. "Change is the sign of growth, vitality & health," he wrote, while recognizing that many modern works were devoid of artistic intention. This realization led him to draw a line between art and "non-art": "Art is the expression by signs of an intellectual state; in painting, the expression of an intellectual perception induced by visual phenomena. Anything lacking in this intention verges on the 'trompe-l'oeil' which is the antithesis of art."[79] These letters also make an argument for the dominant position of Paris in the art world, in contrast to the North American capitals his family seemed to want him to return to. Lyman strongly defended Paris's life-affirming atmosphere and how privileged he was to be studying there:

> A statement of these privileges seems almost too obvious. America *never could have* [Lyman's emphasis] a collection approaching that of The Louvre, unless the Louvre were transfered bodily to America. Then think of all the other musées, the private collections of Durand-Ruel, Vollard, the Norwegian Consul, Stein, Bernheim. Why one El Greco in the Louvre, one Cézanne at Stein's, are worth the entire Metropolitan. Then let mention a few of the artists who have been given small exhibitions this winter alone—Toulouse-Lautrec, Gauguin, Manet, Renoir, Matisse, Valotton, Cézanne, Delacroix, Manguin, Courbet, Nadelmann, Van Dongen, Van Gogh—I have picked out only the notable ones.[80]

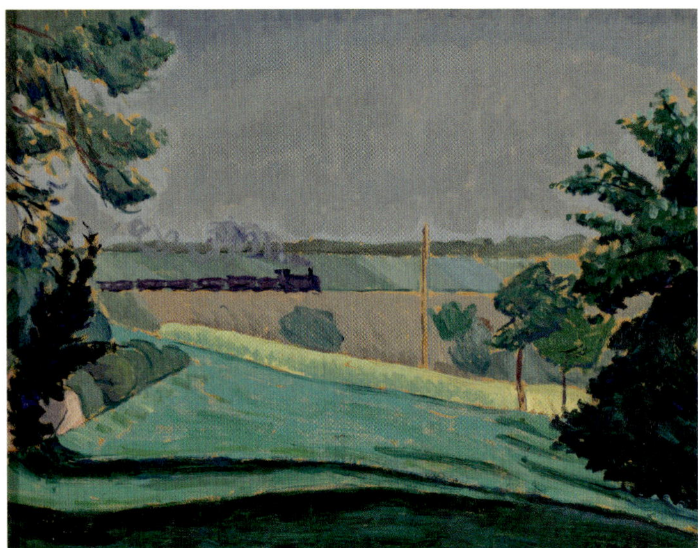

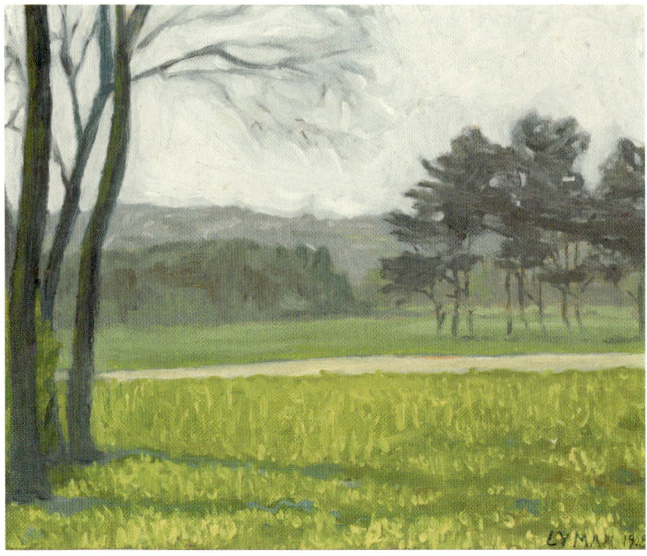

Ten years later, he reiterated his feeling of belonging in the city: "All I believe in and aspire to is here."[81] Paris had not only shaped his thinking about art and life, it had also honed his ability to grasp the issues of modern art from a universal point of view and to defend its principles, both through painting and writing.[82] In contrast to his compatriot Morrice, Lyman was perfectly bilingual; he spoke and argued with ease and self-confidence in French. When he quoted the words of Irish novelist and poet George Moore, "Paris has made me," every word referred to himself.[83] These words found their equivalent artistic expression in the remarkable *Self-portrait* (**CAT. 14**), which he completed at the end of the 1910s and which shows the painter's aesthetic transformation. Lyman was thirty-two at the time. His portrait is one of the first examples of "shock art" in modern Canadian art: the work has become an icon. The abandonment of natural shades in favour of bold colours (pink highlighted with white and purplish-blue for the face, green for the hair and moustache), the contour line that throws the shapes into relief against a background of red-orange shadings, all the elements making up this new and strictly decorative harmony profoundly connect Lyman's work with Matisse's. In Montreal, however, these chromatic harmonies were deemed to be discordant, with Fernand Préfontaine stating in the monthly *Le Nigog*: "My pleasure in seeing [Lyman's] work is spoiled by this use of unpleasant tones."[84] And this was the mouthpiece of the most progressive criticism of the period. This kind of welcome made Lyman decide to stop showing his work in Canada for several years.

What effect did Paris have on Lyman? In his first works, of which only a few have come down to us, the young painter shows a fondness for painting media generously applied on small wooden panels. In this, he followed in the footsteps of Morrice and Clarence Gagnon, both of whom preferred this format. In Lyman's painting, the thick impasto typical of Impressionist painting provided a variety of textures. He made the most of this by using energetic strokes or more uniform shapes. *Early Spring* from 1908 (**CAT. 16**) is mainly composed of horizontal bands intersected by a few trees that give life to the landscape. The vitality of this view of the French countryside, captured in the first clear and vibrant days of the season of renewal, owes a great deal to the expressiveness of the medium and its distinctive handling: the vertical strokes in the foreground give way to the homogeneous

/ **CAT. 15** John Lyman
Swiss Essay No. 1
1911

/ **CAT. 16** John Lyman
Early Spring
1908

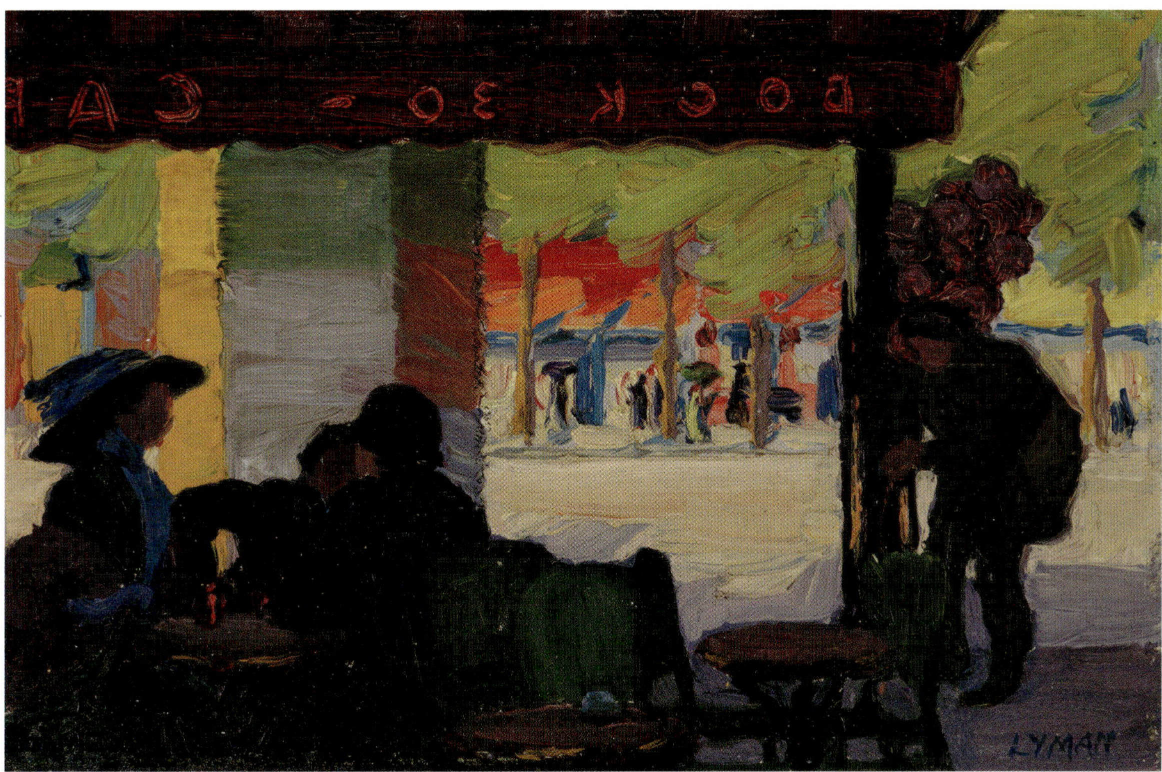

shapes of the road and the middle ground, before the mountains and the sky come to life. Lyman had learned from his first instructor, Marcel-Béronneau, to produce his paintings quickly, forcing him to capture the essence of shapes.[85] The Canadian's works remained imbued with this synthetic spirit, undiminished over time.

Painted about 1909, the small oil painting *Café, Rue Royale, Paris* (**CAT. 17**) also shows a thick application of paint, but this time the chromatic diversity outshines the various textures visible in the spring landscape. This café scene is portrayed against the light, in the shade of an awning that protects a few seated clients and one figure standing in the doorway. Beyond this dark foreground, the light reflects the lively prism colours onto the trees, passersby and storefronts on the other side of the street, before, on the left, turning into geometric shapes that without further detail transmit the sense of light, outside the café, flooding the Rue Royale.

From his trip to Switzerland, where Lyman spent the summer of 1911 with his young wife Corinne Saint-Pierre, daughter of Montreal couturier William Saint-Pierre, the painter brought back a landscape he called *Swiss Essay No. 1* (**CAT. 15**); it shows an uncluttered vision, perfectly in line with what he had learned during his short period at the Académie Matisse. Green dominates this composition, which has strong Cézanne undertones: it is painted with a disconcerting radicalism using diagonal and horizontal planes, and with a minimum of paint. The canvas emits a few bursts of light, but the main source of luminosity lies in a range of greens—emerald, olive and jade—as well as in the landscape's turquoise tones. The train crossing this green space produces a swirling plume of blue smoke, the only flight of fancy in the midst of a structure made up of solid planes, although the painter did handle them in a variety of ways. *Swiss Essay No. 1* is the first of a series of landscapes leaning toward the use of simple plastic techniques, as espoused by Matisse.

/ **CAT. 17** John Lyman
Café, Rue Royale, Paris
About 1909

During the war, Lyman served as a volunteer with the French Red Cross and did almost no painting. This makes it difficult to date very precisely the painting entitled *Beach at Trouville* (CAT. 108), which was exhibited in 1917 at the 34th Spring Exhibition of the Art Association of Montreal. However, the idea for this delightful Trouville beach scene, done in the form of a sketch, might have come from his visits to the north of France in 1909 and 1910, accompanied by his friend, the English painter Matthew Smith, or from a trip there with Corinne in 1911. It is also possible that he painted his recollection of Trouville in Canada, just before exhibiting it; this would explain why 1916 is indicated on the museum label attached to the back of the work, on the occasion of the exhibition. Might he have modified an already well-advanced sketch? If this were the case, it would explain why the Montreal Museum of Fine Arts had dated it from 1911 in the catalogue of the retrospective they gave Lyman in 1963.[86] The mystery remains unsolved.

Beach at Trouville illustrates the delights of the Channel beaches on a beautiful sunny day. The formal unity of the scene stems from the division of the surface into three chromatic planes, the white of the beach in front, the cluster of red- and yellow-striped tents in the middle ground and finally the blue of the sea and sky in the background. They are connected by the vertical motifs of the parasol and the mast flying the French flag. The light and heat of the Normandy beaches veil with a light haze the topmost band, with its boats and clouds. Lyman succeeded in capturing on canvas the sense of pleasure he had experienced on days at the seaside, in the north of France. He shared with Morrice a special affection for beach scenes, whose light he captured on various occasions: on the shore of the Atlantic Ocean, on the French and North-American coastlines, on the shores of Canadian lakes and—at the very end of his life—on the beaches of the Caribbean.

In 1912, the Lymans spent the summer in the Laurentians, and the two views of Dalesville that resulted took his expressive quest still further. They clearly depict the painter's feelings on visiting the leafy-green hamlet dotted with lakes in the township of Chatham, near the small towns of Carillon and Lachute. The hilly

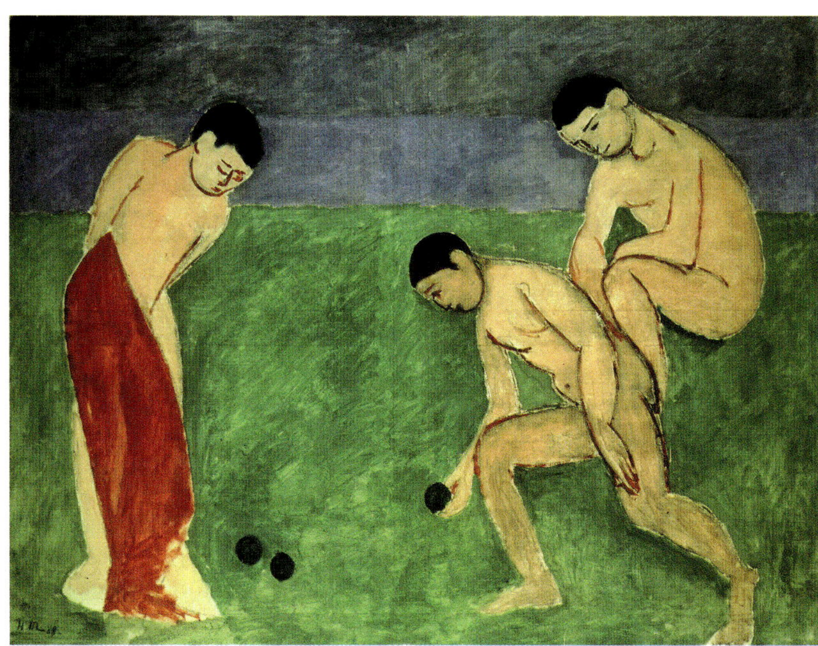

/ **FIG. 2** Henri Matisse
Game of Bowls
1908

/ **CAT. 18** John Lyman
The Airplane
Before 1933

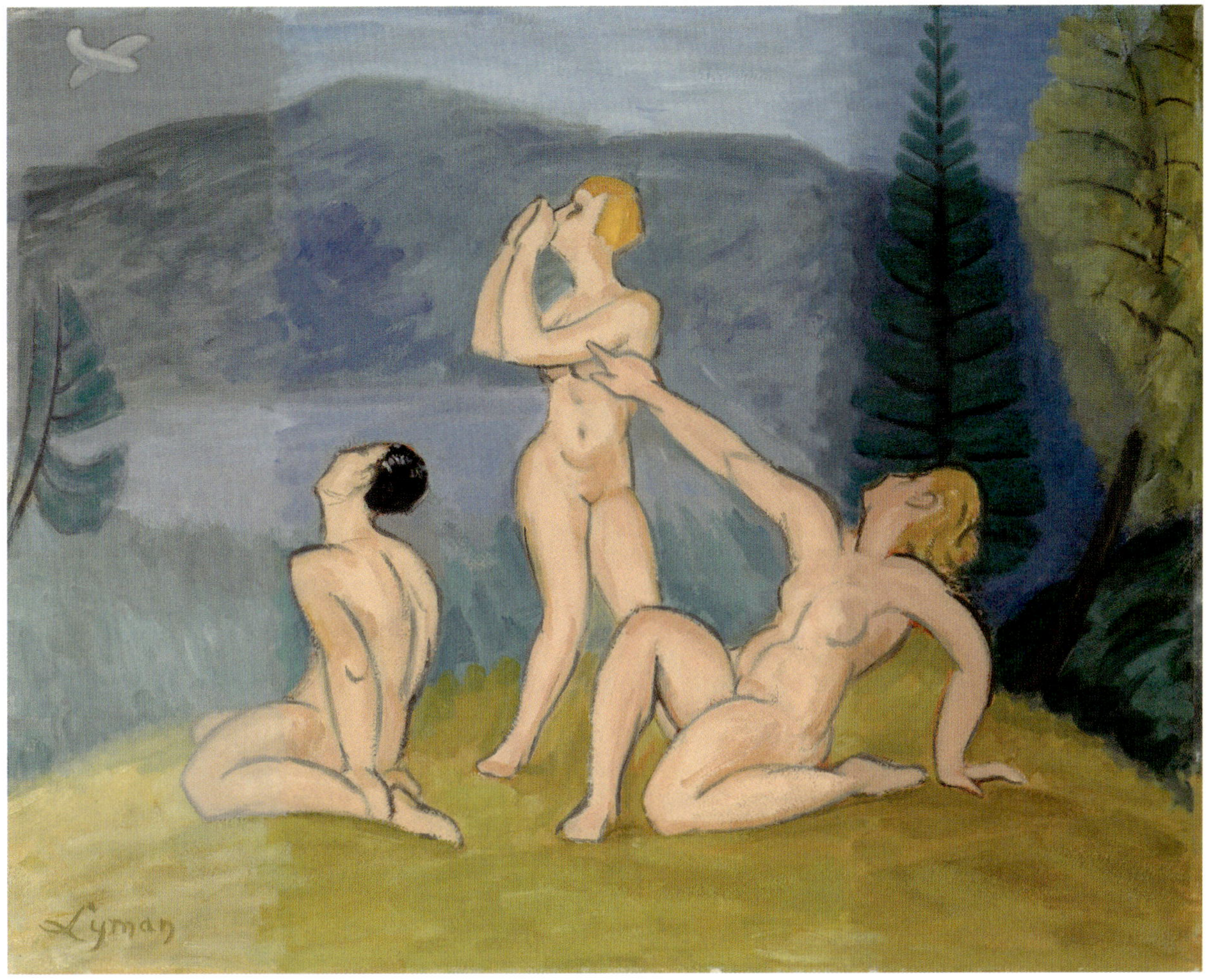

landscape, with barns and houses standing here and there alongside the curves of a blue river, inspired him to use a vigorous style. In *Dalesville* (**CAT. 84**), the painter uses a black contour line to make the tree, shrubs, river and house motifs stand out. He incorporates the support medium by allowing the primed surface of the canvas to show through, in so doing adding to the decorative effect. From this comes light that modulates the colour field, as well as a plastic liveliness in keeping with this inhabited portion of the village, with the road and the river running through it. In *Wild Nature Impromptu, 1st State* (**CAT. 83**), the support medium makes a lesser statement, which does not make the painting any less decorative. In this lakeside landscape, the vegetation is a pretext for simple and stylized motifs—trees evoked by a few black strokes, contour lines framing the mountains—all expressing a sense of immutability and timelessness.

The oil on wood entitled *Westmount in Winter* (**CAT. 86**) is more difficult to approach. It shows a cityscape in brilliant light. Lyman painted it from his father's house on Roslyn Avenue in Westmount[87] during the winter of 1911-1912, when he was in Montreal with Corinne. He brutally depicted the cold season, playing off the powerful contrasts of the white and purplish surface of the snow against the red buildings, with their dark pillars and blue shadows. Applied very liberally with rough strokes, the medium again lets the primed surface of the canvas show through.

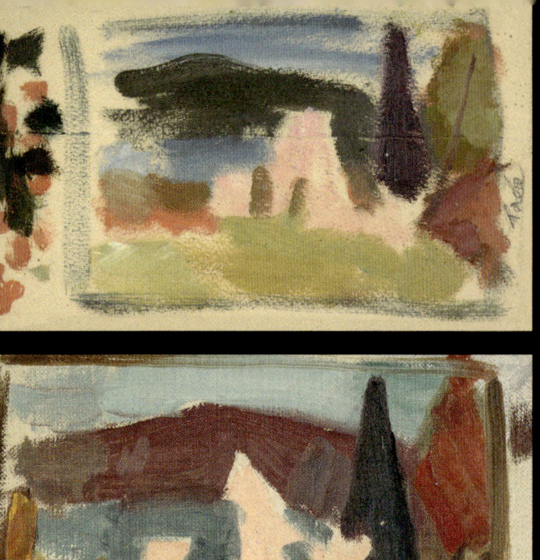
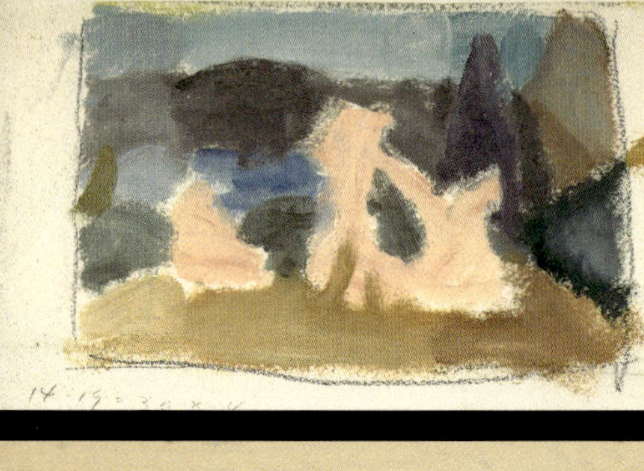
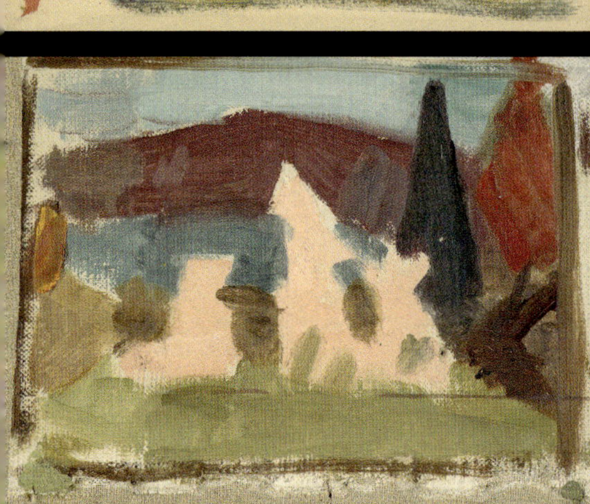
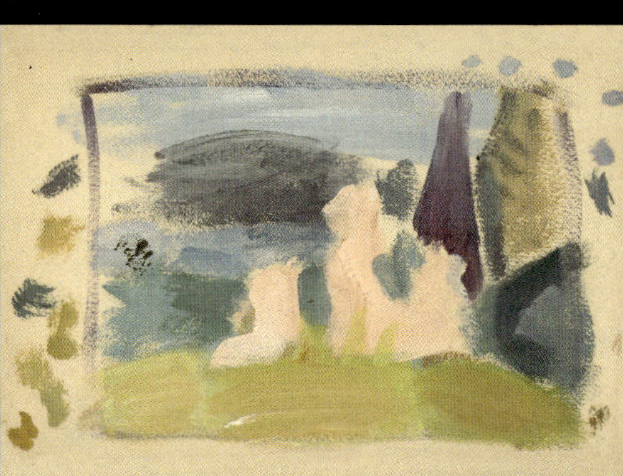
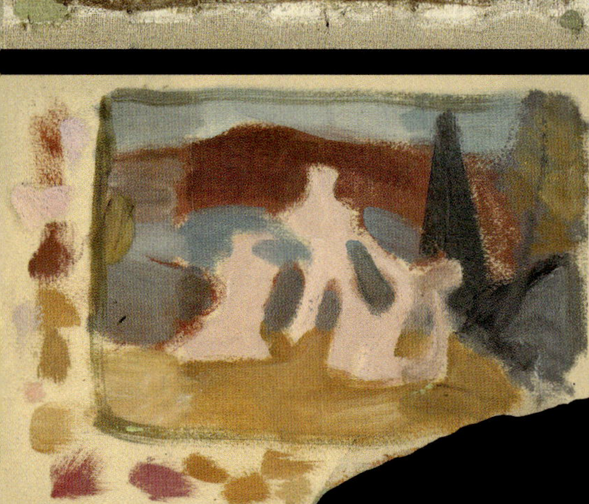
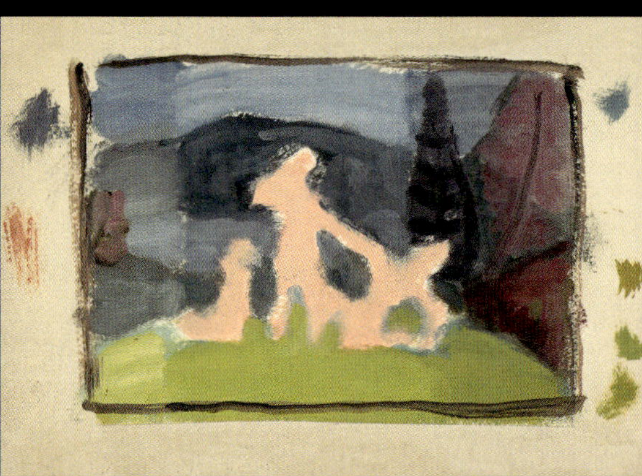
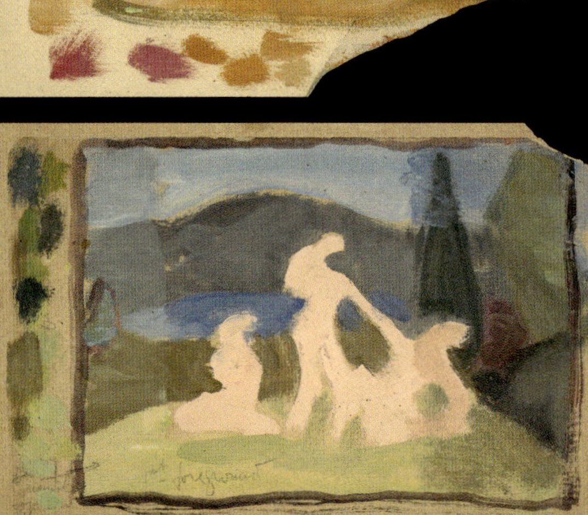
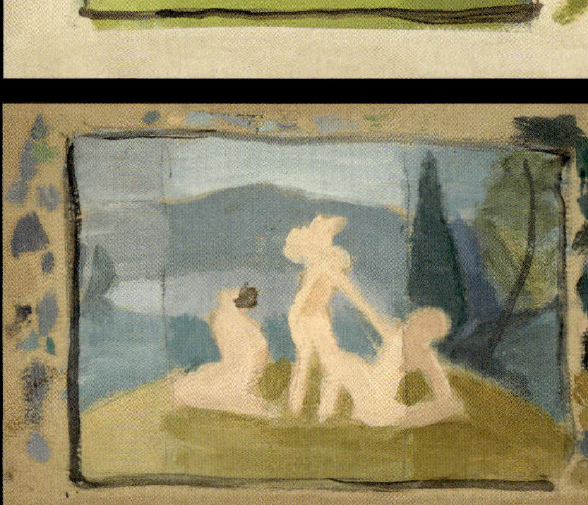

Was the disconcerting composition entitled *The Airplane* (CAT. 18) part of his output in 1912, as art historian Louise Dompierre implies?[88] Publications on Lyman have paid little attention to this atypical, strange and experimental painting. With its stylized mountains, lake and evergreens, wilderness dominates the scene. Lyman may have been illustrating a current theme in this painting, the flight of a plane in the Canadian sky, first attempted by a biplane in 1909. However, this is far from certain, as the model of the plane and the hairstyles of the figures on the right belong to another era (the period between the Wars), as indeed does the painter's signature. On the other hand, it is known that Lyman often signed his canvases long after having created them. Regardless of the year in which it was painted, the subject of *The Airplane* evokes Matisse's decorative paintings of 1908 and 1909, depicting nudes captivated by an object or animal, like *Game of Bowls* (FIG. 2) or *Bathers with a Turtle*. Stylistically, the use of a black outline to draw the three bodies is certainly what brings him closest to Matisse. However, Lyman did not go so far as to reduce the surroundings to coloured bands, like the French painter did; he preferred to place his figures in a lake and mountain setting whose chromatic combinations he had carefully analyzed. This is suggested by eight small recently discovered preparatory sketches for *The Airplane*, painted on cardboard and canvas (CATS. 18.01-08). In the sketches, Lyman arranged his impressions in the form of chromatic shapes that vary depending on the combination of tones—reds and purples or blues and greens. Not satisfied with the result, he divided his composition into three vertical sections, applying to each one a nuanced treatment of colour. The work was presented for the first time in 1933, under the title *The Airplane*, in a group exhibition at the Henry Morgan Gallery in Montreal;[89] in the catalogue, it is accompanied by the comment "sketch for a decorative panel." It is true that its effect supplants the story itself, justifying this designation.

Soon afterwards, in 1913, during an exhibition organized by the Art Association of Montreal, the convictions Lyman had acquired in Paris would be sorely tested. We should mention before going further that the Lyman family had long been connected with this institution; Frederick G. Lyman, the artist's father, had been a member since 1905[90] and his son, John, since 1907. During John's absence, his father had taken on the task of presenting the works his son sent him in 1910 and 1911. John Lyman was exhibited again in 1912, when his work earned him, in the written press, this ironic comment from Léon Lorrain, literary critic for the *Nationaliste* and a journalist with *Le Devoir*: "Canada has a *Cubist*, or perhaps he is really a *Futurist*. His entries consist of four landscapes, bearing respectively the suggestive titles 1, 2, 3, 4, and one portrait. It's simply wonderful! The walls of the Salon des Indépendants in Paris, which have seen a little of everything, have never welcomed anything more advanced in terms of composition, or rather, of decomposition."[91] Although Lorrain's tone was contemptuous, it seems moderate in comparison with the harsh comments awaiting Lyman the following year.

We should remember that at the beginning of 1913 the major trends in modern art arrived in North America on a massive scale. The International Exhibition of Modern Art, known today as the Armory Show, took place in New York from February 17 to March 15, 1913. This huge exhibition of 1,250 works by more than 300 artists

/ CAT. 18.01-08 John Lyman
Studies for "The Airplane"
Before 1933

put on display the most recent developments in art in Europe and the United States. It provided an exceptional showcase for Post-Impressionism. Brought together for the first time on American soil were works by Van Gogh, Cézanne, Gauguin, Matisse and many others. Unleashing the most intense passions, the exhibition caused what can only be called an earthquake.

The weak echoes reported in the Montreal press make it difficult to assess the importance of this event. There was of course the short piece by Arthur Stringer, news correspondent in New York for the weekly of the Anglophone Montreal elite, the *Saturday Mirror*,[92] but it came and went without being noticed. In any case, Stringer was so busy jeering at the Cubist, Futurist and Post-Impressionist works, just as his American colleagues were blithely doing, that he forgot to mention that William Van Horne had loaned his works by Toulouse-Lautrec and Cézanne to the Armory Show.[93]

The shock waves would be felt again in Montreal after the closure of the Armory Show when, at the 30th Spring Exhibition, John Lyman presented 4 paintings among the 500 or so works on display: a landscape (*Wild Nature Impromptu*) **(FIG. 41)**, a portrait (*A Brunette*) **(FIG. 42)**, a circus scene (*Humoresque − The Circus*) and a close-up view of a small house (*Bagatelle − A Cottage*).[94] The rough and uncompromising style of these paintings shocked Montreal's reactionary journalists, who gave them disparaging reviews, drawing freely on the impassioned words of their New York colleagues. With respect to *Wild Nature Impromptu*, a version of our *Wild Nature Impromptu, 1st State* **(CAT. 83)** whose location was not specified,[95] one critic wrote, "It is nothing short of a daub of crude colors on canvas. It suggests nothing; it conveys no idea; it creates nothing; it resembles nothing—except paint. The drawing is wretched; there is absolutely no composition about it; and as for the color-values—well, the colors-scheme is wild enough to drive a true colorist insane."[96]

In arguing that Lyman's composition resembled nothing other than painting itself, the journalist could not have better evoked self-referentiality in a work of art, the very principle of pictorial modernism that Lyman subscribed to. For its part, the *Herald* called into question the judgment of the members of the Art Association of Montreal's executive committee, which notably included Morrice's father, David Morrice: "Are these gentlemen or a majority of them, prepared to declare in public their belief in the artistic principles of Mr. Lyman?"[97] These are just a few examples among many of the furious reception the local press reserved for Lyman and his Post-Impressionist works.[98] His "scandalous" participation was the centrepiece of the event. It encouraged uninterrupted media coverage during the period of the exhibition and contributed to the record crowd of 28,000 visitors in the rooms of the Art Association of Montreal. With his four unfortunate paintings, John Lyman played the role of scapegoat for ignorant critics contemptuous of innovative approaches to art. In the midst of all this turbulence, the name of Matisse was mentioned several times as being part of the dangerous Post-Impressionist group.[99]

Yet, a few voices spoke out in favour of the moderns. The renowned photographer and art critic Harold Mortimer-Lamb denounced the narrow views and the danger of the critics' incompetence for the future of young progressive painters, of whom there were so few in Montreal.[100] In particular, there was the voice of the artist's father, Frederick G. Lyman. In an interview with Ella May of the *Herald,* published on March 27, he came to his son's rescue by staunchly defending his training with Matisse. To the question May asked about John's affinities with the Impressionist movement, he replied, "He [John] doesn't belong to any particular school. He studied in Paris at Julian's Academy, under Jean Paul Laurens and afterwards under Henri Matisse, one of the prominent Paris artists of to-day. Matisse wouldn't have a pupil who attempted to imitate him, but working with Matisse, he sought to catch the spirit with which Matisse produced his powerful paintings."[101] Did this mean that John had succeeded in convincing his father that his ideas on art were correct?

On April 1, in the pages of the *Star,* the newspaper in which critic Samuel Morgan-Powell was at his most virulent in this "battle" against Lyman and Post-Impressionism, the father reiterated his support for his son. In a letter to the editor, he recalled the reaction of the eminent British critic John Ruskin who had spoken out against Whistler's painting before its innovative qualities were recognized in England.[102] On April 15, Lyman also replied to his detractor from Paris, by letter.[103] He set the record straight in terms of the history and nature of what was commonly called Post-Impressionism. Then he reported the success of the moderns outside Canada in the eyes of critics and collectors, especially with regard to Matisse: "This week is being held a show of eleven paintings by Matisse, just brought back from Tangier, eight of which were bought before they could be exhibited at price: between $2,000 and $4,000. His works are to be found in many of great collections of France, Austria, Germany, Russia, etc." The exhibition of Moroccan paintings and sculptures Lyman mentioned in his letter had just opened at the Galerie Bernheim-Jeune in Paris, under the title *Henri Matisse : tableaux du Maroc et sculptures*; it included the famous Moroccan Triptych, commissioned by the Russian Ivan Abramovitch Morosov, comprised of *Landscape Viewed from a Window* (**FIG. 19**), *On the Terrace* and *The Casbah Gate* (**FIG. 40**). This triptych is now preserved in the Pushkin Museum in Moscow.

In this first half of 1913, at the point when Montreal critics were protesting so violently about his works, Lyman demonstrated a well-honed knowledge of the Paris art network. The Galerie Bernheim-Jeune, for example, was one of Morrice's Paris dealers. Moreover, we now know that Morrice was then in North Africa with Matisse. They were in Tangier, where the Canadian painter experienced the shock of the light in that part of the world at a watershed moment in his career. This was actually the second time he had stayed in Tangier with Matisse. However, Lyman said nothing about this in the very blunt letter he sent to the *Montreal Daily Star* in response to the attacks he was the object of and in which he defended Matisse.

If the name Morrice was in the newspapers in the winter of 1913, it was because he was participating—with Lyman—in the 30th Spring Exhibition of the Art Association, where he also received a negative review from Morgan-Powell, albeit to a lesser degree. He presented three paintings, one of which was intimately connected with the Association's history. *The Old Holton House* depicted the building that had occupied the site on Sherbrooke Street where the Maxwell brothers, in 1912, constructed the new building that would become the Montreal Museum of Fine Arts. Morgan-Powell lamented the fact that this winter scene had lost the invigorating qualities of the Impressionist snow scenes done by Morrice's colleagues Maurice Cullen and Marc-Aurèle de Foy Suzor-Coté. The journalist from the *Star*, for whom Impressionism was the most acceptable movement in contemporary painting, attributed this so-called weakness of Morrice's painting to its being done in the studio.[104] Nor was he receptive to the luminous composition *The Beach, Le Pouldu* (National Gallery of Canada), shown at the same time.

"WHAT IS ART, ESSENTIALLY?"

If any doubt remained as to the interest the Art Association's executive committee had in Lyman's work, it was to dissipate rapidly when the institution announced it would exhibit his paintings and drawings in two small rooms, in May 1913. In actual fact, the artist was the beneficiary of the blind faith of the Association's members.[105] Nonetheless, the uproar of the previous month forced him to explain to the public the principles guiding his "enigmatic" approach. He wanted to show the progression of his artistic journey by giving his exhibition a retrospective character.[106] Visitors were invited to follow Lyman's approach from 1908 to 1913. The painter removed all descriptive titles, which perfectly suited the independent and autonomous language of painting and the portrayal of his impressions of nature. Some titles evoked music, like *Colour Fugue* or *Wild Nature Impromptu*, and others, nature, like *Floral Caprice* or *Rural Sensation*, and there were more essays, *French Essay*, *Swiss Essay* and *Canadian Essay*. This way of naming works makes it very difficult today to identify them. Two of them are presented in this catalogue: *Swiss Essay No. 1* (**CAT. 15**) and *Wild Nature Impromptu, 1st State* (**CAT. 83**). There is some doubt as to whether *Café, Rue Royale, Paris* (**CAT. 17**) and *Westmount in Winter* (**CAT. 86**) were exhibited.

The 1913 exhibition was accompanied by a small catalogue,[107] its foreword written in French by Corinne Saint-Pierre Lyman, who asked the eternal and especially pertinent question, in this era of major upheavals: "What is art, essentially?" This one-page text is a thoughtful reflection on the main issues of pictorial modernism. At the heart of Corinne's text lies nature, which art cannot imitate: "Art that looks natural is nonsense; art must be artificial; where imitation ceases, art begins . . . Art is not the story of what we see . . . what determines it is what arises between expression and the inspiring object: imagination, organizing intelligence and personality as well."

Until now, art history has given little weight to this first public statement by a Canadian voice, one that should be considered a manifesto for contemporary art in this country. These principles are similar notably to those defended by Matisse, who had affirmed, in "Notes of a Painter," his desire to "create the image," like Cézanne—that is, to capture the essence of things behind the fleetingness of their appearance. In other words, the "artificial" art that the true artist aspires to, according to Corinne, results from a demanding honesty in the act of painting and the need to organize one's own sensations with respect to nature. However, she warns, the unfamiliarity of the work of art will be surprising at first glance: by turning away from imitation or a "reworking of the past," the work "shock at first sight, in that it is strange, unfamiliar, unintelligible."

Corinne Saint-Pierre could not have chosen her words better. It was true that the works of John G. Lyman shocked people. The definition of art given by the journalist from the *Montreal Daily Star*—just like most of his colleagues[108]—was far removed from Lyman's work. In his review of the special Lyman exhibition, this journalist again deplored the harmful influence of Matisse on the Canadian's works: "The influence of Matisse is written large over the later works. There is the same distortion of limbs in his figures, the same throwing into prominence of brutal and unrestrained sex. It is Mr. Lyman's own business if he wants to do this, but it is the business of others to say that he has failed to do it well." And he added, "But the latest school, especially Matisse and his followers, take a fierce delight as already said in decadent inexistence on the physical elements of sex."[109]

This "critics' incredible savageness," Lyman would recall, compelled him to leave the country:[110] "And then, what confirmed me in my decision to stay in Europe was . . . Morrice. He was not at all understood [by Canadians] and I said to myself: if they don't appreciate him, they cannot appreciate me. He said it was completely useless, that he would never be understood in Canada, and that as for me, it would be better if I never went back."[111] Although he continued until 1920 to participate in the Art Association's annual exhibitions, presenting two or three works a year, John Lyman left Canada that year. That was when his real exile began; it ended in 1931.

TRAVELS, LIGHT AND MODERNISM

The history of modern painting abounds with examples where the experience of travel and encounters with the southern light have led to new formal paths. Simply mention Delacroix, Van Gogh, Gauguin and the Fauves Matisse or Derain and their vibrantly coloured paintings spring to mind. Henri Matisse liked to share every one of his impressions of his travels. The plentiful correspondence he maintained with his friends Albert Marquet and Charles Camoin is packed with observations about the weather, the quality of the light on his arrival or the light he had to leave behind with regret.[112] A northern man, Matisse had experienced the wonder of Mediterranean light in Ajaccio in 1898. After that, he never stopped talking about the various colours and textures of light: fair and golden, erasing shadows in Collioure, melted after rain in Tangier, silvery in Nice, crystal-like in New York, limpid in Oceania, and so on.

Continuing this tradition, Canadians Morrice and Lyman also explored the south, which gave new life to their artistic vision. At a time when expression through colour was laying a new foundation for pictorial modernism, North America offered them the light of Bermuda and the islands of the Caribbean.

We are able to follow their travels through a number of written accounts. Few of them concern James Wilson Morrice, and we have only a few notes and the drawings in his sketchbooks to describe his journeys. This absence of words makes the few comments he left behind about his quest all the more valuable: "Bright colour is what I want. It rains here all the time,"[113] or, "A painter should go south; it cleans your palette for you."[114] In contrast, in the case of John Lyman, we have quite a large number of texts: his correspondence with his father, the diary he kept from 1927 to 1963, the articles he published, as well as the interviews he gave to journalists. Of his own quest, he would say, "Light is everything. It is what reveals to us shapes and their colours. I am not a fan of outdoor painting and the 'effects' of light do not interest me. What attracts me is the quality of the colour determined by the light. The greatest joy in painting is to find light through colour. My fondness for Fauvism is entirely rooted in this."[115]

Beyond words lie the works by both of these artists, whose modernist styles, awash in vivid colours, are evidence of their daring and their aesthetic discoveries.

THE WEST INDIES AND MORRICE'S WANDERINGS

From 1912 to 1914, Morrice lived in Spain and North Africa.[116] After a visit to London, he returned to Montreal. His parents' death and the war that was brewing in Europe delayed his return to France. In February 1915, he headed to the islands of the Caribbean, taking advantage of the invitation of a friend, Richard B. Van Horne, the son of the collector Sir William Van Horne. At the beginning of the century, this businessman had extended his railroad management activities to Cuba, becoming president of the Cuba Company Railroad connecting Santiago to Havana by rail. Morrice, during his Cuban trip, which lasted more than a month, stopped in these two cities, as well as at Camaguey, at the Van Horne residence. He added on an excursion to Kingston, Jamaica (CAT. 76).

From this first trip to the Caribbean, the painter brought back brightly coloured drawings and sketches that provided him with the material to produce several paintings in his Paris studio in May 1915.[117] In Santiago, a port city in the south of Cuba, he fell in love with a colonial-style house with an indigo blue facade, punctuated by orange shutters covering the windows. This building was the inspiration for a highly decorative composition, *House in Santiago, Cuba* (CAT. 19).[118] While the painter had previously favoured close-up planes, as in *Red House, Venice* (CAT. 10), he had never before taken the two-dimensional effect so far in a painting, creating a clear relationship between the horizontal and vertical lines. Thus, the muddy ground, the bench and the first-floor balcony form shapes that echo the long blue and orange rectangles of the facade. The painting's geometrical structure is nonetheless disrupted by the broken lines of the slender tree trunks and the exotic plant, as well as by the figure sitting on the bench. *House in Santiago* appealed to London's Contemporary Art Society, which acquired it in 1916, before donating it to the Tate Gallery in 1924 on the recommendation of Roger Fry.

Houses, Cuba (CAT. 77) depicts a completely different space, very airy, arranged in horizontal bands, from the ground to the sky. In the middle area is a row of low

/ **CAT. 19** James W. Morrice
House in Santiago, Cuba
1915

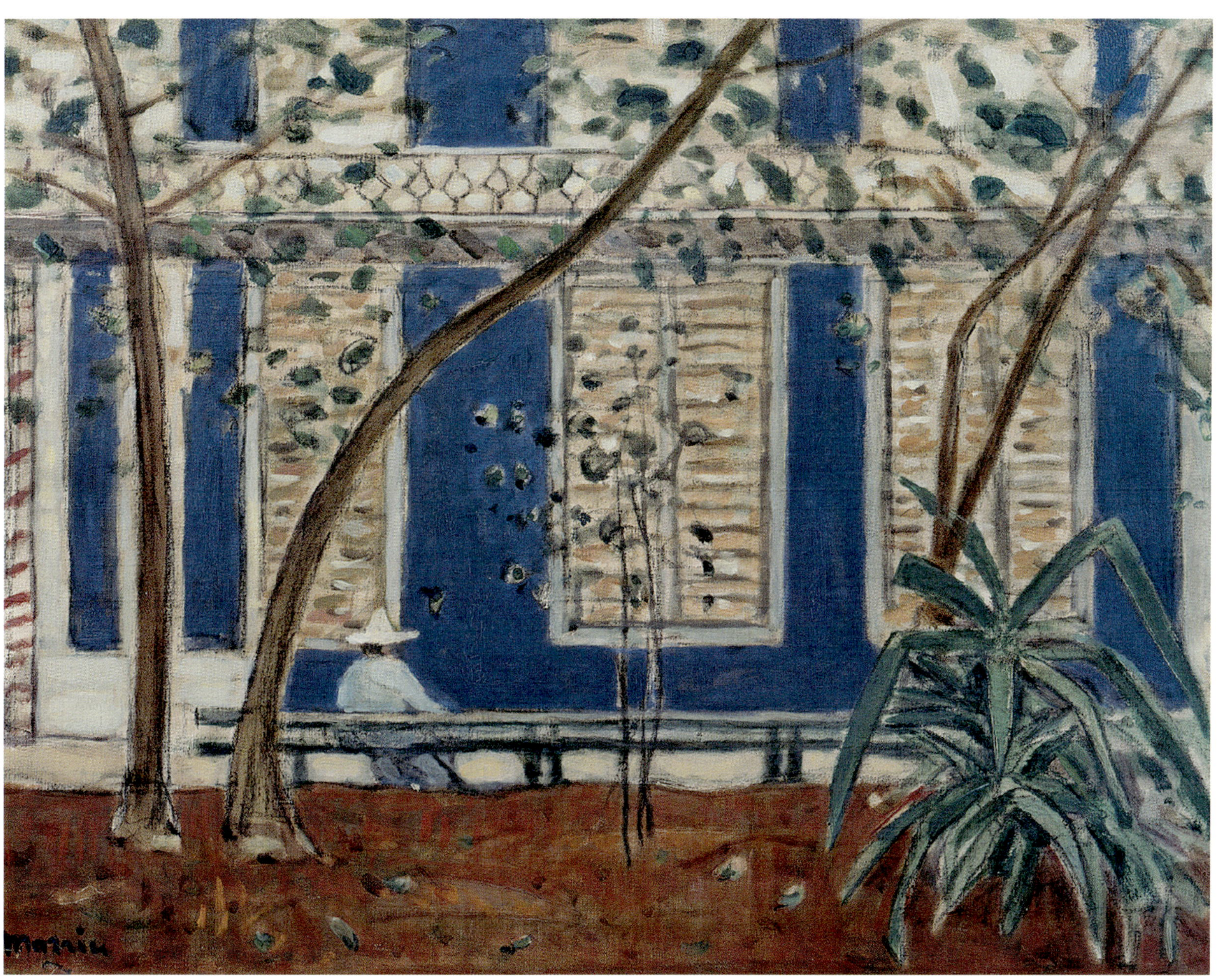

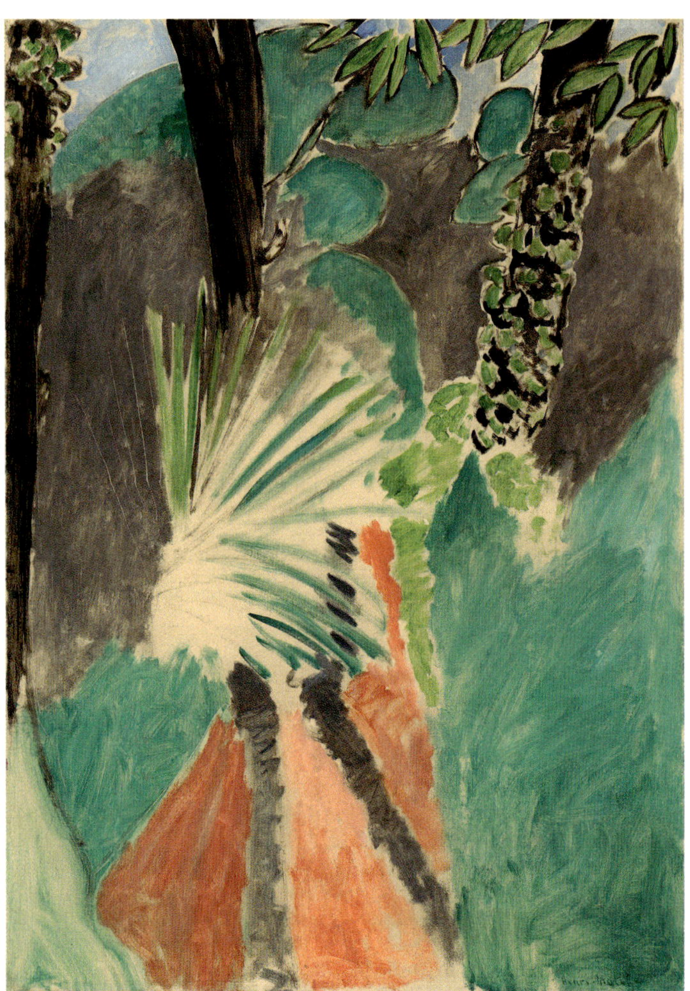 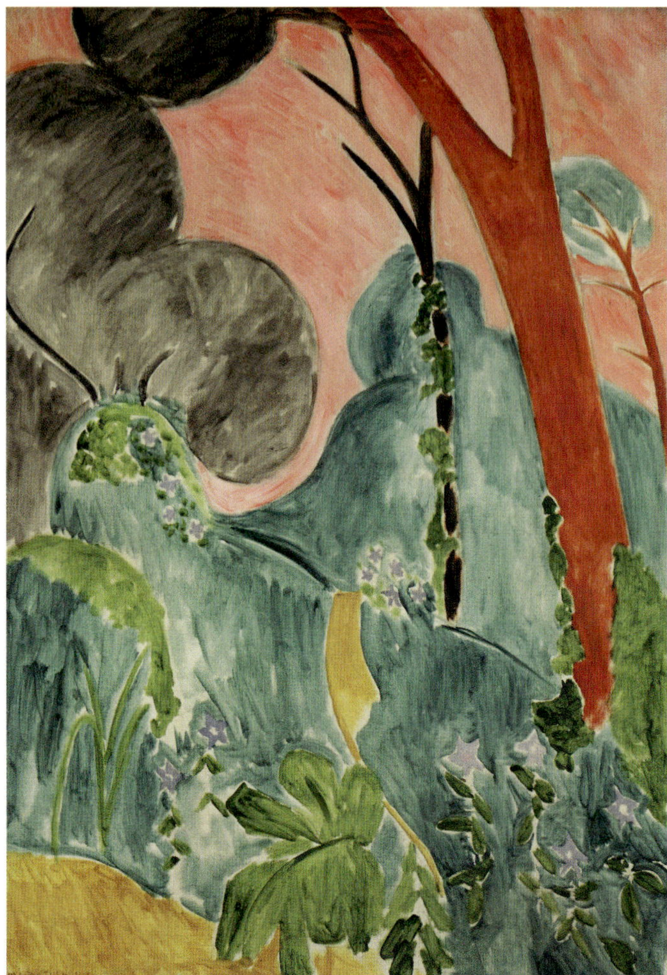

houses with coloured facades, raspberry red and greenish-blue. Their solid treatment contrasts with the speckles on the tiled roofs, the grassy strip, the central tree and the palm tree on the right, its trunk dotted with small brown patches.[119] There are three Cuban men in the middle ground, while a child hunched at the foot of the palm tree holds a red scarf with white polka dots. The painter flecked his garment with blue, thus balancing the chromatic links connecting the foreground to the red facade topped with a blue band, in the middle ground.

While a geometric arrangement of shapes can still be seen in *Houses, Cuba*, this effect has completely disappeared in *Garden in Cuba* (**CAT. 21**), in which nature dominates architecture. Here, Morrice was inspired by the lush vegetation of a city garden. Tropical plants and trees flourish in colours of green and red, forming a screen through which can be seen a few tiny illuminated areas on a white roughcast facade, pierced by windows. The turquoise touches in the sky tint the garment worn by the black woman, seated on a bench on the right. Even more than in the two previous works, Morrice drew his inspiration very faithfully from a study painted *in situ*.[120] He used the same technique, quickly applying his medium by rubbing and scraping, giving the surface an unfinished feeling. The "sketched" effect of this luxuriant bouquet of greenery recalls the sketches of *Palm Leaf, Tangier* and *Periwinkles (Moroccan Garden)* painted by Matisse in 1912 in the gardens of the Villa Brooks in Tangier (**CAT. 20** and **FIG. 3**), which Morrice had seen and liked on his first trip to Morocco.

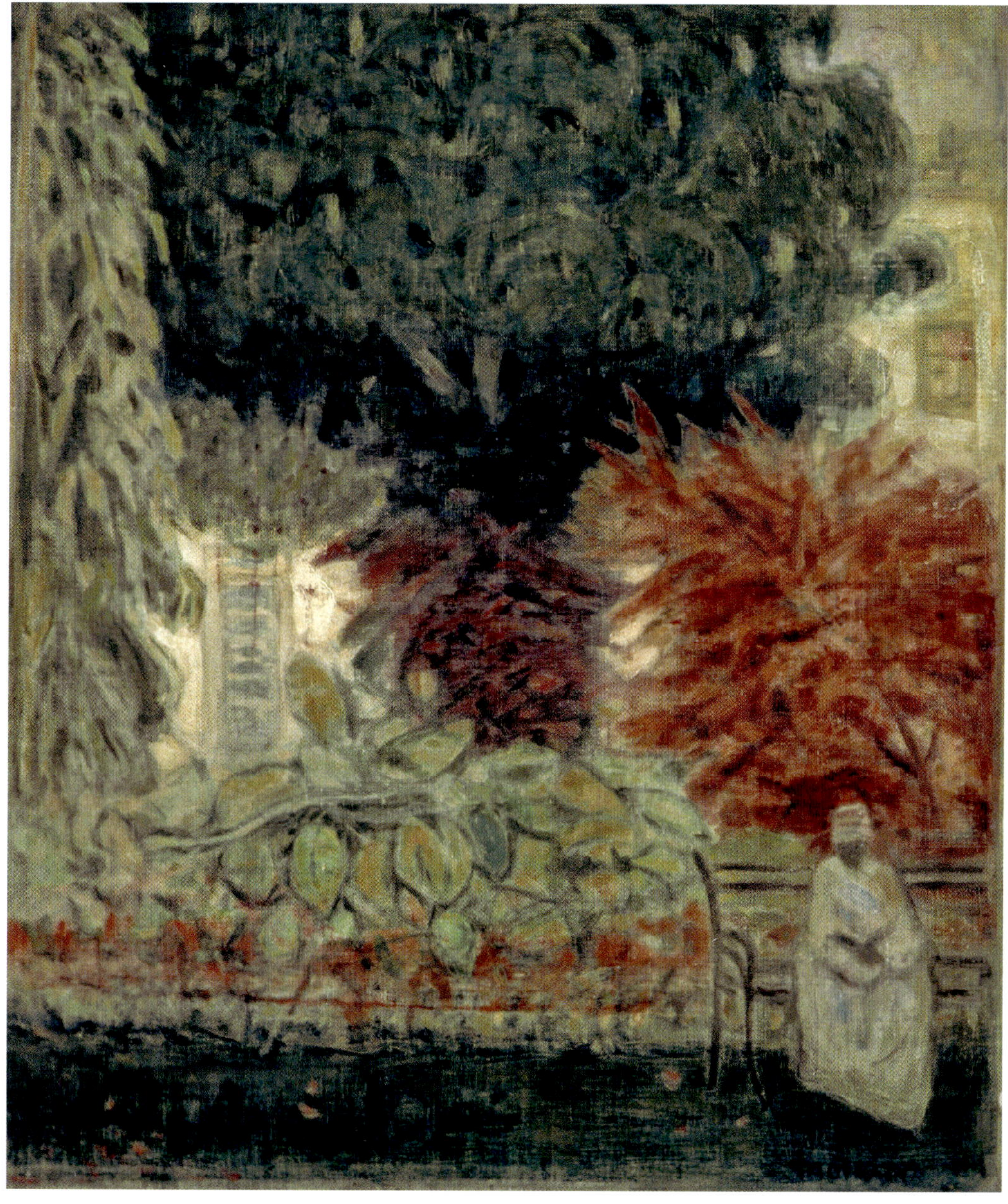

Recent research on Morrice has revealed that, after the First World War, the painter did several paintings using photographs and coloured postcards as sources.[121] He was thus able to continue to produce Cuban scenes after 1915. This was the case for *Café El Pasaje, Havana* **(CAT. 74)**, a work based on a black and white photograph taken in 1915.[122] The real subject is the dazzling light captured from inside the café at the El Pasaje Hotel. Tall arcades open onto the Avenue del Prado, lined with light-coloured houses and yellow trees that stand out against a bright, solid blue sky. This azure blue was new in Morrice's palette of colours, and the painter used it for the first time in the commissions he carried out in 1918 for the Canadian government, as a war artist. This is, in fact, what enables us to date this painting from 1918, after having long believed it had been done in 1915.

Morrice appears to have visited the El Pasaje Hotel; this memory is visible in the marks of charcoal on the surface, in the diluted medium that lets the grain of the canvas show through and in the uniform qualities of the sky and the trees' mottled foliage.

/ CAT. 20 Henri Matisse
Palm Leaf, Tangier
1912

/ FIG. 3 Henri Matisse
Periwinkles (Moroccan Garden)
1912

/ CAT. 21 James W. Morrice
Garden in Cuba
1915

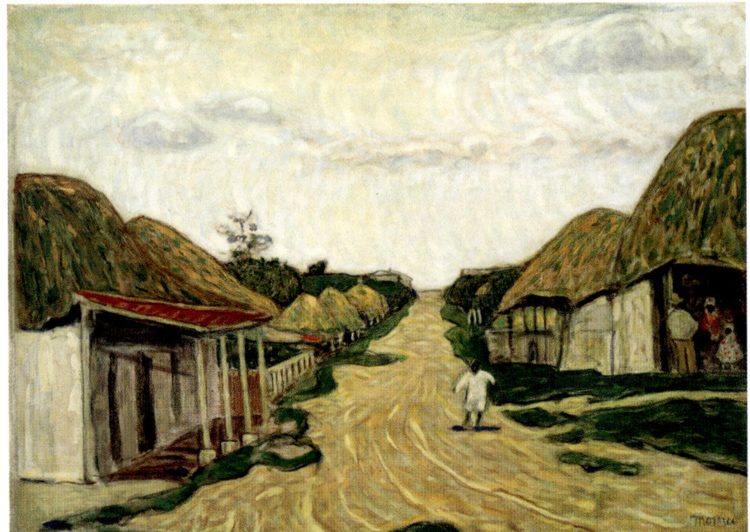

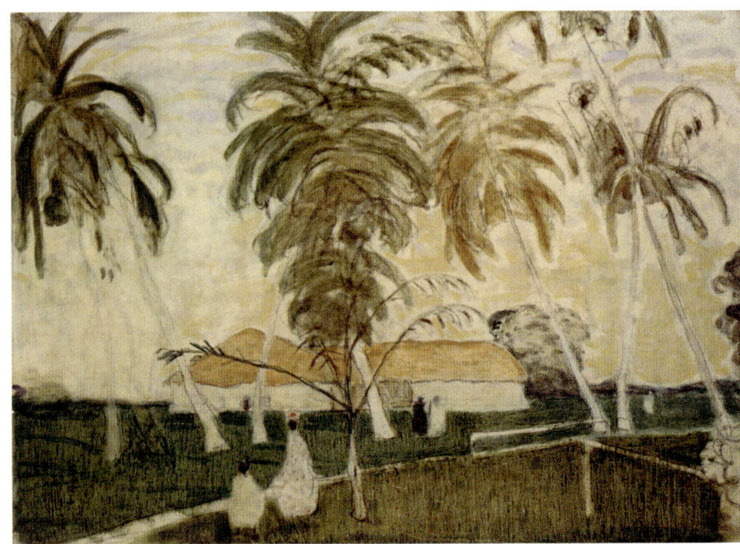

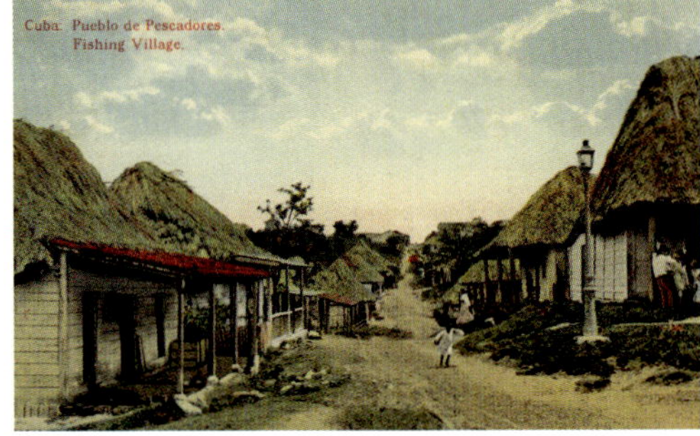

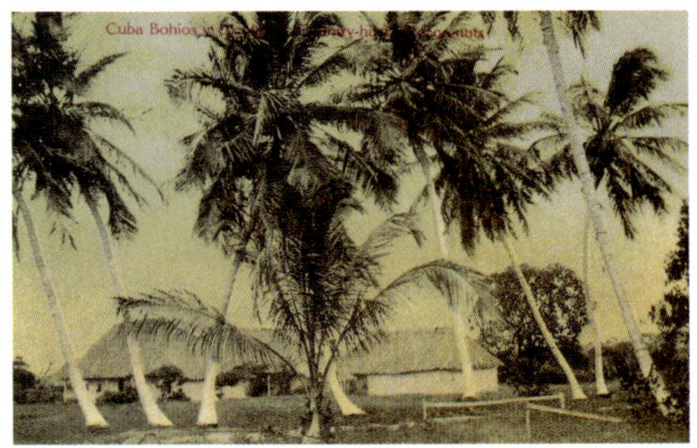

/ **CAT. 22** James W. Morrice
Village Street, West Indies
About 1918-1919

/ **CAT. 23** James W. Morrice
Landscape, West Indies
About 1918-1921

/ **FIG. 4** Jordi, Havana
**Cuba, pueblo de pescadores/
Fishing Village**
Undated

/ **FIG. 5**
**Cuba, bohios y cocoteros/
Country Huts & Cocoa Nuts**
Undated

His composition magnifies the striking effect of the backlight in the photograph. In the painted work, the café's interior contrasts with the exterior. This relationship shows the distance separating Morrice from Bonnard and Matisse, who instead had chosen to systematically eliminate distinct backlighting. In their work, compositions including a window portray the unity of the chromatic space by suppressing the naturalistic effects of shadow and the contrasts between the interior and the exterior (**CAT. 70**). Our painter, on the other hand, even though he gets closer to the window in *Scene in Havana* (**CAT. 73**), gives special importance to the exterior light and takes care to show the backlighting and the limits of the interior space, this time by means of the grey shutter on the left, the ornamental railing and the thin dark-red band at the bottom.

Morrice took up watercolours again when producing his studies at the Picardy front, in February 1918. This technique, which he used as an intermediate step between the printed source and the final composition, gave him a new freedom that can be felt in his paintings. Thus, even before returning to the islands of the Caribbean in February 1921, he produced compositions like *Village Street, West Indies* (**CAT. 22**), *Landscape, West Indies* (**CAT. 23**) and *The Pond, West Indies* (**CAT. 24**). The duplicate visual source (coloured postcard and watercolour), as well as the similar sizes of the three works, suggest that Morrice may have painted them during the same period, perhaps as a triptych. In all three cases, he copied the compositions on the postcards (**FIGS. 4, 5** and **44**), sometimes changing certain elements, like the lamppost on the right that he removed from *Village Street, West Indies*, or the figures he added in the other two paintings. In the first work, Morrice copied the postcard faithfully, using its brilliant colours. A black line restrains the coloured shapes whose many shades are emphasized by unruly strokes. In *The Pond, West Indies* and *Landscape, West Indies*, the painter preferred the translucence of watercolours. The elegant trunks of coconut palms wave their long fronds nonchalantly in the upper part of these compositions, amplifying the effect of

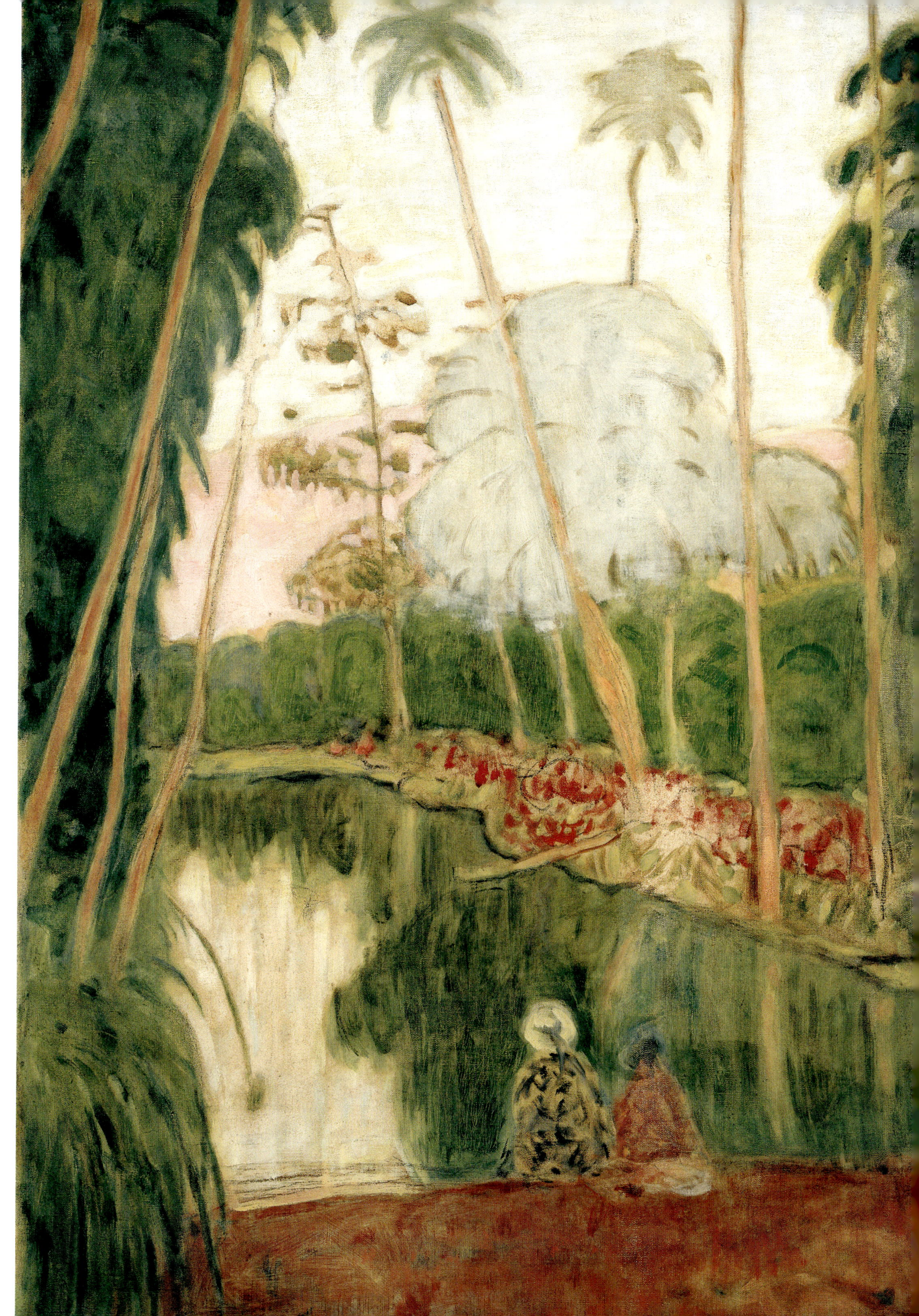

lightness and fluidity emanating from these works. In the scene entitled *Landscape, West Indies*, charcoal and pencil drawing can be seen over the entire surface. It crosses the thinly painted greenish-yellow sky and the ochre and green harmony of the landscape. The only bright colour notes are the pink polka dots on the dress and the vermilion turban worn by the figure. In comparison, *The Pond, West Indies* is a symphony to the glory of light, with its greens, reds, pinks and blues breathing a sense of original purity into this heavenly place.

These three paintings by Morrice were known to John Lyman, who couldn't bear the street scene, considering it to be a failure: "The one time he tried to embrace form, there was nothing there."[123] Only one other work by Morrice, *Landscape, Trinidad* (**CAT. 72**), would earn such a severe judgment from Lyman: "It is forced and posterish, and the colour values ring false."[124] On the other hand, he very much liked the feeling projected by *Landscape, West Indies*, and *The Pond, West Indies*, two works that depict the essential character of the exotic islands and that he bought for his own collection. According to Lyman, Morrice was the brilliant successor to Gauguin.[125]

Morrice returned to the Caribbean in January 1921 for the second and final time. He sailed as far as Trinidad, off the coast of Venezuela. The fifty-six-year-old painter was inspired by Macqueripe Bay, not far from the capital, as well as by the sea, the sandy beaches and the hills, known there as *mornes*, covered with luxuriant vegetation. He would turn them into his freest and simplest paintings (**CATS. 25** and **26**). The freshness and density of memory in *Landscape, Trinidad (Macqueripe Bay)* stem from the solid colour blocks of indigo blue and the green shape of the trees sketched in large dark strokes. This is certainly the painting that best illustrates Morrice's modernist daring. The British art critic Paul George Konody, who had the opportunity to admire *A Bathing Cove, Trinidad* (National Gallery of Canada), a work done in the same spirit, in London in the autumn of 1921, wrote that it "carries Matisse's typical style of calligraphic synthesis further . . . sea and beach and cliffs are reduced by him almost to decoratively arranged symbols."[126]

The painter had achieved a synthesis of form, reducing it to its symbolic value. In "Notes of a Painter," Matisse wrote that an artist "must recognize that when he uses his reason, his picture is an artifice and that when he paints, he must feel that he is copying nature."[127] The art historian Roger Fry, the organizer of the two large Post-Impressionist exhibitions in London in 1910 and 1912, had also clarified this idea of expression and "design" in his writings. For him, what was specific to Post-Impressionism was its ability to understand through form the essential relationships that made up an object. Expressing "the treeness of a tree"[128] was to strip objects of their anecdotal content and all the accidents that get in the way of their unchanging nature. The work becomes a creation of the mind, the vibrant memory of what captivated the painter observing his subject.[129] In the course of his development, Morrice arrived at this unity of chromatic planes and the extreme simplification of details that make his modernist intent perfectly clear. This is the case with *Landscape, Trinidad (Macqueripe Bay)*, which captures the essence of the locale. The great freedom he showed resonated with John Lyman who wrote these admiring words: "With what magic did he evoke this bathing cove in Trinidad while concerning himself so little with describing it, with such nonchalant drawing and such general colour! Could this be his masterpiece?"[130]

Previous page:

/ CAT. 24 James W. Morrice
The Pond, West Indies
About 1920-1922

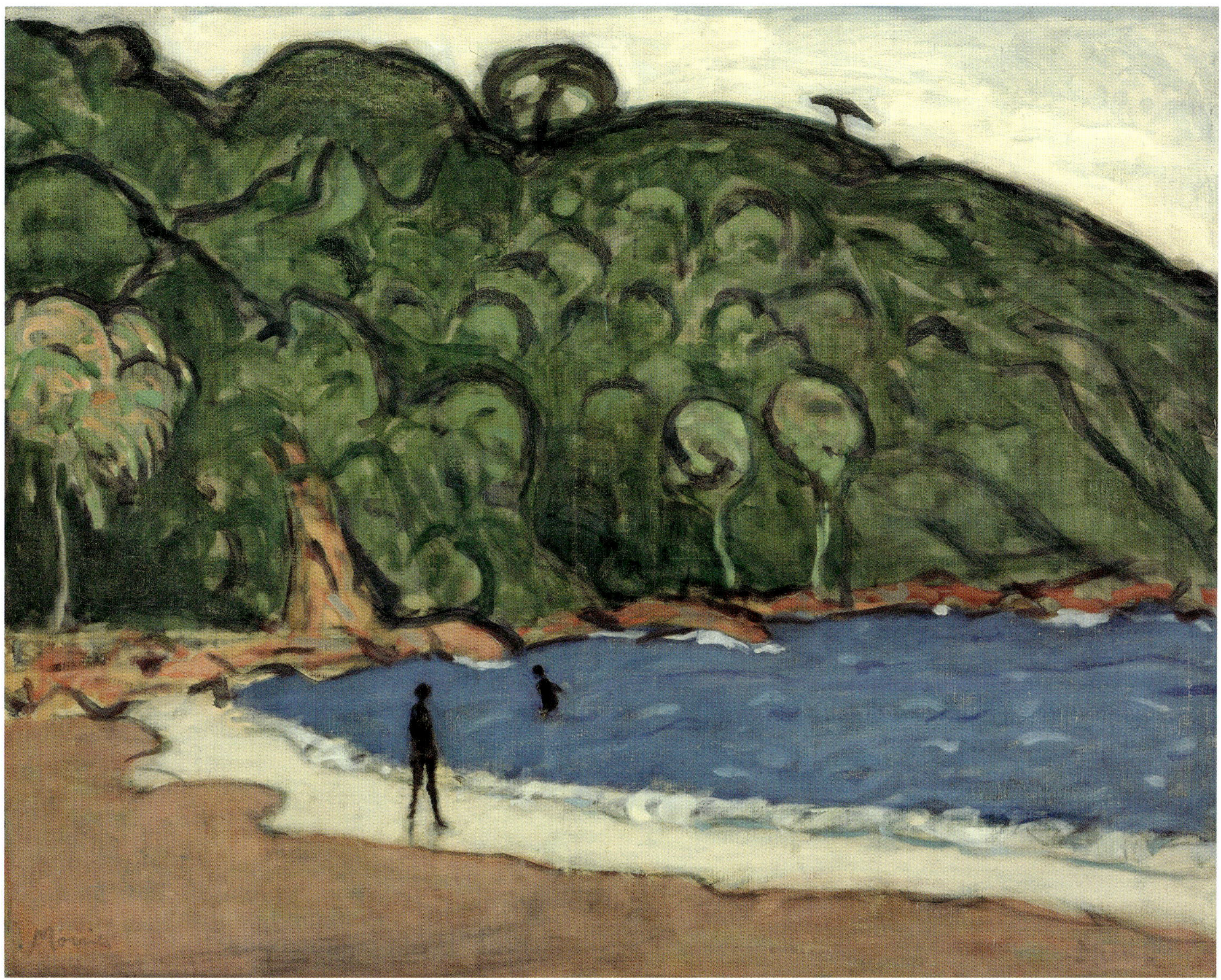

After this final visit to North America, Morrice continued to wander between the south of France, Corsica and Algeria, tirelessly painting, until his final stop in Tunis, where he died on January 1924, in the luminous North Africa so dear to his heart. A few weeks earlier, he had run into John Lyman in Cagnes-sur-Mer, France. By then, ten years had already elapsed since the events of 1913 in Montreal, when the reception of Lyman's works had caused a scandal, wounding the artist and causing him to leave Canada.

LYMAN: THE STRUCTURING LIGHT
OF BERMUDA AND THE MEDITERRANEAN

In this dark period for modern art in Montreal, John Lyman took refuge in Bermuda. At the request of his uncle James Morgan, he agreed to supervise the renovation and enlargement of an eighteenth-century dwelling on his Southlands estate. Shaken by the violent reception of his work in Montreal and in particular deeply disturbed by the disappointment he had caused his father,[131] he was

/ **CAT. 25** James W. Morrice
**Landscape, Trinidad
(Macqueripe Bay)**
1921

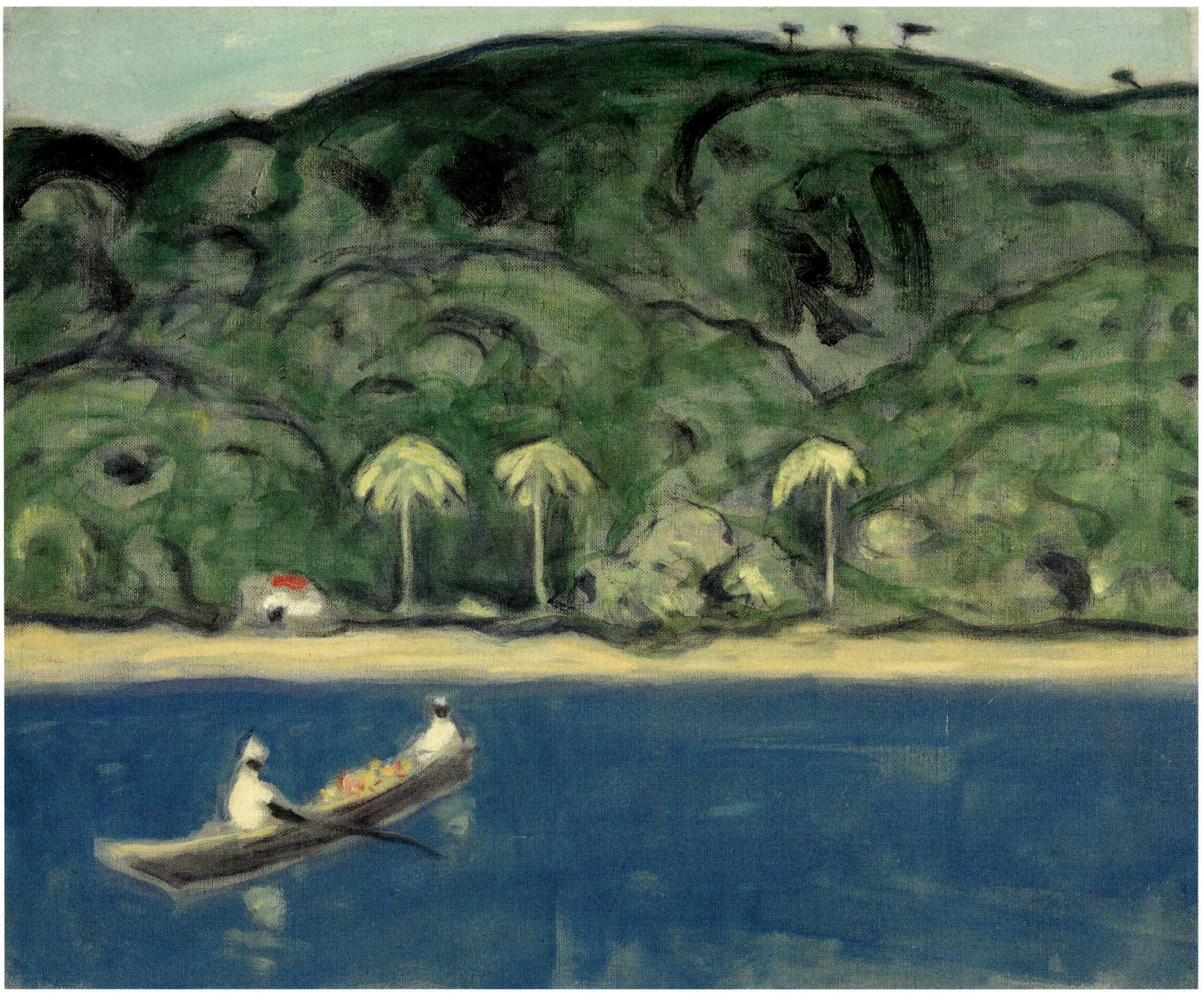

considering giving up art. He nonetheless painted a few landscapes and portraits. Like Morrice, his aesthetic language would be transformed by his contact with these islands.

The work he produced during the winters he spent in Bermuda from 1913 to 1915[132] enabled him to explore various effects, as shown in the two portraits of his wife Corinne. In *Profile of Corinne* (**CAT. 93**), the composition is dominated by the play of coloured shapes—the black of the hair, the pink tone of the skin—using a generous application of paint, in thick and regular layers. The dark and rounded shape of the short hair is offset by the brightness of the white dress with red polka dots. It is very likely to this portrait that the painter was alluding when he wrote to his father, at the beginning of 1914: "I have just finished the portrait I was doing of Corinne. I have been working at it off & on for three months. Rather different from my usual method. I find it hard to keep to original conception fresh for so long a time. I find short sprints more suited to my constitution than long distance races. I am aesthetically short-winded."[133] Using Corinne again as a model, *On the Beach, Bermuda* (**CAT. 107**) echoes the formal simplicity of the preceding portrait. Here,

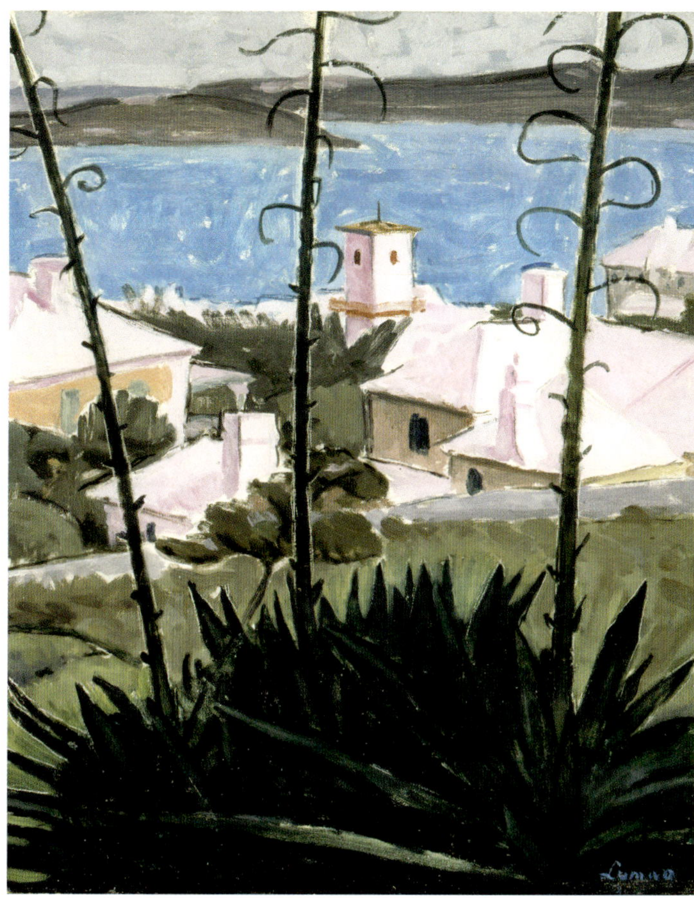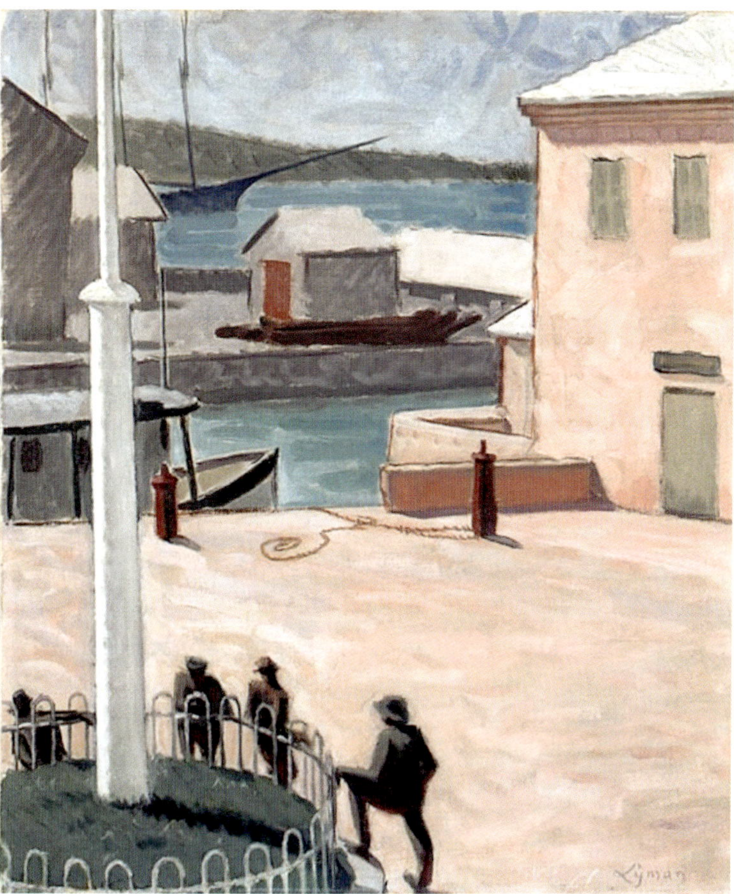

Lyman explored instead a cursive style combined with a thin layer of paint which evokes watercolour. This style was not unfamiliar in the language of the American Post-Impressionists Maurice Prendergast and H. Lyman Saÿen, a close friend of Leo and Gertrude Stein in Paris[134] and a distant uncle of John. He used this same treatment the following summer to paint *The Lawns of Fairfield, Cowansville* (CAT. 85) in Quebec, but he did not venture any further down this path, which was suited to simple effects better suited to drawing than to painting.

The pink of Bermuda's beaches and buildings colours the landscapes he painted during this time, softly blended in *Southlands, Bermuda* (CAT. 78) and *Untitled* (CAT. 79). The island archipelago's gentle light is reflected on the roofs of Saint-George, in the central band of the composition (CAT. 27). Inserted between the overgrown vegetation and the turquoise sea, the small pink and white geometric planes convey the very peaceful and almost unchanging feeling of life in the islands. This sense of calm is felt even more strongly in *Landscape, Bermuda* (FIG. 6). The pink colour is warmed up by red and amber shades that contrast with the blues of the water and sky. Recalling Cézanne and Braque, the work is based on the solid equilibrium of chromatic shapes, one of the foundations of Lyman's plastic vocabulary. This would even lead him to say that his painting was classical. In contrast to the Romantics, who preferred movement and fragility, Lyman claimed to

/ **CAT. 26** James W. Morrice
Fruit Boat, Trinidad
1921

/ **CAT. 27** John Lyman
St. George, Bermuda
About 1913

/ **FIG. 6** John Lyman
Landscape, Bermuda
About 1914

have always sought after balance, so as to transmit though his painting a message of calm.[135] In this he shared the vision of Henri Matisse, who also dreamed of "an art of balance, or purity and serenity, devoid of troubling or depressing subject matter, an art which might be for every mental worker, be he businessman or writer, like an appeasing influence, like a mental soother, something like a good armchair in which to rest from physical fatigue."[136]

After the war, in 1919, John Lyman settled in France, where he lived for a large part of the year, while spending a few months enjoying the hot climate and a cheaper life in Tunisia. Right to the end of his life, just like Morrice and Matisse, he continued his quest for essential form, the idea of "design" put forward by Roger Fry. He succeeded in this by honing his highly structured, solid style—"classical," as he liked to say. What he would later remember of Tunisia was "the character of the cities, so different from those we live in, [of] the architecture [and of] the inhabitants," but he would especially recall "the extraordinary delicacy of the light . . . you only understand it little by little. It surprises you at first, because you had imagined an Orient full of bright colours—and it's not that at all. The light of North Africa is all nuanced, made up of a thousand delicate, pearly reflections that the eye only becomes sensitive to after a certain time."[137]

The coastal cities of Hammamet and Monastir were among the subjects of his Tunisian output, which, as far as we know, does not include any other beach scenes. The painter preferred the simple and massive volumes of walled cities, like Hammamet, whose appearance changed at different times of the day. Like Paul Klee and Auguste Macke, Lyman was seduced by the shapes and contrasting planes of the white medina, which inspired him to paint vigorously constructed compositions. The minaret of the mosque in *Hammamet* (CAT. 28) stands in immaculate whiteness above the city's ramparts, the Casbah, on the seashore. The light shines on the high barrier of crenelated earth made up of wide purplish planes, foiling any attempt to scale the protective wall.

A pure and sharp-edged light also makes the cupolas in *The Marabouts' Tombs, Morocco* (CAT. 60) stand out against the reds and pinks of the surrounding vegetation. This symphony of colours is not found elsewhere in any of Lyman's output from the Maghreb known up to now. These paintings usually contain spaces in shades of ochre or sand, like those that fill the interior of the citadel in *The Monastir Casbah* (CAT. 62) and that are also found in a small brightly coloured painting of women who have come to draw water from the Roman well in the village of Sidi Djedidi, a few kilometres from Hammamet (CAT. 61). The sea can be glimpsed in the distance in three more organic compositions in which trees figure alongside architectural motifs (CATS. 29, 63 and 64). In *View of North Africa*, the isolation of the mausoleum's planes, of the wall in ruins and of the two burnoose-clad figures in the foreground—rendered in Morrice's style—contrasts clearly outlined forms with the shaggy effect of a tree. In *Zaouia, Hammamet*, vegetation reclaims the religious building, which Lyman painted from another point of view in a very attractive watercolour preserved at the Musée national des beaux-arts du Québec (FIG. 7). In *Landscape with House (North African Coast)*, the trees are like a grid: we have to look through the series of trunks and shadows to arrive at the flood

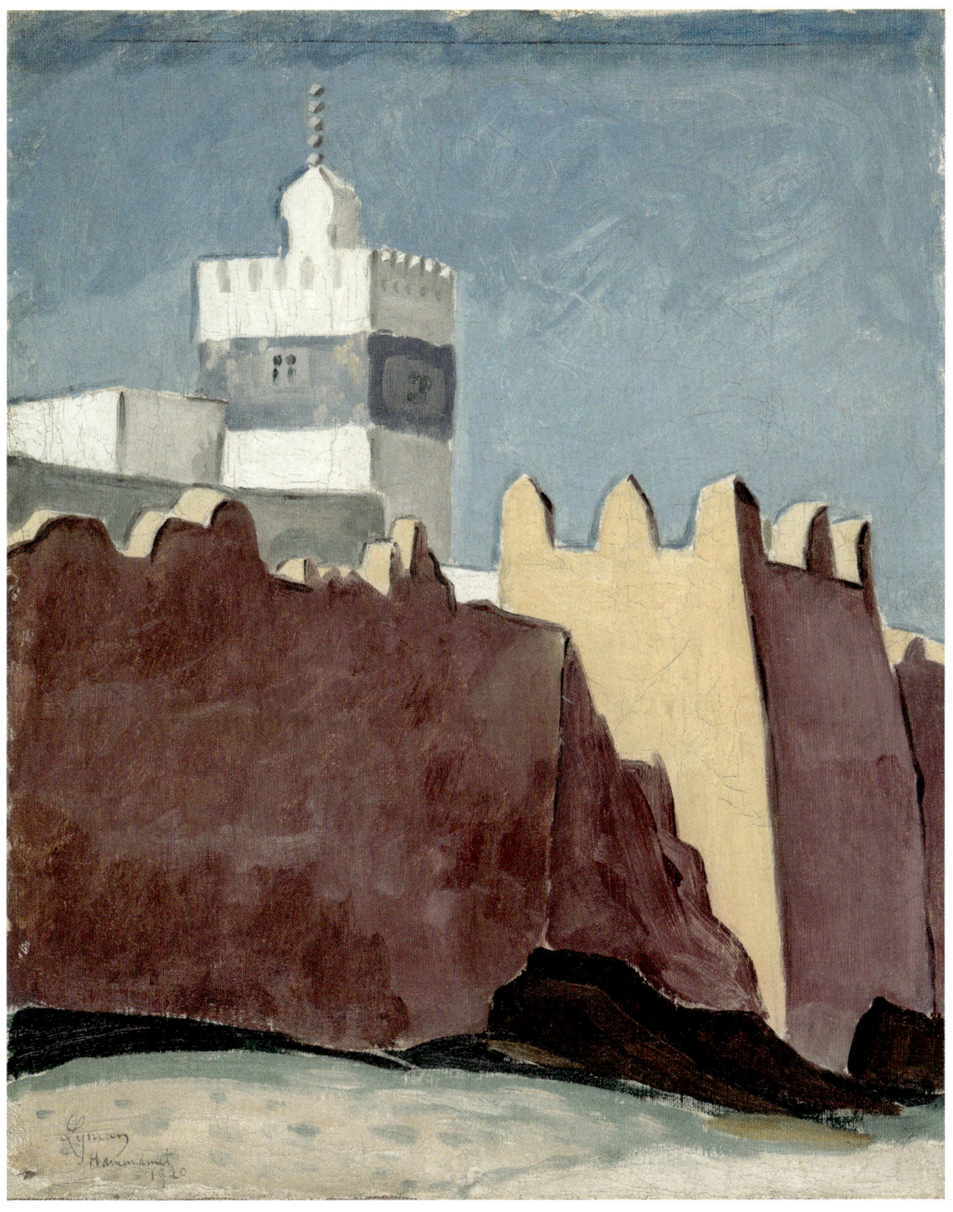

of light that illuminates the field and the seaside house. This organization evokes the magnificent *View of Collioure* that Matisse painted about 1907 or 1908, and which Lyman had perhaps seen when he visited Michael and Sarah Stein. Nonetheless, the comparison shows how much Lyman, in this painting, remained attached to a naturalist vision of landscape.

In 1944, the art critic Robert Élie wrote that the framework of John Lyman's paintings was "always solid, without however being rigid, and that while the painting presents itself like an architectural structure made up of well-defined volumes and planes, it then deepens, until it ends in a completely free game, changing, as indecipherable as life, homogeneous as a living being."[138] This is what we see in the portraits of *Habiba (Young Tunisian Girl)* **(CAT. 30)** and of *The Arab Philosopher* **(CAT. 31)**.

/ **CAT. 28** John Lyman
Hammamet
1920

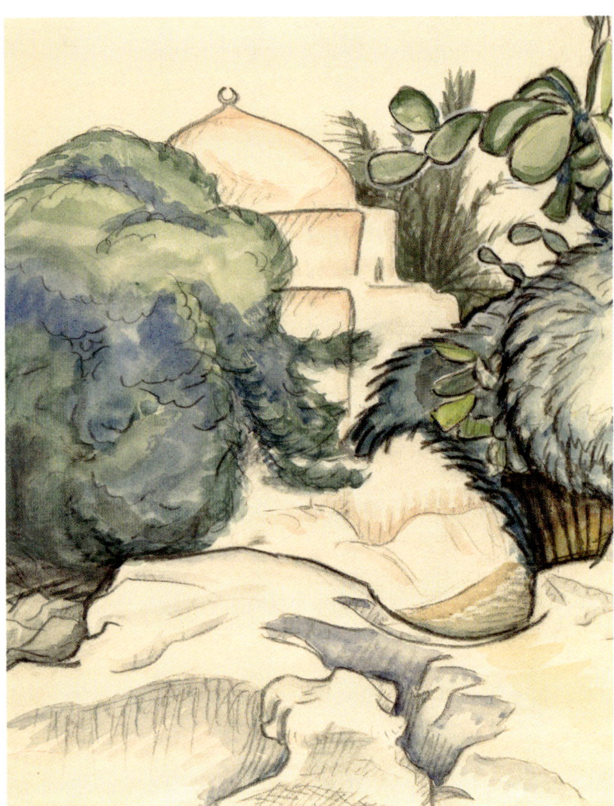

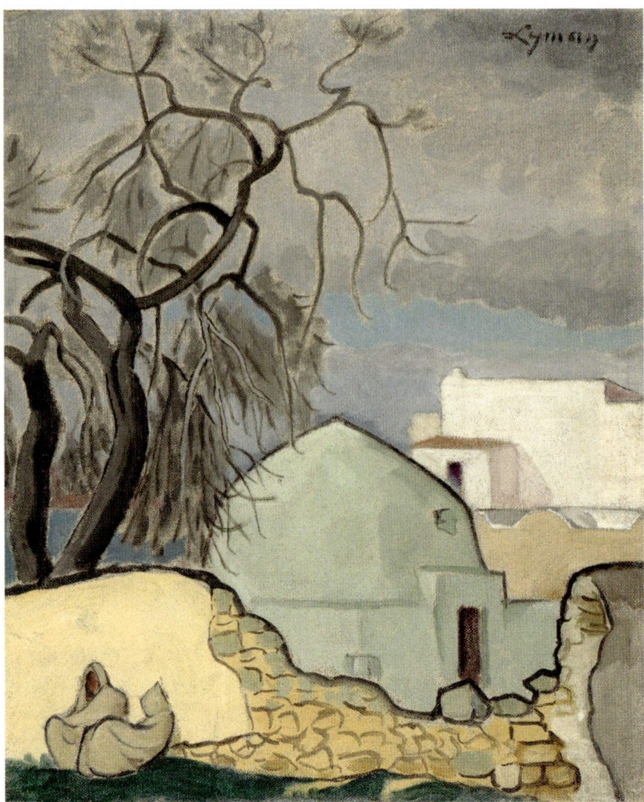

These paintings project a rare expressive intensity, which Lyman achieved by combining geometric structure with a painting style that, using large brushstrokes, gives a rhythm to the background in both portraits. The veil, the *hayek* worn by young Berber women, frames Habiba's pretty round and amber-coloured face and gives the portrait a pyramidal form; this is also the case in *Arab Girl*, preserved at the Agnes Etherington Art Centre in Kingston.

In *The Arab Philosopher*, Lyman gives us a full-length portrait, showing the subject in a meditative pose, legs crossed, his head resting on his left hand. Wearing a turban and oriental slippers, the serious and reflective-looking man is dressed in a burnoose and a dark coat over an immaculately white blouse and trousers. The only decor is an earthenware jar and an ornamental carpet. The background, consisting solely of brushstrokes, is a gradation of purplish colours and contributes to the reflective atmosphere of this remarkable painting. The figure, Tahar Djedidi, was a Tunisian friend of Lyman, and represented for him "a true philosopher," whose "only possession was the infinity of time."[139]

John Lyman's North African works were first exhibited in Paris before being seen in Montreal. Much less present in the salons than his compatriot Morrice had been, Lyman nonetheless had the opportunity to show his work several times in the French capital from 1920 to 1930.[140] The Salon d'Automne was the only one, in 1921 and 1923, to bring together the two painters during their exile, showing Morrice's West Indian landscapes and Lyman's Tunisian landscapes. As always, the Société d'Automne organized a small retrospective of members who had died during the year; this was why, in the autumn of 1924, fourteen works by Morrice were exhibited in its rooms, while only one work, a painting of a nude, was by

/ **FIG. 7** John Lyman
Zaouia, Hammamet
About 1921

/ **CAT. 29** John Lyman
View of North Africa
Between 1920 and 1926

Lyman. Several modern artists had abandoned the salons in favour of other exhibition sites, like the specialized art galleries that were becoming increasingly numerous in the major western capitals. During this period, John Lyman also exhibited at the Salon des Indépendants in 1923 and 1924, as well as at the new Salon des Tuileries, which opened in 1923 and was home to Henri Matisse's works from 1924 to 1954. Rebelling against the Société nationale des beaux-arts, as had the Salon d'Automne in 1903, the Salon des Tuileries wanted to be liberal and eclectic. Artists participated at the invitation of a committee chaired by Albert Besnard. Lyman presented eight works there from 1923 to 1930. In contrast to Morrice, his presence in the Paris salons went unnoticed and the critics remained silent about him. Eyes were turned toward abstraction and the new trends of post-Cubism, Purism, Surrealism and Art Deco.

THE END OF EXILE

In Canada, on the other hand, Montreal's critics and journalists, both French- and English-speaking, praised his work when he exhibited at the Johnson Art Galleries, from October 1 to 15, 1927: "Remarkable exhibition of paintings by Mr. John Lyman,"[141] said *La Presse*; "Canvases Make Definite Appeal," headlined *The Gazette*. Even the *Montreal Star*'s fiery critic, Morgan-Powell, was won over. In his article "John G. Lyman Shows A Remarkable Advance In Painting Pictures" he argued that the painter had abandoned all recklessness and proved that he could now draw and compose.[142]

In this solo show, John Lyman's first in the country since 1913, landscapes were exhibited side by side with intimist scenes like *The Book* (**CAT. 92**),[143] "a marvel," wrote Albert Laberge in *La Presse*.[144] This composition, with its motifs and vibrant colours, turns squarely away from the illusion of naturalism. Its "decorative" effect points straight to Matisse, for whom "decorative" did not have the negative connotation it would acquire over time. He had, after all, declared that "expression and decoration are but one and the same thing, the second term being condensed in the first."[145]

John Lyman would explain that the main reason for his definitive return to Montreal in the autumn of 1931 was the feeling of being an outsider in France: "More and more, I felt that [Canada] was my country, that I belonged to Canada . . . The French landscape called to mind French painters. You could not look at Aix without thinking of Cézanne, whereas here, the landscape was mine, everything was mine, and I could do what I wanted with it."[146] By expressing himself in this way, Lyman was in no way promoting nationalist painting, like that of the Group of Seven, or regionalist painting, which he liked to call "exoticism for consumption on the premises."[147] Lyman's exhibitions in Montreal bear witness to his universal perspective. Thus, in February and March 1931, during his first exhibition at Scott & Sons, the walls were covered with scenes depicting Saint-François, Île d'Orléans, Laval-des-Rapides and Rivière des Mille-Îles, alongside views of Spain and North Africa, and beach scenes like those at Saint-Jean-de-Luz (**CAT. 90**).

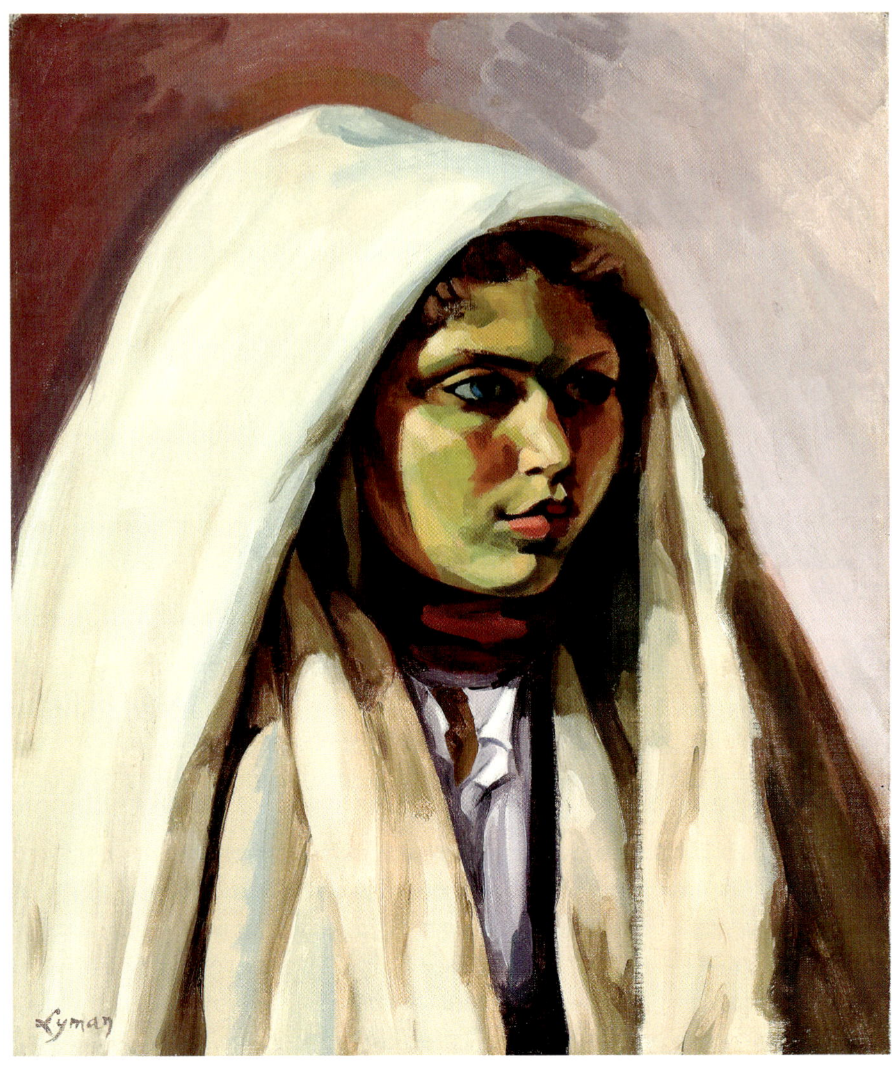

Back in Canada, John Lyman rejoined the art world, not only by exhibiting, but also by taking an interest in young artists, bringing together progressive voices in groups whose values he shared—the Atelier, the Eastern Group and the Contemporary Arts Society—and turning the Montreal apartment where he and Corinne lived into a place for meetings and fertile exchanges on the future of Canadian modernism. The couple's home, well-known for its hospitality, was decorated with "North African rugs, shelves full of leatherbound books and beautiful paintings everywhere, mostly Morrice's and his own."[148] John Lyman became a truly unifying force in his community, involved on several levels, as painter, teacher, art critic and exhibition organizer.

The exile of Lyman and Morrice changed the course of Canadian art history. The sum of their experiences shaped their universal thinking, expressed in the richness of their work: Parisian artistic life, their participation in the large salons, Matisse's teachings and, especially, their many travels were all points of light that would be reflected in the future of art in this country. When John Lyman, in 1945, published his book on James Wilson Morrice and honoured his debt to his older colleague, he concluded with words that could very well be applied to himself: "[Morrice] welcomed influences in conformity with his nature, like all of us, but his independence remained inviolable."[149]

/ CAT. 30 John Lyman
Habiba (Young Tunisian Girl)
About 1922

/ CAT. 31 John Lyman
The Arab Philosopher
Between 1920 and 1926

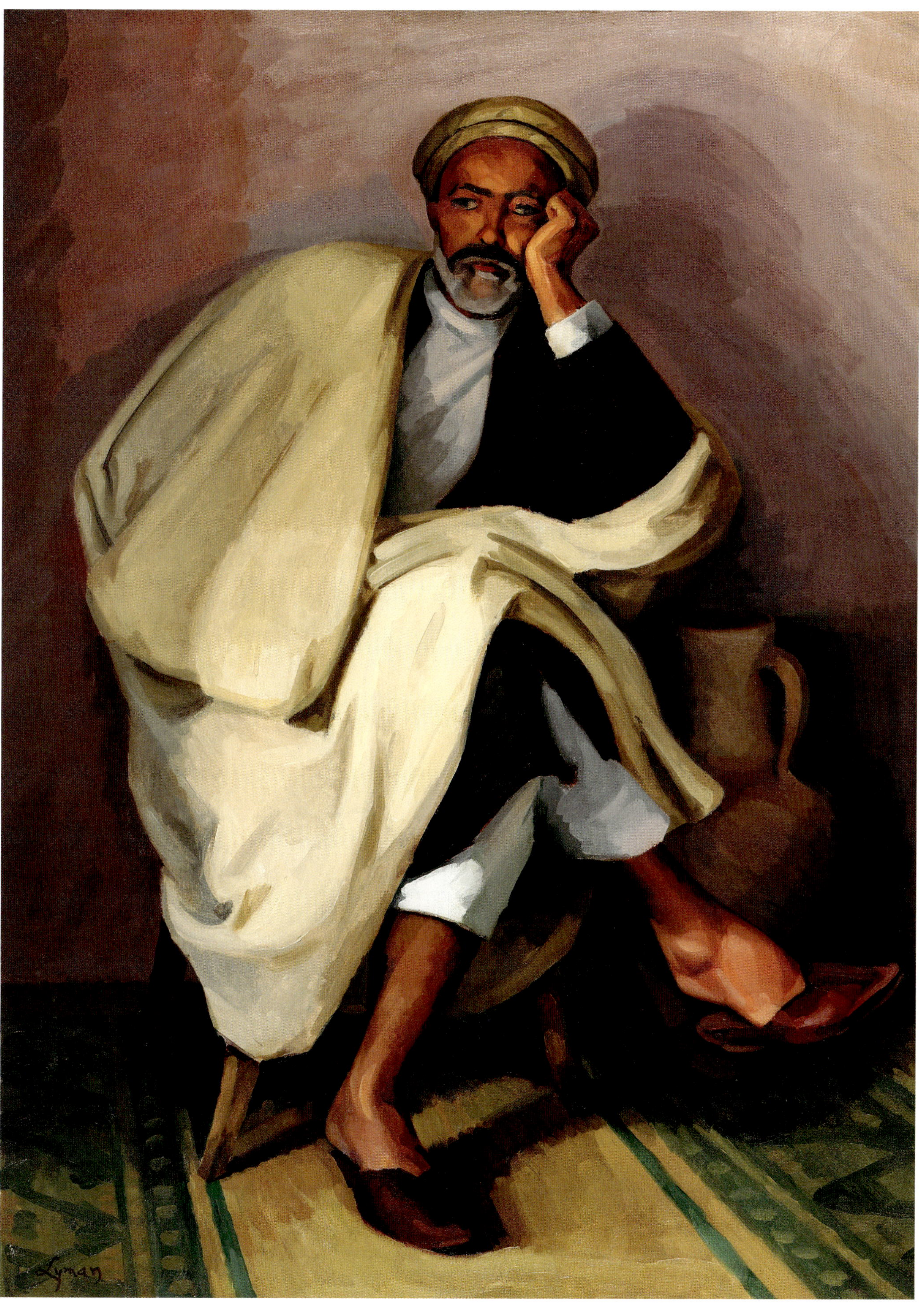

Notes

1. This essay owes a great deal to Lucie Dorais, a Morrice specialist, who placed at my disposal her unpublished research into the artist's work.

2. Except during the winter of 1896-1897, when he stayed in Canada for six months, Morrice came back and stayed for five to eight weeks during the winters of 1899-1900, 1905-1906, 1908-1909, 1911-1912, 1914-1915, in January 1917 and in the winter of 1920-1921. He spent two months in Canada in the summer of 1903.

3. John Lyman, *Morrice* (Montreal: L'Arbre, "Art vivant" series, 1945), p. 10.

4. Ibid.

5. "How are they treating him nowadays over there?" Donald W. Buchanan, "Interview in Montparnasse," *Canadian Art*, vol. 8, no. 2 (Christmas 1950), p. 64.

6. Henri Matisse quoted by Arman Dayot, "Préface," in *Catalogue des tableaux et études par James Wilson Morrice*, exhib. cat. (Paris: Galeries Simonson, 1926), p. 7.

7. See Marc Gauthier's essay in this catalogue, pp. 187-197.

8. Typewritten script of the Guy Viau documentary on John Lyman, *Je vis par les yeux*, 1958, John Lyman fonds, Bibliothèque et Archives nationales du Québec, Montreal, p. 9.

9. Letter from John Lyman to his father, Paris, February 13, 1927, in *Inédits de John Lyman*, texts selected and annotated by Hedwige Asselin (Montreal: Ministère des Affaires culturelles/Bibliothèque nationale du Québec, 1980), p. 213.

10. Sylvain Allaire found the names of some 80 Canadian artists who had exhibited 334 works at the Salon des Artistes français and at the salon that preceded it, from 1870 to 1914. Among these artists were the following: Charles Alexander (1864-1915), Caroline Hélène Armington (1875-1939), Frank Milton Armington (1876-1941), James MacDonald Barnsley (1861-1929), William Blair Bruce (1859-1906), William Brymner (1855-1925), Florence Carlyle (1864-1923), Louis Théodore Dubé (1862-1925), Wyatt Eaton (1849-1896), Allan Aaron Edson (1846-1888), Clarence Gagnon (1881-1941), Charles Paul Gruppe (1860-1940), John Hammond (1843-1939), Robert Harris (1849-1919), Henri Hébert (1884-1950), Louis-Philippe Hébert (1850-1917), Charles Huot (1874-1930), Alexander Young Jackson (1882-1974), Alfred Laliberté (1878-1953), Paul Peel (1860-1992), Sophie Pemberton (1869-1959), George Agnew Reid (1860-1947), John Wentworth Russell (1879-1959), Marc-Aurèle de Foy Suzor-Coté (1869-1937), Frederick Boyd Waters (1879-1924), Percy Franklin Woodcock (1855-1936). Sylvain Allaire, "Les artistes canadiens aux Salons de Paris, de 1870 à 1914," master's thesis, Montreal, Université de Montréal, 1985, p. 20. See also Tobi Bruce and Patrick Shaw Cable, *The French Connection: Canadian Painters at the Paris Salons 1880-1900*, exhib. cat. (Hamilton: Art Gallery of Hamilton, 2011), which adds to this list Mary Alexandra Bell (1864-1951) and Laura Muntz (1860-1930).

11. Dominique Lobstein, "Le Salon de la Société des artistes indépendants : première et unique application de la liberté en art," in Pierre Sanchez, *Dictionnaire des Indépendants* (Dijon: L'Échelle de Jacob, 2003), pp. 13-56.

12. Dominique Lobstein, *Dictionnaire des Indépendants, 1884-1914*, vol. 2. *E-M* (Dijon: L'Échelle de Jacob, 2003), p. 623.

13. In 1923, a similar situation paralyzed the activities of the Société nationale and caused a new disagreement leading to the creation of the Salon des Tuileries, where John Lyman exhibited by invitation in 1923, 1927 and 1930.

14. Pierre Sanchez, "Avertissements," and Olivier Meslay, "Préface," in Pierre Sanchez, *Dictionnaire du Salon d'Automne. Répertoire des exposants et liste des œuvres présentées, 1903-1945* (Dijon: L'Échelle de Jacob, 2006), pp. 9-24.

15. Nicole Cloutier, "Short Note: Morrice 1912," *Journal of Canadian Art History*, vol. 10, no. 2 (1987), pp. 153-159.

16. In the same period, Ontario painter and engraver Donald Shaw MacLaughlan came next after Morrice, with 52 pieces sent to the Salons of the Société des Artistes français and the Nationale from 1899 to 1911. Among the Québécois, Henri Beau participated in the Salons des Artistes français, des Indépendants and d'Automne, with 32 paintings (1893-1907); Marc-Aurèle de Foy Suzor-Coté with 29 paintings, drawings and one sculpture, at the Salon des Artistes français, and one sculpture at the Salon de la Nationale (1894-1911); Clarence Gagnon showed 20 consignments of paintings and one engraving at the Salons des Artistes français and the Nationale (1905-1914); Maurice Cullen showed 17 paintings at the Salon de la Nationale alone (1894-1905); lastly, sculptor Alfred Laliberté was represented at the Salon des Artistes français by 8 pieces of sculpture (1905-1912). We should mention as well that in 1904 Canadian Ernest Percyval Tudor-Hart exhibited at the Salon de la Nationale and the Salon d'Automne. Allaire, "Les artistes canadiens aux Salons de Paris, de 1870 à 1914," pp. 23, 117-122 and 145-146. Finally, the name of William Henry Clapp, who exhibited 4 paintings at the Salon d'Automne in 1906 and 1907, should be added to the list.

17. It is interesting to note that *The Communicant*, Morrice's largest easel painting, done in 1899, was acquired by the American Impressionist William Merrit Chase when it was shown at the Pennsylvania Academy of Fine Arts in Philadelphia in 1900. The painting is now in the collections of the Musée national des beaux-arts du Québec (1978.98).

18. The most recent study of this society is that of Anne-Françoise Ponthus, *La Société Nouvelle (1900-1914). Un réseau d'amis peintres et sculpteurs* [sic] *(Claus, Cottet, Le Sidaner, Martin, Ménard, Simon, Desbois, Meunier, Poupelet, Rodin, Schnegg, Troubetzkoy…)* (Saarbrücken, Germany: Éditions universitaires européennes, 2010), 636 pp. Morrice is discussed on pp. 386-389, and his name is mentioned several times in the annexes.

19. There was one collector of Rodin in Montreal at the end of the nineteenth century: George Alexander Drummond (1829-1910), who had purchased a work by Rodin in Paris in 1891, as well as works by Edgar Degas, Claude Monet and Whistler. Drummond was Scottish by birth, like his friend David Morrice, James's father. Both sat on the board of the Art Association of Montreal, of which Drummond was president in 1896-1897. Janet M. Brooke, "Rodin et le Canada," in *Rodin à Québec*, exhib. cat. (Quebec City: Musée du Québec, 1998), pp. 228-247.

20. Letter from James Morrice to Newton MacTavish, Paris, October 12, 1911.

21. *Quinta Esposizione Internazionale d'Arte della città di Venezia*, exhib. cat. (Venice: Carlo Ferrari, 1903), 159 pp. and 96 ills. [Morrice, p. 64, nos. 37 and 38]; *Sesta Esposizione Arti Visive La Biennale Di Venezia*, exhib. cat. (Venice: Carlo Ferrari, 1905), 165 pp. and 96 ills. [Morrice, p. 36, nos. 29 and 30].

22. In 1904, the French government acquired *Quai des Grands-Augustins*, now in the collections of the Musée d'Orsay (1980-146) and, in 1905, *Au bord de la mer (Saint-Malo)*, a work presumed lost. The Musée des beaux-arts de Lyon purchased *Snow Effect (Sleigh)* in 1906 (cat. 6).

23. Ghislain Clermont, "La réception critique internationale de James Wilson Morrice en 1905," *Revue de l'Université de Moncton*, vol. 26, no. 2 (1993), pp. 83-107.

24. Stéphane Richemond, "Histoire de la Société des Peintres orientalistes français," in Pierre Sanchez, *La Société des Peintres orientalistes français. Répertoire des exposants et liste de leurs œuvres, 1889-1943* (Dijon: L'Échelle de Jacob, 2008), pp. 13-42.

25. The Société held its Salon in February and March at the Grand Palais in Paris.

26. "It is the most interesting exhibition of the year. Somewhat revolutionary at times." Letter from James Wilson Morrice to Newton MacTavish, Paris, August 24, [1909].

27. To read about this exhibition, see Marc Gauthier, "Les Salons parisiens au Canada: l'*Exposition d'art français* de Montréal en 1909," master's thesis, Quebec City, Université Laval, 2011.

28. William Van Horne was the only Montreal collector of his day to step outside the bounds of Impressionism, acquiring works by Toulouse-Lautrec and Paul Cézanne. Van Horne was a member of the consultative committee of *Burlington Magazine* from 1905 to 1915, the year of his death, which Roger Fry so kindly wrote about in an article published in the monthly ("Sir William Van Horne," *The Burlington Magazine*, vol. 28, no. 151 [October 1915], pp. 39-40). See Janet M. Brooke, *Discerning Tastes: Montreal Collectors 1880-1920*, exhib. cat. (Montreal: The Montreal Museum of Fine Arts, 1989), pp. 20-23. In the Van Horne collection, Morrice especially admired a work by El Greco, "one of the most beautiful I've seen," he wrote to Edmund

Morris on April 1, 1913, on his return from Toledo, Spain. *Portrait of a Man of the House of Leiva* by El Greco is now preserved in the collections of the Montreal Museum of Fine Arts (1945.885), bequeathed by Adaline Van Horne.

29. Brooke, "Rodin et le Canada," in *Rodin à Québec*, pp. 228-247.

30. Ibid., p. 234.

31. Gauthier, "Les Salons parisiens au Canada," pp. 122-123.

32. Louis Vauxcelles, "The Art of J. W. Morrice," *The Canadian Magazine*, vol. 34, no. 2 (December 1909), pp. 169-176.

33. "There is to be an exhibition of French art in the Art Gallery here in Montreal next week. I have seen the pictures—most of them I know—good—fairly good but not too good—I think myself we could make an equally good display." Letter from James Wilson Morrice to Edmund Morris, [Montreal], February [3], 1909.

34. "Among the people we met yesterday at the Galerie des Arts are the French Consul [Consul General of France, Joseph de Loynes] and Mr. Morrice, one of Canada's best painters, who has long lived in Paris, but who is currently visiting Montreal." Anonymous, "L'exposition d'art français," *La Presse*, January 27, 1909, p. 13, quoted in Gauthier, "Les Salons parisiens au Canada," p. 70.

35. Letter from James Wilson Morrice to Newton MacTavish, Paris, August 24, [1909].

36. Letter from James Wilson Morrice to Edmund Morris, Paris, February 12, 1911.

37. Letter from James Wilson Morrice to Edmund Morris, Paris, November 8, 1911.

38. Lyman attended the Académie Julian from March 9, 1908, to January 2, 1910, regularly from March 9 to June 7, 1908, from November 9, 1908, to May 17, 1909, and finally from November 9, 1909, to January 2, 1910.

39. On his arrival in Paris in 1890, Morrice had also attended this academy, which he did not seem to enjoy, leaving after four weeks.

40. Letter from John Lyman to his father, [Paris], November 15, 1909. In the following letter sent to his father, dated November 25, Lyman questions Laurens's judgement on drawing.

41. John Lyman, "Art World," *Toronto Saturday Night*, March 6, 1937, p. 16.

42. John Lyman in Fernand Dansereau's film *John Lyman, peintre*, National Film Board, 1959, 28 min 12 s.

43. See Charles C. Hill, *Morrice: A Gift to the Nation – The G. Blair Laing Collection*, exhib. cat. (Ottawa: National Gallery of Canada, 1992), pp. 50 and 51.

44. Lucie Dorais thinks Morrice may have later retouched the 1897 sketch, whose lower section is painted with a thicker paste than the upper section, bringing it in line with the painting's final composition.

45. Maurice Guillemot, "Le Salon de la Société nationale des Beaux-arts," *L'Art et les Artistes*, vol. 5, no. 3 (June 1907), p. 80.

46. Alluding to a poem by Rudyard Kipling about Canada. Letter from J. W. Morrice to Robert Henri, Paris, June 23, [1906], Yale University, Beinecke Rare Book and Manuscript Library, New Haven, Connecticut.

47. *James Wilson Morrice, R.C.A. 1865-1924 Memorial Exhibition*, exhib. cat. (Ottawa: National Gallery of Canada, 1937-1938), no. 2, p. 9. The exhibition was also presented at the Art Gallery of Toronto and the Art Association of Montreal.

48. The sketch preserved by the Art Gallery of Ontario is entitled *Winter Scene, Quebec* (56/27).

49. William R. Watson, *Retrospective: Recollections of a Montreal Art Dealer* (Toronto: University of Toronto Press, 1974), p. 16, reprinted in Hill, *Morrice: A Gift to the Nation*, p. 116.

50. Lucie Dorais, email to the author, September 12, 2013.

51. Lyman, *Morrice*, p. 23.

52. See Hélène Sicotte, "A Canadian in Paris," in *Clarence Gagnon: Dreaming the Landscape*, exhib, cat. (Quebec City/Montreal: Musée national des beaux-arts du Québec/Les Éditions de l'Homme, 2006), pp. 55-93.

53. Lyman quoted by Guy Viau, *Notes biographiques*, MNBAQ library, Lyman file, chapter 2, p. 4.

54. Letter from John Lyman to his father, Paris, May 26, [1909], in *Inédits de John Lyman*, p. 184.

55. Henri Chervet, "Le Salon de la Société Nationale des Beaux-arts," *La Nouvelle Revue* [Paris], May 1, 1909, p. 133.

56. Maurice Hamel, "Les Salons de 1909 – La Société Nationale des Beaux-Arts," *Les Arts* [Paris], (June 1909), p. 16.

57. Louis Vauxcelles, "Le Salon de la Société Nationale," *Gil Blas* [Paris], April 14, 1909, p. [2].

58. Louis Vauxcelles [Louis Mayer], "Le Salon d'Automne," *Gil Blas* [Paris], October 17, 1905, supplement, p. 1. Morrice exhibited four studies at this Salon, three Venetian and one entitled *Les Tuileries*.

59. Lyman, *Morrice*, p. 19.

60. John O'Brian carried out an excellent study of the changes that marked Morrice's aesthetic development as a result of contact with his Irish friend Roderic O'Conor. He shows brilliantly how the latter was a "catalyst" for Morrice's growing interest in Paul Gauguin, Pierre Bonnard and Édouard Vuillard, and how his works reflect the influence of these three painters. John O'Brian, "Morrice, O'Conor, Gauguin, Bonnard et Vuillard," *Revue de l'université de Moncton*, vol. 15, nos. 2-3 (April-December 1982), pp. 9-35.

61. Vauxcelles, "The Art of J. W. Morrice," p. 169.

62. "Comparing me to Whistler is absurd." Letter from James Wilson Morrice to Edmund Morris, Concarneau, December 7, 1909.

63. Vauxcelles, "The Art of J. W. Morrice," p. 176.

64. Letter from James Morrice to Edmund Morris, Paris, 30 January, [1910].

65. *Manet and the Post-Impressionists*, London, Grafton Galleries, from November 8, 1910, to January 15, 1911. Focused on Cézanne, Van Gogh and Gauguin, the three great masters of the movement, Fry's exhibition brought together their successors—Matisse, Picasso, Derain, Friesz, Marquet, de Vlaminck, Puy, Valtat, Manguin, Rouault and many others. Manet's presence linked the movement to the tradition. The second exhibition, *Second Post-Impressionist Exhibition*, presented at the Grafton Galleries from October 5 to December 31, 1912, was organized in a different way, with young British and Russian artists alongside French Post-Impressionists. See Anne-Pascale Bruneau, "Aux sources du post-impressionnisme. Les expositions de 1910 et 1912 aux Grafton Galleries de Londres," *Revue de l'Art*, no. 113 (1996), pp. 7-18.

66. Letter from James Morrice to Edmund Morris, Paris, January 9, [1911].

67. Henri Matisse, "Notes d'un peintre," *La Grande Revue*, t. 53 (December 25, 1908). Translated as "Notes of a Painter" in Alfred H. Barr, *Matisse: His Art and His Public* (London: Secker & Warburg, 1975), p. 121. Subsequent quotes are taken from this publication.

68. "Also from Morrice I learnt more about pictures; and it was he who later advised me to look at Matisse." Clive Bell, *Old Friends: Personal Recollections* (London: Chatto & Windus, 1956), p. 66.

69. Cécile Debray, introduction in Henri Matisse, *Notes d'un peintre* (Paris: Centre Pompidou/Succession H. Matisse, 2012), p. 5.

70. Matisse's participation in this salon, which took place from October 1 to November 8, was in line with small retrospectives dedicated to accomplished or deceased painters presented there since 1904: homage had already been paid to Ingres, Gauguin, Cézanne and Renoir.

71. The names of the jury members were only provided in the catalogue, distributed at the opening of the Salon. "Règlement de l'exposition de 1908 – Admissions," Société du Salon d'Automne, *Catalogue des Ouvrages de Peinture, Sculpture, Dessin, Gravure, Architecture et Art décoratif exposés au Grand Palais des Champs-Élysées*, exhib. cat. (Paris: Librairie Administrative Paul Dupont, 1908), pp. 300-301. The exhibition took place from October 1 to November 8.

72. Matisse's name appears in two ways in the salon catalogues, under the letter M for "Matisse, Henri" and under the letter H for "Henri-Matisse." It may have been the presence of Auguste Matisse at the 1904 Salon d'Automne that made Henri decide to identify himself in this way.

73. Letter from J. W. Morrice to Edmund Morris, Paris, October 23, [1908].

74. Gertrude Stein, *Portraits and Prayers* (New York: Random House, 1934), p. 72.

75. "Nothing new here except the pictures of the 'Cubists' at the Salon d'Automne. This art I am incapable of understanding." Letter from James Morrice to Edmund Morris, Paris, November 8, 1911.

76. Jean Clair, "Les aventures du nerf optique," in *Bonnard*, exhib. cat. (Paris: Centre Georges Pompidou, 1984), p. 18.

77. Letter from James Wilson Morrice to Edmund Morris, Paris, June 20, 1911.

78. Nicole Cloutier, *James Wilson Morrice, 1865-1924*, exhib. cat. (Montreal: The Montreal Museum of Fine Arts, 1985), p. 214.

79. Letter from John Lyman to his father [Frederick Gold Lyman], Paris, May 31, [1910], in *Inédits de John Lyman*, p. 195.

80. He continued, "Perhaps it would interest you to know that all the greatest painters since the XVIIIth century, with a couple of isolated exceptions such as Von Marees & Turner, were more or less by adoption, if not by birth Parisians—Ingres, Delacroix, Millet, Chavannes, Courbet, Manet, Renoir, Cézanne, Whistler, Lautrec, Van Gogh & Gauguin. Naturally their memory & example (with exception of Whistler) flourish greenest here." Letter from John Lyman to his father, Paris, May 20, 1910, in *Inédits de John Lyman*, p. 193.

81. Letter from John Lyman to his father, Paris, August 31, [1919], ibid., p. 205.

82. Louise Dompierre, *John Lyman, 1886-1967*, exhib. cat. (Kingston: Agnes Etherington Art Centre, 1986), pp. 46 and 48.

83. George Moore, *Memoirs of my Dead Life* (1906), quoted in a letter from John Lyman to his father, Paris, August 3, 1919, in *Inédits de John Lyman*, p. 203. Édouard Manet immortalized the writer in a pastel portrait in 1879.

84. Fernand Préfontaine, "La mare aux grenouilles," *Le Nigog*, vol. 1, no. 5 (May 1918), in *Le Nigog. Réimpression à l'identique des 12 numéros: janvier à décembre 1918* (Montreal: Comeau and Nadeau, 1998), p. 170. Préfontaine had seen Lyman's *Self-portrait* at the 35th Exhibition of the Art Association of Montreal in 1918: "Mr. Lyman is a disturbing painter; his two portraits are solidly drawn and have accurate values, but they are unfortunately painted in colours I do not understand. Mr. Lyman, who is an artist, obviously has the right to use whatever colours he wants, but, all the same, my pleasure in seeing his work is spoiled by this use of unpleasant tones."

85. Paul Dumas, "Lyman," *Le Quartier Latin*, vol. 26, no. 11 (December 17, 1943), p. III.

86. *Beach at Trouville* is catalogued at no. 6. in *John Lyman*, exhib. cat., essay by Gilles Corbeil (Montreal: The Montreal Museum of Fine Arts, 1963), n. p.

87. As suggested by Charles C. Hill, *Acquisition Report*, no. 23989, National Gallery of Canada.

88. Dompierre, *John Lyman*, p. 36 (ill.).

89. The exhibition, which was held from the May 1 to 13, 1933, brought together works by the members of the new artists' group, the Atelier (André Biéler, Elizabeth Frost, Georg Holt, John Lyman and Goodridge Roberts), which Lyman established in December 1931, a few months after his return to Montreal. The Atelier's first exhibition had taken place in the spring of 1932 (March 30 to April 9), also at the Henry Morgan Gallery, and included André Biéler, Marc-Aurèle Fortin, Elizabeth Frost, Edwin H. Holgate, Georg Holt and John Lyman.

90. Several members of the Art Association of Montreal had the last name Lyman. The names Frederick and John G., mentioned for the first time in the Association's annual reports in 1905 and 1907, joined those of A. C. Lyman, Arthur Lyman, F. S. Lyman, H. H. Lyman and Walter E. Lyman, who had been members since the end of the nineteenth century. In 1913, there were seven members named Lyman: Arthur, C. Sydney, F. G., Georges, John G., Frederick G. and Walter E. In 1917, John was no longer a member, but his father remained so until his death in 1927.

91. Léon Lorrain, "Le Salon du printemps," *Le Devoir*, March 19, 1912, p. 1.

92. Arthur Stringer, "Arthur Stringer's New York Letter," *The Saturday Mirror* [Montreal], March 8, 1913.

93. *Redhead Sitting in the Garden of Monsieur Forest* and *The Hangover* by Toulouse-Lautrec and *Portrait of Madame Cézanne* by Paul Cézanne. Brooke, *Discerning Tastes*, p. 62.

94. *Bagatelle*, now in a private collection, illustrated the article "Au Salon de Peinture à la Galerie des Arts," *La Presse*, March 29, 1913, p. 16. It can be seen in colour in Dompierre, *John Lyman*, p. IV. The painting entitled *A Brunette*, now lost, illustrated the article by Samuel Morgan-Powell [S.M.P.], "Art and the Post-Impressionists," *The Montreal Daily Star*, March 29, 1913, p. 22. *Wild Nature Impromptu*, also known as *Wild Nature Impromptu, 2nd State*, which we have not traced, was reproduced twice in 1913: Ella May, "'Critics Ignorant' says 'Futurist Supporter,'" *The Montreal Herald*, March 27, 1913; and Morgan-Powell, "Art and the Post-Impressionists," just cited above. *Humoresque – The Circus*, now lost, does not appear in any newspaper.

95. As the reproductions of the second version of *Wild Nature Impromptu* in the *Herald* and the *Star* show, the composition of the work is very similar to the first version, a lake bordered by a field and mountains, dotted with a few trees, with a ribbon of sky across the top. In the second version, the painter allots more space to the sky, which takes up half of the painted surface. The painting is square in shape, in contrast to the first version, which is rectangular.

96. Morgan-Powell, "Art and the Post-Impressionists," p. 22.

97. Anonymous, "Futurist Pictures Cause Stir at Spring Art Exhibit," *The Montreal Daily Herald*, March 26, 1913, p. 3.

98. Michèle Grandbois, "The Challenge of the Nude," in *The Nude in Modern Canadian Art 1920-1950*, exhib. cat. (Quebec City/Paris: Musée national des beaux-arts du Québec/ Somogy Éditions d'Art, 2009), pp. 23-34.

99. May, "'Critics Ignorant' says 'Futurist Supporter,'" p. 2 (ill.); Anonymous, "Artists Divided Over 'Art' Show by the Futurists," *The Montreal Daily Herald*, March 28, 1913, p. 6; Truth [pseud.], "Primal Academism as Best Name for Futurist School," *The Montreal Daily Herald*, March 29, 1913, p. 16.

100. Mortimer-Lamb was pointing very directly at the critic from *The Montreal Daily Star*, Samuel Morgan-Powell. H. Mortimer-Lamb, "Letter From Mr. Lamb," in "Post-Impression Creates Much Discussion Locally," *The Montreal Daily Star*, April 7, 1913; H. Mortimer-Lamb, "Art and Art Critics," in "Letters to the Editor," *The Montreal Daily Star*, April 19, 1913. In Mortimer-Lamb's opinion, John Lyman presented the most modern works, which was not the case of Randolph S. Hewton and A. Y. Jackson, whom critics had wrongly associated with Post-Impressionism.

101. May, "'Critics Ignorant' says 'Futurist Supporter,'" p. 2.

102. "Letters to Editor/Mr. J. G. Lyman's Paintings," *The Montreal Daily Star*, April 1, 1913, p. 10.

103. "Mr. John G. Lyman Writes in Defence of *Post-impressionism*," *The Montreal Daily Star*, May 5, 1913.

104. "Compare his [Cullen's] snow, or that of Mr. Suzor-Coté, with the snow painted by Mr. J. W. Morrice. You have a very fine example of the immense loss in values that results from exclusive studio work . . . Mr. Morrice gives us flat, disappointing tones." S.M.P., "Art Association Exhibition Shows Notable Features," *The Montreal Daily Star*, March 25, 1913.

105. John Lyman would later say that the members of the Art Association had not seen what he was going to exhibit. Lyman in Dansereau, *John Lyman, peintre*.

106. It should be noted that of the 42 paintings identified in the catalogue, only 35 were shown, Samuel Morgan-Powell tells us in his article "Essays, Fugues, Adventures and Improvisation: Extraordinary Display of Crudities and Offensive Things at the Art Gallery," *The Montreal Daily Star*, May 23, 1913, p. 2.

107. *Exhibition of Paintings and Drawings by John G. Lyman in the Galleries of The Art Association*, exhib. cat. (Montreal: Montreal Art Association, 1913), 4 pp.. The exhibition was held from May 21 to May 31.

108. See on this subject the bibliography by Lorne Huston, "The 1913 Spring Exhibition of the Art Association of Montreal: Anatomy of a Public Debate," *Journal of Canadian Art History*, vol. 34, no. 1 (2013), pp. 43-53.

109. M.C.J., "Mr. Lyman Shows Clever Pictures at The Gallery but His Art Lacks Distinction and Is Largely Imitative," *The Montreal Daily Star*, May 21, 1913, p. 2.

110. Dompierre, *John Lyman*, p. 38.

111. John Lyman, script of the film *Je vis par les yeux*, 1958, p. 25, BANQ, quoted in Dompierre, ibid. With regard to his compatriots' incomprehension of his work, Morrice wrote, "Besides I am becoming doubtful about the advisability of sending pictures to Toronto. Nothing is sold (except to our excellent friend MacTavish)—nobody understands them—and it involves great expense. I have not the slightest desire to improve the taste of the Canadian public." Letter from James Wilson Morrice to Edmund Morris, Paris, February 12, 1911.

112. *Correspondance entre Charles Camoin et Henri Matisse*, introduced and annotated by Claudine Grammont (Lausanne: Bibliothèque des Arts/Succession H. Matisse, 1997), 231 pp.; *Matisse-Marquet. Correspondance, 1898-1947*, selected and annotated by Claudine Grammont (Lausanne: La Bibliothèque des Arts, 2008), 195 pp.

113. Letter from James Wilson Morrice to Edmund Morris, Paris November 1, [1912], when he announced his departure for Tangier in November 1912.

114. Muriel Ciolkowska, "Memories of Morrice," *The Canadian Forum*, vol. 6 (November 1925), p. 53.

115. Noël Lajoie, "Propos d'ateliers. Entretien avec John Lyman," *Le Devoir*, December 31, 1955.

116. See Lucie Dorais's essay in this catalogue, which deals with Morrice's visits to the Maghreb, pp. 79-101.

117. "I got some good sketches and I am now working on them." Letter from James Wilson Morrice to Newton MacTavish, Paris, May 26, [1915].

118. The study is preserved at the Montreal Museum of Fine Arts under the title *House in Santiago* (1981.9).

119. The National Gallery of Canada has the *Study for "Houses, Cuba"* (30482), which gives a closer view of the scene. The main differences are the way the elements are drawn, as well as the presence of a fourth figure in the centre, replacing the black child at the foot of the palm tree.

120. The *Study for "Garden in Cuba"* is in the collections of the Art Gallery of Hamilton (81.47).

121. See the updated information and recent discoveries on this issue in Lucie Dorais, *J. W. Morrice as an Armchair Traveller*, manuscript, Ottawa, February 2006, 24 pp. and notes.

122. See Hill, *Morrice: A Gift to the Nation*, pp. 167 and 168.

123. Lyman, *Morrice*, p. 35

124. John Lyman, "The Morrice Retrospective," *The Montrealer*, February 15, 1938, p. 19. In April 1937, the Art Gallery of Ontario had acquired *Landscape, Trinidad* from the Galerie Pierre Matisse.

125. "Since Gauguin's wonderful adventure, no other painter has come to know these islands without being dazzled by the charm of the exotic setting, no one else has so well understood their essential character." Lyman, *Morrice*, p. 35.

126. P. G. Konody, "Art and Artists. The Goupil Gallery Salon," *The Observer* [Aberdeen, UK], November 27, 1921, p. 10.

127. Barr, *Matisse*, p. 122.

128. From the introduction to the catalogue *Manet and the Post-Impressionists*, written by Desmond MacCarthy, based on notes provided by Roger Fry (London: Ballantyne, 1910), p. 9.

129. Matisse explained this idea by referring to the purchase he had just made of a small panel by Seurat, hanging on the wall of his Paris apartment next to a photo of *Jacob Wrestling with the Angel* by Delacroix: "His composition [Delacroix's], is created from all sorts of things, whereas Seurat uses scientifically organized materials more, reproducing and showing us objects constructed by scientific means rather than by signs stemming from feelings. The result, from the point of view of the work, is a positivism, a slightly inert stability in his composition that is not a creation of the mind, but a juxtaposition of objects. You have to get past that barrier to feel the light, colourful and gentle and pure, the highest pleasure." *Correspondance entre Charles Camoin et Henri Matisse*, p. 79.

130. Lyman, *Morrice*, p. 35. This is actually *Landscape, Trinidad (Macqueripe Bay)*, which Lyman wrongly called *A Bathing Cove, Trinidad*, and which he reproduced at the very end of his book (ill. 20).

131. "The reason that I seem so indifferent to painting is that I have been discouraged—not by criticism & opposition—but by your regret to have let me go in for that art, your impatience to see me produce something marketable, & my desire not to complicate your financial burdens." Letter from John Lyman to his father, Cannes, April 4, 1916, in *Inédits de John Lyman*, p. 197.

132. He returned there in the summer of 1918, but this time without doing any painting.

133. Letter from John Lyman to his father, Bermuda, [?] 3rd (1914), in *Inédits de John Lyman*, p. 196.

134. See Peter Morrin, Judith Zilczer and William C. Agee, *The Advent of Modernism: Post-Impressionism and North American Art, 1900-1918*, exhib. cat. (Atlanta: High Museum of Art, 1986), pp. 154-155. John Lyman held this uncle, who had abandoned a flourishing scientific career for modern painting, in high esteem: "Before ever coming here he had made a reputation for himself in science, had gained a competency for life, and had painted decorations in the Capitol at Washington. After spending about three years here, he perceived that he had hitherto had no idea of what art was, and settled down to reside & study. Aside from his admirable work, he has made psychological investigations of great importance." Letter from John Lyman to his father, Paris, May 20, 1910, in *Inédits de John Lyman*, p. 193.

135. Lyman in Dansereau, *John Lyman, peintre*.

136. Barr, *Matisse*, p. 122.

137. Lajoie, "Propos d'ateliers," see note 115 above.

138. Robert Élie, "La peinture. L'œuvre de John Lyman," *La Nouvelle Relève*, vol. 3, no. 3 (March-April 1944), p. 178.

139. List of John Lyman's paintings exhibited at the Art Association of Montreal up to 1935, accompanied by a short biography and notes on the paintings, including *The Arab Philosopher*. Biographical file on the artist at the Montreal Museum of Fine Arts.

140. Except for 1922, 1925 and 1929.

141. [Albert Laberge], "L'Art et les artistes. Remarquable exposition de peintures par John Lyman. Scènes de Tunisie d'un riche coloris et paysages de France et du Canada par un artiste très personnel," *La Presse*, October 8, 1927.

142. "He has abandoned all recklessness; he has given full proof that he can draw and can compose," *The Montreal Star*, October 7, 1927.

143. I want to thank Richard Renlund, who brought this painting to my attention in the fall of 2011.

144. [Albert Laberge], "L'Art et les artistes," see note 141 above.

145. With regard to the "decorative," refer to Henri Matisse, *Écrits et propos sur l'art*, introduced by Dominique Fourcade (Paris: Hermann, 1972), pp. 308 and 309.

146. Dansereau, *John Lyman, peintre*.

147. Ibid.

148. Philip Surrey, "Preface," *John Lyman*, exhib. cat. (Quebec City/Montreal: Musée du Québec/Musée d'art contemporain, 1966), n. p.

149. Lyman, *Morrice*, p. 36.

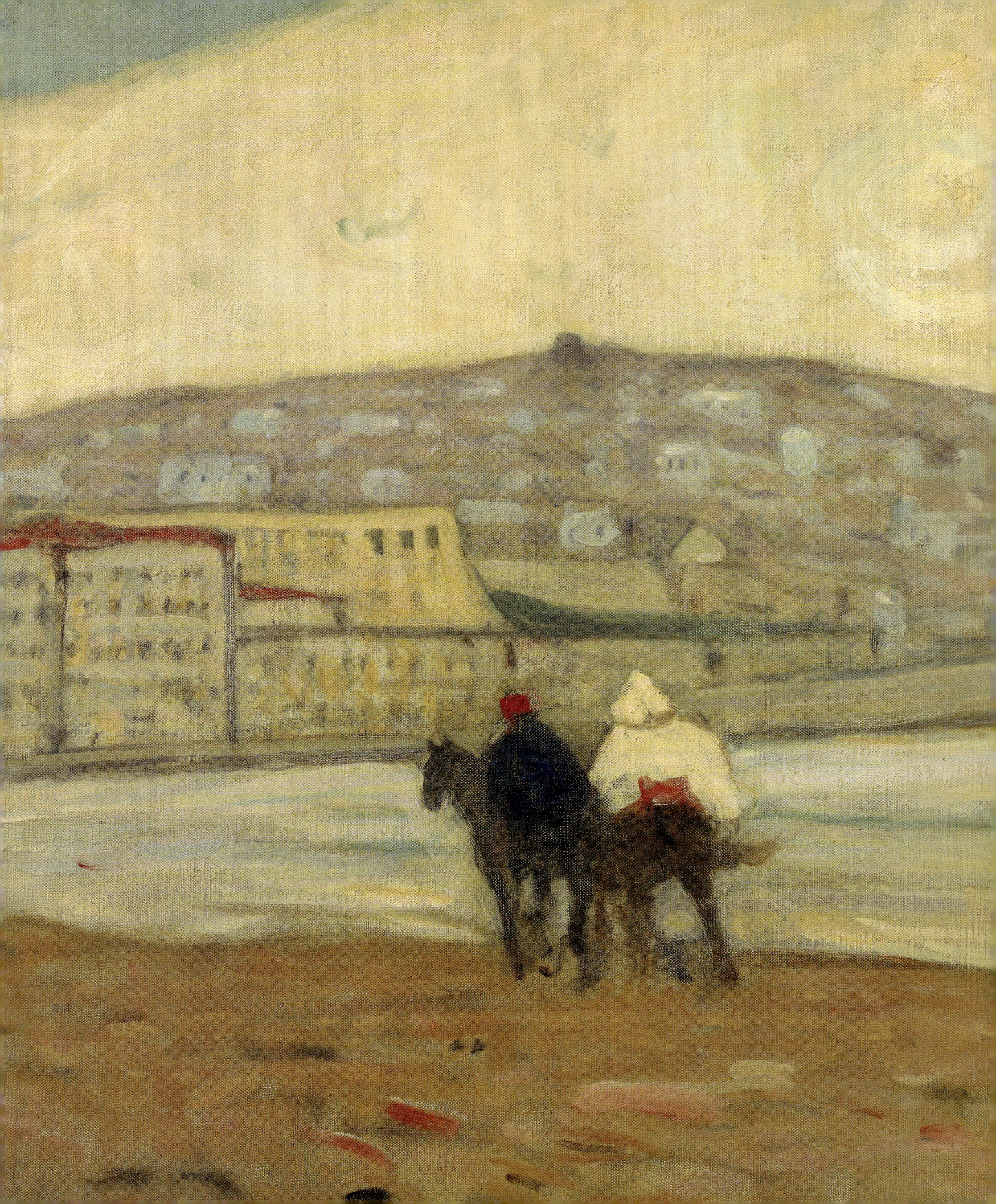

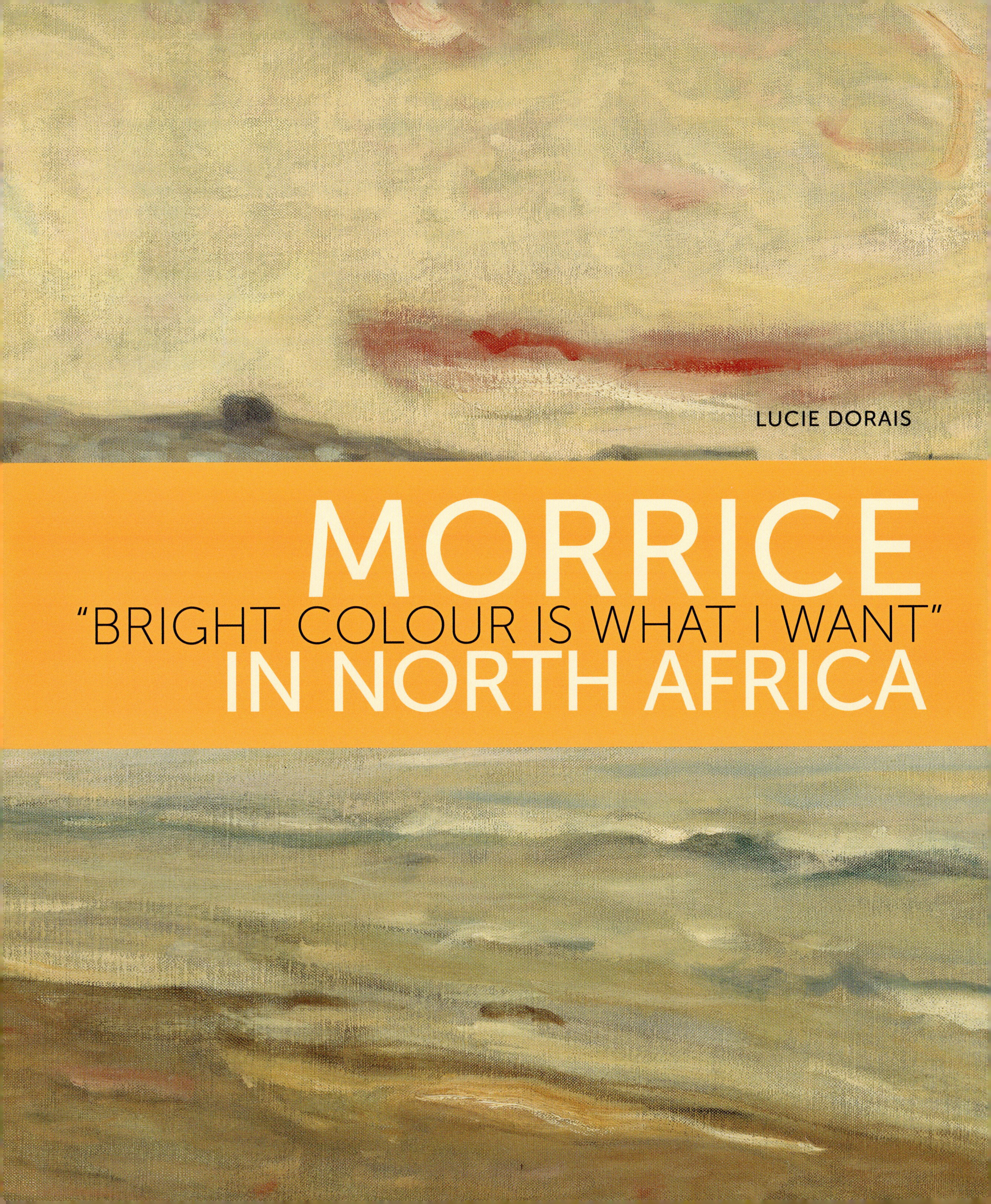

LUCIE DORAIS

MORRICE

"BRIGHT COLOUR IS WHAT I WANT"

IN NORTH AFRICA

Born in Montreal to prosperous Scottish parents and Parisian by adoption, known for his atmospheric, soft-toned landscapes, James Wilson Morrice travelled often, and to increasingly distant destinations, for creative stimulation. In February 1912, he debarked in Tangier; this was his first trip outside of Quebec or Europe, and, as he had two years earlier in Concarneau, he took in the city and the bustling life around him. The French painter Henri Matisse was also staying in Tangier, and the two artists were reunited in the North African city the following winter. So influential were these visits that Morrice subsequently almost completely abandoned European or Quebec subjects. His pursuit of sun-soaked subjects also took him to the West Indies, but it was to North Africa that he returned most often.

Morrice might have discovered the South much earlier, during a stay in Capri about 1894, but he was not yet ready to abandon his Dutch fogs and conventional landscapes inspired by the paintings of Henri Harpignies, even though a few of his sunny views of Capri were so successful that they were long thought to have been painted much later in his career—and in North Africa. Instead, he fell in love with Venice, which he visited during his 1894 trip (CATS. 10 and 11), and the Queen of the Adriatic was long his only Orient: all of the paintings that he sent to the exhibitions of the Peintres orientalistes français, in Paris, in 1904 and 1905, were Venetian. In 1912, having timidly incorporated a bit of Fauvist colour into his works, Morrice was finally ready to take on the sun of North Africa.

Morocco, Algeria and Tunisia—*El-Maghrib* (an Arabic term meaning "land of the setting sun")—had been part of Europeans' imaginary Orient for centuries. These three Muslim countries shared an Arab-Berber culture that, by 1912, was imbued to various degrees with French and, in Morocco, Spanish culture. Morrice visited them all, so it is not always easy to determine where he painted a particular North African subject: is *View of a North African Town* (CAT. 32), for instance, Moroccan or Tunisian? Few postcards were published before the First World War, and those published subsequently bore testimony to the frenzied pace of demolition and construction in the Maghreb, particularly Morocco, after 1920.

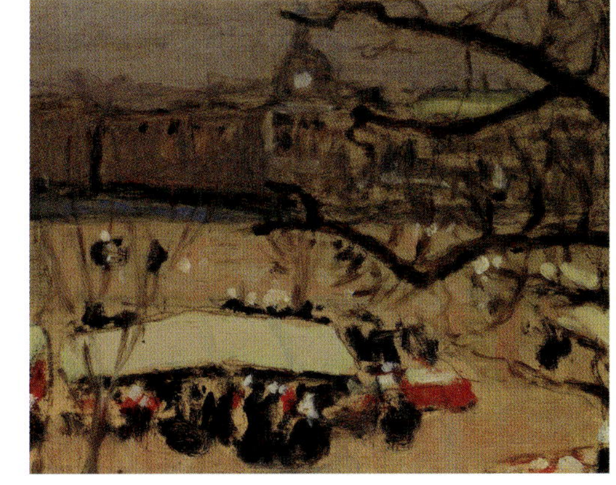

Previous double page:

/ CAT. 33 (DETAIL) James W. Morrice
Tangier
1912

/ FIG. 8 James W. Morrice
Market, Concarneau
About 1909-1910

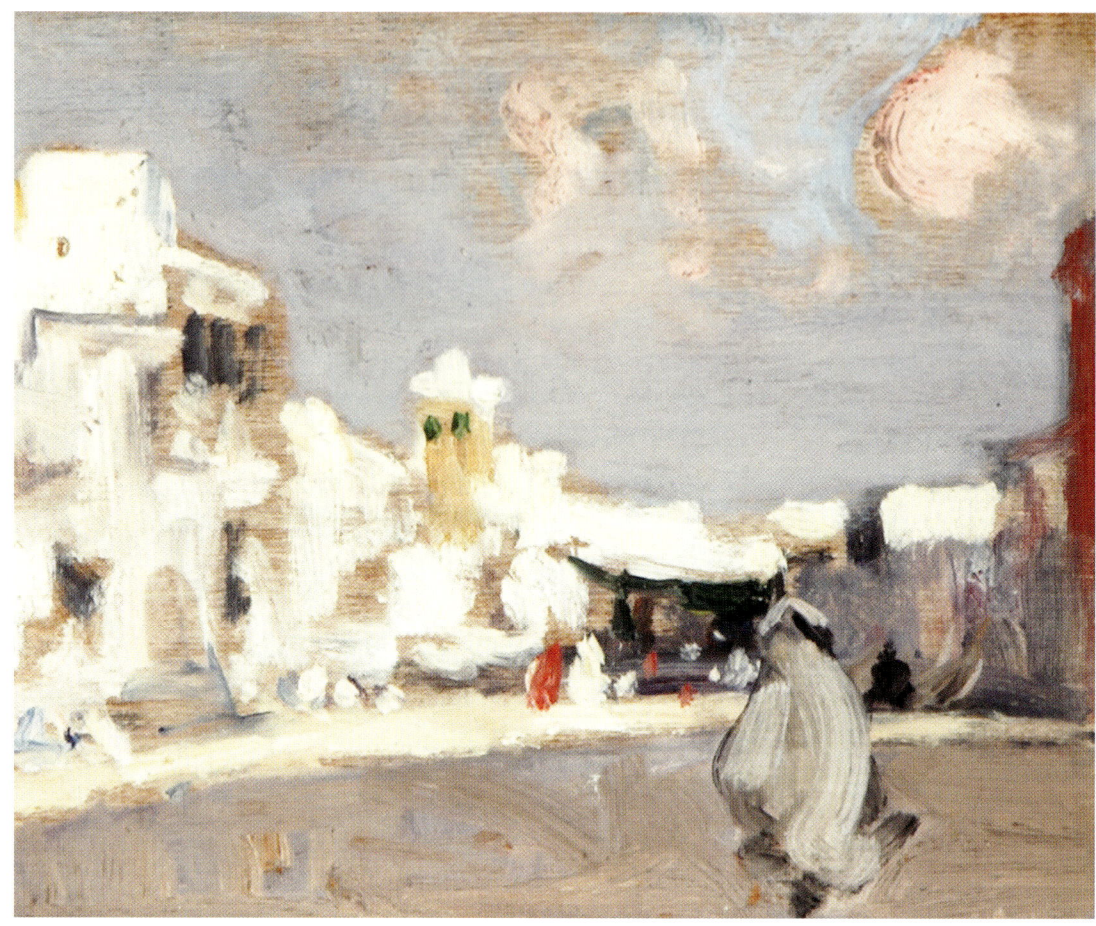

The Marshan hill in Tangier, for example, the probable subject of the painting *Landscape, Tangier* (CAT. 36), was rapidly covered with villas and buildings soon after Morrice visited.

FIRST STAY IN TANGIER

Morrice left for Tangier not from Paris but from Montreal in late January 1912. Arriving in his hometown just before Christmas with a group of paintings that he was planning to show at Scott & Sons, he was perhaps a bit disappointed by the low visibility of his entries in the 1911 Salon d'Automne—which had been dominated by the Cubists, whose work he did not understand.[1] The exhibition in Montreal opened on January 16, but Morrice was in Quebec City and planning to set sail for Gibraltar on February 3.[2] Was he already thinking about Morocco? He departed early, setting sail in New York, with friends, before the end of January.[3] He landed in Gibraltar on February 3 or 11;[4] from there, it took only a few hours to cross the strait.

At the time, Morocco was not yet a tourist destination,[5] but Tangier enjoyed special status due to its proximity to Spain, and travel agencies were beginning to vaunt its charms. The magazine *The Studio* among others recommended the city to painters,[6] and many eagerly took the advice; most of them stayed at the Grand Hôtel Villa de France. Morrice did so, as well as Henri Matisse and his wife, Amélie, who had arrived in late January; and the African-American painter Henry Ossawa Tanner, his wife and the young Australian Hilda Rix, who moved in on February 4.[7]

/ **CAT. 32** James W. Morrice
View of a North African Town
About 1912-1914

/ **FIG. 9** L.L., Paris
Market Scene, Tangier
About 1925?

/ **FIG. 10** A. Cavilla, Tangier
General View from the Grand Zoco
About 1910

The large white hotel, owned by the Davin family, overlooked the Grand Socco open-air market **(FIG. 9)**; the European quarter, still new, was situated behind the hotel, so that the view from hotel's windows was completely "Moorish"—including the bell tower of the Anglican St. Andrew's Church—but one did not hear the muezzin's call to prayer or the cries of the donkey drivers **(FIG. 10)**. At the back of the Grand Socco, the Fez gate marked the entrance to the medina (the old Arab quarter), from which a maze of alleys rose toward the Casbah (seat of the sultanate) topped with a minaret. One could also skirt the medina walls—to the right to go down to the beach or to the left to climb up to the Marshan neighbourhood. The Grand Socco, with its street vendors sitting on the ground and small shops on the perimeter, was overflowing with colourful subjects, and Hilda Rix never ventured farther afield.[8] Morrice painted many pochades there, but it is impossible to determine which date from his first stay, which was not as well documented as the second one; indeed, no sketchbooks or letters to friends have survived. Thus, a few letters from Matisse to his wife, who returned to France on March 31, provide proof that the two artists spent time together in Tangier, which they left together on April 14.

To have an idea of what Morrice did during this first stay, we must look at the four Moroccan paintings that he sent to the 1912 Salon d'Automne (along with a Brittany landscape and a study of a model) and their preparatory sketches, all of which have been preserved. From the beach, he painted a panoramic view of the medina on its hill **(CAT. 33)** that was quite faithful to his sketch (*African Coast*, private coll.), except for the red strip of the setting sun; of the many figures on the beach, he retained only a donkey-driver in a burnoose. His other view of the beach **(CAT. 34)**, a composition structured by horizontal bands that are reminiscent of his *View towards Lévis from Québec* **(CAT. 8)**, is very different; the colour range is the same, but the tonality, natural in the sketch (*By the Sea*, Art Gallery of Hamilton), is much stronger in the painting: can we see the influence of Matisse? In early April, he had shown two of his landscape "sketches" to Morrice, probably two canvases painted in the garden of the private villa belonging to Jack Brooks, who had opened his grand gardens to Matisse **(CAT. 20)**, and perhaps also *Landscape Viewed from a Window* **(FIG. 19)**, in which blue dominates.[9]

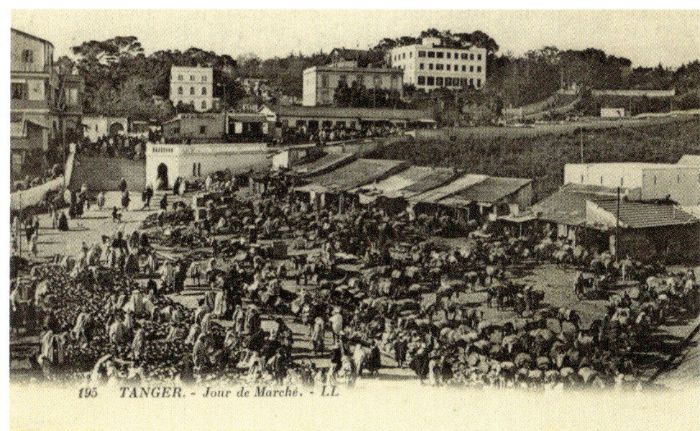

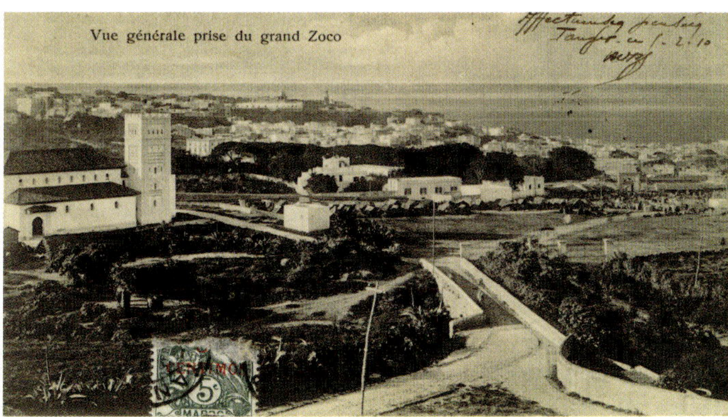

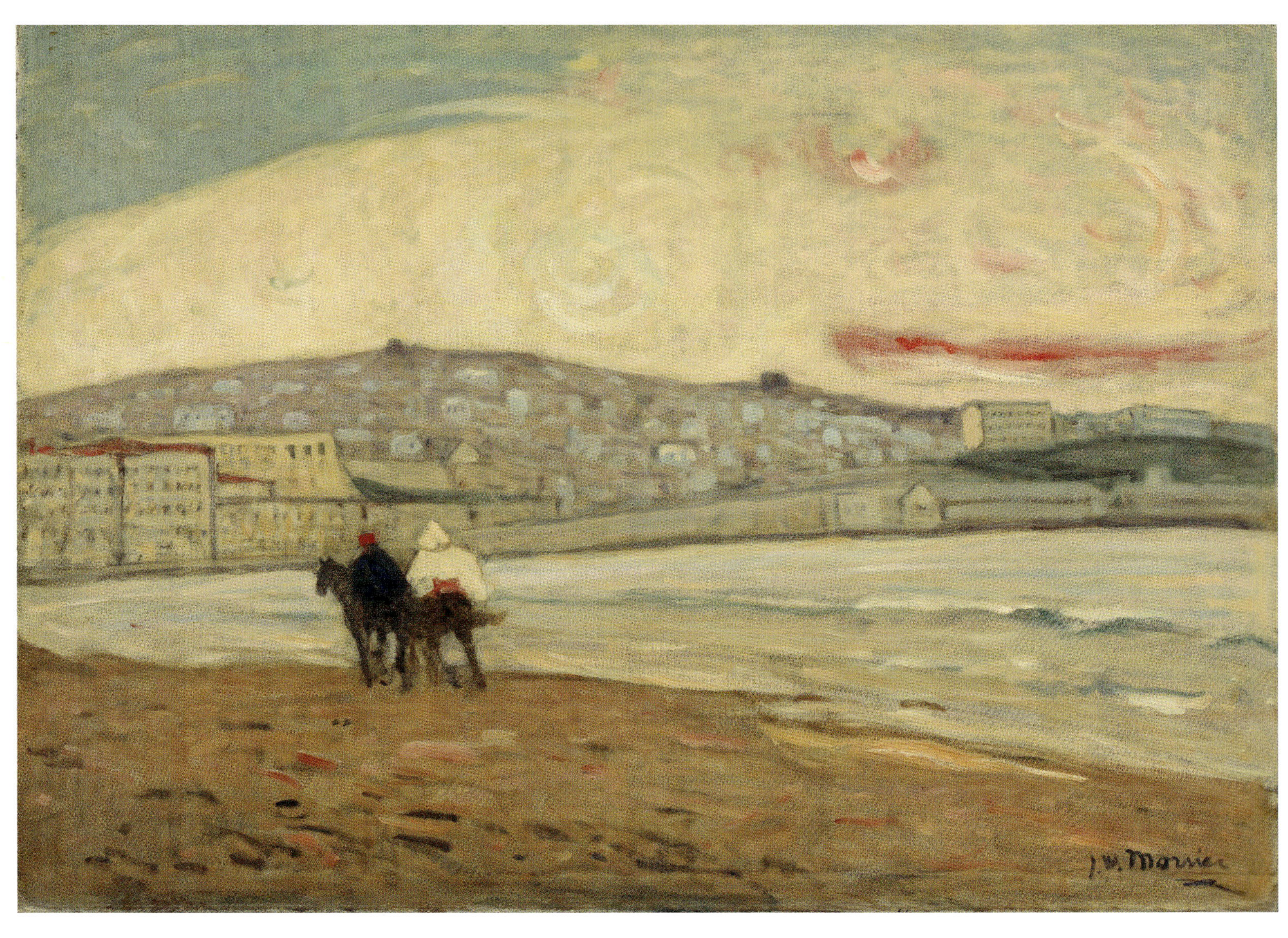

/ **CAT. 33** James W. Morrice
Tangier
1912

/ **CAT. 34** James W. Morrice
Tangier, the Beach
1912

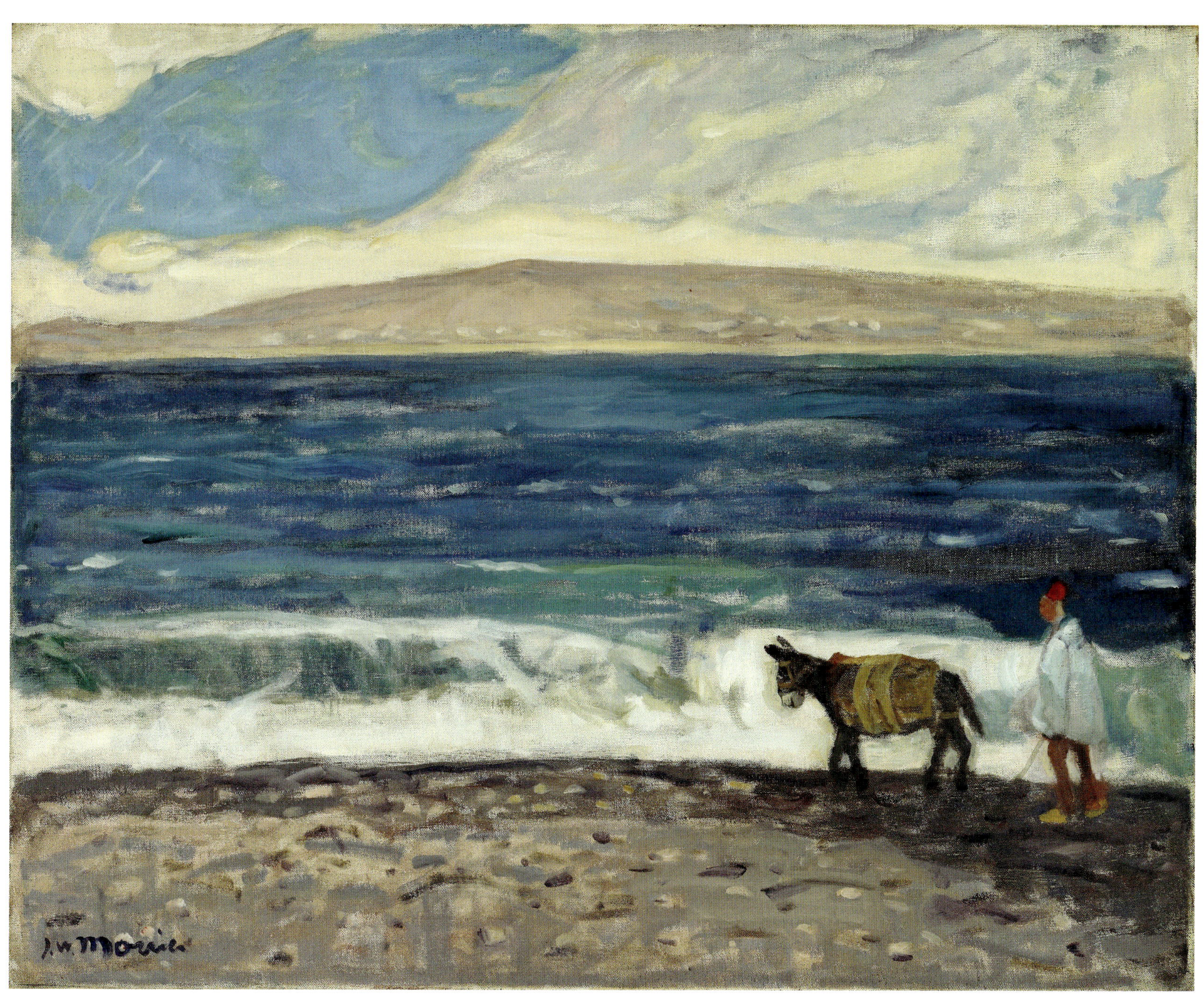

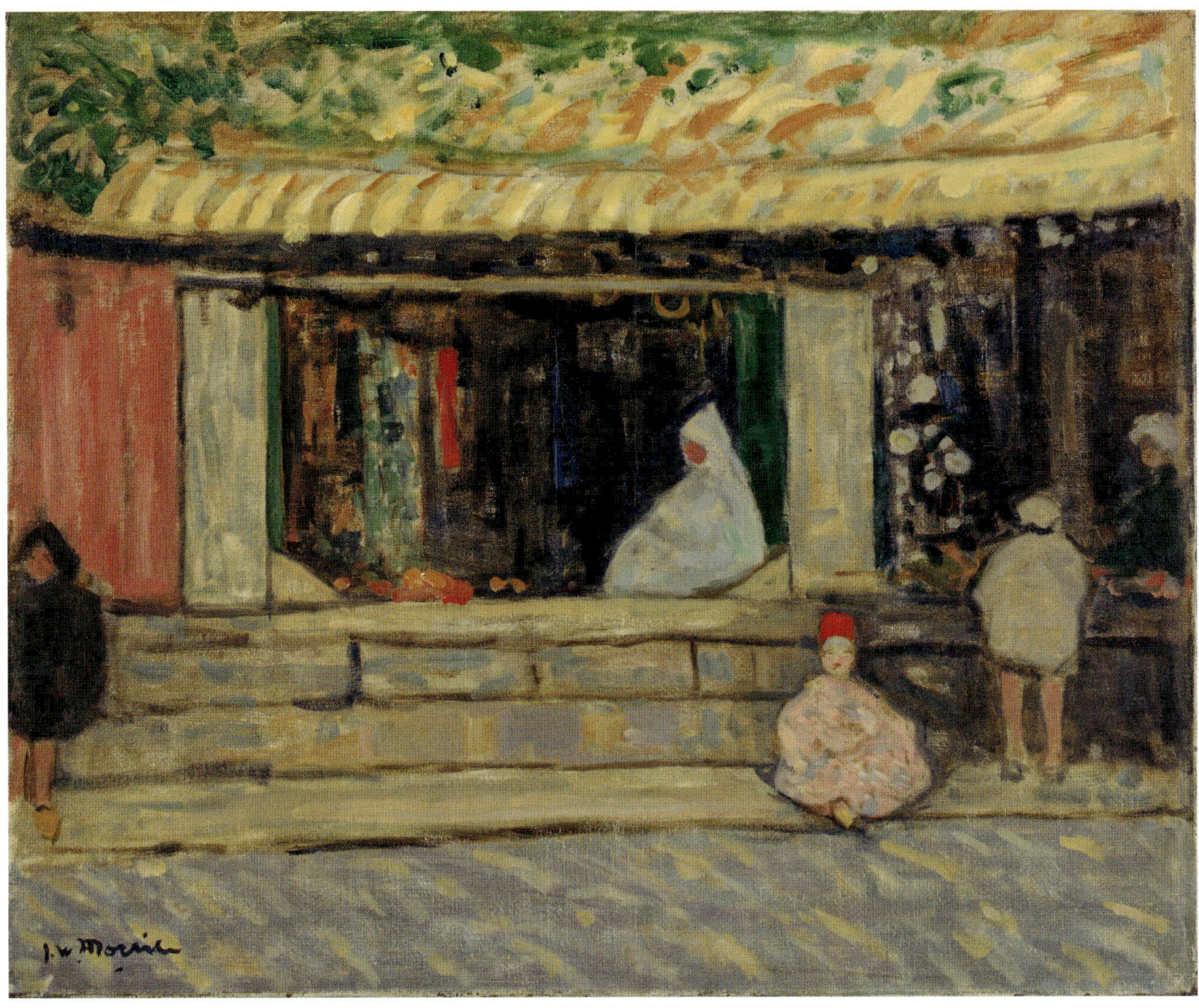

Tangier, Store **(CAT. 35)** reprises the composition and colours of a sketch drawn in the Grand Socco (*Oriental Bazaar*, private coll.). *Landscape, Tangier* **(CAT. 36)**, on the other hand, completely transforms the subject of the sketch as Morrice had painted it from nature: a road rises diagonally up a hill, past an enclosure, a smoking chimney, and a white building; at the top is a marabout (tomb of a saint), some buildings and clumps of trees. Only the summit, slightly less rounded, ties the sketch to the painting, although the building on the right has replaced the marabout on the left and has been replaced by trees. However, the first and second planes are completely different: the road now forms an arabesque, and the few buildings along its sides have been consolidated into a large central band: the grassy foreground, from which three men, seen from the back, contemplate the landscape, is a pure creation, added to bring the background to the surface of

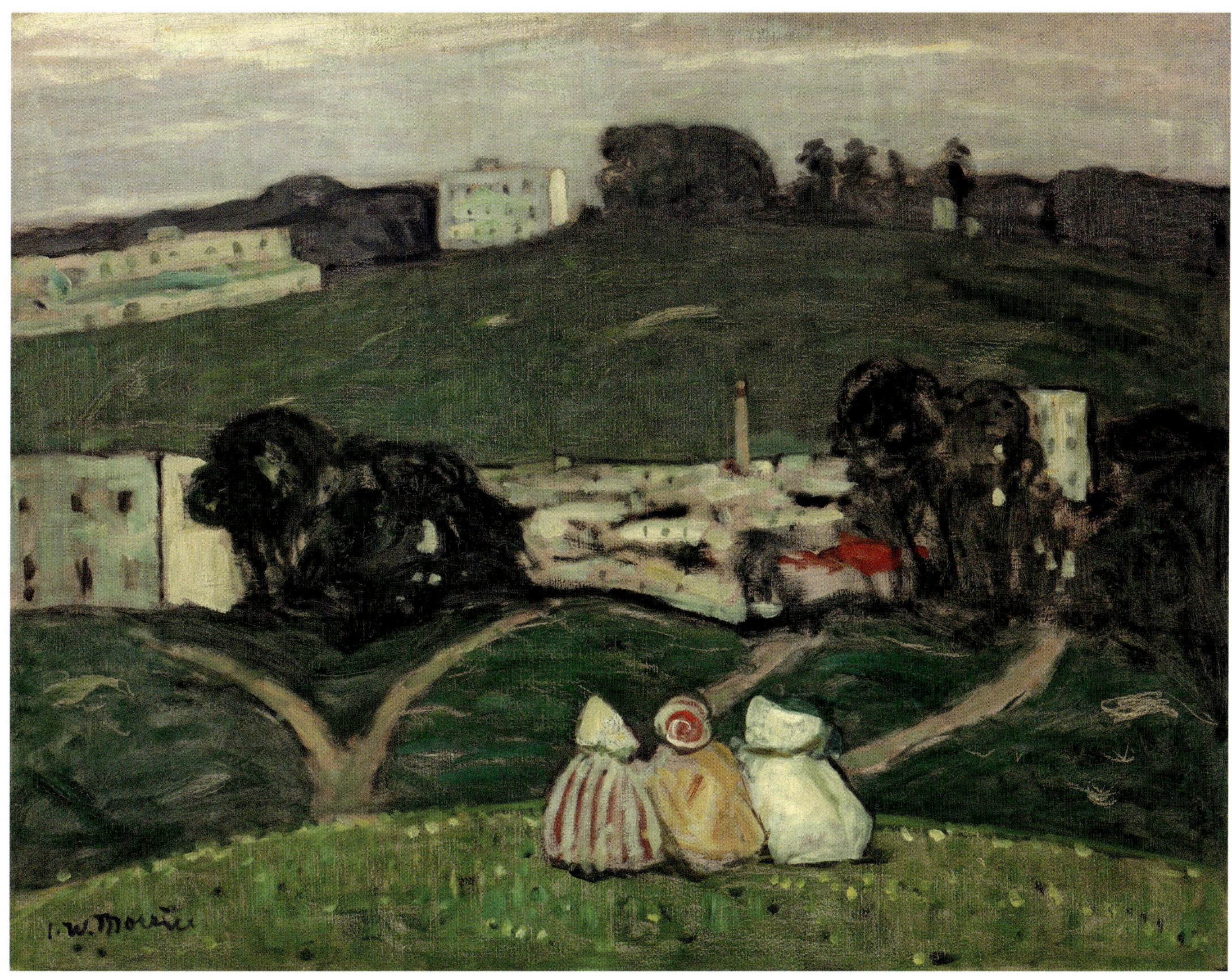

the painting. The harmony of the colours, with the subtle interplay between green and pink, was already suggested in the sketch: in Tangier, the setting sun tinges everything in mauve.

None of these four paintings is situated in the medina: as he had in Concarneau **(FIG. 8)** and Saint-Malo, Morrice preferred the seashore and town squares to narrow alleys. What was new, at least in *Tangier, the Beach* and *Tangier, Store*, was the increased brilliance of the colour and, in *Landscape, Tangier*, the obvious search for a decorative effect. Morrice was just beginning to understand Matisse, but his efforts went unnoticed among the hundreds of paintings at the Salon d'Automne, where the Cubists continued to dominate and abstract art made a first appearance.[10]

/ **CAT. 35** James W. Morrice
Tangier, Store
1912

/ **CAT. 36** James W. Morrice
Landscape, Tangier
1912

SECOND STAY IN TANGIER

As the fall of 1912 was rainy, Morrice decided to return to Tangier for the winter: "Bright colour is what I want," he wrote in a letter.[11] Did he know that Matisse had been there since October 8?[12] Morrice arrived in December,[13] probably from Marseille, and settled once again in the Villa de France. Charles Camoin, a friend of Matisse, was there too; the three artists often ate supper together, but Morrice's strong penchant for whisky disconcerted the Frenchmen.[14] Did they also work side by side? According to Matisse, they spent time together only "outside of working sessions."[15] The previous year, Matisse had painted at Villa Brooks and drew frequently in the medina (which Morrice, as we have seen, seems to have avoided); this time, he worked mainly at the hotel or in the studio of a photographer in the medina.[16] It is not known if Morrice also used this studio close to the Petit Socco, but he painted the gateway of a nearby *fondouk* (caravanserai) **(CAT. 66)**.

We can follow Morrice better during his second stay in Tangier because his sketchbook has been preserved.[17] He found the pretty "house with trellis" at the top of the medina, in front of the Bab-el-Assa gate **(CAT. 37)**. This was and is still today, a café, which Matisse drew many times;[18] he described the spot to his family as follows: "A small marvel . . . painted in bluish whitewash and the ground floor, a little set back, is a palisade of dark blue thin wood upon which sprout enormous dark violet morning glories."[19] Whereas Matisse saw it in sunlight, its morning glories still in bloom, Morrice discovered it under a heavy winter sky, its flowers wilted.

The views painted by the two artists from the windows of their respective rooms at the Villa de France are often cited to prove that they stayed together in Tangier. Matisse brought his version **(FIG. 19)**, begun the previous year, back to finish

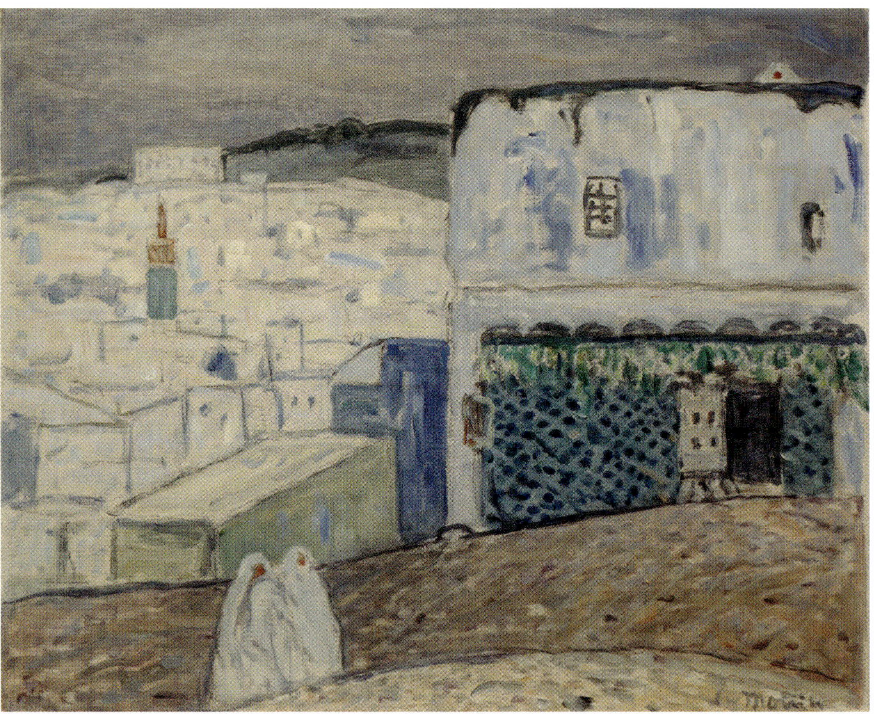

/ CAT. 37 James W. Morrice
Tangier, the Town
1913

/ CAT. 38 James W. Morrice
Waiting for the Boat, Tangier
About 1913

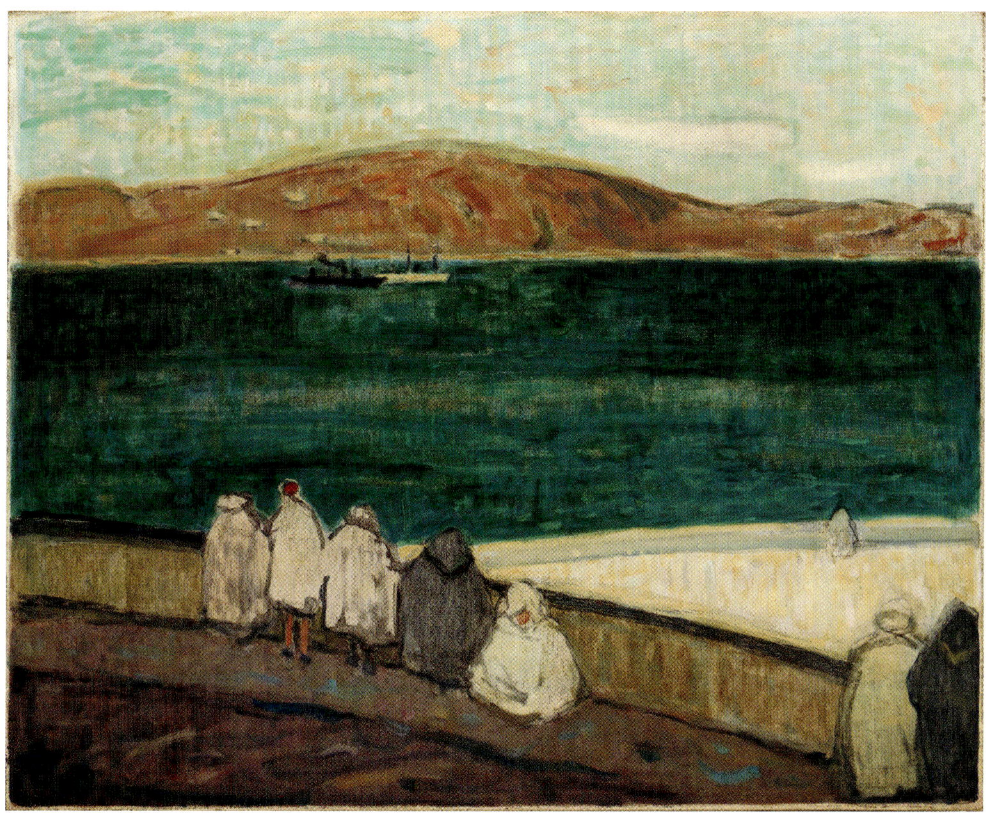

it, whereas Morrice undoubtedly executed his (**CAT. 65**) during his second stay.[20] Morrice could have painted it without reference to Matisse, the theme occurring to him on its own.[21] He had already painted from hotel windows (**FIG. 8** and **CAT. 8**), and he will do so again (**CAT. 76**). But the addition of the window frame and the flower pots, which are absent from the drawing, show that he had probably seen Matisse's painting. That said, he would have borrowed only the motif, as the two versions differ considerably in style and size. As Lyman wrote, "The identical subject. But another world!"[22]

Did Matisse inspire the painting *Tangier, Garden* presented at the 1913 Salon d'Automne and never found? Matisse also comes to mind when we look at the beautiful portrait *Tangier, Dancer* (**CAT. 42**), the subject with her hand resting quietly on a small drum. Because of the weight of tradition, local models were difficult to find; Matisse had to use deception to find Zorah and then convince her to pose,[23] and Morrice found his model in a café frequented by Europeans, as the silhouette in the background on the right indicates. The model's tattoos, real or fake, speak of her Berber origin and, perhaps, her second profession.[24]

Morrice drew and painted, with great verve, many of the medina's gates (**CAT. 47**); he also contemplated Tangier from the Marshan hill (**CAT. 57**) and the beach from the terraces of the Hôtel Continental, above the port (**CAT. 38**). He even visited a nearby marabout (**CAT. 39**). He left Tangier in late February, two weeks after the Matisses but before Camoin, and he spent a week in Gibraltar before returning to Paris.

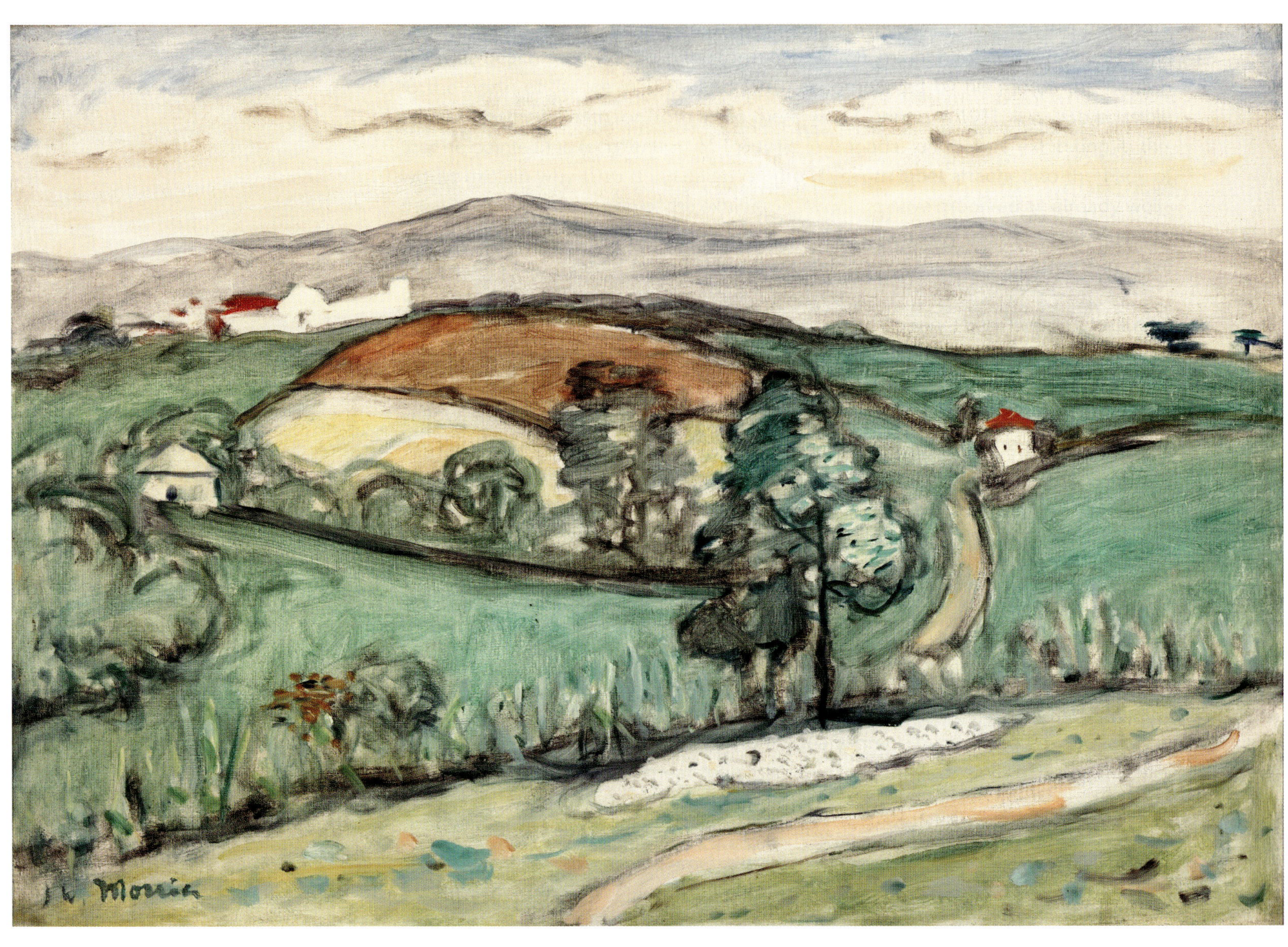

/ CAT. 39 James W. Morrice
Tangier, the Outskirts
1913

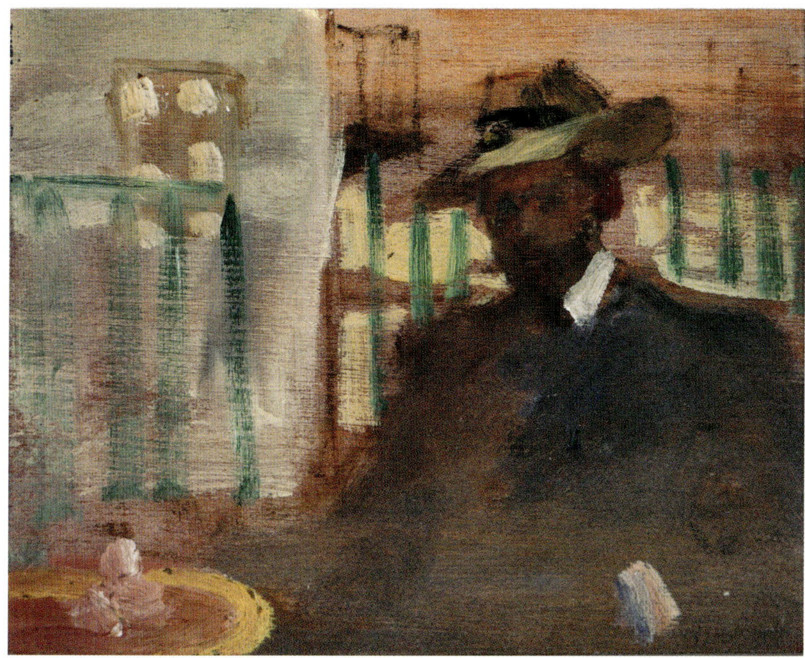

Most of the paintings mentioned above were exhibited at the 1913 Salon d'Automne, complemented by a view of the Rock of Gibraltar **(CAT. 4)**, but only one critic mentioned Morrice, "who is in love with urban landscapes."[25] Unlike the 1912 canvases, in which the colours were brilliant, *Tangier, the Town* **(CAT. 37)** and *View from the Window, Tangier* **(CAT. 65)** are atmospheric studies along the lines of the views of Concarneau **(FIG. 8)**; the weather was to blame! Others, such as *Waiting for the Boat, Tangier* and *Gibraltar*, continue the exploration of decorative effects. In *Tangier, the Outskirts* **(CAT. 39)**, based on a large-format sketch in the collection of the National Gallery of Canada, Morrice used his brushes in a new, freer way. Since his first Moroccan sojourn, quick nervous lines in pencil were becoming more prevalent in his pochades, and other sketches, such as *Tangier* **(CAT. 57)** and *Moonlight on the Bay of Tangier* **(CAT. 54)**, were drawn directly with paint on the wood panel. It was this new manner, very similar to Matisse's, that Morrice transposed into his canvas.

With better information on the details of Morrice's stays in Tangier with Matisse, we can reassess the portrait said to be of Matisse **(FIG. 11)**.[26] Photographs of Matisse dating from 1913 show that he always wore his glasses, and that his bushy red beard was trimmed square. The white house in the pochade, with its stone quoins, immediately evokes Finistère, in southern Brittany, which Morrice visited often between 1905 and 1910. Finally, the technique used for the small portrait, with its delicate frottage, also suggests this period. We do not know the name of the model, but we believe that it is not Matisse in Tangier.

/ **FIG. 11** James W. Morrice
Portrait, said to be of Matisse
Between 1905 and 1910

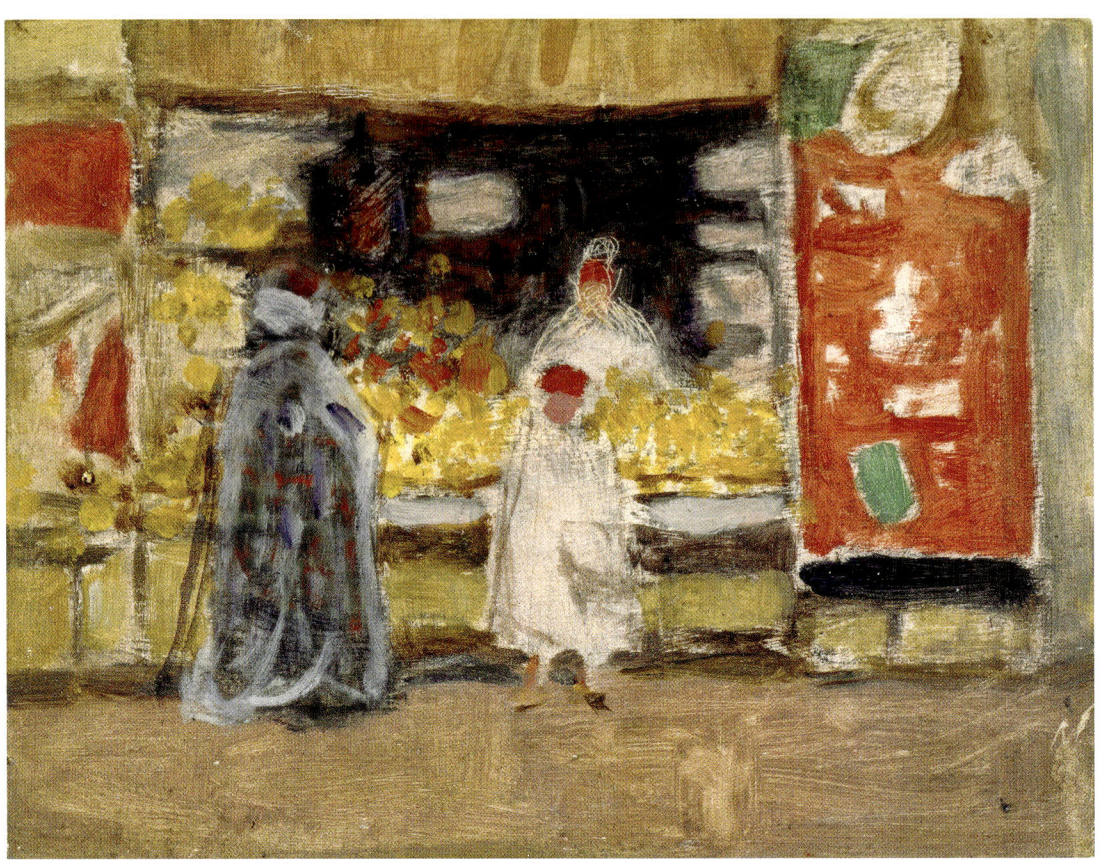

/ **CAT. 40** James W. Morrice
**Bazaar, Study for "Fruit Market,
North Africa (Tunis)"**
1914

DETOURS

Morrice spent the winter of 1913-1914 in Cagnes-sur-Mer, near Nice, with his companion Léa Cadoret, but it was snowing in January, and the call of the Maghreb was too strong: by March, he was in Tunis,[27] which was closer to Nice than Tangier, and also more cosmopolitan. Tunisia had been a French protectorate since 1881, and there were almost as many cafés there as in France, recognizable by their striped awnings (CATS. 53 and 56). The souks in Tunis were more numerous and varied than those in Tangier, and most of them were vaulted over, but, here too, Morrice painted only open spaces. Upon his return to Paris, he will transform three pochades into large-format canvases.

Study for "Afternoon, Tunis" (CAT. 51) and *Tunis Street Scene* (CAT. 59), more drawn than painted—Morrice had primed his wood panel with pale ink to make the task easier—included more details than did the basic drawing found at the very end of the Tangier sketchbook, after the pages devoted to Cagnes.[28] The corresponding paintings, identical in size,[29] are rendered in softer tones than the Tangier canvases; to temper the brilliance of the sun in *Afternoon*, Morrice toned down the sky with a bit of olive, and he painted his *Street Scene* a bit later in the day.

With its bright colours, the sketch for *Fruit Market, North Africa (Tunis)* (CATS. 40 and 41) more closely resembles the Tangier pochades;[30] the customer and the merchant are discussing something, but a young boy looks at us. This boy appears again, with his straw basket, in Morrice's hotel room (CAT. 43); a girl (his sister?) also posed for the artist (CAT. 44). With the same wallpaper in the background, they

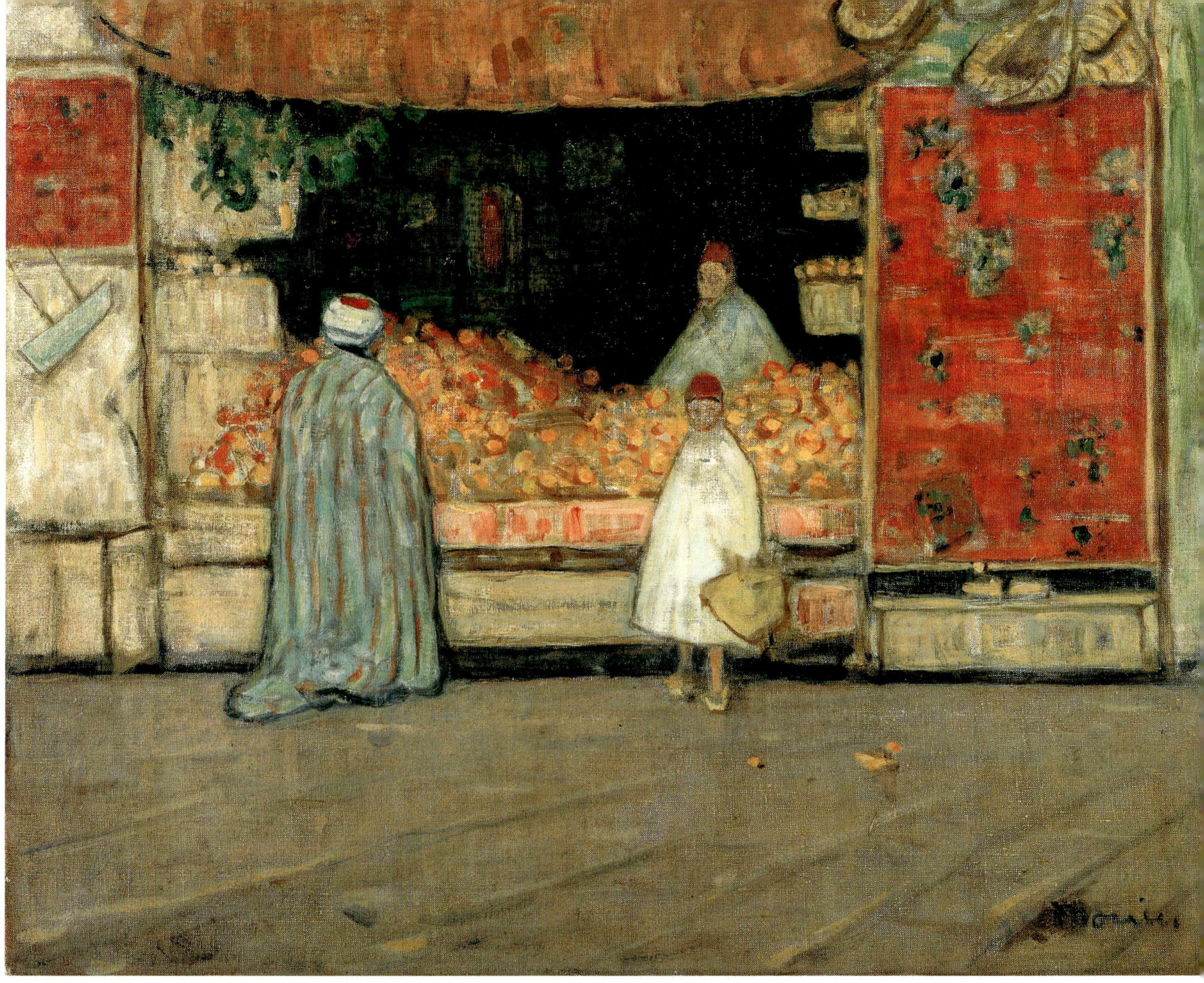

are as firmly seated in their chairs as are Matisse's *Riffian*s[31]—a frontal view rare for Morrice. The colour, applied rapidly and letting the white of the support show through, is also similar to Matisse's technique in his studies of Moroccan models. There, the similarity ends: the *Riffian*s are huge, whereas the portraits of the children are relatively small; Matisse emphasized the quiet strength of his warriors with simple backgrounds, whereas Morrice chose to include more domesticated props (straw basket, flowers) and a decorative environment.

Morrice probably intended his Tunisian paintings to go to the 1914 Salon d'Automne, but the exhibition did not take place due to the outbreak of the First World War. The series of winters in the Maghreb was interrupted, but Morrice discovered another southern destination—Cuba and, briefly, Jamaica—in the spring of 1915. He brought back from these trips pochades with colours that were strong but not vivid, as well as postcards that were to inspire him later. He apparently took no more trips outside of France before the Armistice, except a return to Montreal for the New Year in 1917, when he made the Bordeaux–New York crossing in the company of Corinne and John Lyman;[32] nothing else is known about this trip.

/ CAT. 41 James W. Morrice
Fruit Market, North Africa (Tunis)
1914

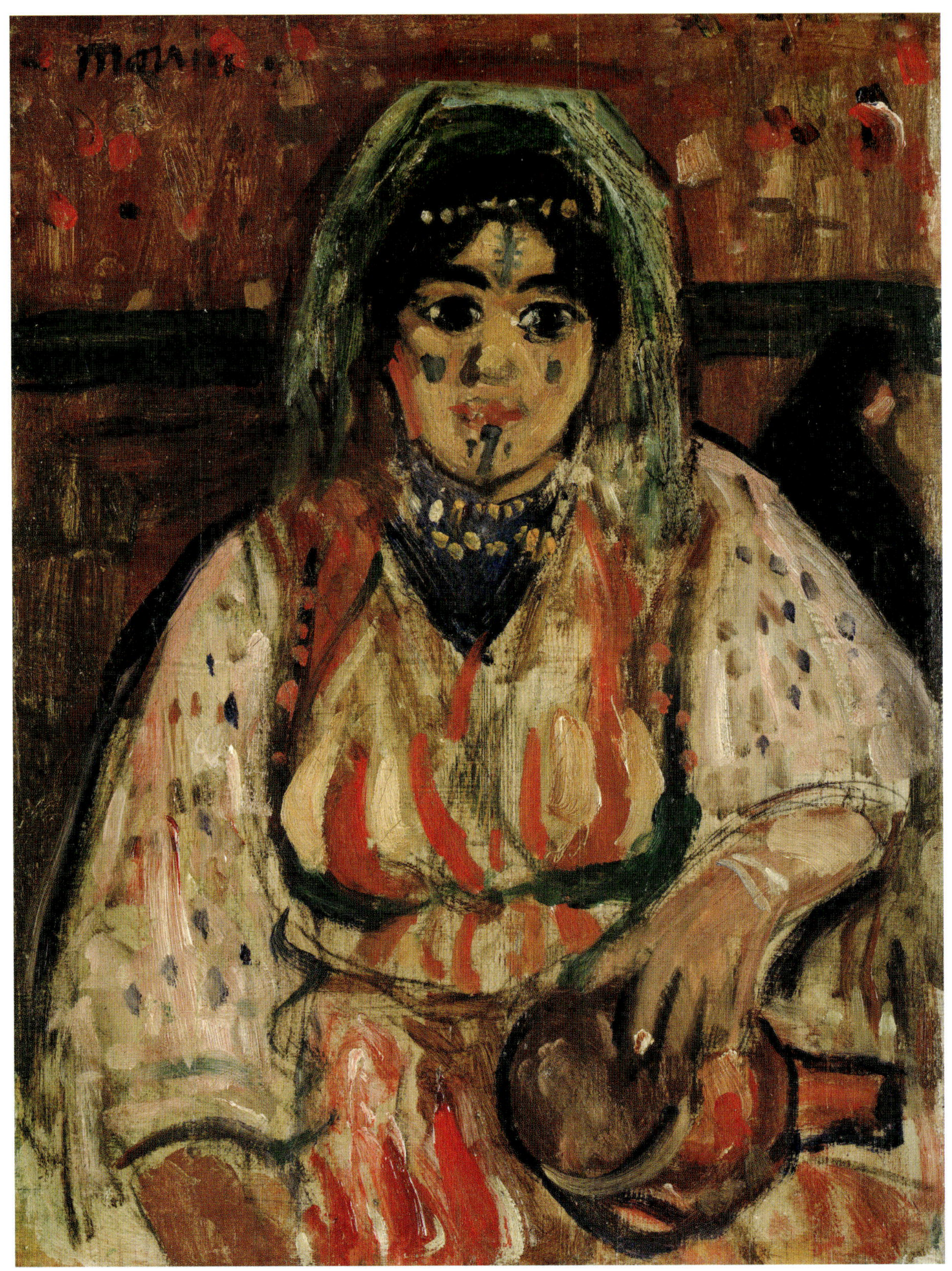
Matisse

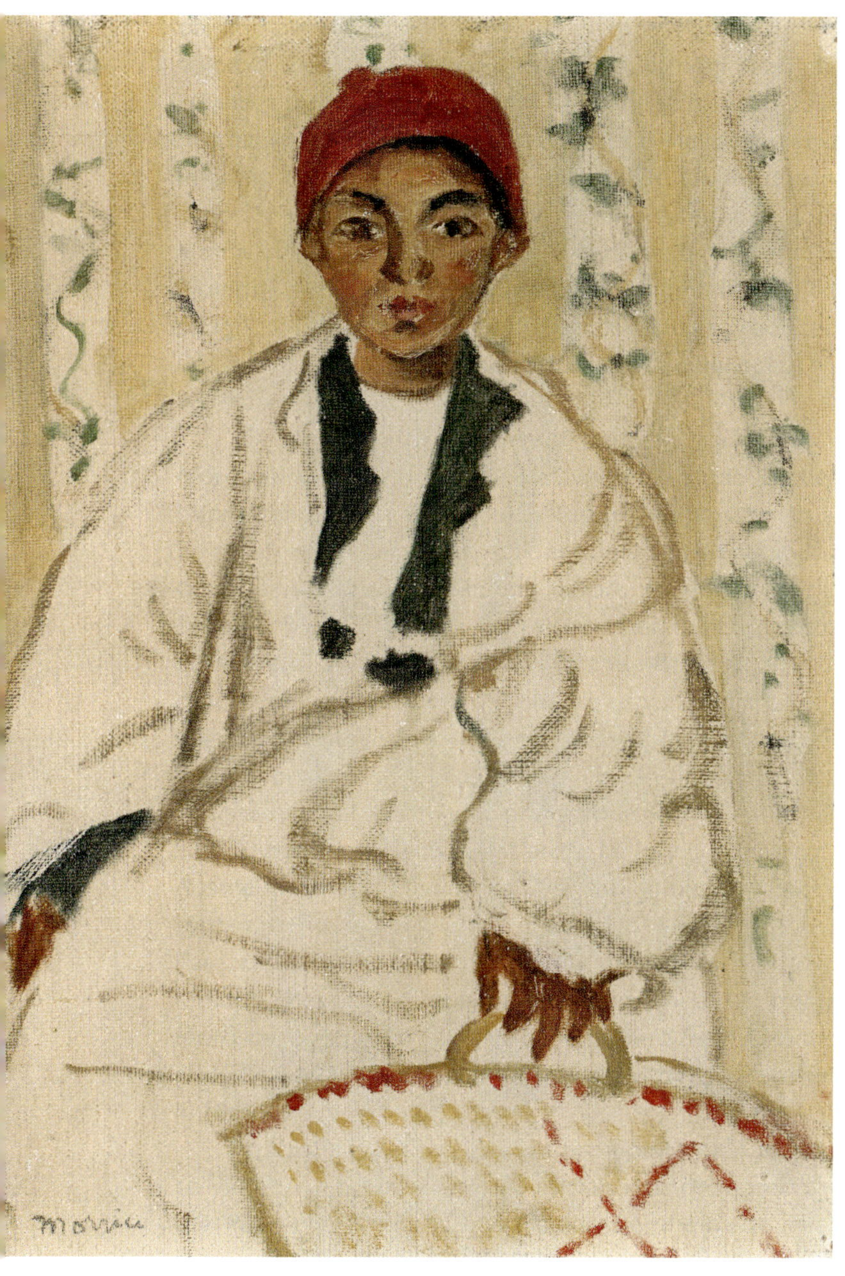

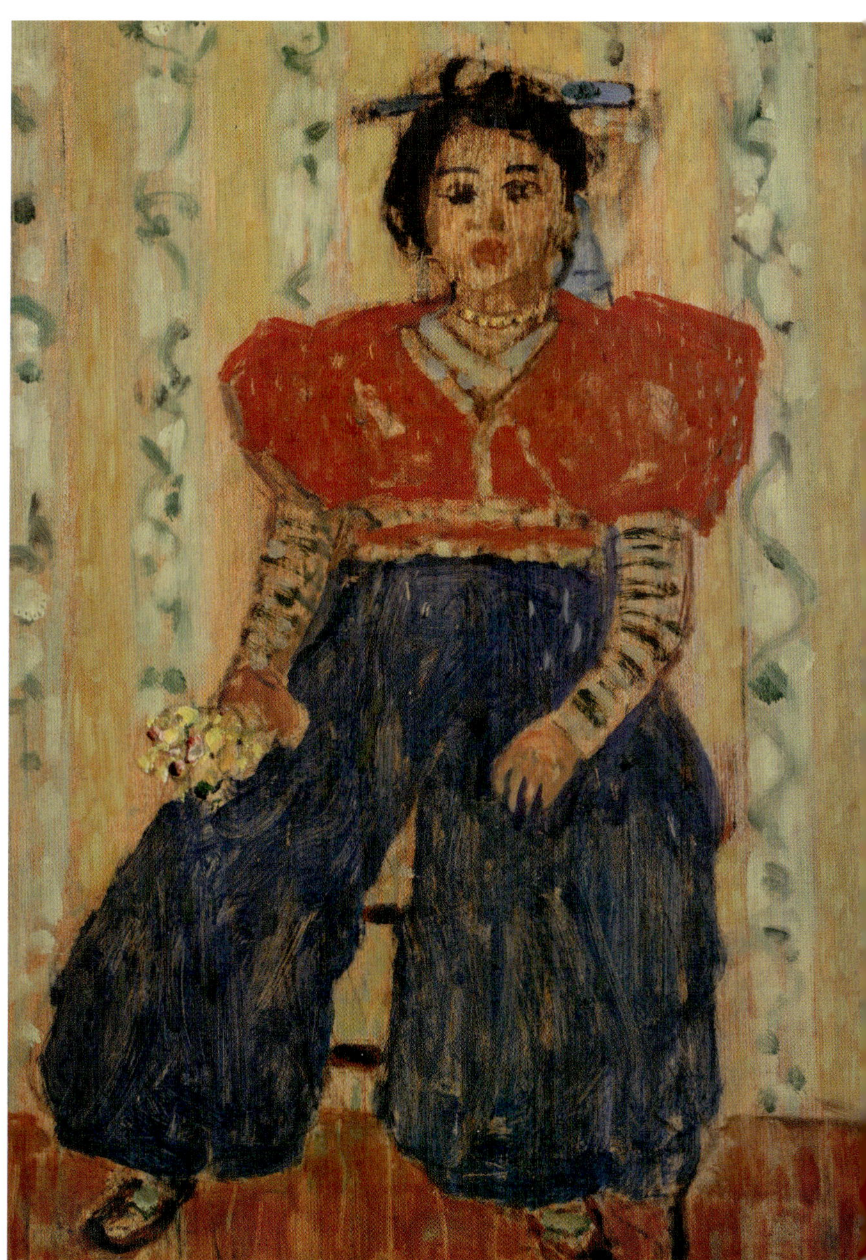

/ **CAT. 42** James W. Morrice
Tangier, Dancer
1913

/ **CAT. 43** James W. Morrice
Seated Arab
1914

/ **CAT. 44** James W. Morrice
Tunisian Girl
1914

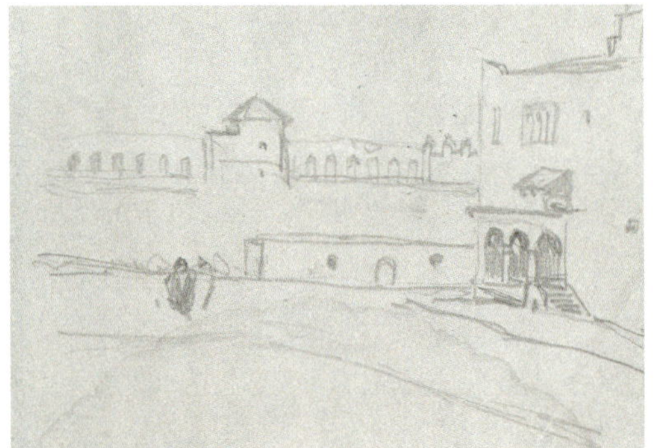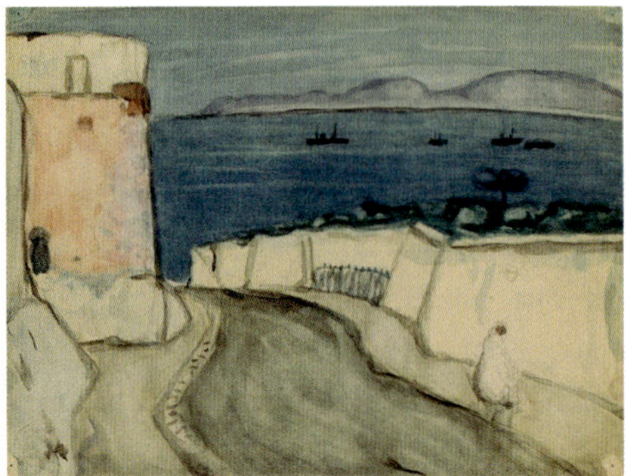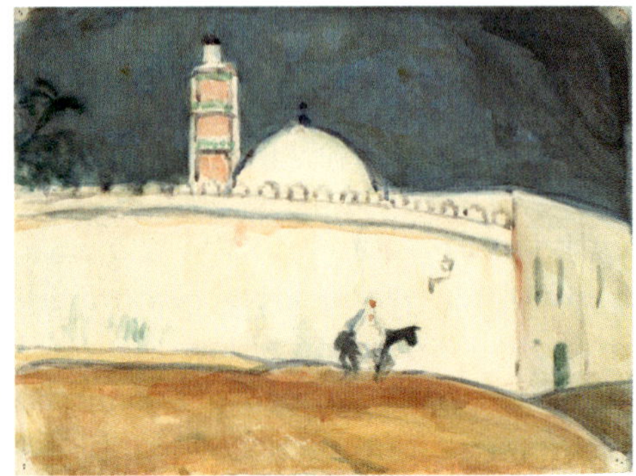

FURTHER SOJOURNS

Morrice returned to Morocco after the war, but the exact date of this voyage, documented by a number of drawings and watercolours, as well as a few paintings, is not known.[33] The country was now almost entirely accessible to visitors, and the transportation system was developing rapidly. Casablanca and Rabat, the capital, will soon be completely redesigned and expanded. Tangier had changed less, but the Grand Socco had been dominated, since 1917, by a minaret, which Morrice included, reducing its scale, in a nocturnal view from the Villa de France.[34] The watercolour sketch, which he now preferred to the sketch on wood, freed his gesture and his imagination, and his compositions were somewhat more dynamic **(FIG. 13)**. Rabat held his attention longer than did Tangier—particularly El-Allou Boulevard, bordering the medina, and its inward-looking Arab houses **(FIG. 12)**. In *Morocco Buildings* **(CAT. 49)**, the only large-format Moroccan canvas he painted after the war, Morrice tempered the austere white facade with light strokes of soft colour and highlighted it with an indigo sky that took little space but whose intensity balanced the composition perfectly.

The flexibility acquired through his use of watercolour is also evident in the magnificent paintings produced from sketches brought back from Trinidad in the spring of 1921 or from printed images, such as the postcards brought back from Cuba in 1915. *Village Street, West Indies* **(CAT. 22)**, very faithful to the original—even including the child caught in the snapshot—is probably the first experiment of this type, whereas the magnificent *The Pond, West Indies* **(CAT. 24)**, once owned by John Lyman, is totally liberated from its source, which supplied only the setting.

In March 1922, Morrice finally discovered the third country of the Maghreb, Algeria, which had been under colonial rule for almost a hundred years. Algiers was a French city, and there was nothing exotic about the Place du Gouvernement, which overlooked the port, except the Mosquée de la Pêcherie **(CATS. 45 and 46)**. Perhaps seeking a less Europeanized area, he visited Constantine.[35] He returned to Algiers the following year, and this time he visited Oran, farther west **(FIG. 14)**.[36] Léa Cadoret, his faithful companion who had always waited for him patiently in France, finally was on the voyage, as she may have been the previous year.[37]

/ **FIG. 12** James W. Morrice
El-Allou Boulevard, Rabat
About 1919-1921

/ **FIG. 13** James W. Morrice
Tangier
About 1919-1921

/ **FIG. 14** James W. Morrice
The Mosque, Oran
Probably 1923

/ **CAT. 45** James W. Morrice
The Mosque, Algiers
1922

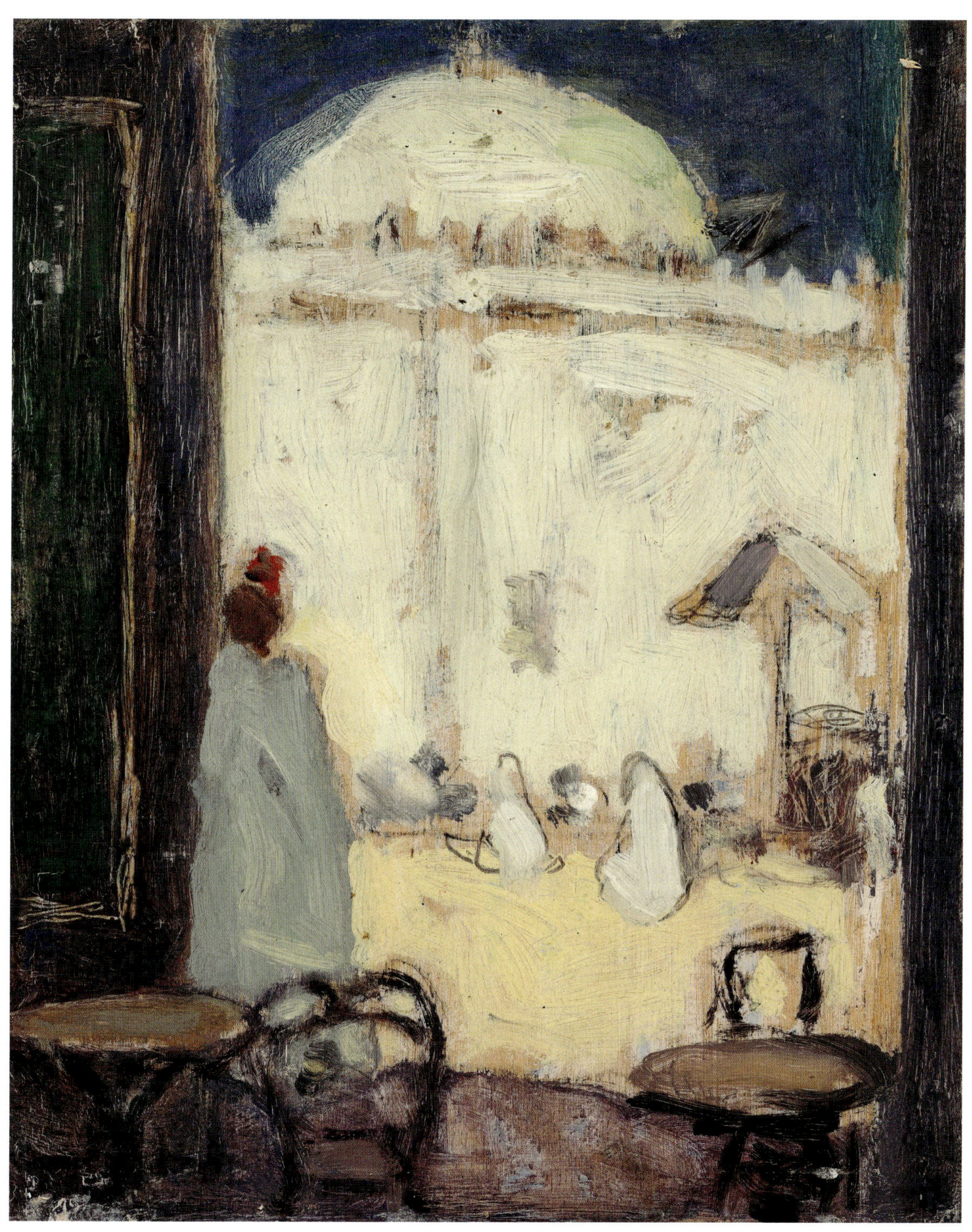

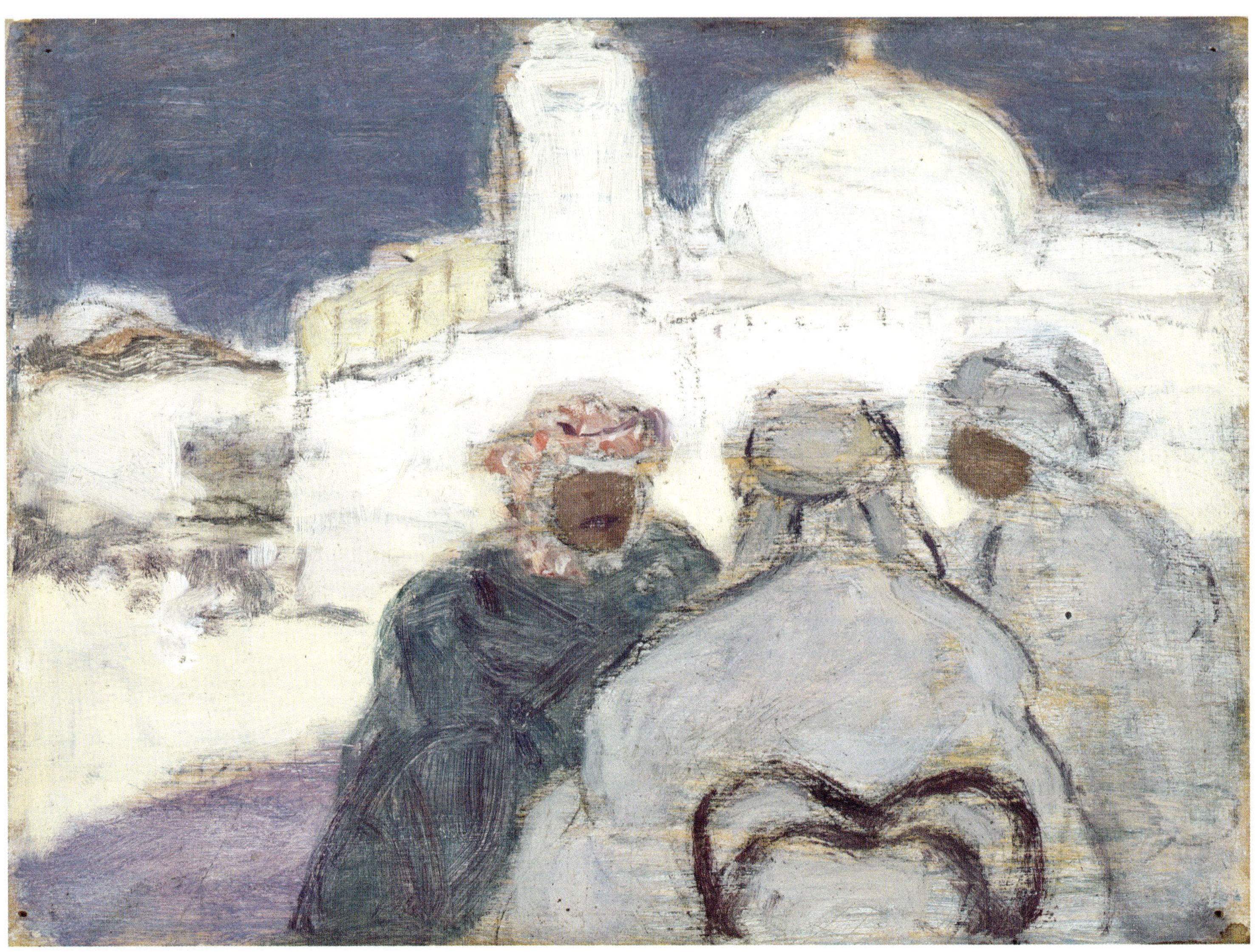

/ **CAT. 46** James W. Morrice
Arabs talking
1922

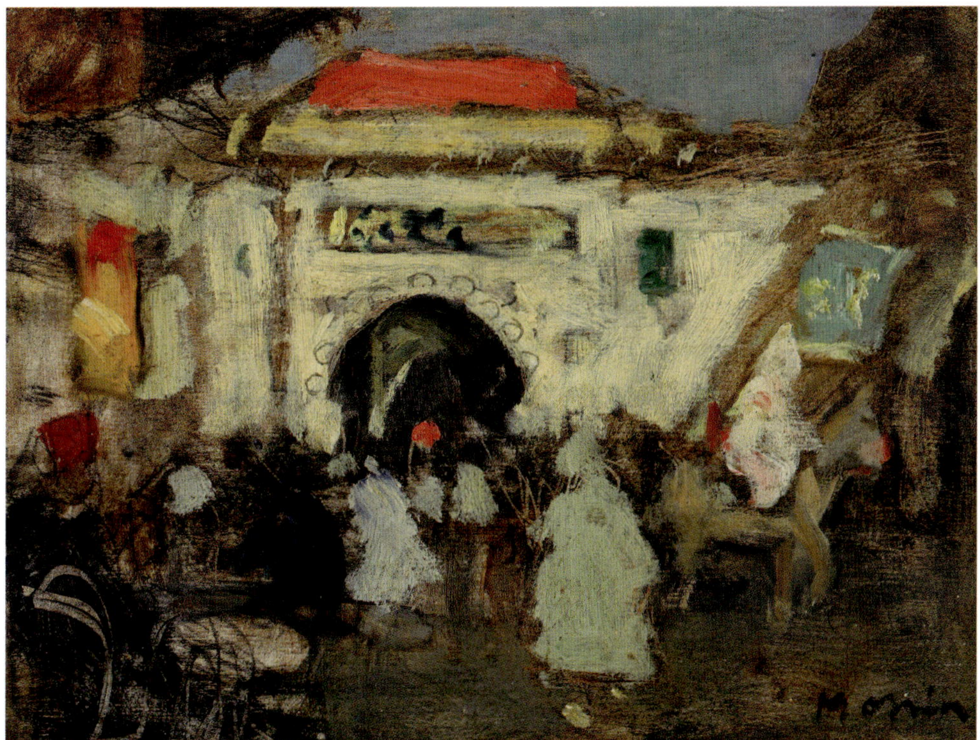

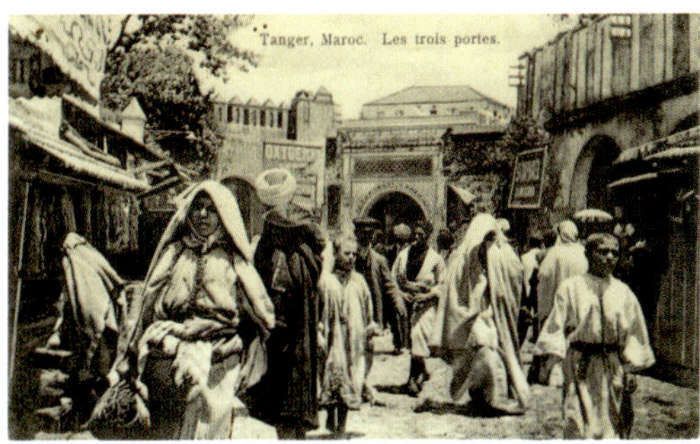

The series of winters in the Maghreb, which continued in Tunis in late December 1923—this time without Léa—was put to a sudden end by the artist's death. He fell ill as he debarked from the ship taking him from Sicily,[38] and he died in Tunis on January 23, 1924; his body still rests in the ground of the North Africa that he so loved.

"A painter should go South; it cleans your palette for you,"[39] Morrice told a journalist friend upon his return from North Africa after the war. There was a change of tone but not really of subject: although the vegetation was more exotic, the buildings white and the people dressed in long robes, the artist saw North Africa as he had seen Quebec City or Concarneau. The long white Maghrebian garment was the perfect clothing for his preferred silhouette, short and a bit rotund, but his Arabs and Berbers were as generic as his Bretons: their costumes situated the landscapes. It was the approach of a *flâneur*—unlike that of the Orientalists, who described, and often judged, the new colonies; paradoxically, Morrice, more and more modern in his style, eliminated all "modern" (European) elements from his compositions,[40] or else he transformed them—for example, the posters seen in a postcard—into dabs of colour (**FIG. 15** and **CAT. 47**). In *The Mosque, Oran* (**FIG. 14**), the mosque, portrayed as isolated between the ochre pavement and the indigo sky, was in reality surrounded by tall European buildings, and he thus "abstracted" it from its context. One can only wonder what path Morrice's art might have taken if death had not overtaken him in Tunis.

/ **CAT. 47** James W. Morrice
A Gate in Tangier
About 1912-1913

/ **FIG. 15** S. J. Nahon, Tangier
Tangier, Morocco: The Three Doors
About 1912

Notes

1. Letter to Edmund Morris, Paris, November 8, [1911]. Art Gallery of Ontario, Toronto, E. P. Taylor Library & Archives, Edmund Morris Fonds.

2. Letter to E. Morris, Quebec City, January 14, [1912]. The *Exhibition of Pictures of James W. Morrice* at W. Scott & Sons, advertised from January 16 to 31 in *The Gazette* (Montreal), received no reviews; the newspapers noted only an exhibition by Mary Ritter Hamilton, whose Paris paintings were on display at the Art Association of Montreal in February (MMFA, *Art Association of Montreal Scrapbooks*, 1912).

3. "Am leaving on Monday with some friends for Tangiers." Letter to E. Morris, Quebec City, "Thursday" [January 18 or 25, 1912].

4. The group probably took the *Cedric* (Wednesday, January 24) or the *Cincinnati* (Tuesday, January 30). See the ads for these liners in *The Gazette* (Montreal), January 17, 1912, and the "Ocean Intelligence" daily chronicle in the *Pittsburgh Gazette*. We do not know the names of Morrice's friends or what they did after they arrived in Tangier.

5. The country had never been conquered but was coveted by France and Germany; a provisional treaty signed by the two powers in November 1911 had just made it a French protectorate, but a number of regions were not yet pacified. The signature of the final treaty in Fez on March 30, 1912, resulted in a brutally repressed uprising.

6. In Karl Baedeker, *The Mediterranean: Seaports and Sea Routes* (Leipzig: Karl Baedeker, 1911), descriptions of Morocco were limited to Tangier (several pages) and a few Atlantic ports (briefly described); these were visited by the artist Robert E. Groves for his article "Morocco as a Winter Sketching Ground," with drawings by the author, in *The Studio*, vol. 45, no. 187 (October 1908), pp. 24-30. See also R. B. Cunninghame, "The Atmosphere of Morocco," illustrated by John Lavery, in Charles Holme, ed., *Sketching Grounds* (London: The Studio, 1909), pp. 143-152.

7. Rix, who was travelling alone, joined up with the American group in Paris. Jeannette Hoorn, *Hilda Rix Nicholas and Elsie Rix's Moroccan Idyll* (Victoria, Australia: Miegunyah Press [Melbourne University], 2012), p. 64.

8. Hoorn, *Hilda Rix Nicholas and Elsie Rix's Moroccan Idyll*, passim.

9. Henri Matisse, letter to his family, April 3, 1912. Exactly which works did Morrice see? The authors of the catalogue *Matisse in Morocco* lean toward *Periwinkles* and *Palm Leaf, Tangier*, but three days earlier Matisse mentioned a "blue" landscape that could be *Acanthus* (Moderna Museet, Stockholm) or *Landscape Viewed from a Window* (of the Villa de France) from the Morosov Triptych. See Jack Cowart, ed., *Matisse in Morocco: The Paintings and Drawings, 1912-1913*, exhib. cat. (Washington: National Gallery, 1990), pp. 42, 70, 82.

10. Louis Vauxcelles noted "his nonchalant distinction and his science of matching colours" ("Le Salon d'Automne," *Gil Blas* [Paris], September 30, 1912, p. [3]), and Thiébault-Sisson, the only to notice the new motif

11. Letter to E. Morris, Paris, November 1, [1912].

12. Perhaps the anecdote reported by Buchanan, and oft repeated, took place during this visit rather than the first one: Morrice apparently "happened" to go to Tangier to find Matisse, whom he admired (Donald W. Buchanan, *James Wilson Morrice: A Biography* [Toronto: The Ryerson Press, 1936], p. 110). Buchanan questioned Matisse in Paris in 1935, but it seems that his notes were not preserved.

13. Letter to E. Morris, "Tangier," January 1, 1913; he was planning to stay a month, if the rain stopped. Four days later, Matisse spoke about good weather and the early blooms (letter to Matthew Prichard, January 4, 1913, quoted by Alfred H. Barr in *Matisse, His Art and His Public* [New York: The Museum of Modern Art, 1951], p. 145).

14. Letter from Charles Camoin to Henri Matisse [Tangier, February 18, 1913], in *Correspondance entre Charles Camoin et Henri Matisse*, introduced and annotated by Claudine Grammont (Lausanne: Bibliothèque des Arts/Succession H. Matisse, 1997), pp. 41-42. Letter from Charles Camoin to Albert Marquet, "Tanger Janvier 1913," in "Correspondance Camoin/Marquet," Appendix, *Charles Camoin: rétrospective 1879-1965*, exhib. cat. (Paris/Marseille: RMN/Musée de Marseille, 1997), p. 222. In contradiction to what is still often written, Marquet was not in Tangier, as he preferred the city in summertime.

15. Letter from Matisse to Armand Dayot, in *Catalogue des tableaux et études par James Wilson Morrice* (Paris: Galeries Simonson, 1926), p. 7.

16. This studio was right in the centre of the medina, near the Assouias mosque. See Hilary Spurling, *Matisse the Master – A Life of Henri Matisse: The Conquest of Colour, 1909-1954* (New York: Knopf, 2005), pp. 127-128. It may have belonged to Léon Davin, who had been living in Tangier since 1880 and was related to the owner of the Villa de France; Mrs. Davin also willingly allowed artists passing through to use the hotel rooms as a studio; see Hoorn, *Hilda Rix Nicholas and Elsie Rix's Moroccan Idyll*, p. 166.

17. MMFA, sketchbook no. 6, Dr.1973.29, also used in Gibraltar (March 1913), Cagnes-sur-Mer (winter 1913-1914) and Tunis (March 1914). It should be noted that this sketchbook contains no drawing linked to the canvases painted following the first stay.

18. Cowart, *Matisse in Morocco*, pp. 141-143 and nos. 58-60. We also see this house in the background in his *Casbah Gate* (fig. 40).

19. Archives Matisse, November [about 8-12], 1912, quoted in ibid., p. 142. Camoin also painted this house in full sunlight (*House with Arbor, Tangier*, see ibid., p. 261).

20. Matisse, *Landscape Viewed from a Window*, 1912-1913 (fig. 19). Morrice's canvas was exhibited at the 1913 Salon d'Automne, and there is a related drawing in sketchbook no. 6, p. 16.

21. Camoin (*View of the English Church, Tangier*, winter 1912-1913, private coll.) and Marquet (*View of Tangier*, summer 1913, private coll.) also painted this view. When Elsie Rix, Hilda's sister, arrived at the Villa de France, she immediately recognized a landscape painted by the Australian artist E. Phillips Fox that she had seen the previous year; she hastily climbed up to the roof to draw the view, to which she included a caption, for her mother (February 9, 1914, drawing reproduced in Hoorn, *Hilda Rix Nicholas and Elsie Rix's Moroccan Idyll*, p. 116; Fox's canvas, painted in 1911, is reproduced on p. 117). Morrice himself drew a sketchier version from the roof, with a detail of the balustrade: sketchbook no. 6, p. 27.

22. John Lyman, "The Morrice Retrospective," *The Montrealer*, February 15, 1938, p. 20; in this article, Lyman recounts how he identified the motif in Morrice's canvas, then titled *View from Window, Cagnes*, by comparing it to a reproduction of Matisse's.

23. Cowart, *Matisse in Morocco*, no. 9 (*Zorah in Yellow*, private coll.), no. 13 (*Zorah on the Terrace*, centre painting of the Morosov Triptych, Pushkin Museum, Moscow, winter 1912-1913) and no. 16 (*Zorah Standing*, 1912, State Hermitage Museum, St. Petersburg).

24. Christelle Taraud, "Jouer avec la marginalité: le cas des filles soumises 'indigènes' du quartier réservé de Casablanca dans les années 1920-1950," *Clio. Histoire, femmes et sociétés*, no. 17, colloquium "ProstituéEs," (2003), p. 75; she cites the many works by Dr. J. Herber, including *Les tatouages des prostituées marocaines* (Paris: Éditions Ernest Leroux, 1919).

25. Adolphe Dervaux, "Notes sur l'Art - Le Salon d'Automne," *La Plume* (Paris), December 1, 1913, p. 248. During this time, the English discovered Morrice: Muriel Ciolkowska, "A Canadian Painter: James Wilson Morrice," *The Studio*, vol. 59, no. 245 (August 1913), pp. 176-183; the most recent work reproduced by the author was the previous year's *Tangier* (cat. 33).

26. Revealed by W. R. Johnston, *James Wilson Morrice, 1865-1924*, exhib. cat. (Montreal: The Montreal Museum of Fine Arts, 1965), no. 136, who does not comment on it. The portrait is reproduced in Cowart et al., *Matisse in Morocco*, p. 258, and in Charles C. Hill, *Morrice: A Gift to the Nation – The G. Blair Laing Collection* (Ottawa: National Gallery of Canada, 1992), p. 153. All of these authors date it "1912-1913," thus from Tangier, because of the title. Hill compares it to the portrait of a child in the same staging, which a dealer situated . . . in Tunis (*Through a Garden Fence*, NGC 30477); the only differences are that the quoins of the house are maroon and we can see the opposite shore. We suspect, here too, a confabulation by the dealer, like so many found in the catalogue of Morrice's works. The back of *Portrait* might give more information (inscription and/or label), but we have not had access to it.

27. Letter from A. Y. [Arthur G.?] Collins to Maurice Cullen, March 12, 1914; Art Gallery of Hamilton, Archives. Morrice's stay preceded by two weeks that of the Swiss artist Paul Klee and his German friend August Macke.

28. Sketchbook no. 6, p. 57, partial drawing of *Tunis Street Scene* (stall, tree, door and window); p. 59, partial drawing of *Afternoon, Tunis* (dome, gate and figures).

29. The canvas painted after *Tunis Street Scene* is not presented here: *Tunis* (previously *Tangier*), Vancouver Art Gallery, 97.49.04, gift of M. and M. M. Young, 1997.

30. The corresponding drawing is found on the first page of sketchbook no. 10, MMFA, Dr.1973.33, also used in London in 1914 and in Cuba in 1915; it also contains the drawing for *Plane Tree and Tent, North Africa* (cat. 53).

31. *Standing Riffian* (State Hermitage Museum, St. Petersburg) and *Seated Riffian* (Barnes Foundation, Philadelphia); Morrice may have seen them in Galerie Bernheim-Jeune, in Paris, in April 1913.

32. "List or Manifest of Alien Passengers for the United States Immigration Officer at Port of Arrival," New York, January 3, 1917; the ship *SS Espagne* had left Bordeaux on December 23 (www.ancestry.ca, accessed June 13, 2007).

33. Drawings in sketchbooks no. 22, MMFA, Dr.1973.45 (also used in Picardie and at Concarneau in 1918) and no. 21, MMFA, Dr.1973.44 (also taken to Trinidad in 1921, then to Corsica and Algeria in 1922); there

might thus have been two trips. One of them may date to the winter of 1919-1920, when the housing crisis and a coal shortage caused a number of artists to leave Paris for the winter; letter from John Lyman to his father, October 10, 1919, Bibliothèque et Archives nationales du Québec, *John Lyman et son œuvre* [microfilm], 1975, section E (bobbin 3). Morrice no longer wrote to his friends after 1915 (Edmund Morris died in 1913), and we are thus deprived of a valuable resource.

34. *Nocturne Landscape*, 26.7 x 33.7 cm, MMFA (in the process of acquisition); see Johnston, *James Wilson Morrice*, no. 96 (ill.). The point of view is higher and more to the right than in his canvas of the winter of 1912-1913.

35. Sketchbook no. 21, pp. 4 and 12, and water-colours; a note from this sketchbook, p. 56, informs us that Morrice was thinking of going farther south to Biskra; Matisse had stayed there briefly in 1906, and the Canadian artist Maurice Cullen, a friend of Morrice, in 1893.

36. Sketchbook no. 19, pp. 26, 28 and 29, 33, 34, and watercolours; this sketchbook was used in Algiers, Dieppe and Sicily, from 1922 until Morrice's death.

37. Sketchbook no. 21, p. 55v: under the heading "1922 Léa" is written "février 1000 Corse / 30 mars 1000 Algiers." And in sketchbook no. 19, p. 71: "Lea Cadoret 8 February 1000 frs 700 for / repairs Kasba" [1923]. These two dates, as well as the different styles of the drawings in the two sketchbooks, prove that Morrice went to Algeria twice.

38. On December 28, in Tunis, everything was fine (postcard to Léa Cadoret, quoted by William R. Johnston, "James Wilson Morrice: A Canadian Abroad," *Apollo*, vol. 87, no. 76 [June 1968], p. 457, note 8, then coll. Léa Cadoret, currently not located), as it was on January 14, when he left Sicily after a two-week stay with the family of his brother Arthur A. (postcard to William Brymner, posted in Palermo on January 14, 1924, Art Gallery of Ontario, E. P. Taylor Library & Archives, Donald W. Buchanan Fonds, gift of K. R. Thomson, 1995). The next day, in Algiers, the Orientalist painter Gustave Lemaître heard that he was "very sick" in Tunis (where he had hosted Paul Klee and August Macke in April 1914), to get information (letter from G[ustave] Lemaître to Madame Jean Alazard, Algiers, January 15, 1924, private coll., France, communicated to Charles C. Hill, NGC, in 1990).

39. Muriel Ciolkowska, "Memories of Morrice," *The Canadian Forum*, November 1925, p. 53.

40. One example: the marabout of *Afternoon, Tunis* (cat. 50) was in fact right downtown, beside the Alleoua gate at the south end of the medina, served by a tramway stop and frequented by horse-drawn carriages (Baedeker, *The Mediterranean: Seaports and Sea Routes*, p. 330); the gate and its marabout have since been demolished to make room for the central bus terminal.

THE EXTRAORDINARY DELICACY OF NORTH AFRICAN LIGHT
PORTFOLIO

Morrice and Lyman made several trips to Morocco, Tunisia and Algeria during the 1910s and 1920s, enthralled by the "extraordinary delicacy" of the light of the Maghreb, the "land of the setting sun" of the Arab world.

In 1912, Morrice was first to cross the Strait of Gibraltar to Tangier, in Morocco, where Matisse was already staying. The two artists spent time together, and they would meet there again the following winter. Seated at a café table, observing the city and its teeming life, Morrice would discreetly take out one of the small wood panels he kept in his jacket pocket. Slowly, with a few strokes of oil paint, he would strive to capture all the subtle variations in the atmosphere.

It was the small town of Hammamet, in Tunisia, that would become Lyman's home port in the early 1920s. Later, he recalled its iridescent light: "You only understand it little by little. It surprises you at first, because you had imagined an Orient full of bright colours—and it's not that at all. The light of North Africa is all nuanced, made up of a thousand delicate, pearly reflections that the eye only becomes sensitive to after a certain time."

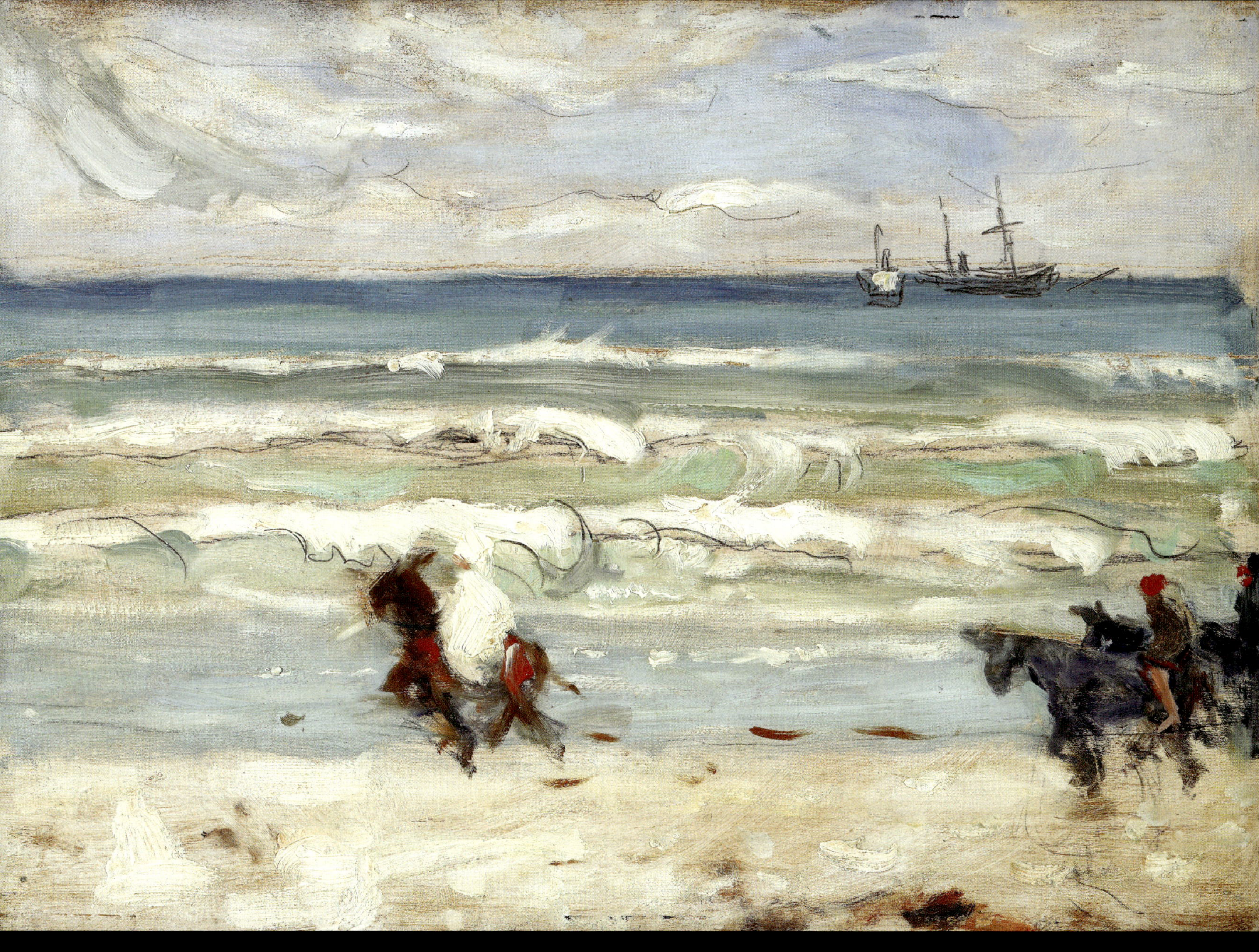

/ CAT. 48 James W. Morrice
Beach Scene, Tangier
1912 or 1913

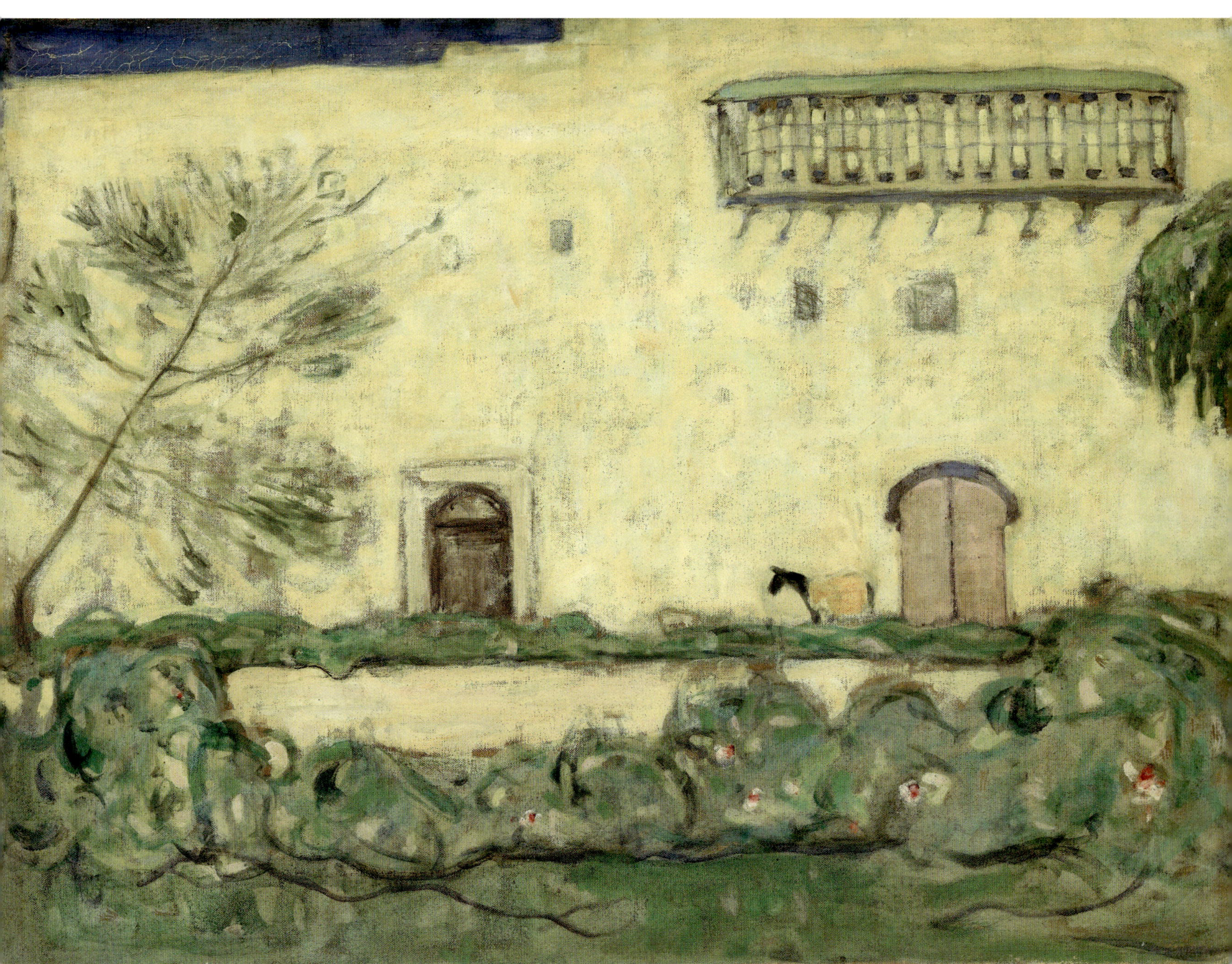

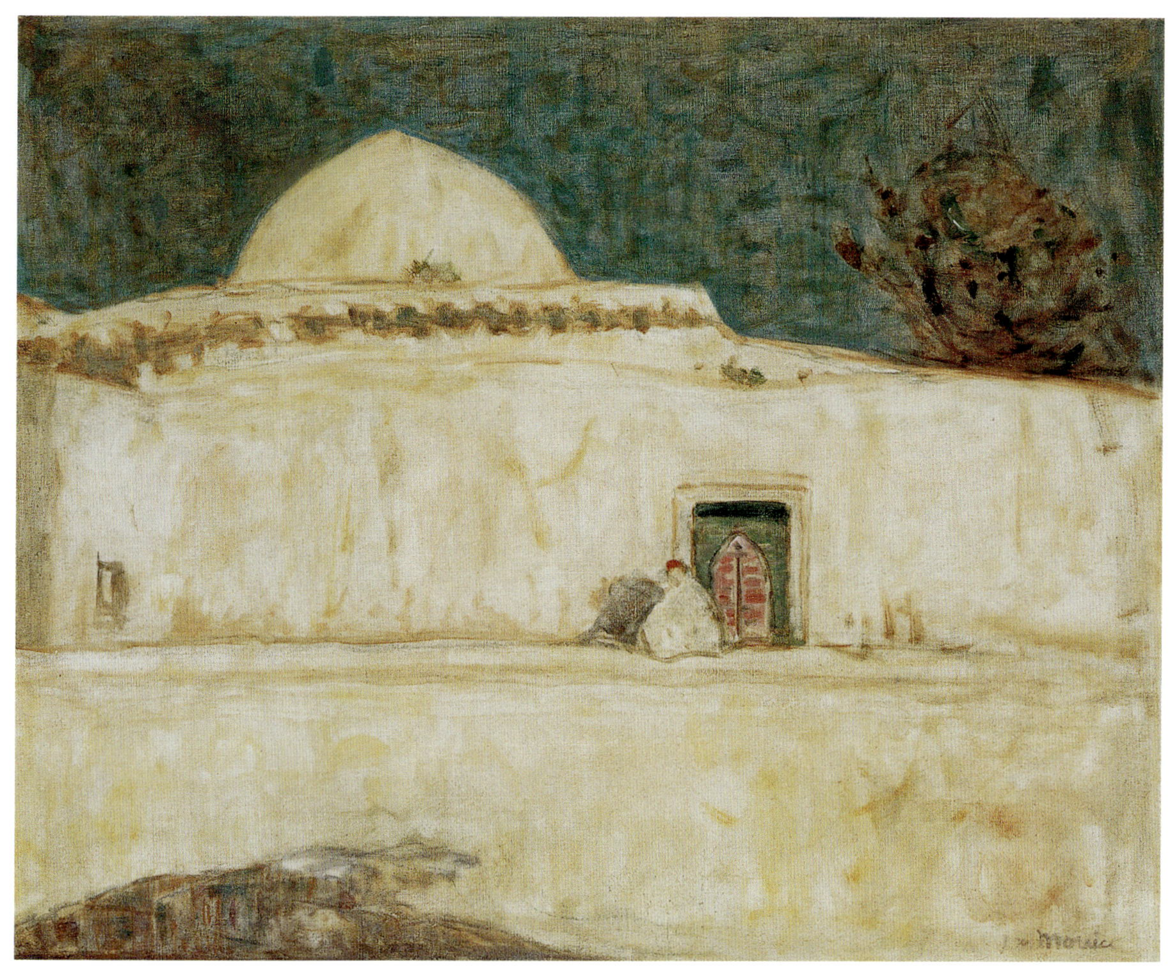

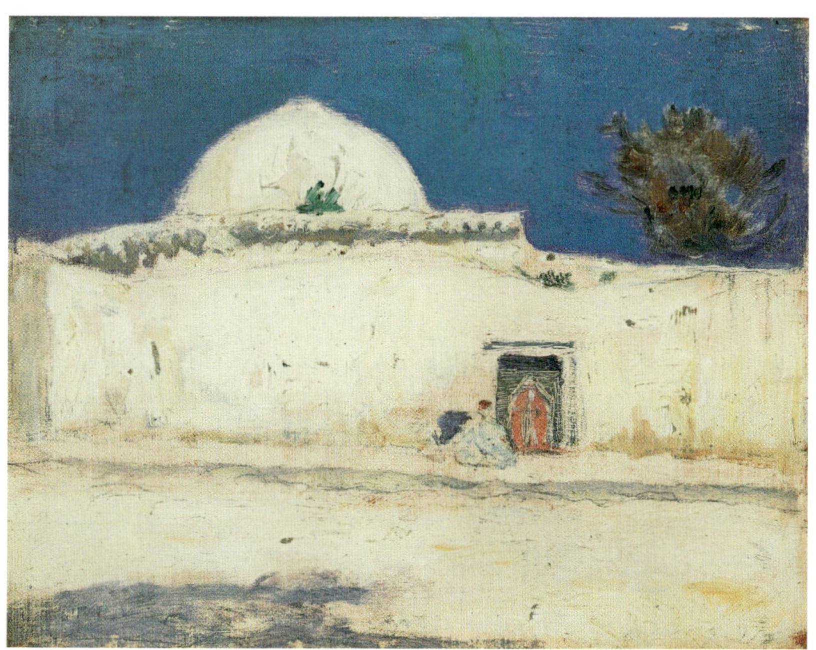

/ CAT. 49 James W. Morrice
Morocco Buildings
About 1919-1921

/ CAT. 50 James W. Morrice
Afternoon, Tunis
1914

/ CAT. 51 James W. Morrice
Study for "Afternoon, Tunis"
1914

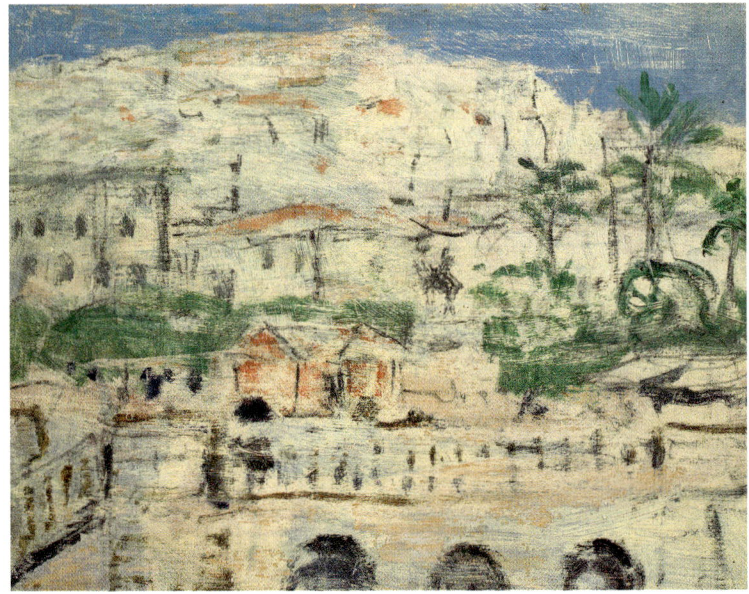

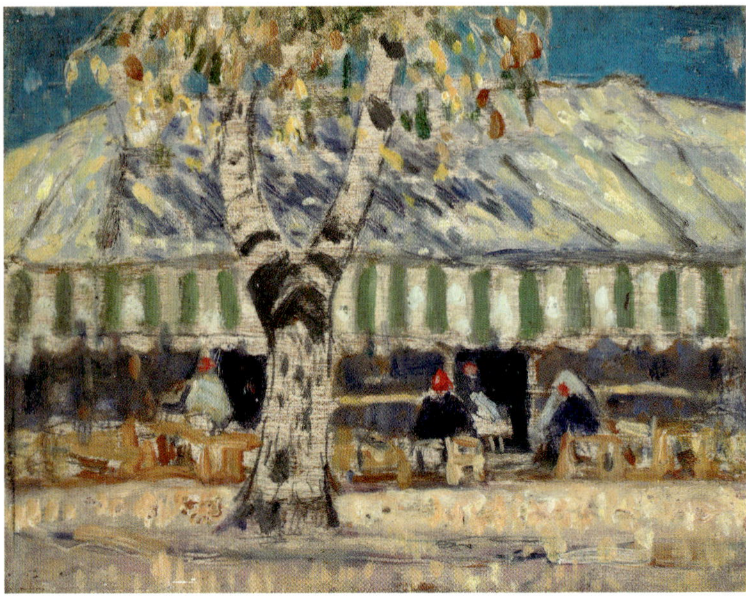

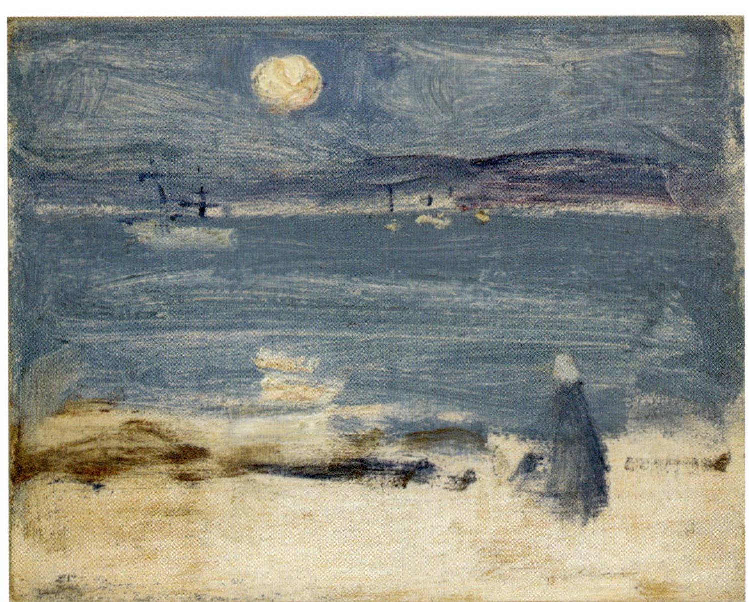

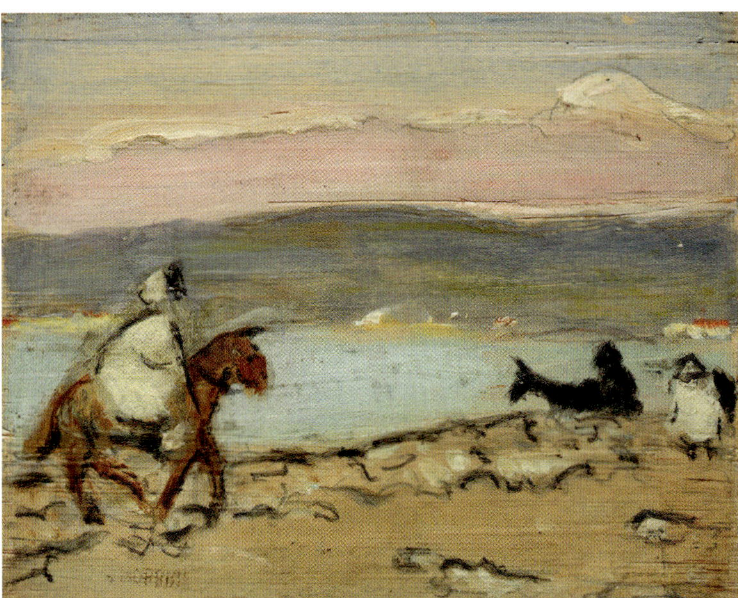

/ CAT. 52 James W. Morrice
Algiers
About 1922-1923

/ CAT. 53 James W. Morrice
Plane Tree and Tent, North Africa
1914

/ CAT. 54 James W. Morrice
Moonlight on the Bay of Tangier
1912 or 1913

/ CAT. 55 James W. Morrice
On the Road, Tangier
1912 or 1913

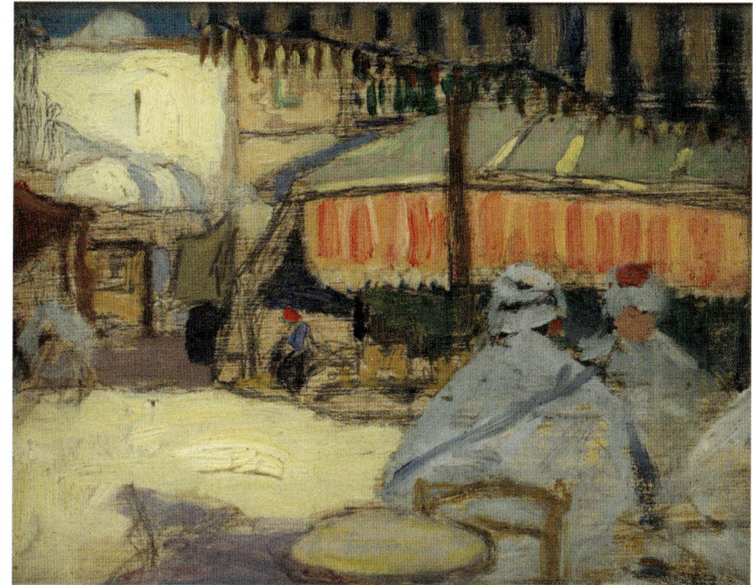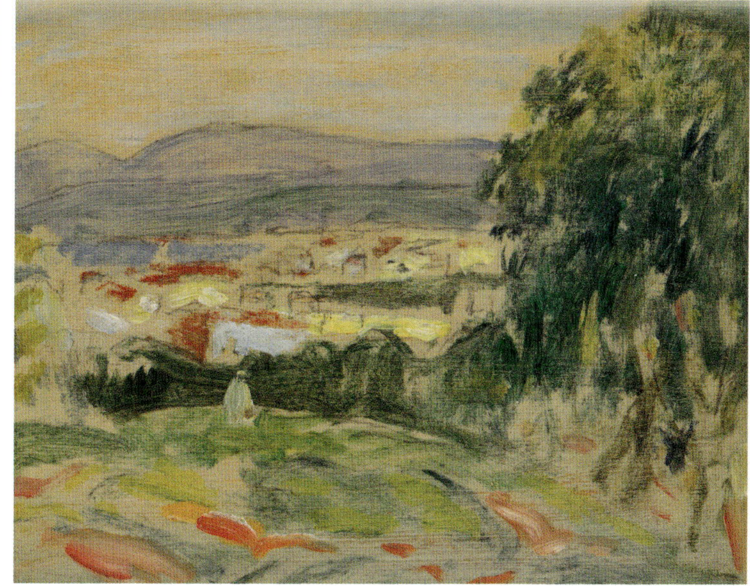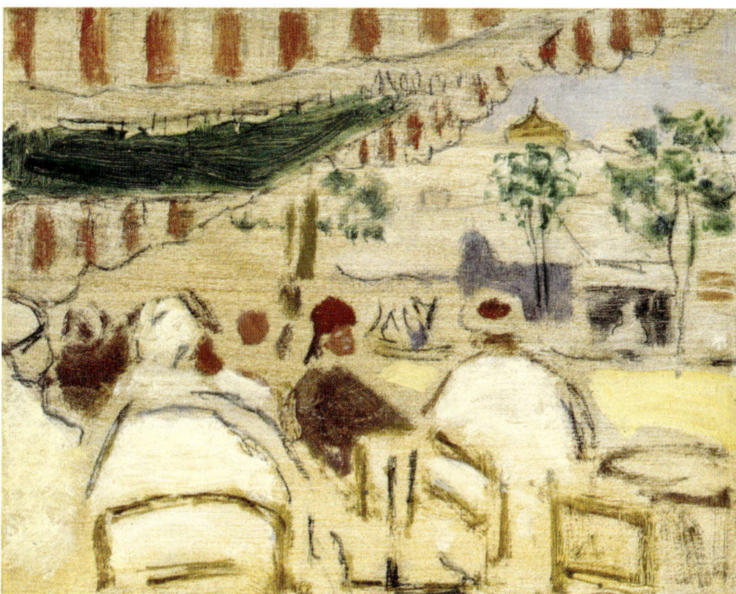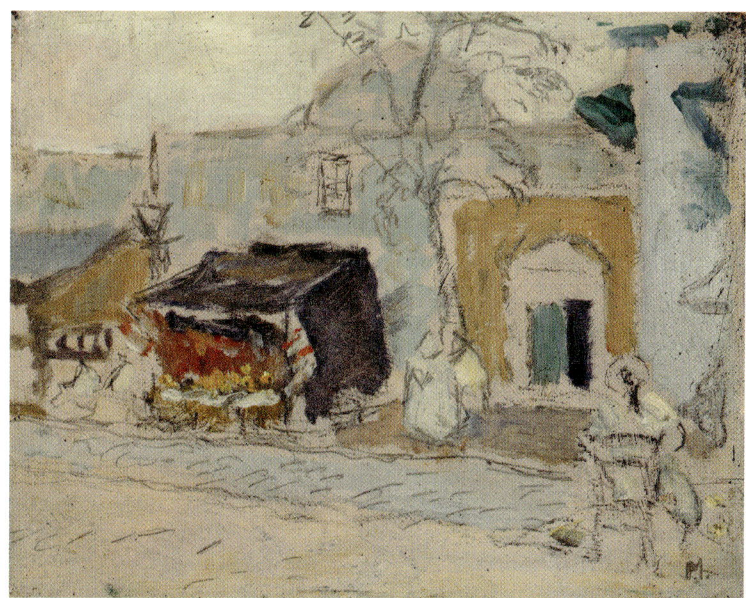

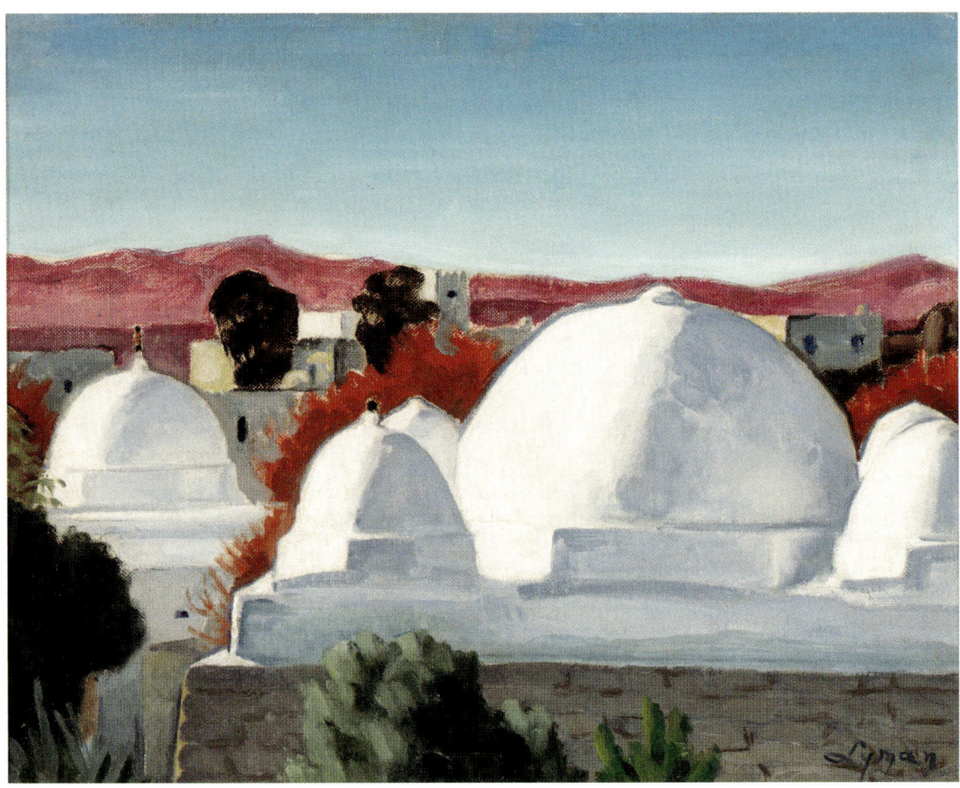 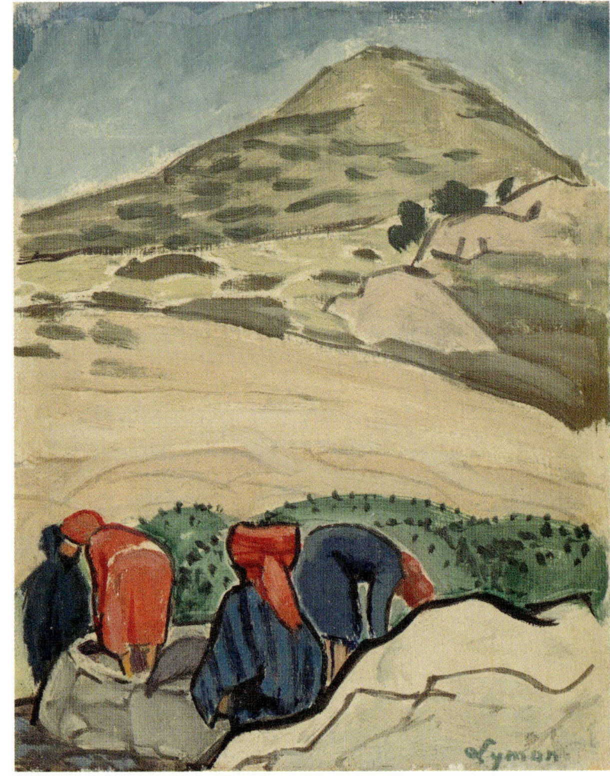

/ **CAT. 60** John Lyman
The Marabouts' Tombs, Morocco
Between 1920 and 1926

/ **CAT. 61** John Lyman
Sidi Djedidi, Tunisia, the Roman Well
About 1921

/ **CAT. 62** John Lyman
The Monastir Casbah
About 1920

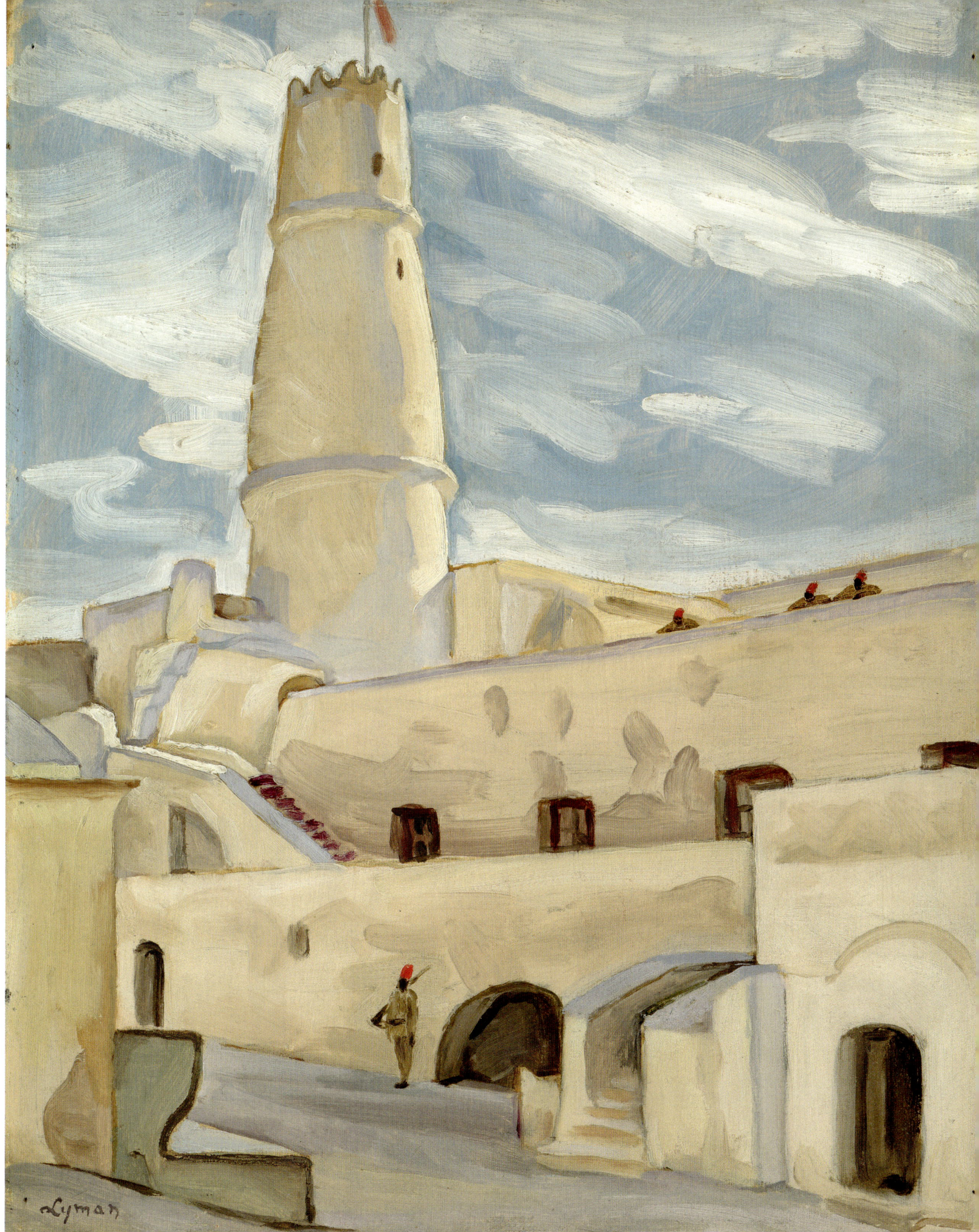
Lyman

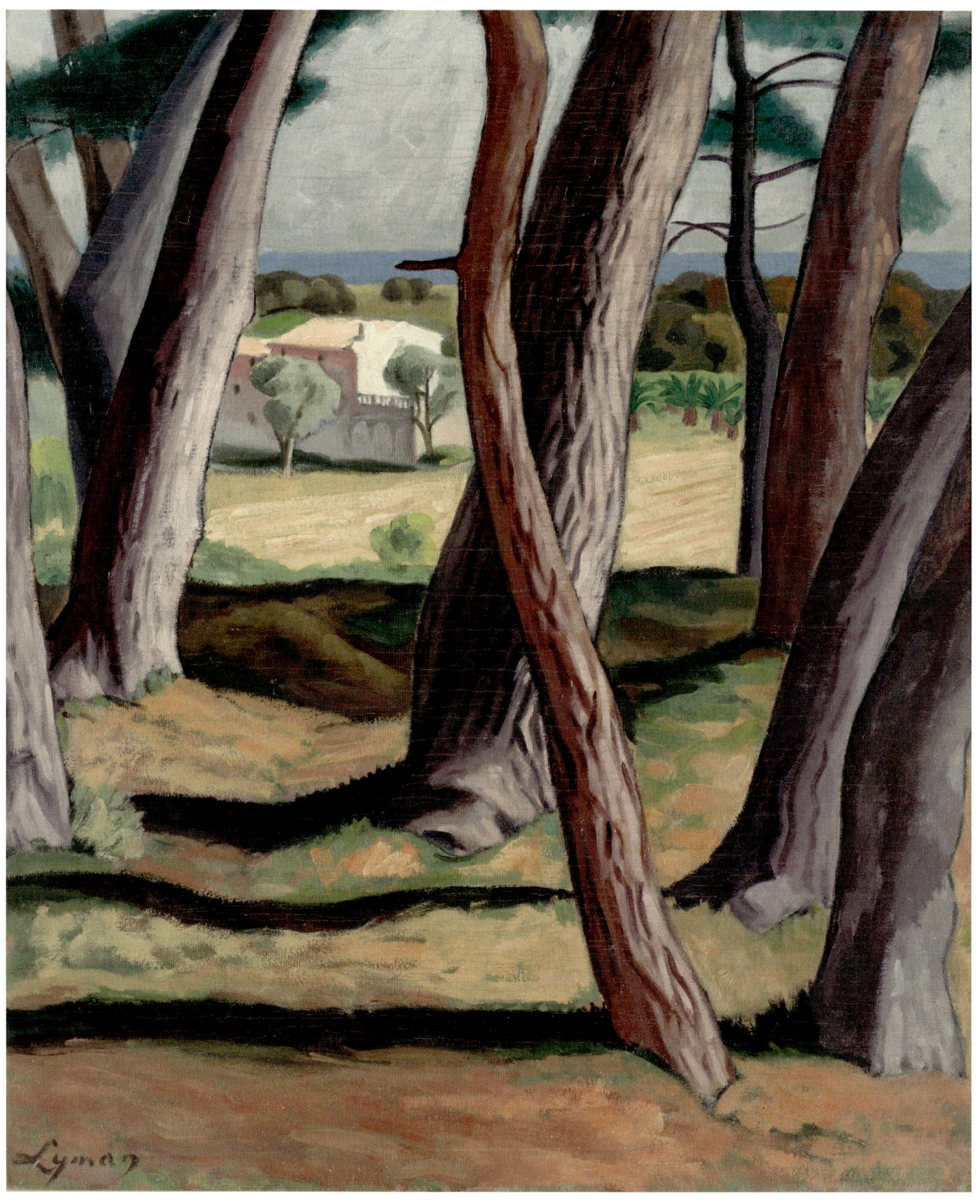
Lyman

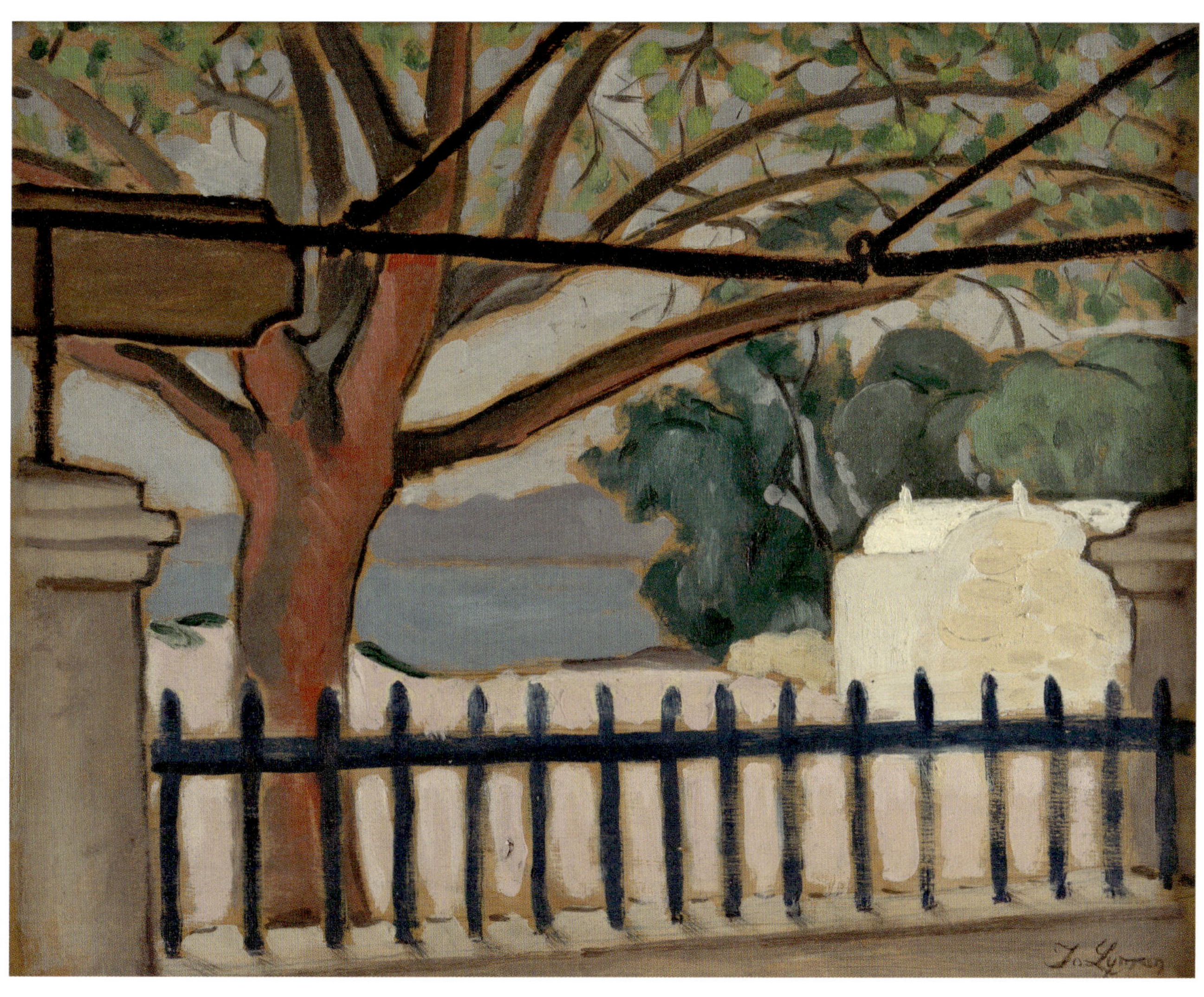

/ CAT. 63 John Lyman
**Landscape with House
(North African Coast)**
Between 1920 and 1926

/ CAT. 64 John Lyman
Zaouia, Hammamet
Between 1920 and 1926

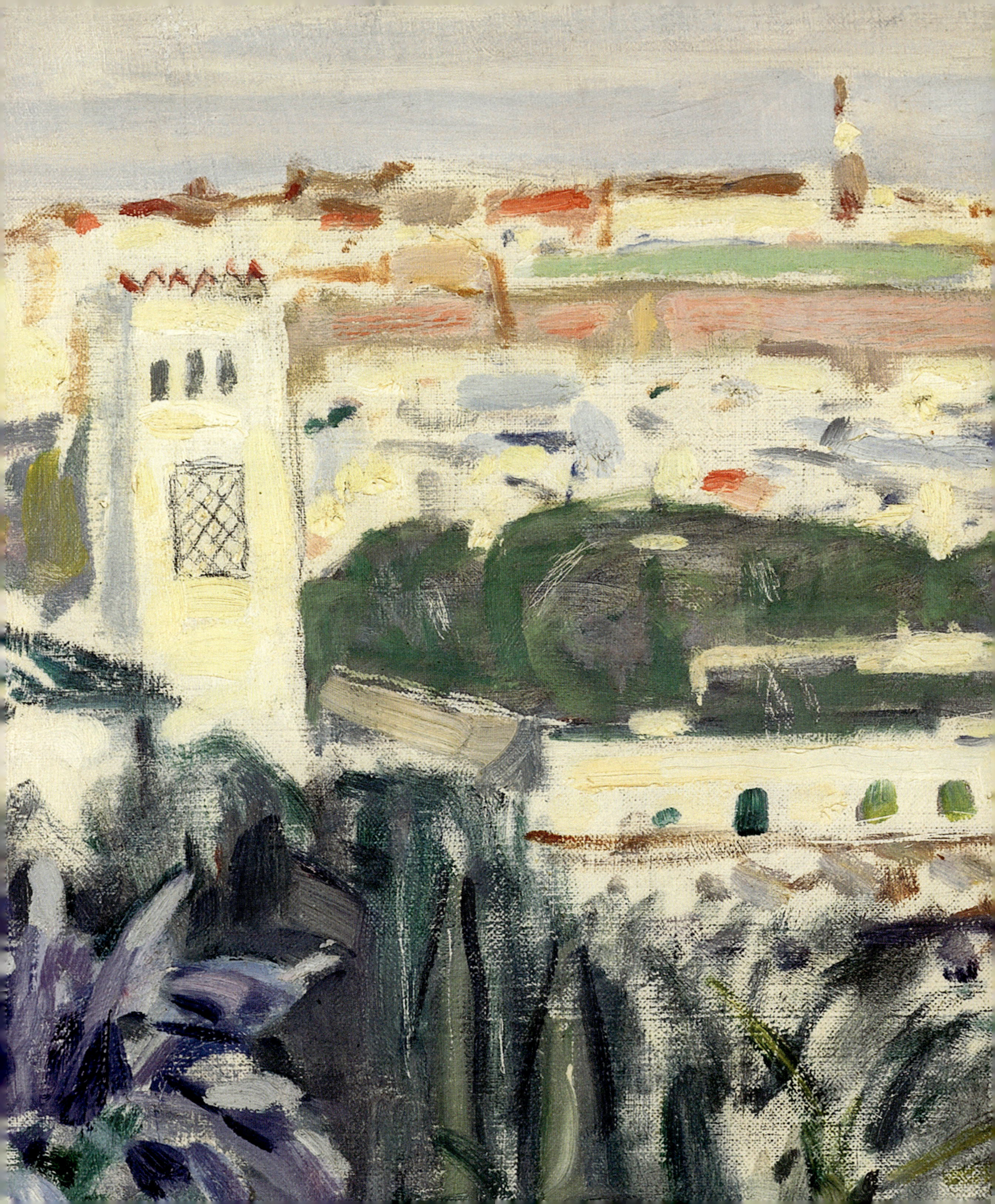

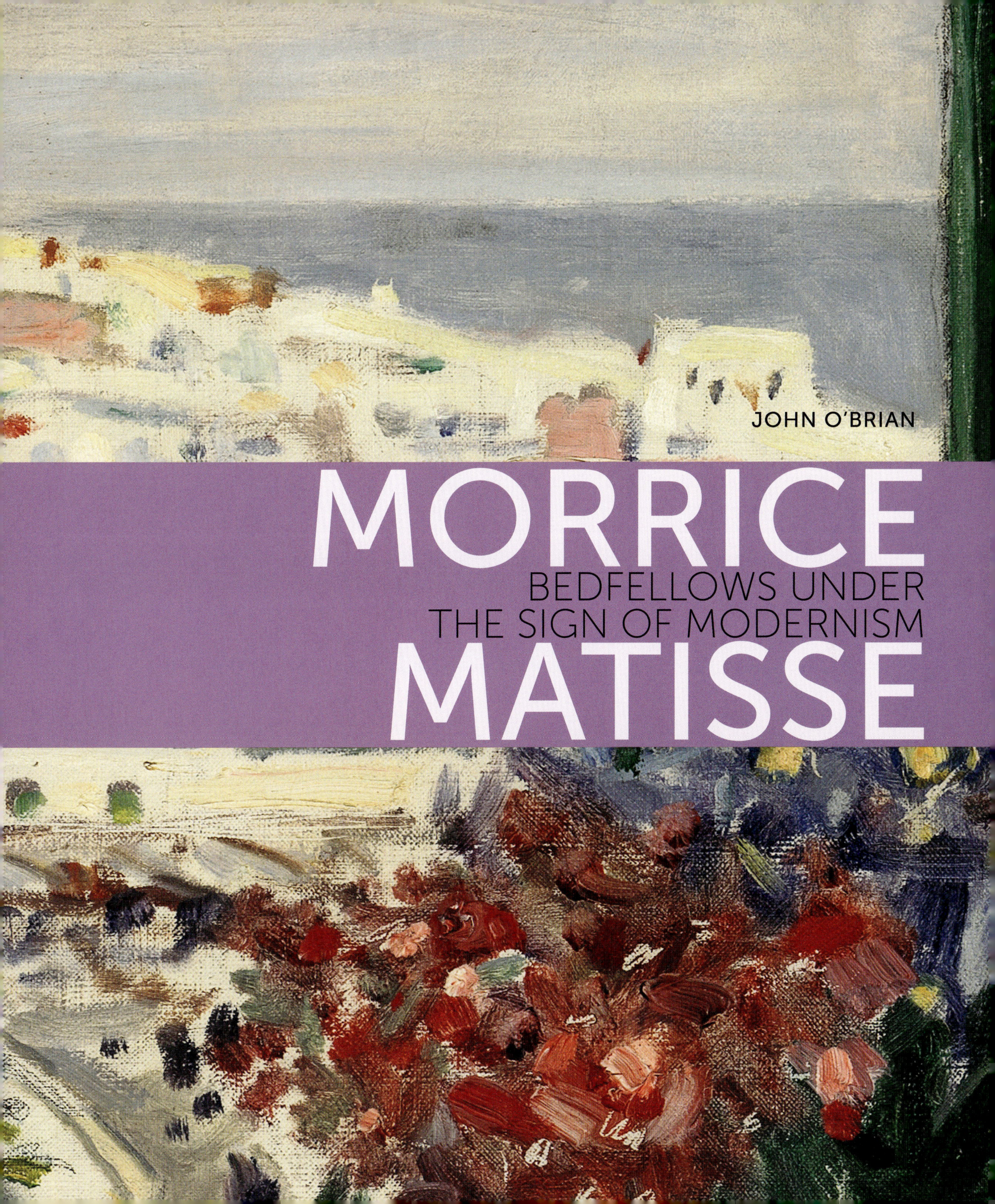

JOHN O'BRIAN

MORRICE
MATISSE

BEDFELLOWS UNDER THE SIGN OF MODERNISM

RECEPTION AND REPUTATION

Henri Matisse and James Wilson Morrice both emphasized the satisfactions of paint over the attractions of subject matter in their work. Critics were quick to recognize these proclivities. In 1909, Louis Vauxcelles, the critic responsible for coining the terms "Fauvism" and "Cubism," described Morrice as "the [North] American painter who has achieved in France and in Paris the most notable and well-merited place in the world of art since the death James McNeill Whistler."[1] In Europe's premier art city, according to Vauxcelles, Morrice had acquired the most significant reputation of any living Canadian or American artist. The critic for *L'Éclair* agreed, declaring that Morrice was "a remarkably gifted painter" and that his "landscapes [were] among the best."[2] *The Ferry, Quebec* **(CAT. 5)** from 1907 is representative of the kind of work Vauxcelles and the critic for *L'Éclair* admired. Using abbreviated notations of colour confined within a narrow tonal range, Morrice depicts a wintry stretch of the St. Lawrence River between the headland of Quebec City and the wharf at Lévis. The canvas is thinly painted in cool blues, greens and greys. In the painting, Morrice flattens the perspective in order to call attention to his mark-making and to the surface of his support.

In the period leading up to the First World War, Morrice occupied a prominent place in literary as well as artistic circles in Paris. Not only was his work favourably reviewed by critics such as Vauxcelles but his company was also sought out by writers.[3] Somerset Maugham, Arnold Bennett and Aleister Crowley found Morrice so captivating that they appropriated his personality and diction for use in their novels. "Hasn't he had too much to drink?" asks someone about the artist Warren in Maugham's *The Magician* (1908). "Much," comes the reply, "but he is always in that condition, and the further he goes from sobriety the more charming he is."[4] Matisse once wrote something similar. After first declaring his admiration for Morrice—"the artist with the delicate eye who delighted in interpreting landscapes of closely related values in soft and muted hues"—Matisse said that he "used to go with him to a café where I drank as many glasses of mineral water as he took glasses of alcool,"[5] adding that the Canadian artist was a friend, "a true gentleman, a good companion, with great wit and humour."[6]

Previous double page:

/ **CAT. 65 (DETAIL)** James W. Morrice
View from the Window, Tangier
1913

The occasion for Matisse's reflections was a 1926 exhibition of Morrice's work organized by the Galeries Simonson, Paris. Morrice had died two years earlier, and the gallery was mounting the exhibition in honour of the artist. Soon after, the Jeu de Paume also recognized Morrice by presenting an exhibition by the National Gallery of Canada, which included a substantial selection of his work.[7] In the years following these two shows, however, Morrice's reputation outside Canada fell as steadily as Matisse's rose. His work was rarely exhibited internationally, except when the Canadian flag was being waved, and historians gradually wrote him out of the narratives of modern art.[8] Morrice became a shadowy figure. Although he had spent the winters of 1912 and 1913 together with Matisse in Tangier, Morocco, Pierre Schneider did not even list Morrice in the index of his exhaustively researched 1984 monograph on Matisse.[9] It was only in 1990, when the National Gallery in Washington mounted *Matisse in Morocco*, an exhibition that travelled to the State Hermitage Museum in St. Petersburg, the Pushkin Museum in Moscow and the Museum of Modern Art in New York that Morrice began to emerge from the obscurity to which he had been relegated. The catalogue of the exhibition opened up a new space for the artist by reproducing half a dozen of his paintings and drawings and comparing them with those of Matisse and Charles Camoin, a friend of both artists who was also in Tangier with them during the second winter, in 1913.[10] Hilary Spurling continued the process of recovery in the second volume of her biography of Matisse. She observed that the three artists had not only sketched together in the streets of the city but had also shared a photographer's studio to work indoors during the rainy season.[11]

In what follows, I want to examine the relationship between Morrice and Matisse in terms of artistic reception. I am equally interested in the asymmetries as in symmetries of their receptions. The first part of the essay covers the period from 1890, when Morrice arrived in Paris, to Morrice's exhibition in 1926 at the Simonson Galleries. The second part covers the period from the 1936 publication of Donald W. Buchanan's foundational biography of Morrice to the National Gallery of Canada's acquisition of Matisse's *Nude on a Yellow Sofa* **(CAT. 71)** in 1958. By coincidence, or not, *Nude on a Yellow Sofa* was executed in the same year that Matisse wrote approvingly about Morrice for the Simonson exhibition.

The two reception histories add up. On the one hand, they tell us about some of the processes by which one artist becomes canonized while another is forgotten except in his own country. This involves thinking about matters of absence and presence as well as about the traces that draw absence and presence together. Traces not only mark the absence of things that were once present, such as the international reputation enjoyed by Morrice when he was alive. The power of the trace lies in its ability to mediate between what is *here* and what is *not here*, and the archive is one place this transaction occurs. As Jacques Derrida has observed, the archive is a place that allows for repetition, memorization and reproduction.[12] In other words, the archive is a place that allows for the investigation of traces, which is difficult in the case of Morrice because most traces left by the artist have disappeared.

On the other hand, the reception histories tell us about bourgeois ambivalence toward modernism in the first half of the twentieth century, about the anxieties produced by modern art within a rapidly shifting world order marked by war and socio-political change. The disinterested gaze with which audiences learned to encounter the paintings of Morrice and Matisse such as *The Ferry, Quebec* and *Nude on a Yellow Sofa* required mastery of a specific way of seeing. As Pierre Bourdieu argues in *Distinction*, "A work of art has meaning and interest only for someone who possesses the cultural competence, that is, the code, into which it is encoded."[13] In the modern period, high culture asserted itself under the sign of disinterested pleasure—pleasure that is purified of pleasure, as Bourdieu puts it—in opposition to desublimated appetites and pleasures. The exercise by audiences of cultural competences and codes conveyed social and class difference. The disinterested gaze with which audiences looked at works by Morrice and Matisse conferred "distinction" on the viewers—and also helped to determine the kinds of reception accorded to the artists' work.[14]

GENERATIONAL SYMMETRIES

Let me begin with some biographical details. Their symmetry helps to explain the nature of Morrice's friendship with Matisse as well as Matisse's attitude to the National Gallery of Canada and its desire to acquire a major painting by him.[15] The two artists were strangely matched, though I do say "strangely." With a nod to Gertrude Stein's description of the Cone sisters, the sibling collectors of modern art from Baltimore,[16] the details are these: that Morrice and Matisse belonged to the same generation, Morrice having been born in 1865 and Matisse four years later; that Morrice's family was wealthy, his father having made a fortune in textiles after emigrating from Scotland, and that Matisse's family was less wealthy, his father having earned his living as a small-town grain merchant; that each was encouraged by his parents to study law, as often happened with young men of some social standing in Canada no less than in France; that Morrice stayed in Toronto after university in 1886 to study law at Osgoode Hall and after one year of courses began articling in 1887, while Matisse was sent to study law in Paris in 1887 and after two years returned home to begin clerking in 1889; that, also in the manner of young men of some social standing, each decided to quit law after several years as having already had enough of it; that, after quitting, each chose to go to Paris to study art; and that during a brief period each had studied at the Académie Julian: Morrice in 1890, and Matisse in 1891.[17]

Beyond these coincidences, there is nothing especially remarkable in these details. The course of action followed by Morrice and Matisse was a course of action followed by other would-be artists from France as well as the rest of Europe and North America, including Maurice Prendergast and Robert Henri from the United States, who attended the Académie Julian about the same time. Julian's was large and its publicity, which included flyers distributed in several

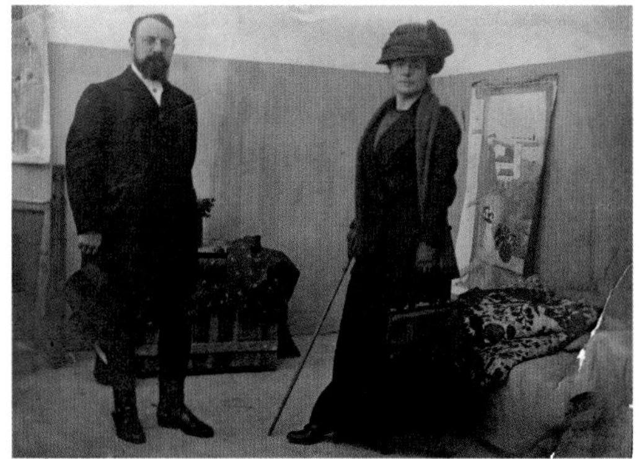

languages, was effective. Charles Fromuth, another American who subsequently became a friend of Morrice, wrote about the place and its inhabitants in his journal in 1890.

> After an inspection of the various ateliers all crowded with students from all nations and without a preference for any of the professors, I chose the largest because one had the choice of two models posing at the same time. It was also nearest to the stairway of exit. Another stimulant of choice was I found a group of students from the Philadelphia Academy.[18]

Even if the two artists had met, Morrice spoke little French, Matisse little English, and the ateliers were packed. It is more likely that they met during the first decade of the twentieth century when Morrice had gained facility in French and was starting to exhibit at the Salon d'Automne. (In 1903, Matisse, Marquet and Rouault, among others, participated in the first Salon d'Automne, as a sign of protest against the conservatism of the official salon.) Morrice's initial showing at the Salon d'Automne was in 1905—a contribution of four small oil panels, three of Venice and one of the Tuileries garden—the same year that Vauxcelles labelled Matisse and his circle "wild beasts" or "fauves."[19] If the two artists did not connect on that occasion, in 1908 they definitely met as jurors on the selection committee for the Salon d'Automne.[20] But there can be no doubt that by 1905 Morrice was already taking careful notice of Matisse's painting. Clive Bell recalled that on an excursion he and Morrice took around Paris—the future art critic informally apprenticed himself to Morrice in the middle years of the decade—the artist advised him to look at Matisse.[21] When Bernard Berenson offered Bell the same advice in Florence in the spring of 1908, it was only a confirmation of what Morrice had urged earlier.[22] Although Berenson changed his opinion of Matisse in later life—Clement Greenberg considered Berenson to have "a radical and peevish miscomprehension of the art of his own age"[23]—Morrice did not.

TANGIER

The two extended moments of intersection in the lives of Morrice and Matisse occurred in Tangier during the winters of 1912 and 1913. The only witness accounts by either artist of their time together in Morocco are by Matisse, both in the memoir written for the 1926 retrospective and in an interview conducted by Buchanan in 1935. The accounts confound expectations as we are conditioned to look for reminiscences about the great by the less great and not the other way around. Apart from Matisse, the most significant witness of their time spent together was Camoin, during the second winter in Tangier.[24] Based on extant letters, especially those of Matisse and Camoin, but including some written by Morrice, I calculate that they were in one another's company for a total of about fifteen weeks over the course of the two winters—a consequential amount of time.[25]

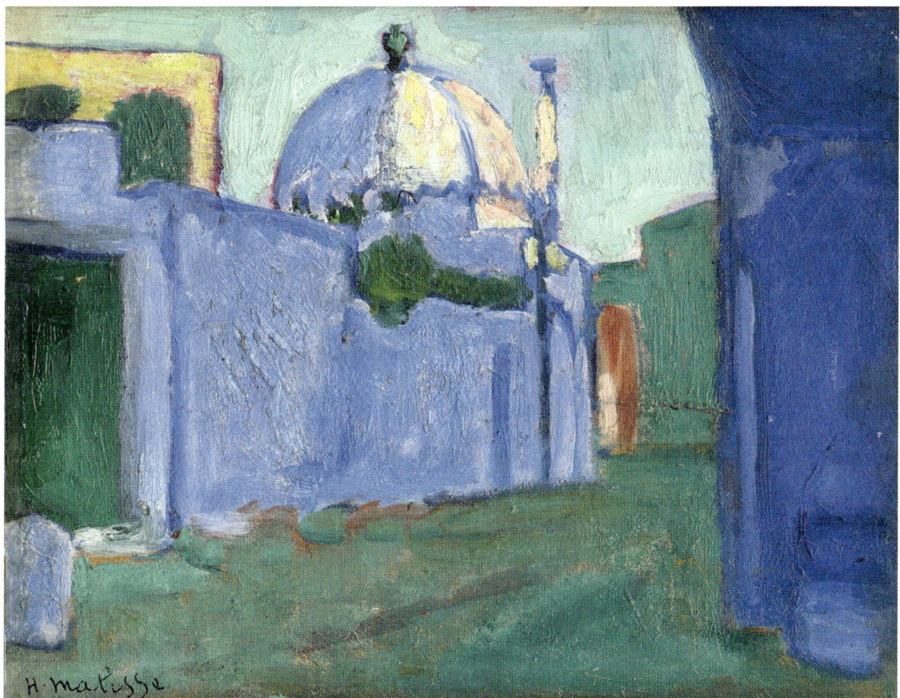 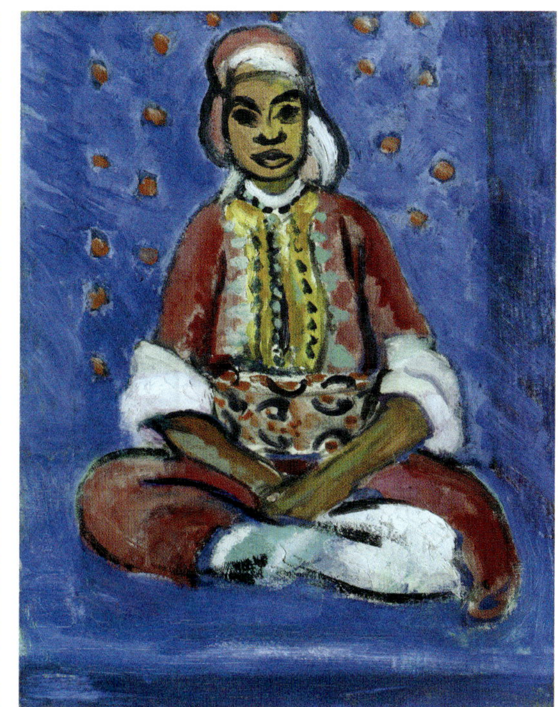

In the years leading up to the First World War, Morroco was a pawn on the imperial chessboard. France had long claimed Morocco as a sphere of influence, and in 1904 it persuaded Britain to officially recognize the claim. German objections to the recognition intensified the level of distrust among the colonial powers and provoked a political crisis, one of several marking the path to the outbreak of war. The 1912 Treaty of Fez, which formalized Morocco as a French protectorate and also gave Spain the right to exploit the country's iron mines, deepened the distrust.[26] At the time, Morrice and Matisse were coming to the end of their first trip to Tangier. On April 1, two days after the treaty was signed, Matisse wrote to Albert Marquet: "It is said that things are very bad in Fez. That there are French workers here destined for Fez. That no one dares send them for fear of attacks, which would make things even more complicated."[27] Looking at the paintings produced that winter by Morrice and Matisse, in which formal concerns of light and colour trump mimetic concerns about what was being depicted, one would be hard pressed to discern that war and insurrection were in the air. But Morocco was an unstable place for foreigners, especially the French, and nationalists singled out French-owned businesses and burned them to the ground. The correspondent for the *Times* of London, Walter Harris, reported that in Fez the "insurgents marched through the streets carrying the severed heads of Frenchmen on pikes."[28] (This may be an exaggeration that reflected prevailing Orientalist attitudes.) In addition to being a correspondent, Harris made it his business to know everyone of importance in Morocco. That included Matisse and Morrice.[29]

/ **FIG. 16** Charles Camoin
Matisse and his wife in Tangier, with *Landscape Viewed from a Window* **in the background**
1913

/ **FIG. 17** Henri Matisse
The Marabout
1912

/ **FIG. 18** Henri Matisse
Girl from Tangier
1912

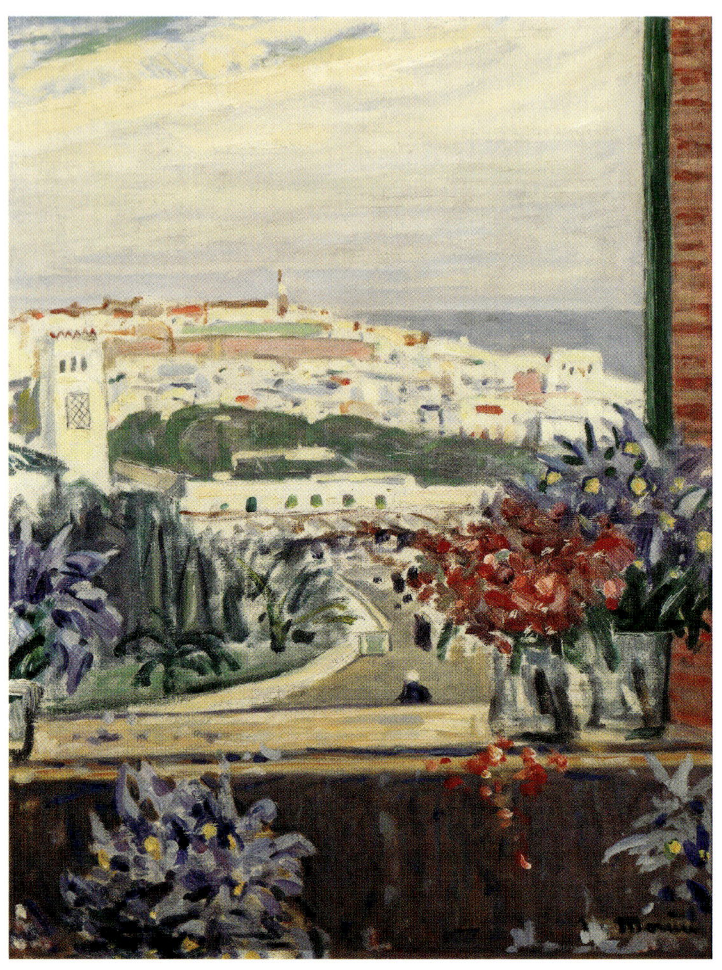

When Matisse remarked in 1926 that Morrice was a *bon camarade*, he was not simply speaking well of the dead. He meant it. Matisse reported that, except during working hours, he and Morrice were always together in Tangier. (Some of the time they were together during working hours as well, as we have seen, sharing a photographer's studio or sketching in the streets with Camoin.) Even allowing for Matisse's habitually long working day, and granting license for exaggeration, that adds up to several months of evenings. What drew them together? A passage from a draft of Buchanan's biography, not included in the published edition of the book, reveals the personal side of Matisse's friendship for Morrice:

> The strange humours of the Canadian, his lovable character, his whimsy and wit, still endear him to Matisse, who recalls with a smile how he would bring him to see his children and how to them he appeared such a strange spectacle, a character apart with odd mannerisms as, for example, the way he had of stuffing the tobacco into his pipe, which always made them laugh.[30]

Morrice's companionship, then, made Matisse smile and his children laugh. He was a character about whom you could tell stories. The demands Matisse put upon

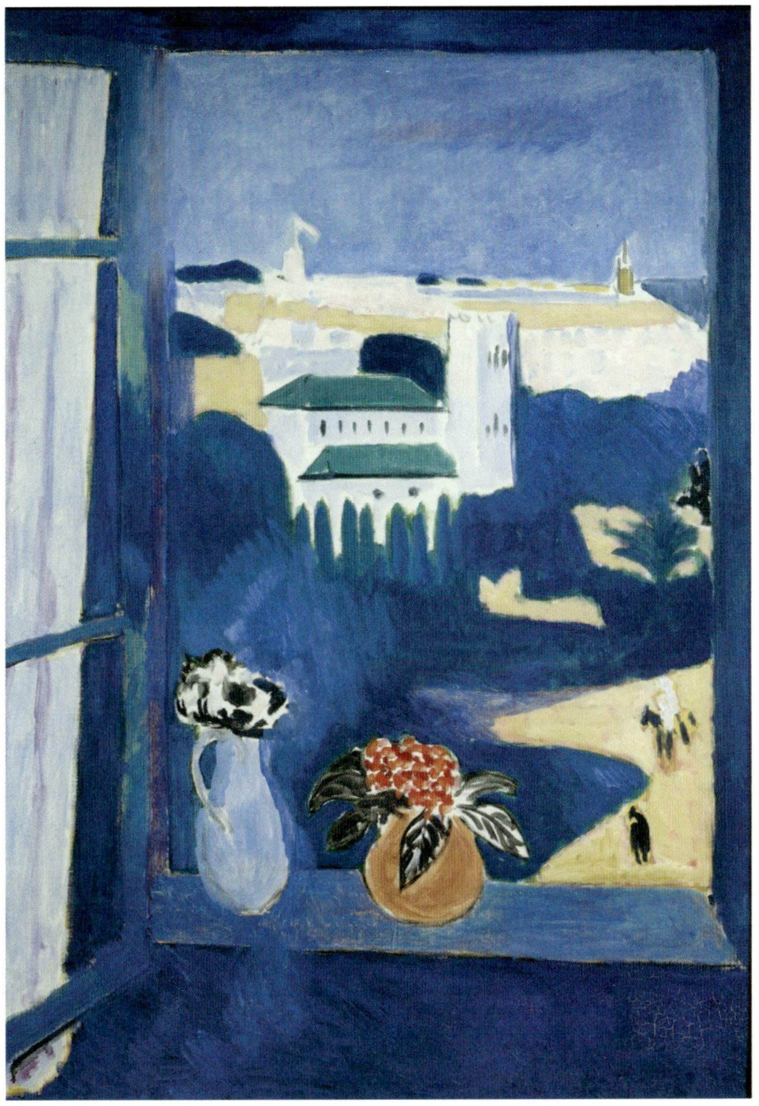

himself in the studio frequently made him anxious, causing sleepless nights, as did the political situation in Morocco. Morrice was an antidote.

In his 1935 interview with Buchanan, Matisse declared that the two artists never talked about art and other artists.[31] We would do well to take this assertion with a grain of salt. In Tangier the two artists visited the studio of the Irish portrait painter John Lavery together—"What lousy painting," Matisse wrote afterwards[32]— and keenly valued having the good opinion of one another's work. Matisse felt slighted by Morrice's reluctance to openly declare his admiration for his painting and wrote to Camoin to express his bruised feelings. Camoin replied immediately: "Morrice talked to me a bit about painting, telling me that, contrary to what you think, he very much likes what you do."[33] They also painted the same view from a window of the Hôtel Villa de France, where they stayed two times (CAT. 65 and FIG. 19).[34] The paintings depict the urban park around the Anglican church of St. Andrew's in Tangier, including the church itself with its tower built in Moroccan style as a copy of a Muslim minaret, rising above the greenery of the park—Matisse painted the park deep blue on the first occasion—and the walls of the Casbah in the distance. A panoramic photograph of the scene taken from a window of the hotel dates from around the same time (FIG. 10), as well as a portrait of the artist and his wife, with the painting hanged to the wall in the background (FIG. 16).

/ **CAT. 65** James W. Morrice
View from the Window, Tangier
1913

/ **FIG. 19** Henri Matisse
Landscape Viewed from a Window
1912-1913

PAINTING PROCEDURES

Matisse worked in pairs and series throughout his career, often painting several versions of the same motif.[35] Sometimes the versions were strikingly different, as was the case with the two paintings executed from the window of the Hôtel Villa de France, where the readable composition and dense application of paint in the first version gives way to the aporia of abstraction and thinly applied primary colours in the second. There was also a large difference in his two portraits of a young Moroccan from the Rif, *Standing Riffian* and *Seated Riffian*. Morrice also worked in pairs from time to time. In *Blanche* **(CAT. 67)** and *Blanche Baume* **(CAT. 68)**, the composition of the paintings is almost identical. In both, the model Blanche Baume occupies the same position on a high-backed sofa while wearing the same hat backed by vertically striped wallpaper. But the colour selections in the paintings are markedly different. The red of the sofa shifts to green from one canvas to the next and the wallpaper from blue to yellow, while the hat shifts from red to blue-grey. Morrice admired the figure paintings of Pierre Bonnard—something of Bonnard's example is present in the two portraits—but *Blanche* and *Blanche Baume* owe a comparable debt to the example of Matisse.[36]

If Morrice was acquainted with Matisse's painting techniques and procedures first hand, the reverse was also true. Matisse once mimicked Morrice's habit of wiping a small wood panel (pochade) across the seat of his trousers to help smooth the surface before painting on it.[37] Oil on panel was a favourite medium of Morrice **(CAT. 66)** as it allowed him to carry a small box, containing his paints and brushes as well as the pochades, fitted neatly into a side pocket of his suit. Not wishing to call attention to himself, Morrice "was never seen to carry visible paint-ing kit," one observer reported.[38] This allowed him to move with the crowd like the *flâneur* he was, while at the same time remaining hidden from it. He would sit at a café table—in the company of Matisse or alone—with his paint box placed un-obtrusively on his lap, looking much like any other patron. For Morrice, the activity of painting was inseparable from his search for pleasure, and he did not hurry the process. Each stroke of pigment was carefully deliberated. He wanted to catch the nuances of light and atmosphere, the subtleties of form and composition, in the most economical way possible. Only two brushstrokes were required for him to represent the band of a hat, for instance, and most of the paint on his pochades is applied so thinly that the warm brown colour of the panel and its wood grain shows through.

In addition to talk of daily affairs, Matisse and Morrice also engaged in banter around the business of art. In different ways, they had performed rather well in their second professions. They had not only received extensive critical attention, Matisse for major and Morrice for minor transgressions against the dominant conventions of painting, but had also been purchased by prominent collectors of modern art.[39] Ivan Morosov, the Russian collector for whom Matisse executed several large Moroccan paintings that are now in the collection of the Pushkin Museum, had purchased a painting by Morrice as early as 1904—four years before he purchased

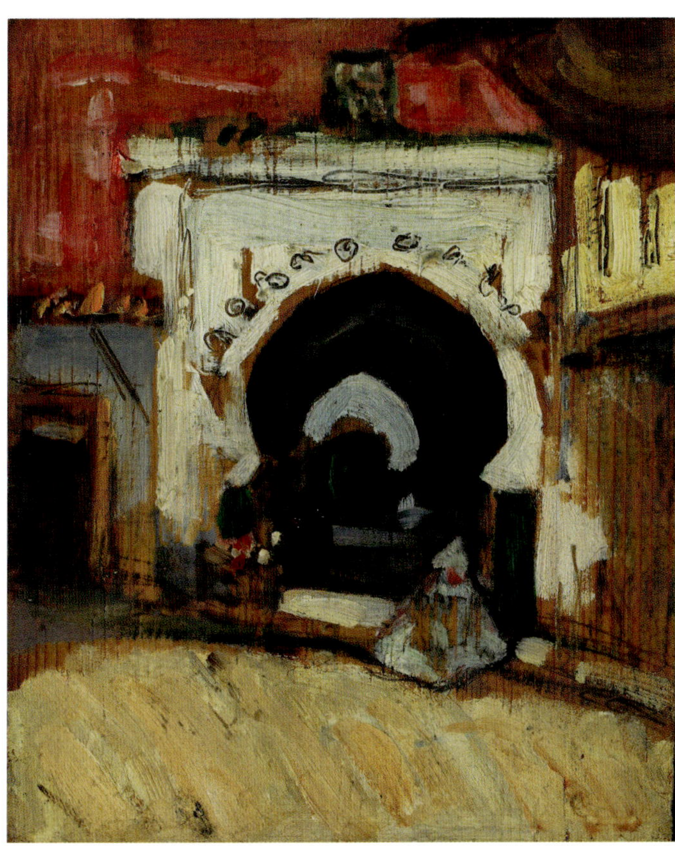

anything by Matisse. There should be no mistaking the shared interests and ambitions of the two painters. Like most artists intent on building careers and reputations in the avant-garde, they knew very well how the marketplace worked and the place played in it by exhibitions and reviews.

Morrice managed his reputation in the United States and Canada less well than in France and Europe. While he regularly sent paintings for exhibition to the Pennsylvania Academy of Fine Arts and the Carnegie Institute—encouraged, it seems, by Maurice Prendergast, Robert Henri and John Sloan—as well as to the Canadian Art Club in Toronto and the Art Association of Montreal, and though the National Gallery of Canada and several of these organizations purchased his work, as did important private collectors such as Albert C. Barnes and William Van Horne, Morrice did not regularly send his best or most recent paintings to exhibitions in North America.[40] More than once, he forwarded work that had been executed ten years earlier, which hardly ingratiated him to collectors. Shortly before the first winter in Tangier, Morrice informed a Canadian correspondent that he had "not the slightest desire to improve the taste of the Canadian public," and that he doubted the advisability of sending any paintings at all to Toronto.[41] The irony is that Morrice did "improve" the taste of Canadian audiences. As his international reputation declined in the years following his death, Canadian audiences were precisely those that most highly valued his work. The faded specter of Morrice's reputation abroad was resisted only by the artist's reception in Canada. It was not until the 1990 exhibition organized by the National Gallery of Art, Washington, that Morrice's paintings started to ghost out of the past into the present.

/ **CAT. 66** James W. Morrice
**Moroccan Town
(Gateway in Tangier)**
About 1913

Next double page:

/ **CAT. 67** James W. Morrice
Blanche
About 1911-1912

/ **CAT. 68** James W. Morrice
Blanche Baume
About 1911-1912

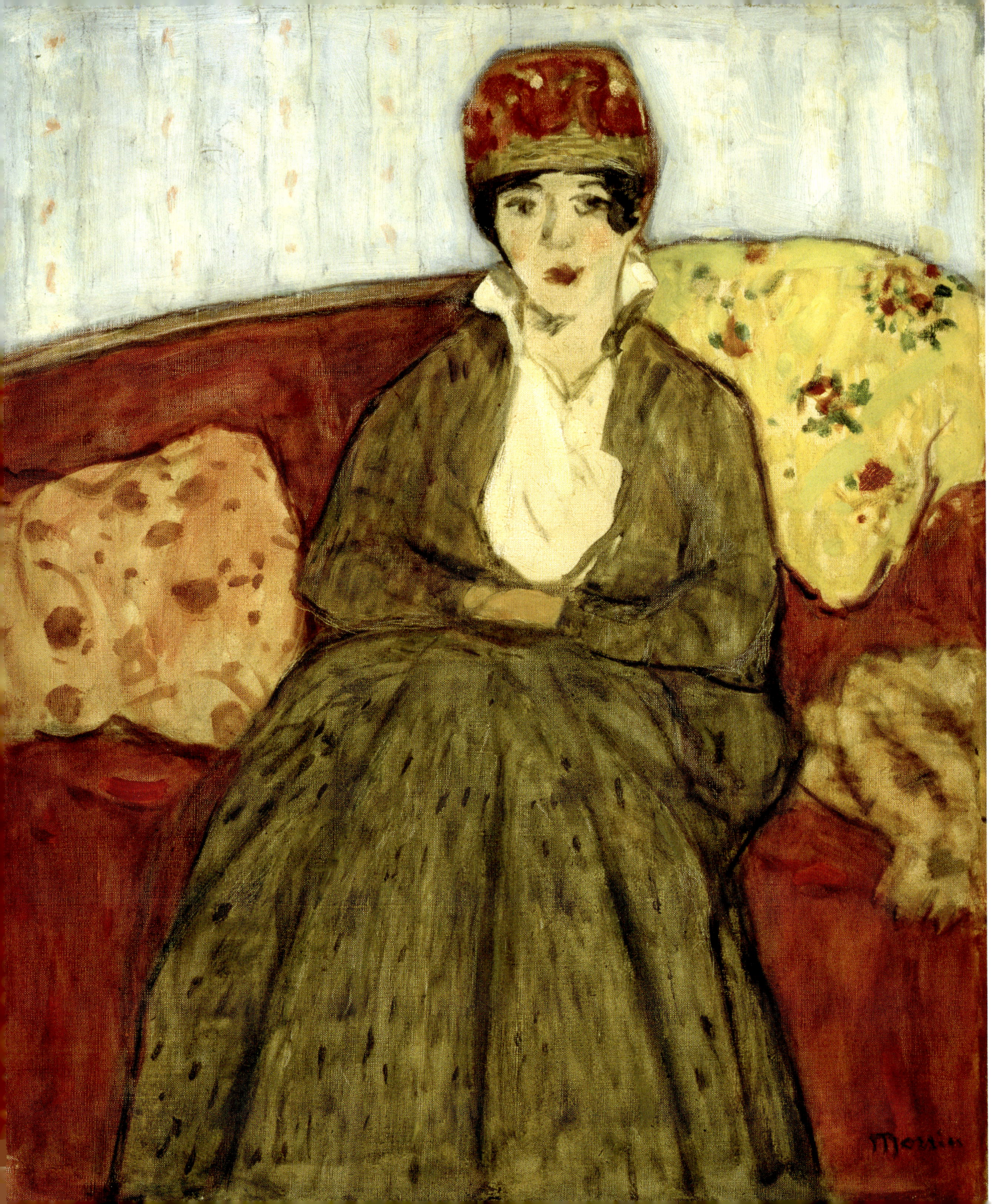

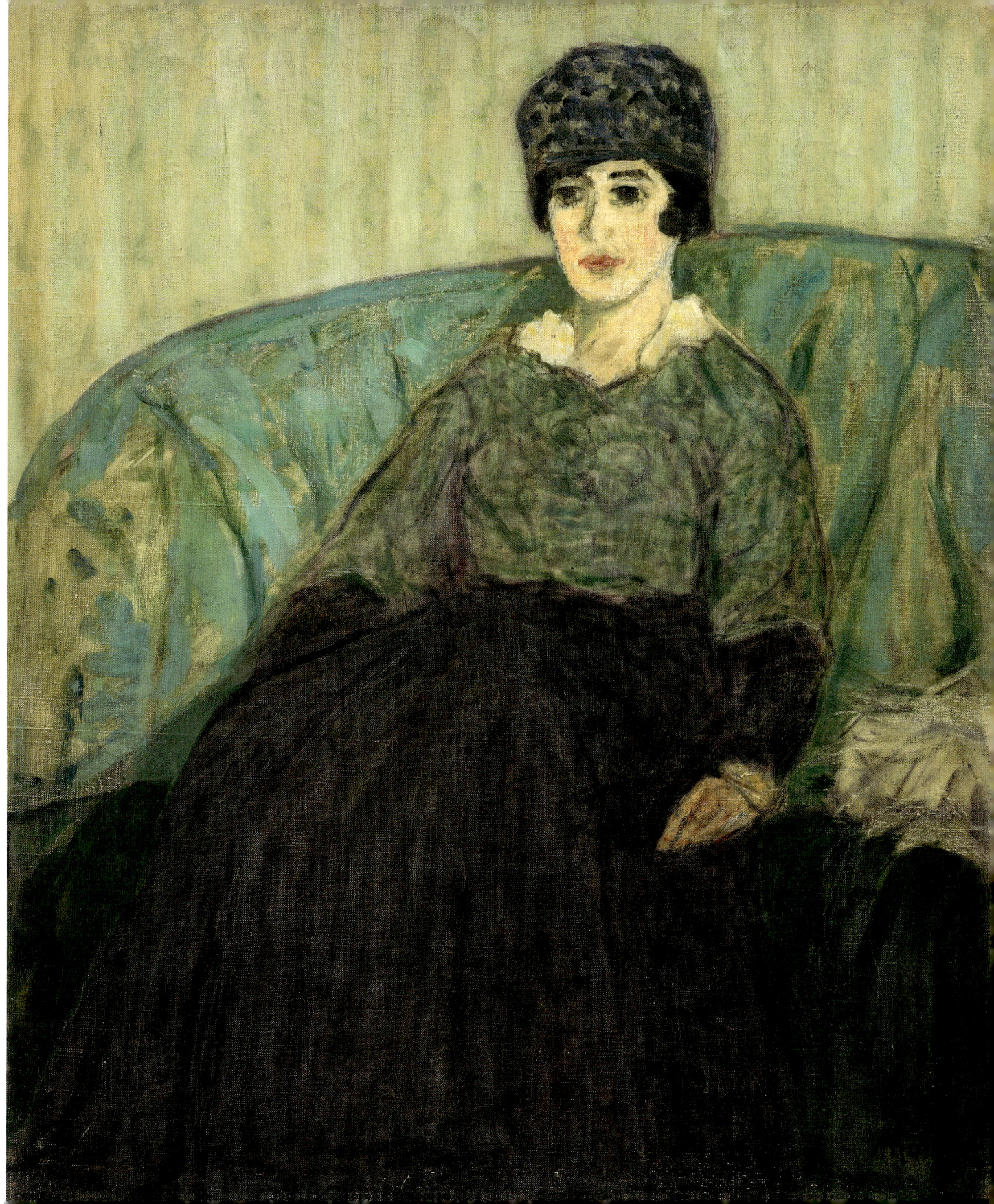

MATISSE IN CANADA

In contrast to Morrice, Matisse managed his reputation in North America as well as any artist in the twentieth century, not excepting Picasso.[42] Some evidence of Matisse's solicitude for his North American reputation is demonstrated by how much longer it took for his art—indeed, for modernism generally—to be accepted in Canada than in the United States. This was despite the example of Morrice's art, and despite the proselytizing for both Morrice and Matisse's work by John Lyman, who was a friend of Morrice and a student of Matisse. Audiences attracted to the nationalist landscape paintings of the Group of Seven balked at the structures of Bourdieu's disinterested gaze. In addition to Morrice and Lyman, the dramatis personae involved in the promotion of Matisse in Canada include Buchanan, who held a variety of positions at the National Gallery; Father M. A. Couturier, the French Catholic priest who spent the Second World War years in exile in Montreal and who was dedicated to promoting modern art, notably the construction of the Matisse chapel in Vence, within the Catholic church; Pierre Matisse, the artist's son and one of his principal dealers in the United States; Anthony Blunt, the influential (and subsequently disgraced) English art historian; and two museum officials with international reputations, James Johnson Sweeney and Charles Sterling.

It is remarkable that until five years before Matisse's death in 1954, no painting or sculpture by him had found its way into public Canadian collections. Paintings had been exhibited in Canada and had met with stock responses picked up from elsewhere. Writing about an exhibition of contemporary French painting held in Montreal in 1936, an exhibition which included work by Bonnard, Raoul Dufy, Fernand Léger and Picasso (represented by *La Vie*, 1903, Cleveland Museum of Art) as well as two paintings by Matisse, the reviewer for *The Montreal Daily Star* described it as "a very interesting show of work which is well known and admired in more progressive places."[43] However, Lyman had spent most of his adult life in "more progressive places" such as France and was less apologetic. He wrote that the exhibition ought to be visited and looked at because it represented "living art . . . I mean art that is a direct outgrowth of the life and thought of our times rather than a pale dilution of some bygone convention."[44] One of the paintings in the exhibition by Matisse, *Large Cliff – Two Rays* (**CAT. 69**) was purchased by Hamilton S. Southam, a friend of Buchanan.[45] It was probably the first Matisse painting to enter a Canadian collection (**FIG. 20**), though it was sold a short time later to a New York dealer.[46]

A phenomenon in Canadian museums well into the 1960s was the appointment of prominent European and American art historians as advisers.[47] These consultants, largely invisible to the outside world, were paid (though sometimes they provided the service without remuneration) to advise the museums on the acquisition of works of art. A similar arrangement existed in other countries with strong cultural and colonial ties to Europe. In Canada, as might be expected, many of the advisers were British.[48] Among the consultants were W. G. Constable, who held a variety of senior posts in Britain and the United States in universities and museums; Phillip Hendy, who was Director of the National Gallery, London,

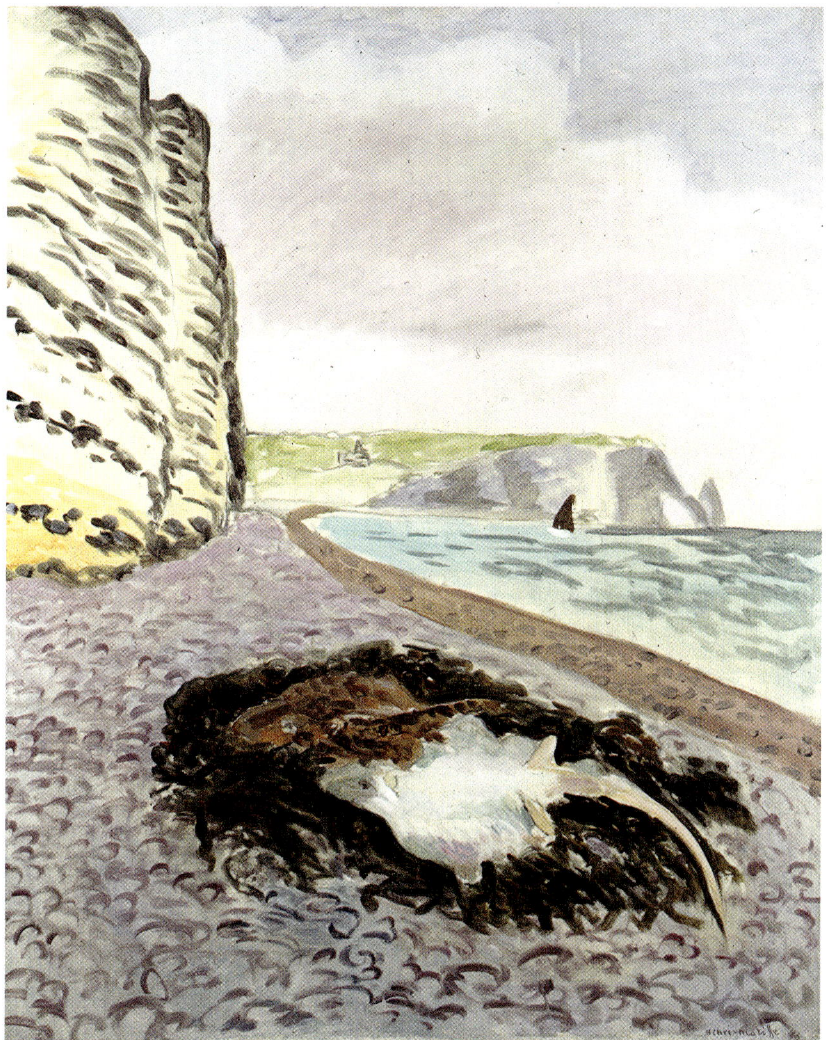

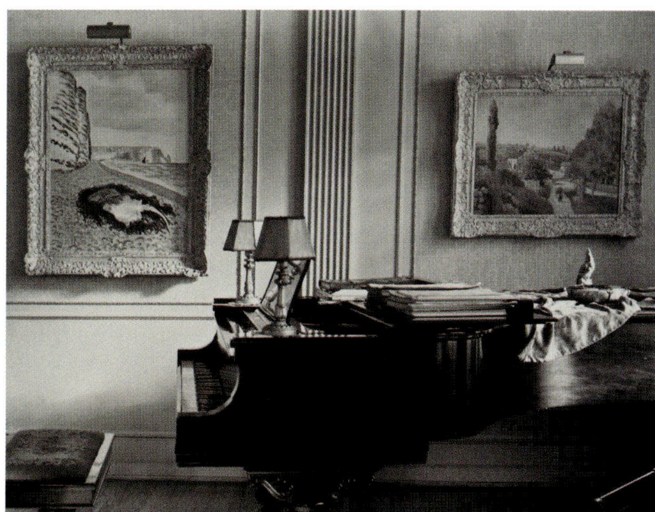

between 1946 and 1967; Paul Oppé, who was Deputy Director of the Victoria and Albert Museum in the years prior to the First World War; and the previously cited Charles Sterling and Anthony Blunt, the latter of whom, at one time or another from 1948 onward advised no less than three Canadian institutions, the Art Gallery of Ontario, the Montreal Museum of Fine Arts and the National Gallery of Canada.[49]

It was on Blunt's advice that in 1949 the Art Gallery of Ontario acquired a major bronze by Matisse, *Jeannette V* **(FIG. 21)**. Blunt was commissioned by the gallery to survey "the Paris situation" and given a modest budget to buy whatever he thought reflected the best value at the time. His assessment of contemporary French art was scathing:

> The young painters, as far as they can be seen and from all I can gather from people I met, are not worth buying. They are either completely abstract (and not as good as their predecessors in this field of 25 years ago), or eclectic imitations of Picasso and Matisse, or neo-expressionists (which does not suit the French temperament), or retardative impressionists, or vulgar.[50]

/ **CAT. 69**　Henri Matisse
Large Cliff – Two Rays
1920

/ **FIG. 20**
Matisse's *Large Cliff* **at the home
of H. S. Southam**
Between 1936 and 1943

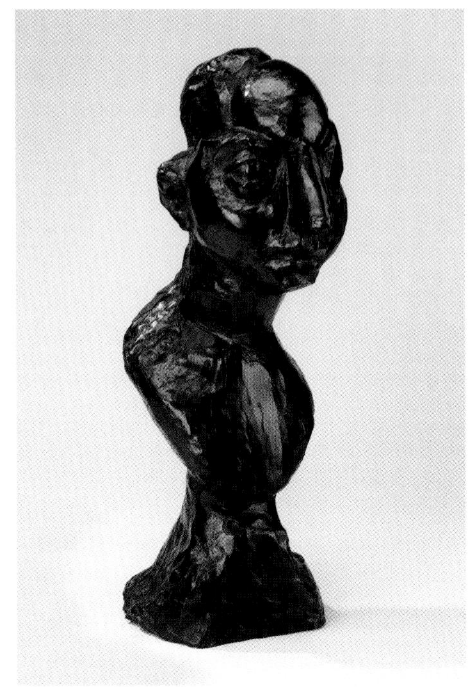

/ **FIG. 21** Henri Matisse
Jeannette V
1916

/ **CAT. 70** Henri Matisse
Seated Woman,
Back Turned to the Open Window
About 1922

Prices of paintings by Picasso and Matisse were too high for the gallery's small budget, so Blunt reported that he had hit upon the solution of instead buying early bronze heads by each artist.[51] The cost to the gallery of acquiring the first sculpture by Matisse to enter a Canadian museum was $1,000—including, Blunt added, the packing and shipping.

It was also in 1949 that the first painting by Matisse entered a Canadian museum. *Seated Woman, Back Turned to the Open Window* (CAT. 70), from the early years of Matisse's Nice period, was acquired by the Montreal Museum of Fine Arts from Durand-Ruel in New York. The canvas came with an impressive provenance. It had belonged to Stephen C. Clark, who in his enthusiasm for the Nice period had assembled by 1930 what Alfred H. Barr considered to be the finest collection anywhere of paintings by Matisse produced since 1917. Barr recognized that this period was characterized by "a less strenuous, more traditional and more popularly acceptable style" than the periods preceding it.[52] It was precisely this more acceptable style that seems to have made work from the period so desirable to private collectors and museum authorities alike, including the authorities at the Montreal museum.

When Buchanan conducted a second interview with Matisse in 1950, the National Gallery of Canada still had not acquired a painting by the artist. Buchanan interviewed Matisse at his apartment in Montparnasse during the summer.[53] He had just come from the Venice Biennale, where Matisse had been awarded the grand prize, and the artist himself had come from Cimiez to ensure that the stained glass for the chapel at Vence was being properly manufactured as well as to consult with Father Couturier about other details relating to the chapel. It was Father Couturier, Buchanan writes in a published account of the interview, who arranged the meeting.[54] With all the attention being paid to Matisse, Buchanan considered himself lucky to be admitted to see him at all. As he correctly observed, Matisse's every move in 1950 was being tracked by magazines as diverse as *Vogue* and *Les Arts*. Only a "favoured few" were granted an audience with the invalided artist, not counting the press, who were regular visitors. Of course, as the co-editor of *Canadian Art*, the ranking arts quarterly in Canada, Buchanan *was* the press and subsequently wrote up his visit with Matisse like everyone else who gained access to the celebrated artist.

According to Buchanan, Matisse immediately asked about Morrice. "How are they treating him nowadays over there?" Matisse demanded.[55] When Buchanan, by way of providing some information, said that the Montreal Museum of Fine Arts had recently opened a special room devoted to his work, Matisse was reportedly pleased. He must also have been pleased to learn that the museum had just purchased his *Seated Woman, Back Turned to the Open Window*.

Matisse was therefore primed when Buchanan stated that the National Gallery of Canada wanted to purchase a major painting by him. He responded that it might be possible for the gallery to buy a painting directly from him and then began to consider which of his works would be most suitable. Matisse's interest in finding the right painting for the collection is reminiscent of the trouble he took to select paintings for Etta Cone, works he knew were destined to go to a museum,

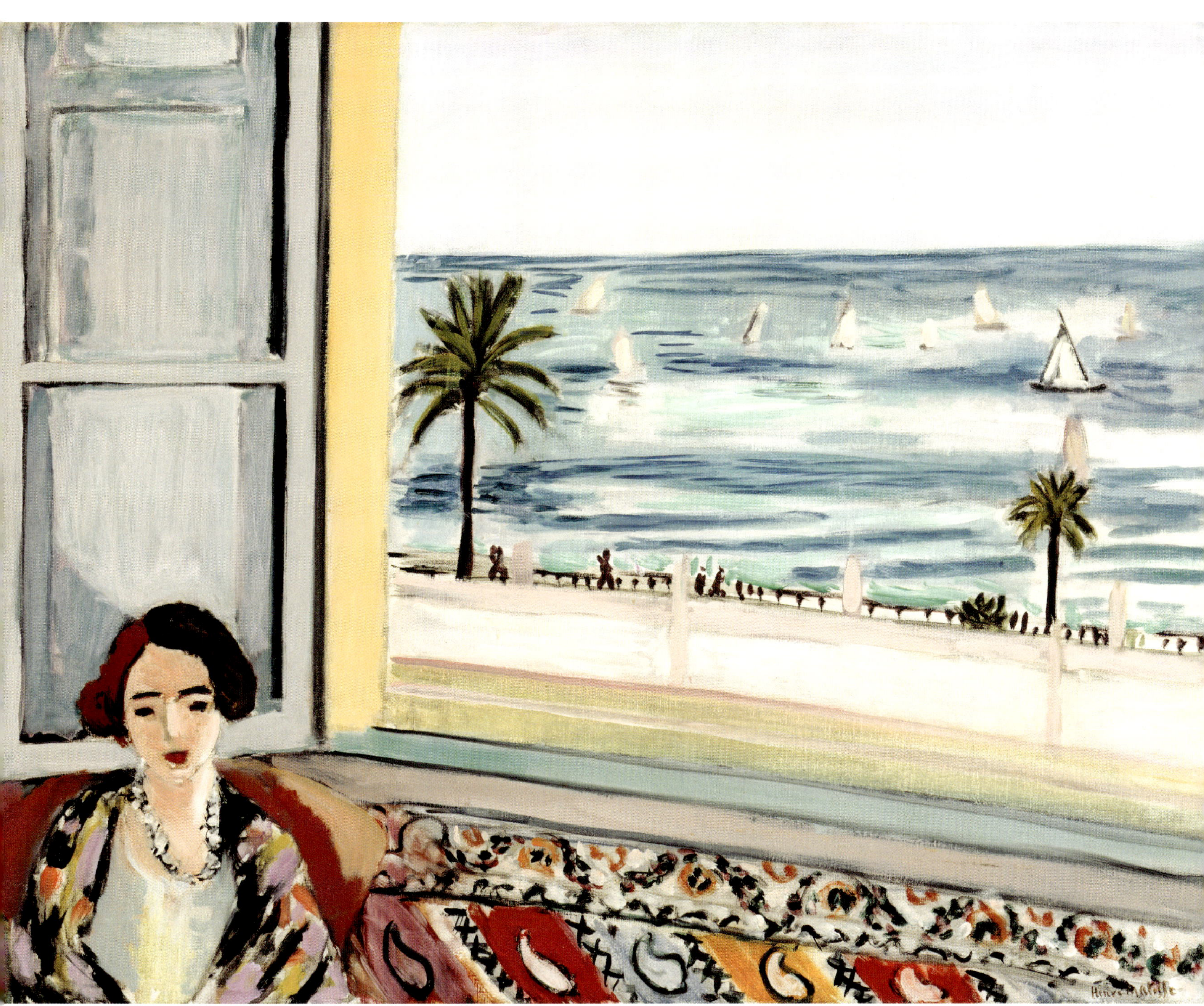

and to persuade her that they were the ones she should have.[56] More than most artists, Matisse had a strong sense of modes and differences within his oeuvre, and of particular categories that were appropriate for certain collections and occasions. One can picture him deciding what would be right for Canada and working through the constrictions faced by the National Gallery.

Since he had already conversed with Buchanan about Morrice, Matisse would certainly have thought about what Morrice had told him of the hostility to modernism in Canada as well as about the dour ingredients of Protestantism and Catholicism in the country. In this regard, he may have been more astute than Blunt in 1948 when Blunt recommended that the National Gallery purchase a Toulouse-Lautrec brothel scene. Blunt wrote to the Director that it was "far from an agreeable picture or an elevating one," but that it did have a "savage vitality"[57]—exactly the characteristics that might be counted on to put it out of favour with the Gallery's trustees. (It was not purchased.) He would also have reflected on the strongest qualities of Morrice's art, in his own words on "landscapes of closely related values" like *Landscape, Tangier* (CAT. 36).[58] He may also have thought of his student, Lyman, and those aspects of Lyman's work that derived from his own example. Finally, he may have returned a thought to the Montreal Museum of Fine Art's recent purchase before declaring to Buchanan that whatever the National Gallery bought it should be "nothing too shocking."[59]

NUDE ON A YELLOW SOFA

Measuring the amount of "shock" that he thought the National Gallery could sustain, Buchanan proposed *Nude on a Yellow Sofa* (CAT. 71), a painting from Matisse's own collection that he had first seen exhibited in Venice. Matisse is reported to have promptly endorsed the suggestion by saying, "Ah yes, that would be the very thing, something solid."[60] And solid the painting is, if by solid we understand Matisse to mean that the modelled darks and lights of the figure give the form density and weight. There is a strong scaffolding to the nude's construction, more than initially meets the eye. It is also solid in the sense that it is carefully conceived and constructed. The painting is heavily reworked in several places, especially around the abdomen and knees where pentimenti are clearly visible, to satisfy the demands of the composition. But "solid" hardly describes the background against which Matisse has positioned the nude. It is comprised of three or four intensely decorative components that are full of commotion: an ornamental screen patterned with a floral design painted in mauve-grey, mauve and black; patches of flooring painted in bright red; and the yellow sofa itself. On at least one level, then, the painting is an exercise in integrating solidity with flatness and monochrome values with incandescent ones.

Matisse painted *Nude on a Yellow Sofa* in 1926, the same year he wrote about Morrice for the Simonson exhibition in Paris. He may or may not have recalled the connection when talking to Buchanan. It is a far less conservative painting than Matisse's remarks to Buchanan, and Buchanan's to his readers in 1950, would

/ CAT. 71 Henri Matisse
Nude on a Yellow Sofa
1926

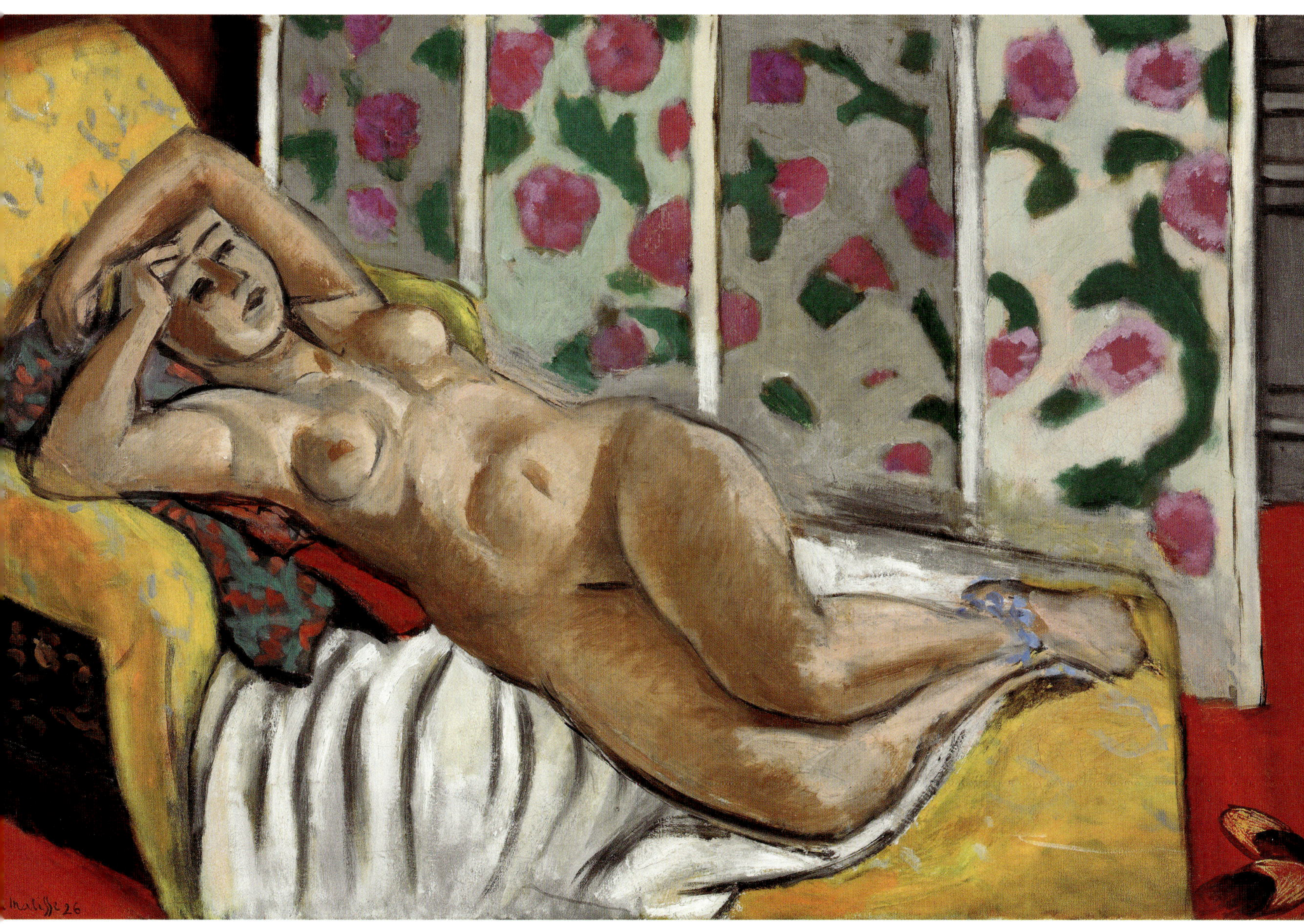

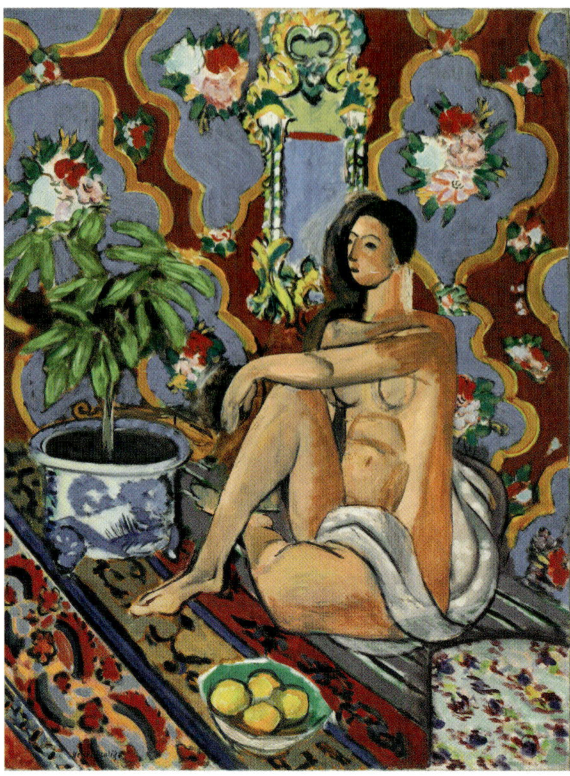

appear to indicate. The canvas stands out from the main run of odalisques and nudes painted by Matisse during the preceding half-dozen years.[61] Although it is not as radically disjunctive as *Decorative Figure on an Ornamental Background* **(FIG. 22)**, painted in the same year, where the nude is made to battle for space against the detonating patterns and colours of the riotous wallpaper and the carpeted floor, as if Matisse were determined to overwhelm the space with a surfeit of decorative matter, nor is it as tranquil and mild as many of the confections that characterize the period in general. For all the luxuriance of its parts—luxuriance of paint and luxuriance of depicted things—for all the harmony of its securely ordered composition, *Nude on a Yellow Sofa* has about it a peculiar tension.

The tension derives from the nude itself. This figure, diagonally pitched on its sofa-pedestal in the manner of Michelangelo's figures for Lorenzo de' Medici's tomb,[62] is an insistent, almost alien form in the flattened and subtly contrived décor of the room. It has an "exaggerated firmness," to borrow from Matisse's description of Maillol's figures, and a gravitational slope that makes its seemingly relaxed position precarious. The figure is peculiarly anti-sensual, anti-picturesque. The area around the upper breast has been gouged and made over, deliberately rendered awkward. The same is true of the way the upper arm falls across the figure's forehead, abruptly levelling the top of the head by squaring it off as in the *Blue Nude* of 1907. These manoeuvres subvert the lassitude implicit in the painting's subject matter and defeat its aura of ease.

Matisse must have recognized the unusual qualities of the painting only after offering it to Buchanan, for he invented a series of excuses not to part with it. On December 4, 1950, he wrote to Buchanan to inform him that he was sorry but the painting could not be sold as it was needed for several exhibitions to which he had agreed to lend works.[63] In October 1951, he again forestalled negotiation by sending a message through the Pierre Matisse Gallery in New York—evidence of the transatlantic role that Matisse *père* expected Matisse *fils* to play—that the timing was not opportune.[64] On January 25, 1952, he wrote a second time, this time admitting that he did not want to sell the painting. "I have very few paintings in my possession and would like to keep for as long as possible those that are most significant to me."[65] Although this may be read simply as an excuse, it is likely that Matisse did place a premium on the painting. Why else would he keep reneging on his commitment to Buchanan?

Even in the face of these rebuffs Buchanan continued pressuring Matisse, finding new ways to lean on him. In the summer of 1952, the National Gallery arranged for Lionello Venturi to pursue the acquisition on its behalf. That too ended in failure. Venturi explained on October 20 that he had been unable to see Matisse, let alone get any indication of whether the 1926 painting or another painting might be available. "I am very sorry not to have been able to do anything to your purpose," he wrote, "but Matisse is a very difficult man."[66] After one more overture in August 1953, this brought to an end the negotiations during Matisse's lifetime. He was determined to hang on to the painting, and nothing would dissuade him otherwise.

For his part, Buchanan was equally determined not to let the painting slip from his grasp. It had been the painting specifically selected by Matisse for the National Gallery, the one joined in Matisse's thoughts with Canada and Morrice. In 1956, two years after Matisse's death, he had the opportunity to see the painting again, this time in the company of Sweeney, then Director of the Guggenheim Museum, and Charles Sterling, Curator at the Louvre. The opportunity was provided by a Matisse retrospective in Paris organized by the Musée national d'art moderne in which there were a dozen paintings from the Matisse estate. Buchanan, Sweeney and Sterling compared the canvas to the other estate paintings and agreed among themselves that it was the best.[67]

Buchanan tried to reopen negotiations with the Pierre Matisse Gallery, but again without success.[68] Then, after nearly eight years of dogged pursuit, he was met with reciprocal interest, and in 1958 the National Gallery purchased *Nude on a Yellow Sofa*. It was, you might think, a triumphant moment. The Gallery had pursued and acquired a major work by one of the canonical figures of twentieth-century art. Moreover, that figure had been pivotal in the introduction of modernism to Canada, in part through his ties with two locally canonical modernists, Morrice and Lyman. But when the painting was put on public display in Ottawa, it occasioned no great fanfare. By the late fifties, few self-respecting museums were without their own representative examples of Matisse's work, and the moment for a vivid public reaction in Canada to an unusual and demanding work by Matisse had passed. In a less extreme way, the lack of response paralleled the silence that accompanied Morrice's work in the decades following his death.

Notes

I first addressed the subject of Morrice and Matisse in lectures delivered at the Art Gallery of Ontario (Philip McCready Memorial Lecture) and the Brooklyn Museum ("Advent of Modernism" symposium) in the late 1980s. Subsequently, I drafted a chapter on the relationship of the two artists for my book *Ruthless Hedonism: The American Reception of Matisse* (Chicago: The University of Chicago Press, 1999), but for reasons of space and coherence it was not included. The present essay draws on material from the orphaned chapter as well as from recent research. I would like to express my gratitude to a dozen curators and archivists, many no longer associated with the institutions cited after their names, for facilitating access to paintings and archives: Nicole Cloutier, The Montreal Museum of Fine Arts; Larissa Doukelskaya and Albert Kostenevich, Hermitage Museum, St. Petersburg; Claude Duthuit, Archives Matisse, Paris; Charles C. Hill and Michael Pantazzi, National Gallery of Canada, Ottawa; Isabelle Monod-Fontaine, Musée national d'art moderne, Paris; Dennis Reid, The Art Gallery of Ontario; and John Elderfield and Rona Roob, The Museum of Modern Art, New York. I would also like to thank Jeff O'Brien, my research assistant, Lucie Dorais, who was particularly helpful on historical matters, as well as T. J. Clark and Diane Gooderham for reading drafts of the essay.

1. Louis Vauxcelles, "The Art of J. W. Morrice," *The Canadian Magazine*, vol. 34, no. 2 (December 1909), p. 169.

2. "Le Salon d'Automne. Quelques notes," *L'Éclair*, September 30, 1909, p. 2.

3. Among French writers, Morrice knew the poet Paul Fort and his circle. In his possession were two volumes of Fort's poems inscribed "à James Wilson Morrice, son admirateur, Paul Fort." The volumes are in the collection of the Montreal Museum of Fine Arts.

4. Somerset Maugham confirmed that he based the figure of Warren in *The Magician* on Morrice. See his correspondence with Donald W. Buchanan, March 31, 1935 (Archives of the National Gallery of Canada, 7.4.C). In addition to Warren, Maugham depicted aspects of Morrice's personality in the poet Cronshaw in *Of Human Bondage* (1915), whose conversation was a mixture of "wisdom and nonsense." Arnold Bennett depicted aspects of Morrice in *Buried Alive* (1910) and *Sacred and Profane Love* (1911), and Aleister Crowley did likewise in his sometimes scatological *Confessions of Aleister Crowley: An Autohagiography* (1929). Morrice encountered this group of writers at Le Chat Blanc, in the Rue d'Odessa, a restaurant frequented by a clique within the Anglo-American community in Paris. Donald W. Buchanan, *James Wilson Morrice – Painter and Nomad: A Biography* (Toronto: The Ryerson Press, 1936), pp. 50-74, tracked down the literary allusions after interviewing some of the regulars. See also John O'Brian, "Morrice –O'Conor, Gauguin, Bonnard et Vuillard," *Revue de l'Université de Moncton*, vol. 15, nos. 2-3 (April-December 1982), pp. 9-34, on Morrice's reputation in this circle.

5. Letter from Henri Matisse to Armand Dayot, quoted at length in *Catalogue des tableaux et études par James Wilson Morrice* (Paris: Galeries Simonson, 1926), pp. 6-7.

6. Matisse to Dayot, ibid.,

7. *Exposition d'art canadien*, at the Galerie du Jeu de Paume, Paris, April 11 to May 11, 1927, organized by the National Gallery of Canada. Included forty-eight works by Morrice.

8. International exhibitions in which Morrice appeared were generally sponsored by Canadian museums or government authorities. See, for example, the Venice Biennale in 1958 and the *OKanada* exhibition in 1982-1983. *OKanada* was a compendium of historical and contemporary art exhibited at the Academie der Künst, Berlin. The exhibition was accompanied by a substantial German-language catalogue and later by an English/French translation. Another international exhibition in which Morrice appeared was *The Advent of Modernism: Post-Impressionism and North American Art, 1900-1918*, organized by Peter Morrin for the High Museum of Art, Atlanta, in 1986. It was also accompanied by a catalogue.

9. Pierre Schneider, *Matisse* (New York: Rizzoli, 1984). However, Jack Flam, *Matisse: The Man and His Art, 1869-1918* (Ithaca: Cornell University Press, 1986), acknowledges Morrice and cites Buchanan's biography.

10. Jack Cowart, ed. *Matisse in Morocco: The Paintings and Drawings, 1912-1913* (Washington: National Gallery of Art, 1990). The exhibition was organized by Jack Cowart and Pierre Schneider.

11. Hilary Spurling, *Matisse the Master – A Life of Henri Matisse: The Conquest of Colour, 1909-1954* (New York: Knopf, 2005), pp. 127-128.

12. Jacques Derrida, *Archive Fever: A Freudian Impression* (Chicago: The University of Chicago Press, 1995), p. 11.

13. Pierre Bourdieu, *Distinction: A Social Critique of the Judgment of Taste,* trans. Richard Nice (Cambridge, Mass.: Harvard University Press, 1984), p. 2. See also Bourdieu, *The Field of Cultural Production: Essays on Art and Literature*, ed. Randal Johnson (New York: Columbia University Press, 1993).

14. Since the publication of *Distinction*, which coincided with the beginning of a rapid expansion in the art market, the exercise of cultural competence exhibited by wealthy collectors has changed. Collectors now assert power and economic advantage in ways that court publicity and celebrity. See the special issue of *Texte Zur Kunst*, no. 83 (September 2011), particularly the article by Steffen Zillig, "The Image of the Collector – From Citoyen to Celebrity," pp. 94-113.

15. The most thorough documentation of Morrice's life and work, in addition to the 1936 biography by Buchanan, is: Lucie Dorais, *J. W. Morrice* (Ottawa: National Gallery of Canada, 1985); Nicole Cloutier, ed., *James Wilson Morrice, 1865-1924*, exhib. cat. (Montreal: The Montreal Museum of Fine Arts, 1985); Charles C. Hill, *Morrice: A Gift to the Nation – The G. Blair Laing Collection*, exhib. cat. (Ottawa: National Gallery of Canada, 1992); and Michèle Grandbois, "James Wilson Morrice et Albert Marquet: Des parcours croisés," in *Marquet au fil de l'eau*, exhib. cat. (Quebec City: Musée national des beaux-arts du Québec, 2003), pp. 85-108. Some important new information, including a trip by Morrice to Morocco after the war, is disclosed by Lucie Dorais, "James Wilson Morrice," in *Canadian Art: The Thomson Collection at the Art Gallery of Ontario* (Toronto: Skylet Publishing/The Art Gallery of Ontario, 2008), pp. 42-53.

16. Gertrude Stein, "Two Women" (1912), reprinted in Brenda Richardson, *Dr. Claribel and Miss Etta: The Cone Collection* (Baltimore: Baltimore Museum of Art, 1984).

17. On Matisse's early movements, see Schneider, *Matisse*, and Hilary Spurling, *Unknown Matisse: A Life of Henri Matisse* (New York: Knopf, 1998). The only firm evidence that Morrice studied at the Académie Julian is from the artist himself. In 1920, at a moment of national self-consciousness following the First World War, Morrice was asked to fill out a questionnaire "for the purpose of making a record of Canadian artists and their works." (Archives of the National Gallery of Canada, James Wilson Morrice file.)

18. Journal of Charles H. Fromuth, vol. 1, Library of Congress, Manuscript Division (MNC 2796), 41; cited in Cloutier, *James Wilson Morrice*, p. 19.

19. Morrice exhibited regularly at the Société nationale des beaux-arts from 1896 to 1911, and in 1920 as well. He exhibited at the Salon d'Automne from 1905 to 1923.

20. Morrice was vice president of the jury for the 1908 Salon d'Automne, a jury on which Matisse also served. See Dorais, *J. W. Morrice*, pp. 16 and 19, and Grandbois, "James Wilson Morrice and Albert Marquet," p. 95 and note 29.

21. Clive Bell, *Old Friends: Personal Recollections* (London: Chatto & Windus, 1956), pp. 66-67 and pp. 156-163. Bell judged Morrice to be "a typical good second-rate painter (first-rate almost)."

22. Bell, *Old Friends*, pp. 158-159.

23. Clement Greenberg, "Review of *Aesthetics and History in the Visual Arts*," *New York Times Book Review* (November 28, 1948), in *The Collected Essays and Criticism*, vol. 2, ed. John O'Brian (Chicago: The University of Chicago Press, 1986), p. 263.

24. See Danièle Giraudy, "Correspondance Henri Matisse – Charles Camoin," *Revue de l'art*, no. 12 (1971), pp. 12-16, and *Correspondance entre Charles Camoin et Henri Matisse*, introduced and annotated by Claudine Grammont (Lausanne: Bibliothèque des Arts/Succession H. Matisse, 1997).

25. When Matisse arrived in Tangier at the end of January 1912, Morrice was still in Montreal visiting friends and family but preparing to depart for North Africa. The artists were together in Tangier from mid-February to mid-April. On the second sojourn, Matisse again preceded Morrice to Morocco and again

left before him. Matisse arrived in Tangier in early October and remained until late February 1913; Morrice arrived in December and stayed until March. See *Correspondance entre Charles Camoin et Henri Matisse* and letters from Morrice to Edmund Morris, Edmund Morris Papers, E. P. Taylor Research Library, Art Gallery of Ontario.

26. C. R. Pennell, *Morocco since 1830: A History* (New York: New York University Press, 2000).

27. Letter from Matisse to Marquet, [Tanger] April 1, 1912, in *Matisse-Marquet. Correspondance, 1898-1947*, texts selected and annotated by Claudine Grammont (Lausanne: Bibliothèque des Arts, 2008), p. 88.

28. Walter Harris, *Times* of London, April 23, 1912.

29. Spurling, *Matisse the Master*, p. 115.

30. Donald W. Buchanan, unpublished passage in the manuscript of *James Wilson Morrice – Painter and Nomad: A Biography*, 1936, Archives of the National Gallery of Canada, 7.4.C.

31. Buchanan, *James Wilson Morrice*, p. 110.

32. Spurling, *Matisse the Master*, p. 109.

33. Camoin wrote to Matisse, after Matisse had already left by boat for Marseille. Giraudy, "Correspondance Henri Matisse – Charles Camoin," p. 15.

34. Morrice painted an oil of the scene, *View from the Window, Tangier* (cat. 65) and Matisse painted two large oils, *Landscape Viewed from a Window* (fig. 19) and *Fenêtre ouverte sur Tanger* (private coll.). Camoin also painted one watercolour from the same sight, *View of the English Church, Tangier* (private coll.).

35. An exhibition held at the Centre Pompidou, Paris, in 2012—*Matisse. Paires et séries*—explored this aspect of Matisse's working method.

36. Cloutier, *James Wilson Morrice*, p. 195.

37. Buchanan, *James Wilson Morrice*, p. 111.

38. Muriel Ciolkowska, "Memories of Morrice," *The Canadian Forum*, vol. 6 (November 1925), p. 52.

39. Typical of the notices received by Morrice's work is that by the critic of *L'Éclair*, September 30, 1909, p. 2, in a review of the Salon d'Automne: "Among 259 foreigners, we point out for various reasons M. Morrice, whose landscapes are among the best and who is a remarkably gifted painter." See also Ghislain Clermont, "Morrice et la critique," *Revue de l'Université de Moncton*, vol. 15, nos. 2-3 (April-December 1982), pp. 25-48.

40. Cloutier, *James Wilson Morrice*, p. 53, charts Morrice's contributions to exhibitions in North America and Europe. Albert Barnes hung the winter scene by Morrice (accession number 2053) above a painting by Prendergast (2076) at his foundation.

41. Letter from Morrice to Edmund Morris, February 12, 1911 (Edmund Morris papers, E. P. Taylor Research Library, Art Gallery of Ontario).

42. See O'Brian, *Ruthless Hedonism*, especially chapters 1-3.

43. "Modern French Pictures by the School of Paris," *The Montreal Daily Star*, October 7, 1936. The exhibition was organized by W. Scott & Sons, Montreal, in conjunction with Alex Reid & Lefevre, London.

44. John Lyman, "The School of Paris," *The Montrealer*, December 15, 1936. Lyman was a catalyst in promoting Matisse's (and Morrice's) brand of modernism in Canada, especially after 1931 when he abandoned his European expatriatism to return to Montreal. Throughout his life, Lyman was rueful about the excoriating criticism he had received from Canadian reviewers in 1913. It was directed at several paintings inflected by Fauvism that he had contributed to the Spring Exhibition of the Art Association of Montreal, and especially at his one-man show in the same place in May of that year.

45. Hamilton Southam delivered a eulogy at Buchanan's funeral in 1966. Shortly before he died, Buchanan and I were separately invited to the same dinner party at Southam's house in Ottawa. Buchanan and Southam controlled the conversation, much of which revolved around the International Fine Arts Exhibition being planned for Expo '67, for which Buchanan was director. There was also discussion of the Matisse painting that Southam had owned.

46. Archives of the National Gallery of Canada, Collector files (H. S. Southam). The painting was sold for Southam in 1943 by the Dominion Gallery in Montreal (confirmed in a conversation between John O'Brian and Dr. Max Stern, December 7, 1985).

47. Sarah A. Stanners is insightful on this topic. See her "Going British and Being Modern in the Visual Art Systems of Canada, 1906-1976," dissertation, Toronto, University of Toronto, 2009.

48. A large number of Canadian artists also looked to Britain for aesthetic guidance. See Christine Boyanoski, *The 1940s: A Decade of Painting in Ontario* (Toronto: The Art Gallery of Ontario, 1984), p. 26.

49. Jean Sutherland Boggs, *The National Gallery of Canada* (Toronto: Oxford University Press, 1971), is informative about the National Gallery's use of advisers and the specific role they played in the museum's acquisitions.

50. Letter from Anthony Blunt to Martin Baldwin, Paris, April 13, 1949 (Curatorial files, Art Gallery of Ontario, Toronto).

51. The complementary Picasso bronze acquired by Blunt was the *Head of Fernande*, 1909 (Zervos II: 573).

52. Alfred H. Barr, Jr., *Matisse: His Art and His Public* (New York: The Museum of Modern Art, 1951), pp. 199-201.

53. Donald W. Buchanan, "Interview in Montparnasse," *Canadian Art*, vol. 8, no. 2 (Christmas 1950), pp. 61-65.

54. Buchanan, "Interview in Montparnasse," pp. 63-64. While in Montreal during the war, Couturier lectured and wrote extensively on modern art, including the work of Matisse; see Marie-Alain Couturier, *Art et Catholicisme* (Montreal: Éditions de l'Arbre, 1941).

55. Buchanan, "Interview in Montparnasse," p. 64.

56. Richardson, *Dr. Claribel and Miss Etta*.

57. Boggs, *The National Gallery of Canada*, p. 42.

58. *Landscape, Tangier* was exhibited at the 1912 Salon d'Automne.

59. Buchanan, "Interview in Montparnasse," p. 64. At the exact moment that *Blue Nude* caused a furor at the New York Armory Show in 1913, Matisse was with Morrice in Tangier.

60. Ibid.

61. See Jack Cowart and Dominique Fourcade, *Henri Matisse: The Early Years in Nice, 1916-1930* (Washington/New York: National Gallery of Art/Harry N. Abrams, 1986) for a selection of Matisse's paintings on the theme of the nude. *Nude on a Yellow Sofa* closely follows the composition of half-a-dozen preceding paintings and drawings, the earliest of which is *Nu allongé*, oil on canvas, 1922, Barnes Foundation, Lower Merion, Pennsylvania.

62. Matisse on several occasions modelled and drew the figures of "Dawn" and "Night"; in 1922 he executed lithographs after them.

63. Letter from Henri Matisse to Donald W. Buchanan, Cimiez, December 4, 1950 (Archives of the National Gallery of Canada, 1.11 M).

64. Memorandum from Donald W. Buchanan to H. O. McCurry, Director, National Gallery of Canada, October 1951 (Archives of the National Gallery of Canada, 1.11 M).

65. Letter from Henri Matisse to Donald W. Buchanan, Cimiez, January 25, 1952 (private coll., Toronto).

66. Letter from Lionello Venturi to H. O. McCurry, Rome, October 20, 1952 (Archives of the National Gallery of Canada, 1.11 M).

67. Report from Buchanan to the acquisition committee of the National Gallery of Canada, January 1958 (Archives of the National Gallery of Canada, 1.11 M).

68. In response to Buchanan's letter of November 19, 1956, Pierre Matisse wrote from New York on November 21: "I do not really know whether, when technical details have been ironed out, I will want to dispose of *Nude on a Yellow Sofa*" (Archives of the National Gallery of Canada, 1.11 F).

ENDLESS SUMMER
PORTFOLIO

The archipelagos of the Atlantic Ocean and the Caribbean Sea were true sanctuaries for our painters in their quest of light and warmth. Lyman was the first to make the journey, following the scandal caused by his Montreal exhibition of 1913. The pinkish Bermudian light brought him fresh inspiration and revived his urge to paint. At the end of his life he settled in Barbados, where he made paintings in warm, contrasting colours.

February 1915: war is roaring through Europe. Morrice sets sail for the "American Mediterranean" and, in Cuba, discovers Havana's cafés, Santiago's colonial architecture and the exotic and luxuriant nature of the largest island in the Caribbean. He brings back from his trip a large quantity of material—drawings, pochades, photographs and postcards—which he used as sources for his work until his second and final Caribbean voyage, to Trinidad, in 1921. The freshness of the light and the calligraphic synthesis and sketch-like quality of his paintings of this period are evocative of Matisse's work in Tangier.

Endless Summer: this was the evocative title chosen for the magnificent exhibition on Canadian artists in the Caribbean, held in 1988 at the McMichael Canadian Art Collection.

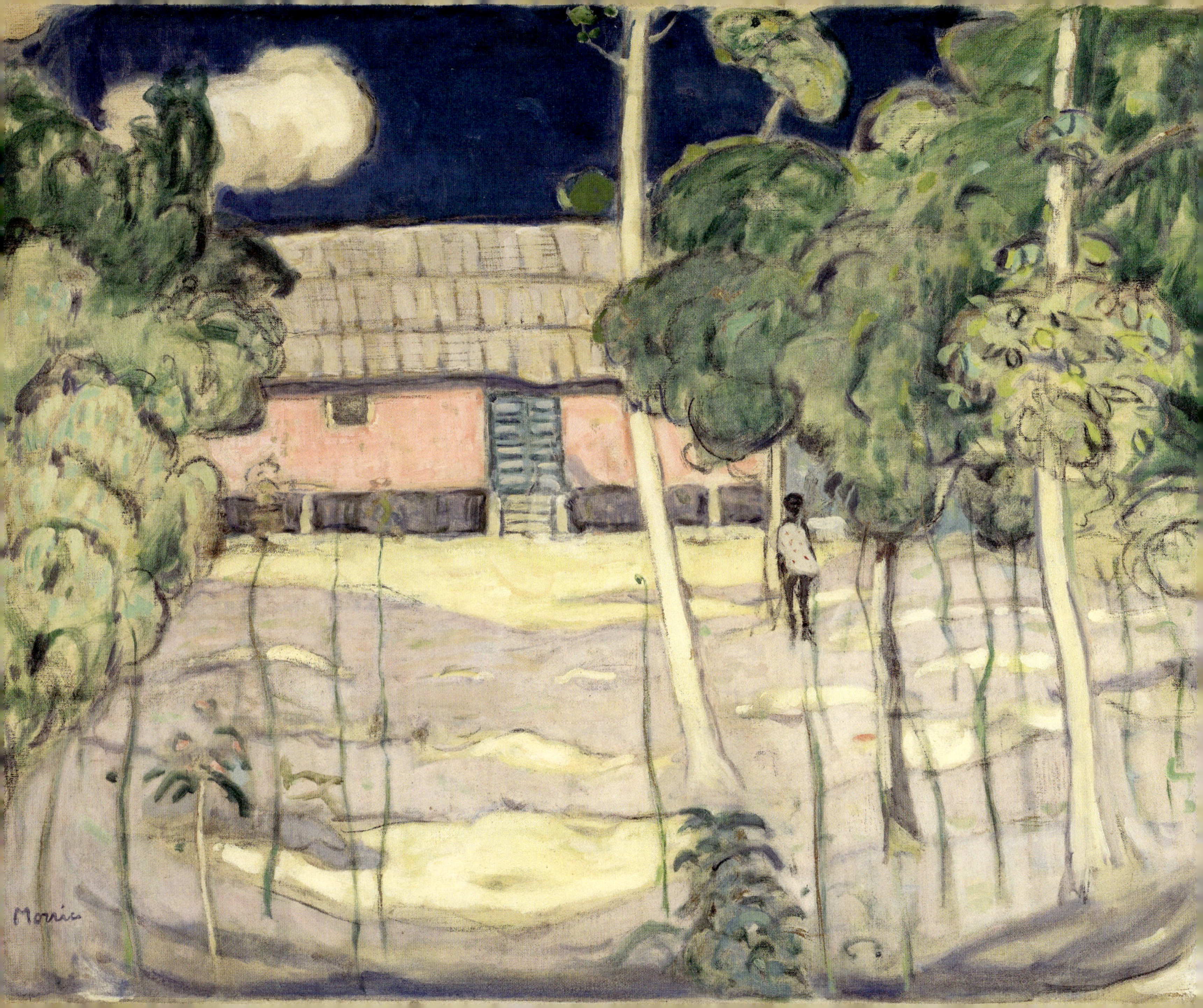

Morrice

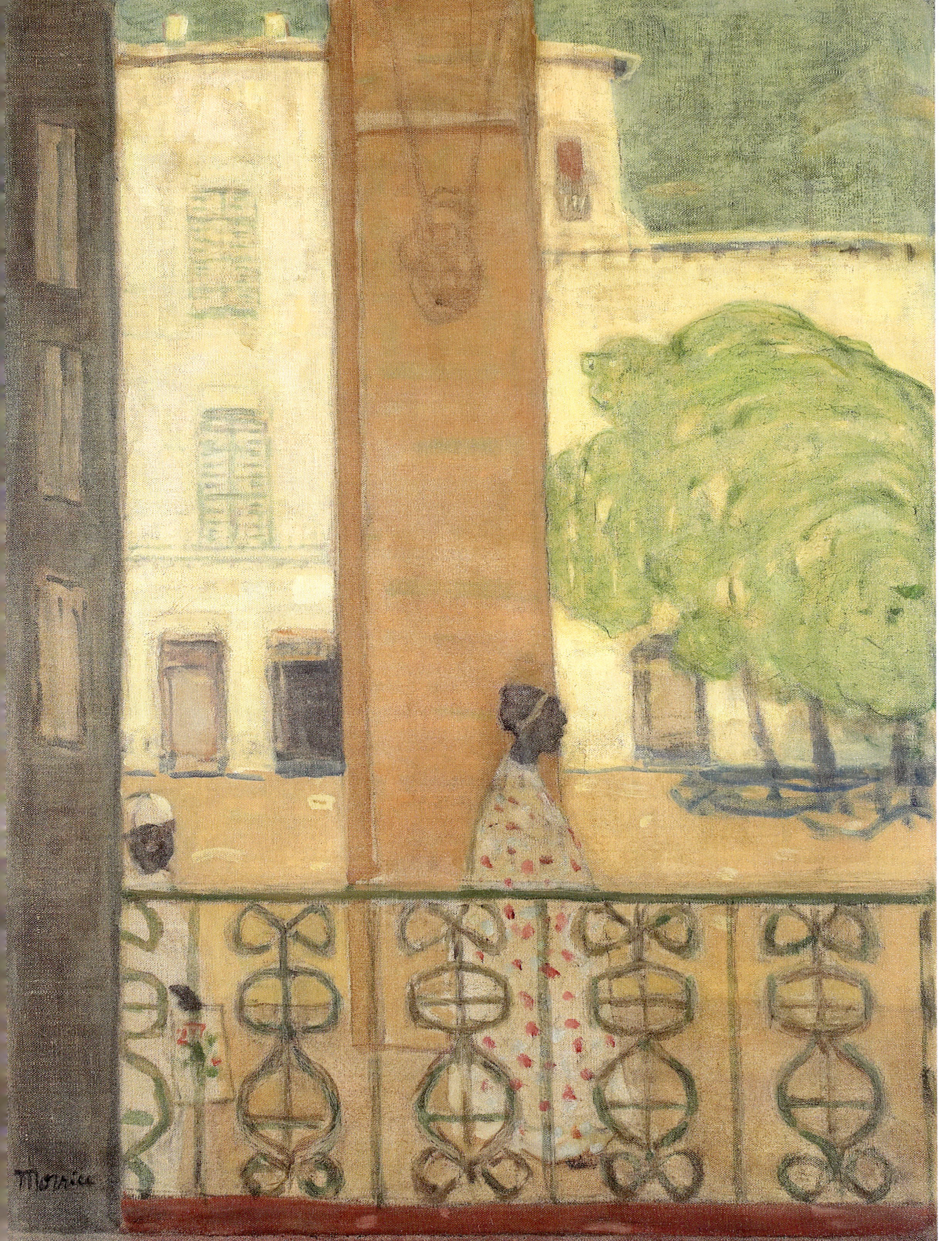
Morrice

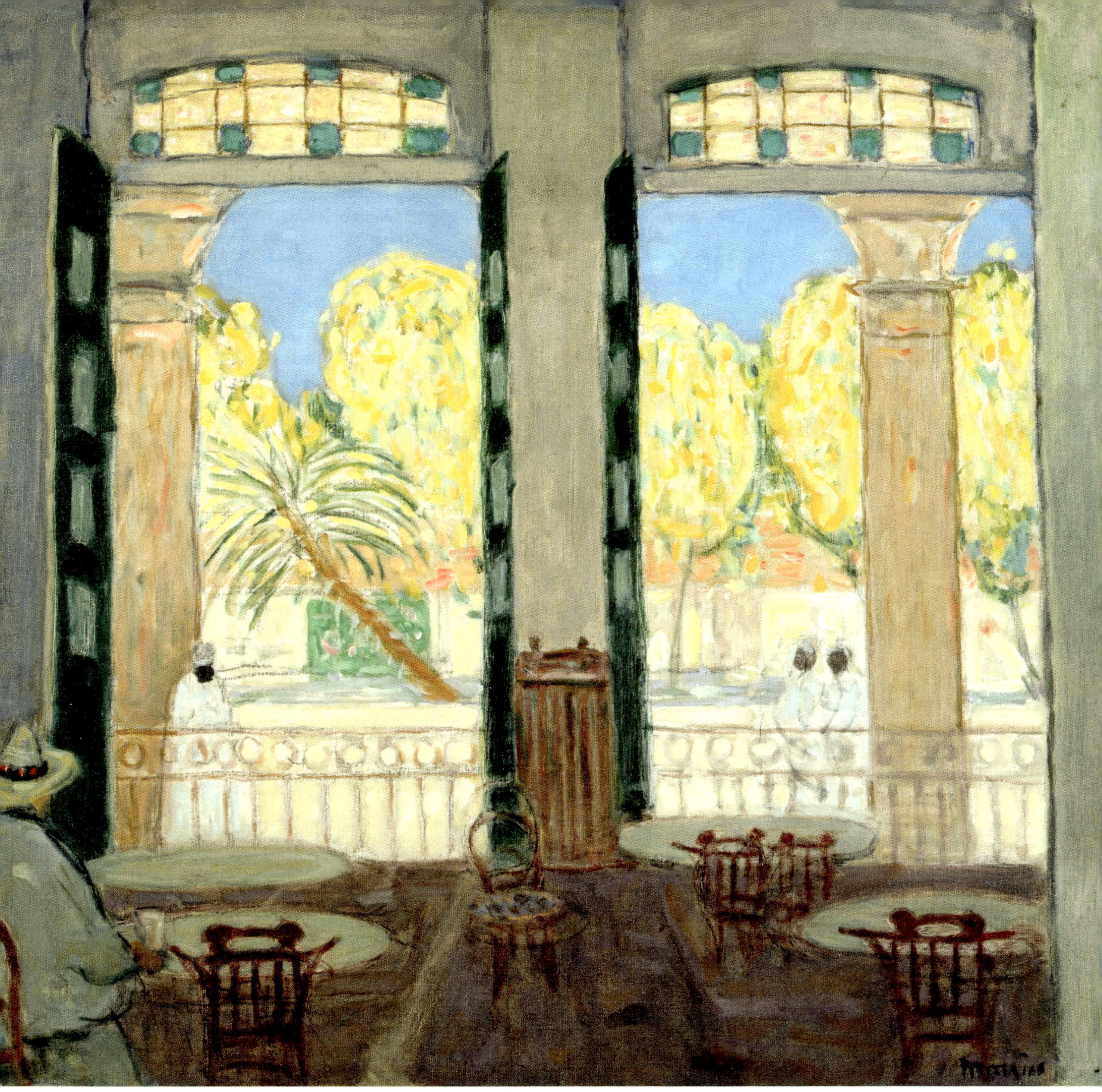

/ CAT. 73 James W. Morrice
Scene in Havana
About 1918-1919

/ CAT. 74 James W. Morrice
Café El Pasaje, Havana
About 1918-1919

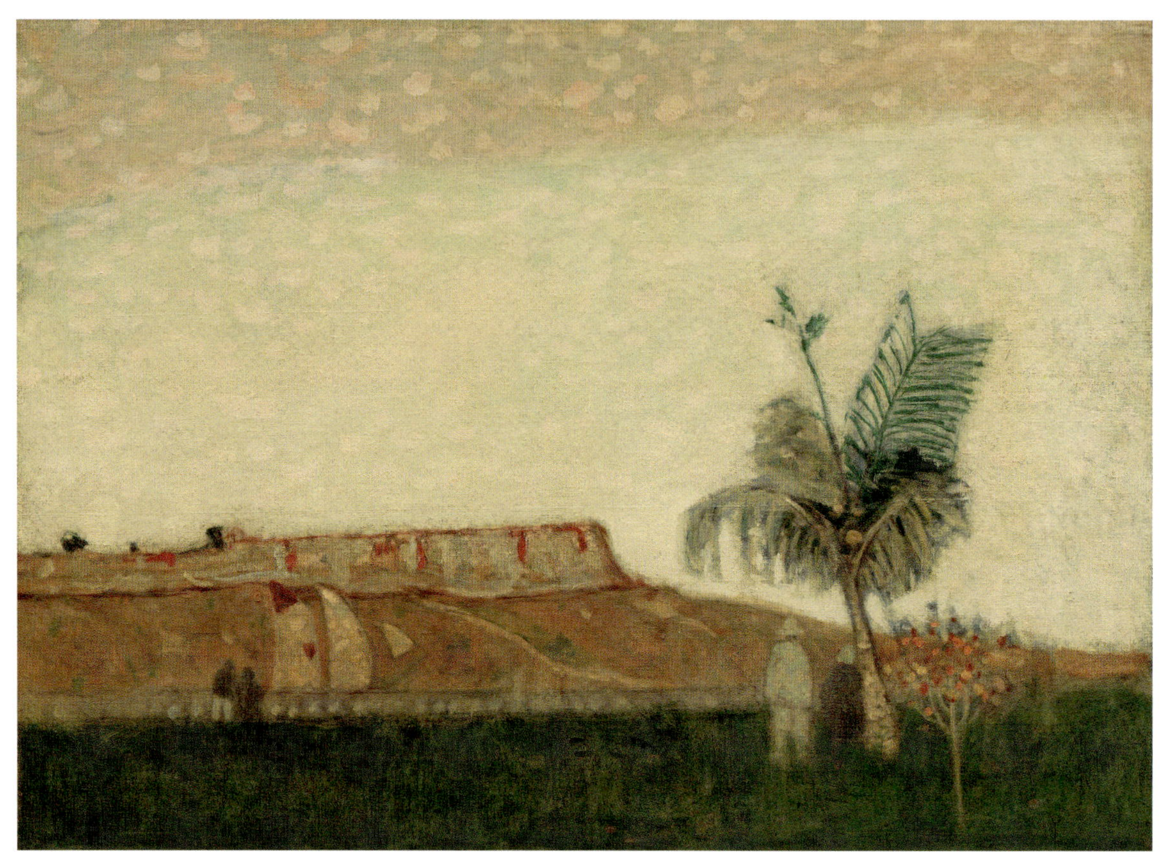

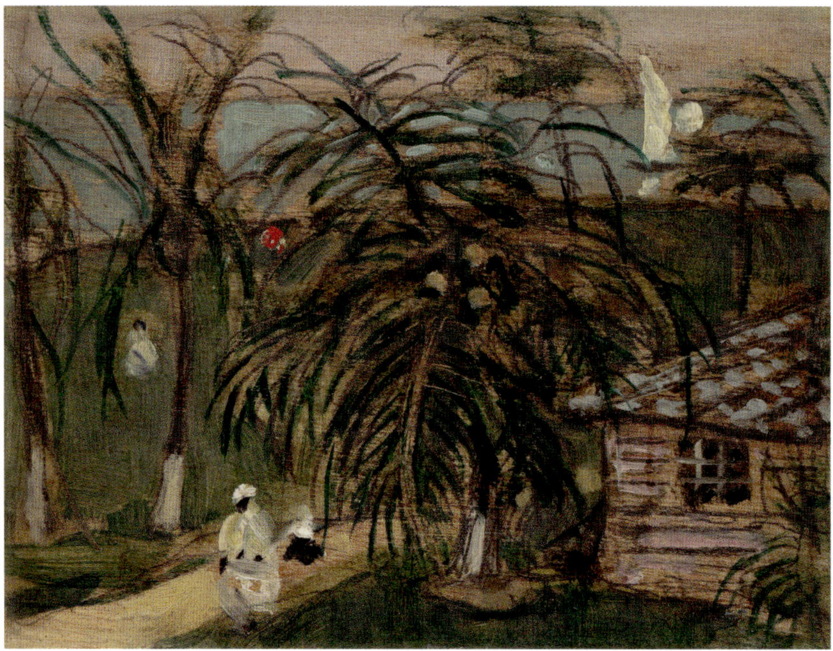

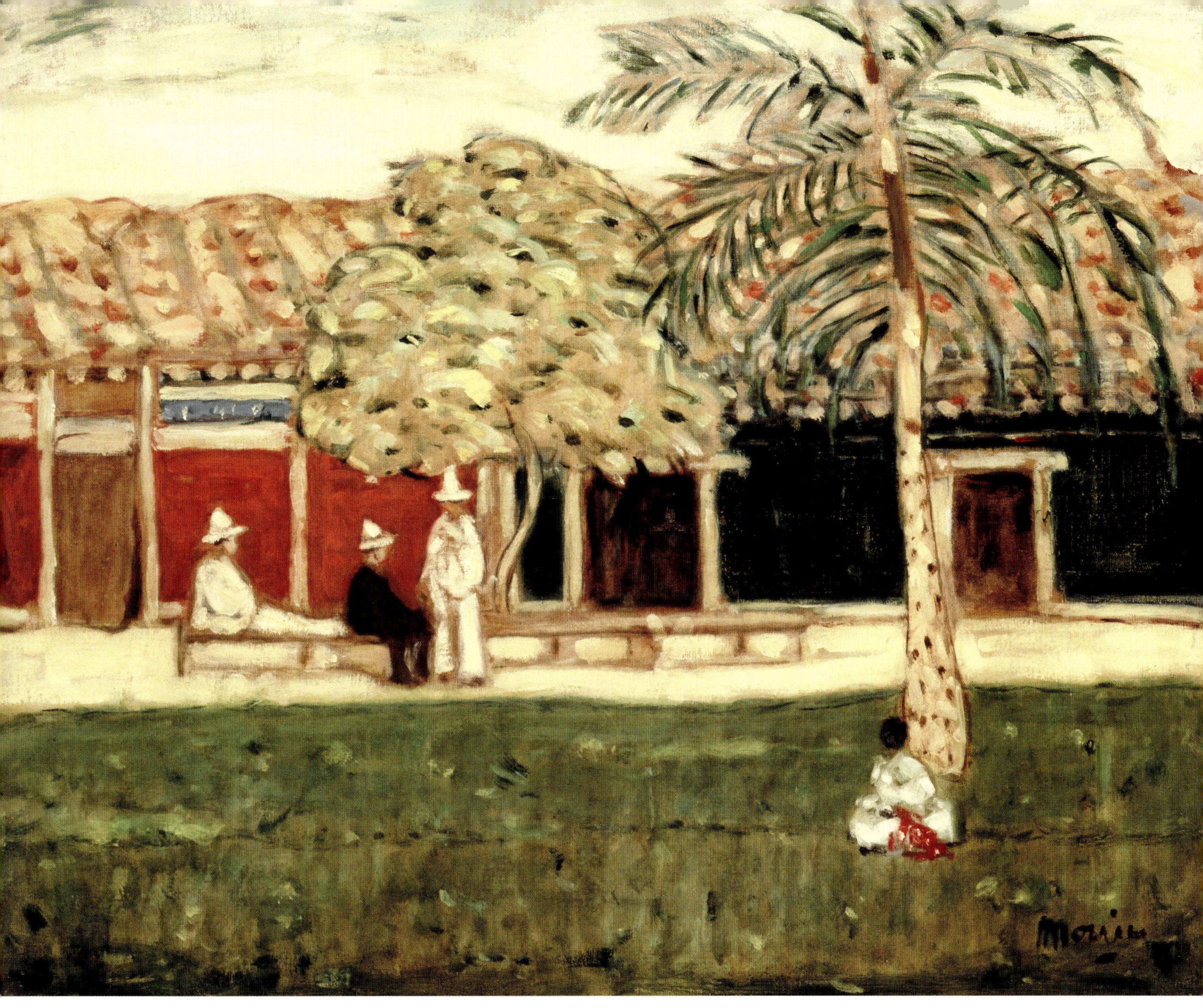

/ CAT. 75 James W. Morrice
Havana, Cuba
1915

/ CAT. 76 James W. Morrice
Jamaica
1915

/ CAT. 77 James W. Morrice
Houses, Cuba
1915

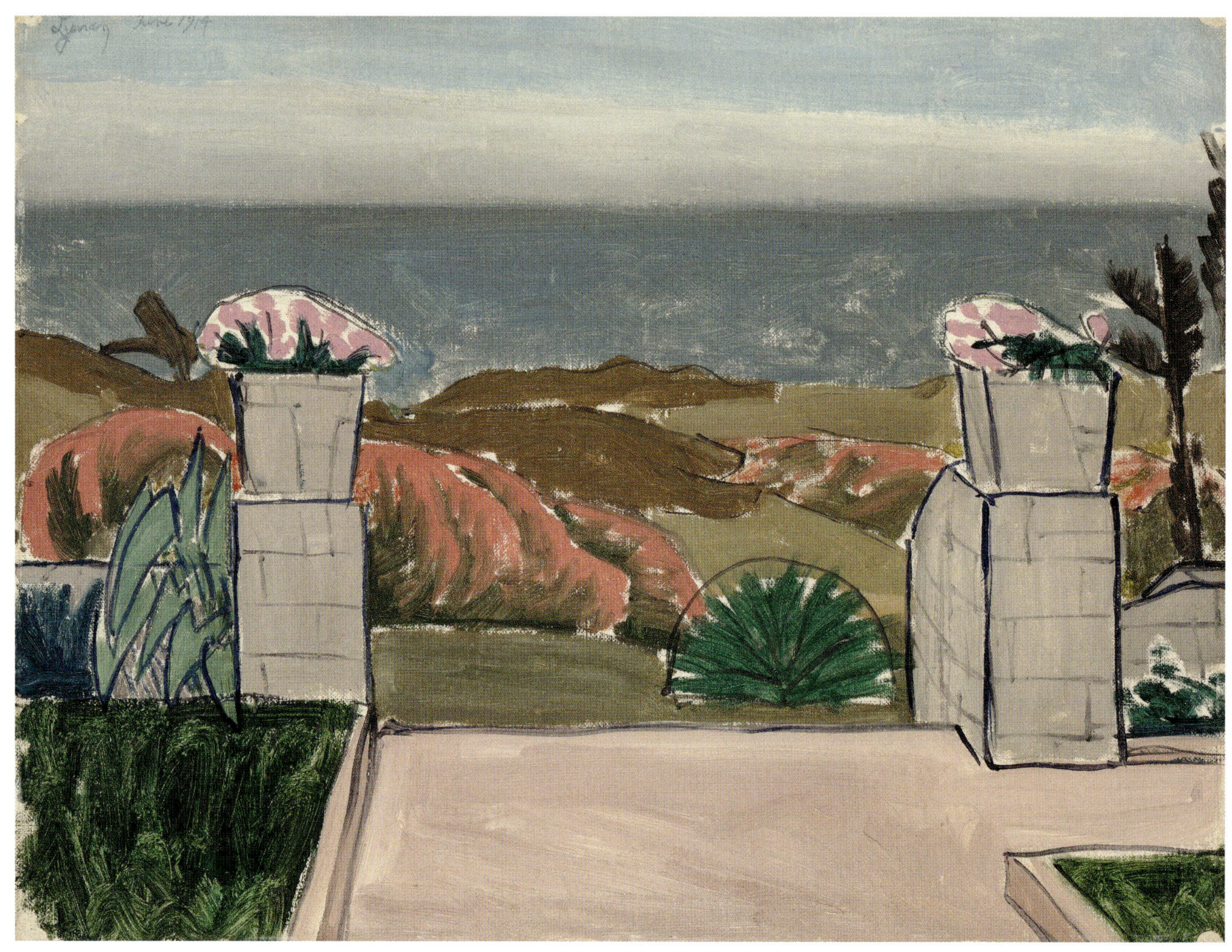

/ CAT. 78 John Lyman
Southlands, Bermuda
1914

/ CAT. 79 John Lyman
Untitled
About 1914-1917

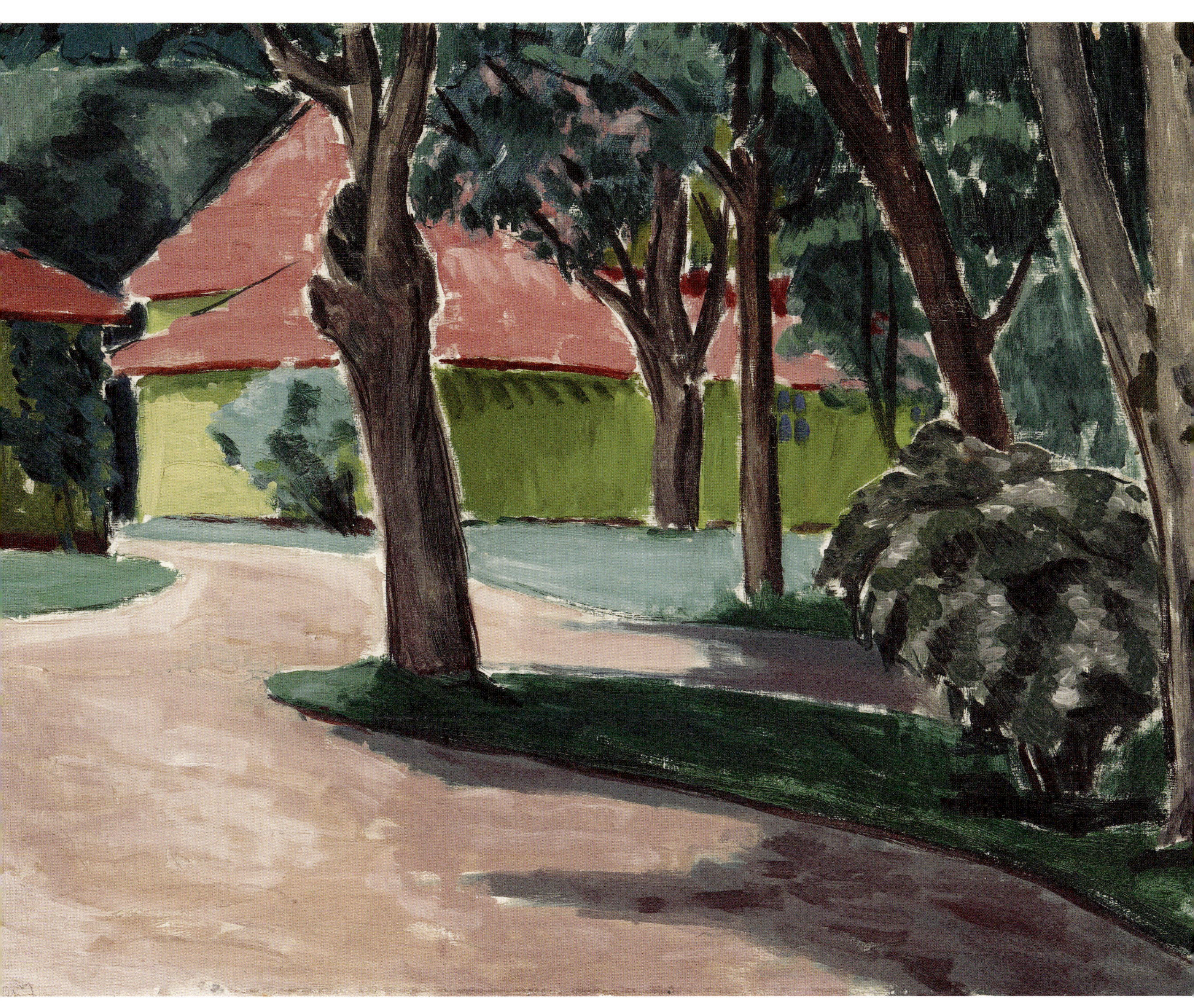

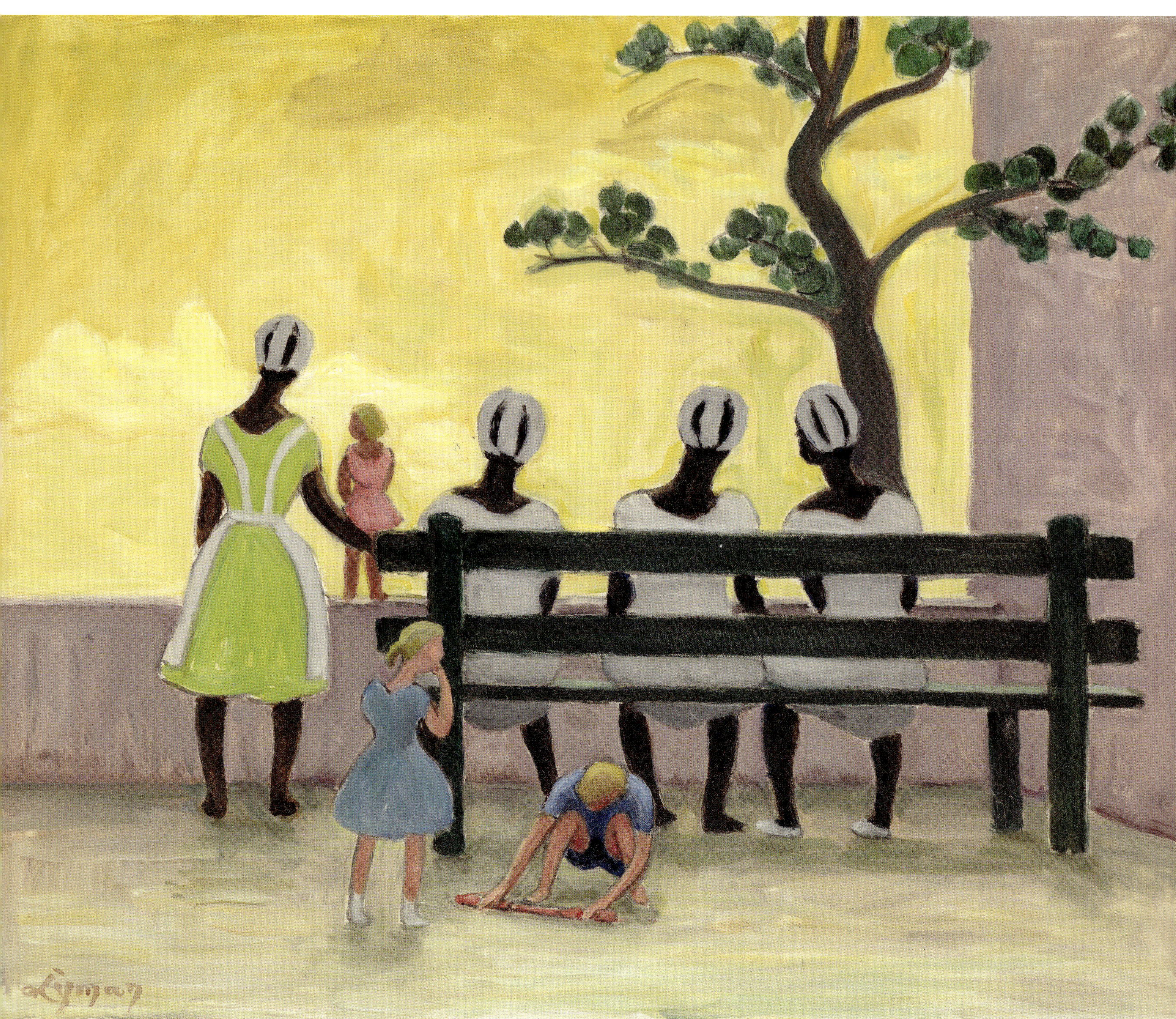

/ CAT. 80 John Lyman
Nannies on the Terrace
1961

/ CAT. 81 John Lyman
The Lobster Trap
1962

/ CAT. 82 John Lyman
Hauling up the Fishing Boat
1962

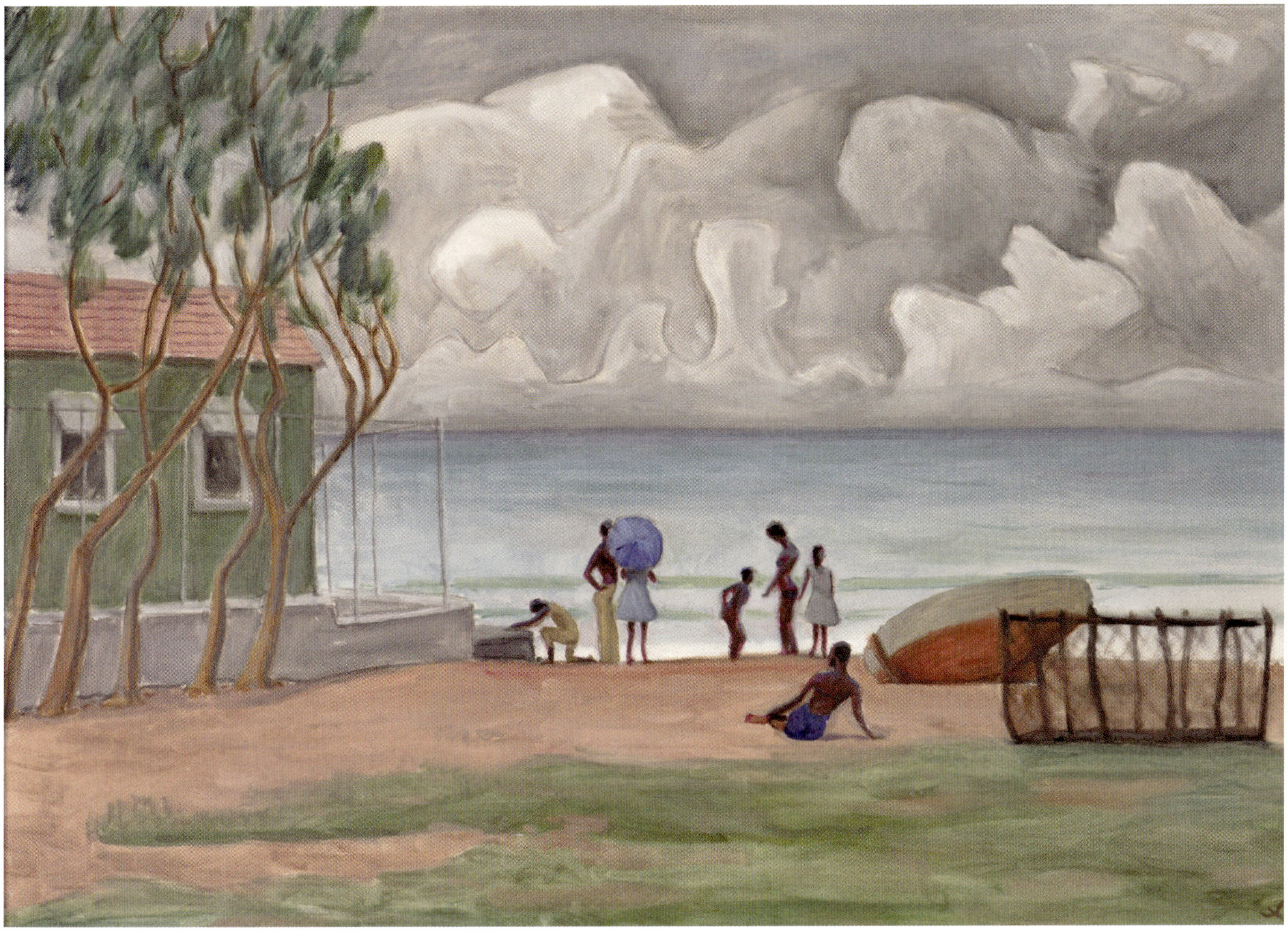

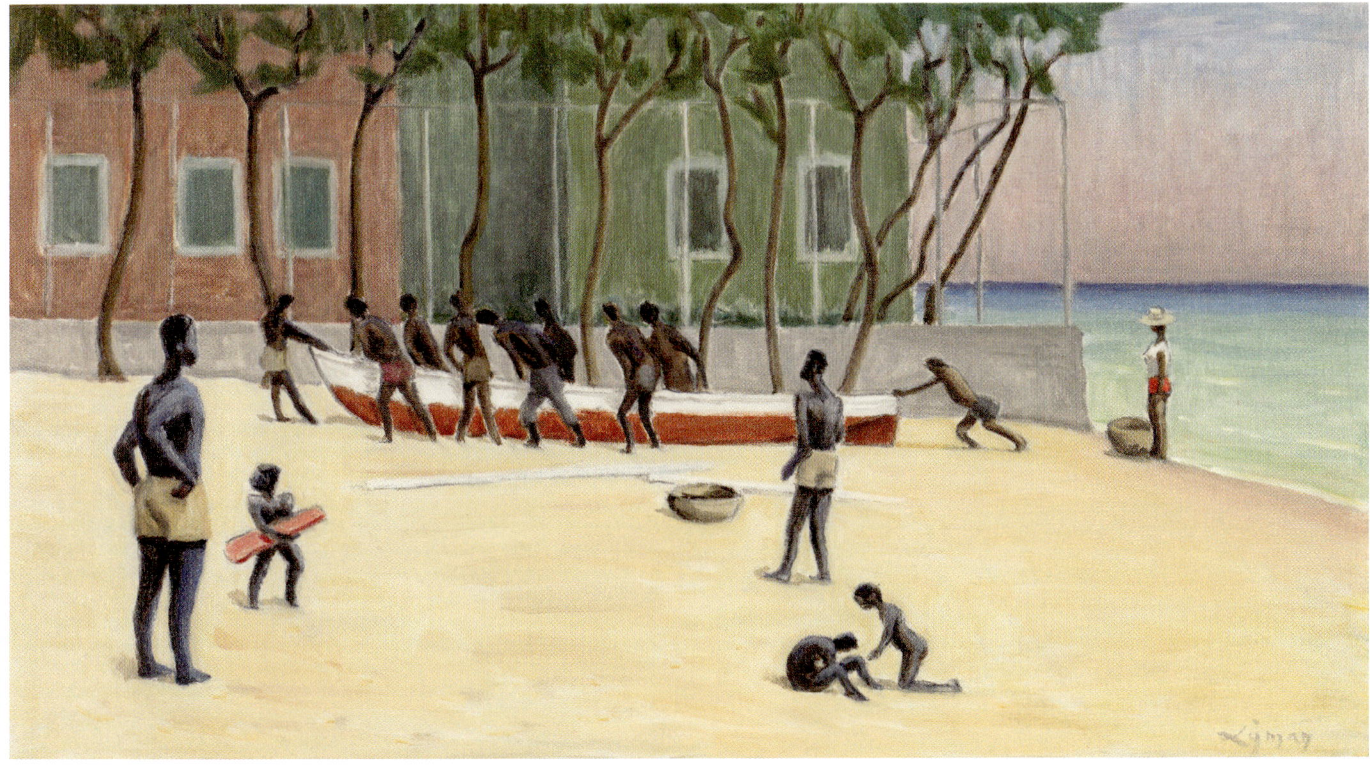

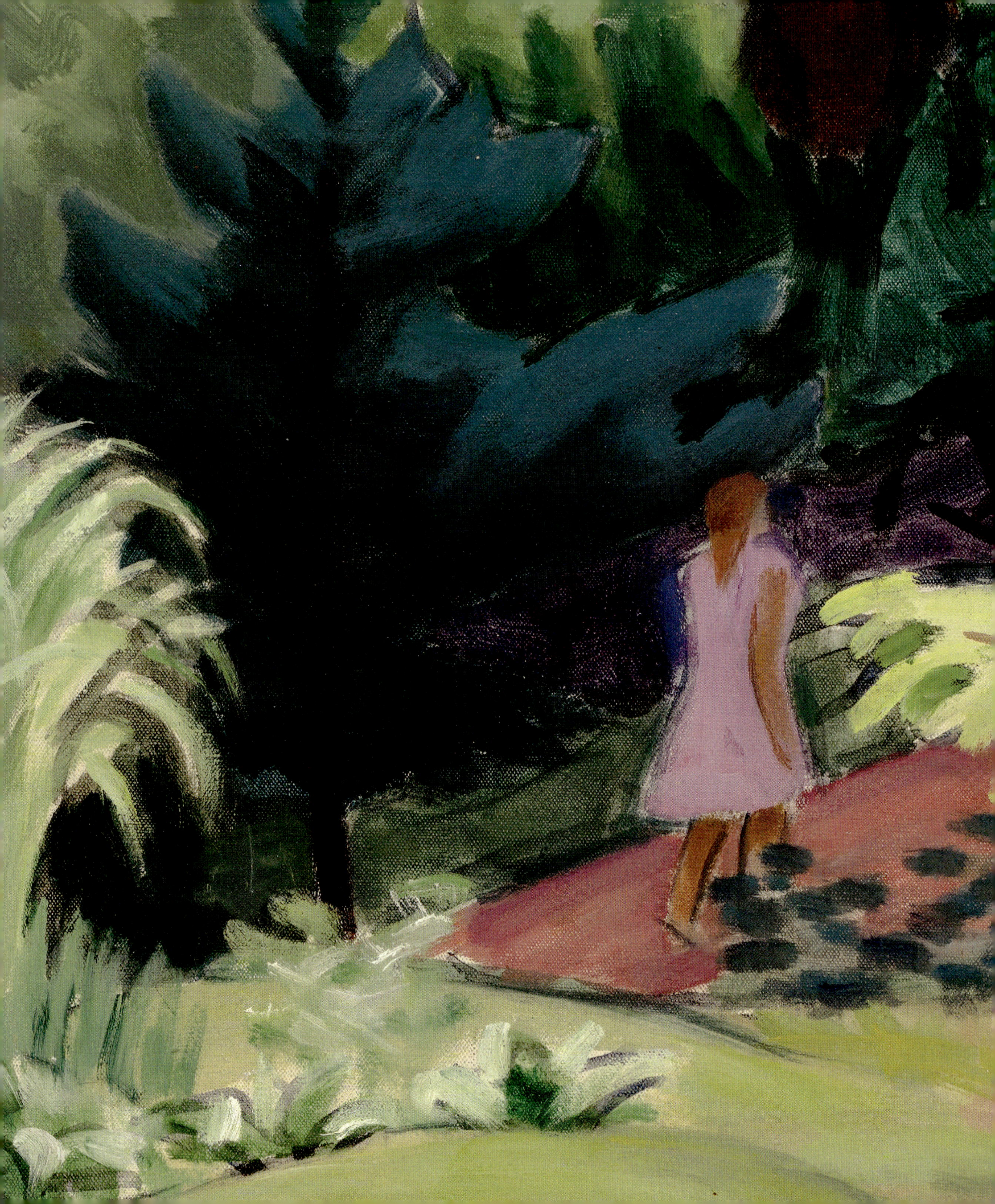

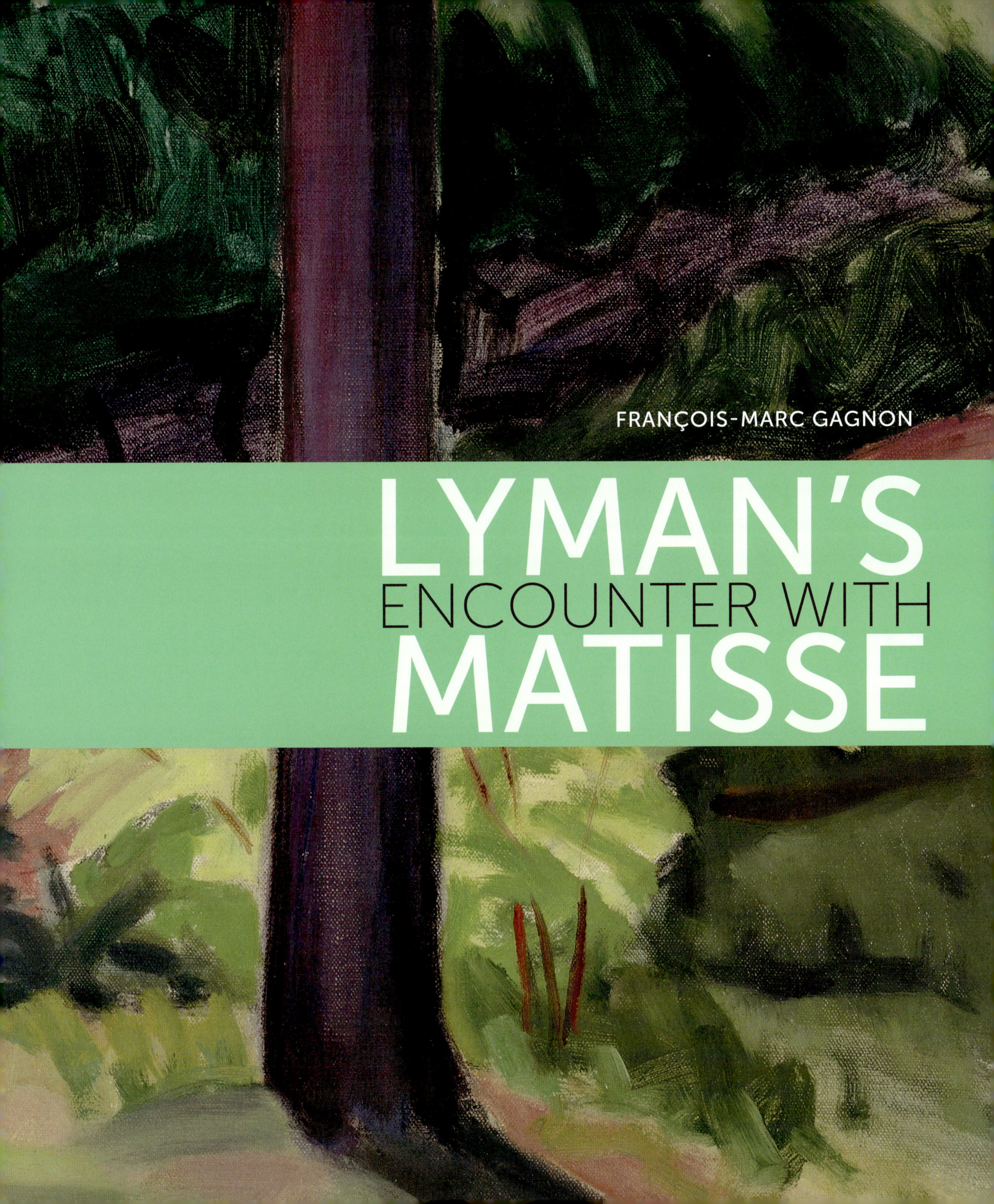

FRANÇOIS-MARC GAGNON

LYMAN'S ENCOUNTER WITH MATISSE

We cannot attempt to shed light on the relationship between John Lyman's and Matisse's painting without referring to the views of the late art critic and art dealer Gilles Corbeil. In the small catalogue published by the Montreal Museum of Fine Arts for Lyman's exhibition there in 1963, Corbeil wrote,

> That it has been said and written—as I have done myself—that Lyman's spirit was related to Matisse's or Bonnard's confuses me. There is such a difference between him and these painters that the very idea of bringing them together seems absurd to me today. In fact, Lyman resembles no one. He forms a complete world on his own, "a world without cracks," as Borduas liked to say about his master, Ozias Leduc.[1]

This remark surprised more than one person. In fact, Corbeil had sought to make a distinction between Lyman and Matisse, especially their respective conceptions of light:

> More a harmonist than a colourist, he [Lyman] is concerned above all with granting light to colour, "with finding light through colour," as he likes to say. At the risk of creating a paradox, I would say that Lyman replaces colour fauvism with light fauvism. This light explodes, beams from everywhere; it is not a natural light, it does not lend itself to the variations of the day; invented by the painter, it becomes pictorial light.

Previous double page:

/ CAT. 88 (DETAIL) John Lyman
Going up the Hill
1952

In Corbeil's view, Lyman's light was cold, implacable, and did not have the same brilliance as Matisse's. We can concede that this is true, at least in some paintings. But how can we not think that Lyman resembled Matisse on a much more important point: his desire to keep to visual language and avoid academic painting—art serving a program other than pictorial? In Fernand Dansereau's film on him, Lyman justified his rejection of the aesthetic of the Group of Seven precisely because the painters of the Group, such as A. Y. Jackson, wanted to define Canadian art as having Canadian subjects:

> Soon after my return [to Canada], Jackson wrote an article in a magazine[2] saying that the future of Canadian painting was to paint in the Far North, as far away as possible, and I wrote a letter in response, saying that it was to penetrate the internal reality.[3] For me, Canadian painting is painting conceived by Canadians. We wouldn't prescribe rocks and Christmas trees as necessary to Canadian painting.[4]

It is easy to find Matisse taking a similar position in favour of the means specific to painting, rather than to more or less picturesque subjects. For instance, in his "Notes of a Painter," originally published in 1908, Matisse wrote, "But the thought of a painter must not be considered as separate from his pictorial means, for the thought is worth no more than its expression by those means, which must be more complete (and by complete I do not mean complicated) the deeper is his thought." Further, he goes on to say,

> What I dream of is an art of balance, or purity and serenity, devoid of troubling or depressing subject matter, an art which might be for every mental worker, be he businessman or writer, like an appeasing influence, like a mental soother, something like a good armchair in which to rest from physical fatigue.[5]

Lyman speaks in analogous terms. When Guy Viau asks him, in Dansereau's film, "What is the message of your painting?" Lyman answers, "I have not deliberately put a message in my painting. I loathed academic painting, but after, looking at my paintings, I think that they all have a message. A message of serenity, I think, it's classic in that sense."[6] This idea has something in common with Matisse's "good armchair"! Lyman wrote, in one of his reviews in *The Montrealer*, "If Matisse's work is seldom an ornament for a given space, it is an ornament for certain needs of our existence, for our need of calm and joy, and in art as in life joy is possibly the hardest thing to confer."[7]

To return to Gilles Corbeil and conclude this introduction to Lyman's manner, Corbeil softens his critique: "It is incontestable that Lyman espouses the initial tenets of the Fauvist aesthetic: the rejection of the impressionist palette, the search for structure, a taste for the arabesque, the omission of local tone, cursive writing, economy of picture, expressive outlines: this is the very basis of his art."[8] Although Lyman is compared to the three masters that he mentioned most often in his presentation of modern art—Cézanne, Renoir and Matisse— it is clear that his own painting gravitated more toward the last than the first two. Thus, the idea of analyzing the connection between Matisse and Lyman is perhaps not hopeless after all!

LYMAN AT THE ACADÉMIE MATISSE

Lyman himself wrote—thought long after the fact—about his first encounters with Matisse:

> My first acquaintance with Matisse's painting was when, in the Spring of 1909, I saw his *Fontainebleau Forest* in the Salon des Indépendants. Its summary intensity haunted my dreams. In the Fall, Matthew Smith and I (we had become friends a year earlier at Étaples) resolved to attend the "Académie Matisse." Nothing could have been less academic than this nest of heretical fledglings, logged in a disused convent under the trees of an ancient garden . . . Students who came to him to learn modern tricks got no encouragement. "Learn to walk on the ground before you try the tight-rope" was his constant reminder. Continental art teachers seldom criticise oftener than once a week; Matisse visited us only once a fortnight, and then his criticism usually took the form of a long chat about fundamental principles, and qualities. We were about fifteen in the school . . . Once Matisse invited us to his house at Issy-les-Moulineaux, the house with the large studio, where, besides the two versions of *La Desserte*, the *Red Interior*, and dozens of other well-known pictures, he painted *The Dance*, which was there at the time. Later I came to know the model with the glowing skin (we nicknamed her the Italian Sunset) whom Matisse had taken south with him in the Summer, and who, posing among green pines against the Mediterranean blue, had suggested the colour of *The Dance*. That was the last year of the "Académie Matisse."[9]

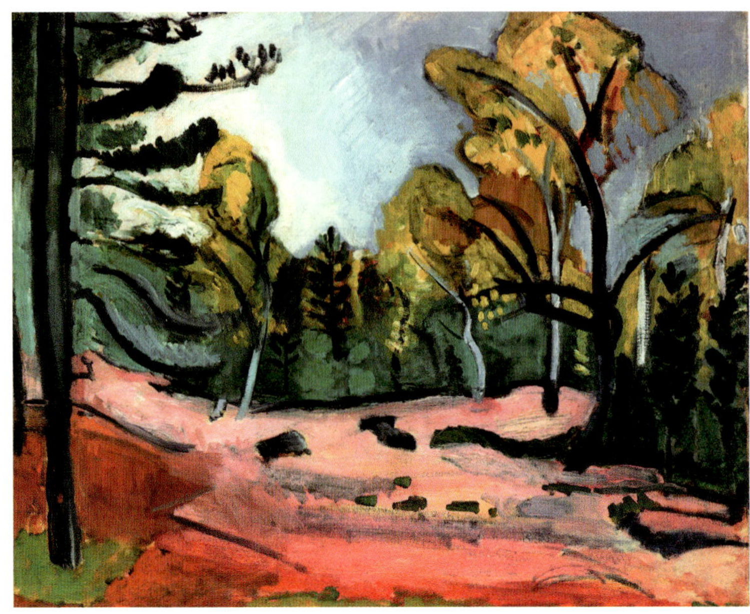

This text calls for a careful analysis. The painting by Matisse to which Lyman alludes first and that he says he saw at the 1909 Salon des Indépendants may be one that was recently on display at Christie's: *Autumn Landscape: Forest of Fontainebleau* **(FIG. 23)**.

A check of the exhibition catalogue shows that the work in question does not seem to have been presented in the 25th exhibition of the Société des Artistes indépendants, at the Jardin des Tuileries. Instead, Matisse apparently exhibited *The Girl with Green Eyes* (no. 1099) and *Spanish Woman with a Tambourine* (no. 1100), as well as two "studies" (nos. 783 and 784). Was Lyman's memory faulty? Evidence found by Wanda de Guébriant, manager of the Archives Matisse, shows that we must believe Lyman, despite the exhibition catalogue! At the 1909 Salon des Indépendants, the dispatches were limited to two works per artist. Matisse wanted to circumvent this obligation by showing his "studies" (nos. 783 and 784) under the name "Henri-Matisse" and his paintings *The Girl with Green Eyes* and *Spanish Woman with a Tambourine* (both for sale) under the name "Matisse-Henri." Yet, in a letter dated March 16, Russian collector Sergei Ivanovich Shchukin wrote, "I like *Spanish Woman* a great deal, and I am impatiently waiting for Mr. Fénéon's letter with regard to price." On March 27 (two days after the Salon opened), Shchukin told Matisse that he had "bought [his] *Spanish Woman* from Bernheim for 5000 F." Thus, it was then that *Autumn Landscape: Forest of Fontainebleau* replaced *Spanish Woman* at the Salon. In a letter to Shchukin, dated April 9, 1909, Matisse himself wrote, "I exhibited at the Salon des Indépendants the portrait with green eyes and Mrs. Stein's Fontainebleau landscape."[10] Lyman thus was correct when he said that he had seen *Autumn Landscape* at the show in 1909. He would see it again at the Steins' home in the spring of 1910; I shall return to this.

Was *Autumn Landscape: Forest of Fontainebleau* a sort of "trigger" for Lyman, spurring him to break definitively with academic painting?[11] At the Académie Julian, and especially in the view of Jean Paul Laurens, Lyman's master, landscape was almost nonexistent; at most, it might serve as background for the historical compositions that fascinated Laurens. If we believe a letter that Lyman wrote to his father on November 15, 1909, he did not make much of a splash at Julian: "My last esquisse at Julian's took about 37th place, next to the last."[12] It must be said that Laurens was particularly disastrous as an art teacher: "He insists on his conception of the subject rather than setting a premium on individual and personal conception." Tired of the arbitrary way he was being treated, Lyman added, "I don't intend to waste my time doing any more esquisses which forfeit their right to a critique because they are the result of my sentiment rather than J.-P's."

Although this remark does not give us an indication of when exactly Lyman entered the Académie Matisse, it gives us an idea of his reasons for leaving Laurens. A biography of Matthew Smith supplies more information on Smith's arrival at the Académie Matisse:

> After two years there [at the Slade School in London] he [Smith] made an escape to Brittany . . . Then he escaped further, to Paris, where he joined the school of Henri Matisse. After a month, however, the master abandoned it, and the pupils' attempt to run the school without him lasted only another month. This was in 1910.[13]

Another biographer of Smith theorizes that he entered the Académie Matisse only in April 1910.[14] If Lyman followed him, we should conclude that Smith and Lyman attended the Académie Matisse for only three months: April, May and June 1910 (the last month without the master).

It is surprising, given the impact that this stay at the Académie Matisse had on Lyman's opening to modern art, that he did not mention it in his correspondence with his father. A recent discovery may help to qualify this statement. In a letter dated April 14, 1910, Lyman wrote to his father,

> About going home, I was thinking that it would be best not to go too early so that I could be very little help, and then you will want me for all the interior work and finishing up. I think it will be best to stay on at school now as long as I can, and then feel free to stay on as long as you want me. What so you say? Smith has just come in for tea before going to the croquis class, so I must stop.[15]

Curiously, someone (it is not Lyman's handwriting) added the word "Matisse" just above the world "school": "I think it will be best to stay on at the /Matisse/ school." We might therefore conjecture that as of April 14, Lyman and Smith had been at the Académie Matisse for two weeks.

At this time, the academy had left the Couvent des Oiseaux, located at 84, rue de Sèvres, almost at the corner of the Boulevard des Invalides. The government had sold the convent in 1904 and the building was slated for demolition, which took place in 1909. In the spring of 1908, Matisse and his family had moved to the Hôtel Biron (the former Couvent du Sacré-Coeur), at 33, boulevard des Invalides, at the corner of the Rue de Varenne. He had his studio there, and he transformed the convent's former refectory into the academy. The Hôtel Biron, which was home to the

Rodin museum starting in 1916, was in the middle of gardens that had been left overgrown. It is hard to imagine how it was then when one looks at it today, with its magnificent French-style gardens and its restored and transformed buildings, but at the time, the Hôtel Biron, unoccupied for several years, was falling into ruin and also slated for demolition. A number of artists had found refuge there, the best known of whom were Jean Cocteau, Isadora Duncan, Auguste Rodin, Rainer Maria Rilke, and Matisse and his family.

It is surprising that Lyman spoke of only some fifteen students at the Académie Matisse during this period, unless this indicates that he was part of a smaller group that worked there in the afternoons.[16] We have no way of knowing. One thing is certain: in a 1909 photograph of Matisse and his students, there were more than double that number (FIG. 38). Lyman remembered the names of some of them: "Edward Bruce" (probably Patrick Henry Bruce, who later turned to Cubism); Per Lasson Krogh, a Norwegian painter usually known for his large mural in the Security Council chamber of the United Nations building in New York; Hans Marsilius Purrmann, a German painter who was a friend of Matisse and very involved in the foundation of the academy; and other German and Scandinavian artists.

According to Lyman, Matisse did not critique the students' paintings every week, as was the habit in rival institutions of the same type. He came every fifteen days[17] and, using one of his students' paintings as a pretext, pronounced general considerations on art and its principles. We know that he did not encourage them to imitate his style. An idea of the content of Matisse's discourse can be garnered by consulting his "Notes of a Painter," cited above. He explained elsewhere his methods and intentions:

> I thought that it would be good to have young artists avoid the path that I had had to take myself. So I took the initiative of opening [in 1908] an academy in a convent on Rue de Sèvres [Couvent des Oiseaux], which I then moved [in the spring of that year] to Sacré-Coeur [convent] [Hôtel Biron], to a site that was where Lycée Buffon is today.[18] Numerous students applied. I did my best, above all, to instil a sense of tradition in them. I don't have to tell you how disappointed my students were to see a master, reputed to be revolutionary, repeat to them Courbet's words: "I simply wanted to draw forth, from a complete acquaintance with tradition, the reasoned and independent sense of my own individuality."[19]

In his 1955 article, Lyman mentions visiting Matisse in Issy-les-Moulineaux, where Matisse had been living since September 1909. He does not mention having seen either version (blue or red) of *The Dessert* or the painting that he called *Red Interior*, probably *The Red Studio,* but he visited the studio where *The Red Studio*

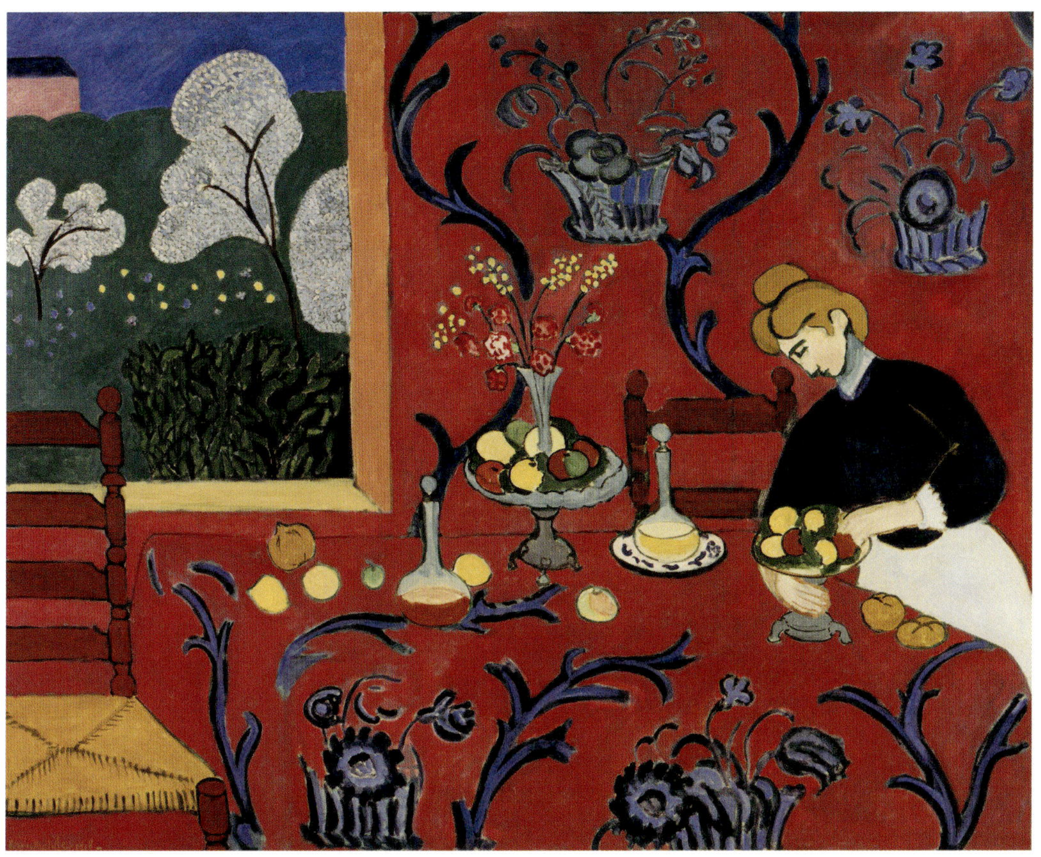

was to be painted in autumn 1911, after his stay at the Académie Matisse. Contrary to what Lyman might have thought, *The Dessert* was not painted there. Painted first in blue in June 1908,[20] then repainted in red when the artist returned from Germany in July 1908 **(FIG. 24)**, it dated from before Matisse's move to Issy. At the time of Lyman's visit to Matisse's studio, this painting had already been in Moscow for several months, in the hands of Shchukin, who had bought it directly from Matisse in August 1908.

On the other hand, it is very possible that Lyman saw one of the versions of *Dance* in the spring of 1910. What immediately comes to mind is the sketch painted in March 1909, at the Boulevard des Invalides, which ended up in the Museum of Modern Art in New York. In fact, preserved at the State Hermitage Museum is a work titled *Still Life with "Dance,"* dated 1909, which incorporates the version at the MoMA. But more likely Lyman saw the definitive version destined to adorn Shchukin's staircase in Moscow **(FIG. 25)**; this one was painted at Issy-les-Moulineaux and it was still there after Lyman's visit, as evidenced by another painting by Matisse in two versions dated 1912, which includes *Dance* (Shchukin version) in the background.[21] It was only in August 1912 that *Dance* finally adorned Shchukin's staircase.

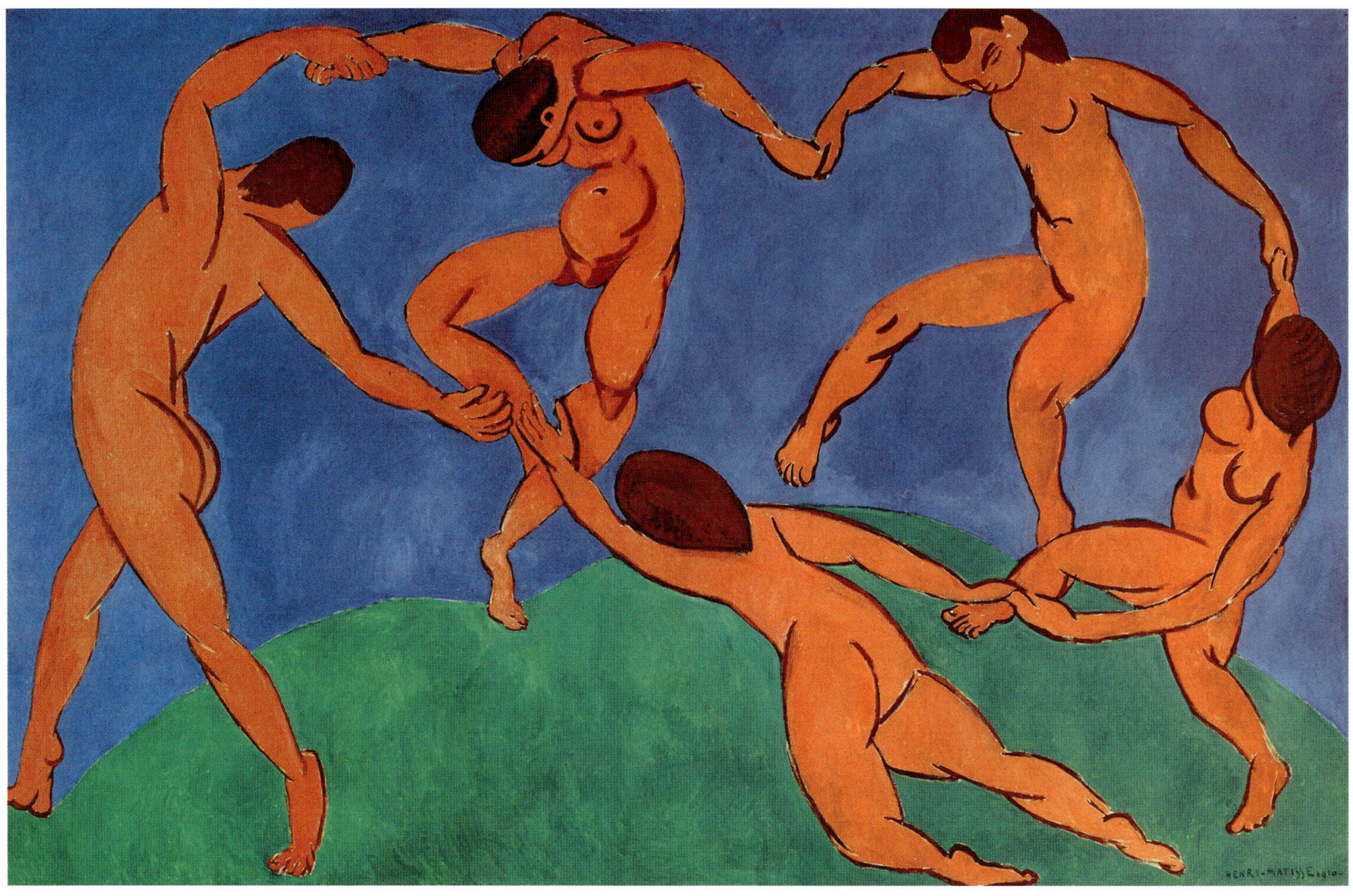

/ **FIG. 25** Henri Matisse
Dance
1909-1910

Finally, we note Lyman's allusion to Matisse's model Loulou Brouty, who spent the entire summer of 1909 with the Matisses in Cavalière, a small fishing village on the Mediterranean between Nice and Toulon. Everyone liked Brouty. She played with the children, provided company for Amélie and took swimming lessons with Henri between painting sessions. She was a refreshingly unpretentious Parisian with black hair, feline features and a body so tanned by the Midi sun that Matisse's students, as Lyman reported, had nicknamed her the "Italian sunset." She posed for *Woman in Green* **(FIG. 26)**, another canvas purchased by Shchukin.

It is thus not surprising that, on the occasion of the debates provoked by his exhibition in Montreal in 1913, Lyman told the journalists at the *Star* that they did not know what they were talking about when they discussed Matisse and Post-Impressionism:

> I know Mr. Matisse personally and have seen most of his work, which is almost as good a source of knowledge as an inference from an article in *Le Temps*. I know that is NOT SO MUCH his early as his late work that has been bought for many great private collections in Europe; I know that examples of his work of EVERY year are to be found in these collections.[22]

LYMAN AT THE STEINS'

When we try to retrace Lyman's early contact with Matisse's paintings, we must not neglect the fact that he attended the salon of collectors Michael and Sarah Stein, at 58, rue Madame in Paris. During one of these visits he would have seen once again *Autumn Landscape: Forest of Fontainebleau*, presented at the 1909 Salon des Indépendants and purchased by the Steins, as mentioned above. Lyman would have accompanied his cousin, the painter and inventor Henry Lyman Saÿen, Henry Morgan's godson, to the Steins' home in December 1909. In May 1910, Lyman wrote that he was visiting the Steins almost every week and that their residence was "filled with a perhaps unrivalled collection of modern masters, and a wealth of beautiful things, furniture, books, photos, and documents of all kinds."[23]

Henry Lyman Saÿen is an interesting figure. He was married to Jeannette Hope, a fashion designer at Wanamaker, a famous Philadelphia department store. Her boss, Rodman Wanamaker, financed their trip to Paris in 1906, hoping that she would bring back news of the latest fashions. For a time, Henry was a partner of Charles Cottet, founder of the Bande noire, a group of painters who had chosen a very dark palette, in reaction to the luminous colours of the Post-Impressionists. But after meeting Leo and Gertrude Stein and discovering their collection, Saÿen parted ways with Cottet and moved into the enemy camp. His art rapidly evolved toward Fauvism. He became a regular guest at parties hosted by Michael and Sarah Stein. Lyman could not have had a better introduction to them.

There is no doubt that Lyman was able to complement his knowledge of Matisse's painting at the Steins'. He saw numerous important paintings there: the famous *Portrait of Madame Matisse*, known as *The Green Line,* from 1905; a sketch for *The Joy of Life*, from the winter of 1905-1906; *Pink Onions*, from 1906; *Self-portrait*, also from 1906 **(FIG. 37)**; and even the sketch for *Luxury*, from 1907, lent by Matisse to his friends the Steins.

We do not know whether Lyman visited Matisse's exhibition held from February 14 to February 22, 1910, at Bernheim-Jeune, as Morrice did. One thing is certain: a good third of the sixty-five paintings in this retrospective came from the Steins.

IN NICE

Lyman alluded to at least two visits to Matisse's studio in Nice after the war. The first must have been in the early 1920s, as he recounts having found Matisse on the balcony of a hotel room on the Promenade des Anglais, painting *Festival of Flowers*. Lyman remembered that as Matisse painted he was "keeping time with his brush"; but he also noted that was not very impressed with the result: "The looping brushwork did not produce a very good picture. He was just having fun."[24] We do know, however, that no fewer than five of Matisse's paintings are titled *Festival of Flowers*: three dated 1921, one dated 1922 and one probably from 1923 **(FIG. 27)**.[25] All of them portrayed the "Battle of Flowers," a sort of competition of floats and brass bands parading from Promenade des Anglais to Promenade de la Jetée to celebrate the

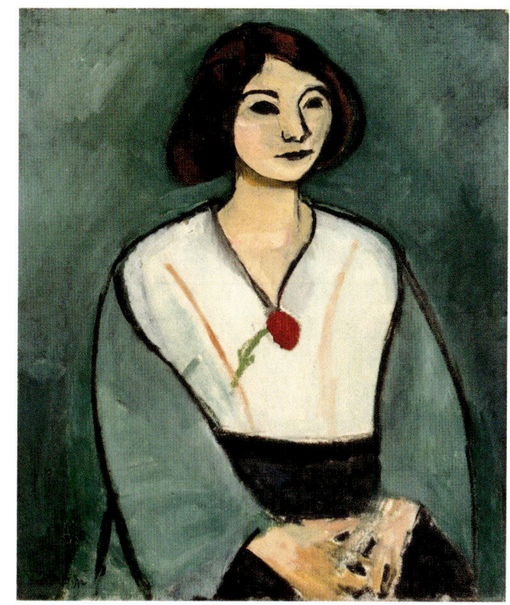

/ **FIG. 26** Henri Matisse
Woman in Green
1909

Mardi Gras. In the 1923 version, Matisse portrayed his daughter, Marguerite, and his model Henriette Darricarrère watching the spectacle from the third-floor balcony of his hotel. A palm tree to the right and a point jutting into the sea (Saint-Jean-Cap-Ferrat) on the left frame the composition.

In 1922, Lyman purchased a villa in Cagnes-sur-Mer, near Nice, and came into contact once again with Matisse, who, as Jack Cowart has established,[26] had left the Hôtel de la Méditerranée to take up more permanent residence on Place Charles-Félix, thus becoming a resident of Nice. Lyman wrote about this visit in one of his articles in the *Montrealer* in December 1938: "Henri Matisse's *Odalisk with Red Trousers* is a joyous triumph of colour. It is a typical work of the 20's when he was in full possession of his means and had disciplined his audacious experiment into perfect harmony."[27] This is a valuable hint on the context of Lyman's second visit to Matisse's studio. It was no longer the Festival of Flowers that now preoccupied Matisse, but the series of Odalisques **(FIG. 28)**, the most famous of which is probably *Odalisque Seated with Arms Raised, Green Striped Chair*, from 1923, now in the Chester Dale Collection at the National Gallery of Art in Washington. Lyman continued,

> It was about this time that I last visited him in his studio at Nice. He showed me picture after picture, and I said nothing. That is what looking at painting ought to do to you—shut you up. When we talk about it we are really talking around it—about what is not painting, and a Matisse is all painting, as pure painting as ever existed.[28]

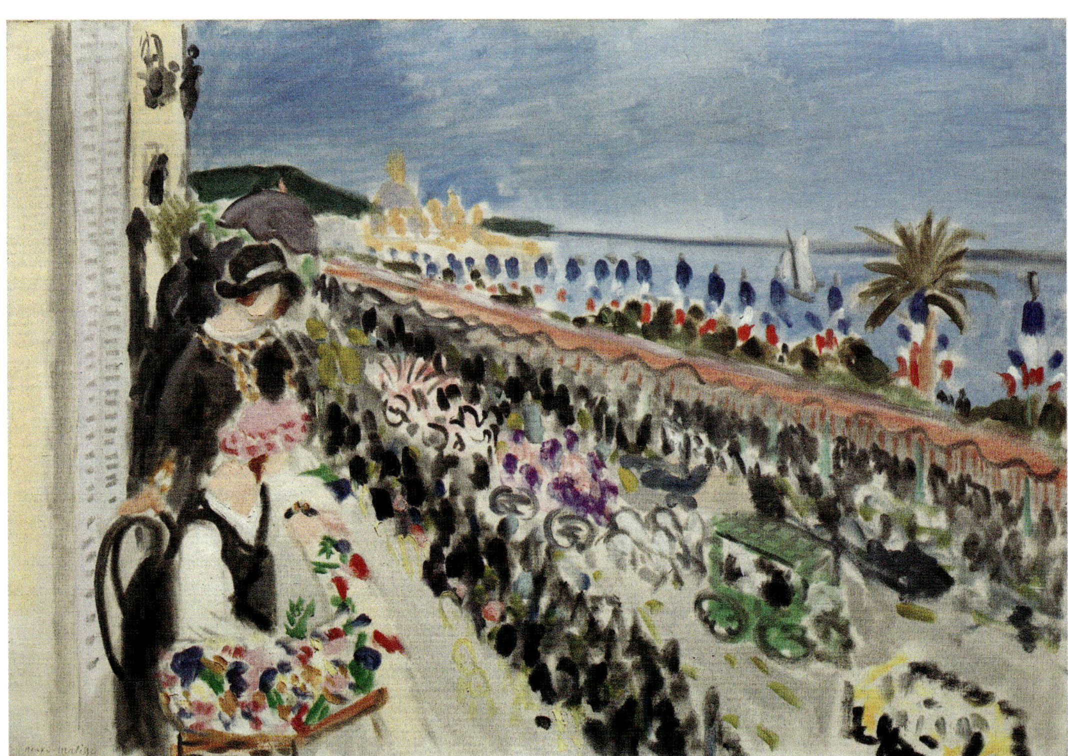

/ **FIG. 27** Henri Matisse
Festival of Flowers, Nice
1923

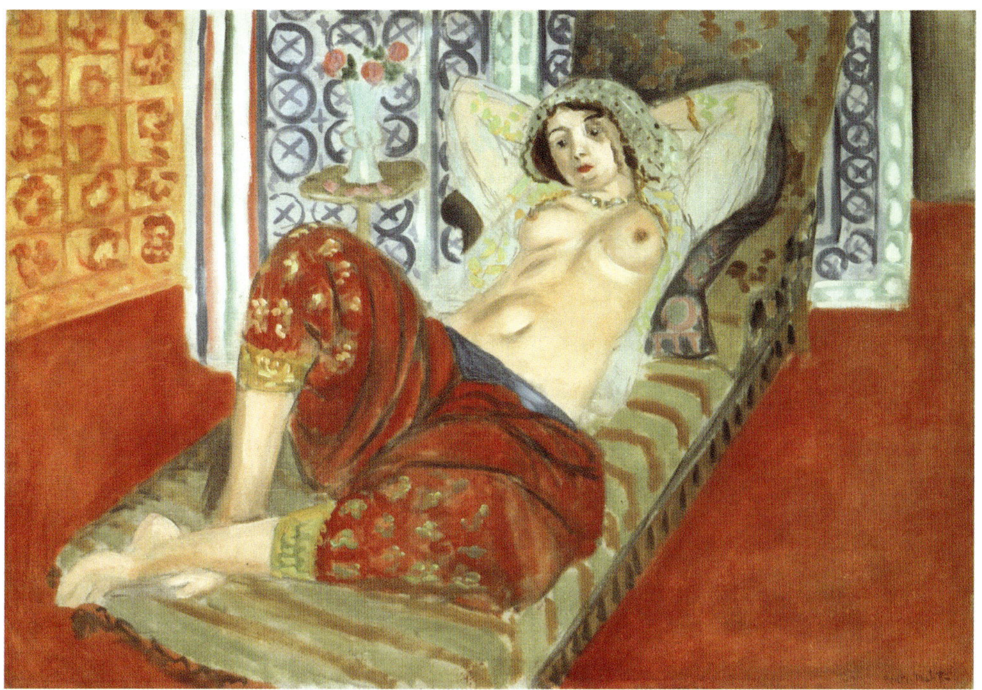

Lyman apparently returned to this visit in "Adieu, Matisse," written in 1955:

> When we returned to the Côte d'Azur couple of years later, he had moved to that spacious, high-ceilinged apartment with great windows overlooking Les Ponchettes and the bay. We went there to pay our respects, and he showed us all his recent work, canvas after canvas. Words were soon obliterated from my mind by the sight of so much lyric splendor. Matisse must have understood for he did not seem in the least put out by my failure to exclaim.[29]

MATISSE IN LYMAN'S ART CRITICISM

In parallel with his painting activities, Lyman wanted to bring together Canadian painters not tainted by "academism," and for this purpose he founded the Contemporary Arts Society in 1939. He also took on the mission of introducing the general public to modern art, the art of its times, and he became a columnist in *The Montrealer*,[30] a local magazine modelled on *The New Yorker*. Some of the passages quoted above are from his columns. Lyman also kept a journal[31] in which he often wrote reviews of exhibitions that he had seen and gave his opinion on the development of his own art.

Curiously, Lyman did not refer often to Matisse in his reviews in *The Montrealer*[32] or in his journal. When he did mention him, it was generally in relation not to his own painting but to the writings of Roger Fry, Clive Bell, John Dewey or Élie Faure, or in reference to other artists, such as Morrice, Matthew Smith and Raoul Dufy.

/ FIG. 28 Henri Matisse
Odalisque in Red Trousers
1921

Lyman proved to be particularly interested in the ideas of the two great defenders of the School of Paris in England, Clive Bell and Roger Fry, and in their theory of "significant form" and "pure art," which he applied to Matisse:

> I am not saying that the pure painting is the only kind that has virtue. I take these things as they come and I do not believe in theoretical platforms for art. Painting has carried auras of innumerable kinds, and perhaps, or even certainly, that of Matisse has its aura, but it is one that has no counterpart in words. It is as nearly pure painting as some of Blake's stanzas are pure poetry.[33]

This notion of "aura," which Lyman did not describe in detail, certainly had a link with light, and no doubt he sought his own light in his painting, as did Matisse. He remained silent, however, on the similarities between his own painting and Matisse's.

Was he more open to the topic when, instead of writing about critics, he was writing about painters? Not really. Here, for example, is what he says about James Wilson Morrice and Raoul Dufy. He begins by stating that Morrice's work offers a certain continuity that is generally not acknowledged by critics, because of his more recent, freer paintings, and then he talks about his influences, including Matisse:

> The greatest change after first period and from then on one can only measure road covered between early and latest works. The greater change after the very early manner. Owed to Whistler by two-dimensional "arrangement" rather than the balanced value of chiaroscuro or an architecture of line and form. To the Impressionists the vivacity of quality of lighting and the interdependence of reflection. To Matisse the bolder accent of impressionism of sentiment (as opposed to impressionism of senses). But latter must not be overestimated.[34]

We might wonder whether he would not have liked to apply the same reservation concerning the influence of Matisse's painting to his own work as he had done to Morrice's.

On Dufy, Lyman is more categorical:

> Back in the first years of the century [Dufy] was painting like anybody else in the aftermath of Impressionism, very much indeed like Matisse at the same period, and it was from Matisse that he was to get his revelation, as one artist always gets it from another, and not from sticks and stones, or snow and jack-pines. It was from one of the latter's paintings in the Salon of 1905. "Before this picture," relates Dufy, "I understood all the new reason for painting, and impressionist realism lost his charm for me in the contemplation of the miracle of imagination introduced into drawing and colour. I understood immediately the new mechanism."[35]

After that, Lyman comments, Dufy became a "decorator." His fabrics, ceramics, tapestries, lithographs, woodcuts (Lyman cites Dufy's prints for Guillaume Apollinaire's *The Bestiary*), even his murals for the Paris World Fair are evidence of this, in Lyman's view.

It goes without saying that what Lyman was saying about Dufy could also apply to his own work. His style did not come solely from observation of nature, as is too easily believed. In contrast to the conviction of the Group of Seven—mentioned above, through the words of group member A. Y. Jackson—Lyman believed that art came from art. The members of the Group of Seven would, in the end, admit the impact that an exhibition of contemporary Scandinavian art presented in the winter of 1912-1913 at the Buffalo Fair Arts Academy—which we know that L. Harris and J. E. McDonald attended—had on their conception of what Canadian painting should be. Only in April 1931, looking back at the event during a lecture on Scandinavian art given at the Art Gallery of Toronto, did J. E. MacDonald admit that when they had visited the exhibition the two artists had said to themselves, "This is what we want to do with Canada!"[36] Even in their view, authentic painting came in part from a dialogue in images with other painters, and not from the spectacle of nature alone.

In fact, Lyman wrote more about Renoir and Cézanne than Matisse as founders of modernism. In this, he revealed himself to be a disciple of Clive Bell and Roger Fry, both of whom were of the opinion that Matisse ranked behind these two giants of modernist painting. But once more, it is important not to go by words alone. The evidence of Lyman's paintings must also be discussed.

THE EVIDENCE OF THE PAINTINGS

LIGHT

The first thing to determine is in what way Lyman's conception of light is similar to Matisse's. As Gilles Corbeil sensed, this connection is not so obvious. Matisse always seemed to make more luminous paintings than did Lyman, who liked grey skies rather than views in full sun. But if one looks beyond appearances to a more conceptual level, it becomes clear that the two artists shared a certain aversion to light that changes all the time as clouds pass and to variations in lighting at different times of day. What Matisse went to find in Morocco was stable, constant light that would allow him to paint without fear that a sudden change in luminosity would force him to adapt his idea and relegate the construction of his subject to second priority. He had complained about such circumstances in a letter to Marquet, written toward the end of his stay in Tangier: "The light is superb, but the weather changes too much."[37] And, again to Marquet: "I'm unhappy with my trip from the point of view of the weather, so variable. How annoying."[38] In this, Fauvism was unlike Impressionism; the Impressionists were always partial to tiny changes in atmospheric luminosity, as exemplified by Monet's *Haystacks*, *Cathedrals* and *Poplars*, in which he tried to evoke the fleeting qualities of nature rather than its permanence.

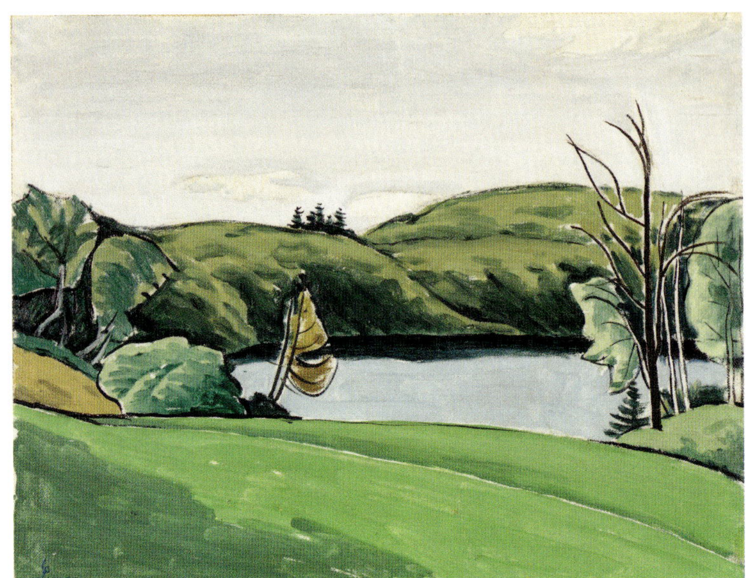

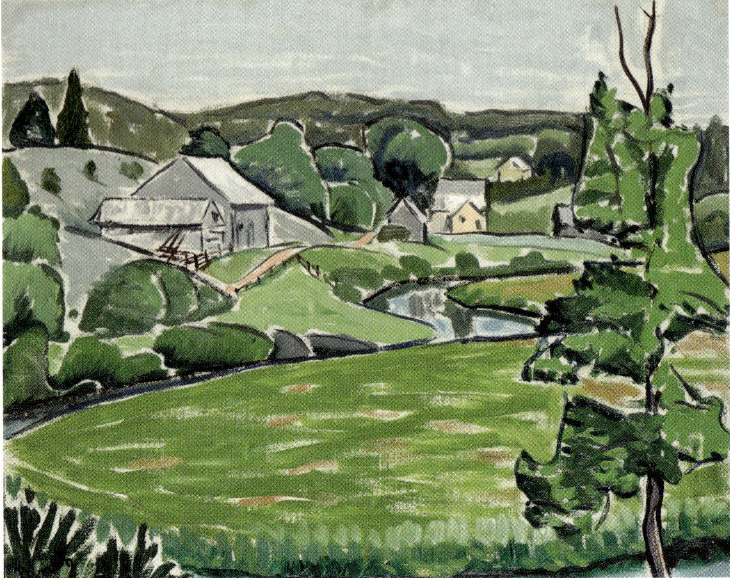

It seems that Lyman had a similar concern for stability. Of course, his reference was no longer to the Moroccan sun, and he did not complain about the "grey weather" as Matisse did, but he saw in the Canadian sky—which had in common with its African counterpart that it could provide stable, almost unchanging lighting, although, of course, not as bright—the possibility for great latitude in the construction of a painting. One can find a number of examples in Lyman's work, particularly his landscapes.

Wild Nature Impromptu, 1st State (**CAT. 83**)[39] is typical in this regard. Under a grey sky with a few clouds, the green foreground, as well as the lake and hills in the background, gives an impression of immutability or permanence disrupted by passing shadows, similar to paintings by Marc-Aurèle Fortin. In painting the small tree in the centre and the branches to the right *in front of* the background, Lyman plays on the two-dimensionality of the support and asks the eye to re-establish the planes in their natural succession. Moreover, the visible brushstrokes in Lyman's paintings make more tangible his respect for the pictorial surface, while suggesting the painter's presence in the painting.

THE PICTURESQUE AND THE PICTORIAL

Matisse made a clear distinction between the picturesque and the pictorial. "Picturesque," the original meaning of which is "worthy of being painted," designates a subject that is impressed upon the painter without him wondering about its relevance or quality. "Here is what is to be painted!" he exclaims, as Delacroix did in Algiers. The exoticism, the unique nature of the scene, the costumes, the architecture of the Casbah, the narrow alleys—all of this was so new and seductive that the painter believed that simply rendering what he saw would make his painting. The subject was "ready-made," so to speak. In contrast to the picturesque, the

/ **CAT. 83** John Lyman
Wild Nature Impromptu, 1st State
1912

/ **CAT. 84** John Lyman
Dalesville
1912

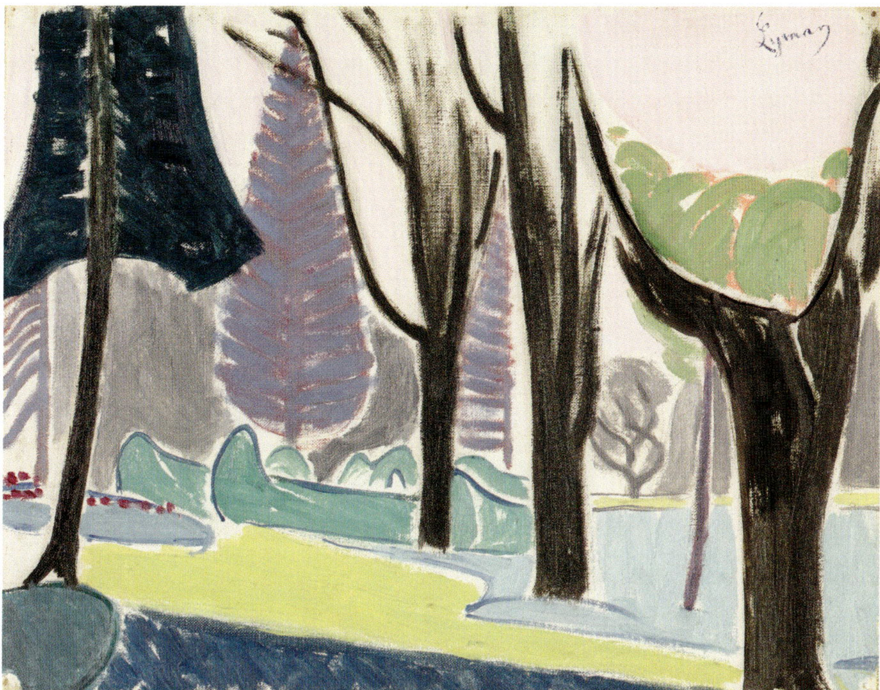

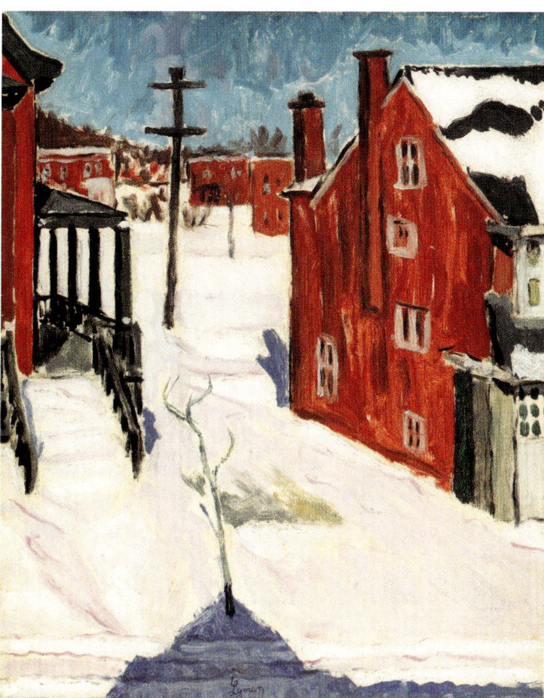

pictorial takes nothing for granted. The painter has his vision and he maintains it even against the seductiveness of the subject, which serves for only half of the work. Many things considered self-propagating or distracting must be sacrificed so that the artist retains only the idea. Matisse did not want to yield to Orientalism, although he was enthusiastic about Islamic art and odalisques.

It is natural to think that Lyman would agree with Matisse on this distinction, as he had always shunned picturesque subjects, including the wild landscape of northern Ontario that so enchanted the Group of Seven. Nothing was further from Lyman's mind than the romantic idea of the sublime landscape of high mountains that seduced Lawren Harris and J. E. MacDonald. Even a subject that might at least suggest exoticism, such as *Zaouia, Hammamet*, in Tunisia (CAT. 64),[40] is treated with extreme restraint. The tree and fence in the foreground draw more attention than do the buildings with cupolas farther back on the right, even though the title indicates that they are the main subject of the painting.

A curious landscape called *Westmount in Winter* (CAT. 86), acquired by the National Gallery of Canada in 1981, illustrates even more clearly Lyman's rejection of the picturesque. The foreground is occupied by the blue shadow of the roof of a house that we do not see but that ineluctably leads the gaze toward a telegraph pole in the centre of the composition. Furthermore, the style of the houses, which we see only from the back or sides, tends to refute the idea that Westmount was a particularly wealthy, opulent neighbourhood. Here, on the contrary, the snow covers everything under the blue sky, and the area seems unexpectedly ordinary.

/ CAT. 85 John Lyman
The Lawns of Fairfield, Cowansville
1914

/ CAT. 86 John Lyman
Westmount in Winter
1912

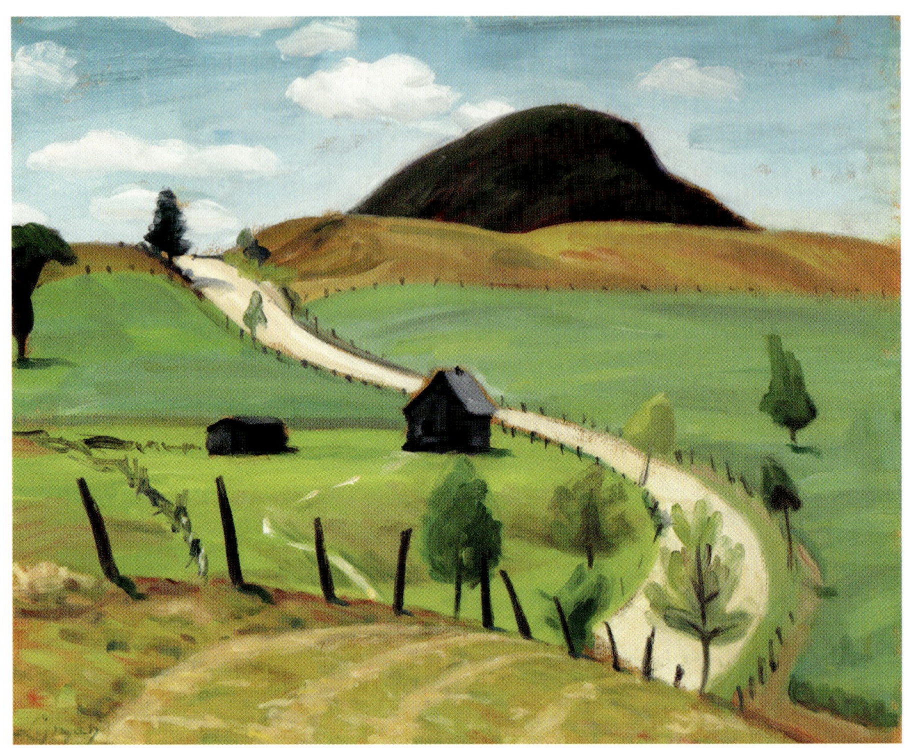

THE DECORATIVE

A very strong aspect of Matisse's art, which Lyman seems to have been less concerned with, is the tendency toward the decorative, which Matisse developed in contact with Asian applied arts (carpets, vases, garments and other items). The importance of decoration to Matisse is even more remarkable because he was thus resisting both the widespread idea that decoration was of interest only in the minor arts and the current dominated by Cubism, which was reaffirming the idea of representation—albeit burst into multiple facets—of the outside world. Thus, Matisse's taste for decorative surfaces contradicted, in a way, Lyman's interest in Cézanne and his mastery of the construction of volumes.

It seems that Lyman's desire to construct landscapes sometimes took precedence over any leanings toward the decorative. Some of his landscapes do not sacrifice depth to surface effects. The foreground might be occupied by a fence—for example, in *Going up the Hill* (CAT. 88) and *Greenery III* (CAT. 89)—as if to better mark the place from which we enter the pictorial space. One can see an equivalent *repoussoir* plane in Cézanne's still lifes, which enables viewers to situate themselves in relation to the subject by showing them the edge of the table on which the objects in the painting are placed.

/ **CAT. 87** John Lyman
Road at La Conception
1934-1935

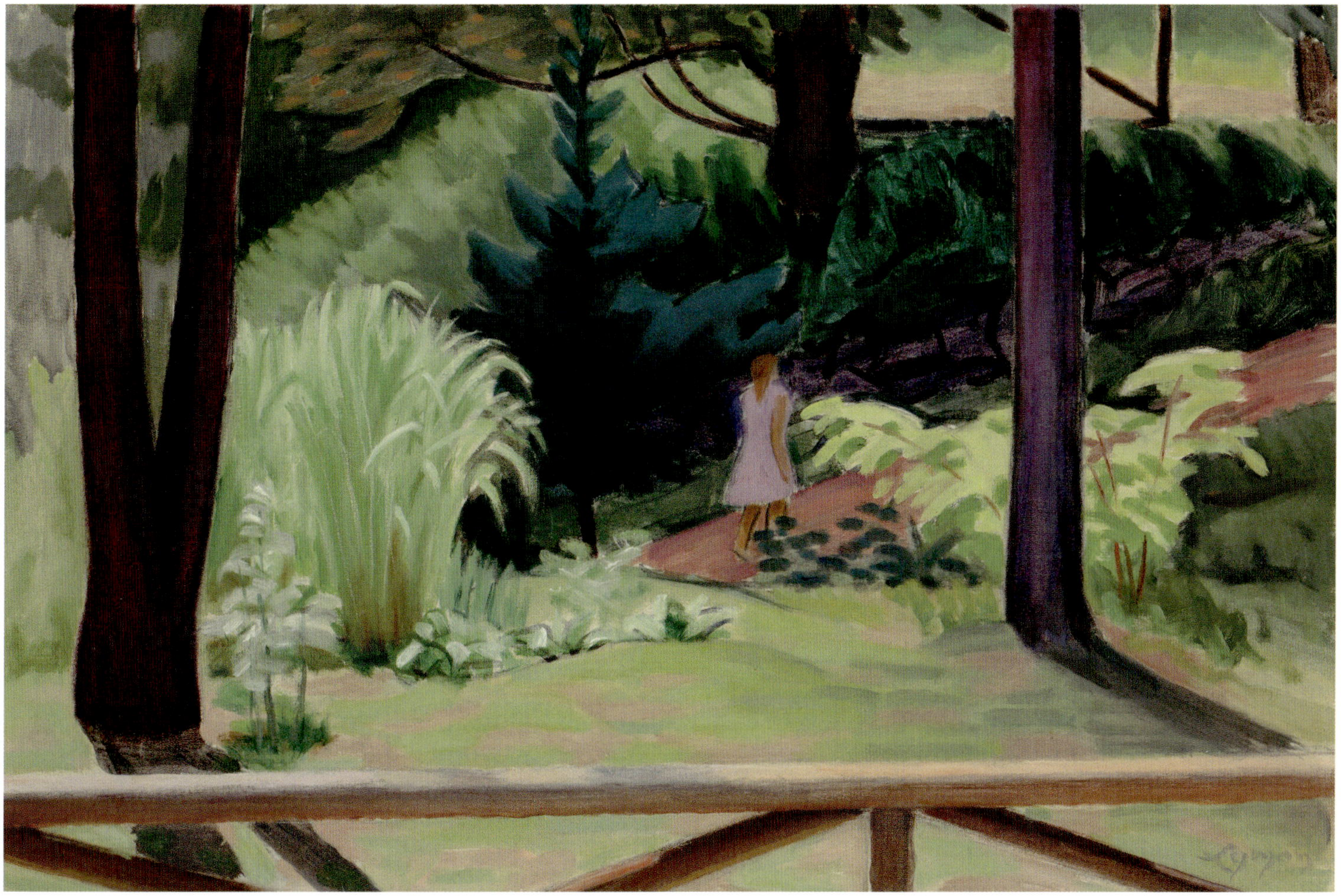

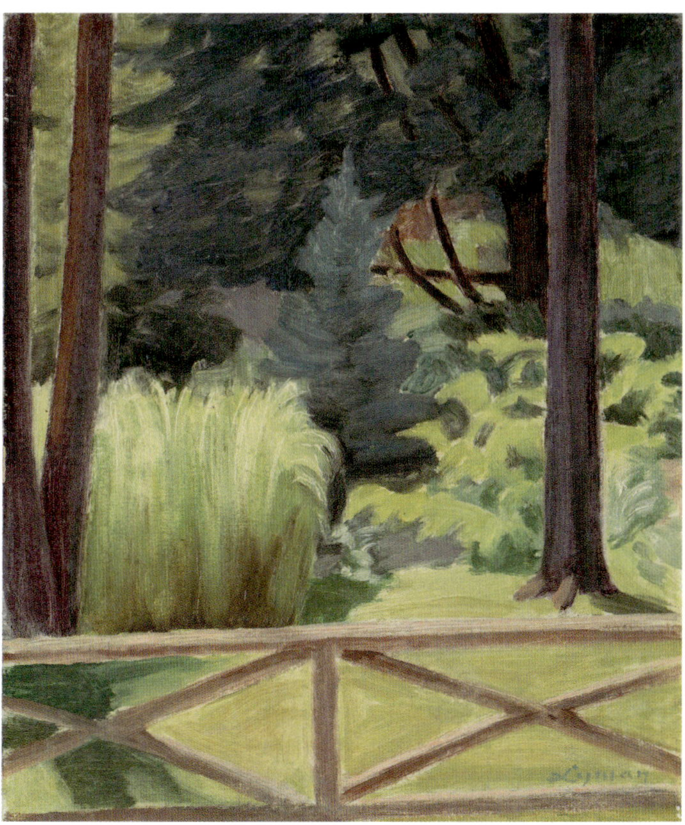

/ **CAT. 88** John Lyman
Going up the Hill
1952

/ **CAT. 89** John Lyman
Greenery III
1947

Once this border is crossed, a landscape, a woodland and a path on which a girl is walking are revealed, bathed in light. The composition is then closed in by the dark mass of trees and the suggestion of another clearing beyond. But even when Lyman does not make use of several layers of articulations like this, the succession of planes in the space is clear. The fence keeps viewers at a distance that they must not cross in order to properly see the painting, which is thus defined as a fragment of space.

Many things are going on in the small landscape called *St. George, Bermuda* (CAT. 27). A thorny plant occupies the foreground, and three of its branches stick out and cross the entire composition. The background shows an exterior of a coastal village, and the horizon of the ocean is situated very high, almost three-quarters up the surface of the painting. The succession of planes is strongly articulated by colour: dark green, pale green, white and pink, and then blue. Lyman thus sometimes resists the idea of a landscape treated purely decoratively in the plane.

Even the paintings in the series of the beach at Saint-Jean-de-Luz (CAT. 90) force the figures into the function of articulating the space in various planes that spread as far as the ocean and beyond. Lyman observes the rules of spatial recession very carefully by assigning a specific size to each figure, including those swimming and diving, in the background of the composition.

Nevertheless, the purely decorative end of the spectrum always remained a temptation for Lyman. The habit of keeping in reserve, as in *Dalesville* (CAT. 84), the parts that will be occupied by a tree to the right or the shrubs in the rest of the composition, seem, at first glance, to contradict the effects of perspective that one would expect in a landscape of this type. The surface takes pride of place, and when one says "surface," one deliberately says ornament, decoration. The same effect, pushed even further, is seen in *The Lawns of Fairfield, Cowansville* (CAT. 85), in which the trees are flattened, their branches and trunks treated as lines, and the colour is applied without nuance, as it came out of the tube.

/ **CAT. 90** John Lyman
On the Beach (Saint-Jean-de-Luz)
1929-1930

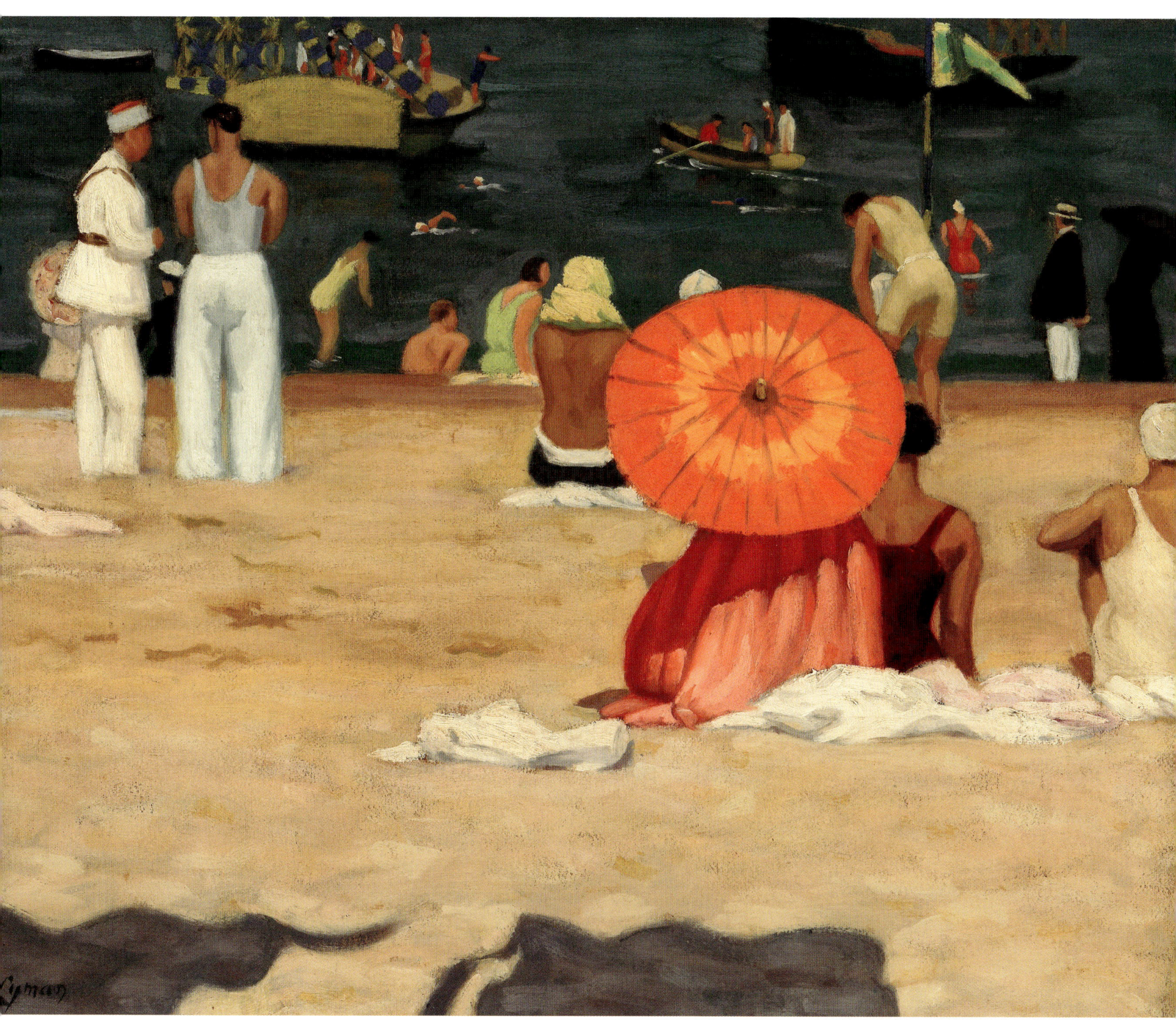

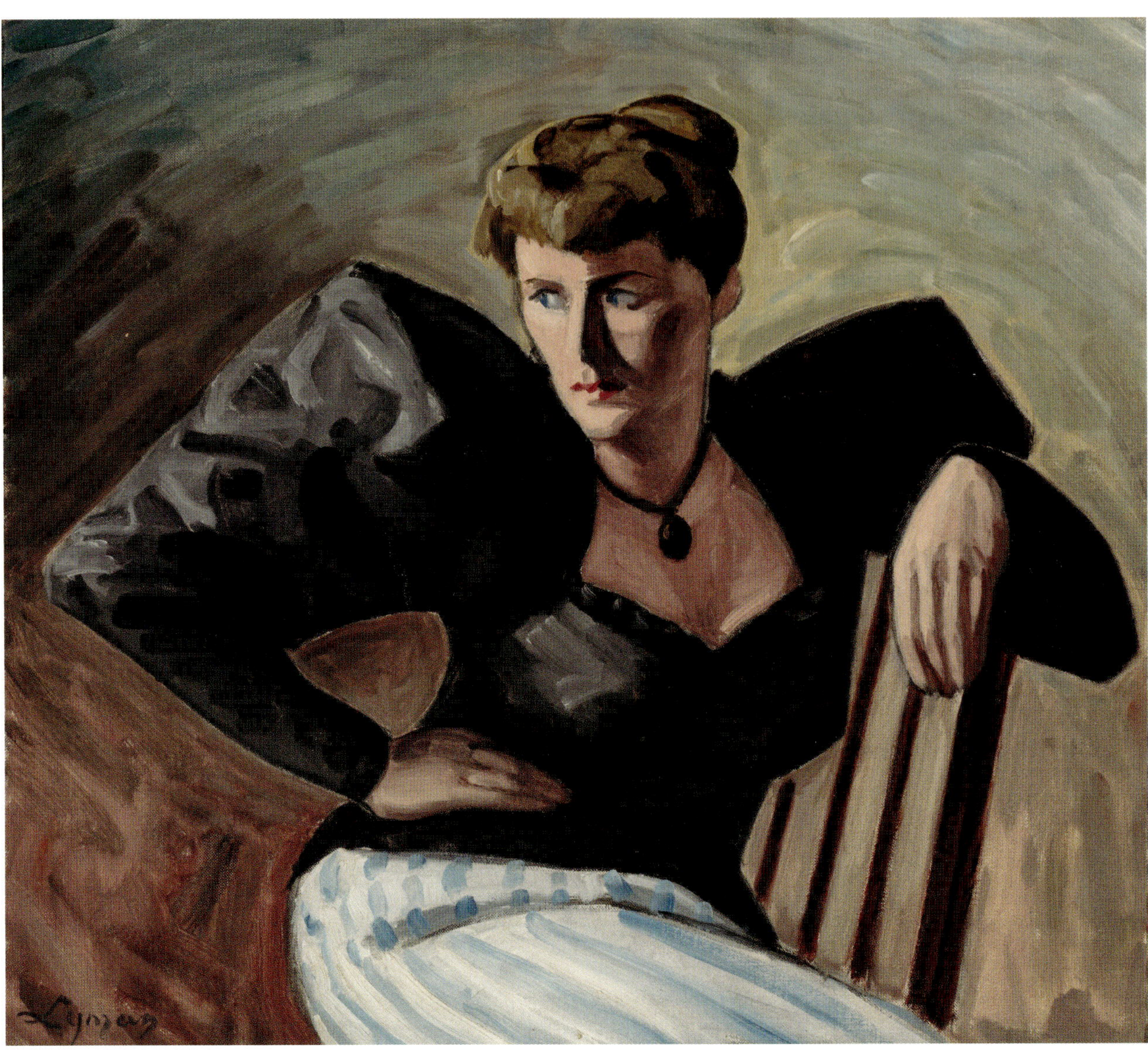

FIGURES

The other end of the spectrum of Lyman's inspiration—marked by Cézanne's influence—is also a counterpoint to the decorative tendency. This extreme takes him to the human figure.

What is striking about Lyman's exotic figures is their "sculptural" construction. *Habiba (Young Tunisian Girl)* **(CAT. 30)** illustrates this tendency perfectly. In this beautiful portrait of a Maghreb woman, Lyman is concerned no longer with respecting the two-dimensionality of the support but, on the contrary, with affirming the presence of a volume. The three-quarters view of the model, the strong contrast in lighting between the two sides of the face and the large veil covering her head situate the figure in a three-dimensional space, even the viewer's space. The same qualities are evident in *Portrait of Dr. Dumas* (about 1944, National Gallery of Canada), perhaps even more strongly. Here, the brushstrokes give us an opportunity to observe the painter's masterful control of the lighting on the volumes. The result is an affirmation of the physical presence of the model, to the detriment of analysis of his psychology. The painting is about pure exteriority.

/ **CAT. 91** John Lyman
Jori Smith in Costume
1936

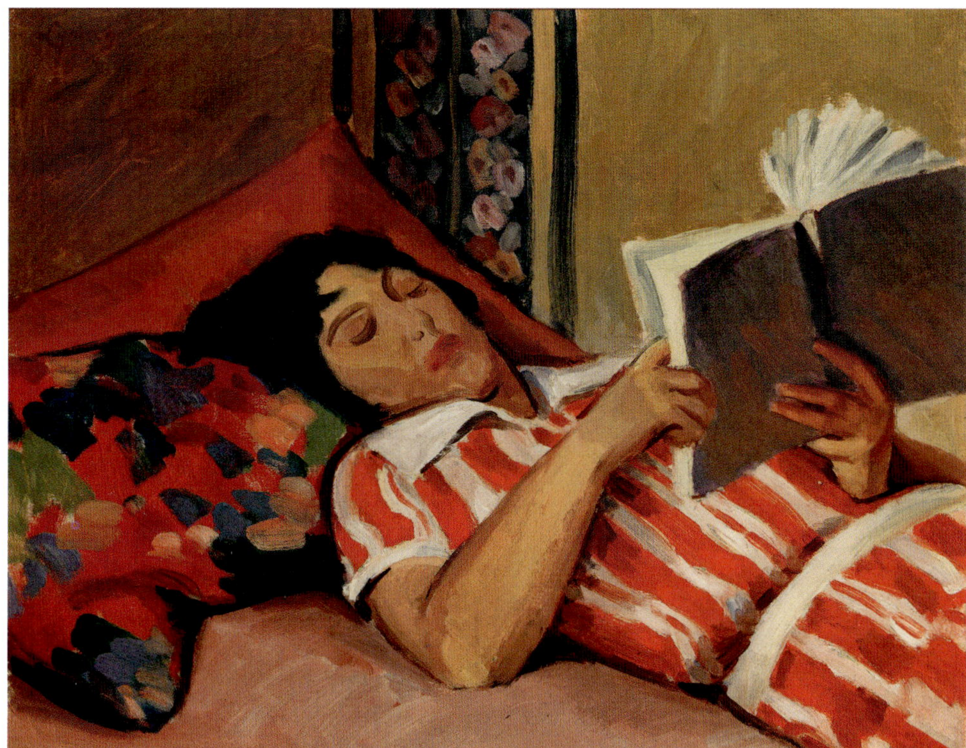

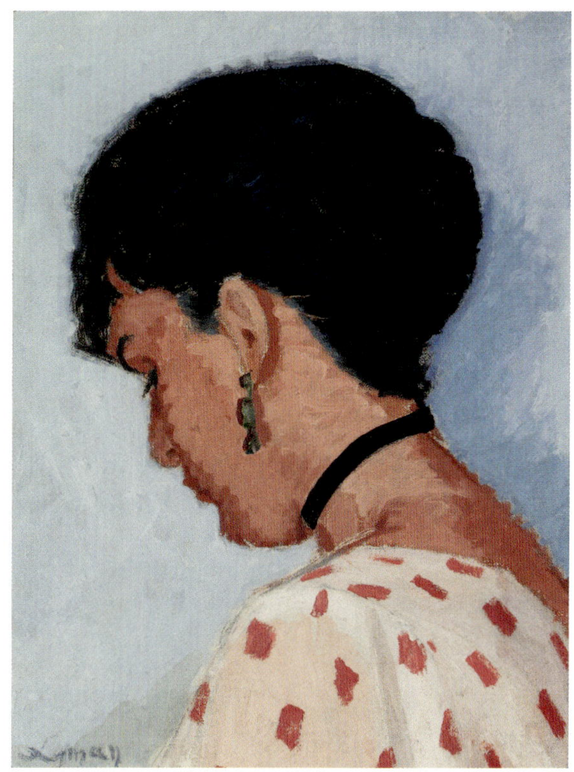

Lyman's portraits of women, such as *Portrait of Marcelle* (**CAT. 98**), are just as impenetrable. Marcelle holds a book that she is not reading and seems to stare straight ahead, into the distance. It is probably not inappropriate to liken this portrait to Matisse's *Woman in Green*, mentioned earlier. One could say the same of *Jori Smith in Costume* (**CAT. 91**), even though the rather extravagant "costume" makes us forget the simplicity of the pose. Nor does *The Book* (**CAT. 92**), showing a woman in a striped dress lying on her back and reading, give us access to the figure's inner world. In fact, this is true of all portrayals of readers absorbed in their book. Unaware of the world around them, completely absorbed in the imaginary world of their book, they become in fact a pure spectacle for the person looking at the painting, as they push the viewer out of their world.[41]

Thus, Lyman had a strong tendency to treat his figures with a code of pure exteriority. The paradox of this production, which seems fundamentally very close to abstraction, is that it came from a painter who, at least in his writings, was not very drawn—and that is putting it mildly—to the abstract art of his time. He saw abstraction as an easy way out, a way to avoid the solid construction of a figurative painting:

> You cannot get somewhere in figurative painting without having a truly unique personality; in abstract painting, unusual technique is enough. And all of the technical possibilities are quickly exploited, but one never exhausts the world, or nature. Don't answer that the non-figurative painter also draws on nature; he has ceased to do so long since, or at least it is much less important than the suggestions that come from the inventions of others, from comical documents about nature and from accidents in manipulation of materials.[42]

/ **CAT. 92** John Lyman
The Book
About 1925

/ **CAT. 93** John Lyman
Profile of Corinne
1913-1914

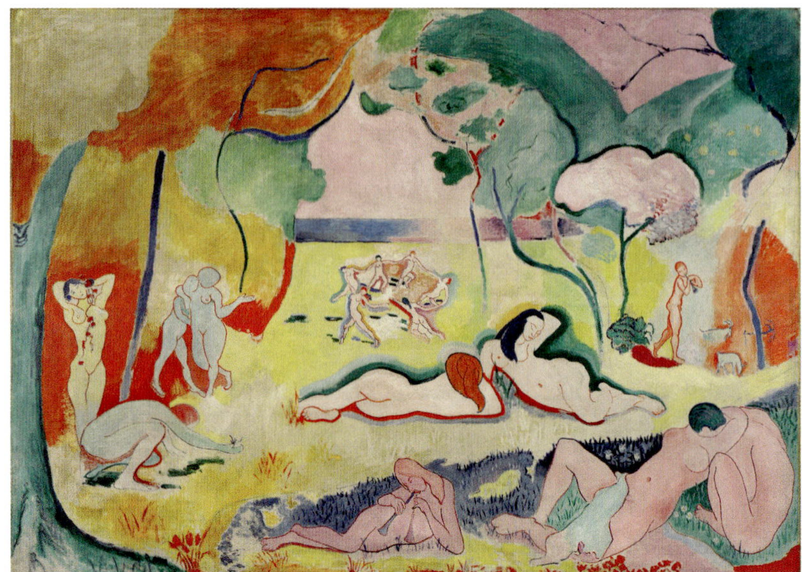

It goes without saying that these criticisms could be applied to figurative painters just as easily. Did Lyman's mistrust of abstraction blind him to his own efforts to abstract "accidents"—to use the old philosophical term—from the figure, preserving only its quality of ontological presence, so striking in his paintings of figures?

The same careful construction is found in the scenes in which Lyman features one or more full-length figures. One can see in *Indolent Youth* (CAT. 97) an attempt at a male odalisque. But, unlike Matisse's odalisque paintings, nothing is invested in the setting; the figure, defined by a firm, confident line, dominates. The same might apply to *Orientale* (CAT. 96), in the National Gallery of Canada collection, which presents a true odalisque. Again, the setting is almost bare, in spite of the tambourine and the striped sofa on which she is stretched out. There is none of the profusion of decorative fabrics, or allusion to Moroccan or Islamic art, that is found in Matisse's paintings of the same subject.[43]

In *Sunbathing II* (CAT. 114)—for which there exists a complete series of oil sketches preserved at the Musée national des beaux-arts du Québec (CATS. 114.01-09) and the Montreal Museum of Fine Arts—three figures seem immersed in their inner world, or inaccessible to us. The black woman in the foreground seems to be asleep; the blonde woman behind her turns her back to us; and in the background, the frame cuts off the face of the third figure. The rest of the painting is devoted to spatial organization through the diagonals of the docks. Implementation of the idea for this painting must have excited Lyman, if we judge by the preparatory sketches that have been preserved. These documents are interesting because they enable us to enter the painter's mind, so to speak, to attend to the many choices that he had and to his final decision-making process—in other words, to the creative spirit behind the very act of creation.

Finally, we can see in Lyman's *Bathers* (CAT. 94) a personal version of Matisse's *The Joy of Life* (FIG. 29)—except that Lyman did not turn to mythology to express the idea. For him, it was enough to imagine a scene with bathers.

/ **FIG. 29** Henri Matisse
The Joy of Life
1905-1906

/ **CAT. 94** John Lyman
Bathers
1933-1934

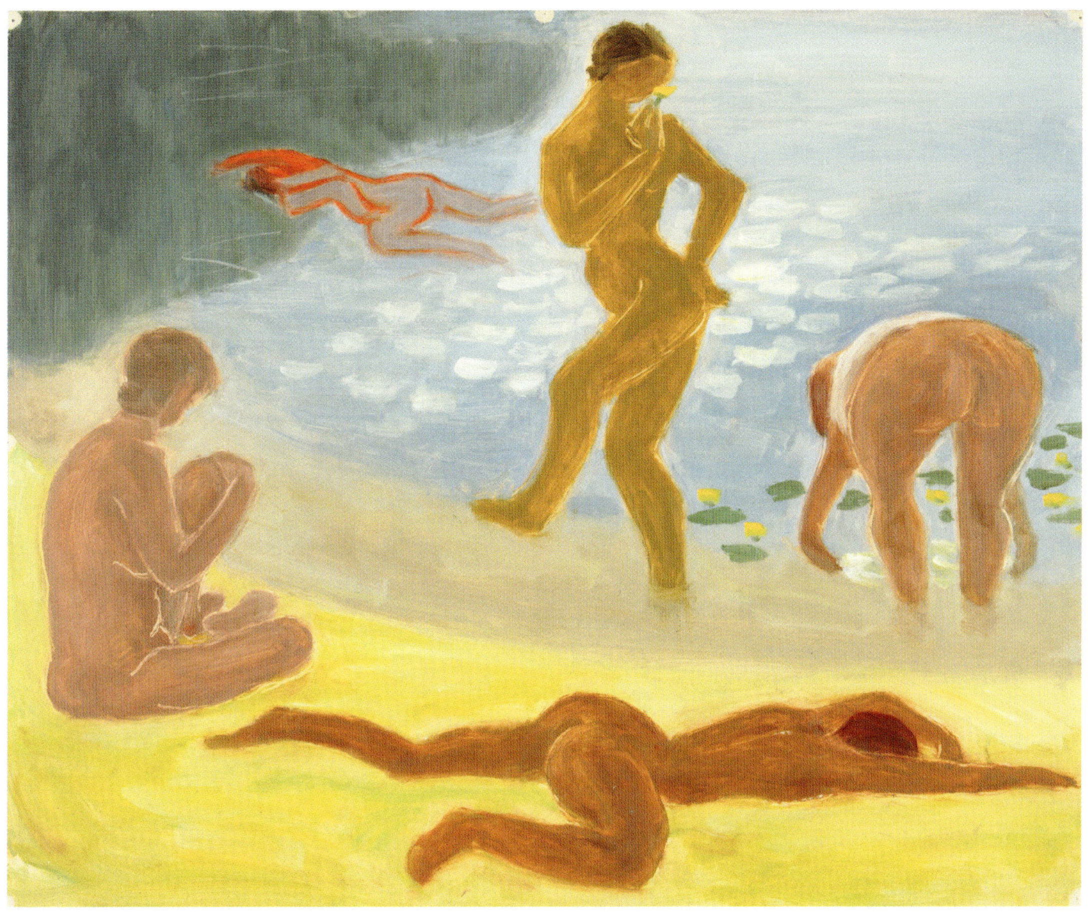

We can thus revisit Gilles Corbeil's skepticism regarding the links between Lyman and Matisse. The dialogue between the two painters must have been constant and profound, even if Lyman also felt Cézanne's influence from time to time. Lyman subscribed to Fauvism because of his taste for solidly constructed paintings, sacrificing the changing effects of luminosity, appreciating decorative effects and rejecting the picturesque, even in countries as exotic as Tunisia and Morocco. Following James Wilson Morrice, whom he admired greatly, Lyman embodied, in the development of Canadian painting, the "missing link" of Fauvism, between the Impressionism of Clarence Gagnon, the early-twentieth-century painter bitterly opposed to everything that had followed Impressionism, and the Cubism of Alfred Pellan, who had spent fourteen years in Paris in contact with all of the avant-gardes. Though remaining faithful to his own form of figuration, his taste for strict construction and his discreet colour palette, Lyman was able to understand that "living art," unlike "academic art," had to adopt the vocabulary of its times. His friendship with and respect for Paul-Émile Borduas, who produced non-figurative art starting in the 1940s—influenced by his reading of Breton and by Surrealism, a movement for which Lyman had little affinity—is proof of this. As the poet and great promoter of Automatisme, Claude Gauvreau, would remark, even the young painters gathered around Borduas saw in him a strong ally who would open to them the doors to the Contemporary Arts Society, which he had founded. Lyman's work, which presaged the advent of abstract art, remains the best affirmation of the need for construction in the figurative painting.

Notes

1. *John Lyman*, exhib. cat., essay by Gilles Corbeil (in French) (Montreal: The Montreal Museum of Fine Arts, 1963). This catalogue was published on the occasion on an exhibition held at Montreal Museum of Fine Arts from September 5 to September 29, 1963, then at the National Gallery of Canada from October 4 to October 27, and finally at the Art Gallery of Hamilton from November 8 to December 1.

2. I was not able to find the article by A. Y. Jackson, or Lyman's reply, but it was a position that Jackson had always taken, especially leading up to his excursion with L. Harris to the Far North in 1931.

3. Without referring directly to Jackson's writing, Lyman wrote in 1932, "In dealing with the painting of Canadians it is quite customary to create an inherent confusion in terms between the two distinct ideas of the manifestations of Canadian nature, and the manifestations of nature to a Canadian, of the physical representation of Canada and the Canadianism of an artist" (*The Canadian Forum* [Toronto], vol. 12, no. 140 [May 1932], pp. 313-314). I am grateful to M. Grandbois for this valuable reference.

4. Fernand Dansereau, *John Lyman, peintre*, film, National Film Board, 1959, 28 min 12 s.

5. Henri Matisse, "Notes of a Painter," in Alfred H. Barr, *Matisse: His Art and His Public* (London: Secker & Warburg, 1975), p. 122. First published under the title "Notes d'un peintre," in *La Grande Revue*, December 25, 1908.

6. Dansereau, *John Lyman, peintre*.

7. John Lyman, "Art. The Eastern Group – French and Dutch Moderns – At the Art Association," *The Montrealer*, December 1, 1938.

8. Corbeil, in *John Lyman*.

9. John Lyman, "Adieu, Matisse," *Canadian Art*, vol. 12, no. 2 (winter 1955), pp. 44-45.

10. I am grateful to Wanda de Guébriant, director of the Archives Matisse, for sharing this correspondence with me.

11. I am grateful to M. Grandbois for these details on *Autumn Landscape: Forest of Fontainebleau*, recently on view at Christie's and acquired by collectors a few months before the major exhibition *The Steins Collect: Matisse, Picasso, and the Parisian Avant-Garde*, presented at the Grand Palais in Paris, the San Francisco Museum of Art, and the Metropolitan Museum of Art in New York, between October 2011 and June 2012.

12. Letter from John Lyman to his father, [Paris], November 15, 1909.

13. Philip Hendy, *Matthew Smith* (Harmondsworth, Middlesex, England: Penguin Books, 1944), p. 7.

14. Malcolm Yorke, *Matthew Smith: His Life and Reputation* (London/Boston: Faber and Faber, 1997), p. 68.

15. Letter from John Lyman to his father, Paris, Thursday, April 14, [1910], John Lyman Fonds, Bibliothèque et Archives nationales du Québec, Montreal.

16. As Hilary Spurling notes in *Matisse the Master – A Life of Henri Matisse: The Conquest of Colour, 1909-1954* (New York: Knopf, 2005), pp. 12-14, regarding Sarah Stein.

17. At least during the time when Lyman attended the academy. The previous year, Matisse saw his students every Saturday.

18. Probably rather the Lycée Victor-Duruy; the Lycée Buffon is in the 15th arrondissement.

19. Henri Matisse, *Écrits et propos sur l'art*, introduced by Dominique Fourcade (Paris: Hermann, 1992 [1972]), pp. 85-86.

20. The blue version of *The Dessert* was exhibited at the 1908 Salon d'Automne as *Decorative Panel for a Dining Room*. Known through a black-and-white photograph reproduced in Barr, *Matisse*, p. 344. Barr also reproduced in this book a section of the textile that was used for the background of the painting, as well as several other canvases, including *Portrait of Greta Moll*. See Hilary Spurling and Jack Flam, *Matisse, His Art and His Textiles: The Fabric of Dreams* (London: Royal Academy of Arts, 2004).

21. See Barr, *Matisse*, p. 132 ff, and the reproductions of the two versions of *Nasturtiums with "Dance,"* pp. 382 and 383.

22. "Mr. John G. Lyman in defense of Post Impressionist Painting," *The Star* (Montreal), May 17, 1913.

23. Letter from Lyman to his father, May 20, 1910, in *Inédits de John Lyman*, texts selected and annotated by Hedwidge Asselin (Montreal: Bibliothèque nationale du Québec, 1980), p. 193.

24. Lyman, "Adieu, Matisse," p. 45.

25. Alfred H. Barr mentioned that two of them had already been taken into American collections: one to the Cleveland Museum of Art and the other to the Baltimore Museum of Art. See Barr, *Matisse*, p. 210.

26. Jack Cowart, "The Place of Silvered Light: An Expanded, Illustrated Chronology of Matisse in the South of France, 1916-1932," in Jack Cowart and Dominique Fourcade, *Henri Matisse: The Early Years in Nice, 1916-1930* (Washington/New York: National Gallery of Art/Harry N. Abrams, 1987), pp. 28-32.

27. Lyman, "Art. The Eastern Group," pp. 32-33.

28. John Lyman, "Peintres modernes français et hollandais," quoted without further reference in Paul Dumas, *Lyman* (Montreal: L'Arbre, "Art vivant" series, 1945), pp. 31-32 (translation in original); it was probably from his article "Art. The Eastern Group."

29. Lyman, "Adieu, Matisse," pp. 44-45.

30. Louise Déry devoted her master's thesis to Lyman's reviews in *The Montrealer*. See Louise Déry, "L'influence de la critique d'art de John Lyman dans le milieu artistique québécois," master's thesis, Quebec City, Université Laval, 1982.

31. Published in *Inédits de John Lyman*.

32. In her thesis, Déry counted Lyman's references to Matisse in his articles for *The Montrealer—*fewer than ten—and noted the works by Matisse reproduced: *Large Cliff – Two Rays*, a painting executed in the summer of 1920 in Étretat (cat. 69), in his article of October 30, 1930; *Pianist and Still Life*, from 1924 (Kunstmuseum, Bern), in his article of October 15, 1937; *Window at Tangier*, from 1912, in his article of February 15, 1938; and *Odalisque in Red Trousers*, in his article of December 1, 1938. Lyman had probably seen this last painting during his visits to Matisse's home in Nice.

33. Lyman, "Art: The Eastern Group," p. 33.

34. *Inédits de John Lyman*, p. 41.

35. John Lyman, "*Dufy, Improvisatore* chez Scott & Sons," *The Montrealer*, February 15, 1939, pp. 20-21.

36. See Dennis Reid, *Le Groupe des Sept/The Group of Seven*, exhib. cat. (Ottawa: National Gallery of Canada, 1970), p. 32.

37. Postcard dated April 6, 1912, Archives Marquet, quoted in Jack Cowart, ed., *Matisse in Morocco: The Paintings and Drawings, 1912-1913*, exhib. cat. (Washington: National Gallery of Art, 1990), p. 52, note 8.

38. Postcard dated April 2, 1912, Archives Marquet, quoted in Cowart, ibid., note 9.

39. In using the term "wild nature" in 1912, Lyman could not have been referring to the Group of Seven, whose fame began to spread only in 1920.

40. A *zaouia* is a Muslim religious building.

41. Here, I am following the ideas of Michael Fried, *Absorption and Theatricality: Painting and Beholder in the Age of Diderot* (Chicago/London: University of Chicago Press, 1988 [1980]), who studied the theme of reading. See also Stefan Bollmann, *Reading Women* (London/New York: Merrell, 2005), more relevant to this painting.

42. *Inédits de John Lyman*, p. 156.

43. See, for comparison, *Nude on a Yellow Sofa* (cat. 71), a Matisse presented in our exhibition. Matisse closes the background of his composition with a four-section screen with floral motifs.

DECORATIVE PAINTING
PORTFOLIO

The portraits, still lifes and nudes presented in this section all share the preoccupation with decorative harmonies that characterizes studio painting. Henri Matisse considered the terms "expression" and "decoration" to be synonymous. Fascinated by Persian carpets and Oriental fabrics, by the shape of objects and the contrasts between textures, he saw composition as "the art of arranging in a decorative manner the diverse elements at the painter's command to express his feelings."

In a decorative painting approach, nothing is incidental or unconnected, everything sustains the whole and is sustained by it. This conception is diametrically opposed to the reductive quality that the notion of decorative painting has today.

The principle defended by Matisse is in fact reflected in all the works in this catalogue, regardless of genre. The decorative approach renounces realism and naturalism—even Impressionism—to capture the essence of form, or what the painter saw "below the surface, beyond appearances, what is permanent and durable," John Lyman remarked, following his master.

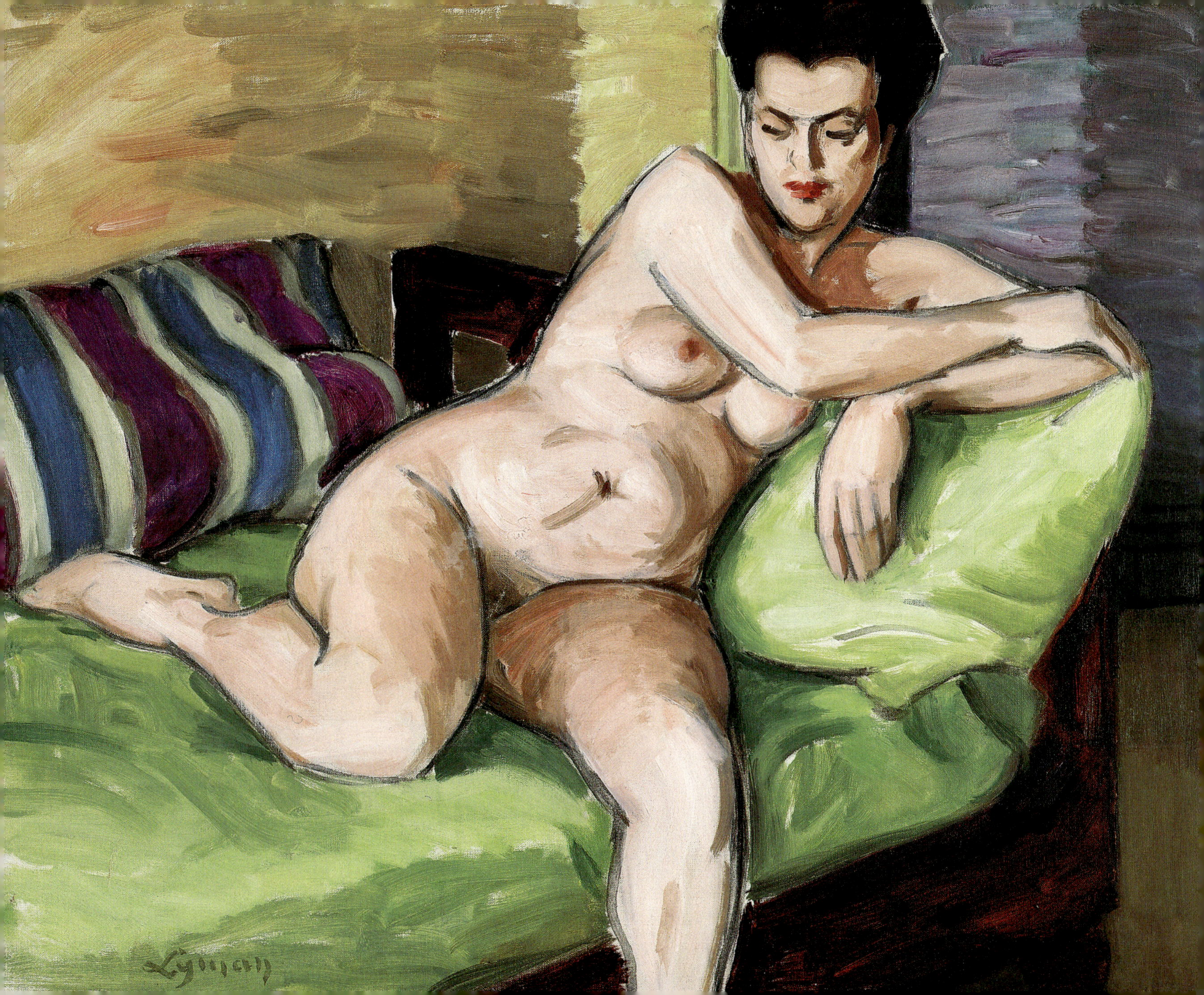
Lyman

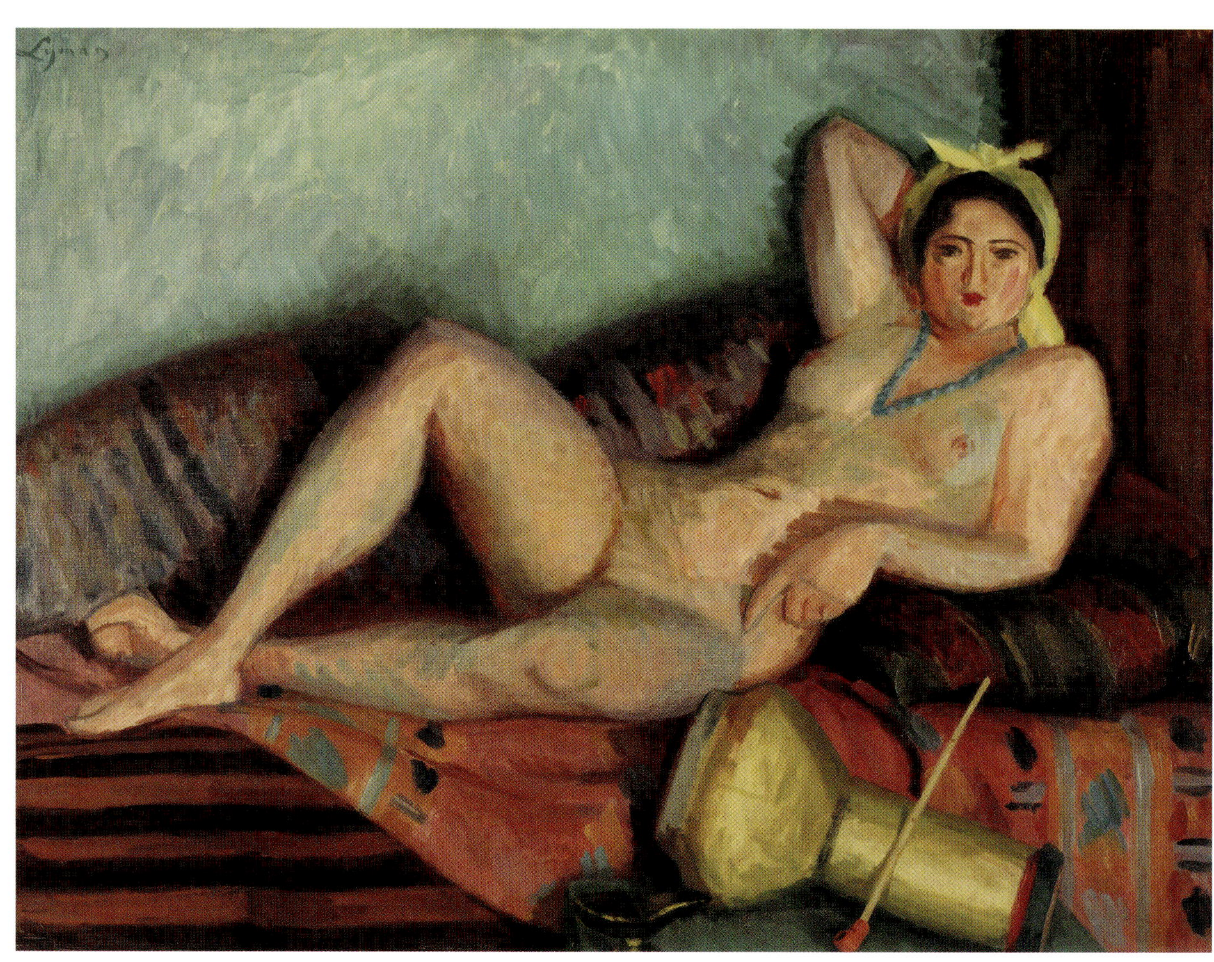

/ CAT. 96 John Lyman
Orientale
About 1924

/ CAT. 97 John Lyman
Indolent Youth
About 1922

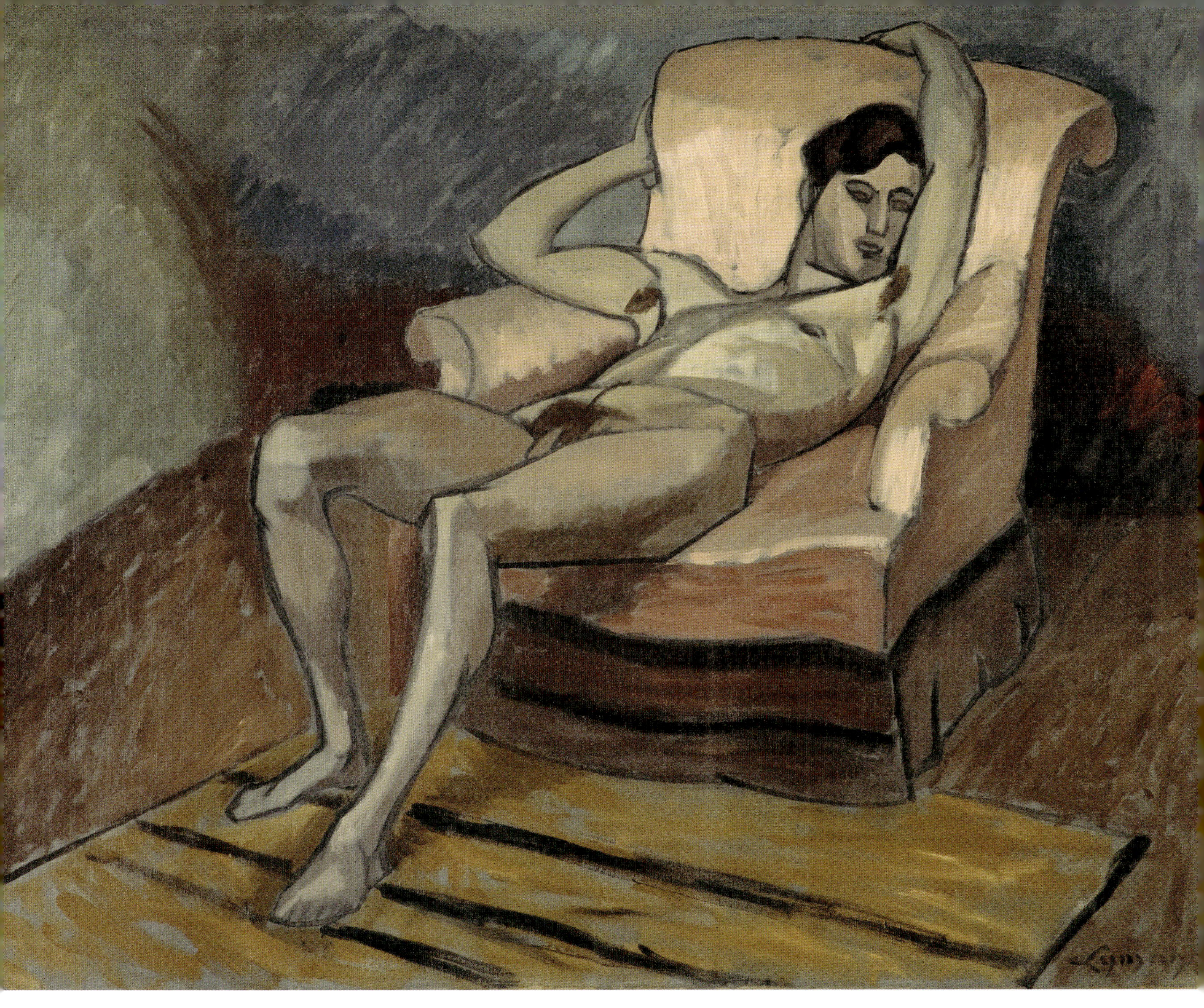

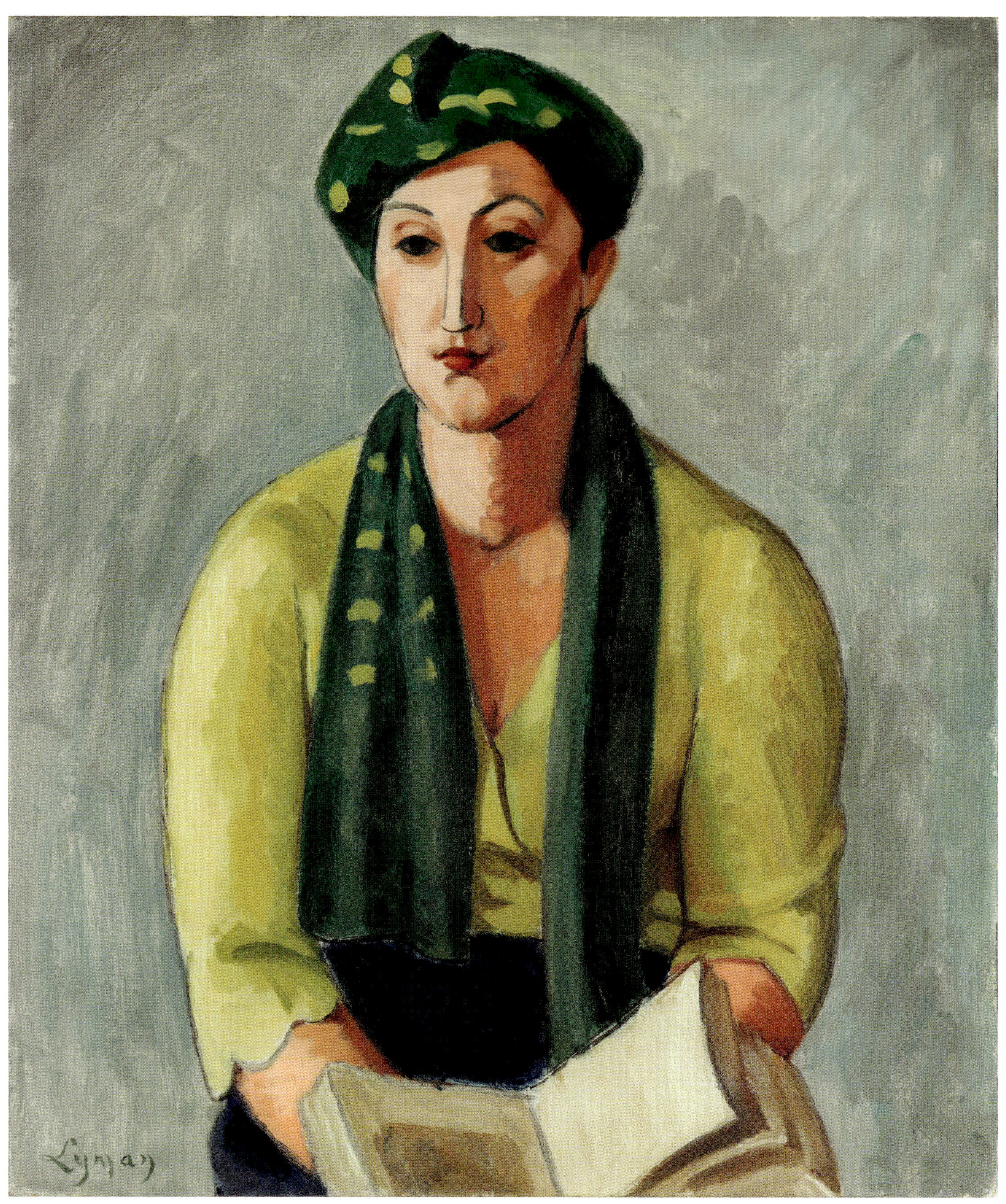

Lyman

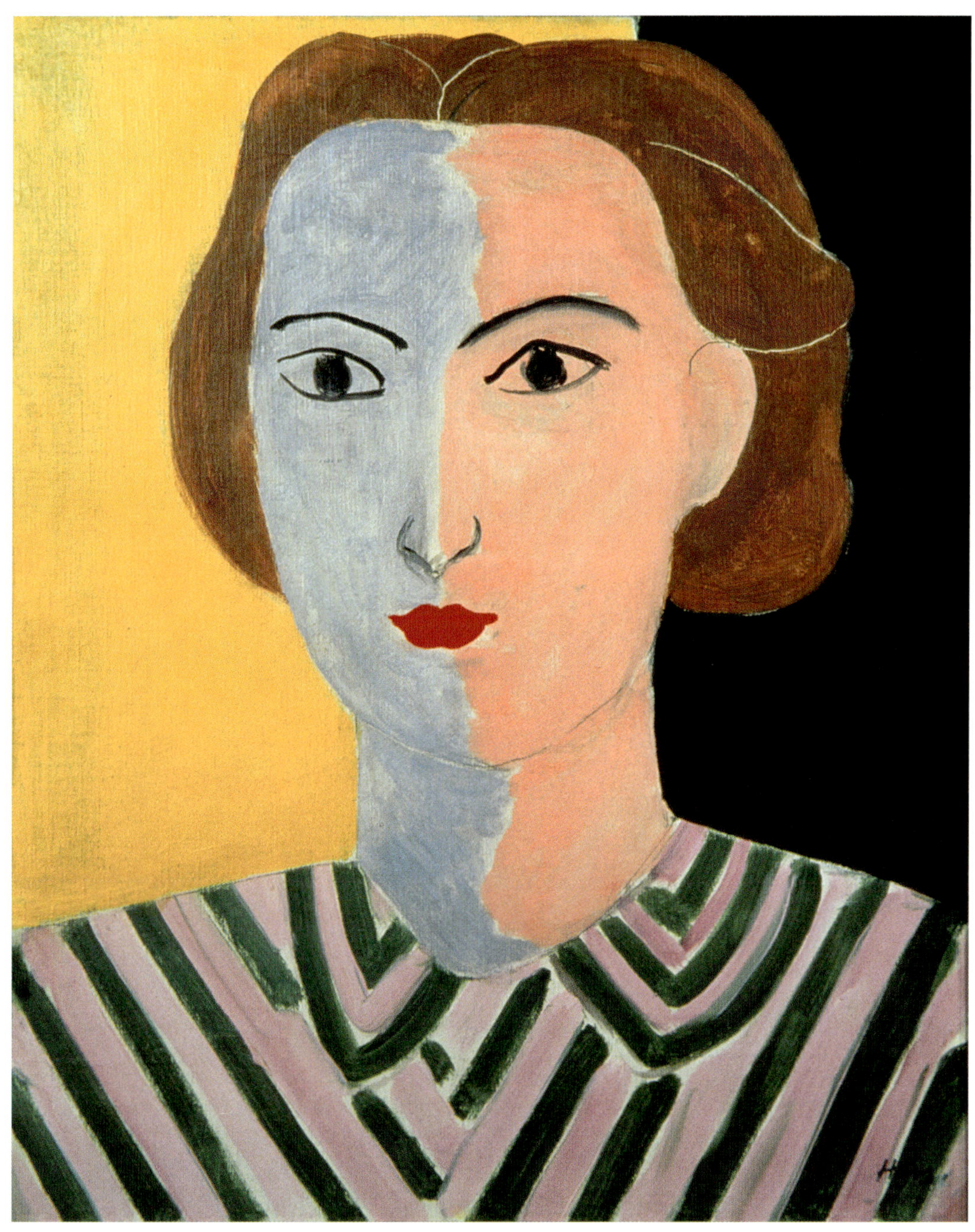

/ CAT. 98 John Lyman
Portrait of Marcelle
About 1935

/ CAT. 99 Henri Matisse
Portrait with Pink and Blue Face
1936-1937

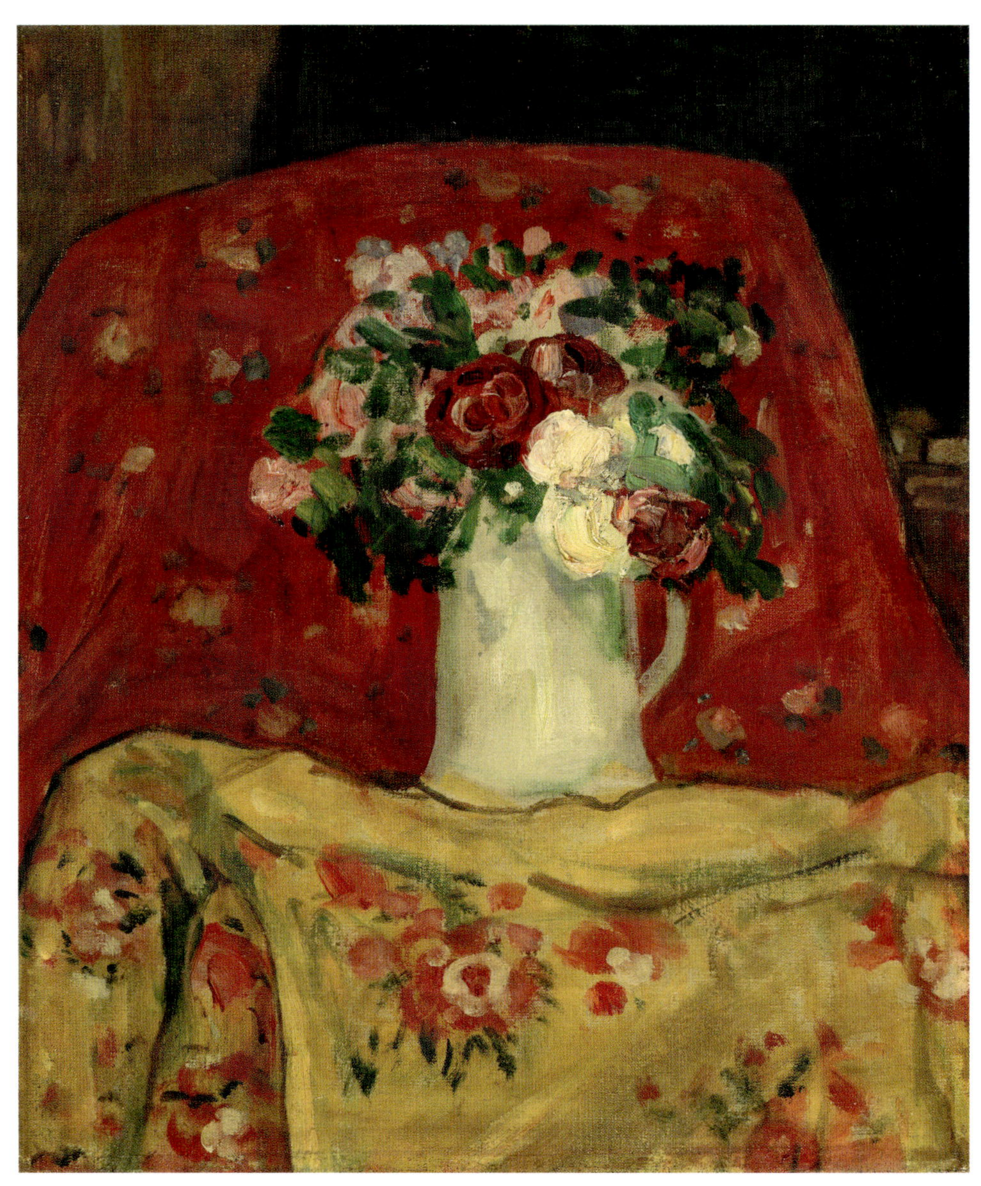

/ CAT. 100 James W. Morrice
Flowers
About 1911-1912

/ CAT. 101 James W. Morrice
Nude with a Feather
About 1911

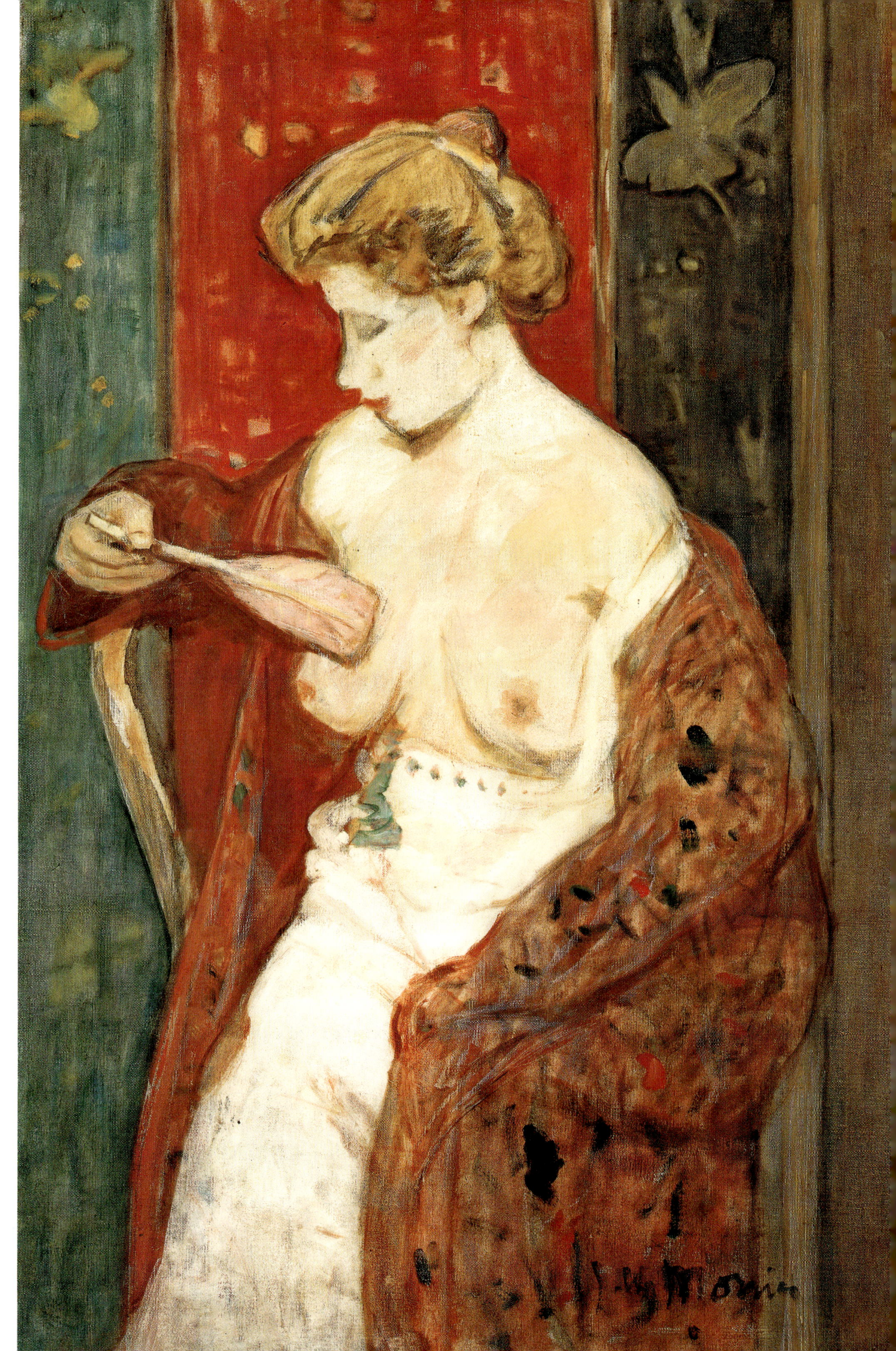

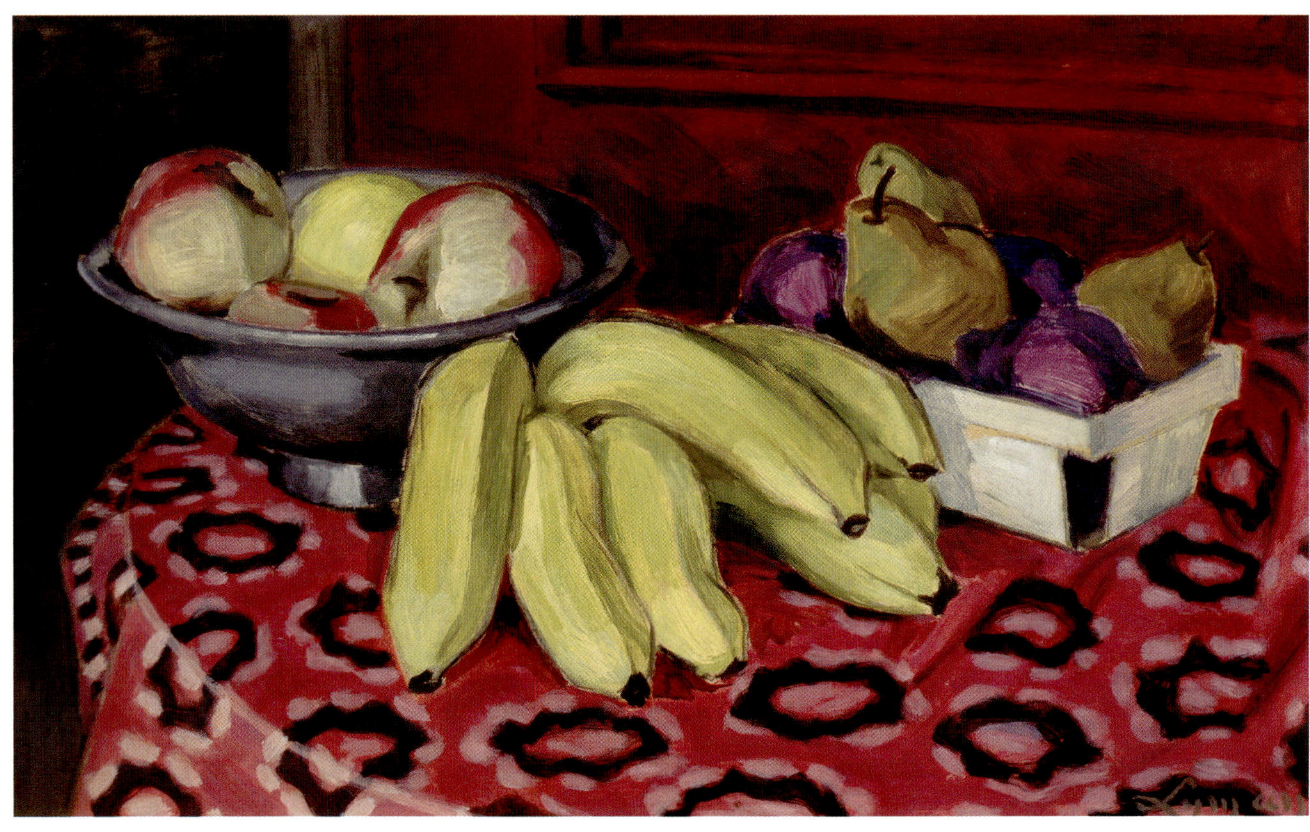

/ **CAT. 102** John Lyman
Still Life with Fruit
1946

/ **CAT. 103** Henri Matisse
Anemones and Peach Blossoms
1944

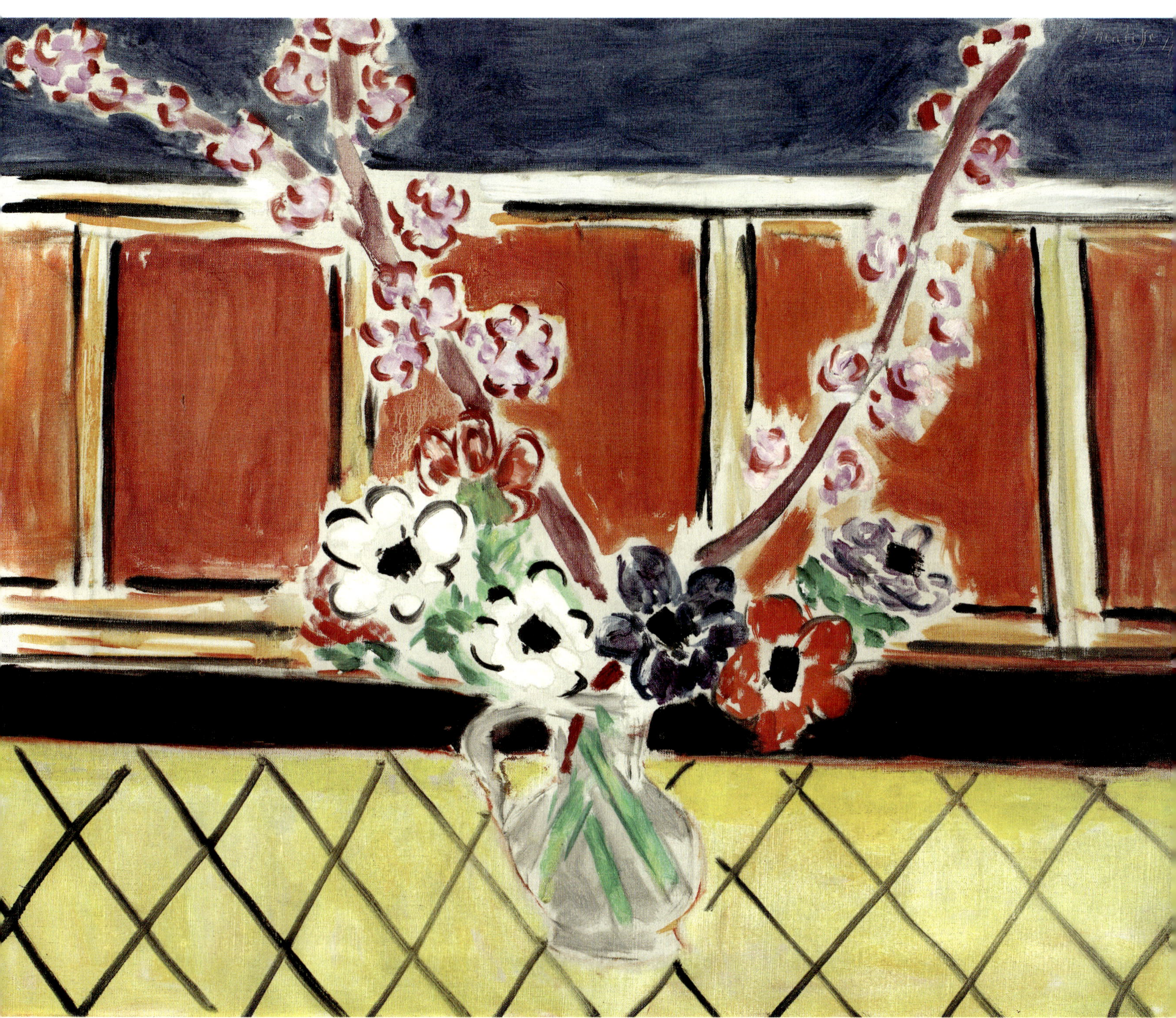

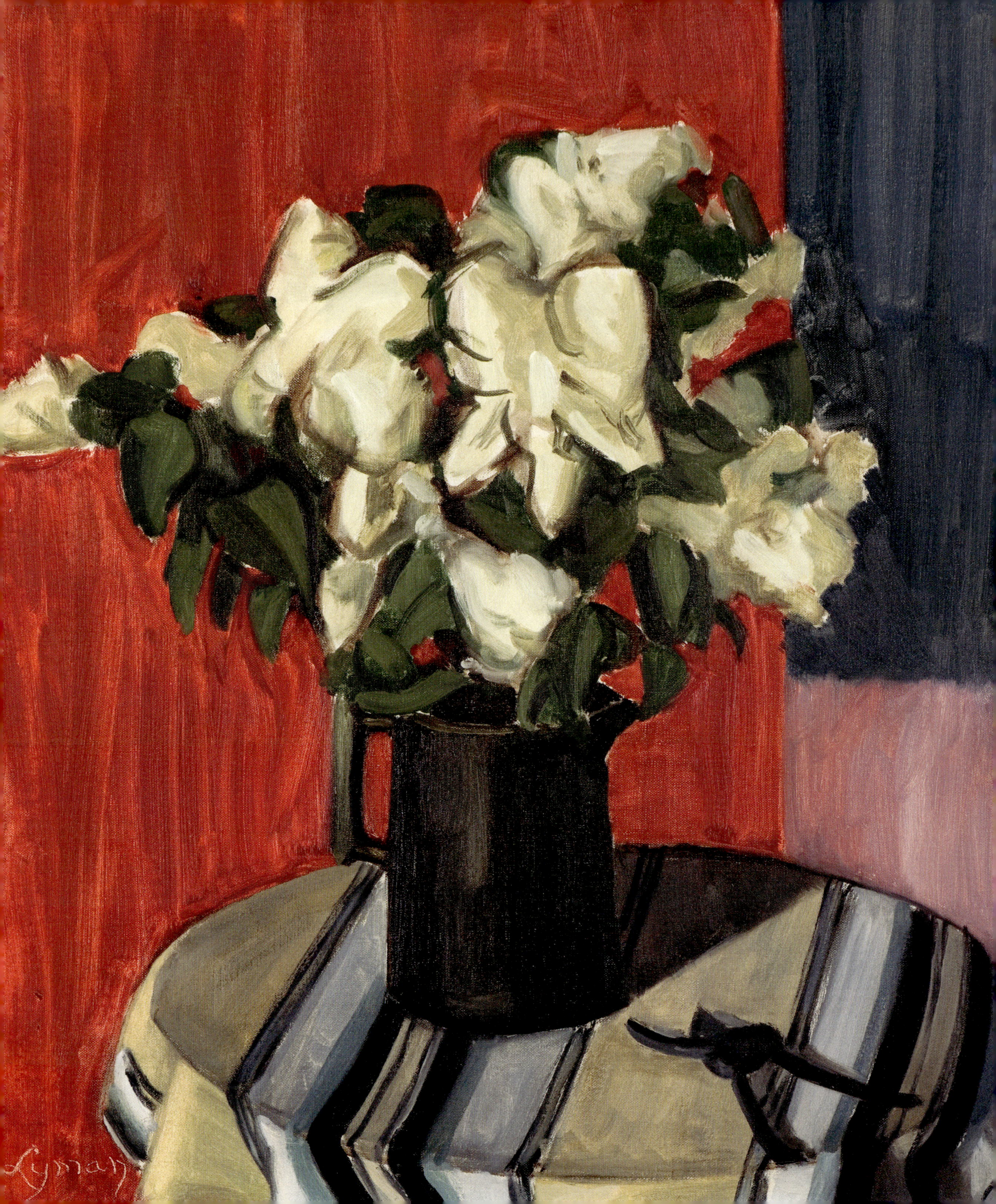
Lyman

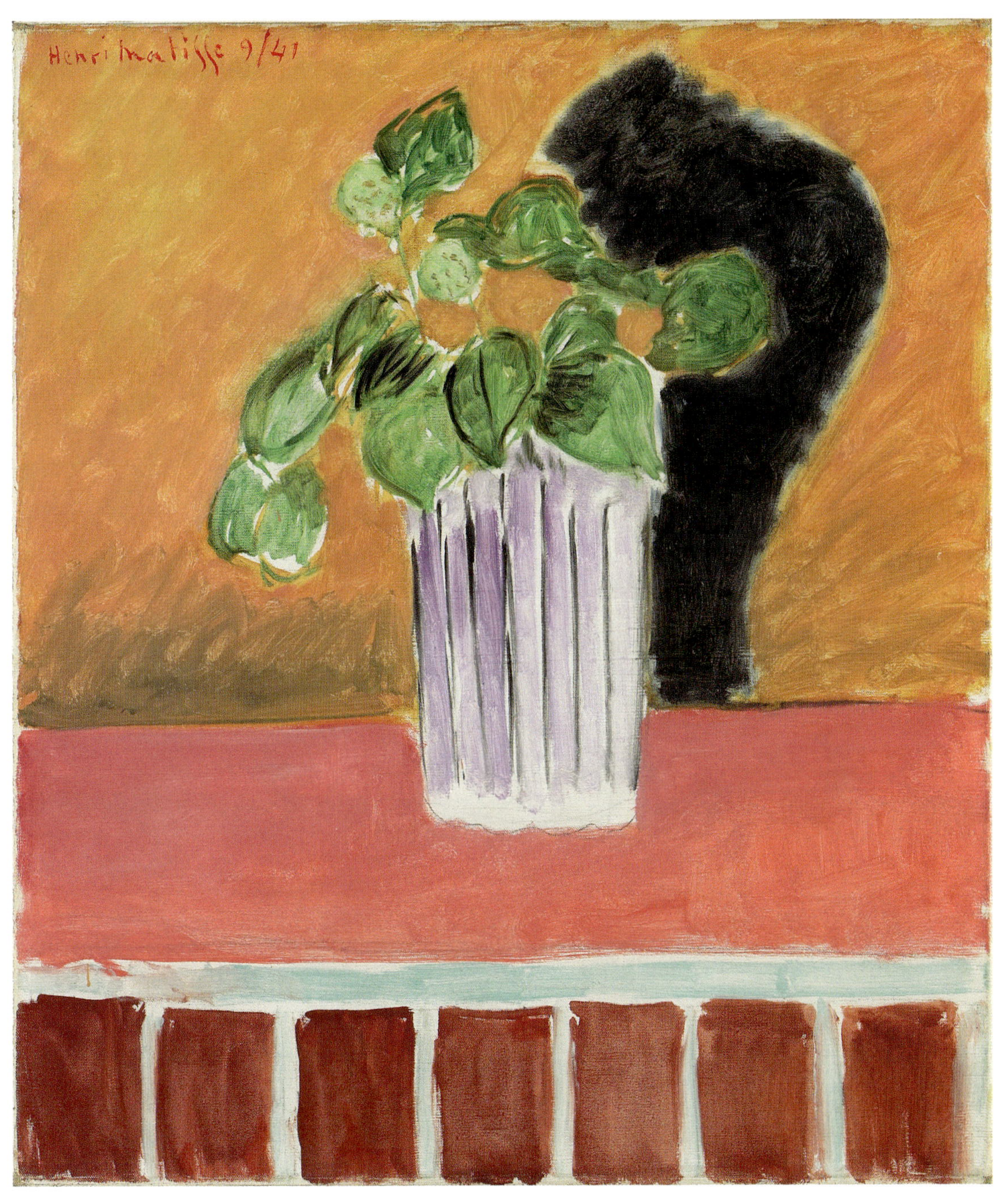

/ **CAT. 104** John Lyman
White Lilacs
1954

/ **CAT. 105** Henri Matisse
Ivy Branch
1941

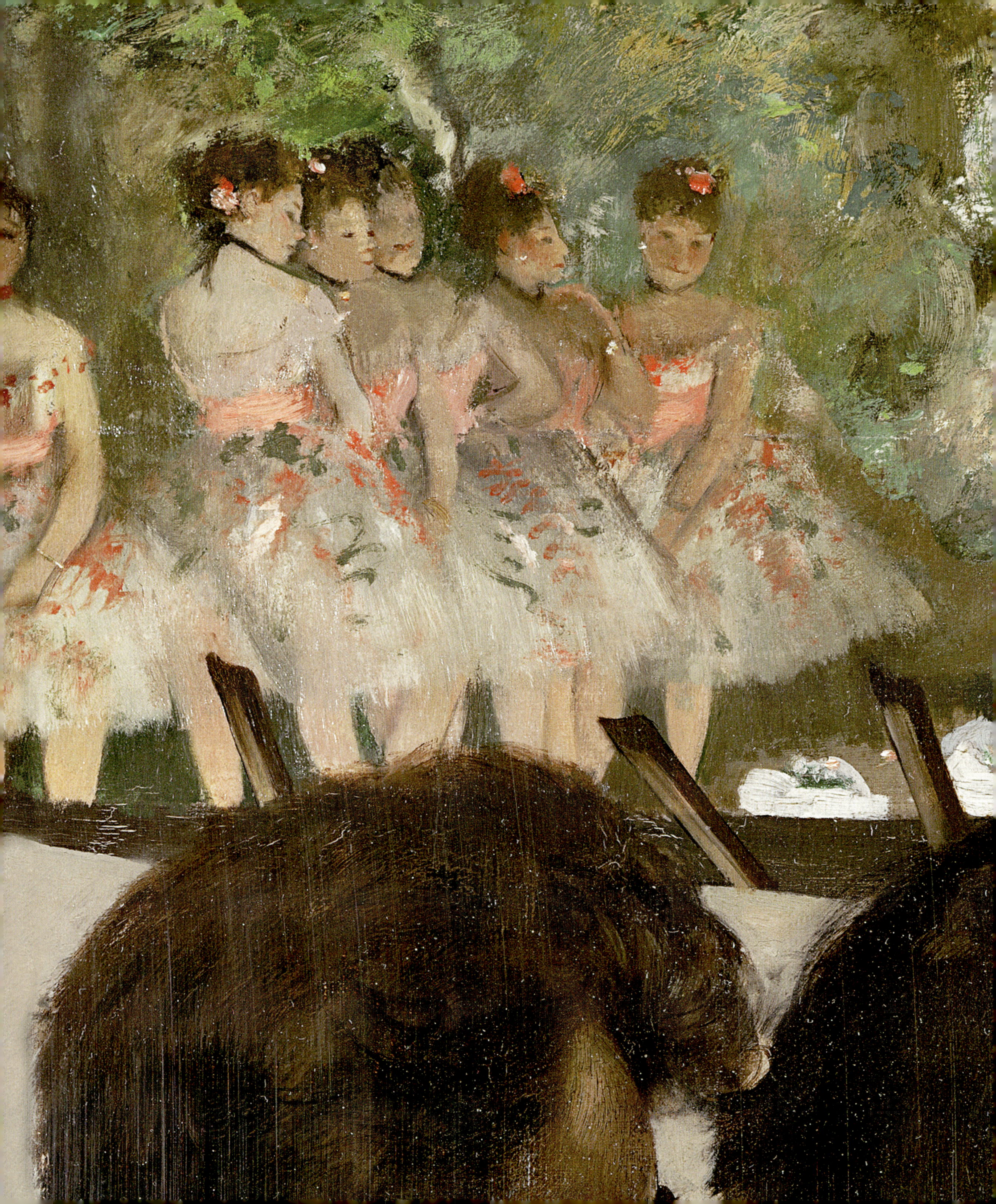

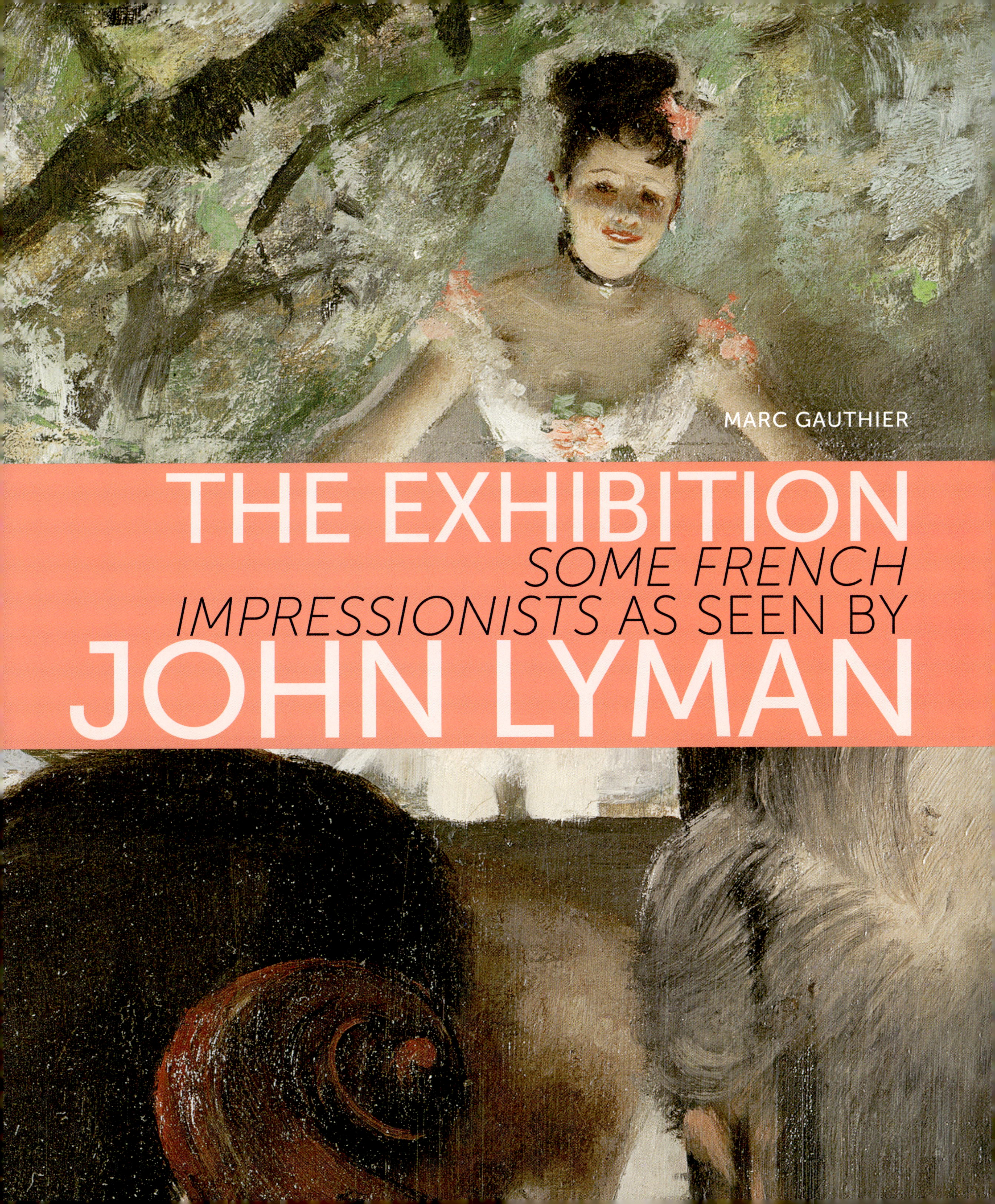

MARC GAUTHIER

THE EXHIBITION
SOME FRENCH IMPRESSIONISTS AS SEEN BY
JOHN LYMAN

In an interview with Guy Viau in 1959, John Lyman talked about his early career.[1] Asked about "a circumstance" that may have encouraged him to become a painter, he recalled an Impressionist exhibition organized in Montreal a half-century earlier. The impact had been immediate: "It really moved me. For me, it was a new vision, a new reality. I took anything, book illustrations, photographs, and after that, I made paintings with the colour decomposed into separate marks. I was burning up with it. I think that's what truly got me started."[2] The exhibition to which Lyman was referring was called *Some French Impressionists*. Presented at the Art Association of Montreal during the last two weeks of February 1906, it included twenty-nine canvases painted by twelve artists associated with Impressionism, including Édouard Manet, Claude Monet and Auguste Renoir.[3]

There are many questions about this exhibition. Which paintings did Lyman see in 1906 that excited him so much? Why was Paul Durand-Ruel, the dealer in Impressionist works, interested in presenting this group of paintings in Montreal? Was it a first experiment with the genre? Finally, although these works had a definite impact on the young Lyman, how did the public and Montreal art critics react to the event? Here, I will attempt to provide some answers to these questions.

THE PAINTINGS ON DISPLAY

When Lyman visited the Art Association of Montreal galleries in February 1906, two exhibitions were being presented. On display in the "old gallery" were vases, pottery and two stained-glass windows by Tiffany, and in the "new gallery" were works by Impressionist painters.[4] *Some French Impressionists* offered an overview of the movement, presenting two or three paintings by each artist. These works had a huge effect on the nineteen-year-old Lyman. As he admired the portraits, land-scapes, interiors, and racetrack and opera scenes, his view of painting changed. I shall try to better understand the event, even though only a few of these canvases have been identified with certainty.

Previous double page:

/ **FIG. 33 (DETAIL)** Edgar Degas
Orchestra Musicians
1871-1874

Manet was represented by two works painted a few months apart. His *Portrait of Faure as Hamlet* was part of a series of portraits painted in the Spanish manner, in which a standing figure emerges from a tonal background. The bright colours are concentrated on the face, accentuating its expressiveness. In the other work, *Before the Mirror* (FIG. 30), Manet used a different technique. The motif of a woman at her toilette, recurrent in his paintings, enabled him to portray his model in a moment of privacy. On the chromatic level, he used a light, luminous palette. Most of the volumes are created by masses of colour, although lines accentuate certain forms (the hollow of the right hip, the right hand, the contour of the mirror frame). The broad brushstrokes in the mirror only suggest the reflection.[5]

Three of Monet's paintings were in the Montreal exhibition. *Cliff Walk at Pourville* (1882, location unknown) portrayed Val Saint-Nicolas, situated in the Norman town of Pourville, near Dieppe.[6] The painter used pure colours to portray his subject. Massive black triangles create zones of shadow, and their uniformity

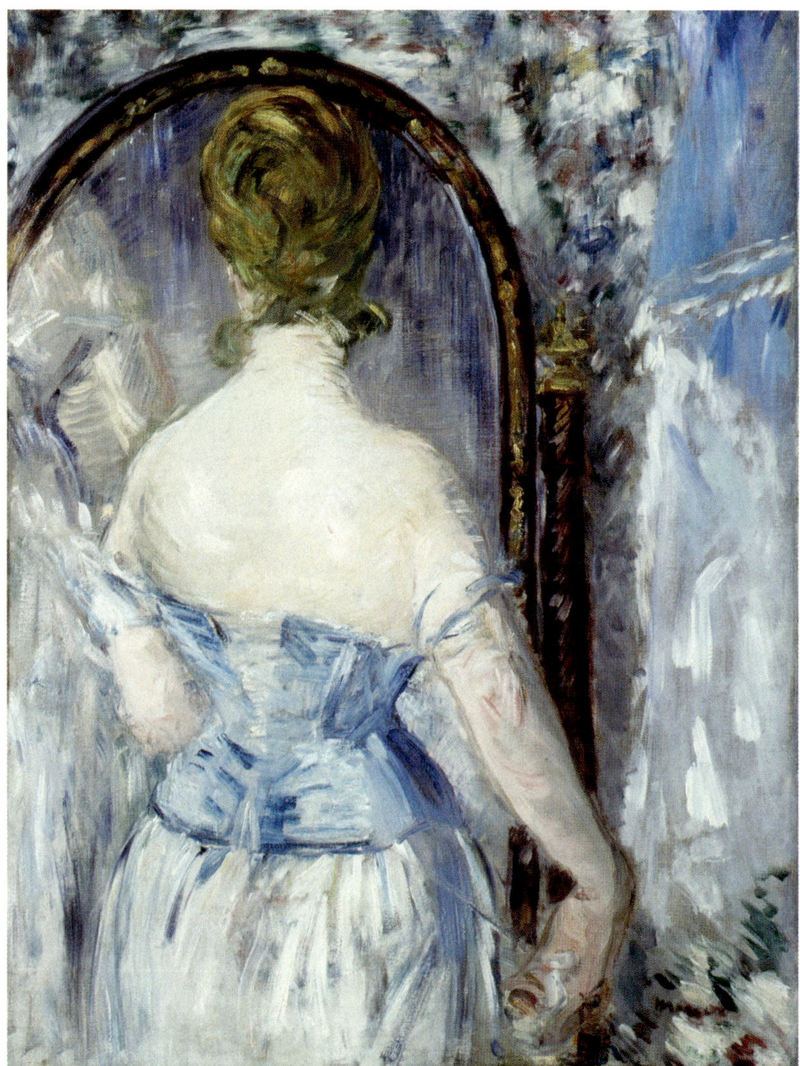

/ **FIG. 30** Édouard Manet
Before the Mirror
1876

/ **FIG. 31** Auguste Renoir
Fog on Guernsey
1883

/ **FIG. 32** Camille Pissarro
**The Saint-Sever Bridge,
Rouen: Mist**
1896

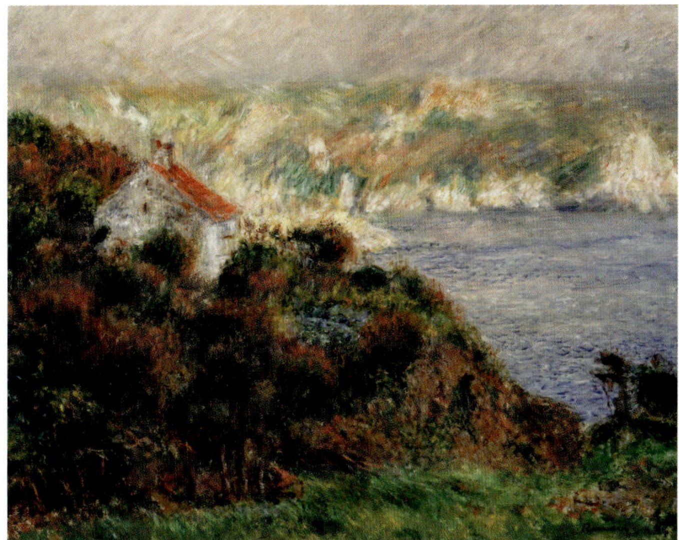
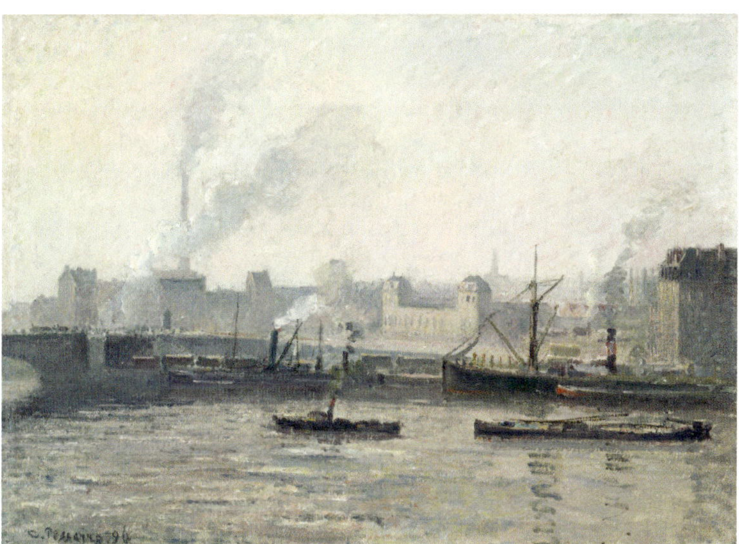

accentuates the flattened foreground. *Islands at Port-Villez* (1883, private coll., France) was painted a few months later.[7] The third painting had a different dynamic. Part of a series on views of London, *The Houses of Parliament, Sunset* (1903, private coll., United States) offered an example of Monet's latest production.[8]

Two reading scenes and a landscape by Renoir were on display in Montreal. In *Fog on Guernsey* **(FIG. 31)**, painted during a stay on the Channel island in the summer of 1883, Renoir revisited a subject popular among artists, Moulin Huet Bay.[9] Three paintings by Camille Pissarro were also on view: *Orchard in Louveciennes, Spring* (1870, location unknown), *The Fields of Éragny, Flowering Apple Tree* (1885, private coll., Japan) and *The Saint-Sever Bridge, Rouen: Mist* **(FIG. 32)**.[10] In these landscapes, the painter used very visible brushstrokes. The palette is light and luminous in the first two paintings and darker in the last one. In addition, two paintings by Edgar Degas were shown in the exhibition. A scene of a horse race is identified by the generic title *Race Horses*. The opera theme in the other painting is evoked by its title, *Orchestra Musicians* **(FIG. 33)**.[11] Finally, Mary Cassatt[12] and Alfred Sisley[13] completed this representative survey of French Impressionism. In these two cases, stylistic affinities took precedence over the artists' country of origin, as one was American, and the other English.[14]

The other paintings in the exhibition have not been identified. We know only that ten paintings by five painters—Albert André, Georges D'Espagnat, Gustave Loiseau, Maxime Maufra and Henry Moret—were presented. Supported by the art dealer Paul Durand-Ruel and following the Impressionist manner, these painters were considered by Monet and Renoir to be their artistic heirs.[15] Most of them lived in Brittany and normally painted canvases dominated by bright colours. This production, though not without merit, remained on the margins of the new currents in art that emerged in France at the turn of the twentieth century. The painter Émile Bernard described Henry Moret as "a peaceful, sincere revolutionary"[16]—an expression that could apply to all of these artists. Due to a lack of reviews in the

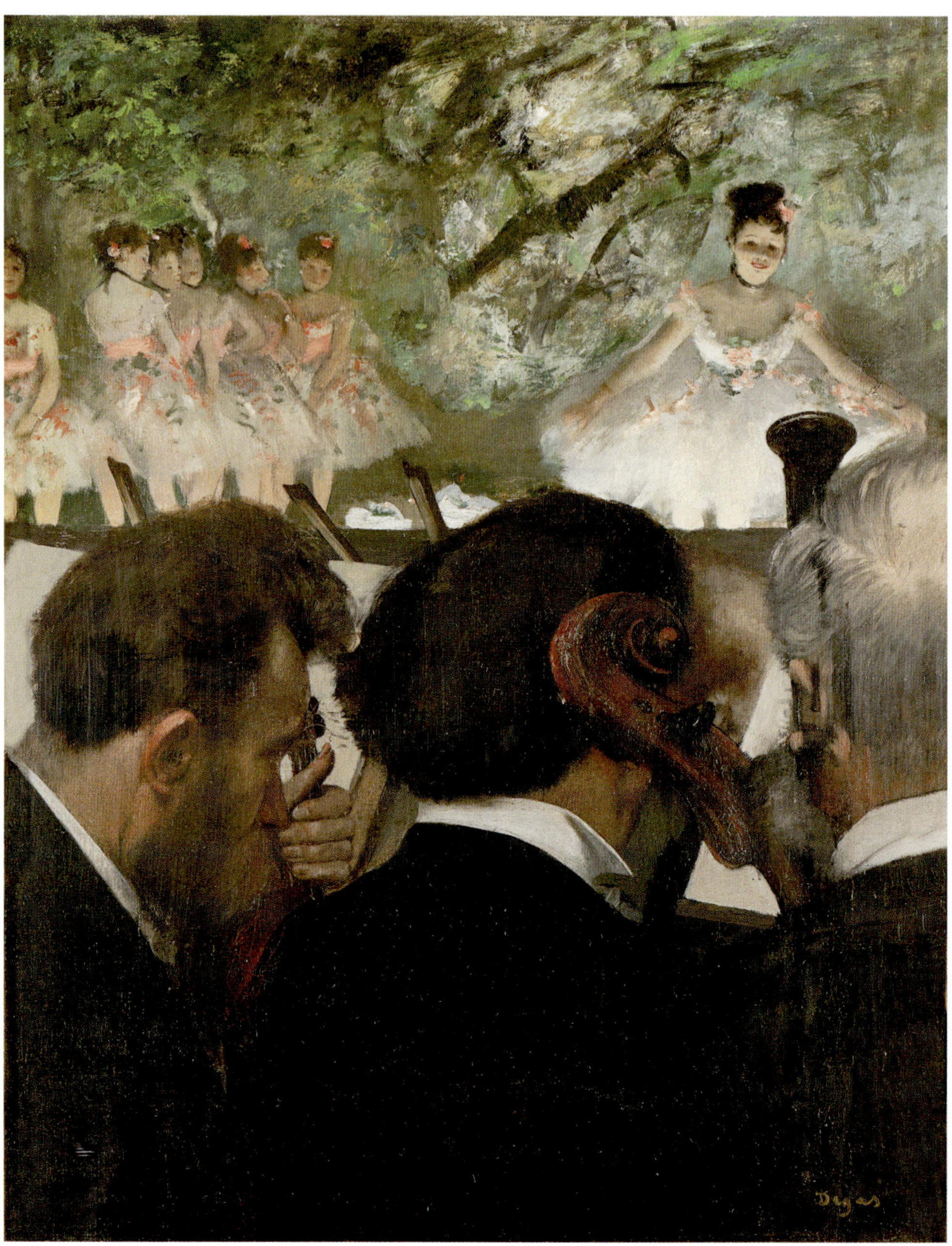

local press and the current state of the research, it is risky to try to identify which of their works were exhibited in Montreal. There is a single exception: one journalist considered Moret's *Cliffs near Morgat, Finistère* a "gem"[17] in the exhibition. It was described in greater detail, and I shall return to this.

A FIRST IN MONTREAL?

When interviewed decades after the event, Lyman expressed the view that *Some French Impressionists* had been an anomaly in the Montreal art landscape: "It was truly curious in Montreal at the time, because it was really the first time that we became aware of this school here."[18] This statement is not strictly accurate. In fact, this

/ **FIG. 33** Edgar Degas
Orchestra Musicians
1871-1874

was not the first appearance of Impressionism in the city; there had been French Impressionist works in Montreal since the early 1890s. The first Canadian to acquire an Impressionist canvas was Sir George A. Drummond, an influential businessman associated with the Bank of Montreal, who made his purchase in Europe on June 27, 1889.[19] Montreal collections were enhanced with several more Impressionist paintings between 1891 and 1911.[20]

Occasionally, these paintings left the premises of their owners—gathered in the Art Association of Montreal—to appear in loan exhibitions.[21] Before 1906, impressionist works were displayed twice in such events, in 1895 and 1897.[22] On the other hand, Sir William Van Horne, vice-president and general manager of the Canadian Pacific Railway, purchased works and quickly resold them, in 1892, without ever having them displayed in public.[23] The low profile of Impressionism in Montreal raises important questions about the popularity of the movement in the city.

Exhibitions of French Impressionism in Montreal were not limited, however, to works lent by collectors. In fact, the city's art dealers regularly partnered with their foreign colleagues for commercial purposes. In this context, in November 1892 the gallery W. Scott & Sons hosted a consignment of Impressionist canvases from Durand-Ruel's New York branch.[24] The experiment was repeated in March 1896.[25] Paintings by Monet and Pissarro were apparently also sent to Montreal in the winter of 1899.[26]

At the time when *Some French Impressionists* was being organized, French Impressionism had thus been rarely displayed or discussed in Montreal.[27] As a consequence, this exhibition of twenty-nine paintings seems surprising. What was Durand-Ruel's goal, given that there was so little interest in Impressionism? In 1906, the dealer's project could be understood as being relevant both on a global and local level. On the global level, Durand-Ruel made abundant use of exhibitions as a means of promoting the artists in his gallery.[28] At the time, he was heavily promoting French Impressionism in North American cities.[29] This activity was part of a broader perspective, as the visibility of Impressionism was rising in the English-speaking world as a whole.[30] In this sense, *Some French Impressionists* had an educational mission, and none of the works was for sale.[31]

On the local level, the number of collectors supporting the Montreal market had grown during the first decade of the twentieth century. To Sir George A. Drummond and Sir William Van Horne were added other businessmen, such as James Ross and Richard B. Angus.[32] To pique their curiosity, the dealer provided a high market value works—the insurance on them was $56,600[33]—and portraying familiar subjects.[34] He was personally involved, as he sent the works directly to the Art Association of Montreal, without the intermediary of a local dealer such as W. Scott & Sons. He did the same in 1907, when thirteen etchings by Cassatt belonging to his firm were shown in the Art Association's third exhibition of prints.[35] This strategy was abandoned after a final attempt in 1909 for the *Exhibition of French Art*.[36]

AN OPPORTUNITY TO ASSESS FRENCH IMPRESSIONISM

According to Lyman, *Some French Impressionists* made few ripples in Montreal. In 1959, when he was asked, "What effect did the exhibition have on the public?" he answered, "None that I know of. Very few people, probably, took an interest in it. And for the general public, in the end, the paintings must have seemed incomprehensible and appalling, as they did in the first Impressionist exhibitions in Paris."[37] Lyman's comment must be clarified, as almost 2,600 people visited the exhibition in 1906.[38] The event also received a fairly favourable critical reception in the press.

As a general rule, Montreal journalists of the time recognized the place that Impressionism occupied in art history and acknowledged the esteem in which its painters were held. For instance, Alfred Sisley was considered a "great impressionist landscape painter"[39] in 1899, the year of his death. During the 1906 exhibition, Manet, Renoir, Degas and Monet were called "giants of this school."[40] A few years later, Monet's essential role was underlined again.[41]

On the pictorial level, the response was less categorical. The negative reaction to Impressionist painters' pictorial innovations at the time of their first public showing was referred to on a number of occasions by Montreal critics. These artists had suffered the derision,[42] even the wrath, of their elders.[43] However, by 1906, their manner of painting was solidly inscribed in the art landscape. Their work had found its audience[44] and seen some success.[45]

Some French Impressionists provided an opportunity to assess this "technique," as the local press termed it. In all of the reviews, the emphasis was placed on this aspect, and more precisely on the transfer of chromatic mixing from the painter's palette to the beholder's eye. The *Montreal Daily Star* journalist summarized it in these terms: "Instead of the colors being mixed upon the palette, they were juxtaposed upon the canvas itself, the effect being that the colors blended at a certain distance, giving a particularly sparkling and brilliant effect."[46] The process was detailed in the description of Moret's *Cliffs near Morgat, Finistère*:

> Step up to this one of Moret's and you will notice splotches of pure green and blue, with dashes of red and orange in the foreground. Splotches, that is what it is with your nose against the canvas. But walk off to some distance and look at it: a fairy scene, great rocky cliffs looming up from a sea that is more exquisite than words can paint, a tiny crescent of beach, and a riotous green foreground. It is a bright, beautiful day with a mistiness in the air that veils the distant cliffs. The sea is a dream of loveliness. And there is a mystery and charm about the scene that passes description. Everyone who loves the sea will realize it. One of those perfect fleeting moments in nature when the supernatural seems to mingle with the natural. If you can read all this into this picture of Moret's you have begun to comprehend the impressionistic movement.[47]

The *Montreal Daily Witness* editorialist used the occasion of the exhibition to re-mind readers that Impressionism was already a quarter-century old and had given rise to Pointillism.[48] He wondered whether the movement would last, and he came to an ambivalent conclusion: "To this the answer must be yes and no." On the one hand, he claimed that half of the paintings would not have been accepted at a local exhibition if they had been by Canadian artists, for juries would have rejected them,[49] due to their leaning toward the "old style of work." On the other hand, the author noted that the Impressionists had gained respectability over the decades and that their vision had expanded the field of painting. Furthermore, he noted, all artistic expression has merit. Finally, he encouraged visitors not to reject the art on display out of hand: "It is to be expected, in the case of the present exhibition, that many will require a little time in which to become sympathetic."

Although critics brought issues to the fore, a certain wariness toward the movement lingered. *La Patrie* invited its readers to visit the exhibition because of the discussion it would generate.[50] The *Montreal Daily Star* wondered about the reaction of educated viewers, whose preference for faithful reproduction of reality led them to call the Impressionists' chromatic experiments "such a daub."[51] Given this negative attitude, the author concluded, "One must go with an open, receptive mind."[52] Despite such appeals, the Montreal public was known to be conservative, and this was reflected as far away as New York.[53]

In 1906, when the young John Lyman visited *Some French Impressionists*, he was taking part in a seminal moment in Canada's exposure to French Impressionism. As one aspect of Durand-Ruel's increased activity in the English-speaking world, the arrival of this exhibition in the galleries of the Art Association of Montreal allowed for a critical assessment of the art movement. Although the painters' status and pictorial advances were beyond doubt, the posterity of their technique and its reception by the public were challenged. Whereas the conservatism of Montrealers led to a fear of failure, the journalistic discourse remained open with regard to innovations, noting, on many occasions, the decomposition of the subject with separate brushstrokes and the use of bright colours. According to Lyman, these characteristics of Impressionism were to contribute to his decision to become a painter.

Notes

1. I am grateful to Michèle Grandbois and Didier Prioul for the comments they made on this text.

2. Fernand Dansereau, *John Lyman, peintre*, film, National Film Board, 1959, 28 min.

3. *A Catalogue of the Works of Some French Impressionists Which Will Be on View at the Art Gallery, From the 12th Until the 28th February, 1906* (Montreal: Art Association of Montreal, 1906).

4. "Loan Exhibition," *The Gazette*, February 13, 1906, p. 7.

5. Analyzing *A Bar at the Folies-Bergères*, Carol Armstrong maintains that the contrast between a figure painted flatly in the foreground and its reflection with imprecise contours signals Berthe Morisot's influence on Manet (Carol Armstrong, "Facturing Femininity: Manet's 'Before the Mirror,'" *October*, vol. 74 [autumn 1995], p. 101). *Before the Mirror* falls within this dynamic, which lasted several years. It should be noted that no painting by Berthe Morisot was on display in Montreal in 1906.

6. This painting is identified as no. 757 in Daniel Wildenstein's catalogue raisonné. It was sold at Christie's on May 12, 1999, and its current location is unknown. See Daniel Wildenstein, *Monet: Catalogue raisonné*, 4 vols. (Cologne: Taschen/Wildenstein Institute, 1996). For auction sales, see Christie's, "Auction Results: Impressionist and 19th Century Art (Evening Sale). Sale 9088. Lot 16," http://www.christies.com/lotfinder/paintings/claude-monet-bords-de-la-falaise-1686642-details.aspx (accessed July 1, 2013).

7. Wildenstein, *Monet*, no. 841.

8. Ibid., no. 1604.

9. John House, *Renoir, 1841-1919* (Saint-Pierre-Port, Guernsey: Guernsey Museum & Art Gallery, 1989), pp. 4-6.

10. These works correspond, respectively, to nos. 160, 792 and 1143 in Wildenstein's catalogue raisonné. The last painting, identified as *St. Sever Bridge, Foggy Weather* in the 1906 catalogue and related to *The Saint-Sever Bridge, Rouen: Mist*, was briefly mentioned in the Montreal press ("this Rouen street bathed in moonlight by Pissaro [sic]"). Although the painting located in North Carolina portrays a bridge in foggy weather rather than a street in moonlight, I have retained the attribution in the catalogue raisonné due to the brevity of the citation in the newspaper. See Joachim Pissarro and Claire Durand-Ruel Snollaerts, *Pissarro. Catalogue critique des peintures*, 2 vols. (Paris: Skira/Wildenstein Institute, 2005). For the mention in the press, see "Expositions d'art," *La Patrie*, February 13, 1906, p. 4.

11. The presence of this painting in Montreal in 1906 is mentioned in Jean Sutherland Boggs, ed., *Degas* (Paris: Réunion des musées nationaux, 1988), pp. 164-165. I would like to thank Didier Prioul for supplying this reference.

12. Mary Cassatt was represented by three paintings. Because the subject of mother and child is ubiquitous in her work, the painting *Mother and Child* is practically impossible to identify. A work titled *The Caress* (1902, Smithsonian American Art Museum, Washington) is identified in the catalogue raisonné by Adelyne Dohme Breeskin at no. 393. This may be the work that was exhibited in Montreal. Finally, *Young Woman Reading in a Garden* might correspond to *Lydia Reading in a Garden* (1880, The Art Institute of Chicago). For the catalogue raisonné, see Adelyne Dohme Breeskin, *Mary Cassatt: A Catalogue Raisonné of the Oils, Pastels, Watercolors, and Drawings* (Washington: Smithsonian Institution, 1979).

13. The three landscapes by Alfred Sisley take up subjects that he portrayed often: Saint-Mammès and Marne. As they were not described in the press, it is difficult to identify them.

14. The Montreal press noted this dynamic. See "The Impressionists at Art Gallery," *The Montreal Daily Star*, February 14, 1906, p. 3, and "Loan Exhibition," *The Gazette*, see note 4 above.

15. François Daulte, *Les Post-impressionnistes de la galerie Durand-Ruel* (Geneva: Galerie des Granges, 1973).

16. "Moret," in Sophie Monneret, *L'Impressionnisme et son époque. Dictionnaire international. Noms propres, A à T* (Paris: Robert Laffont, "Bouquins" imprint, 1979), p. 593.

17. "The Impressionists at Art Gallery," *The Montreal Daily Star*, see note 14 above.

18. Dansereau, *John Lyman, peintre*, 3 min 45 sec.

19. Janet M. Brooke, *Discerning Tastes: Montreal Collectors, 1880-1920*, exhib. cat. (Montreal: The Montreal Museum of Fine Arts, 1989), p. 141.

20. Ibid.

21. More than thirty loan exhibitions were organized by the Art Association of Montreal between 1860 and 1915.

22. Works by Mary Cassatt, Claude Monet, Camille Pissarro and Auguste Renoir were on display in 1895. See *Eighteenth Loan Exhibition of Paintings Held in the New Gallery* (Montreal: Art Association of Montreal, 1895). Two years later, a pastel by Auguste Renoir was exhibited again. See *19th Loan Exhibition, Water-Colours and Pastels – In the Art Gallery, Phillips Square* (Montreal: Art Association of Montreal, 1897).

23. Brooke, *Discerning Tastes*, p. 135.

24. Hélène Sicotte, "L'implantation de la galerie d'art à Montréal : le cas de W. Scott & Sons, 1859-1914. Comment la révision du concept d'œuvre d'art autorisa la spécialisation du commerce d'art," 2 vols., dissertation, Montreal, Université du Québec à Montréal, 2003, p. 295.

25. Ibid., p. 301.

26. This information is drawn from these artists' catalogues raisonnés. In both cases, the information came from the Durand-Ruel archives. No mention of the exhibition was found in *The Montreal Daily Star* or *The Gazette* between January and April 1899. See Pissarro and Durand-Ruel Snollaerts, *Pissarro*, p. 364, and Wildenstein, *Monet*, p. 1018.

27. The notable exceptions were the lectures given by William Brymner in 1896 and 1897. See Alicia Boutilier and Paul Maréchal, eds., *William Brymner: Artist, Teacher, Colleague*, exhib. cat. (Kingston: Agnes Etherington Art Centre, 2010), pp. 131-149.

28. Caroline Durand-Ruel Godfroy, "Paul Durand-Ruel's Marketing Practices," *Van Gogh Museum Journal* (2000), p. 86.

29. The dealer used touring exhibitions as a tool. For instance, *Paintings by the French Impressionists* travelled around the United States between 1907 and 1909 with stops in eight cities, including Milwaukee, Cincinnati and St. Louis. An account of the exhibition halls of the Albright Art Gallery in Buffalo in December 1907 listed more than seventy works. Of these, nine paintings had titles identical to works presented in Montreal in 1906. Our current state of knowledge does not enable us to know whether Montreal was an exploratory version of this touring exhibition. On the touring exhibition, see Wildenstein, *Monet*, p. 1019. A reference to a touring exhibition of Degas's works is also mentioned in the compilation by Phaedra Siebert, "Appendix: Selected Degas Exhibitions in America," in David A. Brenneman and Ann Dumas, *Degas and America: The Early Collectors*, exhib. cat. (Atlanta/Minneapolis/New York: High Museum of Art/Minneapolis Institute of Art, 2000), p. 248. On the works at the Albright Art Gallery, see "French Impressionism at the Albright Gallery," *Academy Notes*, vol. 3, no. 7 (December 1907), pp. 113-119.

30. The first English-language book devoted to Impressionism was published in 1903 in London. Titled *The French Impressionists*, it was a translation of *L'Impressionnisme, son histoire, son esthétique, ses maîtres* by Camille Mauclair. The introduction to *Some French Impressionists* drew on Mauclair's comprehension of the art movement. On the importance of this book in the English-speaking world, see the entry "Mauclair" in Monneret, *L'Impressionnisme et son époque*, p. 510. See Camille Mauclair, *The French Impressionists, 1860-1900* (London/New York: Duckworth/E. P. Dutton, 1903).

31. Copy of the letter from John B. Abbott to Durand-Ruel, January 12, 1906, Archives of the Montreal Museum of Fine Arts, Letter Book no. 5 (1902-1916), p. 389.

32. Brooke, *Discerning Tastes*, pp. 25-30.

33. Manet's *Portrait of Faure as Hamlet* was the most expensive work; it was valued at $10,000.

It was followed by Manet's other painting, *Before the Mirror*, and the two paintings by Degas. At the other extreme, the works by Albert André, Georges d'Espagnat, Gustave Loiseau, Maxime Maufra and Henry Moret were each worth $300 or less. Archives of the Montreal Museum of Fine Arts, *Art Association of Montreal Scrapbooks*, vol. 5 (1902-1908), pp. 168-169.

34. Among the works purchased then resold by Sir William Van Horne mentioned above were two of girls reading by Renoir and a landscape of the Marne river by Alfred Sisley. Similar works were on display in Montreal in 1906. The information available today does not enable us to know if these were the same paintings that Durand-Ruel put on tour again. On Renoir, see nos. 983 and 1402 in Guy-Patrice Dauberville and Michel Dauberville, *Renoir. Catalogue raisonné des tableaux, pastels, dessins et aquarelles, 1882-1894. Tome II* (Paris: Éditions Bernheim-Jeune, 2009). On Sisley, see no. 426 in François Daulte, *Alfred Sisley. Catalogue raisonné de l'œuvre peint* (Lausanne: Éditions Durand-Ruel, 1959).

35. The works by Mary Cassatt correspond to numbers 45 to 57 in the catalogue. See *A Catalogue of the Third Exhibition of Works in Black and White at the Art Gallery* (Montreal: Art Association of Montreal, 1907), p. 12.

36. Marc Gauthier, "Les Salons parisiens au Canada: l'*Exposition d'art français* de Montréal en 1909," 2 vols., master's thesis, Quebec City, Université Laval, 2011, p. 30.

37. Dansereau, *John Lyman, peintre*, 4 min 15 sec.

38. This was a clearly higher attendance than for the loan exhibitions in 1905 and 1907, and double the number of visits to the exhibition of works by Daubigny and Corot lent by Chapman in December 1906. On the other hand, all of these events had lower attendance than did the annual exhibitions devoted to contemporary Canadian artists, while the 1905 *Coronation Picture Exhibition* was visited by more than 16,000 people. See the annual reports of the Art Association of Montreal, 1905-1907, Archives of the Montreal Museum of Fine Arts.

39. "Personals," *The Montreal Daily Star*, February 17, 1899, p. 7.

40. "Loan Exhibition," *The Gazette*, see note 4 above.

41. B. K. S., "Startling Surprise in Store for Art Lovers in French Exhibition," *The Montreal Daily Herald*, January 30, 1909, p. 10.

42. "Loan Exhibition," *The Gazette*, see note 4 above.

43. "Impressionist Act," *The Montreal Daily Star*, February 13, 1906, p. 10.

44. Ibid.

45. "Loan Exhibition," *The Gazette*, see note 4 above.

46. "Impressionist Act," *The Montreal Daily Star*, see note 43 above.

47. "The Impressionists at Art Gallery," *The Montreal Daily Star*, see note 14 above.

48. "What is Art?," *The Montreal Daily Witness*, February 12, 1906, p. 6. All quotations in the paragraph come from this article.

49. This line of thought became more widely discussed over time. In 1913, debate arose in the Montreal newspapers about paintings by Canadian artists, notably Lyman's works. See Lorne Huston, "The 1913 Spring Exhibition of the Art Association of Montreal: Anatomy of a Public Debate," *Journal of Canadian Art History/Annales d'histoire de l'art canadien*, vol. 34, no. 1 (2013), pp. 12-55.

50. "Expositions d'art," *La Patrie*, see note 10 above.

51. "The Impressionists at Art Gallery," *The Montreal Daily Star*, see note 14 above.

52. Ibid.

53. "Canadian Art Notes," *American Art News*, March 3, 1906, p. 4.

THE MARVEL OF WATER
PORTFOLIO

Water, whether ocean, sea, river, lake or stream, offers a spectacle of infinite variety. Our artists honoured it throughout their peregrinations, from the English Channel and the Mediterranean to the shores of the Windward Islands.

Lyman admired his compatriot's handling of the element. "In every climate," he wrote, "Morrice conjured the marvel of water; at every stage of his work, it enlivens by its presence—and more often still by its atmosphere—the artist's finest canvases, which are filled with its colour and its vapour."

This attraction to water was shared by Lyman, who was especially struck by the expressive power of beaches swarming with bathers and dotted with striped tents, brilliantly coloured umbrellas and parasols. Ever preoccupied with order and balance, he modulated his vision with a diversity of chromatic combinations.

When he returned home to Montreal in 1931, Lyman reclaimed the Canadian landscape, interpreting it according to the principles of pictorial simplification and synthesis that were fundamental to his art.

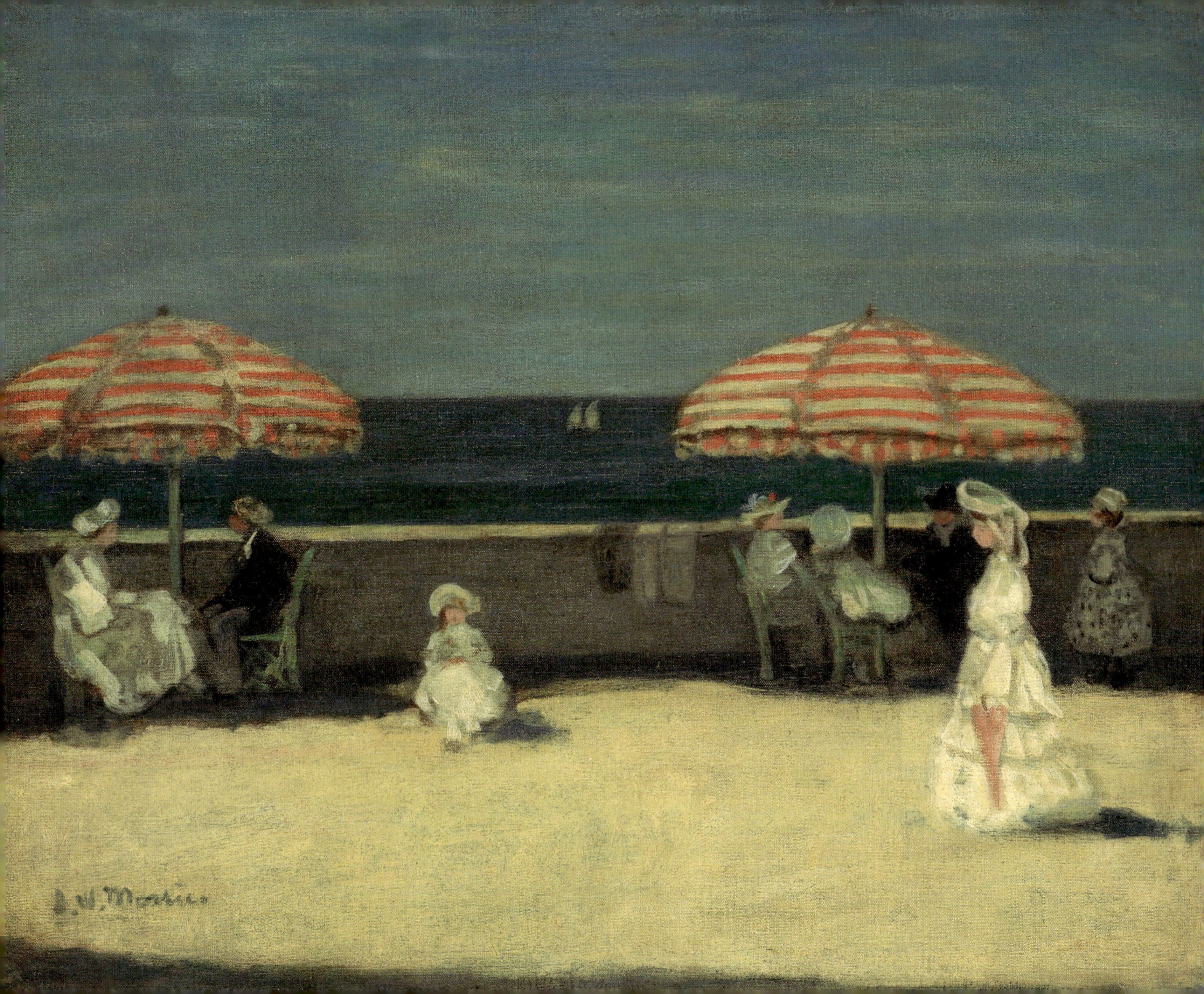

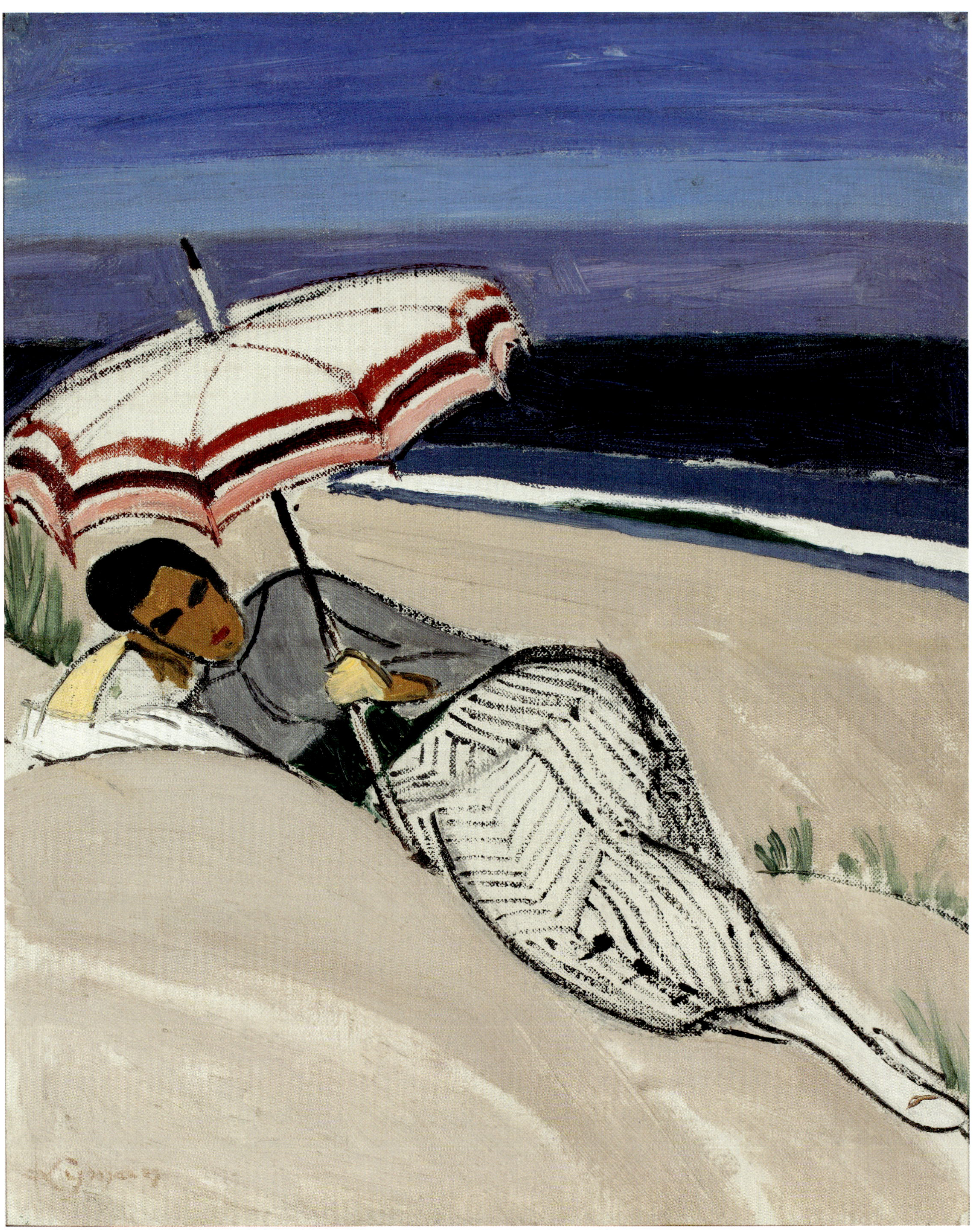

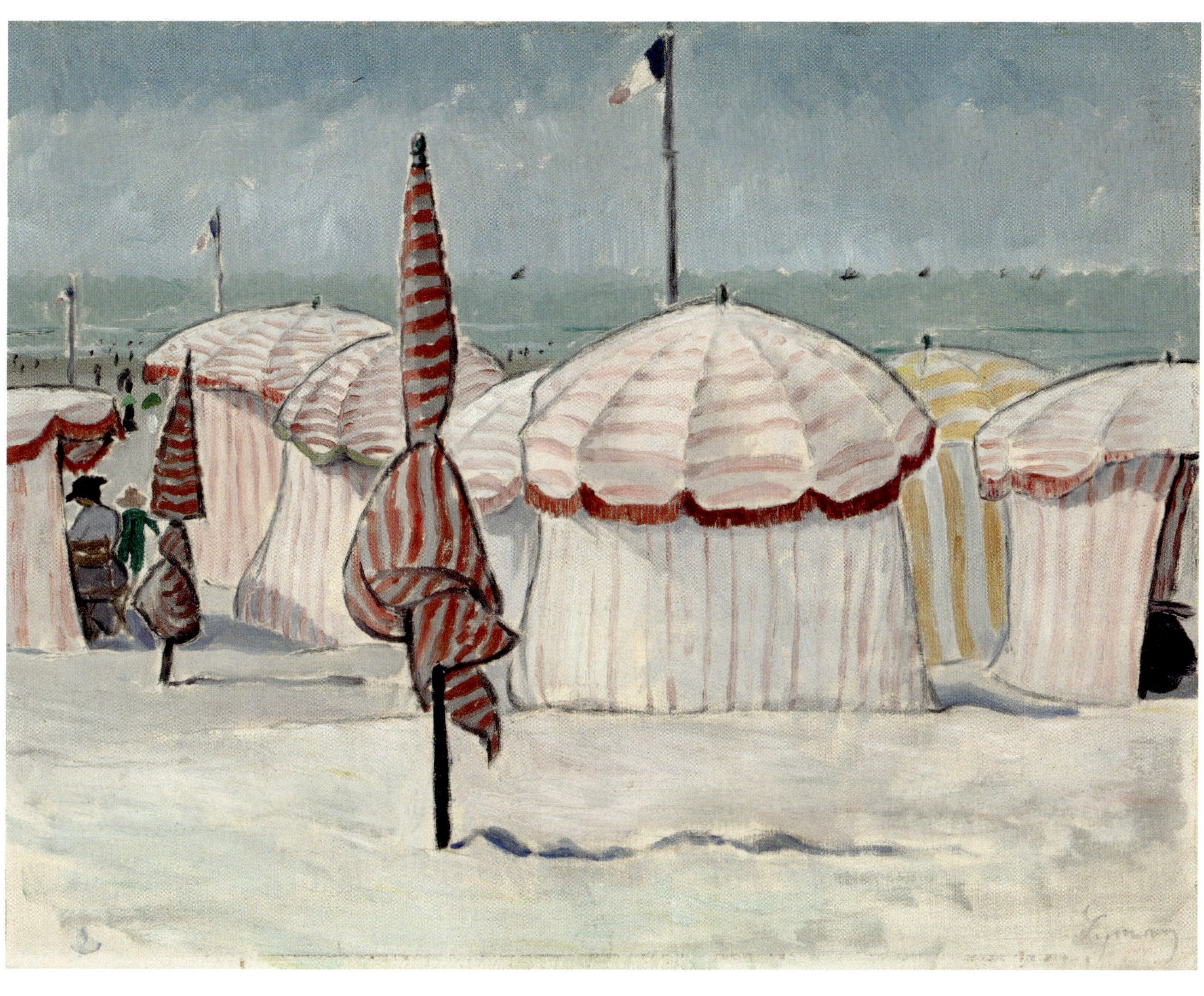

/ CAT. 107 John Lyman
On the Beach, Bermuda
1913

/ CAT. 108 John Lyman
Beach at Trouville
Between 1911 and 1916

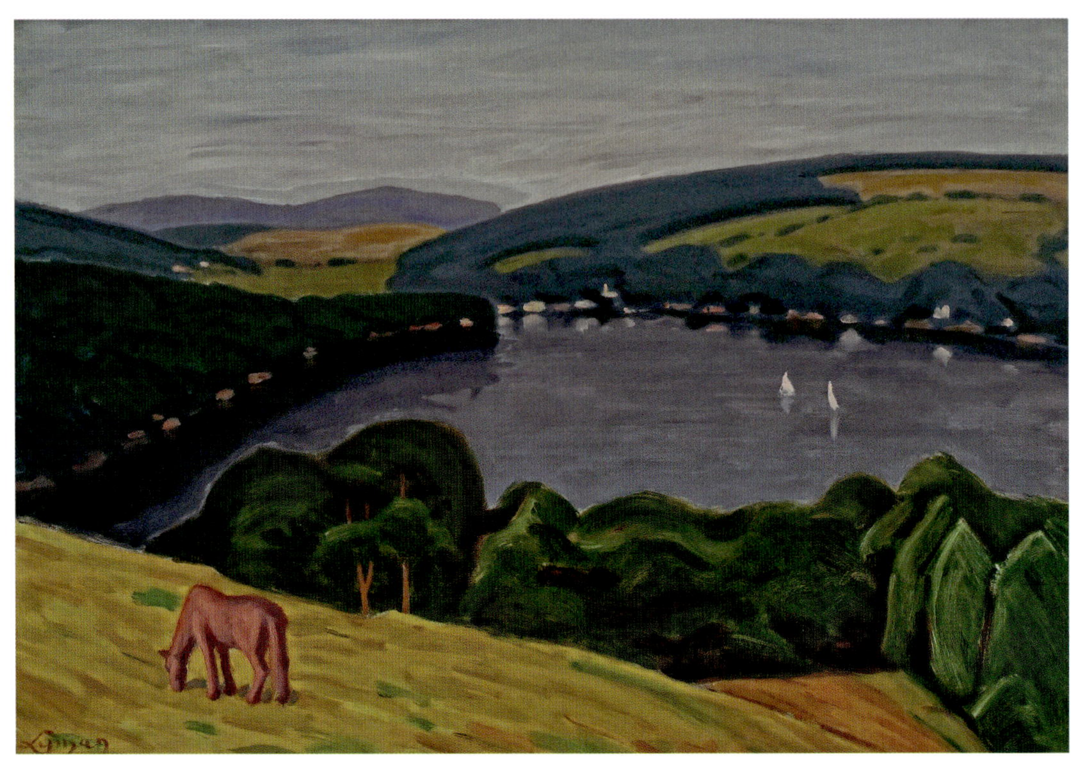

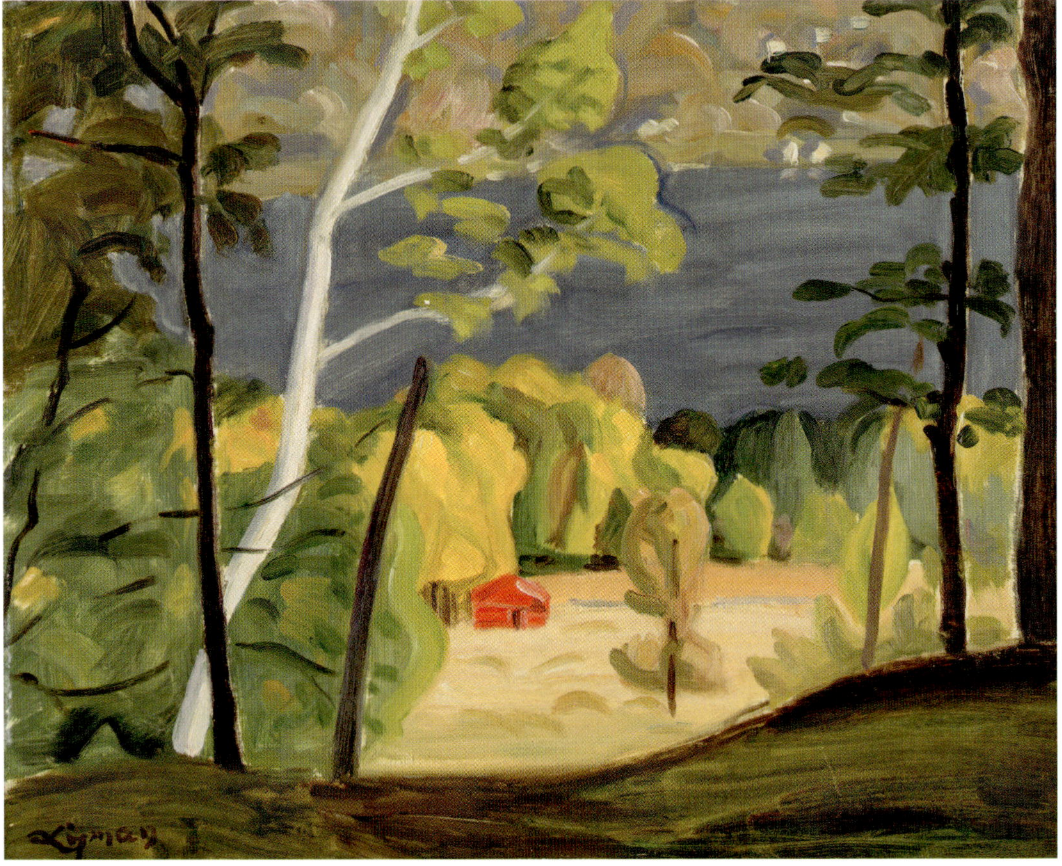

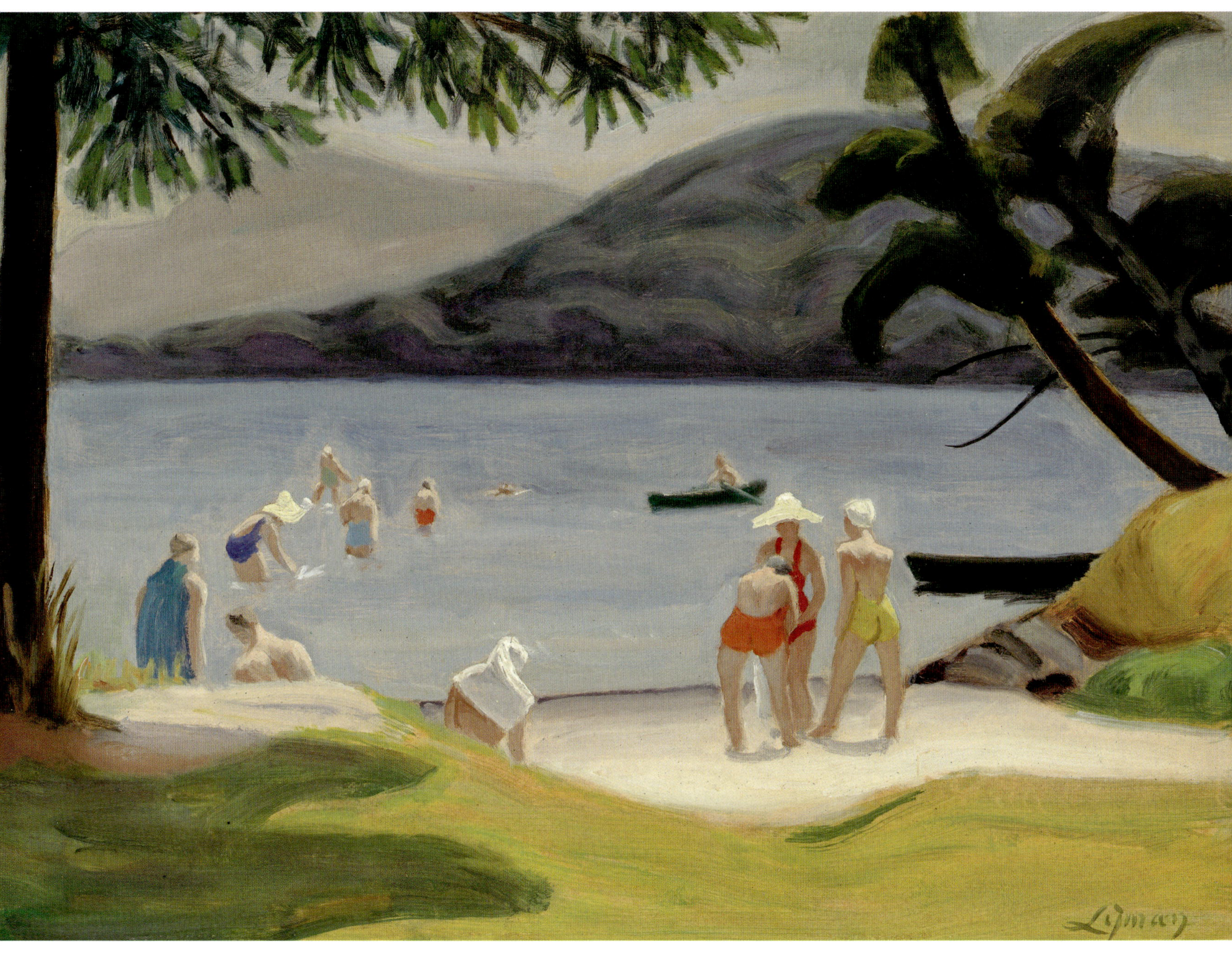

/ CAT. 109 John Lyman
Massawippi Lake
1933

/ CAT. 110 John Lyman
The Red Cabin at Lake Massawippi
1945

/ CAT. 111 John Lyman
Bathing Beach, Lake Ouimet
About 1939

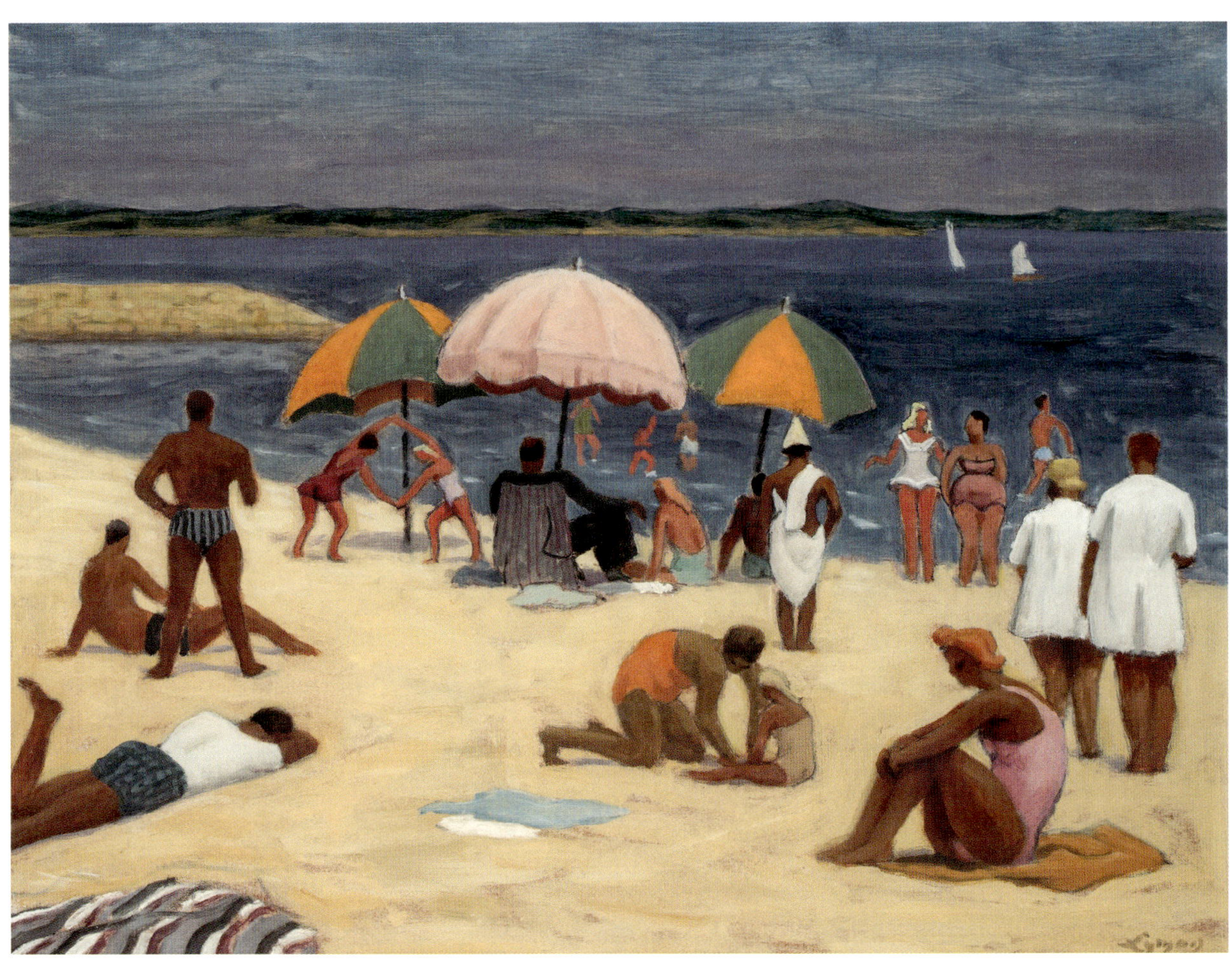

/ CAT. 112 John Lyman
Beach Scene
1957

/ CAT. 113 John Lyman
The Yacht Club, North Hatley
1948

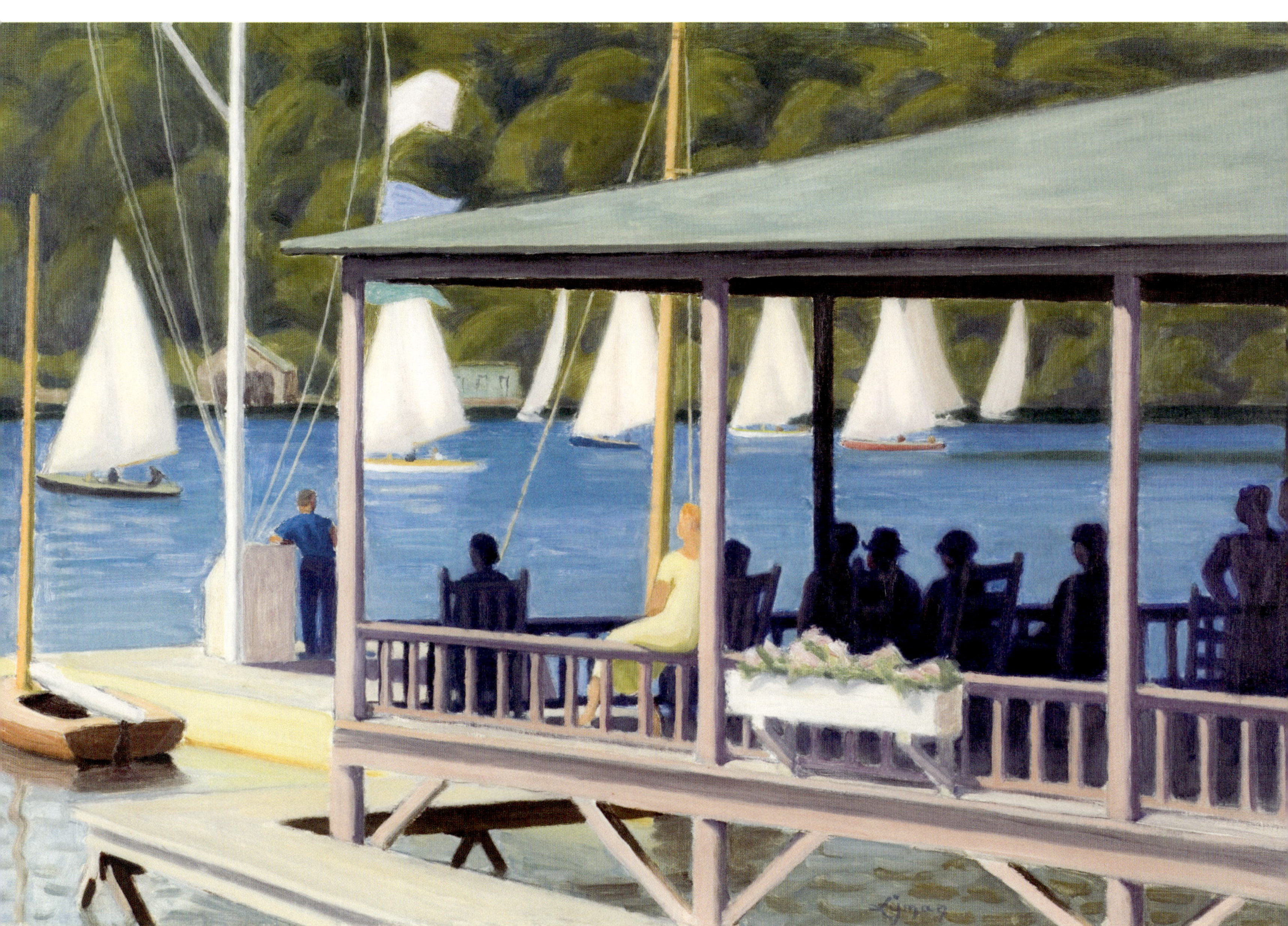

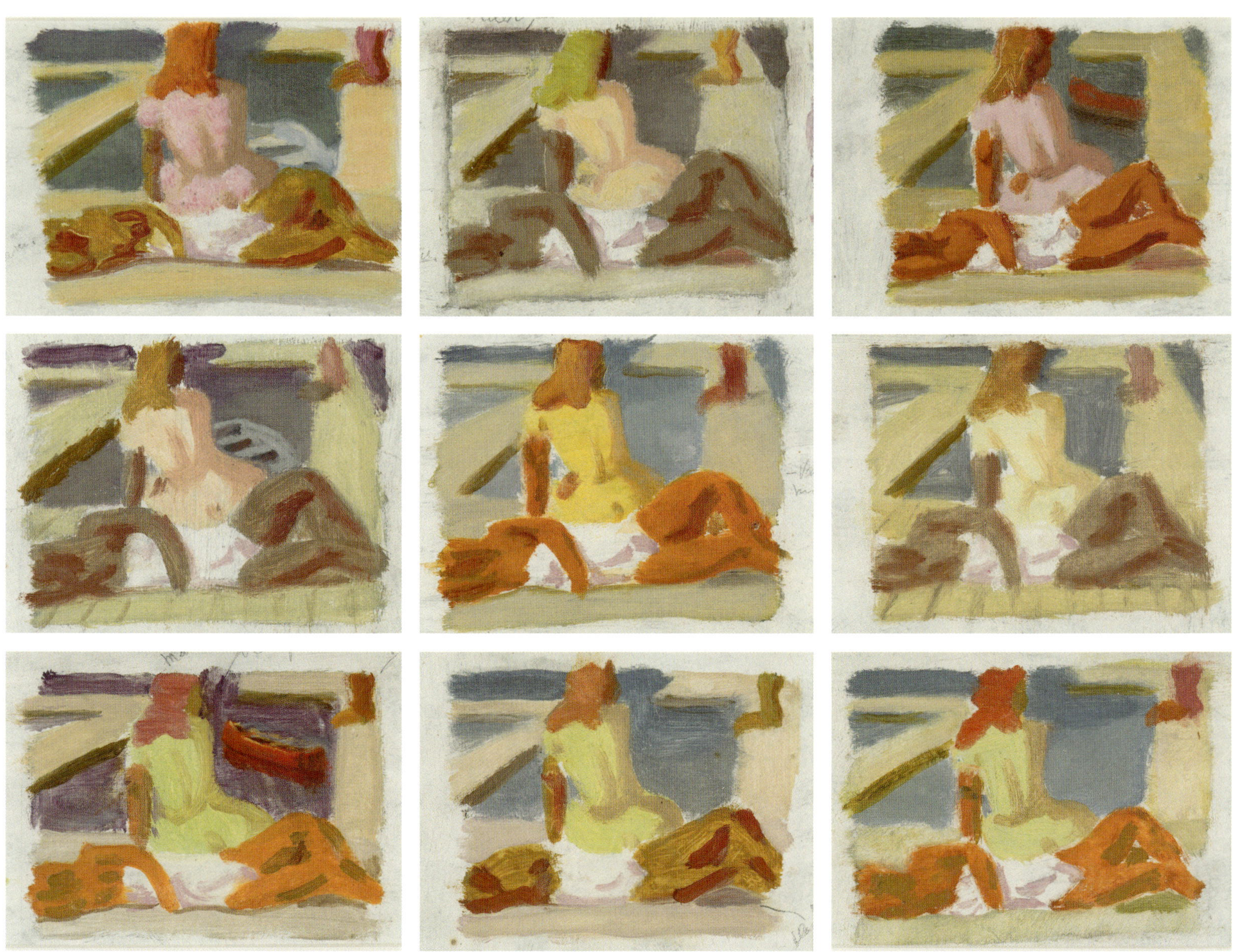

/ CAT. 114.01-09 John Lyman
Studies for "Sunbathing I and II"
About 1955

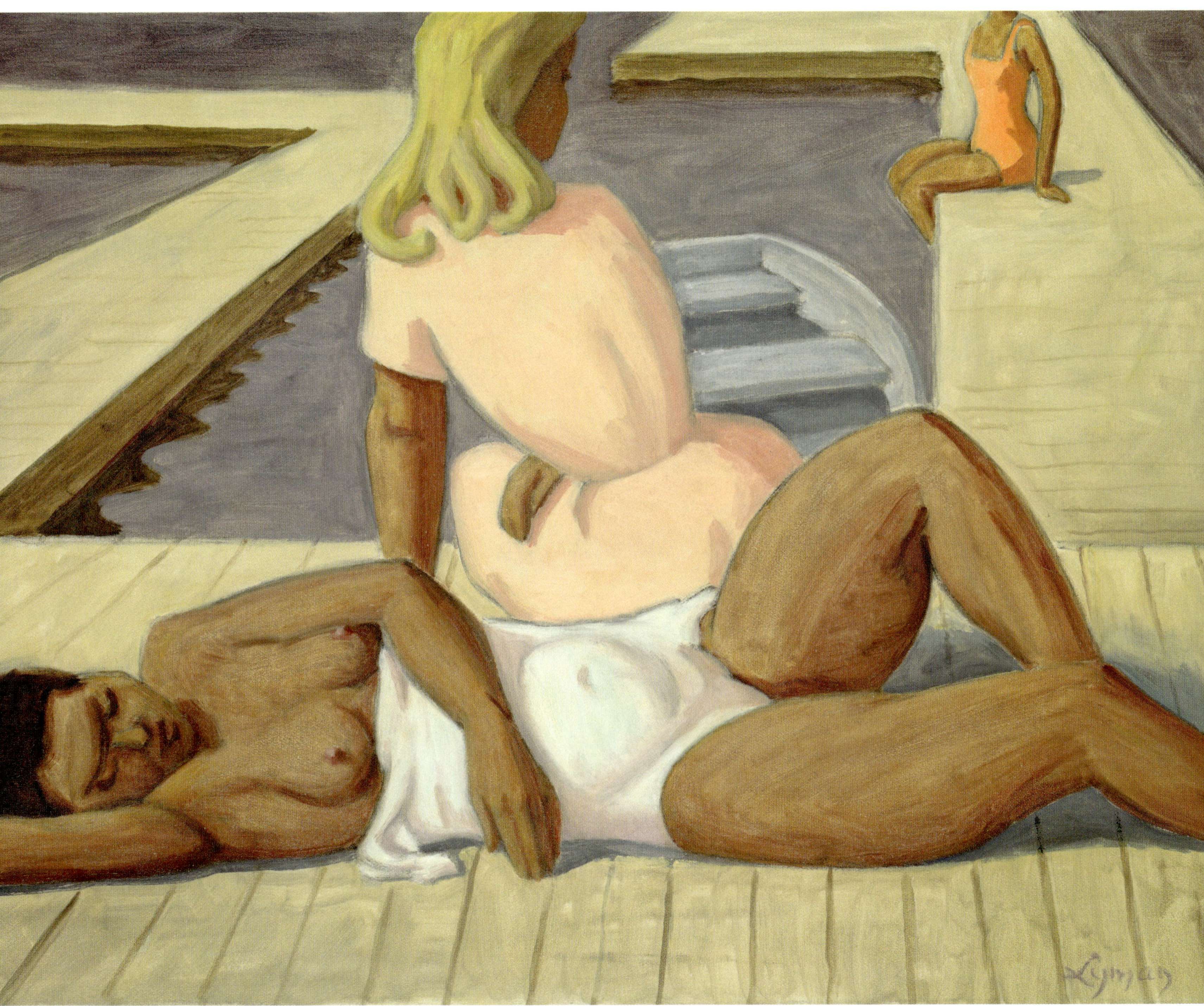

/ CAT. 114 John Lyman
Sunbathing II
1960

RICHARD FOISY AND MICHÈLE GRANDBOIS

MORRICE LYMAN MATISSE

INTERTWINING JOURNEYS

CHRONOLOGY

1865   **August 10**

Birth of James Wilson **Morrice** in Montreal; his father, a Presbyterian Scot, would make his fortune in the textile industry and become a benefactor of education and the arts.

1869   **December 31**

Birth of Henri **Matisse** in Cateau-Cambrésis, in the region of Nord-Pas-de-Calais (France), the son of a grain merchant.

1886   **September 29**

Birth of John **Lyman** in Biddeford, Maine, the son of a pharmaceutical products wholesaler who, in the same year, settles in Montreal. His wife would die in 1889, when their son was three years old.

1889   **December 14**

At the age of twenty-four, **Morrice** sails on the *Aurania* from New York to Liverpool.[1] In the fall, he earned a law degree at Osgoode Hall in Toronto and was admitted to the Bar of Ontario. The previous year, he took part for the first time in the joint exhibition of the Ontario Society of Artists and the Royal Canadian Academy of Arts, in Toronto. In 1889, he exhibits for the first time at the Spring Exhibition of the Art Association of Montreal (AAM), while showing again with the Ontario Society of Artists, all apparently without any training from any professor. Impassioned by the arts, he gives up the law.

1890   **January 20-March 10**

Morrice attends morning sessions at the Académie Julian.[2] He is in the class of Jules Lefebvre (1836-1911), renowned for his female nudes, and Benjamin Constant (1845-1902), an Orientalist and portrait painter. Like many foreigners enrolled at the Académie Julian, he lives at the Hôtel de l'Univers et du Portugal, at 10, rue Croix-des-Petits-Champs, just steps away from the Palais-Royal.

Summer

Morrice stays at a resort in Saint-Malo, his first destination in Brittany, where he would often return. "It was on a grey day or under an obscured sun that he discovered the ports and beaches of Brittany and Normandy."[3]

The same year, during a period of convalescence, Henri **Matisse**, a notary's clerk in Saint-Quentin, discovers his vocation while reading a treatise on painting. He is twenty-one years old and paints his first canvases. His father opposes this new direction, but his mother secretly encourages him.

1891   **October 5**

To prepare for the examination for admission to the École des beaux-arts, **Matisse** enrolls in the Académie Julian (left bank studio) where he would remain for one year. First, he studies with William Bouguereau (1825-1905), among the most influential, wealthiest academic painters of the country, who tells him, "You will never know how to draw." Then, he studies with Gabriel Ferrier (1847-1914) with whom the situation hardly improves.

1892   **April**

Morrice lives at 9, rue Campagne-Première, in the Montparnasse district; it is perhaps at this time, or shortly beforehand, that he takes lessons from the landscape painter Henri Harpignies (1819-1916). "The old artist taught drawing and painting and also required his students to sketch outdoors."[4]

October

Matisse enrols in evening courses at the École des arts décoratifs to earn a teaching diploma. There, he becomes acquainted with Albert Marquet (1875-1947) and Henri Manguin (1874-1949).

Matisse enters the studio of Gustave Moreau (1826-1898) at the École des beaux-arts as an auditing student. He would stay on for six years, until the master's death. In this same studio, Manguin would join him in 1894, and Marquet in 1895. Charles Camoin (1879-1965), with whom **Matisse** would maintain a long friendship, entered the studio in 1898.

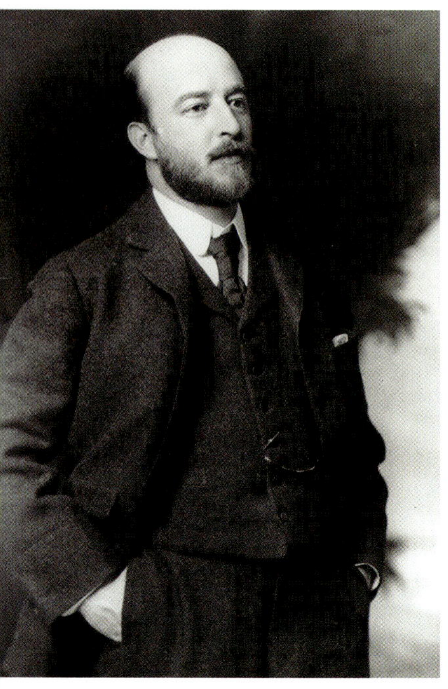

/ **FIG. 34** William Notman & Son
James W. Morrice
1900

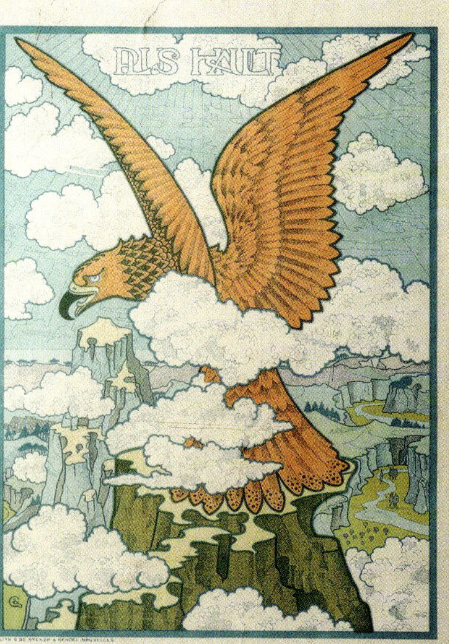

/ **FIG. 35** Gisbert Combaz
**Poster for an exhibition
of La Libre Esthétique**
1900

1894 **Morrice** discovers Italy during a long journey he is thought to have taken during that year; he visits Venice, where he would often return, and Capri, which he never visited again.

1895 **May 2**
Jean-François Raffaëlli (1850-1924), a French painter having participated, at the invitation of Edgar Degas, in the Impressionist exhibitions of 1880 and 1881, gives a lecture on Impressionism in Montreal for the members of the AAM. In the fall, it would be followed by an exhibition of Impressionist paintings taken from Montreal collections. The lecture and the exhibition are the first public events associated with the Impressionist movement in Canada.

Summer
In the company of the painter Émile Auguste Wéry (1868-1935), a neighbour across the hall from his new apartment at 19, quai Saint-Michel, **Matisse** makes his first trip to Brittany, at Belle-Île and Beuzec-Cap-Sizun. "And soon I was seduced by the brilliance of pure colour. I returned from my voyage with a passion for the colours of the rainbow."[5]

1896 **April 25-June 30**
For the first time, **Matisse** and **Morrice** exhibit at the Salon de la Société nationale des beaux-arts (SNBA), at Champ-de-Mars. **Matisse** is immediately elected an associate member, as the president, Pierre Puvis de Chavannes (1824-1898) had argued in his favour. **Matisse** exhibits four works: two *Desserts*, a *Studio Interior* and a *Woman Reading*, while **Morrice** exhibits a *Nocturne*. **Matisse** would stop exhibiting there after 1899, whereas **Morrice** would continue until 1911.

Summer
Morrice and **Matisse** journey in Brittany: **Morrice** in Saint-Malo and Cancale, in the north; **Matisse** in Belle-Île, Pointe du Raz and Pont-Aven, in the south. The two painters had not yet met.

1898 **January 8**
Matisse marries Amélie Pareyre. Honeymoon in London, on the advice of Camille Pissarro (1830-1903), to see the works of William Turner (1775-1851).

February
Matisse is in Ajaccio, Corsica, where he experiences "[his] great fascination with the South."[6] "Everything is brilliant, all is colour, and all is light."[7]

1899 **October 2**
Morrice moves into 45, quai des Grands-Augustins, less than five hundred feet from 19, quai Saint-Michel, where **Matisse** has resided for four years. **Morrice** paints in one of the rooms of his apartment overlooking the quay. "His modest dwelling, filled with canvases and trunks always prepared for departures, was furnished with the bare essentials."[8]

1900 **March 1-30**
Morrice takes part for the first time in the exhibition of La Libre Esthétique in Brussels (fig. 35) where his works would be shown again in 1902, 1905 and 1908. **Matisse** would exhibit there beginning in 1906.

Spring-Summer
John **Lyman**, soon to turn fourteen years of age, goes on a voyage to Europe with his father. They visit Naples, Rome, Florence, Paris and London. In Paris, they visit the World's Fair, then the Salon des Artistes français where the young boy notices the nudes. He has his portrait done by the American Stephen Seymour Thomas (1865-1956)—a friend of John's father—who earned a gold medal at the Salon des Artistes français and a bronze medal at the World's Fair.

"When as a boy I was first taken to Paris . . . I (and the grown-ups I knew) little dreamt the Universal Exhibition of 1900 had given official recognition to the impressionists and post-impressionists, and from that year another school would be dated. It was in perfect innocence of such things that we visited the Grand Palais, which had just been built to house the centennial exhibition of French art, including Cézanne, Renoir and Gauguin. I remember we brought back a picture postcard of a painting by some disciple of Cabanel that attracted the crowd, which card, if I had it still, would be a treasured keepsake of Paris, Paul Morand recalls in his book '1900.' It represented three nude Danaës who, by their upper-class, middle-class and lower-class beauty as well as by the colour of their hair, symbolized the gold, silver and copper coins that rained upon them. They had the loveliest poses and highly pomaded skins, but nothing under their skins."[9]

Lyman draws and paints in watercolour with his cousin F. Cleveland Morgan (1881-1962) who would become an important collector of decorative art and prints and one of the principal patrons of the AAM, where he would later become curator of decorative art, in the capacity of a volunteer.

1901   **Summer**
Morrice travels in Italy (cat. 11), this time with the painter and etcher Joseph Pennell (1857-1926), a close friend and biographer of Whistler (1834-1903).[10]

1902   **Spring**
Morrice is elected an associate member of the Société nationale des beaux-arts.

1903   **October 31-December 6**
Matisse participates in the brand new Salon d'Automne that opens its doors at the Petit Palais.[11] The salon only exhibits previously unseen works.

"The opening of the Salon d'Automne, in 1903, was splendid. Alongside a Gauguin retrospective,[12] alongside the works of Redon and Bonnard, which **Morrice** already held in high esteem,[13] one witnessed the sudden appearance of the revolutionary techniques of Rouault, **Matisse**, Derain,[14] of all those that propelled the emergence of these gentlemen of the Institute, but who would themselves be called the 'Fauves'."[15]

1904   **Spring**
The Russian industrialist Ivan Abramovitch Morosov (1871-1921) acquires his first painting by **Morrice**, *Street Fair, Montmartre*, dated 1898, purchased at the Salon de la Société nationale des beaux-arts. Today, the work is in the State Hermitage Museum in St. Petersburg. Morosov would acquire his first **Matisse**, a flower piece, in 1907, at the Galerie Bernheim-Jeune.

June 1-18
First solo exhibition of **Matisse** at the Galerie Ambroise Vollard.

Since settling in Paris, **Morrice** mainly frequents the Anglo-American community, linked to the English end-of-century movement, the Aesthetic Movement. He advises young, aspiring modernists such as Clive Bell (1881-1964), a future member of the Bloomsbury Group, to take note of **Matisse**: "Also, from **Morrice**, I learnt more about pictures; and it was he who later advised me to look at **Matisse**."[16]

The British novelist and art critic Arnold Bennett (1867-1931), who had moved to France in March 1903 and would stay there until February 1913, befriends **Morrice**.[17]

The British playwright and novelist Somerset Maugham (1874-1965), who had settled in Paris—where he was born—in 1904 for a period of two years, makes the acquaintance of **Morrice**. In 1908, in London, Maugham publishes his novel *The Magician*, in which he personifies **Morrice** in the character of Warren: "He has the most fascinating sense of colour in the world, and the more intoxicated he is, the more beautiful and delicate is his painting."[18]

Morrice and the Irish painter Roderic O'Conor (1860-1940), from the École de Pont-Aven—a friend of Gauguin,[19] Clive Bell and Somerset Maugham—become regular patrons of the Chat Blanc, a café-restaurant in the Rue d'Odessa in Paris. They are soon joined by Bell as well as other foreign writers, painters, sculptors and students.

1905   **Morrice** is forty and has lived in France for fifteen years. The influence of his painting peaks: 11 exhibitions held in 5 countries, although none in Canada. Critics review his works in 115 articles, including about 50 that mention his participation in the Salon de la SNBA and 20 that reference the Salon d'Automne.[20]

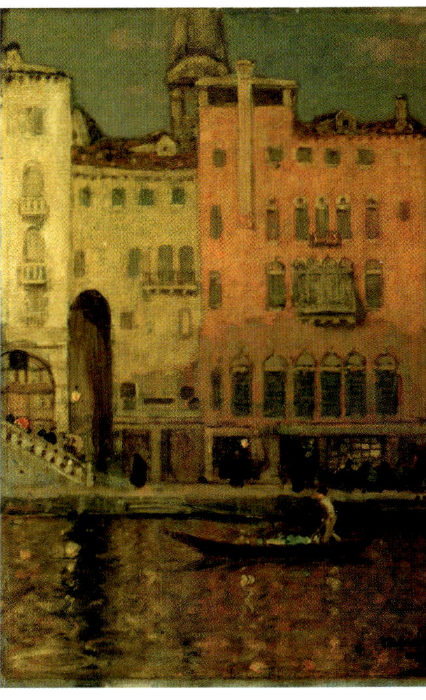

/ **CAT. 11** James W. Morrice
Venice at the Golden Hour
About 1901-1902

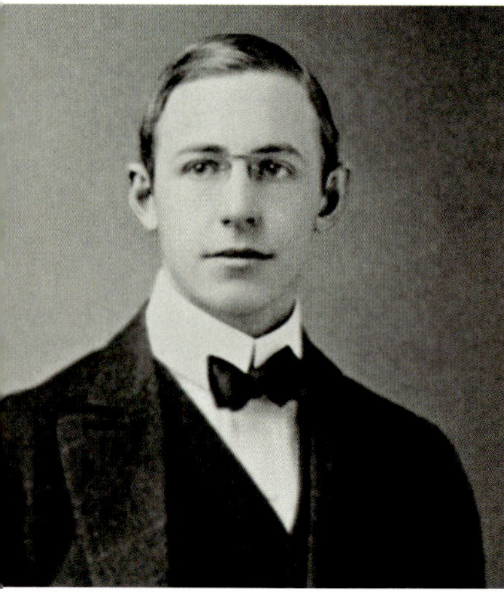

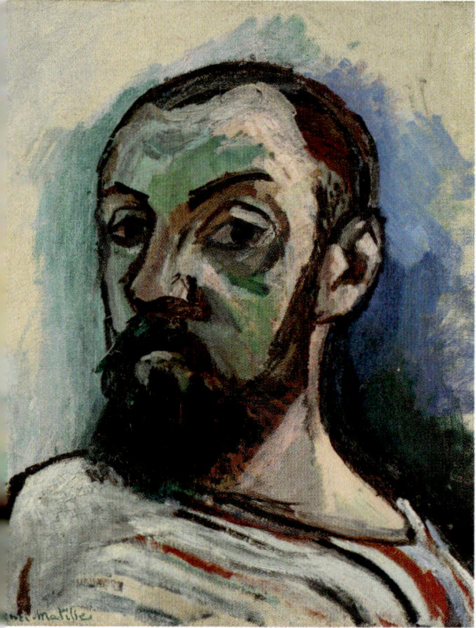

Lyman is nineteen and studying at McGill University in Montreal, intending to become a writer. His classmate Guy Drummond, son of Sir George A. Drummond (1829-1910), invites him to come to see the works of Boudin, Constable, Corot, Daubigny, Degas, Monet, Rembrandt, Rodin, Turner, Whistler, Raffaëlli, Valadon and others that embellish the walls of his parents' opulent residence.

October 18-November 25
Morrice makes his debut at the 3rd Salon d'Automne, at the Grand Palais. He exhibits four works in salle VI which earn him critical acclaim for these "tiny, precious wonders" and again for these "two Venetian notes [that] may discourage all the other Salon exhibitors from painting!"[21]

Next door, in salle VII, which the critic Louis Vauxcelles would call the room of the "Fauves,"[22] the highly colourful works of Charles Camoin, André Derain, Pierre Girieux, Charles Manguin, Albert Marquet, **Matisse** and Maurice de Vlaminck create a scandal.

The same Louis Vauxcelles gives his opinion of the work of **Morrice** in *Gil Blas*: "A small, peaceful corner for intimate works, pretty, discreet paintings that soothe tired or dazzled eyes . . . No radiance, but taste . . . M. **Morrice** [takes us] to Venice, or to the beach; his three small works are gems that Boudin would have loved."[23]

At this salon, **Matisse**, who is thirty-five, is looked to as an elder and group leader of the Atelier Moreau. With works such as the portrait of his wife, *Woman with a Hat*, the first acquisition of a **Matisse** by Léo and Gertrude Stein, he attracts brutal reviews and becomes the laughingstock among visitors: "He is certainly the best laughed-at man in the Salon . . . All day long you will find a crowd of people round his pictures, hustling one another to get a close view. People burst out laughing, look up the pictures in their catalogues, laugh again scornfully—the ladies toss their heads—and walk away." The anonymous author of this article acknowledges, however, that "Mr. **Maticce's** [*sic*] colours are wonderfully bright, and they are artfully arranged." He immediately continues commenting on the participation of **Morrice** by exclaiming: "I like his work extremely!"[24]

Morrice would later assert that the Salon d'Automne was the most interesting exhibition of the year, at times somewhat revolutionary, but that contained the most original works.[25]

1906   **February 12-28**
Lyman visits the exhibition *Some French Impressionists* presented at the Art Association of Montreal, which persuades him to become a painter. Organized by the Galerie Durand-Ruel de Paris,[26] it features twenty-nine paintings by Manet, Degas, Monet, Renoir, Pissarro, Sisley, Cassatt, d'Espagnat, André, Moret, Maufra and Loiseau.[27] Years later, **Lyman** would recall: "It was a tremendous shock to me."[28] What particularly struck him about the Impressionists, was "this extraordinary . . . quality of light."[29]

That winter, **Morrice** stays in Montreal, at least until February 18. He may have attended this exhibition. **Lyman** is not yet familiar with the work of **Morrice**.

Matisse embarks on his first journey to North Africa, to Biskra, Algeria; the following year, he would paint *Blue Nude (Souvenir of Biskra)*.

1907   **Spring**
Lyman once again travels to Paris with his father. The painter Seymour Thomas, whom they meet again there, encourages the young man to take up painting and persuades his father to allow him to study with Pierre Marcel-Béronneau (1869-1937), a symbolist painter and a former student of Gustave Moreau, whose studio is located in the *impasse* Ronsin, where Thomas had his own atelier. **Lyman**'s father agrees. "If he had really wanted to object to my choice of painting as a career, he would not have done what he did,"[30] **Lyman** would later acknowledge.

Lyman arrives at Marcel-Béronneau's studio at the end of the academic year; he would only stay for six weeks. He appreciates the teaching, which urges a student to work ever more quickly, to grasp the essential and not to linger over details. Afterwards, he spends four weeks in Brittany, in particular at Saint-Jean-du-Doigt with the Thomas family, where he paints his first landscapes in oil.

April

On visiting the Salon de la SNBA, **Lyman** discovers **Morrice**. He is fascinated by *The Ferry*, now known as the *The Ferry, Quebec* (cat. 5). "Having just arrived [in Paris], I walked to the Salon de la Société nationale, in the company of an American friend . . . he drew my attention to the opening of a man named James Wilson **Morrice**, who was, apparently, my compatriot. There was a painting—it represented the St. Lawrence bearing ice—of an almost awkward and unfinished appearance among all these offhand or overdone styles: it was the only painting at the Salon that I would remember . . . the admiration I would always feel for him dated from this moment. I would [not] meet the man until a few years later."[31]

Summer

Matisse sets off on a journey in Italy. He sees Giotto's frescoes in Padua, Duccio's in Siena, Piero della Francesca's in Arezzo and visits Venice. In Florence, he and his wife stay with the Steins, at their villa in Fiesole.

Fall

Lyman is enrolled at the Royal College of Art in South Kensington, London, where, on the advice of his father, he is studying architectural design to prepare for a profession as an architect or interior decorator. With only one remaining trimester, he would soon abandon this undertaking to devote himself to painting.

Morosov acquires his first painting by **Matisse** from Bernheim-Jeune. He also acquires, perhaps from the same dealer, a second painting by **Morrice**, *Landscape with River and Boats*, today in the State Hermitage Museum in St. Petersburg.

December

Sergei Shchukin (1854-1936), Russian textile merchant and collector, discovers the work of **Matisse** in the home of Gertrude Stein, in the Rue de Fleurus. He would commission several paintings from the artist, who would specifically create for him the renowned *Dance*.

1908   January

In response to the requests of Sarah Stein, the wife of Michael Stein, brother of Gertrude, and of some of their friends, **Matisse** opens an academy in the former Couvent des Oiseaux, Rue de Sèvres, mere steps away from the Boulevard du Montparnasse, where he had been living since October 1905. In the spring, the Couvent des Oiseaux having been sold, **Matisse** occupies a pavilion located in the garden of the former Couvent du Sacré-Cœur (formerly the Hôtel Biron, today the Musée Rodin), at 33, boulevard des Invalides, at the corner of the Rue de Babylone. His academy is located in the old dining hall of the convent. The Académie **Matisse** would close its doors in June 1910.

Hans Purrmann described the difficult trials to which **Matisse** would subject his students, after they had begun to shed their stylistic tics and mannerisms: "He would strip each work down to its bare essence, examine what was left for any trace of individual expression, and then devote himself to strengthening this residuum."[32]

"Also specific to his teaching was his insistent referencing of Cézanne. He stressed Cézanne's 'unsurpassed meticulous execution,' the architectonic plasticity of his painting placed on the same footing as that of archaic Greece . . . **Matisse** peppered his discourse on painting with frequent references to a musical model and during sessions would not hesitate to have classical music played on the small harmonium in the atelier."[33]

January 12

From London, **Lyman** writes to his father to inform him that he has decided to become a painter: "Whatever branch of art I may specialize in, I am going to do it as an artist, not as a craftsman, and the training of the artist in me can go on apace without my making any decision as to which method of expression I shall adopt."[34]

January 18

Lyman sees three paintings by **Morrice**, among which *Evening, The Lido, Venice*, better known as *Venice, Looking Out over the Lagoon* (cat. 12), at the New Gallery in London, where the 8th Exhibition of the International Society of Sculptors, Painters and Gravers is being held.

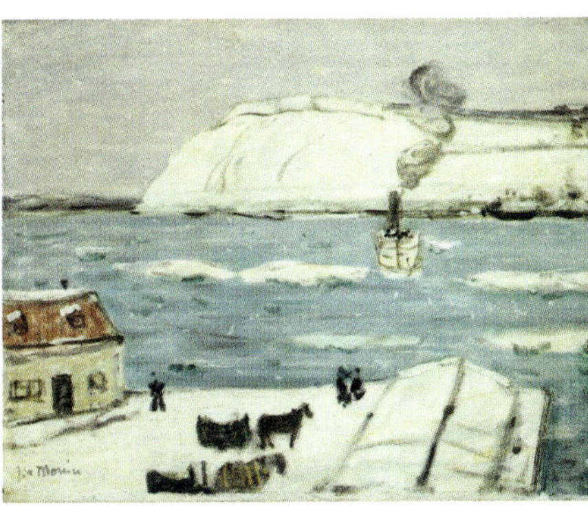

/ CAT. 5 James W. Morrice
The Ferry, Quebec
1907

February 22

Morrice tells his friend, the Canadian painter Edmund Morris,[35] that he has become a member of the Société Nouvelle: "I have [been] made a member of the Société Nouvelle the principal members are Blanche, Cottet, Simon, Dauchez, La Touche. We have an exhibition next month. I will send you the catalogue and also catalogues of other exhibitions."[36]

March

Lyman is back in Paris. He enters the Académie Julian upon the recommendation of Seymour Thomas. He would stay on from March 9, 1908, to January 2, 1910, taking more or less prolonged periods of absence in summer and fall 1909.[37] His teacher is Jean Paul Laurens (1838-1921). "Laurens . . . required, as compositions, subjects of history and Greek mythology that had to be subjected to the most academic of rules."[38] "The first time that I made a composition that did not follow the rules of the academy, he threw it on the floor."[39]

April 6-25

First exhibition of **Matisse** in America, in New York, at the Little Galleries of the Photo Secession, 291, Fifth Avenue, managed by the photographer Alfred Stieglitz (1864-1946). Photographer Edward Steichen (1879-1973) who had met **Matisse** in February in Paris, organized the exhibition, which includes drawings, watercolours, lithographs and etchings.

April-September

Morrice and Marquet are vice-presidents of the jury in the painting section of the 6th Salon d'Automne. Presided over by Henri Lebasque (1865-1937), this jury was formed in April and began operating in September. Among the members are **Matisse**, Georges Rouault and the Irishman John Lavery (1856-1941).[40] **Matisse** shows 11 paintings, 13 sculptures and 6 drawings, an ensemble somewhat reminiscent of the salon's small retrospectives, particularly those of previous years devoted to Gauguin, Cézanne and Renoir. **Morrice** exhibits 5 paintings and one study.

The growing rivalry between the "Picassoists" and the "Matissists" crystallized when Georges Braque's paintings of l'Estaque were rejected by the jury.[41] In history's generally accepted version, **Matisse** told the critic Louis Vauxcelles: "Braque has just sent in a painting made of little cubes," and, asked to describe the painting, "he took a piece of paper and in three seconds sketched two ascending, converging lines surrounding the said cubes."[42] The day after the salon closed, on November 8, Braque presented twenty-seven paintings at the Henry Kahnweiler gallery, an exhibition that marked the beginnings of Cubism.

"At the Salon d'Automne, a critic from the *Gazette des beaux-arts* wrote that the two main trends were 'the intuition of Mr. **Matisse** opposed to the traditional, methodical art of Maurice Denis.' And that these two trends divided artists into two camps. **Morrice** quickly made his preferences known."[43]

"[That year] **Morrice** . . . would tell Clive Bell . . . as the two men stood before a group of works by **Matisse**, that contrary to popular opinion, **Matisse** did not need to be put into a padded cell,[44] but that he was good, very good."[45]

Fall

Following a brief stay in Montreal, **Lyman** returns to Paris and resumes his studies at Julian. He has a studio at 83, boulevard du Montparnasse.[46]

December 25

Matisse publishes his "Notes d'un peintre," accompanied by several reproductions, in *La Grande Revue*. The text is published under the aegis of George Desvallières (1861-1950), a friend of Maurice Denis, vice-president of the Salon d'Automne, recognized critic at *La Grande Revue*, committed Catholic, renowned painter, former member of Gustave Moreau's studio and a defender of the young school since the scandal of the Fauves in 1905. The "Notes d'un peintre" would influence **Lyman**.

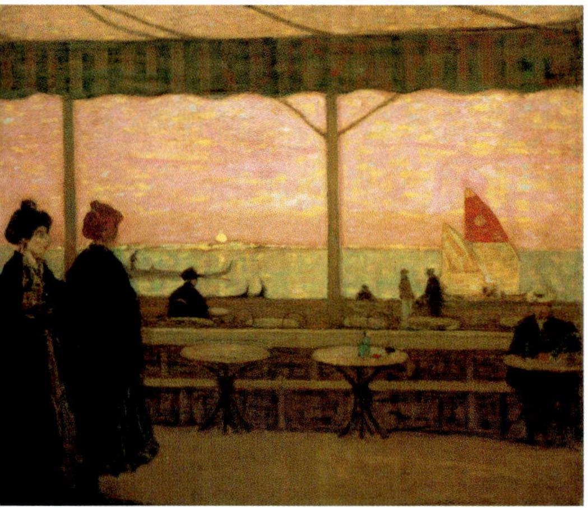

/ **CAT. 12** James W. Morrice
**Venice, Looking Out
over the Lagoon**
About 1904

During the year
Publication of *Modern Art*, the English translation of the influential work first published in German in 1904 by the German critic Julius Meier-Graefe, in which Van Gogh, Gauguin and Cézanne are described as "expressionists," the heirs of Manet who renewed his revolutionary initiative. The term "expressionist" was chosen to distinguish these artists from the Impressionists. In 1910, Roger Fry preferred to use the term "post-impressionist" to indicate that these painters came after the Impressionists.

1909

February
Morrice, in Montreal, writes to his friend Edmund Morris:

"There is to be an exhibition of French Art in the Art Gallery here in Montreal next week. I have seen the pictures—most of them I know good—fairly good but not too good—I think myself we could make an equally good display. Am working like a slave on snow pictures and will write again in a couple of days."[47]

The exhibition of French art at the AAM opens January 30 and closes on March 1. **Matisse**, like many other artists of the avant-garde, is not included in this exhibition.

March 25-May 2
At the Salon des Indépendants, **Lyman** sees *Autumn Landscape: Forest of Fontainebleau* (fig. 23) by **Matisse** which makes a strong impression on him: "My first acquaintance with **Matisse**'s painting was when, in the Spring of 1909, I saw his *Fontainebleau Forest* in the Salon des Indépendants.[48] Its summary intensity haunted my dreams."[49] "Some had already spoken to me about **Matisse**, but this was the first time I saw his paintings, and I was alone when I saw them."[50]

This encounter with the painting of **Matisse** persuades him to study with this artist.[51]

April 2-24
At the AAM Exhibition in Montreal, **Morrice** is awarded the Jessie Dow prize[52] for *Regatta, Saint-Malo*. Shortly before this exhibition, the National Gallery of Canada had acquired *Quai des Grands-Augustins, Paris*, the first work by **Morrice** to be included in Canadian public collections.[53]

April 15-June 30
Lyman admires the works of **Morrice** at the Salon de la SNBA, works he describes as "pure painting poetry." He is impressed by two Quebec subjects: *Entrance to a Quebec Village* (cat. 7) and a view of Lévis from the Dufferin Terrace in Quebec City (cat. 8).

Summer
Lyman is in Étaples, at Pas-de-Calais, where the painter Seymour Thomas is renting a villa, but **Lyman** prefers to stay at the hotel. That is where he meets the English painter Matthew Smith (1879-1959) who would become one of his friends.[54]

November
Lyman attends, for one of the last times, the class of Jean Paul Laurens at the Académie Julian:

"My last esquisse at Julian's took about 37th place, next to the last . . . Anything high in key invokes his censure to such a degree that he doesn't even criticize its composition; air and light in an esquisse are sufficient to make him throw it on the floor and sunlight in a canvas gives him an apoplexy. The subject this time was Herod's death. Unfortunately I was [foolish] enough to conceive of the affair as happening in the sunlight . . . I don't intend to waste my time doing any more esquisses which forfeit their right to a critique because they are the result of my sentiment rather than J.-P.'s. It is my business to try to develop my personality rather than to repress it every time it comes into play."[55]

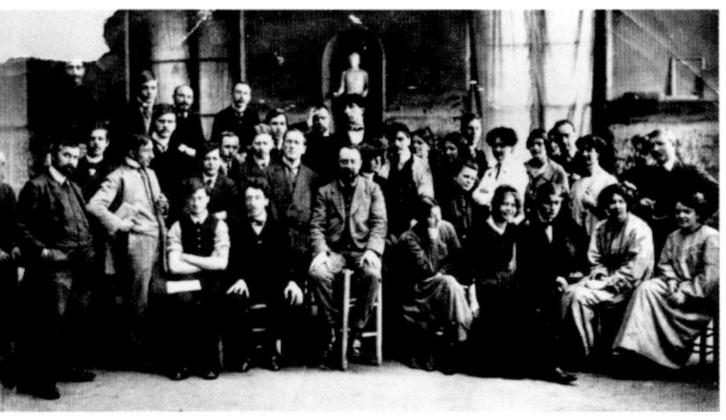

Lyman would soon leave the Académie Julian for the Académie Colarossi, at 10, rue de la Grande-Chaumière, where he again encountered Matthew Smith: "We would meet every evening, from 5 to 7, at Colarossi, at the Grande Chaumière. We would pay 50 centimes for a model. We no longer went to Julian."[56]

Of the various spring salons in Paris, **Lyman** preferred the Salon d'Automne de 1909, "in fact more vital and full of conviction,"[57] in agreement with **Morrice** who had expressed the same opinion: "It is the most interesting exhibition of the year—somewhat revolutionary at times."[58]

December

The Canadian Magazine publishes "The Art of J. W. **Morrice**" by Louis Vauxcelles, the first article about the artist in a journal in Canada:

"Since the death of James MacNeill Whistler, J. W. **Morrice** is unquestionably the American[59] painter who has achieved in France and at Paris (where he participates regularly in all the important exhibitions) the most notable and well-merited place in the world of art . . . J. W. **Morrice** is neither a portraitist nor landscapist—simply a painter, and one of the best of to-day."[60]

In December, **Lyman** accompanies his cousin Henry Lyman Saÿen (1875-1918), godson of Henry Morgan, to visit Gertrude Stein.[61] This was the first in a series of visits that would occur on a weekly basis in the early months of 1910. **Lyman** writes that he would visit nearly every week in theirs studios "filled with a perhaps unrivalled collection of modern masters, and a wealth of beautiful things, furniture, books, photos, and documents of all kinds."[62]

1910

January 10

John **Lyman** and Matthew Smith leave Étaples where they had spent a portion of the Christmas holidays and settle in Paris, in a hotel on the Rue Jean-Bart.[63] At the time, Paris was flooded by the high waters of the Seine.

January 14

Lyman unsuccessfully attempts to see **Morrice**. **Morrice** was in Concarneau where he had a studio and where he had been staying from mid-November 1909 to early June 1910, slipping away from time to time to go to Paris. Although he returned to Paris on January 15, he was forced to stay at a hotel as well, because of the flooding.

January 30

Morrice, in a letter, talks about the Cézanne exhibition on in Paris:[64]

"There is a fine show of Cézanne's pictures on now. Fine work almost criminally fine. I once disliked some of his pictures but I now like them all. His is the savage work that one would expect to come from America—but it is always France that produces anything emphatic in art."[65] At this exhibition, **Matisse** contributed a painting entitled *Three Bathers*.

February 14-22

Morrice likely attends the large **Matisse** exhibition at the Galerie Bernheim-Jeune, which features sixty-five canvases and twenty-five drawings in a most comprehensive retrospective. The reviews are "uncommonly abusive."[66]

February 27-March 20

Second **Matisse** exhibition in New York, at the 291 Gallery, originally called the Little Galleries of the Photo Secession: exhibition of drawings, etchings and watercolours, with one lithograph and one painting. Favourable reception.

April 4-23

Although still in Paris, **Lyman** exhibits for the first time in Montreal, at the AAM Spring Exhibition, three paintings on a marine theme, which his father had proposed to the jury. **Morrice**, participating for the ninth time in this exhibition, shows four Saint-Malo scenes.[67]

April-May

Along with Matthew Smith, **Lyman** attends the Académie Matisse,[68] then located in the Couvent du Sacré-Cœur. He usually goes to the morning sessions.

Recollections of Matthew Smith:
"The school had a very pleasant atmosphere. There were long windows looking onto a garden which we walked about in during the rests. Students who wished to have a criticism left their drawing or canvas on the easel, while the others carefully hid them. We all followed **Matisse** around to each student's work and listened to what he said. I do not remember very much, as at that time I had very little French. I remember him going up to a Signorelli drawing pinned on the wall (a drawing of four nude figures, two male and two female, a very beautiful drawing) and running his finger down the drawing in several places, saying 'Voilà l'architecture.' This impressed me very much, for up to that time in London I had only heard of construction, and I felt 'l'architecture' had a more aesthetic value."[69]

Recollections of John **Lyman**:
"Nothing could have been less academic than this nest of heretical fledglings, logged in a disused convent under the trees of an ancient garden . . . We were about fifteen in the school. There was Edward Bruce, Per Kro[h]g, the Norwegian painter, Hans Purrmann, other Germans, other Scandinavians."[70]

"He did not give criticism to each student. He would take the canvas of one student or another as a point of departure for holding forth. He would not tolerate superficial things, merely decorative abbreviations. Students who came to him to learn modern tricks got no encouragement . . . He would always tell us that one had to learn to walk on the ground before trying the tight-rope, to always seek character, the truth, and that if that led to deformation, it had to be done unconsciously, to better render it."[71]

Throughout his lifetime, **Lyman** would often recollect **Matisse**: "The man impressed me far less than his painting."[72] "I was never really able to become close to him in his ways. It was only much later that I understood."[73] "What I always liked was the classicism, the measure, the order, especially the balance . . . That is why artists like **Matisse**, like Maillol, delighted me so much, because at the time, to me they represented classicism, balance."[74]

Spring
Matisse invites his students to visit him at his atelier at Issy-les-Moulineaux. **Lyman** remembers: "He talked about craft all the time . . . serious, solemn, precise, at all times wanting to preserve his lucidity, eyes wide open on the world, imposing upon himself an invariable schedule and perfecting his syntheses with sustained effort."[75]

May
Morrice indicates **Lyman's** Parisian address ("83 Boul Montparnasse") in his sketchbook no. 15, page 57v, with the note "Arrives Concarneau May 13." **Lyman** spends a few weeks in Concarneau in May 1910 but does not manage to meet with **Morrice**.[76]

Late May
Lyman, ill, interrupts his studies, and then returns to Canada during the month of June.

June 6
In preparation for the *Manet and the Post-Impressionists* exhibition, Roger Fry visits **Matisse's** atelier at à Issy-les-Moulineaux. There he sees *Dance II*, in progress.

June
End of the Académie Matisse: "What a relief!" writes [**Matisse**] to Biette, "I took it far too seriously."[77]

Fall
Back in Montreal, **Lyman** becomes engaged to Corinne Saint-Pierre (1890-1967), the daughter of renowned couturier William Saint-Pierre.

November 8, 1910-January 15, 1911
Manet and the Post-Impressionists, an exhibition curated by Roger Fry, assisted by Desmond MacCarthy, is presented at the Grafton Gallery in London (228 paintings). The presence of the triumvirate Cézanne-Van Gogh-Gauguin had a strong impact:

"The show aimed at no gradual infiltration, but—bang! An assault along the whole academic front of art."[78] The poster featured the names of Manet, Cézanne, Gauguin, Van Gogh, plus those of Picasso and **Matisse**, who were each represented by two or three paintings.

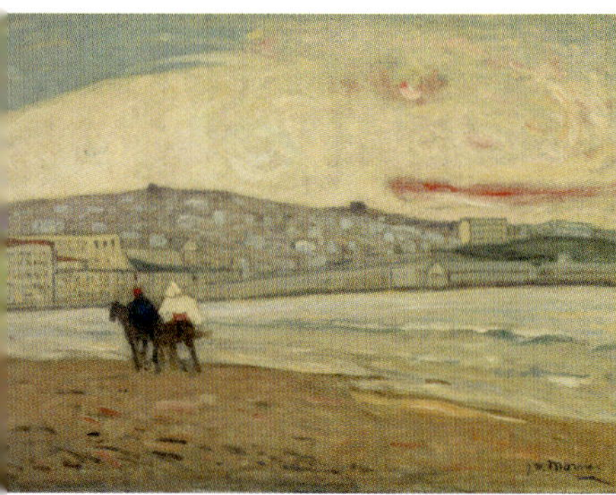

Fry had not chosen any contemporary Cubist paintings, not wishing to shock the public too much. About this show, **Morrice** writes: "There was some excitement in London last month over the exhibition called the Post Impressionists. Everybody laughed and jeered but with a few exceptions it consisted of good things. Art that will last."[79]

December 2
Matisse considers a working trip to Tangier, in Morocco. From Sevilla, in Spain, he writes to his wife: "What do you think of my idea of staying on for another month to work in Sevilla, Granada or Tangier?"[80]

1911

Spring-Summer
On April 8, **Lyman** marries Corinne Saint-Pierre in Plattsburgh, in the United States. They then leave for New York and Europe (France, Switzerland, Germany).

The couple meets **Matisse** in Paris on the occasion of the Salon des Indépendants which is held from April 21 to June 13 and where the first major Cubist group show takes place, which causes a scandal. The critics designate Picasso as the instigator. **Lyman** recalls: "At the time, there was an exhibition in Paris where exhibited . . . there was Picasso. He [**Matisse**] criticized them, he asked me questions, he compared his works and the others. He was very worried." Corinne Saint-Pierre also remembers **Matisse**: "That spring, there were many exhibitions in Paris. He did not talk to me about one painter, he did not have an admiring word to say about a single one of the painters who exhibited, not one word of praise."[81]

Lyman again encounters Matthew Smith, as well as Gertrude Stein, and he takes Corinne to visit her.[82] In Switzerland, **Lyman**, who had not painted for a year, resumes working. He returns to Normandy, to Varengeville-sur-Mer, with Matthew Smith. At the end of the summer, the Lymans return to Canada.

June 20
Morrice writes to Edmund Morris that the Salon de la SNBA had not been interesting this year, but that there had been a few very good modern art exhibitions by virtually unknown artists, particularly Bonnard "who is the best man here now—since Gauguin died."[83] Bonnard had just exhibited with Bernheim-Jeune, showing drawings as well as twenty-seven paintings, including three panels entitled *The Mediterranean*, commissioned by Ivan Morosov.

October 23-November 10
Matisse is in Russia with Shchukin. In Moscow, they pay a visit to Morosov whose collection then contained two works by **Morrice** and one by **Matisse**.

November 8
Morrice writes that he has four paintings at the Salon d'Automne de Paris (October 1-November 8), where nothing new has happened apart from the presence of the Cubists who have stirred up very heated debate: "This art I am incapable of understanding."[84]

1912

January 14
Morrice writes to Edmund Morris that he has arrived in Quebec City and that on February 3 he would be embarking on a ship bound for Gibraltar.[85]

January 29
Matisse and his wife, Amélie, arrive in Tangier. They would stay at the Hôtel Villa de France.

Early February
Morrice encounters **Matisse** in Tangier and moves into the same hotel. Apart from sharing meals, they each work alone, meeting at the end of the day. **Morrice** and **Matisse** would stay in Tangier until April. During this stay, Tangier experienced six consecutive weeks of rain.

March 14-April 6
The critic of *Le Devoir* ridicules the contributions of John **Lyman** at the AAM Spring Exhibition: "Canada has a *cubist*, unless he is a *futurist*[86] . . . The walls of the Salon des Indépendants in Paris, which have borne all sorts of things, have never sported anything so advanced in terms of composition, or rather, decomposition."[87]

/ CAT. 33 James W. Morrice
Tangier
1912

Otherwise, the participation of James Wilson **Morrice** in the same exhibition earns him praise from the critic at *The Gazette*: "A luminous nocturne is the canvas *Venice, Night*, by Mr. J. W. **Morrice**. With his usual richness of tone the artist shows beneath a dark sky of velvety depth."[88] Other critics notice instead *Palazzo Dario*, a Venetian painting of 1906, more colourful: "Nothing more beautiful . . . has ever been exhibited by Mr. **Morrice**."[89] The critic at *La Presse* takes a rest from the "eccentricities" [of **Lyman**], considering the paintings of Clarence Gagnon and **Morrice**.[90] At the time, **Morrice** had lost interest in this event and left it up to his dealer Scott & Sons to choose the works to be presented from his inventory.

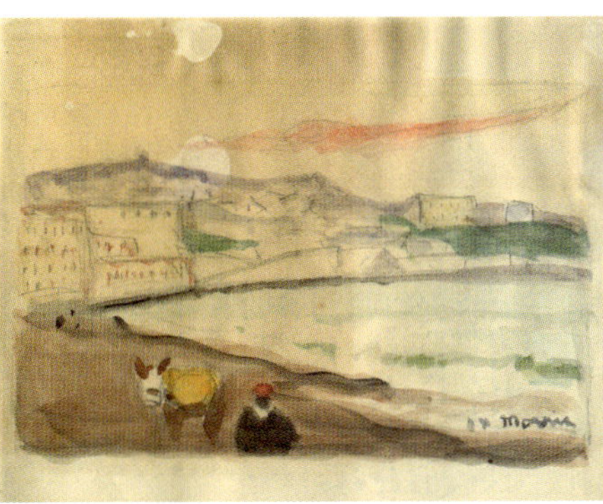

April 3

Matisse writes to his wife, who had left Tangier on March 31, to say that **Morrice** had seen two of his landscape sketches—probably *Periwinkles (Moroccan Garden)* (fig. 3) and *Palm Leaf, Tangier* (cat. 20)—and that he had liked them very much.

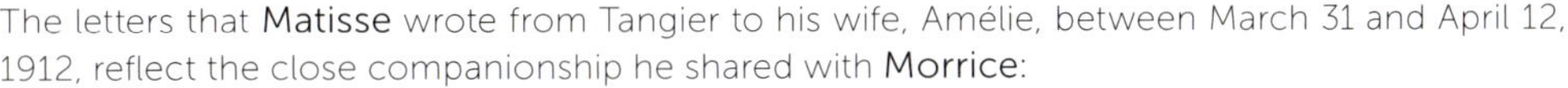

The letters that **Matisse** wrote from Tangier to his wife, Amélie, between March 31 and April 12, 1912, reflect the close companionship he shared with **Morrice**:

"Had lunch with **Morrice** who went off to work."

> Letter to Amélie, Tangier, Sunday, 5 p.m. [March 31, 1912]

"After lunch, Mlle Davin told me that I would work in the studio where Tranchant [Maurice Tranchant (1869-1944)] was and then that the young Arab girl could come without being seen. She wanted to take a photo of **Morrice** and me to send to you, but the sun hid behind the clouds, and she put it off until tomorrow. So I went up to rest from three until half-past four, then I went to find information about ship departures. They all leave on Saturday, Sunday or Tuesday. We will likely leave on those days. **Morrice** has made up his mind. Then I saw the moon rise over the sea, magnificently. I went to meet **Morrice** at the café and I went up to dine with him. The moonlight is magnificent this evening."

> Letter to Amélie, Monday, 7 p.m. [April 1, 1912]

"If I were feeling up to it, perhaps I would stay to do the Morosoff landscape, I did not talk about it with **Morrice** who expects to leave Tuesday on the German ship, much more chic than yours." Post-scriptum: "**Morrice** saw the two landscape sketches, he found them very pleasing."

> Letter to Amélie, April 3, 1912

"Yesterday afternoon **Morrice** and I went to have tea at Lavery's.[91] What bad painting . . . What will I do? **Morrice** thinks he will leave on Tuesday. If I were feeling up to it, I would like to work. Perhaps I should go with him to C, it is fairly close there to Paris[92] and the weather might be good, which would allow me to do the Morosoff painting. On the other hand, life is tranquil here, except for such changeable weather."

> Letter to Amélie [April 5, 1912]

"Today I am going to lunch with **Morrice** at Lavery's. We do not know, **Morrice** and I, when we wil leave. For I returned to see the Broux garden, it is quite beautiful, the white bindweed is starting to bloom, the plains are studded with the yellow flowers that you know, the acacia is in blossom, it is spring. If I am on form, it is worth my while to stay."

> Letter to Amélie, Saturday, April 6, 1912

"I am leaving on Sunday with **Morrice**. So on Thursday I will be in Issy with my family."

> Postcard to Mrs. Matisse, Tuesday, April 9, 1912

"I gave your regards to **Morrice**."

> Letter to Amélie, April 10, 1912

"**Morrice** is making a drawing for Mlle Davin in her album, I am waiting for him to finish so I can do the same."

> Letter to Amélie, Friday, 3 o'clock [April 12, 1912]

/ **FIG. 39** James W. Morrice
Miss Davin Notebook, folio 44
1912

April 14

Matisse and **Morrice** leave Tangier for Marseille and return to Paris. During this first sojourn of two and a half months in Tangier, **Matisse** painted *Vase of Irises, View of the Bay of Tangier, Basket of Oranges, Acanthus, Periwinkles* (fig. 3), *Palm Leaf, Tangier* (cat. 20), *Amido* and *Zorah in Yellow*. He also probably painted *The Marabout* (fig. 17), *Moroccan Woman*, perhaps *Zorah Seated* and sketched *Landscape Viewed from a Window* (fig. 19). **Morrice** brings back mainly pochades that he reworked over the summer in Paris and shows four paintings inspired by Tangier at the Salon d'Automne in the same year.

May 16

Lyman participates in the founding of the Arts Club of Montreal at Maurice Cullen's studio in Beaver Hall Square.[93] Besides **Lyman** and Cullen, Herbert Raine, A. W. Kilgour, E. J. Cox, Charles Simpson, J. C. Franchère, Charles Gill, Sidney Carter and G. Horne Russell also take part.

August

After spending a part of the summer in Quebec—in Dalesville, near Lachute—to paint, **Lyman** leaves again for France. While in New York, he and his wife stop in at the 291 Gallery where they discover Gertrude Stein's articles on **Matisse** and Picasso in the journal *Camera Work*.[94]

After visiting Paris, they spend the winter of 1912-1913 in Saint-Jean-de-Luz. **Lyman** reads Nietzsche and writes a great deal. "He was torn. He would write things, then he would not want to paint, but he could not help himself,"[95] his wife would recall.

October 1-November 8

At the Salon d'Automne in Paris, **Morrice** exhibits six paintings, including four of Tangier—*Tangier; Tangier, the Beach; Tangier, Store* and *Landscape, Tangier* (cats. 33-36)—while **Matisse** shows *Nasturtiums with "Dance,"* completed between his two voyages to Tangier that year, and *Corner of the Artist's Studio*.

October 5-December 31

Second Post-Impressionist Exhibition: British, French and Russian Artists organized by Roger Fry at the Grafton Gallery in London. The exhibition was intended to be representative of the most recent developments in modern art, with the Cubist works of Picasso (13 oils and 3 drawings) and a selection of paintings (19) and sculptures of **Matisse**.

October 8

Matisse arrives in Tangier for his second stay. Charles Camoin arrives in late November in the company of Mrs. Matisse, and **Morrice** during the month of December: "Bright colour is what I want."[96] All four stay at the Hôtel Villa de France. **Matisse** recalls: "Apart from working sessions, we were always together."[97] Clive Bell writes: "Once again they were together in North Africa. **Matisse** appreciated the painting of **Morrice** and found him charming, but I think he found his habits unsettling. He did not like it, I think, when Arab boys would follow **Morrice** in the street, shouting "Whisky! Whisky!"[98]

1913

January

When the January rains begins, **Matisse** rents a well-lit photographer's studio, in the centre of the town, overlooking the bay. He, **Morrice** and Camoin may have met together there, as suggested in a later letter from Camoin to **Matisse**: "I still think of, with regret, our gallivanting about Tangier, at the Moorish café, at your studio at the photographer's, and the fellow **Morrice** who would zigzag around in the large dining room. All that is so long ago, damn it!"[99]

Matisse brought back his *Landscape Viewed from a Window* (fig. 19) from Paris to complete it. **Morrice** painted his canvas entitled *View from the Window, Tangier* (cat. 65) during this second trip. In his book on **Morrice** (1945), **Lyman** would compare the two works: "Also there is no real resemblance between his painting [that of **Morrice**] and that of **Matisse**. Better than any commentary, the two painters have left us, as if intentionally, to deprive us of any possible illusion, compositions with identical subjects. Like **Matisse**, **Morrice** placed

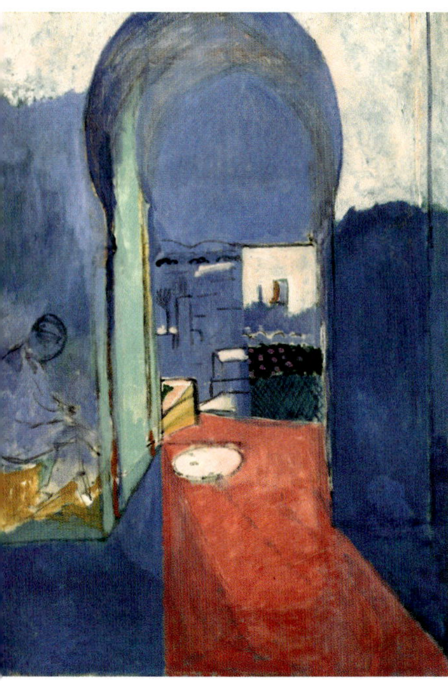

/ **FIG. 40** Henri Matisse
The Casbah Gate
1912-1913

pots of flowers on the sill of his *View from the Window*, beyond these are the same buildings and gardens, in the midst of the same city flanked by the sea . . . but another world. In that of **Matisse** everything is subordinated to an arabesque farm which, like a French garden, proposes to the mind certain formal certainties; that of **Morrice** is similar to an English garden, which, not imposing a fixed form on nature, prompts the soul to dream."[100]

Mid-February

Matisse leaves Tangier. Camoin and **Morrice** stay on for a few more weeks. **Morrice** leaves in early March for Gibraltar, then Paris.

Matisse's recollections of **Morrice**:

"About fifteen years ago [*sic*], I spent two winters in Tangier in the company of **Morrice**. You know the artist with the delicate eye who delighted in interpreting landscapes of closely related values in soft and muted hues . . . As a man, he was a true gentleman, a good companion, with great wit and humour. He had, as everyone knows, an unfortunate passion for whisky. Nevertheless, apart from working sessions, we were always together. I used to go with him to a café where I drank as many glasses of mineral water as he took glasses of alcool . . . I do not know what more to tell you. He was Canadian of Scottish origin, from a wealthy family, he himself was very rich, but he did not display his wealth. He was always travelling over hill and dale, a little like a migrating bird, but with no fixed landing place."[101]

These recollections would later be commented on by John **Lyman** who would present a greater contrast between the two painters, going so far as "to doubt that this contact was very intimate . . . Moreover, this is reflected in the distantly polite tone in which **Matisse** wrote his recollections of our 'gentleman' on the occasion of a posthumous exhibition. The Frenchman liked profound discussions of aesthetics, for which the Canadian had neither the facility of expression (his French was mediocre) nor the spirit to sustain. It is odd to envisage the encounter of these two men whose outer appearance did not reveal, at first glance, opposing temperaments."[102]

February 17–March 15

Matisse prompts outrage at the Armory Show, in New York, then in Chicago (March 24–April 15) and in Boston (April 28–May 18). It was the first time that the works of the modern artists Cézanne, Gauguin, Rouault, **Matisse** and many others were seen together in North America.

February 18

Camoin writes to **Matisse**: "**Morrice**, between whiskies, in one of his lucid moments, spoke to me of painting, telling me that contrary to what you believe, he really likes what you do. He asked me if he could see my paintings and I was a bit surprised about his preferences."[103]

March 26–April 16

In Montreal, **Lyman** shows four works at the AAM Spring Exhibition: *Humoresque – The Circus*; *A Brunette*; *Wild Nature Impromptu;* and *Bagatelle – A Cottage*. Genuine shock erupts in the Montreal press (fig. 41) who associate him with Post-Impressionism and more specifically, with **Matisse**.[104]

On March 29 (fig. 42), the critic Samuel Morgan-Powell writes that **Matisse** is a madman and that London was busy "laughing to this day about the latest fantasy of **Matisse**," adding that "if Montreal joins with London and laughs about it, the fad will soon pass."[105]

March–June

Morrice and **Matisse** are assembled side by side on the walls of Prima Esposizione Internazionale d'Arte della Secessione (First International Exhibition of Secession Art) in Rome, with *The Terrace, Quebec* and *Goldfish*.

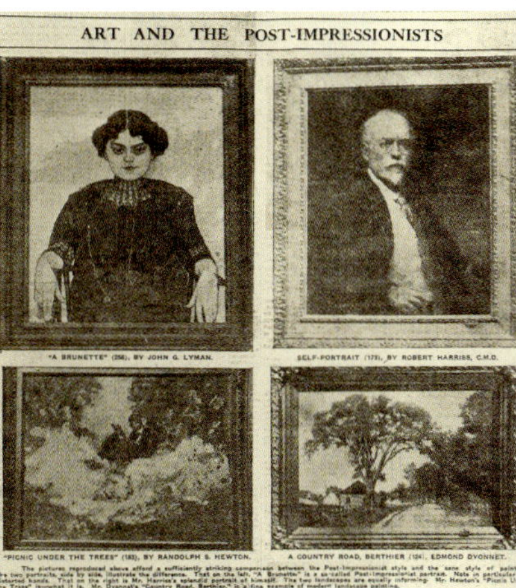

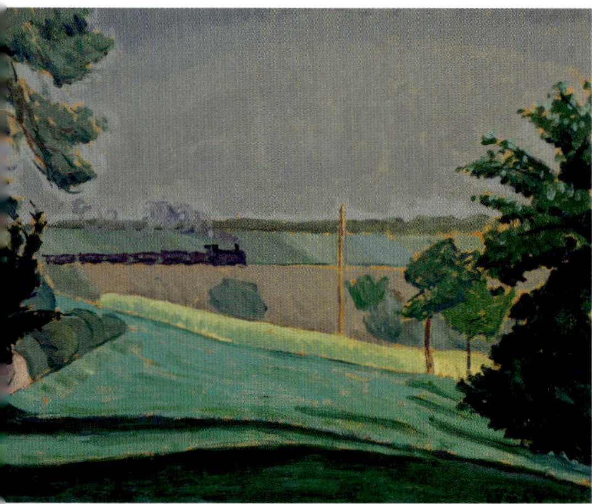

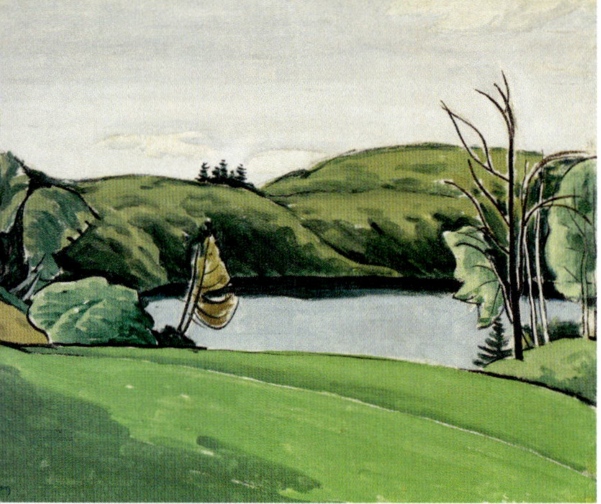

April 5-May 17

In London, at the Exhibition of the International Society of Sculptors, Painters and Gravers,[106] **Morrice** shows three paintings of Tangier: *Tangier* (cat. 33), *Tangier, the Beach* (cat. 34) and *Tangier at Night* (location unknown).

April 14-19

At Bernheim-Jeune, **Matisse** exhibits fourteen paintings, drawings and sculptures brought back from his stay in Morocco. Only three paintings are for sale, the others belonging to Shchukin and to Morosov.

Lyman attends this exhibition and then returns to Montreal. **Morrice** likely also attends.

May 1-3

A response from **Lyman** (sent from Paris on April 15) to the article of March 29 by Samuel Morgan-Powell is published in *The Montreal Star* of May 1. **Lyman** defends **Matisse**:

"London, glibly asserts S.M.P., is laughing, and 'Paris—sane artistic Paris—takes **Matisse** as it does most imitators.' Anyone who consults the articles that appeared in many London journals during the Post Impressionist exhibitions of the last two years, can assure himself that there are many who intend to laugh last and best. Many pictures from these shows were bought for English collections; and as for Paris—scarcely a remaining work of the dead Post Impressionists can be found on the market at any price. This week is being held a show of eleven paintings by **Matisse**, just brought back from Tangiers, eight of which were bought before they could be exhibited at prices between \$2,000 and \$4,000. His works are to be found in many of the great private collections of France, Austria, Germany, Russia, etc. I may also add that if S.M.P. had gone a little deeper into his New York journalistic literature, he would know that over two hundred Post Impressionists works were bought at the first exhibition held here recently."[107]

On May 3, **Lyman** writes to the secretary of the AAM, J. B. Abbott, to request a room for a solo exhibition of ten days. The director, Mr. Meredith, gives his approval on May 5, without even having seen the paintings the artist intends to show.

May 17

Another response from **Lyman**, in which he indicates that he is personally acquainted with **Matisse**, is published in *The Montreal Star*:

"I said that eight out of the eleven pictures done by **Matisse** last winter were bought at prices between \$2,000 and \$4,000 before they could be exhibited. Some were bought for the collection of a Russian, which at his death is to become the property of the Moscow Municipal Gallery. I said I was in a position to know. I know Mr. **Matisse** personally and I have seen most of his work which is almost as good a source of knowledge as is an inference from an article in *Le Temps*. I know that it is NOT SO MUCH his early as his late work that has been bought for many great private collections in Europe; I know that examples of his work of EVERY year up to including 1913 are to be found in these collections; I know, having seen it, that the work he did when a student at l'École des beaux-arts is far more what he called extreme Post Impressionism than anything ever seen in this city; with all of which I find difficulty in reconciling the assurance, 'that it is the sane work of **Matisse** before he allied himself with the Post Impressionist School, that bought up for great private collection.' But the great joke is that I also know Mr. Stein, of whose article the quoted fragment is suppose to damn **Matisse**, and who owns at least 29 canvases by **Matisse** and other Post Impressionists."[108]

May 21-31

The controversy surrounding **Lyman** reignites when the painter shows forty-two works at his first solo exhibition at the AAM. "At the opening, everyone was laughing," the painter would recall.[109] The free style and the musical titles of the paintings and drawings trigger a storm of invective in the Montreal press who repeat its attacks on "futurism" and "Post-Impressionism."[110] Two of these works are in our exhibition: *Swiss Essay No. 1* (cat. 15) and *Wild Nature Impromptu, 1st State* (cat. 83).

Foreword to the *Exhibition of Paintings and Drawings by John G. **Lyman***, presented at the AAM from May 21 to May 31, 1913.

What is art, essentially?

Contemplation is a faculty that we westerners lack; we would not do as the Hindu disciple who, having asked his master a question and the master having answered: "Go think about it for seven years, you will then come to tell me that your request was futile," returned after seven years to ask him for seven more to reflect further; the time having lapsed, the disciple then admitted to his master that his question had not been worth asking.

Yet who among you, painters, composers, dancers, poets, musicians, indeed all of you who merely chatter, has doggedly given direct consideration to this problem: "What is art, essentially?" Who among you has found a practical, if not perfect hypothesis, before hazarding a judgment about a work of art? Art? Many inadequate, flashy things can be said, such as: the story of the adventures of the human soul . . . but more progress can be made by saying what art is not.

Art is not an imitation of nature; for those who think it so, it cannot have much importance. Evidently! To imitate is to reproduce; yet man cannot reproduce what he cannot produce. If art were supposed to be natural, the painter of imitation marble would be first among artists, and the shorthand of a Crown Court trial the masterpiece of drama. If art were supposed to be natural, Phidias, Michelangelo, Rembrandt and El Greco would fall short in that they remain themselves and they do not resemble each other.

Art that looks natural is nonsense; art must be artificial; where imitation ceases, art begins; seek its definitive condition in what lies beyond. Art is not the story of what we see, but of what we think about what we see; what determines it is what arises between expression and the inspiring object: imagination, organizing intelligence and personality as well. If an artist's contemporary personality is appreciable to you on the first, second or sixtieth sight, you can be certain that it is merely banal. You do not presume to grasp, even with your twenty-five centuries of education, the ultimate power of Hera of Samos? Thus, how far less capable you would be of understanding, in passing, without effort, the most intimate meaning of the art of your generation or that of your children's! Few of us really see; we merely have visual habits, steeped in the entire past that we have inherited; thus if a work of art is not merely a reworking of this past, it inevitably must shock at first sight, in that it is strange, unfamiliar, unintelligible; only trailblazers will perceive a meaning in it, then, little by little, it will enter into forming future intelligence.

"If art must be obscure, then at least it should be beautiful!" you exclaim.

And... what is beauty?

Ask ancient Plato, no one ever phrased it better: "Beauty is the splendour of truth."

Ask the critics! It is not in the nature of these oracles to be content with half-truths of infinite human wisdom, and they will never be reduced to saying, as did Flaubert's Sphinx: "I have thought so hard, I have nothing left to say."

Those who merely wish to seek a narcotic in art to procure a sweet and vague somnolence, or a sweetmeat to satisfy an emptiness of mind, must not stop here: they will only find a bitter concoction of life's corrosive juices.

Corinne St. P. Lyman.

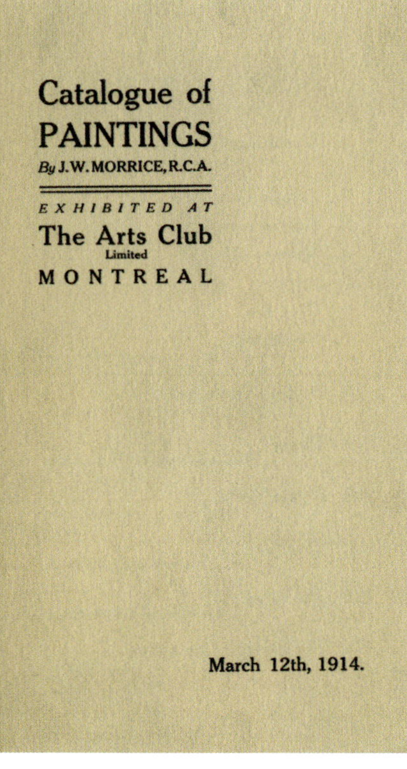

/ **FIG. 43** Cover of the catalogue of Morrice's exhibition at the Arts Club of Montreal
1914

Summer
Shaken by the storm of criticism unleashed by his exhibition, **Lyman** returns to Paris.

November 15, 1913-January 5, 1914
In Paris, at the Salon d'Automne, **Morrice** exhibits a Gibraltar landscape, four Tangier landscapes and a portrait: *Gibraltar* (cat. 4); *Tangier, the Outskirts* (cat. 39); *Tangier, the Town* (cat. 37); *View from the Window, Tangier* (cat. 65); *Tangier, Garden* (location unknown); and *Tangier, Dancer* (cat. 42).

Fall
Lyman returns to Montreal[111] and leaves in November for Bermuda, where he would spend winter. He supervises the construction of a house for one of his uncles. He paints and writes about the history of Bermuda.

1914

January
Although he keeps his studio in Issy-les-Moulineaux, **Matisse** moves back to Paris, at 19, quai Saint-Michel, on the floor above his former studio which he had vacated in October 1905 and which is now occupied by Albert Marquet.

March 12
The Arts Club of Montreal, founded in 1912 by Maurice Cullen, holds an exhibition of the works of **Morrice** (fig. 43).[112]

Spring
Morrice spends the winter in Cagnes and a few weeks in Tunis, North Africa.

Summer
Lyman stays in Cowansville, in the Eastern Townships, in the Georgian style house called "Fairfield" purchased by his father. His relations with his father scarcely improve.

August 2
Start of the First World War.

August 11
Morrice leaves Paris, visits friends in London, in particular the Pennell couple whom he has known for several years:

"James **Morrice**, who thought, if he had a wife, he would not have stirred from Paris, but to be shut up in his studio alone after eight o'clock in the evening[113] was too much for his nerves. He was almost as depressed as my husband over the whole tragedy and we did what we could to help him with our sympathy and company, for we were both extremely fond of him."[114]

He also sees Clive Bell who relates: "He had come to London, perhaps a little panic-stricken, but he did not stay long; for he found, so he told me, that the only thing to be done in an English winter was to sit indoors drinking whisky: 'it was always like that' he added."[115]

October
Having stayed with his family in Collioure since September, **Matisse** returns to Paris, as his studio in Issy is partially occupied by French officers.

November
On his return to Paris, **Morrice** sees that the city has closed down, deprived of its nightlife.[116] Following the death of his mother on November 26, he departs for Canada. His father, David Morrice, would die less than a month later on December 19.

Morrice remains in Canada until mid-February 1915. He had not returned there for three years.

Clive Bell relates that, in contrast to the perception of **Lyman**, the art of **Matisse** had a growing influence on **Morrice**: "The art of **Matisse** had considerable influence on that of **Morrice**. This is much to the credit of the latter; for he was already a mature and fairly successful painter in another style. He preserved an open mind and sensibility, and was capable of profiting by new methods and a younger man's vision."[117]

Winter 1914-1915
Lyman is in Bermuda. He spends little time painting.

1915

January 20-February 27
Third **Matisse** exhibition in New York City, at the Montross Gallery, organized by Walter Pach, who met the painter in Paris the preceding fall. **Morrice**, who was spending a few days in New York City en route to Cuba, may have seen it, since he often frequented Fred J. Gregg, who wrote the catalogue.[118]

February 1
In Montreal, **Lyman** and his wife, Corinne, become involved with the Red Cross.

Mid-February to Mid-April
Morrice leaves Montreal for Cuba with Richard B. Van Horne, son of Sir William Van Horne (1843-1915), who had built the rail network on the island. They spend a few days in New York City, sleep in Washington on the 23rd and embark on a ship bound for New Orleans. **Morrice** stays for over a month in Cuba, sketching in cafés and the streets of Havana and Santiago. He brings back postcards which will serve as models for some paintings (fig. 44). Leaving Santiago, he stops over in Kingston, Jamaica. He finally leaves Havana on April 9 for New York and then takes a passenger liner bound for Bordeaux.[119]

Spring
In New York, **Lyman** attempts to join the U.S. army as a U.S. citizen, then the Canadian army, but he is discharged for health reasons.

May
In Paris, **Morrice** hosts Roger Fry. Fry writes to Clive Bell: "My dear Clive . . . I've been seeing a good deal of Barne,[120] **Morrice** and O'Conor, whom I like quite a lot. They are often talking of you and your ideas. I've bought an O'Conor whose recent work I like a lot—and I hope to get a **Morrice**, though he's nothing at the moment that'll quite do."[121]

August
Morrice travels to Toulouse, Bayonne and Carcassonne.[122]

October 1915-March 1916
Lyman and his wife, Corinne, return to France, in the service of the French Red Cross. They are posted to Cannes then to the military hospital in Marseille.[123]

1916

April
Lyman experiences a period of crisis because of the disappointment of his father, upon whom he is still financially dependent:

"The reason that I seem so indifferent to painting is that I have been discouraged—not by criticism and opposition—but by your regret to have let me go in for that art, your impatience to see me produce something marketable, and my desire not to complicate your financial burdens. You want to know what I am doing and thinking, I have to tell you the truth. With my mentality it was totally impossible for me to degrade myself to doing a mock, pot-boiling art, and so I turned to literature, in which it is easier to find profit for a mediocre, though sincere talent, in the hope of reconciling art and income."[124]

"What has seriously troubled me has been a seeming lack of interest in painting."[125]

Summer
Lyman, ill, abandons his volunteer work at the military hospital in Marseille.

Matisse spends most of the year in Paris, apart from a few visits to Issy. Over the summer, he makes short trips to Marseille and Nice. Roger Fry visits him in early July.

During the year
The Contemporary Art Society in London (founded in 1910 to acquire the works of living artists) purchases a recent work by **Morrice**, *House in Santiago, Cuba* (cat. 19). The Society would show the painting in exhibitions at the Leicester Art Gallery in fall 1919 (with **Matisse** and Maillol), in London at the Grosvenor House in June-July 1923 and then at the Tate Gallery in 1924.[126]

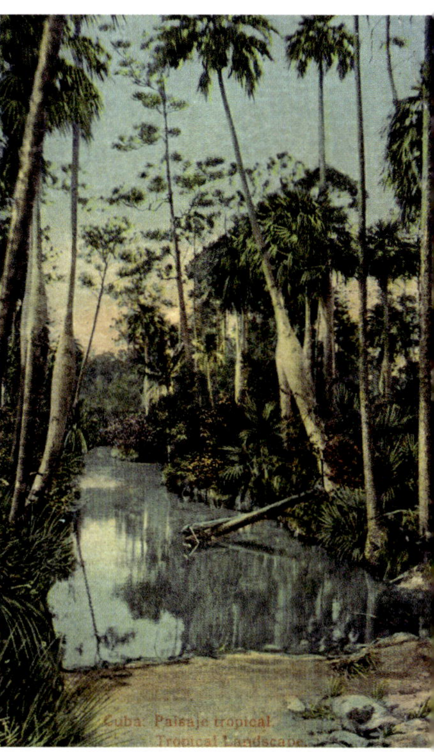

/ **FIG. 44** Jordi, Havana
**Cuba, paisaje tropical/
Tropical Landscape**
Undated

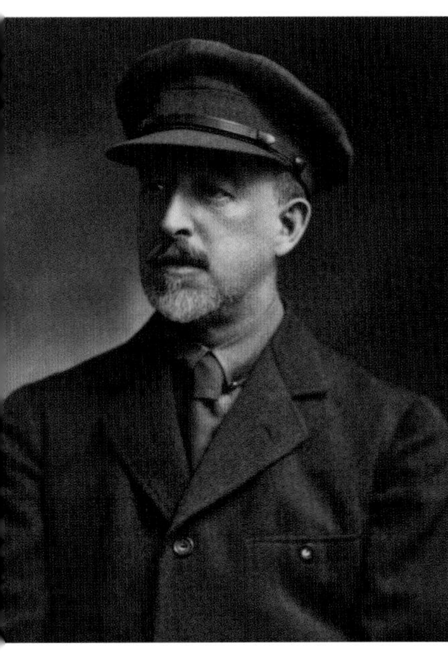

1917

January 4
Morrice, **Lyman** and Corinne arrive in New York, on their way to Montreal. The trio had left Bordeaux on December 23 aboard the *SS Espagne*.[127]

March 22-April 14
Lyman, who had painted very little since the outbreak of the war, nevertheless shows two works at the AAM. **Morrice** no longer exhibits there.

November
Morrice moved to 23, quai de la Tournelle, not far and on the same bank of the river as the Quai des Grands-Augustins that he had been forced to vacate. Léa Cadoret remembers: "A closer, more convenient studio could have been rented, Quai Saint-Michel, in the building where Henri **Matisse** and Albert Marquet had their studios, but **Morrice** refused to take this apartment, because he wanted to paint alone, in isolation."[128]

December
Matisse settles in Nice, at the Hôtel Beau Rivage. He would pay several visits to Renoir who lives nearby at Cagnes-sur-Mer.

1918

February
Morrice spends a few weeks at the Picardy front (fig. 45). He gathers material for the large mural painting commissioned by Lord Beaverbrook on behalf of the Canadian War Memorials (now the Canadian War Museum, Ottawa),[129] that he would paint in Concarneau during the summer.[130] He draws inspiration both from the sketches he brought back from the front and on photographs.

April 4-27
Lyman exhibits a *Portrait* and his self-portrait (cat. 14) at the AAM Spring Exhibition. Once again his painting disconcerts the critics, even in the Montreal avant-garde review *Le Nigog*: "Mr. **Lyman** is a disturbing painter; his two portraits are solidly drawn and have accurate values, but they are unfortunately painted in colours I do not understand. Mr. **Lyman**, who is an artist, obviously has the right to use whatever colours he wants, but, all the same, my pleasure in seeing his work is spoiled by this use of unpleasant tones."[131]

June
Lyman returns to Paris where he attempts to see **Morrice** again. **Lyman** notes that the works of **Matisse** are selling at high prices.

November 11
End of the war. **Morrice** is in Paris. **Lyman** is in Los Angeles, where his father now lives. He travels to Provincetown and to Pasadena, in the suburbs of Los Angeles, sketching and completing a few paintings and watercolours.

November or December
Matisse leaves Paris and returns to Nice where he stays at the Hôtel de la Méditerranée, 13, promenade des Anglais.

1919

Clive Bell, who has not seen **Morrice** since 1914, attempts to meet him Paris: "When I returned to Paris in 1919 I tried to find **Morrice**. No one seemed to know where he was; only it was thought that he was rarely in town."[132] As will be seen later, **Morrice** had resumed his travels.

June
Returning to Paris, **Lyman** resides at 68, rue d'Assas, and he has a studio in the Rue de la Grande-Chaumière.

July 20-August 3
Lyman rents a studio in Grez-sur-Loing, near Nemours, where his friend the painter Matthew Smith has a house: "I hope that my short stay here will start me firmly on the road to painting."[133]

/ FIG. 45 Eugène Pirou, Paris
J. W. Morrice in uniform
About 1918

September
Lyman and Corinne leave for Hammamet in Tunisia where they rent a villa and where they would spend winters until 1922. **Lyman** painted a great deal there, appreciating the "soft, pearly, delicate" aspect of the colours.[134] Perhaps during that winter **Morrice** returns to Morocco, revisiting Tangier, but staying mainly in Rabat.

1920

March 25-April 17
Lyman exhibits at the AAM Spring Exhibition for the last time before 1928.

October 15-December 12
Lyman shows three works at the Salon d'Automne in Paris. This is his first exhibition in France. His address is now 18, rue Boissonade. **Matisse** is at this salon.

1921

January 22-March 3
Following a stay in Quebec, **Morrice** leaves on the *SS Mégantic* from New York for Trinidad, in the Caribbean, where he arrives on February 6. He paints mainly in Macqueripe Bay, leaving for France on the *SS St. Raphael* on March 3.

Summer
Lyman buys the Villa Blanche at Cagnes-sur-Mer, in southeastern France, where Renoir died two years earlier. He turns the stables into a studio and paints a great deal:[135] he completes the portrait of his father during his visit to France and it is also during this time that he paints *Indolent Youth* (cat. 97).[136]

Before September
In the company of Corinne, **Lyman** pays a visit to **Matisse** in Nice,[137] at the Hôtel de la Méditerranée:

"It was about this time that I last visited him in his studio at Nice. He showed me picture after picture, and I said nothing.[138] That is what looking at painting ought to do to you—shut you up . . . If **Matisse**'s work is seldom an ornament for a given space, it is an ornament for certain needs of our existence, for our need of calm and joy, and in art as in life joy is possibly the hardest thing to confer."[139]

"On a visit to Nice, we found him [**Matisse**] on the balcony of the hotel room on the Promenade des Anglais (where he did most of his work between 1917 and 1920) painting 'La Fête des Fleurs à Nice.' In an unusually playful mood, he was swinging his brush in time with the band music. The looping brushwork did not produce a very good picture. He was just having fun."[140]

Fall
Morrice and **Matisse** exhibit at the Goupil Gallery Salon in London. This gives the British art critic Paul George Konody (1872-1933)[141] an opportunity to take stock of the advances in British art and French art:

"Ten years ago, at the First Post-Impressionist Exhibition, Cézanne and Van Gogh were derided as lunatics and incompetent bunglers. To-day, at the Goupil Gallery, Van Gogh's 'Flower-piece' (N° 69) hangs peacefully with a Nicholson and a Wilson Steer, and will not strike anybody as abnormal or eccentric. Even **Matisse** has lost the power to shock. His 'Sur l'herbe' (N° 213) will be calmly judged as an uninspired and rather dull performance, which can cause neither surprise nor anger nor enthusiasm. Indeed, the Canadian, J. W. **Morrice**, in his 'Paysage Trinidad' (N° 193), carries **Matisse**'s typical style of calligraphic synthesis further: sea and beach and cliffs are reduced by him almost to decoratively arranged symbols."[142]

November 1-December 20
Lyman and **Morrice** both exhibit at the Salon d'Automne in Paris; one presents Tunisian subjects, the other, West Indian subjects.

1922

January
Morrice buys a villa for Léa Cadoret at Cagnes-sur-Mer,[143] and he notes the address of **Lyman** in his sketchbook no. 21 (inside the lower cover board). **Lyman** and **Morrice** now each have a villa in the Cagnes countryside and are thus close to **Matisse** who lives not far from Nice.

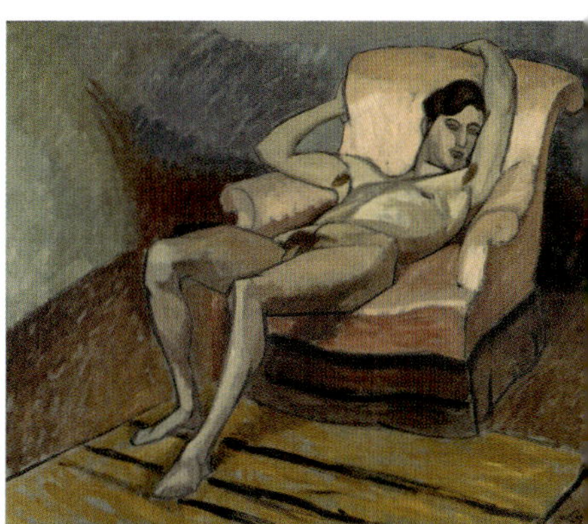

/ **CAT. 97** John Lyman
Indolent Youth
About 1922

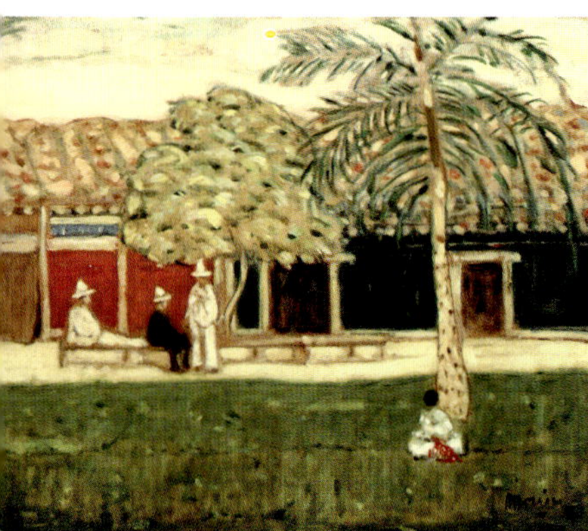

February-April
Morrice travels to Corsica (Bastia) and Algeria (Algiers and Constantine). "**Morrice's** evolution of watercolour treatment is daring . . . he explores in depth the Fauvist lines characteristic of works such as *La Danse* (1909) and *La Musique* (1910) by **Matisse**."[144]

1923

February 10-March 11
Lyman exhibits at the Salon des Artistes indépendants in Paris.

February
Morrice again visits Algeria (Algiers, Oran).

May-June
Lyman participates for the first time in the new Salon des Tuileries in Paris.

November 1-December 16
Lyman and **Morrice** exhibit at the Salon d'Automne.

December 25
Morrice spends Christmas in Cagnes-sur-Mer where he again encounters **Lyman**. He had previously confided in Corinne and told her that there was no hope for him to win any respect in Canada. **Lyman** would later write that **Morrice** had confirmed this through his decision to remain in Europe: "He was not at all understood [by Canadians] and I said to myself: if they don't appreciate him, they cannot appreciate me. He said it was completely useless, that he would never be understood in Canada, and that as for me, it would be better if I never went back."[145]

December 28
Morrice is in Tunis.

1924

January
Morrice stays in Palermo, in Sicily, then returns to Tunis. He enters hospital where he dies on January 23 and is interred at the Christian cemetery of Bab-Saadoun. His body (and the monument) were moved in 1967 to the Borgel cemetery.

November 1-December 14
Lyman exhibits at the Salon d'Automne. At the same salon, Dunoyer de Segonzac (1884-1974) holds a commemorative exhibition for James Wilson **Morrice**. It is a small show of fourteen canvases from private Parisian collections that Clive Bell praised highly, indicating his preference for the paintings of his Impressionist period: "To my mind, [his] best period. The art of **Morrice**, before he came under the influence of **Matisse**, was essentially impressionist—late impressionist. His pictures are full of impressionist paganism, delight in life and adoration of Paris."[146]

1925

January 16-February 15
*Memorial Exhibition of Paintings by the Late James W. **Morrice**, R.C.A.*, at the AAM, where 111 works of **Morrice** are shown, including forty works loaned by Canadian collectors.

1926

January 9-23
*Tableaux et études par James-Wilson **Morrice*** exhibition, featuring fifty-three works, at the Galeries Simonson de Paris, 19, rue de Caumartin (cat. 77). The works are from French public and private collections, as well as from the artist's studio, including a number for sale.[147] The catalogue is prefaced by the critic Armand Dayot (1851-1934) who cites **Matisse**'s reminiscences of the Canadian painter.[148]

Summer
Lyman rents a villa in Ascain, near Saint-Jean-de-Luz, in southwestern France.

November 5-December 19
Lyman and **Matisse** take part in the Salon d'Automne.

1927

May
Lyman and **Matisse** participate in the Salon des Tuileries.[149]

/ CAT. 77 James W. Morrice
Houses, Cuba
1915

Summer
Lyman is in Montreal: "Before even the flattest Quebec landscape I feel that I have more to say than before the magnificent sites of Europe. Two years ago, should have thought this statement impossible."[150]

Lyman begins his research on **Morrice**. His book, the only one he would publish, would not appear until 1945.

October 1-15
Exhibition of Recent Paintings and Drawings by John **Lyman** at the Johnson Art Galleries in Montreal (thirty-three works). The subjects painted are inspired by Quebec, French and Tunisian landscapes, with some portraits. No sales. His worst detractor in 1913, Samuel Morgan-Powell, highly praised this exhibition:

"Living abroad most of his time, one might have expected that Mr. **Lyman** would be strongly influence by modern European schools. Yet it seems to me that in his Eastern sketches, at all events, he retains a strong individuality. His painting of scenery in and around Hammamet, Tunisia, is marked by an originality of handling in both landscape and figure work that invites examination . . . One might cite other examples that combine to indicate the genuine artistic progress of this artist, who has always had the courage of his convictions and who has fought his own fight towards his own ideals—with a success that I, for one, welcome with genuine enthusiasm."[151]

Fall
Lyman again leaves Montreal for Paris.

December
Lyman's father dies in Pasadena, California. After the settlement of the estate, **Lyman** and Corinne return to France.

1928　**March 22-April 15**
After an eight-year absence, **Lyman** participates in the AAM Spring Exhibition.

1930　**February 25-July 31**
Matisse leaves for Tahiti. On March 5, he disembarks for the first time in New York, admiring the city's "crystalline light."[152] "It is grand and majestic like the sea." On March 9, he travels to Chicago where he visits the Art Institute. He then journeys by train to Los Angeles where he arrives on March 13: "An immense version of the Côte d'Azur,"[153] then he goes to San Francisco where a number of artists invite him to a banquet. On the 21st, he embarks on the *Tahiti*, and on the 29th, he arrives in Papeete. Following a moment of enthusiasm— "I think everything is marvellous: landscape, trees, flowers and people"—his interest wanes: "Pictorially, the country says nothing to me."[154] He visits the Leeward Islands, Bora-Bora, Moorea and Tuamotu, then makes the return journey on a ship sailing through Panama, Martinique and Guadeloupe, and arrives in Marseille on July 31: "Did absolutely nothing."[155] It would only be some years later that the effect of this Polynesian voyage would be reflected in his work, particularly in his production of paper cutouts in the 1940s.

June
Lyman is invited to exhibit in the Salon des Tuileries. Despite the mention of two works in the catalogue, *Portrait du pianiste R-M* and *Cavalier andalou*, they were not shown because they had been water damaged.[156]

September
On the occasion of a second voyage to the United States, on a visit to Pittsburgh, invited as a member of the jury for the Carnegie Prize, that he had been awarded in 1927, **Matisse** visits the Barnes Foundation in Merion where some of his works are shown. The jury is composed of Homer St-Gaudins, Ross Moffett, the Canadian Horatio Walker, Glynn Philpot, Henri **Matisse**, Karl Sterrer and Bernard Karfiol (fig. 46). Dr. Albert C. Barnes asks **Matisse** to create a mural decoration for the grand gallery of his foundation (*The Dance*).

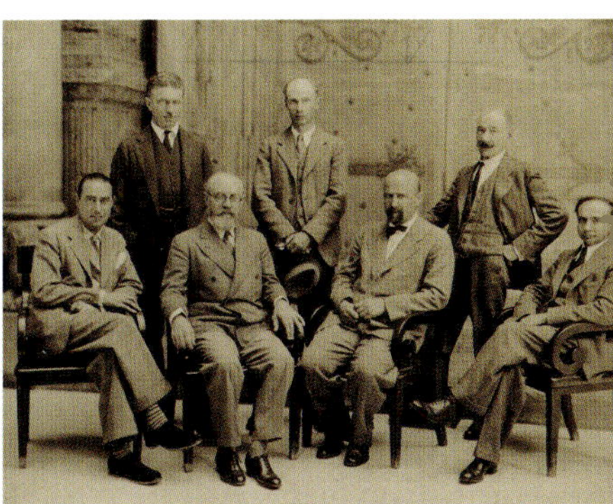

/ **FIG. 46** Ralph W. Johnston
Group portrait of the Carnegie International Jury of Awards
1930

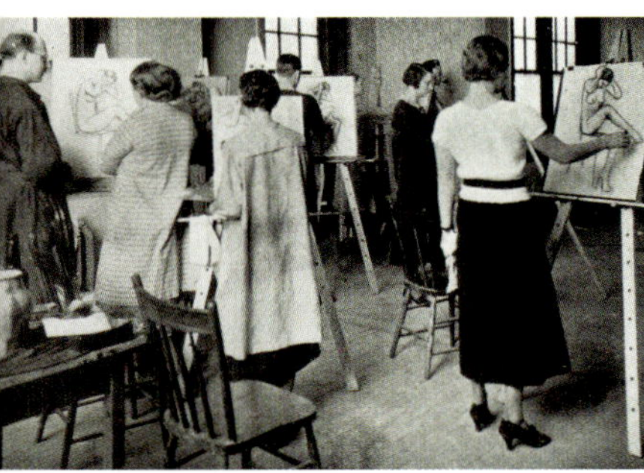

October 13
Lyman writes in his *Journal* that he went to visit Arthur Morrice, the painter's brother, and saw a good number of pochades and paintings. His rediscovery of the work of **Morrice** prompts the following reflection: "The painter who works with pleasure is an amateur. The real painter works with anguish. Painting is a drug to him: he hates it but cannot leave it alone."[157]

December
Matisse returns to Merion, thus making his fifth trans-Atlantic crossing in twelve months. The voyage includes a visit to Miss Etta Cone of Baltimore, one of his major collectors.

1931

February 21-March 4
Exhibition of Paintings by John **Lyman** at Scott & Sons gallery (thirty-nine paintings). Observing his Canadian, Spanish and French subjects, including his magnificent beach scenes at Saint-Jean-de-Luz, a critic speaks of "striking" works.[158]

September 28
Lyman is forty-five. Cheered by the positive reception of his last two Montreal exhibitions at the Johnson Art Galleries and at Scott & Sons, and sensing that mentalities had evolved,[159] he returns to Montreal, "my mind made up by the desire to live where I feel at home,"[160] he said.

November 17
Lyman founds the Atelier group, "a School of Drawing, Painting, Sculpture" that brings together students and professional artists (fig. 47). Joining the other founding members— André Biéler, Elizabeth Frost, Hazen Sise and George Holt—are former members of the Beaver Hall Group, active in the 1920s, including Edwin Holgate, Prudence Heward, Randolph Hewton, Mabel May, Lilias Newton and Anne Savage.[161] The association would soon be considered a "small group of free thinkers."[162]

Lyman introduces his students to the works of Ingres, Cézanne and **Matisse**, as well as to the *Journal* of Delacroix.[163]

1932

March 29-April 9
First exhibition of the Atelier group on the fifth floor of Henry Morgan's department store, featuring the works of André Biéler, Marc-Aurèle Fortin, Elizabeth Frost, Edwin Holgate, George Holt and John **Lyman**. The Atelier joins with McGill University to give night classes.

During this period, the **Lyman** couple receives guests in their home every Friday night and attends the Atelier every Wednesday evening.

1933

May 1-13
Second exhibition of the Atelier at Morgan's, featuring André Biéler, Elizabeth Frost, George Holt, John **Lyman** and Goodridge Roberts. A malicious article in the *Gazette* presents the group as a "questionable and likely subversive organization,"[164] which results in its exclusion by McGill University and later, its dissolution.

1934

December
French Paintings by the Impressionists and Modern Artists at Scott & Sons (held jointly with Alex Reid & Lefevre, Ltd., London) includes one work by **Matisse**: *La Lecture (Woman Reading,* 1924). The catalogue presents an illustration of this painting and another of Pierre Bonnard's *La Table garnie (Table Laid for Dessert),* Renoir's *La Couseuse (The Seamstress)* and Vincent Van Gogh's *Portrait of Père Tanguy.*

In an article entitled "From Monet to **Matisse**," **Lyman** seizes this first opportunity to comment on a work of his former teacher in a Montreal exhibition:[165]

"It is a good thing to think of poetry when we are looking at pictures. When Lawrence speaks in one of his poems of 'spurty little goats' he evokes with these three words so vivid an image that any further comment would only serve to dull it. **Matisse** is an example of this kind of elliptical statement. His maxim is: 'Whatever is not necessary is harmful.' It has been his aim to keep the vivacity of refreshment for the eyes. If you should see a **Matisse** or a Bonnard or a Dufy upside down in a far corner of the room, it would arrest your attention.

/ FIG. 47
A group of students at the Atelier, with John Lyman at left
Photograph reproduced in *Canadian Passing Show,* February 1933

Just why is not easy to say. We could explain some of the reasons, but we could never fathom all of them. After all, what painting has to say can only be well said in paint . . . While **Matisse** was a student at the École des beaux-arts under Gustave Moreau, that extraordinary teacher, who formed a number of the best contemporary French painters, he spent much time in the Louvre copying Raphael, Poussin, Chardin and the great Dutchmen. And the lesson they taught him led him to break away from the impressionist trend. As he himself once said, it would be a mistake to suppose that there is a break in continuity between the old and the modern painters."[166]

1936

March 15

First article by **Lyman**, "Renoir and His Contemporaries," appears in the semi-monthly review *The Montrealer* in which, until 1942, he would publish more than forty art criticism articles dealing with Canadian and European painters.

May 14-28

First and only solo exhibition of **Lyman** in New York, at the Valentine Gallery, where Henri **Matisse** had previously shown in 1927 and in 1928-1929, and where his son Pierre had worked in 1925 and 1926 on the organization of contemporary French art exhibitions.[167] The Canadian's exhibition includes twenty-five paintings: portraits, landscapes, still life and nudes completed since 1913. The American monthly *The Art Digest* covers the exhibition in its June issue, citing excerpts from critics, in particular:

"Carlyle Burrows in the *New York Herald Tribune* said that **Lyman**'s paintings 'follow a natural trend for the most part and are very simple, unaffected things . . . the portraits and figures are somewhat decorative in color, though realistic in essence. **Matisse** seems to have left little impression on him.' But Malcolm Vaughan of the *New York American* felt that 'these landscapes and figure pieces have been turned out with energy and a certain decorative skill, such as a **Matisse** pupil might be expected to produce.' Although Mr. Vaughan perceived that **Lyman**'s paintings were 'attractively rich in hue,' he wished that 'their richness were more a matter of deep feeling than strong coloring.'"[168]

October

The *Exhibition of Modern French Paintings: The School of Paris*, held at Scott & Sons (jointly organized with Alex Reid & Lefevre, Ltd., London), presents two works by **Matisse**: *Femme nue agenouillée*, from 1925, and *Large Cliff – Two Rays*, from 1920 (cat. 69). A new opportunity for **Lyman** to express his views of **Matisse**: "The arabesque-like quality of Henri **Matisse** involving what is unfortunately called deformation . . . No one can overlook the magician **Matisse**, who, in an occidental way, has united the splendour and simplicity of Persian miniatures."[169] The painting *Large Cliff – Two Rays* is purchased by the major Canadian collector and patron Hamilton S. Southam (1916-2008). This is likely the first **Matisse** painting to have been acquired in a Canadian collection.

In *La Relève*, Hector de Saint-Denys Garneau[170] writes about the very same exhibition: "**Matisse**—Impression: I stand before an exquisite improvisation. No immutable will, or preconceived design. I stand before a predisposition, an exquisite aptitude for song, for making colour and smoothness sing. I stand before a poetic state where the most enchanting colour sways in receptiveness . . . And I witness the fulfilment of this painting, its birth. It is organized in a marvellous freedom, not according to a preconceived architecture, but under cover of vision, this gaze that understands and disposes, guided here by marvellous tact, by exquisite taste, an exquisite sense of the relations of mass and of colours. Fully spontaneous tact, on a very intelligent and conscious background, in the choice and the juxtaposition of shades, in the balance of the design . . . The art of **Matisse** renders us particularly present, through a constant supposition, the perceptible prism, and the principle of transposition where it draws its continuity. It is not, in this sense, without affinity with that of a Debussy."[171]

On the other hand, the critic Reynald, far less receptive, writes in *La Presse*: "**Matisse**—curious painter—gave his *Femme nue agenouillée* two dark eyes that cast a racy gaze and a fleeting mystery in a dull face and such a vivid red covering her feet that this splotch eagerly stops the spectator. He excels at making a rag into a song note. But one

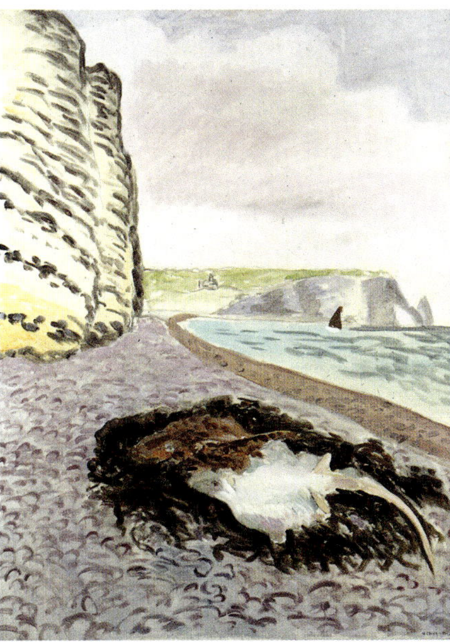

/ **CAT. 69** Henri Matisse
Large Cliff – Two Rays
1920

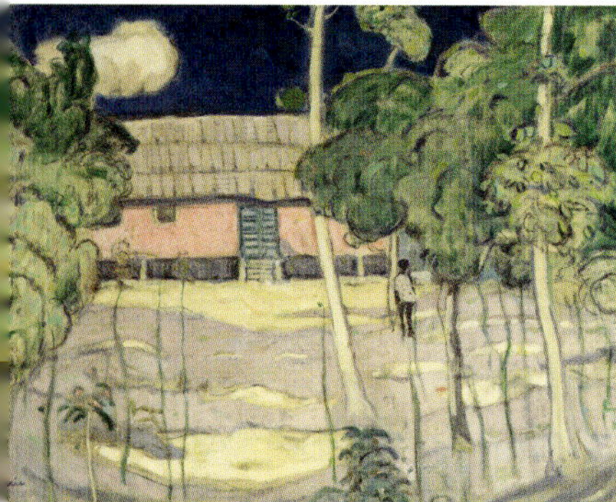

that does not linger for very long . . . A chalky beach, painted in a few furious brushstrokes, is called *Large Cliff – Two Rays*; why 'two' since there there are nothing but brutal strokes in the entire scene?"[172]

December 18

Lyman, who learned of the publication of Buchanan's book on **Morrice**, writes to Eric Brown, director of the National Gallery of Canada: "[It would be] time to organize a really representative retrospective of **Morrice**'s best work. I think that if **Morrice**'s soul is to be established beyond question in his proper place in the public estimation, it would be a splendid thing for art in general in this country."[173] This project would be carried out on November 25 of the following year.

1937

January 15

Lyman comments on *James Wilson Morrice – Painter and Nomad: A Biography*, by Donald W. Buchanan, published by The Ryerson Press, Toronto, in November 1936:

"He [**Morrice**] took the sensitive eye of the impressionists but not their rationalization. To the post-impressionists he owed something of his power of intuitive synthesis but he could not use their stricter sense of construction. The plastic sense that flourishes in France was alien to him. All this Buchanan has made clear. But in discussing the possible influence of **Matisse** he uses interchangeably the words pattern and design. Of course no real painting is pattern. Pure pattern would be wall-paper. Nevertheless the work of such men as Whistler and **Morrice** can be abstracted in pattern without total loss. Even though used with decorative intent, **Matisse**'s constructive design cannot be reduced to pattern. To me the two words typify in a measure the vast difference between the two painters."[174]

February 3-19

At the Arts Club, **Lyman** organizes an exhibition of eleven painters—Alexander Bercovitch, Fritz Brandtner, Prudence Heward, Jack Humphrey, John **Lyman**, Mabel Lockerby, Jean Palardy, Goodridge Roberts, Sarah Robertson, Jori (Marjorie) Smith and Marian Scott—who propose "works in which generally 'advanced,' at times somewhat disconcerting trends are emerging,"[175] according to critical opinion.

This exhibition is a prelude to the founding of the Eastern Group of Painters the following year by **Lyman**.

February 6-20

Lyman's solo exhibition at Scott & Sons (forty-two works).

March 1-31

Morrice exhibition at Scott & Sons (twenty-four works).[176] **Lyman** regrets that no nudes are shown:

"The only side of his work not represented is his nudes. Strange to say not a single one of them is owned in Canada. One wonders why the human body is in such disgrace among us. But I fear my question is not very ingenuous. Some people will certainly aver that the reason is elsewhere, that **Morrice** was an inferior painter of nudes. Not unless he was an inferior painter tout court."[177]

March 29

Pierre Matisse, the son of Henri, who has operated a gallery in New York since 1931, offers to sell to the Art Gallery of Toronto (now the Art Gallery of Ontario) two works by James Wilson **Morrice** sent from Paris. In his letter to Martin Baldwin, the museum curator, Pierre Matisse writes: "I am taking the pleasure to send you the enclosed reproductions of two paintings by J. W. **Morrice**, a Canadian painter who used to be a very good friend of my father."[178] The two works are *Fishing Boats*, now at the National Gallery of Canada, and *Landscape, Trinidad* (cat. 72).

March

Saint-Denys Garneau writes an essay (unpublished) in which he draws a parallel between **Lyman** and **Morrice** whose two exhibitions are in progress:

"It seems to me that the painting of **Lyman** provides a striking example of the dissociation between technique and poetry. In many places, his work takes on an ascetic character, of a rigorous exercise in which a reasonable direction assumes a large part. Several canvases seem to have been approached independently of what we call inspiration, a still existing reality despite the distancing from romanticism . . . We do not sense, as in the work of **Morrice** currently showing at the same Scott galleries, this constant relationship to reality, to nature, this exceptional fraternity, which allows constant exchanges of light, shadow, of all colours, the extremely delicate and tender sensibility of the eye and of intelligence . . . On the contrary, the art of **Lyman** seems to me to be grounded more strongly in the imagination. It often imposes an abrupt departure, an initial break with natural reality. And the constructions that it makes are, to a certain extent, abstract . . . It is also founded on a very accurate and strong observation of harmonic relationships. With **Morrice**, there is always a very sensitive fantasy that guides the construction. With **Lyman**, the construction begins in a relation grasped in reality and transposed, so to speak, from the outset, and taken as the basis for the entire construction."[179]

June 12–October 31
Lyman is the only painter to represent Canada at the Pan-American Exposition in Dallas, Texas, with the portrait of *Jori Smith in Costume* (cat. 91).

October 15
Scott & Sons presents the *French Painting* exhibition. It is divided into three parts: the Pre-Impressionists (Corot, Boudin, Jongkind), the Impressionists (Degas, Sisley, Pissarro, Cézanne, Renoir, Redon, Toulouse-Lautrec, Gauguin) and the School of Paris (Bonnard, **Matisse**, Derain, Dufy, Picasso, Modigliani, Utrillo, Vuillard, Lurçat). **Lyman** comments: "There is a characteristic **Matisse** entitled *Pianist and Still Life*. It is because these objects impress so little their literal identity that this familiar scene becomes a decorative enchantment."[180]

November 15
Lyman announces that the annual *French and Dutch Paintings* exhibition was to open on November 18 at the Johnson Art Galleries. Among the artists represented (Corot, Courbet, Sisley, Modigliani, Bonnard, Derain, Dufy, Utrillo et Van Dongen), **Matisse** is included.[181]

November 25–December 27
The National Gallery of Canada presents the *Memorial Exhibition of J. W. Morrice*, a travelling exhibition that would go to Toronto in January 1938 and conclude in Montreal the following February. The exhibit regroups 131 paintings. **Lyman** loans *The Negress* (Thomson Collection, Art Gallery of Ontario) and *The Pond, West Indies* (cat. 24); William Saint-Pierre loans *Landscape, West Indies* (cat. 23).

1938 November 26–December 10
First exhibition of the Eastern Group of Painters at Scott & Sons, set up by **Lyman** the preceding spring,[182] which includes Alexander Bercovitch, Eric Goldberg, Jack Humphrey,[183] John **Lyman**, Goodridge Roberts and Jori Smith. **Lyman** writes:

"These painters have very divergent personalities yet have something unmistakable in common. You cannot nail it with an 'ism; you cannot pin on any of them a fashion. They are not busy about being on their own time or following any line—self-conscious regionalism, formalized pattern or social comment. They are not racing after the band-wagon of the 'Canadian scene.' That was once good ballyhoo to get people away from foreign stereotypes, but to-day it is just sentimental rhetoric . . . What the group has affirmatively rather eludes definition. I should say they are after the 'fell' of life, the savour of things."[184]

December 1
The *Modern French and Dutch Painters* exhibition, presented at the Johnson Art Galleries, includes, alongside Corot, Courbet, Sisley, Modigliani, Bonnard, Derain, Dufy, Utrillo and Van Dongen, a work by **Matisse**, *Odalisque in Red Trousers* (fig. 28). Comment by **Lyman**: "Henri **Matisse**'s *Odalisk with Red Trousers* is a joyous triumph of colour. It is a typical work

/ CAT. 91 John Lyman
Jori Smith in Costume
1936

of the 20's when he was in full possession of his means and had disciplined his audacious experiments into perfect harmony . . . If **Matisse**'s work is seldom an ornament for a given space, it is an ornament for certain needs of our existence, for our need of calm and joy, and in art as in life joy is possibly the hardest thing to confer."[185]

1939

January

Lyman praises *Drawings by French Sculptors*, an exhibition prepared by the National Gallery of Canada and shown at the AAM. His article is illustrated with a drawing by Henri **Matisse**, a portrait of a young girl.[186]

February 15

Lyman founds the Contemporary Arts Society, Montreal, which replaces the Eastern Group of Painters, which it expands. This association "whose purpose will be to defend professional interests and to assert the vitality of the modern movement in the arts"[187] would be at the heart of artistic activity in Montreal in the 1940s where it would trigger a real renewal. It would be active until November 18, 1948. **Lyman** serves as president until 1945, with, as vice-president, Paul-Émile Borduas (1905-1960). The latter shares with **Lyman** the same admiration for **Matisse** "rich in such a breadth of teachings."[188]

Commenting on the *Dufy, Improvisatore* exhibition at Scott & Sons, **Lyman** relates, with regard to Dufy, an experience recalling a perception he had 1909 while contemplating *Autumn Landscape: Forest of Fontainebleau* by **Matisse**:

"Back in the first years of the century he was painting like anybody else in the aftermath of Impressionism, very much indeed like **Matisse** at the same period, and it was from **Matisse** that he was to get his revelation, as one artist always gets it from another, and not from sticks and stones, or snow and jack-pines. It was from one of the latter's paintings [*Luxe, calme et volupté*] in the Salon of 1905."[189]

April 2

Lyman exhibits at the Faculty Club of McGill University (thirty-six paintings).

April 29

At the Pen and Pencil Club in Montreal, the painter Clarence Gagnon (1886-1942) gives a reactionary lecture entitled "The Grand Bluff of Modernistic Art" in which he reviles Cézanne, **Matisse**, Picasso and "their disciples," very faithfully drawing on an article by Gelett Burgless, "The Wild Men of Paris," published in the *Architectural Record* magazine in May 1910.

"**Matisse**," says Gagnon, "being as mild a man as ever tordured [*sic*] the human form or debauched a palette, paints in a burst of emotion and usually comes to an end of his enthusiasm before he has attained beauty, but alas! When he paints his wife with a broad stripe of green down her nose, though it startlingly suggests her, it is punishment to have made her appear so to you always. He teaches you to see her in a strange and terrible aspect. He has taught you her body. But fearful as it is, it is alive, awfully alive! The other jokers have left him out of sight in the runaway from beauty."[190]

John **Lyman** would respond in May in *The Standard*, denouncing Gagnon's racist remarks and accusing him of sharing the same ideas about modern art as the Nazis. He takes delight in recalling that this slanderous attitude toward modernism existed a quarter of a century ago in Europe and that this point of view was now outmoded.[191]

May 13-28

First exhibition under the patronage of the Contemporary Arts Society, shown at the AAM: *Art of Our Day*, composed of foreign contemporary paintings from private collections in Montreal and that include, in particular, the works of Derain, Dufy, Feininger, Kandinsky (three abstractions), Lhote, Modigliani, Utrillo, Vlaminck and Zadkine. No works by **Matisse**.

September 1

Start of the Second World War. Despite an offer made to him, **Matisse** refuses to leave France: "If everything that has value flees France, what will remain of France?"[192]

November
At the Watson Art Galleries, the *Exhibition of XIX and XX Century French Painting* (jointly organized with the Galerie Jacques Dubourg, Paris, and Alex Reid & Lefevre, London) includes Puvis de Chavannes, Gauguin, Cézanne, Renoir, Seurat, Sisley, Toulouse-Lautrec, Redon, Bonnard, Modigliani, Braque, Utrillo, Picasso, **Matisse**, Derain, Marquet and Segonzac.[193]

December 15-30
First exhibition of the members of the Contemporary Arts Society at the Frank Stevens Gallery of Montreal. Among the artists represented: Fritz Brandtner, Paul-Émile Borduas, Louise Gadbois, John **Lyman**, Louis Muhlstock, Goodridge Roberts and Philip Surrey.

The 1940s

Lyman's organizational efforts bear fruit and his ideas, which he spreads through teaching, newspapers and lectures, are recognized by a large public. His art acquires great visibility and is well received, both by critics and collectors. The success led Canadian museums to acquire their first works by the artist, namely the Musée national des beaux-arts du Québec in 1944, the Montreal Museum of Fine Arts in 1949 and the National Gallery of Canada in 1955.

1941   April 26-May 3
Lyman is part of the *Première Exposition des Indépendants*, organized by the Dominican friar Marie-Alain Couturier (1897-1954) and presented at the Palais Montcalm in Quebec City. The exhibitors are Paul-Émile Borduas, Mary Bouchard, Stanley Cosgrove, Louise Gadbois, Éric Goldberg, John **Lyman** (cat. 14), Louis Muhlstock, Alfred Pellan, Goodridge Roberts, Jori Smith and Philip Surrey. A great defender of, among others, **Matisse**, Father Couturier, in exile in New York since the start of the war, makes frequent journeys to Quebec where he gives lectures, teaches and organizes exhibitions. He encounters certain difficulties in his desire to make **Matisse** well known: one evening when he planned to show slides of the works of this painter to the students of the École des beaux-arts de Montréal, the director Charles Maillard, very conservative, cut off the electricity.[194]

May 16-28
The same exhibition is held in Montreal at Morgan's.

1942   January 11-14
Lyman is part of the *Exposition des maîtres de la peinture moderne*, organized by Father Wilfrid Corbeil at the Séminaire de Joliette, in the company of Paul-Émile Borduas, Marc-Aurèle Fortin, Louise Gadbois, Alfred Pellan and Goodridge Roberts.

February 5-March 8
At the AAM, the *Loan Exhibition of Masterpieces of Painting*,[195] for the benefit of the sailors of the Allied merchant navies, includes **Matisse**'s *The Dream* reproduced in the catalogue. The exhibition, divided into "national schools" (French, English, Dutch, Italian, Spanish), brings together the works of the Old Masters (Titian, Tintoretto, Chardin), the Realists (Courbet and Daumier), the Impressionists (Renoir, Degas) and Post-Impressionists (Cézanne, Gauguin, Derain, Renoir, etc.). It provides **Lyman** with the opportunity to summarize the history of recent art. He evokes **Matisse** and the small painting *The Dream* in these terms:

"The years of doubt produced by reaction the purest art—outside music—the Occident has seen, but they are directly reflected in Picasso's instability of form and **Matisse**'s mobile arabesques. **Matisse** found his answer in putting his whole faith in meanings that pertain to painting alone. The decorative majesty of even his small simple canvas called *The Dreamer* [*sic*] must stir a region deeper than the mind."[196]

1944   March 18-April 1
Lyman retrospective exhibition at the Dominion Gallery (fifty-four paintings).

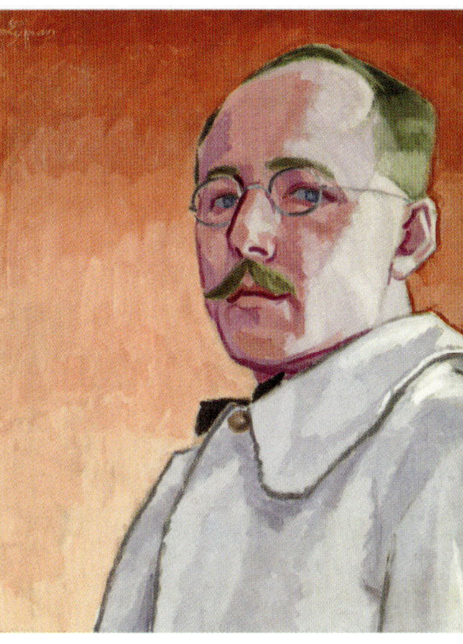

/ **CAT. 14** John Lyman
Self-portrait
1918

November
The Éditions de L'Arbre publishes a monograph on John **Lyman** by Paul Dumas (1928-2005) in its "Art vivant" series. Dumas, a collector, author and art critic, recalls **Matisse**'s influence on **Lyman**: "From **[Matisse]** he retained a taste for luminous colour and limpid subject matter. The influence of **Matisse** is reflected in some of the works of his youth in which the planes are indicated through vast monochrome surfaces and volumes burst forth through the effect of a cursive, nervous line."[197]

1945 August
The Éditions de L'Arbre publishes *Morrice* by **Lyman** in its "Art vivant" series. **Lyman**, who composed directly in French, evokes **Morrice**'s "original personality, which did not stray off course, but pushed ahead in a single, straight, continual movement,"[198] as well as his affection for **Matisse**, "enamoured of sensual logic,"[199] and Dunoyer de Segonzac's account of their friendship: "**Matisse** was also very fond of him."[200]

1947 March 15
Regarding a proposed exhibition of Quebec artists in Paris, **Lyman** writes to tell Father Couturier that he must decline his participation and that of his friends because of a misunderstanding linked to the composition of this show: "We are not taken with the idea that [Maurice] Gagnon will continue to represent the exhibition as mainly Pellanian and Borduasian . . . with a bit of filler." Father Couturier responds by assuring him of the fondness he bears toward him: "And surely you may also guess what your friendship, faithful and discerning, has represented for me throughout these recent years." He tells him that he doubts the planned exhibition for Paris will take place: "The conditions prepared by the Quebec authorities appear to me to be unacceptable." The project never came to fruition.[201]

During the year
Irène Legendre (1904-1992), painter, printmaker, sculptor and professor who was trained in Europe and the United States, publishes her *Petite histoire de l'art moderne* in which **Matisse** is one of the most oft-cited names:

"**Matisse**, the greatest among them [the Fauves], proved to be an unsurpassable colourist. His passion for colour quieted, or rather, became ordered, producing nothing but symphonies of ever perfect taste. His style, composed of arabesques and supple lines, owes to an extremely certain instinct. In a major exhibition of portraits at the Museum of Modern Art in New York, which brought together celebrated artists of both continents, two paintings shone in the forefront: a **Matisse** and a Chagall. The **Matisse** was a portrait of Miss Yvonne Landsberg.[202] A large painting, more abstract than usual, without well-defined colour in which the face emerges in multiple, repeated curves. The freedom with which this painting was executed, the energy, and the grandeur of the design compel admiration. There is something of the French spirit that prevails. We are fascinated."[203]

1948 February 13
In the wake of controversial elections at the Contemporary Arts Society, Paul-Émile Borduas breaks with **Lyman**, especially "considering the unintentional, but real insult [occasioned by his] critic of the text"[204] of the *Refus global*, the manifesto of the Automatistes that would be launched the following August.

June 10, 1948-May 31, 1949
The transatlantic presence of **Matisse**, which had continued to become ever more firmly established since his first exhibition in New York in 1908, extends throughout the United States with a travelling exhibition of drawings in major U.S. cities. At the same time, an important retrospective is held at the Philadelphia Museum of Art. **Matisse** regularly exhibits paintings and drawings in the gallery of his son Pierre in New York.

July
End of the Contemporary Arts Society of Montreal.

1949-1958

After being appointed Adjunct Professor (1949), then Associate Professor (1950), **Lyman** holds the position of Chairman of the Department of Fine Arts at McGill University from 1952 to 1956 and continues to teach until his retirement in 1958, at the age of seventy-two.

From 1950, nearly every page of **Lyman**'s *Journal* is filled with bitterness. The entry of October 10 of that year is particularly representative of his state of mind, mixed with interesting critical reflection:

"I have never followed the fashion in painting, but rather recoiled from it; I have never cultivated a manner, that mimicry of style. This is why, although when I was young I was thought scandalously 'modern,' today I am generally called a conservative, and even sometimes taken for an academic by those for whom modernism means nothing but popular patterns of abstraction of neo-primitivism. The so-called abstract & non-representational movements were genuine enough, for they were founded on an intuition of nature, but latterly they have simply become an easy way out for those who understand nothing & cannot attract attention any other way."[205]

"One wonders why so many painters seek at all costs to be among the very latest, as though they were fashion designers or milliners, when all of history demonstrates that an artist who too accurately represents the taste of his generation will certainly be rejected by posterity. On the other hand, it is often he who, in the eyes of his contemporaries, least conforms to fashion who survives the era, who even becomes representative of that era. There have been great reactionary masters—or who appeared as such, as in rapids where eddies form, which seem to move upstream."[206]

"The real subject of a painting is how you paint it, not what you paint. The meaning of art is deeper than subject-matter which is only something equivalent to the sculptor's armature. The artist chooses the subject that will enable him to carry out (instinctive) intent. Subject-matter—all subject-matter—belongs to every body. There is no original subject: what is personal is what adheres to it in its passage through the artist's mind."[207]

1950   **December**
Morrice's biographer, Donald W. Buchanan, who had met **Matisse** in 1935 to prepare his work for publication in 1936, publishes in *Canadian Art* his recent conversation with the French artist, a meeting facilitated by Father Couturier:

"Well, Father Couturier instructed me so sent a polite note requesting an appointment; also he, himself, would put in a word for me. So all this was done, and then I waited two days for a reply, then three days and finally a week. Thursday night arrived and with it the realization that on Friday night I had to leave for London and Canada. Early Friday morning, the porter knocked on my door. There was a phone number for me to call; it turned out to be a message from **Matisse**'s secretary. Could I come over that morning and if so, how soon? Ten o'clock? And so it was arranged. That left an hour for me to pace my room and rehearse in the best French I could muster all the questions I wanted to ask. For **Matisse**, I knew, didn't speak English. Precisely at ten, I crossed the street and took the elevator to the top floor center. The secretary, an intelligent and capable looking young woman, let me in and there, sitting up in bed, with a tight green and white woollen night-cap on his head, was **Matisse**.

What I noticed first was the vitality of his face, which was strong and at the same time mellow in expression. But above all it was his kindly eyes which seemed to be his most memorable feature.

He welcomed me cordially, said he recollected my visit fifteen years ago when I had been seeking information for use in my biography of James Wilson **Morrice**. 'How are they treating him nowadays over there?' he asked, and seemed happy when I explained that the Montreal Museum of Fine Arts had recently opened a special **Morrice** room devoted to an excellent collection of this master's work."[208]

1954   **November 3**
Death of **Matisse** in Nice.

1955

Early in the year
Lyman pays tribute to **Matisse**:

"He was always a great believer in regular work, and at that time his strict daily routine was: 8 to 9 a.m., violin; 9 to 12, model for painting; after lunch, a short stroll, then model again for drawing; a light supper, a stroll and bed, with a book (perhaps a classic or Mallarmé or Valéry) by his bed-side in case he woke up in the night. The only variation was on Sunday afternoon, when he went to play chamber music with friends.

But few things could distract him from his work. His hand could not remain "silent" for long: soon his pencil was at play. Nature was his constant source and reference, no matter how much its particular aspects were modified to suit his general conception. While he worked he had the feeling that he was copying nature and that every deviation was for the purpose of expressing it more completely.

There is no phase of his work that does not bear witness to his intention. Even in his latest painting, where his synthesis approaches abstraction, every form and colour chord has the ring of truth, awakening prolonged echoes of recognition. Untouched by the doubts and withdrawals that afflict the age, his art is not a refusal but an affirmation of life."[209]

1956

February 5
Lyman notes with regard to the retrospective of Canadian artist David Milne (1882-1953): "He certainly deserved it more than any of the others (except, of course, **Morrice**) who have been given one. At first glance very pleasing, even charming, but it soon begins to wear a little thin. There is considerable sensibility, but it is delicate and superficial, remains on the surface, does not penetrate. In other words, in **Matisse**'s phrase, it lacks density."[210]

1957-1958

On retiring from McGill University, **Lyman** spends the winter of 1957-1958 in Bermuda where he completes a dozen paintings based on sketches. In 1959, He and Corinne, who love Bermuda, buy a house there; from now on, they spend all their winters there. **Lyman** often visits other islands, including Trinidad, where **Morrice** had painted.

1958

November 26
Radio-Canada television, as part of the series "Profils et paysages," broadcasts a National Film Board documentary about John **Lyman**, *Je vis par les yeux* (conversations with Guy Viau), directed by Fernand Dansereau. The documentary would be made into a film entitled *John Lyman, peintre* the following year.

1963

September 5-29
The Montreal Museum of Fine Arts holds an important travelling retrospective exhibition on **Lyman**, comprising sixty-two works.

1966

November 23-December 19
In turn, the Musée du Québec (now the Musée national des beaux-arts du Québec) presents **Lyman**, a retrospective of 188 works, that would become a travelling exhibition. The catalogue is prefaced by Philip Surrey, former member of the Eastern Group of Painters.

1967

May 26
Lyman dies in Barbados.

November 13
Death of Corinne Saint-Pierre Lyman in Montreal.

Notes

1. Anonymous, "Passengers for Europe," *The Evening Telegram* [New York], December 14, 1889, p. 6 ["The Aurania has . . . J. W. Morrice"].

2. Information excerpted from the *Livre de comptabilité des élèves, 31 Rue du Dragon, Atelier de droite, Année 1890* (63 AS 4), archives of the Académie Julian, Archives nationales de France, Pierrefitte-sur-Seine. It rectifies an error perpetuated in a mention of James Wilson Morrice in the *Catalogue général des élèves* (63 AS 1) which describes him as an American attending the Académie Julian from 1888 to 1890: "D Morrice J. W. 88-90 – 10 C des P. Champs – Américain." Morrice's attendance at the Académie Julian was limited to four weeks (January 20-27, February 3-10, February 17-24 and March 3-10, 1890). In the *Grand livre des élèves, Atelier Boulanger & J. Lefebvre / Atelier J. P. Laurens & Benjamin Constant* (63 AS 9), one sheet contains over forty signatures, including the signature of Morrice, preceded by those of the Canadians Maurice Cullen (1866-1934) and Joseph-Charles Franchère (1866-1921), and afterwards, the note, "I ask Messrs. J. Lefebvre & Benj. Constant to admit me as a student in their studio."

3. John Lyman, *Morrice* (Montreal: L'Arbre, "Art vivant" series, 1945), p. 23.

4. Nicole Cloutier, ed., *James Wilson Morrice, 1865-1924*, exhib. cat. (Montreal: The Montreal Museum of Fine Arts, 1985), p. 20.

5. Henri Matisse, *Écrits et propos sur l'art*, introduced by Dominique Fourcade (Paris: Hermann, "Savoir : sur l'art" series, 1972), p. 82.

6. Raymond Escholier, *Matisse, ce vivant* (Paris: Librairie Arthème Fayard, 1956), pp. 40-41.

7. Matisse, cited by Xavier Girard, in *Matisse, une splendeur inouïe* (Paris: Gallimard, "Découvertes Gallimard Peinture" series, 1993), p. 30.

8. Lyman, *Morrice*, p. 18. "Ascetic. Lives very simply. No furniture, carpets, etc., trunks always prepared for departure. But loves fine food, good wine, and clothing of quality, elegance. Would drink a great deal, stay up late, and joke. Intermittent cheerfulness 'as a Scot can be cheerful.' Travelled alone, did not talk." Lyman, cited by Guy Viau, in *Notes biographiques*, MNBAQ library, Lyman file, not dated [likely 1957], chapter 5, p. 14.

9. John Lyman, "The School of Paris," *The Montrealer*, October 30, 1936, p. 19.

10. Charles C. Hill, *Morrice: A Gift to the Nation – The G. Blair Laing* Collection, exhib. cat. (Ottawa: National Gallery of Canada, 1992), p. 87. Letter from Morrice, June 1, [1902], to Joseph Pennell in which he recalls this voyage. See also Cloutier, *James Wilson Morrice*, p. 27, p. 39 note 92. On Pennell, see *Whistler 1834-1903*, exhib. cat. (Paris: Musée d'Orsay, 1995), 335 pages.

11. In 1904, the Salon d'Automne moves to the Grand Palais.

12. Paul Gauguin (1848-1903) had just died in the Marquesas Islands, on May 8, 1903.

13. The first solo exhibition of Pierre Bonnard (1867-1947) took place in 1896, at the Galerie Durand-Ruel. The second and the third were held in 1906, at Ambroise Vollard and at Bernheim-Jeune. Between these two dates, Bonnard participated every year in various group exhibitions, with the Nabis of which he was a member or at the Salon des Indépendants or in different galleries.

14. André Derain (1880-1954) only exhibited for the first time at the Salon d'Automne in 1905.

15. Lyman, *Morrice*, p. 30. It was at the 1905 Salon d'Automne of that certain painters, including Matisse, were given the epithet "Fauves."

16. "From Morrice I learnt to enjoy Paris: to be sure I was a willing pupil. Also from Morrice I learnt more about pictures; and it was he who later advised me to look at Matisse. Here I cannot be sure of dates; but certainly it was before . . . the spring of 1908." Clive Bell, *Old Friends: Personal Recollections* (London: Chatto & Windus, 1956), p. 158. Clive Bell was an art critic and historian, co-founder of the Bloomsbury Group, co-organizer with Roger Fry of the second Post-Impressionist Exhibition in London, in 1912, and brother-in-law of Virginia Woolf, as he married her sister, Vanessa, a painter.

17. In 1908, Bennett would make Morrice one of the characters in his novel *Buried Alive*. "He would write everything down and, later, would use these notes for his novels, so that they appeared to be directly copied from life." André Gide, "Arnold Bennet" [1931], in *Essais critiques* (Paris: Gallimard, Bibliothèque de La Pléiade, 1999), p. 887.

18. Cited in Hill, *Morrice: A Gift to the Nation*, p. 21.

19. See *Gauguin et l'École de Pont-Aven*, exhib. cat. (Paris: Bibliothèque nationale, 1989), pp. 105-107.

20. In the year 1905, Morrice participates in the Annual Exhibition of the International Society of Sculptors, Painters and Gravers in London (January 9-February 11), which travelled to Manchester, Burnley and Bradford in the spring; in the 13th exhibition of the Société des Peintres orientalistes français, Paris (February 12-March 12); in the 12th exhibition of La Libre Esthétique, Brussels (February 1-March 23); in the annual exhibition of the American Art Association of Paris (March 2-25); in the Salon de la Société nationale des beaux-arts, Paris (April 15-June 30), over the course of which some fifty critics underscored his participation; in the Venice Biennial (April 22-October 31); in the Annual Exhibition of the Walker Art Gallery, Liverpool (September 18-January 6, 1906); in the Salon d'Automne, Paris (October 18-November 25); and in the 10th Annual Exhibition of the Carnegie Institute, Pittsburgh (November 2-January 1, 1906). Lucie Dorais completes the list with the following two exhibitions: the Tombola des Filets Bleus, Concarneau (September 10-14); and the 5th Private Showing at the Charles Rivaud gallery, Paris (December 5-January 10, 1906).

21. These comments are those of Gustave Babin, in *L'Écho de Paris*, October 17, 1905, p. 2; and François Monod, in *Art et décoration*, December 18, 1905, p. 206.

22. "In the centre of the room, a child's torso, and a small marble bust of Albert Marque, modelled with refined knowledge. The candour of these busts surprises in the midst of an orgy of pure tones: Donatello among the wild beasts." Louis Vauxcelles, "Le Salon d'Automne," *Gil Blas*, October 17, 1905, suppl. p. [2]. The sculptor Albert Marque (1872-1939) is not be confused with the painter Albert Marquet (1875-1947).

23. Ibid., p. [1].

24. Anonymous, "Notes from Paris," *Truth*, 23 November, 1905, p. 1296.

25. Letter from Morrice to Newton MacTavish, August 24, 1910. Cited in Donald W. Buchanan, *James Wilson Morrice – Painter and Nomad: A Biography* (Toronto: The Ryerson Press, 1936), p. 109. Morrice's correspondence with MacTavish is held at the North York Public Library, Toronto, Canadiana Collection. Journalist, art critic and art historian, Newton MacTavish (1875-1941) paid a visit to Morrice in Paris in 1910. He was one of the founders of the Arts and Letters Club of Toronto in 1908. From 1906 to 1926, he was the publisher of *The Canadian Magazine*.

26. Durand-Ruel presented a few similar exhibitions, notably in London and in the United States. He was encouraged to come to Canada because of the interest shown in the Impressionists by two Canadian collectors, George A. Drummond and William Van Horne. Since 1889, Raffaëlli, Degas, Monet, Sisley, Pissarro, Renoir, Mary Cassat and Toulouse-Lautrec had featured in these two Montreal collections. See Janet M. Brooke, *Discerning Taste: Montreal Collectors, 1880-1920*, exhib. cat. (Montreal: The Montreal Museum of Fine Arts, 1989), p. 137.

27. See the essay by Marc Gauthier in the present catalogue.

28. Typescript of the documentary on John Lyman, *Je vis par les yeux*, conversations with Guy Viau, directed by Fernand Dansereau, National Film Board of Canada, 1958, John Lyman fonds, Bibliothèque et Archives nationales du Québec, Montreal, p. 9. Cited in Louise Dompierre, *John Lyman, 1886-1967*, exhib. cat. (Kingston: Agnes Etherington Art Centre, 1986), p. 24.

29. Ibid., p. 9.

30. Lyman, cited by Viau, in *Notes biographiques*, chapter 5, p. 14.

31. Lyman, *Morrice*, p. 9.

32. Hilary Spurling, *Matisse the Master – A Life of Henri Matisse: The Conquest of Colour, 1909-1954* (New York: Knopf, 1999), pp. 22-23.

33. Claudine Grammont, "Matisse comme religion. Les *Mike Stein* et Matisse, 1908-1918," in *Matisse, Cézanne, Picasso . . . L'aventure des Stein*, exhib. cat. (Paris: RMN-Grand Palais, 2011), p. 226.

34. *Inédits de John Lyman*, texts selected and annotated by Hedwidge Asselin (Montreal: Ministère des Affaires culturelles/Bibliothèque nationale du Québec, 1980), p. 181.

35. Edmund Morris (1871-1913) founded the Canadian Art Club, in 1907 in Toronto, modelling it after Whistler's International Society of Sculptors, Painters and Gravers. The Canadian organization encouraged expatriate artists like Horatio Walker and James Wilson Morrice to exhibit in their country. The agency ceased operations in 1915, two years after the death of Edmund Morris.

36. Letter to Edmund Morris, Paris, February 22, 1908, *Morris Papers*, Art Gallery of Ontario (AGO), Toronto.

37. "Biddefort en Maine Leymann [the "e" is crossed through] (John) / USA 7 rue de Mezieres / Atelier J.P.L. / 4 sem mat 9 mars-5 avril 1908 / et un chevalet 31″ / Mars 1908 16-23-30 / 4 sem. mat. 6 avril-3 mai 1908 25″ / Avril 08 6-13-20-27 / 11 mai 4 sem mat 11 mai-7 juin 1908 25″ / Mai 08 1-25 / (9 nov.08) 3 mois mat. 9 nov. 08-9 février 09 75″ / Nov 08-9-16-30 [crossed through] En cas de retour 2 mois à remettre / Mars 09.22-29 / Avril 09-5-12-19 / Mai 09-3-10-17 / Nov 09-8-15-22-29 / (15 nov. 09) 4 sem mat 8 nov-5 dec 09 25″ / X^bre [Decembre] 09-6-13-27 / (11 X^bre 09) 4 sem mat 6 Xbre 09 − 2 janvier 1910 25″," *Livre des élèves 1907-1909 / Ateliers / Jean Paul Laurens / Baschet Royer / Schommer Gervais / Verlet*, No. O, p. 264 (63 AS 6), archives of the Académie Julian, Archives nationales de France, Pierrefitte-sur-Seine.

38. Typescript of the documentary *Je vis par les yeux*, pp. 29-30.

39. Lyman, cited by Viau, in *Notes biographiques*, chapter 1, p. 16.

40. The names of the jury members, appointed for one year, were randomly drawn during the general assembly held at the Grand Palais on Wednesday, April 8, 1908, at 4 p.m. The jury was active from September 15 to September 18, following reception of the works at the Grand Palais on September 7, 8 and 9. A columnist who was visiting the jury mentioned a division between "right" ("watered down impressionists") and "left" ("that delights in the verve of the Fauves"). Le Diable Boiteux, "Le Boulevard – Jury de peinture," *Gil Blas*, September 17, 1908, p. [1].

41. Gertrude Stein recalls that at the time, André Derain and Georges Braque rallied around Picasso and that the hostility between "Picassoists" and "Matissists" grew acrimonious. Gertrude Stein, *Portraits and Prayers* (New York: Random House, 1934), p. 72.

42. Louis Vauxcelles, preface to the catalogue of the exhibition *Les Fauves, l'Atelier Gustave Moreau* (Paris: 1934). Apollinaire, who would publish *Les Peintres cubistes* in 1913, writes: "As for the word 'Cubist' or 'Cubism,' . . . it originates with Matisse and was used with regard to a painting by Braque. It was used in conversation by 1908" (Letter to Roger Allard, September 17, 1918, in Apollinaire, *Œuvres en prose complètes* [Paris: Gallimard, Bibliothèque de la Pléiade, 1991], p. 1518). According to John Golding (in *Le Cubisme* [Paris: Le Livre de poche, 1965], p. 62, note 6), the anecdote about Matisse's comments was related on September 30, 1911, in *L'Intransigeant*, leading up to the Cubists' participation in the Salon d'Automne and repeated in June 1912 in *La Revue française*, following the Cubists' participation in the Salon des Indépendants.

43. Buchanan, *James Wilson Morrice – Painter and Nomad*, pp. 109-110. Of course, Morrice's preferences ran to Matisse.

44. In other words, a psychiatric hospital.

45. Buchanan, *James Wilson Morrice. Painter and Nomad*, p. 144.

46. Guy Viau, "Chronology," in *John Lyman*, exhib. cat. (Montreal: The Montreal Museum of Fine Arts, 1963), n.p.

47. Letter to Edmund Morris, Paris, February [3], 1909, *Morris Papers*, AGO.

48. *Autumn Landscape: Forest of Fontainebleau* is not recorded in the catalogue of the Salon des Indépendants. Two days after the Salon opening, the work replaced the painting *Spanish Woman with a Tambourine*, which had just been sold to the Russian collector Shchukin. At the time, the Fontainebleau landscape belonged to Gertrude Stein, as confirmed in a letter from Matisse to Shchukin on April 9, 1909: "At the Salon des Indépendants, I exhibited the portrait with the green eyes and Madam Stein's Fontainebleau landscape." Information provided by Wanda de Guébriant, Archives Matisse, Paris.

49. John Lyman, "Adieu, Matisse," *Canadian Art*, vol. 12, no. 2 (winter 1955), pp. 44-45.

50. Lyman, cited by Viau, in *Notes biographiques*, chapter 2, p. 4.

51. Malcom Yorke, *Matthew Smith: His Life and Reputation* (London: Faber and Faber, 1997), p. 60: "Lyman had attended the spring Salon des Indépendants in 1909 and been impressed with a Matisse landscape, so it was presumably he who suggested their next move: they [Lyman and Matthew Smith] would enroll in the school of Henri Matisse."

52. From 1908 to 1965, the AAM (now the Montreal Museum of Fine Arts), during its annual spring exhibition, awarded the Jessie Dow Prize, which recognized the excellence of an oil or watercolour painting (extended to sculpture after 1957). Considered the most prestigious Canadian art award it was also the longest running.

53. Scott & Sons had organized a small private exhibition of Morrice's works. Morrice points out the sales to Edmund Morris in a letter dated February [9], 1909: "four sold and one to the Government."

54. Viau, "Chronology," in *John Lyman*, n.p.

55. Letter to his father, November 15, [1909], in *Inédits de John Lyman*, p. 189.

56. Lyman, cited by Viau, in *Notes biographiques*, chapter 2, p. 10.

57. Letter to his father, October 11, [1909], in *Inédits de John Lyman*, p. 187.

58. Letter to Newton MacTavish, August 24, [1909], North York Public Library, Toronto, Canadiana Collection.

59. "Although Mr. Morrice is a Canadian, a native of Montreal, Mr. Vauxcelles gives to the word 'American' its trans-Atlantic significance." (Editor's note, *The Canadian Magazine*.)

60. Louis Vauxcelles, "The Art of J. W. Morrice," *The Canadian Magazine*, vol. 34, no. 2 (December 1909), pp. 169-176.

61. In 1906, the Americans H. Lyman Saÿen and his wife, Jeannette Hope Saÿen, settle in Paris where they worked on fashion catalogues for the Wanamaker's department store. Over the eight years they spent in Paris, they became the close friends of Gertrude and Leo Stein. See Barbara A. Wolanin, "H. Lyman Saÿen" in Peter Morrin, Judith Zilczer and William c. Agee, *The Advent of Modernism: Post-Impressionism and North American Art, 1900-1918*, exhib. cat. (Atlanta: High Museum of Art, 1986), p. 155.

62. Letter to his father, May 20, 1910, in *Inédits de John Lyman*, p. 193.

63. Yorke, *Matthew Smith*, p. 60.

64. *Exposition Cézanne 1837-1906*, January 10-January 22, 1910, at Bernheim-Jeune.

65. Letter to Edmund Morris, January 30, 1910, *Morris Papers*, AGO.

66. Guillaume Apollinaire, cited in Claude Laugier and Isabelle Monod Fontaine, *Henri Matisse, 1904-1917*, exhib. cat. (Paris: Centre Georges Pompidou, 1993), p. 93. Only Jacques Rivière, in *La Nouvelle Revue Française*, gave a favourable opinion: "Matisse's colour shines with intellectual splendour."

67. Morrice stopped taking part in AAM exhibitions after 1916 and Lyman's participation, interrupted between 1921 and 1927, and thereafter irregular, ceased after 1955.

68. John Lyman asserted on many occasions that he and Matthew Smith had entered the Académie Matisse in fall 1909, the Academy closing its doors in June 1910: "In the fall, Matthew Smith and I (we had become friends a year earlier at Étaples) resolved to attend the 'Académie Matisse' . . . That was the last year of the 'Académie Matisse.'" (Lyman, "Adieu, Matisse," p. 44). The Académie Matisse did not keep a register of students. Some of the students were not really enrolled and only attended on a casual basis (Grammont, "Matisse comme religion," in *Matisse, Cézanne, Picasso . . . L'aventure des Stein*, p. 228, note 44). We know that in fall 1909, Lyman was still attending the Académie Julian, then transferred to the Académie Colarossi. In the absence of other documents, and since Matthew Smith only returned to Paris with Lyman in January 1910, and since Smith's biographer suggests April 1910 as the date of their enrolment in the Académie Matisse ("It was in this building [Hôtel Biron] that Smith and Lyman enrolled, probably in April 1910." Yorke, *Matthew Smith*, p. 61.), we accept this date.

69. Matthew Smith, cited in ibid.

70. Typescript, *Je vis par les yeux*, p. 9, cited in Dompierre, *John Lyman, 1886-1967*, pp. 16-17.

71. Ibid., p. 28.

72. Lyman, cited by Viau, in *Notes biographiques*, chapter 2, p. 5.

73. Ibid., chapter 2, p. 10.

74. Ibid., chapter 4, p. 3.

75. Lyman, *Morrice*, pp. 32-33.

76. Letter to his father, May 20, 1910, in *Inédits de John Lyman*, p. 192.

77. Laugier and Monod Fontaine, *Henri Matisse, 1904-1917*, p. 93, in which this letter is erroneously dated March 1910. Spurling, in *Matisse the Master*, p. 50, restores the correct date of June 1910 and completes the quotation.

78. Desmond MacCarthy, "The Art-Quake of 1910," *The Listener*, February 1, 1943.

79. Letter to Edmund Morris, Paris, January 9, 1911, *Morris Papers*, AGO.

80. Spurling, *Matisse the Master*, p. 66.

81. John Lyman and Corinne Saint-Pierre, cited by Viau, in *Notes biographiques*, chapter 2, p. 8.

82. Lyman, cited par Viau, ibid., chapter 3, p. 3.

83. Letter to Edmund Morris, Paris, June 20, 1911, *Morris Papers*, AGO.

84. Letter to Edmund Morris, Paris, November 8, 1911, *Morris Papers*, AGO.

85. Letter to Edmund Morris, Quebec City, January 14, [1912], *Morris Papers*, AGO. According to Lucie Dorais, Morrice landed in Gibraltar on Friday, February 3, or Sunday, February 11.

86. The first exhibition of the *Peintres futuristes italiens* in Paris had just taken place on February 5-24, at the Galerie Bernheim-Jeune.

87. Léon Lorrain, "Le Salon du Printemps," *Le Devoir*, March 19, 1912, p. 1.

88. Anonymous, "Art Opening, a Social Event," *The Gazette*, March 15, 1912, p. 4.

89. A. C., "Pictures Shown at Spring Exhibition at the Art Gallery Reach a High Level," *The Montreal Star*, March 15, 1912, p. 6.

90. Anonymous, "L'exposition de peintures," *La Presse*, March 23, 1912, p. 20.

91. In Tangier, Matisse and Morrice visited the Irish painter John Lavery, who had also attended Bouguereau's studio at the Académie Julian and who was now vice-president of the International Society of Sculptors, Painters and Gravers of London, where Morrice had been exhibiting since 1901.

92. Likely Concarneau, where Morrice kept a studio.

93. Sylvia Antoniou, *Maurice Cullen*, exhib. cat. (Kingston: Agnes Etherington Art Centre, 1982), p. 54, note 116.

94. Lyman and Corinne Saint-Pierre, cited by Viau, in *Notes biographiques*, chapter 3, p. 3. See also Laugier and Monod Fontaine, *Henri Matisse, 1904-1917*, p. 103.

95. Corinne Saint-Pierre, cited by Viau, in *Notes biographiques*, chapter 4, p. 2.

96. This was how Morrice announced that he would leave for Tangier the following month to spend the winter there. Letter to Edmund Morris, Paris, November 1, [1912], *Morris Papers*, AGO.

97. *Catalogue des tableaux et études par James-Wilson Morrice, exposés Galeries Simonson*, foreword by Armand Dayot, exhib. cat. (Paris: Galeries Simonson, 1926), 11 pages.

98. Bell, *Old Friends*, p. 168. Lucie Dorais suggests that Bell repeated the anecdote that he had read in Donald W. Buchanan's 1936 biography (p. 111). Donald W. Buchanan got it directly from Matisse. Bell had received Buchanan's book and Lyman's book about Morrice (1945) in August 1955 from David Morrice. Letter from David R. Morrice to Clive Bell, August 2, 1955, *Charleston Papers*, King's College, Cambridge.

99. Letter from Charles Camoin to Henri Matisse, February 7, 1945, in *Correspondance entre Charles Camoin et Henri Matisse*, introduced and annotated by Claudine Grammont (Lausanne: La Bibliothèque des Arts/Succession H. Matisse, 1997), p. 214.

100. Lyman, *Morrice*, p. 33.

101. Letter from Henri Matisse to Armand Dayot, undated [late 1925], in *Catalogue des tableaux et études par James-Wilson Morrice, exposés Galeries Simonson*, pp. 6-7. The ellipses in this text suggest that Armand Dayot had made cuts to the original text by Matisse.

102. Lyman, *Morrice*, p. 32. Later, Lyman would add, "For two years, they were always together [Morrice et Matisse], they were constantly seen together," John Lyman, cited by Viau, in *Notes biographiques*, chapter 2, p. 8.

103. *Correspondance entre Charles Camoin et Henri Matisse*, pp. 41-42; Cloutier, *James Wilson Morrice, 1865-1924*, p. 35, note 161.

104. See Lorne Huston, "The 1913 Spring Exhibition of the Art Association of Montreal: Anatomy of a Public Debate," *Journal of Canadian Art History*, vol. 34, no. 1 (2013), pp. 13-52.

105. Samuel Morgan-Powell, in *The Montreal Star*, cited in Buchanan, *James Wilson Morrice – Painter and Nomad*, p. 120.

106. Matisse exhibited with the London International Society of Sculptors, Painters and Gravers in 1910, 1912, 1919 and 1928.

107. "To The Editor: Mr. John G. Lyman Writes in Defence of 'Post-Impressionism,'" *The Montreal Daily Star*, May 1, 1913, p. 10.

108. "To The Editor: Mr. John G. Lyman in Defence of Post Impressionist Painting," *The Montreal Daily Star*, May 17, 1913, p. 12.

109. Lyman, cited by Viau, in *Notes biographiques*, chapter 3, p. 5.

110. In 1911, when William Henry Clapp (1879-1954) returned to Montreal having adopted the Pointillist technique, he earned the scorn of critics. As Lyman would do in 1913, Clapp left Canada in 1915. He lived in Cuba for two years before moving to California, where he lived the rest of his life.

111. According to Viau, *Notes biographiques*, chapter 4, p. 6, and Dompierre, *John Lyman, 1886-1967*, p. 216.

112. Morrice's first non-commercial exhibition in Canada. There was an exhibition at Scott & Sons from January 16 to January 30, 1912, with no catalogue.

113. During the First World War, the curfew in Paris started at about 8 or 9 p.m.

114. Letter from Elizabeth R. Pennell, the wife of the American etcher Joseph Pennell, to Donald W. Buchanan, August 29, 1935, AGO, Edward P. Taylor Library and Archives, D. Buchanan fonds.

115. Bell, *Old Friends*, p. 168.

116. Letter from James Wilson Morrice to Joseph Pennell, November 19, 1914. Washington, Library of Congress, Joseph and Elizabeth Robins Pennell Collection, box 248.

117. Bell, *Old Friends*, p. 157. Bell also writes that, during the war, Morrice often saw Matisse. Is this information reliable? The total absence of documents in the Archives Matisse suggests the contrary and that Morrice and Matisse did not see each other very often after their departure from Morocco.

118. Letter from James Wilson Morrice to Newton MacTavish, Washington, February 23, 1915, North York Public Library, Toronto, Canadiana Collection.

119. The entry "Havana to St. Nazaire / April 18 / Transatlantic," found in sketchbook no. 10, p. 37, is merely a note, since Morrice had left earlier, perhaps because of the heat. *List or Manifest of the Alien Passengers for the United States Immigration Officer at Port of Arrival*, New York, April 13, 1915; the immigration agent added "*SS Rochambeau*" in lead pencil the passenger liner's home port was Le Havre, but on April 4, 1915, and for the entire duration of the war, it was transferred to Bordeaux.

120. This was the painter George Hume Barne (1882-1931), a former acquaintance during the Chat Blanc period who owned *Tangier, Dancer* (cat. 42) by Morrice, a work purchased by Michel Doyon at Christie's, London, in 1991.

121. Denys Sutton, *Letters of Roger Fry*, vol. 2 (London: Chatto & Windus, 1972), p. 385. Further on, Sutton describes Morrice as being "a friend of Matisse" and "on close terms with Clive Bell," p. 739.

122. Letter from James Wilson Morrice to Newton MacTavish, September 13, [1915], North York Public Library, Toronto, Canadiana Collection.

123. In 1921, they would be awarded the 1914-1918 Commemorative war medal (France).

124. Letter to his father, Cannes, April 4, 1916, in *Inédits de John Lyman*, p. 197.

125. Letter to his father, April 23, 1916, in ibid.

126. Ronald Alley, *Catalogue of The Tate Gallery's Collection of Modern Art other than Works by British Artists* (London: Tate Gallery/Sotheby Parke-Bernet, 1981), p. 543.

127. *List or Manifest of the Alien Passengers for the United States Immigration Officer at Port of Arrival*, New York, January 3, 1917.

128. Buchanan, *James Wilson Morrice – Painter and Nomad*, pp. 86-87.

129. Hill, *Morrice: A Gift to the Nation*, 1992, p. 173.

130. "Then the war came. The poet leading a peaceful life, donned khaki, was sent to the front, and assigned to make a decoration for the Canadian War Museum. What was expected of such an inconsequential commission? He compromised by painting the troop departing in a snowfall on a muddy road: a large, arid panel, neither painting nor document. Let's say no more." Lyman, *Morrice*, p. 34.

131. Fernand Préfontaine, "La mare aux grenouilles," *Le Nigog* (May 1918), p. 170.

132. Bell, *Old Friends*, p. 168.

133. Letter to his father, Grez-sur-Loing, July 20, 1919, in *Inédits de John Lyman*, p. 203.

134. Lyman, cited by Viau, in *Notes biographiques*, chapter 4, p. 8.

135. Ibid., chapter 5, p. 14.

136. Ibid.

137. In September 1921, Matisse leaves the Hôtel de la Méditerranée to take an apartment at 1, place Charles Félix, at the edge of the flower market, Cours Saleya, in Nice.

138. "I was so taken with his paintings that I could not utter a word." Lyman, cited by Viau, in *Notes biographiques*, chapter 2, p. 10.

139. John Lyman, "The Eastern Group – French and Dutch Moderns – At the Art Association," *The Montrealer*, December 1, 1938, pp. 32-33. Cited in French by Paul Dumas, *Lyman*, (Montreal, L'Arbre, "Art vivant," series, 1944), pp. 31-32.

140. Lyman, "Adieu, Matisse," p. 45.

141. P. G. Konody, art critic at *The Observer* and the *Daily Mail* assessed Morrice's art: "With Van Gogh he shares the intensity of the mood realized . . . with Gauguin the distinguished sense of simplified decorative design," Buchanan, *James Wilson Morrice – Painter and Nomad*, p. 129.

142. P. G. Konody, "Art and Artists. The Goupil Gallery Salon," *The Observer* [Aberdeen, UK], November 27, 1921, p. 10.

143. G. Blair Laing, *Morrice: A Great Canadian Artist Rediscovered* (Toronto: McClelland and Stewart, 1984), p. 142.

144. Irene Szylinger, "Morrice and Matisse," paper given at the University of Toronto in 1979, cited in Nicole Cloutier, *James Wilson Morrice, 1865-1924*, p. 87, note 19.

145. Typescript of *Je vis par les yeux*, p. 25, cited in Dompierre, *John Lyman, 1886-1967*, p. 38.

146. Clive Bell, "Autumn Shows in Paris," *Vogue*, vol. 64, December 1924, p. 45. H. S. Ciolkowski would later write: "In 1924, a dozen paintings by Morrice were hung in the back of an obscure room at the Salon d'Automne. It would have been more appropriate to do nothing." H. S. Ciolkowski, "James Wilson Morrice," *L'Art et les artistes* [Paris], December 1925, p. 94.

147. Clarence Gagnon commented on a copy of the National Gallery of Canada catalogue: "The Moorish, Tunis and West Indies pictures are very fine, very fresh and vivid coloring . . . They are expensive in francs but extremely cheap in dollars. It will be a terrible mistake if the National Gallery does not get all they can buy. Those loans belong to Art Critics and real connoisseurs who are holding on to them most jealously."

148. See above the insert of 1913.

149. Matisse exhibits a *Dancer* that is not listed in the catalogue but is reproduced to illustrate an article by Charensol in *L'Art vivant*, May 1, 1927.

150. Lyman, *Journal*, August 3, 1927 in *Inédits de John Lyman*, p. 39.

151. Samuel Morgan-Powell, "John G. Lyman Shows a Remarquable Advance in Painting Pictures," *The Montreal Daily Star*, October 7, 1927, p. 6.

152. Matisse, *Écrits et propos sur l'art*, p. 104.

153. Pierre Schneider, *Matisse* (Paris: Flammarion, 2002 [new edition]), p. 607.

154. Ibid., p. 609.

155. Ibid.

156. "June 13th. Varnishing day of Salon des Tuileries. La pagaille! A hundred or two canvases not yet hung, amongst which mine, obliterated with spattered mud. C. [Corinne] phone me to come & withdraw them. The Secretary: 'Mais je vous assure, Monsieur, je ne suis personnellement responsable en rien. Je ne suis qu'un simple travailleur, moi.' No one is ever responsible for anything in France. The Sec'y.: 'Ce n'est pas de notre faute s'il a plu!!!' Nor if there was no roof over the Salon. The Sec'y.: 'Faites-nous une réclamation écrite, voilà comment il faut procéder. Exposez-nous votre demande, nous enquêterons, nous constituerons un dossier (!), ensuite le comité l'examinera et statuera dessus.' This passion for paperasserie! However (probably because I made no claim to refund of dues) I managed to withdraw the canvases without giving them too much discursory pleasure. The portrait of Mendes is in a sorry state. We can never really come to understanding with the French. They attach very little importance to acts and very great importance to words, while we give the preponderance to what one does, not says. The 23 years that I know them leave me farther from them than at the beginning, and the Lord knows I began not only with an open mind but with prejudice in their favour. They have a few very superior qualities, but they have almost all the every-day traits that I most despise: mercenary, niggardly, rapacious, petty, jealous, pettifogging, slovenly, slanderous, tricky—more or less & in varying combinations. The last word the sec'y: 'Évidemment, si on n'est pas du petit comité...!'" In *Inédits de John Lyman*, pp. 97-98.

157. Ibid., p. 100.

158. Anonymous, "John Lyman Shows Striking Works," *The Gazette*, February 24, 1931, p. 4.

159. Lyman said: "Although I had just arrived, I started to see that something was fermenting." Viau, in *Notes biographiques*, chapter 5, p. 15.

160. Ibid.

161. Esther Trépanier, *Peinture et modernité au Québec, 1919-1939* (Quebec City: Éditions Nota Bene, 1998), p. 114, note 15. An exhibition of the Beaver Hall painters will be presented in 2015 at the Montreal Museum of Fine Arts.

162 Anonymous, *The Montreal Star*, March 30, 1932, p. 14, cited in Frances K. Smith, *André Biéler: un artiste et son époque* (Quebec City: Les Presses de l'Université Laval, 2006), p. 152.

163. Charles Hill, *Peinture canadienne des années trente*, exhib. cat. (Ottawa: National Gallery of Canada, 1975), p. 125.

164. Anonymous, "Five Painters Hold Show at Morgan's," *The Gazette*, May 2, 1933, p. 6, cited in Frances K. Smith, *André Biéler*, p. 153. It is observed that Lyman has just as many difficulties with his school as Matisse had with his academy, which had been described as an insane asylum: "I know, like you, that this master of painting has opened a studio, that he attracts people from the the North, that he has acquired a following and that he exploits, to his advantage, no small number of insane persons." Léopold Rude, "Le Salon d'Automne," *Gil Blas*, September 30, 1910, cited in Laugier and Monod Fontaine, *Henri Matisse, 1904-1917*, p. 463.

165. Among the exhibited works were Renoir's *Madame Henriot*, Dufy's *Casino of Nice* and Modigliani's *Portrait of Morgan Russell*.

166. John Lyman, "From Monet to Matisse," *Bridle and Golfer*, December 1934, pp. 18-19, 38, 42.

167. John O'Brian, *Ruthless Hedonism: The American Reception of Matisse* (Chicago: The University of Chicago Press, 1999), p. 47.

168. Anonymous, "Lyman of Canada Has New York Exhibit," *The Art Digest*, June 1, 1936, p. 39.

169. John Lyman, "The School of Paris," *The Montrealer*, October 30, 1936, pp. 18-20.

170. In 1937, the poet and writer Saint-Denys Garneau (1912-1943) published his only collection of poetry, *Regards et jeux dans l'espace*, highly modernist in style, reflecting his training at the Beaux-Arts in 1926-1927 and his ongoing practice of painting.

171. Hector de Saint-Denys Garneau, "Peintres français à la Galerie Scott," *La Relève*, December 1936, pp. 45-50, republished in Hector de Saint-Denys Garneau, *Œuvres en prose*, critical edition by Gisèle Huot (Montreal, Fides, 1995), pp. 104-105.

172. Reynald [Ephrem-Réginald Bertrand], "Le modernisme issu de Paris. Du Picasso de la période bleue à Raoul Dufy, aux galeries Scott," *La Presse*, October 10, 1936, p. 25, cited in Hector de Saint-Denys Garneau, *Œuvres en prose*.

173. Letter to Eric Brown, December 18, 1936. Copy in the "Morrice Memorial Exhibition" file, 1937, folder 1, Ottawa, Library and Archives of the National Gallery of Canada.

174. John Lyman, "Morrice, The Master Incognito," *The Montrealer*, January 15, 1937, p. 19.

175. Reynald, "Belle couleur et probité du métier. Clarence Gagnon à l'Arts Club . . .," *La Presse*, February 27, 1937, p. 54. See also Robert Ayre, "Two Exhibitions," *The Montrealer*, February 1937, p. 24.

176. Reynald, "Les paysages de Robert Tancrède – Rétrospective J. W. Morrice chez Scott," *La Presse*, March 6, 1937, p. 46.

177. John Lyman, "Morrice – The Shadow and the Substance," *The Montrealer*, March 15, 1937, pp. 22-23.

178. Letter from Pierre Matisse to Martin Baldwin, April 28, 1937, work file for *Landscape, Trinidad* (2417), AGO.

179. Hector de Saint-Denys Garneau, "John L[yman] suite," *Œuvres en prose*, pp. 686-687.

180. John Lyman, "Art (The French Show)," *The Montrealer*, October 15, 1937, p. 15. Critic Henri Girard paid attention instead to Matisse's *Paysage montagneux aux environs de Nice*. See Henri Girard, "Peinture française," *Le Canada*, October 19, 1937, p. 2.

181. John Lyman, "Modern Art in the Community," *The Montrealer*, November 15, 1937, p. 33.

182. Hill, *Peinture canadienne des années trente*, p. 131.

183. Humphrey would be replaced by Philip Surrey in 1940.

184. John Lyman, "The Eastern Group – French and Dutch Moderns – At the Art Association," *The Montrealer*, December 1, 1938, pp. 32-33.

185. Ibid.

186. John Lyman, "Drawings – Art and the Stomach," *The Montrealer*, January 1, 1939, p. 22.

187. Press release issued by the Contemporary Arts Society, cited in François-Marc Gagnon, *Paul-Émile Borduas, biographie critique et analyse de l'œuvre* (Montreal: Fides, 1978), p. 81.

188. Paul-Émile Borduas, *Projections libérantes* (1949), in *Écrits I*, scholarly edition by André-G. Bourassa, Jean Fisette and Gilles Lapointe (Montreal: Les Presses de l'Université de Montréal, "Bibliothèque du Nouveau Monde" series, 1987), p. 442. During his studies in Paris in 1928-1930, Borduas attended several exhibitions that featured the works of Matisse. See François-Marc Gagnon, *Paul-Émile Borduas*, p. 38.

189. John Lyman, "*Dufy, Improvisatore* chez Scott & Sons," *The Montrealer*, February 15, 1939, pp. 20-21.

190. Clarence Gagnon, "The Grand Bluff of Modernistic Art," read at the 50th anniversary banquet of the Pen and Pencil Club, April 29, 1939, pp. 10-11, reproduced in Renée Marthe Millette, *Clarence A. Gagnon. Un cas de résistance à la modernité*, Master's thesis, Montreal: Université de Montréal, 1995, 117 pages and appendices.

191. John Lyman, "Gagnon's Talk On Art Draws Spirited Reply," *The Standard*, May 6, 1939, p. 6.

192. Letter from Henri Matisse to his son Pierre Matisse, September 1, 1940, cited in Schneider, *Matisse*, pp. 737-738.

193. John Lyman, "No Hysteria – Art and War – On the Calendar," *The Montrealer,* November 1, 1939, p. 18.

194. Anecdote related by Simone Aubry-Beaulieu (1917-2006), in an interview with Richard Foisy on October 26, 1993, as she was describing her studies at the École des beaux-arts de Montréal in the early 1940s.

195. Lyman wrote the English-language entries for the 139 works in this catalogue, while professor Allard wrote the French-language entries.

196. John Lyman, "Possession of the World – Masterpieces of Painting at the Museum of Fine Arts," *The Montrealer*, February 1942, n.p.

197. Dumas, *Lyman*, p. 12.

198. Lyman, *Morrice*, p. 15.

199. Ibid., p. 28.

200. Ibid., p. 36.

201. *Inédits de John Lyman*, pp. 114-115.

202. The *Portrait of Yvonne Landsberg* dates from 1914. It is reproduced in Schneider, *Matisse*, p. 324, and is now located in the Philadelphia Museum of Art.

203. Irène Legendre, *Petite histoire de l'art moderne*, preface by Amédée Ozenfant and sixteen inserts ([Quebec City]: [Ateliers du "Soleil"], 1947), p. 51. A drawing by Matisse, *Jeune Fille à la blouse roumaine*, reproduced and inserted between pages 130 and 131.

204. Letter to John Lyman, February 13, 1948, in Paul Émile Borduas, *Écrits II, 1923-1953*, vol. 1, scholarly edition by André-G. Bourassa and Gilles Lapointe (Montreal: Les Presses de l'Université de Montréal: "Bibliothèque du Nouveau Monde," series 1997), pp. 231-232.

205. Lyman, *Journal*, October 10, 1950, in *Inédits de John Lyman*, pp. 126-127.

206. In French in the text of the *Journal*.

207. *Inédits de John Lyman*, pp. 126-127.

208. Donald W. Buchanan, "Interview in Montparnasse," *Canadian Art*, vol. 8, no. 2 (Christmas 1950), p. 64.

209. Lyman, "Adieu, Matisse," pp. 45-46.

210. John Lyman, *Journal*, February 5, 1956, in *Inédits de John Lyman*, p. 146.

LIST OF EXHIBITED WORKS

This list includes the works by James Wilson Morrice, John Lyman and Henri Matisse shown in the exhibition. The works of each artist are listed separately, in chronological order. The section devoted to James Wilson Morrice lists the paintings first, followed by the pochades.

In general, the title given to each work is the one under which it was exhibited or published for the first time, or under which it is best known.

In the dates, "about" has been employed in cases where a work was not dated by the artist and there is no known source indicating an exact year of execution.

JAMES WILSON MORRICE (Montreal, Quebec, Canada, 1865 – Tunis, Tunisia, 1924)

Venice at the Golden Hour
About 1901-1902
Oil on canvas
65.4 × 46.3 cm
The Montreal Museum of Fine Arts,
Gwendolen Rutherfurd Caverhill
Bequest (1949.1005)
CAT. 11

**Venice, Looking Out over
the Lagoon**
About 1904
Oil on canvas mounted
on aluminum
60.6 × 73.9 cm
The Montreal Museum of Fine Arts,
gift of James Wilson Morrice Estate
(1925.334)
CAT. 12

Snow Effect (Sleigh)
1906
Oil on canvas
61 × 50.5 cm
Musée des beaux-arts de Lyon (B-772)
CAT. 6

Dieppe
About 1906
Oil on canvas
50.3 × 61.2 cm
National Gallery of Canada, Ottawa,
gift of G. Blair Laing, Toronto, 1989
(30445)
CAT. 106

Red House, Venice
About 1906
Oil on canvas
64.1 × 49.5 cm
The Montreal Museum of Fine Arts,
gift of James Wilson Morrice Estate
(1925.335)
CAT. 10

Autumn
Also known as
Jardin du Luxembourg
1906-1907
Oil on canvas
73.6 × 60.9 cm
A. K. Prakash Collection
CAT. 9

The Ferry, Quebec
1907
Oil on canvas
62 × 81.7 cm
National Gallery of Canada, Ottawa,
purchase 1938 (4301)
CAT. 5

Entrance to a Quebec Village
1909
Oil on canvas
59.7 × 80 cm
Private collection
CAT. 7

View towards Lévis from Québec
1909
Oil on canvas
60.3 × 80 cm
Private collection
CAT. 8

Nude with a Feather
About 1911
Oil on canvas
81.2 × 54.5 cm
The Montreal Museum of Fine Arts,
F. Eleanore Morrice Bequest (1981.65)
CAT. 101

Blanche
About 1911-1912
Oil on canvas
62.1 × 50.8 cm
The Montreal Museum of Fine Arts,
gift of Dr. G. R. McCall (1978.32)
CAT. 67

Blanche Baume
About 1911-1912
Oil on canvas
61.2 × 50.5 cm
National Gallery of Canada, Ottawa,
gift of G. Blair Laing, Toronto, 1989
(30479)
CAT. 68

Flowers
About 1911-1912
Oil on canvas
46 × 38 cm
National Gallery of Canada, Ottawa,
Vincent Massey Bequest, 1968 (15536
CAT. 100

Tangier
1912
Oil on canvas
66 × 93 cm
Musée national des beaux-arts
du Québec, purchase 1925-1926
(1934.467)
CAT. 33

Tangier, Store
1912
Oil on canvas
55 × 65.7 cm
Musée national des beaux-arts
du Québec, purchase 1925-1926
(1934.579)
CAT. 35

Tangier, the Beach
1912
Oil on canvas
59.8 × 72.7 cm
The Thomson Collection at
The Art Gallery of Ontario (103743)
CAT. 34

Landscape, Tangier
1912
Oil on canvas
65.5 × 81.7 cm
National Gallery of Canada,
Ottawa, purchase 1953 (6108)
CAT. 36

Olympia
About 1912
Oil on canvas
82.3 × 61 cm
National Gallery of Canada,
Ottawa, purchase 1957 (6671)
CAT. 13

Beach Scene, Tangier
1912 or 1913
Oil and graphite on wood
22.6 × 31.5 cm
Art Gallery of Ontario, Toronto,
purchased with funds from the
Laidlaw Foundation, 1981 (81/162)
CAT. 48

Gibraltar
1913
Oil on canvas
66 × 81.2 cm
Art Gallery of Ontario, Toronto,
gift of Mr. and Mrs. W. F. McLean,
Toronto, in memory of Mr. and
Mrs. S. G. Bennett, 1989 (89/112)
CAT. 4

Rock of Gibraltar
1913
Oil on canvas
28.2 × 31.5 cm
Pierre Lassonde Collection
CAT. 1

Tangier, Dancer
1913
Oil on wood
33 × 23.8 cm
Michel Doyon Estate
CAT. 42

View from the Window, Tangier
1913
Oil on canvas
62 × 46 cm
Private collection
CAT. 65

Tangier, the Town
1913
Oil on canvas
53.3 × 64.8 cm
Private collection, Alberta
CAT. 37

Tangier, the Outskirts
1913
Oil on canvas
50.8 × 72.4 cm
Private collection
CAT. 39

Waiting for the Boat, Tangier
About 1913
Oil on canvas
59.7 × 73.7 cm
Private collection
CAT. 38

Afternoon, Tunis
1914
Oil on canvas
54.3 × 64.7 cm
The Montreal Museum of Fine Arts,
purchase, John W. Tempest Fund
(1915.130)
CAT. 50

Seated Arab
1914
Oil on canvas
32 × 22.5 cm
Private collection
CAT. 43

Tunisian Girl
1914
Oil on wood
36 × 27 cm
Private collection
CAT. 44

**Fruit Market,
North Africa (Tunis)**
1914
Oil on canvas
50.4 × 61.3 × 1.9 cm
The Montreal Museum of Fine Arts,
David R. Morrice Bequest
(1981.10)
CAT. 41

Garden in Cuba
1915
Oil on canvas
65.3 × 54.2 × 2.5 cm
The Montreal Museum of
Fine Arts, gift of Linda Sloss,
in memory of her parents,
Duncan and Hylda Hodgson
(1999.12)
CAT. 21

Havana, Cuba
Also known as *Jamaica*
1915
Oil on canvas
53.3 × 72.6 cm
Vancouver Art Gallery,
gift of Mr. Maurice and
Mrs. Mary Margaret Young
(97.49.3)
CAT. 75

House in Santiago, Cuba
1915
Oil on canvas
54 × 64.8 cm
Tate Gallery, London (3842)
CAT. 19

Houses, Cuba
1915
Oil on canvas
50.8 × 60.9 cm
The Montreal Museum of Fine Arts,
purchase, William Gilman Cheney
Bequest (1939.670)
CAT. 77

Café El Pasaje, Havana
About 1918-1919
Oil on canvas
65.8 × 67 cm
National Gallery of Canada, Ottawa,
gift of G. Blair Laing, Toronto, 1989
(30401)
CAT. 74

Village Street, West Indies
About 1918-1919
Oil on canvas
60.6 × 81.7 × 2.5 cm
The Montreal Museum of Fine Arts,
purchase, William Gilman Cheney
Bequest (1939.685)
CAT. 22

Scene in Havana
About 1918-1919
Oil on canvas
72.4 × 53.7 cm
Art Gallery of Ontario, Toronto,
purchase, with assistance from
Wintario, 1977 (77/10)
CAT. 73

Landscape, West Indies
About 1918-1921
Oil on canvas
59.7 × 81.3 cm
Power Corporation of Canada
(2000.071.1)
CAT. 23

Morocco Buildings
About 1919-1921
Oil on canvas
60 × 81.5 cm
The Thomson Collection at The Art
Gallery of Ontario (103745)
CAT. 49

The Pond, West Indies
About 1920-1922
Oil on canvas
81.5 × 54.8 cm
The Montreal Museum of Fine
Arts, gift of the Louise and Bernard
Lamarre family (1998.29)
CAT. 24

Fruit Boat, Trinidad
1921
Oil on canvas
38.3 × 46.5 cm
National Gallery of Canada,
Ottawa, gift of G. Blair Laing,
Toronto, 1989 (30459)
CAT. 26

**Landscape, Trinidad
(Macqueripe Bay)**
1921
Oil on canvas
65.8 × 81 cm
National Gallery of Canada,
Ottawa, purchase 1938 (4302)
CAT. 25

Landscape, Trinidad
About 1921
Oil on canvas
74.6 × 92.7 cm
Art Gallery of Ontario, Toronto,
purchase 1937 (2417)
CAT. 72

POCHADES

**Moonlight on
the Bay of Tangier**
1912 or 1913
Oil on wood
12 × 15.2 cm
A. K. Prakash Collection
CAT. 54

On the Road, Tangier
1912 or 1913
Oil on wood
12.3 × 15.5 cm
Vancouver Art Gallery,
gift of Maurice and Mary
Margaret Young (97.49.08)
CAT. 55

Tangier
1912 or 1913
Oil on wood
13.3 × 17.2 cm
A. K. Prakash Collection
CAT. 57

A Gate in Tangier
About 1912-1913
Oil and graphite on wood
13.1 × 17 cm
National Gallery of Canada,
Ottawa, gift of G. Blair Laing,
Toronto, 1989 (30474)
CAT. 47

View of a North African Town
About 1912-1914
Oil on wood
12.2 × 15 cm
Art Gallery of Hamilton,
David R. Morrice Bequest,
1978 (78.48)
CAT. 32

**Moroccan Town
(Gateway in Tangier)**
About 1913
Oil on wood
17 × 13.3 cm
The Thomson Collection
at The Art Gallery of Ontario
(103787)
CAT. 66

At the Café, Tunis
1914
Oil on wood
12 × 14.5 cm
The Montreal Museum of Fine Arts,
Dr. Max Stern Bequest (1988.23)
CAT. 58

**Bazaar, Study for "Fruit Market,
North Africa (Tunis)"**
1914
Oil on wood
13.3 × 17.1 cm
The Montreal Museum of Fine Arts,
gift of James Wilson Morrice Estate
(1925.340d)
CAT. 40

Study for "Afternoon, Tunis"
1914
Oil and graphite on wood
13.3 × 16.8 cm
The Montreal Museum of Fine Arts,
gift of Mrs. Alan G. Law (1925.340b)
CAT. 51

Plane Tree and Tent, North Africa
1914
Oil and graphite on wood
13.2 × 17 cm
National Gallery of Canada, Ottawa,
gift of G. Blair Laing, Toronto, 1989
(30426)
CAT. 53

Café Scene, Tunis
1914
Oil on wood
13.3 × 17.5 cm
A. K. Prakash Collection
CAT. 56

Tunis Street Scene
1914
Oil on wood
12.4 × 15.4 cm
Musée national des beaux-arts
du Québec, purchase (1953.213)
CAT. 59

Jamaica
1915
Oil on wood
12.7 × 16.5 cm
A. K. Prakash Collection
CAT. 76

Arabs Talking
1922
Oil on wood
13.2 × 17.1 cm
The Montreal Museum of Fine Arts,
gift of James Wilson Morrice Estate
(1925.341a)
CAT. 46

The Mosque, Algiers
1922
Oil on wood
17 × 13.4 cm
National Gallery of Canada, Ottawa,
purchase 1925 (3191)
CAT. 45

Algiers
About 1922-1923
Oil and graphite on wood
12.9 × 16.3 cm
National Gallery of Canada, Ottawa, gift
of G. Blair Laing, Toronto, 1989 (30456)
CAT. 52

JOHN LYMAN (Biddeford, Maine, USA, 1886 – Kingsley, Barbados, 1967)

Early Spring
1908
Oil on wood
21.8 × 24.4 cm
Private collection
CAT. 16

Café, Rue Royale, Paris
About 1909
Oil on wood
11 × 18 cm
Musée national des beaux-arts du
Québec, gift of Mrs. John Lyman
Estate (1970.498)
CAT. 17

Swiss Essay No. 1
Also known as *Swiss Landscape*
1911
Oil on wood
32.2 × 41 cm
Private collection
CAT. 15

Beach at Trouville
Between 1911 and 1916
Oil on wood
32.3 × 41 cm
Private collection
CAT. 108

Dalesville
1912
Oil on canvas mounted on Plexiglas
32 × 39.5 cm
Musée national des beaux-arts du
Québec, gift of Mrs. John Lyman
Estate (1970.500)
CAT. 84

Wild Nature Impromptu, 1st State
1912
Oil on canvas mounted on cardboard
32 × 40.5 cm
Musée national des beaux-arts du
Québec, gift of Mrs. John Lyman
Estate (1970.499)
CAT. 83

Westmount in Winter
1912
Oil on wood
40.8 × 32.4 cm
National Gallery of Canada, Ottawa,
purchase 1981 (23989)
CAT. 86

On the Beach, Bermuda
1913
Oil on canvas mounted on wood
40.8 × 32.4 cm
Lavalin Collection of the
Musée d'art contemporain de
Montréal (A 92 995 P 1)
CAT. 107

St. George, Bermuda
About 1913
Oil on wood
40.6 × 33 cm
The Montreal Museum of Fine Arts,
gift of Dr. J. Douglas Morgan in
memory of his brother, Harold M.
Morgan (1952.1069)
CAT. 27

Profile of Corinne
1913-1914
Oil on canvas mounted
on cardboard
35 × 26 cm
Lavalin Collection of the Musée
d'art contemporain de Montréal
(A 92 1050 P 1)
CAT. 93

**The Lawns of Fairfield,
Cowansville**
1914
Oil on canvas mounted
on cardboard
32.2 × 40.5 cm
Musée national des beaux-arts du
Québec, gift of Mrs. John Lyman
Estate (1970.510)
CAT. 85

Southlands, Bermuda
1914
Oil on canvas mounted
on cardboard
32 × 41 cm
Private collection
CAT. 78

Untitled
About 1914-1917
Oil on wood
32 × 41 cm
The Montreal Museum
of Fine Arts, gift of the
Fournelle family (2011.22)
CAT. 79

Self-portrait
1918
Oil on canvas
73 × 60.3 cm
Musée national des beaux-arts du
Québec, purchase (1944.59)
Conservation treatment by the
Centre de conservation du Québec
CAT. 14

Hammamet
1920
Oil on canvas
40.7 × 32.2 cm
Private collection
CAT. 28

The Monastir Casbah
About 1920
Oil on wood
41 × 32.3 cm
Gordon Lenko and Lucie
Charbonneau Collection
CAT. 62

**Landscape with House
(North African Coast)**
Between 1920 and 1926
Oil on canvas
65 × 54.5 cm
Private collection
CAT. 63

The Arab Philosopher
Between 1920 and 1926
Oil on canvas
91 × 65 cm
National Gallery of Canada, Ottawa,
purchase 2002 (41082)
CAT. 31

The Marabouts' Tombs, Morocco
Between 1920 and 1926
Oil on canvas mounted
on cardboard
33.2 × 40.6 cm
Private collection
CAT. 60

View of North Africa
Between 1920 and 1926
Oil on canvas mounted
on cardboard
41 × 33.2 cm
Private collection
CAT. 29

Zaouia, Hammamet
Between 1920 and 1926
Oil on wood
31.4 × 41 cm
Musée national des beaux-arts du
Québec, gift of Mrs. John Lyman
Estate (1970.501)
CAT. 64

**Sidi Djedidi, Tunisia,
the Roman Well**
About 1921
Oil on wood
17 × 14 cm
Musée national des beaux-arts du
Québec, gift of Mrs. John Lyman
Estate (1970.504)
CAT. 61

Habiba (Young Tunisian Girl)
About 1922
Oil on canvas
54.6 × 45.8 cm
The Montreal Museum of Fine Arts,
gift of Germaine M. Black Estate
(1955.1112)
CAT. 30

Indolent Youth
About 1922
Oil on canvas
74 × 91.9 cm
Musée national des beaux-arts
du Québec, gift of Gilles Corbeil
(1979.194)
CAT. 97

Jardin du Luxembourg
Also known as
Le Jardin and *Le Luxembourg*
About 1923
Oil on cardboard
33 × 41 cm
Private collection
CAT. 2

Jardin du Luxembourg II
About 1923
Oil on cardboard
33 × 40.8 cm
Private collection
CAT. 3

Orientale
About 1924
Oil on canvas
66 × 85.1 cm
National Gallery of Canada,
Ottawa, purchase 1978 (18943)
CAT. 96

The Book
About 1925
Oil on wood
31.7 × 39.4 cm
Private collection
CAT. 92

On the Beach (Saint-Jean-de-Luz)
1929-1930
Oil on paper mounted on canvas
45.6 × 55.5 × 2.4 cm
National Gallery of Canada,
Ottawa, gift of the Max Stern
Estate, 1988, in accordance
with his wishes (30182)
CAT. 90

The Airplane
Before 1933
Oil on canvas
69.3 × 84 cm
Private collection
CAT. 18

Studies for "The Airplane"
Before 1933
Oil on cardboard (7);
oil on canvas (1)
9.8 × 17.9 cm; 15.6 × 21 cm;
13.8 × 17.5 cm; 11.5 × 17.8 cm;
13.4 × 17.9 cm; 12.2 × 21.5 cm;
13.8 × 21.4 cm; 14 × 21.4 cm
Private collection
CAT. 18.01-08

Massawippi Lake
1933
Oil on canvas
61 × 86.8 cm
Winnipeg Art Gallery, gift of
Mr. Peter Dobush (G-65-148)
CAT. 109

Bathers
1933-1934
Oil on cardboard
50.8 × 61 cm
Musée national des beaux-arts du
Québec, gift of Mrs. John Lyman
Estate (1970.509)
CAT. 94

Road at La Conception
1934-1935
Oil on wood
38 × 45.5 cm
Dr. Richard Renlund Collection
CAT. 87

Portrait of Marcelle
About 1935
Oil on canvas
60.7 × 50.5 cm
Art Gallery of Ontario, Toronto,
purchase, with assistance from
Wintario, 1978 (78/15)
CAT. 98

Jori Smith in Costume
1936
Oil on canvas
50.8 × 55.9 cm
Private collection
CAT. 91

Bathing Beach, Lake Ouimet
About 1939
Oil on cardboard
33 × 46 cm
Jean-Pierre Valentin Collection
CAT. 111

The Red Cabin at Lake Massawippi
1945
Oil on cardboard
37.5 × 46 cm
Musée national des beaux-arts
du Québec, gift of
Mrs. John Lyman Estate
(1970.515)
CAT. 110

Still Life with Fruit
1946
Oil on canvas
41.2 × 64 cm
Power Corporation of Canada
CAT. 102

Greenery III
1947
Oil on cardboard
45 × 38 cm
Musée national des beaux-arts du
Québec, gift of Mrs. John Lyman
Estate (1970.519)
CAT. 89

Rose
About 1947
Oil on canvas
56 × 69 × 1.5 cm
The Montreal Museum
of Fine Arts, purchase (1948.966)
CAT. 95

The Yacht Club, North Hatley
1948
Oil on canvas
65.5 × 95.5 cm
Agnes Etherington Art Centre,
Queen's University, Kingston
CAT. 113

Going up the Hill
1952
Oil on canvas
52.8 × 76 cm
Musée national des beaux-arts du
Québec, gift of Mrs. John Lyman
Estate (1970.526)
CAT. 88

White Lilacs
1954
Oil on canvas
61 × 50.8 cm
Agnes Etherington Art Centre,
Queen's University, Kingston
CAT. 104

Studies for "Sunbathing I and II"
About 1955
Oil on cardboard (9)
13 × 16 cm; 16.7 × 18 cm;
16.4 × 17 cm; 14.2 × 18 cm;
16.5 × 16 cm; 14 × 16.4 cm;
12.2 × 16 cm; 13 × 16 cm;
12.2 × 16 cm
Musée national des beaux-arts du
Québec, gift of Mrs. John Lyman
Estate (1970.560.01-09)
CAT. 114.01-09

Beach Scene
1957
Oil on Masonite
50.8 × 66 cm
Private collection
CAT. 112

Sunbathing II
1960
Oil on canvas
61 × 76.2 cm
Musée national des beaux-arts
du Québec, gift of
Mrs. John Lyman Estate
(1970.537)
CAT. 114

Nannies on the Terrace
1961
Oil on canvas
51.4 × 61.5 cm
Private collection
CAT. 80

The Lobster Trap
1962
Oil on canvas
61.5 × 92 cm
Musée national des beaux-arts du
Québec, gift of André and Gillian
Valiquette (2009.266)
CAT. 81

Hauling up the Fishing Boat
1962
Oil on canvas
45.7 × 91.4 cm
LMC Health Care Collection
CAT. 82

HENRI MATISSE (Le Cateau-Cambrésis, France, 1869 – Nice, France, 1954)

Palm Leaf, Tangier
1912
Oil on canvas
117.5 × 81.9 cm
National Gallery of Art, Washington,
Chester Dale Fund (1978.73.1)
CAT. 20

Large Cliff – Two Rays
1920
Oil on canvas
93 × 73 cm
Norton Museum of Art, West Palm
Beach, Florida, bequest of R. H.
Norton
CAT. 69

**Seated Woman, Back Turned
to the Open Window**
About 1922
Oil on canvas
73.3 × 92.5 cm
The Montreal Museum of Fine Arts,
purchase, John W. Tempest Fund
(1949.1015)
CAT. 70

Nude on a Yellow Sofa
1926
Oil on canvas
55.1 × 80.8 cm
National Gallery of Canada, Ottawa,
purchase 1958 (6971)
CAT. 71

Portrait with Pink and Blue Face
1936-1937
Oil on canvas
42 × 33.3 cm
Musée d'art contemporain
de Montréal (A 76 2 P 1)
CAT. 99

Ivy Branch
1941
Oil on canvas
55.8 × 46.6 cm
Art Gallery of Ontario, Toronto,
gift of Sam and Ayala Zacks, 1970
(71/249)
CAT. 105

Anemones and Peach Blossoms
1944
Oil on canvas
54 × 65 cm
Detroit Institute of Arts, gift of the
Josephine F. Ford Estate (2005.62)
CAT. 103

LIST OF FIGURES

OTHER PAINTINGS

Edgar Degas
Orchestra Musicians
1871-1874
Oil on canvas
69 × 49 cm
Städtische Galerie im Städelschen
Kunstinstitut, Frankfurt am Main
FIG. 33

Édouard Manet
Before the Mirror
1876
Oil on canvas
92.1 × 71.4 cm
Solomon R. Guggenheim Museum,
New York, Thannhauser Collection,
Gift, Justin K. Thannhauser, 1978
FIG. 30

Camille Pissarro
The Saint-Sever Bridge, Rouen: Mist
1896
Oil on canvas
60.3 × 87 cm
North Carolina Museum of Art,
Raleigh, gift of Wachovia Bank and
Trust Co.
FIG. 32

Auguste Renoir
Fog on Guernsey
1883
Oil on canvas
53.3 × 65.1 cm
Cincinnati Art Museum, John J.
Emery Endowment and The Edwin
and Virginia Irwin Memorial
FIG. 31

PHOTOGRAPHS

Charles Camoin
**Matisse and his wife in Tangier,
with *Landscape Viewed from a
Window* in the background**
1913
Photographic print
Archives Matisse, Paris
FIG. 16

William Notman & Son
James Wilson Morrice
1900
Gelatin silver print
17 × 12 cm
McCord Museum, Montreal
FIG. 34

Eugène Pirou, Paris
J. W. Morrice in uniform
About 1918
Platinum print
National Film Board of Canada
FIG. 45

Ralph W. Johnston
**Group portrait of the Carnegie
International Jury of Awards**
1930
Photographic print
19 × 25 cm
Smithsonian Institution, Archives of
American Art, Forbes Watson Papers
FIG. 46

John Lyman
1905
Photograph shown in the film *Je vis
par les yeux* (1959)
National Film Board of Canada
FIG. 36

Henri Matisse's studio
1909
Photographic print
Archives Matisse, Paris
FIG. 38

A group of students at the Atelier,
with John Lyman at left
Photograph reproduced in *Canadian
Passing Show*, February 1933
FIG. 47

Matisse's *Large Cliff* at the home
of H. S. Southam
Between 1936 and 1943
Photographic print
National Gallery of Canada, Ottawa,
Archives
FIG. 20

POSTCARDS

A. Cavilla, Tangier
General View from the Grand Zoco
About 1910
Postcard
Lucie Dorais Collection
FIG. 10

Jordi, Havana
**Cuba, pueblo de pescadores/
Fishing Village**
Undated
Postcard
Lucie Dorais Collection
FIG. 4

Jordi, Havana
**Cuba, paisaje tropical/
Tropical Landscape**
Undated
Postcard
Lucie Dorais Collection
FIG. 44

L. L., Paris
Market Scene, Tangier
About 1925?
Postcard
Lucie Dorais Collection
FIG. 9

S. J. Nahon, Tangier
Tangier, Morocco: The Three Doors
About 1912
Postcard
Lucie Dorais Collection
FIG. 15

**Cuba, bohios y cocoteros/
Country Huts & Cocoa Nuts**
Undated
Postcard
Lucie Dorais Collection
FIG. 5

DOCUMENTS

Gisbert Combaz
**Poster for an exhibition
of La Libre Esthétique**
1900
Lithograph
73.4 × 42.2 cm
Royal Institute for Cultural
Heritage, Brussels
FIG. 35

**Reproduction of *Wild Nature
Impromptu* by John Lyman in
The Montreal Herald, March 27,
1913, p. 2**
Bibliothèque de l'Assemblée
nationale, Quebec City
FIG. 41

**Reproduction of *A Brunette*
by John Lyman in *The Montreal
Daily Star*, March 29, 1913, p. 22**
Bibliothèque de l'Assemblée
nationale, Quebec City
FIG. 42

**Cover of the catalogue of Morrice's
exhibition at the Arts Club of
Montreal**
1914
The Montreal Museum of Fine Arts,
Archives, Arts Club Fonds
FIG. 43

SELECTED BIBLIOGRAPHY

BOOKS AND ARTICLES

BELL, Clive. *Since Cézanne*. New York: Harcourt, Brace and Co., 1922 (Kessinger Legacy Reprints).
__________. *Old Friends: Personal Recollections*. London: Chatto & Windus, 1956.

BOUTILIER, Alicia. "'To Encourage Others': H. S. Southam and His Collection." In *Inspirational: The Collection of H. S. Southam*, exhib. cat. Hamilton: Art Gallery of Hamilton, 2009, pp. 8-58.

BUCHANAN, Donald W. *James Wilson Morrice - Painter and Nomad: A Biography*. Toronto: The Ryerson Press, 1936.

CIOLKOWSKA, Muriel. "Memories of Morrice." *The Canadian Forum*, vol. 6 (November 1925), pp. 52-53.

CLERMONT, Ghislain. "La réception critique internationale de James Wilson Morrice en 1905." *Revue de l'Université de Moncton*, vol. 26, no. 2 (1993), pp. 83-107.

COGEVAL, Guy, et al. *Le Musée des beaux-arts, Montréal/The Montreal Museum of Fine Arts*. Montreal/Paris: The Montreal Museum of Fine Arts/RMN/BNP Paribas, 2001.

COWART, Jack, and Dominique FOURCADE. *Henri Matisse: The Early Years in Nice, 1916-1930*. Washington/New York: National Gallery of Art/Harry N. Abrams, 1986.

DEBRAY, Cécile. *Henri Matisse, 1869-1954*. Paris: Centre Pompidou, "Monographies" series, 2011.

DES GAGNIERS, Jean. *Morrice*. Ottawa: Éditions du Pélican, 1971.

DORAIS, Lucie. "Deux moments dans la vie et l'œuvre de James Wilson Morrice." *Bulletin 30/1977*. Ottawa: National Gallery of Canada, 1978, pp. 19-35.
__________. *J. W. Morrice*. Ottawa: National Gallery of Canada, 1985.
__________. "Morrice et la figure humaine"/"Morrice and the Human Figure." In CLOUTIER, 1985, pp. 63-72.
__________. "James Wilson Morrice." In *Canadian Art: The Thomson Collection at the Art Gallery of Ontario*. Toronto: Skylet Publishing/The Art Gallery of Ontario, 2008, pp. 42-53.

DUMAS, Paul. *Lyman*. Montreal: L'Arbre, "Art vivant" series, 1944.

ELDERFIELD, John, William S. LIEBERMAN and Riva CASTLEMAN. *Matisse in the Collection of the Museum of Modern Art*. New York: The Museum of Modern Art, 1978.

ESCHOLIER, Raymond. *Matisse, ce vivant*. Paris: Librairie Arthème Fayard, 1956.

ÉTHIER-BLAIS, Jean. "James Wilson Morrice." *Vie des Arts*, no. 73 (winter 1973-1974), pp. 41-44.

FOURNET, Claude. *Matisse-Terre-Lumière*. Paris: Galilée, 1985.

GIRARD, Xavier. *Matisse, une splendeur inouïe*. Paris: Gallimard, "Découvertes Gallimard Peinture" series, 1993.
__________. *Matisse, Nice, 1917-1954*. Paris: Assouline, 1996.

GLEDHILL, John. *Matthew Smith: Catalogue Raisonné of the Oil Paintings*. London: Ashgate, 2009.

GRAMMONT, Claudine. "Chronique d'un scandale annoncé." In *Les Fauves et la critique*, exhib. cat. Turin/Lodève: Palazzo Bricherasio/Musée de Lodève/Electa, 1999, pp. 21-36.

HALLIDAY, Francis, and John RUSSELL. *Matthew Smith*. London: George Allen and Unwin, 1962.

HUSTON, Lorne. "The 1913 Spring Exhibition of the Art Association of Montreal: Anatomy of a Public Debate." *Journal of Canadian Art History/Annales d'histoire de l'art canadien*, vol. 34, no. 1 (2013), pp. 12-55.

KAREL, David. *André Biéler ou le choc des cultures*. Quebec City: Les Presses de l'Université Laval, 2003.

LAING, G. Blair. *Morrice: A Great Canadian Artist Rediscovered*. Toronto: McClelland and Stewart, 1984.

LARSEN, Wayne. *James Wilson Morrice: Painter of Light and Shadow*. Toronto: Dundurn Press, 2008.

LEBLOND, Marius-Ary. *Peintres de races*. Brussels: G. Van Oest & Cie, 1909.

LEMAIRE, Gérard-Georges. *Un thé au Bloomsbury. L'art autour de Virginia Woolf*. Paris: Henri Veyrier, 1990.

LYMAN, John. "Morrice, the Master Incognito." *The Montrealer*, January 15, 1937, pp. 18-20.
__________. "Mr. Gagnon on Morrice." *The Montrealer*, March 1, 1938, p. 21.
__________. *Morrice*. Montreal: L'Arbre, "Art vivant" series, 1945.
__________. "Adieu, Matisse." *Canadian Art*, vol. 12, no. 2 (winter 1955), pp. 44-46.

MARTINET, Jean-Claude, and Guy WILDENSTEIN. *Marquet. L'Afrique du Nord. Catalogue de l'œuvre peint*. Paris: Skira/Seuil/Wildenstein Institute, 2001.

O'BRIAN, John. "Morrice – O'Conor, Gauguin, Bonnard et Vuillard." *Revue de l'Université de Moncton*, vol. 15, nos. 2-3 (April-December 1982), pp. 9-34.
__________. "Morrice ou la quête du plaisir"/"Morrice's Pleasures (1900-1914)." In CLOUTIER, 1985, pp. 89-97.
__________. *Ruthless Hedonism: The American Reception of Matisse*. Chicago: The University of Chicago Press, 1999.

PLEYNET, Marcelin. *Henri Matisse*. Paris: Gallimard, "Folio essais" series, 1990.

SCHNEIDER, Pierre. *Matisse*. New York: Rizzoli, 1984.

SPURLING, Hilary. *Unknown Matisse: A Life of Henri Matisse*. New York: Knopf, 1998.
__________. *Matisse the Master – A Life of Henri Matisse: The Conquest of Colour, 1909-1954*. New York: Knopf, 1999.

SZYLINGER, Irene. "Les aquarelles de James Wilson Morrice"/"A Brief Analysis of the Watercolours." In CLOUTIER, 1985, pp. 79-88.

TRÉPANIER, Esther. *Peinture et modernité au Québec, 1919-1939*. Quebec City: Nota bene, 1998.

VAUXCELLES, Louis. "The Art of J. W. Morrice." *The Canadian Magazine*, vol. 34, no. 2 (December 1909), pp. 169-176.

YORKE, Malcolm. *Matthew Smith: His Life and Reputation*. London: Faber and Faber, 1997.

EXHIBITION CATALOGUES

Memorial Exhibition of Paintings by the Late James W. Morrice, R.C.A. Montreal: Art Association of Montreal, 1925.

Catalogue des tableaux et études par James Wilson Morrice. Foreword by Armand Dayot. Paris: Galeries Simonson, 1926.

Exhibition of Paintings by J. W. Morrice. Montreal: W. Scott & Sons, 1937.

ALAOUI, Brahim, ed. *Le Maroc de Matisse.* Paris: Institut du Monde Arabe/Gallimard, 1999.

BISHOP, Janet, Cécile DEBRAY and Rebecca RABINOW, eds. *The Steins Collect: Matisse, Picasso, and the Parisian Avant-Garde,* San Francisco/New Haven: San Francisco Museum of Modern Art/Yale University Press, 2011.

BROOKE, Janet M. *Le Goût de l'art. Les collectionneurs montréalais, 1880-1920/ Discerning Tastes: Montreal Collectors 1880-1920.* Montreal: The Montreal Museum of Fine Arts, 1989.

BRUCE, Tobi, and Patrick SHAW CABLE. *The French Connection: Canadian Painters at the Paris Salons, 1880-1900.* Hamilton: Art Gallery of Hamilton, 2011.

CADIZ TOPP, Elizabeth. *L'Été sans fin. Les artistes canadiens aux Antilles/ Endless Summer: Canadian Artists in the Caribbean.* Kleinburg: McMichael Canadian Art Collection, 1988.

CLOUTIER, Nicole, ed. *James Wilson Morrice 1865-1924.* Montreal: The Montreal Museum of Fine Arts, 1985.

COWART, Jack, ed. *Matisse in Morocco: The Paintings and Drawings, 1912-1913.* Washington: National Gallery of Art, 1990.

D'ALESSANDRO, Stephanie, and John ELDERFIELD. *Matisse: Radical Invention, 1913-1917.* Chicago: The Art Institute of Chicago, 2010.

DEBRAY, Cécile, ed. *Matisse. Paires et séries.* Paris: Centre Pompidou, 2012.

DEPARPE, Patrice, ed. *Matisse, la couleur découpée. Une donation révélatrice.* Paris/Le Cateau Cambrésis: Somogy Éditions d'Art/Musée départemental Matisse, 2013.

DOMPIERRE, Louise. *John Lyman, 1886-1967.* Kingston: Agnes Etherington Art Centre, 1986.

GRANDBOIS, Michèle, Anna HUDSON and Esther TRÉPANIER. *Le Nu dans l'art moderne canadien, 1920-1950/The Nude in Modern Canadian Art 1920-1950.* Quebec City/Paris: Musée national des beaux-arts du Québec/Somogy Éditions d'Art, 2009.

HILL, Charles C. *Morrice. Un don à la patrie. La collection G. Blair Laing/ Morrice: A Gift to the Nation - The G. Blair Laing Collection.* Ottawa: National Gallery of Canada, 1992.

JOHNSTON, W. R. *James Wilson Morrice, 1865-1924.* Montreal: The Montreal Museum of Fine Arts, 1965.

LANGDALE, Cecily. *Charles Conder, Robert Henri, James Morrice, Maurice Prendergast: The Formative Years, Paris 1890s.* New York: Davis and Long, 1975.

MOREAULT, Michel, Édith-Anne PAGEOT and Jacques DES ROCHERS, eds. *Max Stern, marchand et mécène à Montréal/Max Stern: Montreal Dealer and Patron.* Montreal: The Montreal Museum of Fine Arts/Leonard & Bina Ellen Art Gallery, Concordia University, 2004.

MORRIN, Peter, Judith ZILCZER and William C. AGEE. *The Advent of Modernism: Post-Impressionism and North American Art, 1900-1918.* Atlanta: High Museum of Art, 1986.

MURRAY, Joan. *La Naissance de la modernité : le post-impressionnisme au Canada d'environ 1900 à 1920/The Birth of the Modern: Post-Impressionism in Canadian Art, c. 1900-1920.* Oshawa: The Robert McLaughlin Gallery, 2002.

NELSON, Charmaine. *Le Regard de l'autre : artistes canadiens blancs – sujets féminins noirs/Through An-Other's Eyes: White Canadian Artists – Black Female Subjects.* Oshawa: The Robert McLaughlin Gallery, 1998.

RÉGNIER, Gérard, ed. *Bonnard.* Paris: Centre Pompidou, 1984.

REID, Dennis. *James Wilson Morrice, 1865-1924.* Introduced by Denys Sutton. Bordeaux/Paris: Musée des beaux-arts de Bordeaux/Durand-Ruel, 1968.

RUBIN, William. *Picasso and Braque: Pionneering Cubism.* New York: The Museum of Modern Art, 1989.

SCHNEIDER, Pierre, ed. *Henri Matisse. Exposition du centenaire.* Paris: RMN, 1970.

SERRANO, Véronique, and Claudine GRAMMONT, eds. *Charles Camoin. Rétrospective, 1879-1965.* Lausanne: Fondation de l'Hermitage/RMN/Musées de Marseille, 1997.

SUTTON, Denys. "The Canadian Nomad." In *James Wilson Morrice, 1865-1924.* Vancouver: Vancouver Art Gallery, 1977.

VIAU, Guy. *Lyman.* Montreal: Dominion Gallery, 1963.

ARTISTS' WRITINGS AND CORRESPONDENCE

LYMAN, John. *John Lyman,* exhib. cat. Extracts from newspaper articles and interviews; essay by Gilles Corbeil. Montreal: The Montreal Museum of Fine Arts, 1963.
__________. *Inédits de John Lyman.* Texts selected and annotated by Hedwidge Asselin. Montreal: Ministère des Affaires culturelles/Bibliothèque nationale du Québec, 1980.

MATISSE, Henri. *Écrits et propos sur l'art.* Introduced by Dominique Fourcade. Paris: Hermann, "Savoir : sur l'art" series, 1972.
__________. *Notes d'un peintre.* Introduced by Cécile Debray. Paris: Centre Pompidou/Succession H. Matisse, 2012.

MATISSE, Henri, and Charles CAMOIN. *Correspondance entre Charles Camoin et Henri Matisse.* Introduced and annotated by Claudine Grammont. Lausanne: Bibliothèque des Arts/Succession H. Matisse, 1997.

MATISSE, Henri, and Albert MARQUET. *Matisse-Marquet. Correspondance, 1898-1947.* Selected and annotated by Claudine Grammont. Lausanne: Bibliothèque des Arts, 2008.

INDEX OF NAMES AND TITLES

THE AUTHORS

Lucie Dorais
Art historian, a specialist on the work of James Wilson Morrice,
author of the catalogue raisonné (forthcoming) and a number
of other publications on the artist.

Richard Foisy
Independent researcher in the fields of literature and art history, founding director
of the Centre de recherche sur l'atelier de L'Arche et son époque,
Montréal, 1900-1925.

François-Marc Gagnon
Professor Emeritus at the Université de Montréal, renowned for his
research on Paul-Émile Borduas and the Automatistes,
recipient of the 2010 Prix Gérard-Morisset

Marc Gauthier
Doctoral candidate in art history at Université Laval. His thesis focuses
on Montreal art exhibitions around the turn of the twentieth century.

Michèle Grandbois
Holder of a Ph.D. in history, Curator of Modern Art at
the Musée national des beaux-arts du Québec.

John O'Brian
Professor of art history at the University of British Columbia,
author of *Ruthless Hedonism* (1999), a book on the North American
reception of Matisse's work.

PROJECT DIRECTOR Anne Eschapasse, MNBAQ
CURATOR MICHÈLE Grandbois, MNBAQ
MANAGING EDITOR André Gilbert, MNBAQ
IMAGE PERMISSIONS Phyllis Smith, MNBAQ
COPY EDITOR Louise Gauthier
TRANSLATION Judith Terry (pp. 1-19, 244-256), Barbara Sandilands (pp. 20-77), Käthe Roth (pp. 78-101, 146-173, 187-197), Carolyn Perkes (pp. 208-243)

GRAPHIC DESIGN Christine Hébert
COMPUTER GRAPHICS Johanne Lemay and Chantal Landry
IMAGE PROCESSING Mélanie Sabourin and Johanne Lemay

Cover: James W. Morrice, *Fruit Market, North Africa (Tunis)*, 1914 (cat. 41, detail)

PHOTO CREDITS
Archives Henri Matisse (D.R.): figs. 16, 17, 38, 39
Art Gallery of Ontario: cats. 4, 34, 48, 49, 66, 72, 73, 98, 105, fig. 21
Art Resource, NY: figs. 2, 25, 28
The Barnes Foundation (2014): fig. 29
The Bridgeman Art Library, NY: cat. 103, fig. 31
Jean de Calan: cat. 43
Christie's Images/The Bridgeman Art Library: fig. 23
Bernard Clark: cats. 104, 113
Cleveland Museum of Art: fig. 27
AC Cooper (Colour) Ltd., London: cats. 44, 65
Michael Cullen/TPG Digital Art Services: cats. 7, 38
John Dean Photographs: cat. 92
Toni Hafkenscheid: cat. 39
Heffel: cat. 87
Eric Lessing/Art Resource, NY: fig. 33
McCord Museum: fig. 34
Philippe Migeat/CNAC/MNAM/Distr. RMN-Grand Palais/Art Resource, NY: figs. 1, 22
MNBAQ/Jean-Guy Kérouac: cat. 97
MNBAQ/Idra Labrie: cats. 2, 3, 17, 18, 28, 29, 37, 42, 62, 78, 80, 81, 88, 108, 111, 114, fig. 7
MNBAQ/Denis Legendre: cats. 1, 14, 15, 16, 33, 35, 60, 61, 63, 64, 82, 83, 84, 85, 89, 91, 94, 110, figs. 41, 42
MoMA/SCALA/Art Resource, NY: fig. 3
The Montreal Museum of Fine Arts: cats. 11, 41, 70, 99, fig. 43

The Montreal Museum of Fine Arts/Marilyn Aitken: cat. 95
The Montreal Museum of Fine Arts/Christine Guest: cats. 27, 30, 51, 79
The Montreal Museum of Fine Arts/Brian Merrett: cats. 10, 12, 21, 22, 24, 40, 46, 50, 58, 67, 77, 101
Musée de Grenoble: fig. 18
Roch Nadeau: cat. 112
National Gallery of Canada: cats. 5, 13, 25, 26, 31, 36, 45, 47, 52, 53, 68, 71, 74, 86, 90, 96, 100, 106, figs. 6, 13, 14, 20
North Carolina Museum of Art, Raleigh: fig. 32
The Pushkin State Museum of Fine Arts, Moscow: figs. 19, 40
Royal Institute for Cultural Heritage, Brussels: fig. 35
Smithsonian Institution, Archives of American Art: fig. 46
The Solomon R. Guggenheim Foundation/Art Resource, NY: fig. 30
The State Hermitage Museum, St. Petersburg/ Vladimir Terebenin, Leonard Kheifets, Yuri Molodkovets: figs. 24, 26
Statens Museum for Kunst, Copenhagen: fig. 37
Studio Basset: cat. 6
Tate Gallery, London: cat. 19
Richard-Max Tremblay: cats. 8, 93, 107
Winnipeg Art Gallery/Ernest Mayer: cat. 109

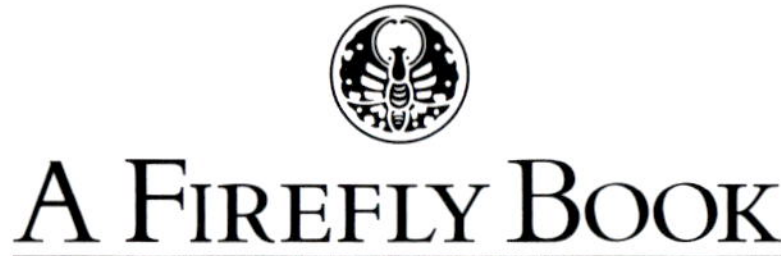

A FIREFLY BOOK

Published by Firefly Books Ltd. 2014

Published originally under the title: *Morrice et Lyman en compagnie de Matisse*
Copyright © 2014 Editions de L'Homme, division of Groupe Sogides Inc. (Montreal, Quebec, Canada)
Henri Matisse artworks © Estate of Henri Matisse/SODRAC (2014)

First printing

Publisher Cataloging-in-Publication Data (U.S.)

A CIP record for this title is available from the Library of Congress

Library and Archives Canada Cataloguing in Publication

Morrice et Lyman en compagnie de Matisse. English
Morrice and Lyman in the company of Matisse / Essays by Lucie Dorais, Richard Foisy, François-Marc Gagnon, Marc Gauthier, Michèle Grandbois & John O'Brian

«Published originally under the title: Morrice et Lyman en Compagnie de Matisse, copyright © 2014 Editions de L'Homme, division de Groupe Sogides Inc. Montreal, Quebec, Canada)» — title page verso.

This publication accompanies the exhibition «Morrice and Lyman: In the Company of Matisse» to be held at the Musée National des Beaux-arts du Québec, and at the McMichael Canadian Art Collection in fall 2014.

Includes bibliographical references and index.

Contents: Introduction / Michèle Grandbois — The light of exile : Morrice and Lyman / Michèle Grandbois — Morrice and Matisse : bedfellows under the sign of modernism / John O'Brian — Morrice in North Africa / Lucie Dorais — Lyman and Matisse / François-Marc Gagnon — Lyman and the shock of light / Marc Gauthier — Crossed paths / Michèle Grandbois & Richard Foisy — Appendices.

ISBN 978-1-77085-493-2 (bound)

1. Morrice, James Wilson, 1865-1924 — Exhibitions. 2. Lyman, John, 1886-1967 — Exhibitions. 3. Matisse, Henri, 1869-1954 — Exhibitions. 4. Matisse, Henri, 1869-1954 — Influence — Exhibitions. 5. Painting, Canadian — 20th century — Exhibitions. 6. Painting, French — 20th century — Exhibitions. 7. Painters — Canada — Historiography — Exhibitions. 8. Painters — France — Historiography — Exhibitions. I. McMichael Canadian Art Collection, host institution. II. Musée national des beaux-arts du Québec, host institution III. Grandbois, Michèle, 1954– . Light of exile. IV. McMichael Canadian Art Collection. V. Musée national des beaux-arts du Québec. VI. Title.

ND245.5.M62M6713 2014   759.11   C2014-903375-3

Published in the United States by Firefly Books (U.S.) Inc.
P.O. Box 1338, Ellicott Station
Buffalo, New York 14205

Published in Canada by Firefly Books Ltd.
50 Staples Avenue, Unit 1
Richmond Hill, Ontario L4B 0A7

Printed in Canada

MUSÉE NATIONAL DES BEAUX-ARTS DU QUÉBEC
Parc des Champs-de-Bataille
Québec (Québec) G1R 5H3
www.mnbaq.org

The Musée national des beaux-arts du Québec is a government corporation funded by the Ministère de la Culture et des Communications du Québec.

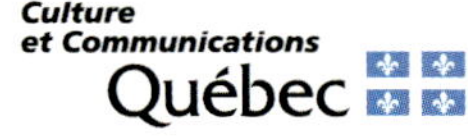